Complementary Methods
for Research in Education
2nd Edition

Complementary Methods
for Research in Education
2nd Edition

Edited by

Richard M. Jaeger

American Educational
Research Association
Washington, DC

American Educational Research Association
1230 17th Street, NW
Washington, DC 20036-3078
202-223-9485

Contents

Preface to the Second Edition

Most of the chapters in this book were introduced in an audio tape series titled *Alternative Methodologies in Educational Research* in 1978. Sponsored by the Committee on Research Training of the American Educational Research Association, the tape series was intended to address the overemphasis on quantitative research methods, to the exclusion or neglect of methods that emphasize verbal portrayals of findings or observational techniques and methods based on naturalistic inquiry, that was common in textbooks on educational research methods at the time. The Committee concluded that a series of audio tapes, each devoted to a single method of disciplined inquiry in education and accompanied by supplementary materials in print form, might significantly enlarge the set of resources available to instructors and students in introductory educational research courses. Many textbooks on educational research methods treat quantitative research procedures quite thoroughly; experimental methods, correlational procedures, quasi-experimental methods, and other procedures that are grounded in psychology and, to some degree, sociology, receive considerable emphasis. Survey research procedures and historical inquiry methods are also addressed in many basic texts, but with comparative superficiality. Some of the methods described in this book, such as case study methodology or aesthetic inquiry in education, will not be found at all in many traditional texts.

The success of the audio tape series resulted in a number of requests from members of the Association for a textbook that was based on the tape scripts. Each author of a tape agreed to revise and update his script, to transform it into a chapter that was suitable for visual (rather than auditory) presentation, and to select and introduce one or more "readings" from the educational research literature that exemplified sound application of the research method discussed in the chapter. Thus the first edition of this book, published in 1988, mirrored the audio tape series but provided additional material through which students could view first hand exemplary applications of the research methods described in the principal chapters of the book.

In the near-decade since the first edition of this book was published, the landscape of educational research methods has changed materially. Although quantitative approaches to disciplined inquiry in education are still employed quite frequently, the publication of research that is totally devoid of quantitative summarization and analysis is now quite common. The American Educational Research Association's journals now abound with reports on case studies, inquiry that incorporates ethnographic procedures, historical accounts, hermeneutic analyses, "thick" description, and narrative accounts—often with excerpts from transcripts of interviews or of discourse among research subjects.

Nonetheless, the distinctions among research methods that were identified for the original tape series are, for the most part, still relevant and useful today, and most are present in this second edition.

Seven of the eight major sections of the first edition of this book have been retained. The authors of chapters on the nature of disciplined inquiry in education (Lee Shulman), historical methods in educational research (Carl Kaestle), ethnographic research in education (Harry Wolcott), case study methods in educational research (Robert Stake), survey research methods in education (Richard Jaeger), comparative experimental methods in educational research (Andrew Porter), and quasi-experimental methods in educational research (Gene Glass) have updated their original writings and their introductions to selected readings by recognizing progress in the development and application of these methodologies over the last decade. The bibliographic material presented in each chapter has been made current, and recent methodological advances have been noted through modifications of narrative and study materials provided at the end of each chapter. The authors of several of these chapters also have selected exemplars of the application of the methods described in their chapters that are different from those selected for the first edition.

Two new chapters and one new section grace this second edition of *Complementary Methods for Research in Education*. The section titled "Philosophic Inquiry Methods in Education" contains a new chapter by Professor Maxine Greene of Columbia University. Titled "A Philosopher Looks at Qualitative Research," the chapter provides an excellent contrasting of the empirico-deductive premises that undergird quantitative inquiry methods and the historical and logical bases of qualitative approaches to research on education. The evolution of thought underlying qualitative inquiry through the decades is presented succinctly and clearly, as is the recognition that inquiry is rarely, if ever, apolitical. Historically, the right to engage in inquiry on education has been narrowly prescribed, and legitimate voice was granted solely to members of an elite who embraced a singular canon. Maxine Greene effectively traces evolution of thought that has given warrant to a far more inclusive body of researchers.

An entirely new section of the book, authored by Tom Barone of Arizona State University and Elliot Eisner of Stanford University, introduces the aesthetic in educational inquiry. In a chapter titled "Arts-Based Educational Research," Barone and Eisner identify and describe the qualities of narrative products of inquiry that make them "arts-based." They also grapple with the critical but necessarily sticky problem of legitimacy and propose criteria by which products of aesthetic inquiry on education should be evaluated and judged. The juxtaposition of their proposals and the evaluative criteria advanced in this book's chapters on inquiry methods grounded in a logical positivist philosophy of science—experimental research, quasi-experimental research, survey research—provides grist for deep reflection and intense debate. In the field of educational and psychological measurement, Samuel Messick (1989) suggested that attention to the consequences of use of a measurement tool (such as a test) was an integral part of the validation of that tool. Without specific reference, but extending Messick's notion, Barone and Eisner suggest that the ultimate test of the validity of a research product is its contribution to the improvement and advancement of education. This notion contrasts sharply with more traditional definitions of validity that incorporate accuracy of prediction and congruence with accepted theory.

In his chapter on the nature of disciplined inquiry in education, Lee Shulman advances the readily confirmed hypothesis that choice of a method of inquiry involves more than determination of the way in which a given research question will be answered. To a great degree, it also determines the nature of the research question that will be asked. Ethnographic researchers and experimental researchers, for example, ask very different research questions. If students are exposed only to more quantitatively grounded researchers and research questions, they will lose more than knowledge of a set of research techniques, or a particular approach to research. They will fail to learn about the wide range of topics and questions for inquiry typically posed by those who engage in naturalistic inquiry. Moreover, they will never consider alternatives to the logical positivist philosophy of science that forms the foundation of classical quantitative, analytic methods.

In a period when inquiry in education lends itself to a richly diverse collection of methods and techniques, it is virtually impossible for a single individual to develop expertise in each. If one or two authors were to attempt to develop a text on educational research methods with the breadth and depth provided here, the task would be formidable indeed. Fortunately, the American Educational Research Association was able to call on accomplished and recognized specialists in each of the research methods represented in the book. Tom Barone and Elliot Eisner, the coauthors of the chapter on aesthetic approaches to inquiry, have produced extensive bodies of work that exemplify and illuminate the application of that mode of discovery. Eisner also is recognized for his introduction and development of the conniseurship approach to educational evaluation. Gene Glass, author of the chapter on quasi-experimental procedures, has published widely on those methods; in particular, he was senior author of a book on time-series analysis, the principal focus of his chapter. Maxine Green is among the nation's most distinguished philosophers of education. Her contributions to that literature are viewed as fundamental to study of the discipline. Carl F. Kaestle is a historian as well as an educator, and is the author of several volumes on the history of education, the methodological focus of his chapter. Andrew C. Porter, senior author of the chapter on experimental research methods, has made extensive contributions to the journal literature on the statistics of education, including the development of methods for analyzing data collected in experiments in which measurement is less than perfectly reliable. He currently directs one of the nation's most respected and productive university-based centers on educational research. Lee S. Shulman prepared the initial chapter of this volume, on the nature of disciplined inquiry in education. Given Shulman's research in such diverse arenas as educational psychology, the education of teachers, curriculum theory, and medical education, it is fitting that he attempt to encapsulate the commonalities and contrasts among diverse methods of inquiry in education. Shulman has been President of the National Academy of Education, a select body of the nation's most distinguished contributors to educational inquiry, and will soon lead the Carnegie Foundation for the Advancement of Teaching, an institution that has made possible major advances in our knowledge of effective teaching and ways to foster its development. Robert Stake, author of the chapter on case study method, is best known, perhaps, for his fundamental work in the theory of educational evaluation. Among myriad contributions in a decades-long record of significant research contribution, he codirected a study of education in the sciences in public schools throughout the United States that is reported in a collection of 11 case studies of science education in 11 different school systems. Harry Wolcott, who prepared the chapter on ethnographic methods in educational research, is both an anthropologist and an educational researcher. His published works include ethnographies of several peoples, with a focus on the role of education in those cultures. I wrote the chapter on survey research methods in education. I have directed a number of local, statewide, and nationwide survey research studies and I am the author of a book on sampling methods for research in education and the social sciences—a topic that is integral to sound survey research.

It is gratifying to know that the first edition of this book, and the audio tape series that preceded it, have been found useful by students and instructors of courses on educational research methods and of courses that incorporate discussion of inquiry in education. I sincerely hope that this second edition will enjoy similar acceptance and use. Readers should know that the contributors to this volume have enjoyed and will enjoy only the extrinsic compensation that comes from the knowledge that their work is appreciated and used to the benefit of generations of students of educational research who follow in their footsteps and build upon the foundation they have provided. All royalties have been waived, and profit, if any, from sales of this book are used to sponsor the Professional Development and Training Program of the American Educational Research Association. The chapter authors are thus owed not only my gratitude, but that of all readers and users of this book.

In its earlier and present forms, this book has benefitted substantially from the varied contributions of many colleagues. I would like to express my appreciation to Peter Airasian, John Christian Busch, Geraldine Clifford, Frederick Erickson, Bruce Hall, John Hills, Kenneth Hopkins, James Impara, Thomas Knapp, Ray Rist, Todd Rogers, Richard Shavelson, George Spindler, David Tyack, and James Wardrop for assisting in the review of one or more of the original chapters. Cynthia Cole provided substantial editorial assistance and many helpful suggestions on the overall organization of the first edition of the book, and a number of her ideas are reflected in this edition as well. I would also like to thank several hundred graduate students in education and the social sciences at the University of North Carolina-Greensboro, Virginia Polytechnic Institute and State University, and the University of Wisconsin-Madison for their careful and thoughtful responses to chapter drafts and study materials, and for a wealth of suggestions on how to improve the pedagogical value of the text. And finally, it is a pleasure to acknowledge the continuing support and contribution of Dr. William Russell, Executive Director of the American Educational Research Association, and of Thomas Campbell of that organization. Mr. Campbell provided diligent and perceptive editing of the entire volume. Without them, this book would still be an idea, smoldering on the back burner of my imagination.

Richard M. Jaeger
Greensboro, North Carolina

A Note to Instructors

This book, the audio tapes that compose the series entitled *Alternative Methodologies in Educational Research,* and the *Study Guide* that accompanies the tape series provide a set of instructional materials for courses that include the study of educational research methods. The audio tape series parallels all but two of the chapters in this second edition of *Complementary Methods for Research in Education.* As noted in the Preface, the chapter on philosophic inquiry methods in this edition of the book is new. The audio tape on that topic in the *Alternative Methodologies* tape series, and the chapter on that topic in the first edition of the book, were written by Michael Scriven. Students will surely benefit from exposure to the very different perspective on the topic that Scriven provides. The chapter on aesthetic inquiry methods by Barone and Eisner has no parallel in the first edition of this book, or in the audio tape series that preceded it.

All of these materials were designed for use in graduate-level courses on the methodology of educational research. Because the materials are modular, they can be used in many ways, and their usefulness transcends courses devoted solely to the study of research methodology. Beyond the introductory section on the nature of disciplined inquiry in education, the remaining sections of this book are virtually independent. Therefore, selected portions of the book could be used in courses devoted to specific methods of research or to specific research perspectives, such as qualitative inquiry methods. In addition, the book provides a set of readings on educational research that could be used independently of the chapters on method.

The audio tapes in the *Alternative Methodologies in Educational Research* series mirror seven of the nine sections on method contained in this book. It is thus possible to have students reinforce their reading of those seven sections by listening to the same authors describe the features of a methodological approach, using somewhat different language. The *Study Guide* that accompanies the audio tape series contains one section for each audio tape, and is available either as an entire manuscript or in individual modules associated with each tape.

Each section of the *Study Guide* contains a detailed topic outline of the material presented in its associated audio tape. Each section also contains a set of study questions and an annotated bibliography (albeit limited to references now almost 2 decades old) to the literature introduced by its associated tape. Some *Study Guide* sections contain exercises, short examples of specific research methods applied to real or fictitious problems, illustrative published materials, and in one section (quasi-experimental research methods) graphical material that is essential to understanding the associated audio tape. The audio tapes and corresponding *Study Guide* sections are available either individually or as a complete series from:

Publications Sales
American Educational Research Association
Alternative Methodologies Tape Series
1230 17th Street, NW
Washington, DC 20036

Some Thoughts on Ways to Use These Materials

This book and the associated audio tape series could be used either to structure an entire course, or to enrich units devoted to particular methods contained in a course with some other principal focus—such as a graduate course in educational psychology or a graduate course on the sociology of education.

If you decide to use this book as your primary text in a course on education research methods, you might want to supplement your lectures by playing associated audio tapes during your class. You could interrupt the audio tapes as necessary, to emphasize and direct a discussion of key points. You could also use the exemplary readings in this book as a focus for discussion of the application of various research methods. You might want to place the audio tape series in your institution's library or media center, and have students listen to the tapes outside of class. You could ask students to prepare answers to selected study questions in this book or the *Study Guide* for discussion during your class, or as homework assignments, to be submitted to you for review and grading.

Another approach to the use of these materials would be to treat the audio tape series as a voluntary reference source that students could use on their own in your institution's library or media center. You could then use this book as a primary or supplementary text. Rather than playing the audio tapes during your class or using them for assigned listening, you could make the tapes and the *Study Guide* available to students whose optimum learning modality is auditory rather than visual, or to students whose prior research background requires them to supplement your assigned work. Even if you choose to play the audio tapes during your class, you might want to place them in your institution's library or media center so that students can hear them again. Having the opportunity to listen to the tapes at their own pace, with the ability to start and stop the tapes, or to review specific sections would enhance the learning of many students.

Materials listed in the bibliographies at the end of each chapter on method in this book and in the *Study Guides* could be placed in the reserve section of your institution's library to ensure ready access by interested students, even if you do not assign additional readings from these lists.

A Note to Students

The materials contained in this book and an associated series of audio tapes entitled *Alternative Methodologies in Educational Research* have been designed to provide you with an efficient, interesting, and painless introduction to powerful and widely used methods of inquiry in education. Following are some hints on ways you can use these materials most effectively.

1. If you are using this book as a text in a course on research methods in education, ask your instructor to place the *Alternative Methodologies in Educational Research* audio tape series in your institution's library or media center. Seven of the nine chapters on method contained in this book were developed originally as scripts of these audio tapes, and the tapes present the essential ideas in those chapters from a slightly different perspective. Two chapters—the one on philosophic inquiry methods by Maxine Greene and the one on aesthetic approaches to inquiry on education by Tom Barone and Elliot Eisner—are new to the second edition of this book and have no parallels in the audio tape series. Although the tape series includes a tape on philosophic inquiry methods, it was written by a different author (Professor Michael Scriven) and offers a very different perspective on that approach to inquiry in education than does the current chapter by Maxine Greene. It is useful and informative, and you would find the audio tape by Scriven to be a worthwhile investment of your time.

2. A *Study Guide* accompanies the audio tape series and contains a section that corresponds to each tape. Each section of the *Study Guide* contains a detailed outline of its corresponding tape designed to help you understand what you are about to hear when you listen to the tape. Prior to reading a chapter in this book that introduces a method of inquiry that is a part of the tape series, you might want to listen to the corresponding audio tape, so as to gain some advance knowledge of the key ideas in the chapter. If you choose to study in this way, review the content outlined in the *Study Guide* before you listen to the associated tape. Then as you listen to the tape, follow along on the outline, to keep in mind where you've been and where you're going next. You'll find that the outline will help focus your attention on the most important concepts presented in the tape and contained in the corresponding chapter. It will aid your recall as well.

3. You will find a series of study questions at the end of each chapter on method in this book, and in each *Study Guide* section. Try to answer these questions shortly after you finish reading a chapter or listening to an audio tape, regardless of whether your instructor assigns them. The questions will help you assess what you know, what you should ask your instructor, and what you

should try to remember. You might also find the study questions helpful when you are reviewing key concepts prior to an examination.

4. Each section in this book contains an annotated bibliography of important references on a method of disciplined inquiry in education. Use these references to supplement what you learn from the examples provided in this book, in the audio tapes, and in the *Study Guide*. Most of the bibliographies contain specific suggestions on what to read first and what to read after you know a bit more about the method of inquiry discussed in the chapter or on a tape. Typically, the bibliographies divide references among introductory sources, advanced sources, and sources that treat special topics within a methodological area. You can do a better job of learning almost any subject if you expose yourself to the views and ideas of several authors. Therefore, set a personal goal of reading at least two sources in the bibliographies provided at the end of each chapter on a method of inquiry.

5. Following each paper in this book that introduces a method of inquiry, you will find one or more selections from the educational research literature. These selections illustrate at least one use of the method you have just studied. They are preceded by a brief introduction in which the author tells you why the selection is important and what you should look for when you read it. When you read these introductions, be sure to take note of the most important points you should learn from the selections that follow.

6. In some sections of the *Study Guide* you will find actual problems that you can complete. These problems are designed to give you first-hand experience in applying the concepts introduced in an associated audio tape or in a corresponding section of this book. Try to work the problems while the information you have gained from this book or an audio tape is fresh in your mind. You can profitably return to the problems and your solutions when you are reviewing for examinations.

7. If you use the audio tapes in the *Alternative Methodologies in Educational Research* series as a supplement to your reading, encourage your instructor to place the tapes in a location that will allow you to listen to them at your own pace, and to start and stop the tapes as you wish. Then listen to the tapes in "bite-size chunks" rather than all at once. After you have listened to the material corresponding to a major section of the outline provided in the *Study Guide*, stop the tape, think about what you've just heard, and write down any questions you'd like to discuss with your instructor. Then listen to the next section.

8. The section of the *Study Guide* that accompanies the audio tape on quasi-experimental research methods, entitled "Quasi-Experimental Research Methods: Time Series Experiments" contains graphical material that you must have in view while you listen to the tape. If you do not have this material in front of you, much of the tape will make no sense at all. So ask for the Study Guide when you get the quasi-experimental methods tape.

9. Researchers who use methods that involve collection and analysis of numerical information—such as experimental methods, quasi-experimental methods, and survey methods—often hold a fundamentally different philo-

sophic view of the nature of truth and reality than do researchers who make use of naturalistic methods—such as case study methods, ethnographic methods, aesthetic methods, and historical methods. So choice of a method of inquiry by a professional researcher might reflect far more than mere selection of a technique. Ask your instructor to describe this distinction, and to introduce you to alternative philosophies of science that underlie disciplined inquiry in education and the social sciences.

Section I
The Nature of Disciplined Inquiry in Education

Disciplines of Inquiry in Education:
A New Overview

Lee S. Shulman
Stanford University
and
The Carnegie Foundation for the Advancement of Teaching

Prologue

More than 15 years have passed since the original version of this chapter was first published, initially as the script for an audiotape, then as an article in the *Educational Researcher*, and finally as the opening chapter in the first edition of this volume. I attempted to provide an introduction to and overview of the field of educational research, offering a perspective that might be helpful for those encountering the field for the first time. I doubt that any of the first edition's authors could foresee at the time how rapidly our field would grow during the next decade and a half or how radically certain aspects of the field would undergo change.

The original version of this chapter apparently has been helpful to many readers over the years; hence my decision to retain the basic organization of the chapter. However, I have tried to indicate where our field has changed and the directions in which it continues to develop. I have no illusions that we can blithely call these changes evidence of progress or growth. Although we have learned a great deal about the educational process and its improvement over the last decade, many of the world's most pressing educational problems remain intractable.

I will begin the chapter by offering a set of dimensions along which we can examine the variety of research methods that are part of the repertoire of educational research. Using these dimensions—problems, investigators, methods, settings, and purposes—we will be able to map the ways in which educational inquiries develop. I will then turn to the topic with which the original chapter began: How can we distinguish research from other forms of human activity in which we explore or investigate the world around us and then write or speak about our insights to others? How, if at all, is the work of the research scholar distinguishable from that of the journalist or the playwright? What are the unique functions of scholars, and how can we best understand their obligations as members of research communities? After a discussion of the concept of disciplined inquiry, I will examine the variety of ways in which scholars frame their questions in disciplinary terms, illustrating these orientations by drawing examples of a variety of different approaches to research that can be conducted around a single problem area: the topic of reading. From these examples, we will begin to see that good research is a matter not of finding the one best method but of carefully framing that question most important to the investigator and the field and then identifying a disciplined way in which to inquire into it that will enlighten both the scholar and his or her community.

Conducting a good study is certainly essential, but it is not enough. It is a serious accomplishment to become wiser or more discerning about a particular problem or issue. It is another to claim that your work has more general value beyond the immediate circumstances of your particular setting or investigation. Thus, I will address the challenge of generalizability, the degree to which a scholar can claim that his or her work can be used to support more general claims about the nature of learning, teaching, development, school finance, and the like. We will see that generalizability is a central issue for all forms of inquiry, from the case study to the national survey.

Next I will examine the ways in which one's preferred modes of research often reflect political or ideological dispositions. This is not a flaw of research; indeed, it is an essential feature of all scholarship that the research practitioner should learn to recognize and acknowledge if he or she is not to develop an unearned air of objective omnipotence or blind faith in putatively dispassionate inquiry. I will examine this issue by reviewing the history of two opposing styles of psychological research in education: experimental and correlational research.

I will also discuss the continuing distinction between quantitative and qualitative inquiry in education and the bases on which scholars can elect to conduct their research in one or some combination of these ways. Much of the current volume is dedicated to explicating the character of many forms of qualitative and quantitative inquiry. I conclude the chapter by looking back over the ways educational research has changed in recent decades. Whether these changes are part of a long-term trajectory of investigation, with the immediate past serving as a harbinger of the immediate future, or whether we are witnessing a pendulum swing rather than a progressive continuum is quite simply impossible to predict. Let us, then, proceed with our dimensions of analysis.

Dimensions of Analysis

There are at least five dimensions that define the research agenda of education: research purposes, research problems, research settings, research investigators, and research methods. Taken together, they serve as a set of commonplaces for discussing educational research. One can envision the interaction of the dimensions by imagining a general mapping sentence for describing any particular educational investigation. In any study, a scholar or investigator frames a problem or issue to investigate using particular methods or procedures in certain settings in accord with particular purposes. Are the problems theoretical or practical? Are the investigators social scientists or practitioners? Are the settings real schools or psychological research laboratories? Are the methods experimental or anthropological? Are the purposes descriptions of current conditions or an exploration of fundamental theory? As we explore these kinds of questions, we will find ourselves developing contrasting portraits of research in education.

First, there are the *problems, topics, or issues* that constitute the subject matter of research. Educational research changes as a function of which kinds of problems are deemed most important to pursue or most legitimate to support. For a long time, many of the core problems and topics were defined by the fundamental psychological processes of learning, such as memory, transfer, and problem solving. The research problems were expected to be general (e.g., How does learning, per se, occur?) rather than focused on the subjects of the school curriculum (e.g., How do students' prior conceptions of conservation affect their learning of physics?). Moreover, even those who opted to study basic general processes looked almost exclusively at the nature of learning, not considering teaching a proper topic of investigation. In more recent years, the problems for educational research have extended broadly into issues of educational practice, as well as expanding rapidly into issues of education policy. Thus, the first question to ask regarding educational research is, What is it about? What questions does it ask? What problems does it address?

Second, a field of study is defined by the *settings* in which the research is conducted. For many years, the settings for much of educational research were psychological laboratories that could be carefully controlled or classrooms that had been made over to resemble laboratories as closely as possible. Other studies were conducted with carefully designed questionnaires, inventories, or interviews susceptible to the same strategies for achieving control that operate in laboratory settings. In contrast, attempting to study the learning of a school subject within the buzzing, blooming confusion of an ordinary classroom with its own teacher might have seemed unbearably daunting to an earlier generation of educational scholars. Indeed, traditional social scientists conducting educational research often argued that if the setting for an investigation were a particular real classroom with its own real teacher, it would be impossible to generalize from its characteristics to those of classrooms in general. However, they reasoned, if the setting for research looked like no classroom in particular (as would a laboratory or simulated setting), then safer generalizations could be proposed. The challenge of selecting research settings has been paramount in the recent history of educational research.

A third element is the background and training of the *investigators* who conduct educational research. Traditionally, these scholars have been exclusively disciplinary specialists such as psychologists, historians, philosophers, or sociologists. In the modern era, investigators increasingly include a wider range of social scientists (including anthropologists, linguists, and economists) in addition to humanists and subject-matter specialists. Their efforts now include aesthetic criticisms as well as econometric models. Moreover, many of these investigators now collaboratively study classroom life in partnership with active classroom teachers. In addition, a growing number of investigations are conducted by teachers who study their own work in their own classrooms. Thus, the practitioner as investigator has become more commonplace in our day.

A fourth element involves the *methods* of research. For many decades, these methods were dictated by psychology and its own two "disciplines," experimental and correlational methods (about which I will have more to say later in this chapter). Increasingly in the modern era, the methods associated with other disciplines have been introduced into educational scholarship. These include the ethnographic methods of anthropology, discourse analysis procedures from linguistics and sociolinguistics, "think-aloud" and other forms of protocol analysis from cognitive science, and many others. Thus, the traditional procedures of educational research have been augmented by a variety of qualitative or field research methods, often reported in the form of case studies. In addition, a new generation of quantitative strategies has been spawned, ranging from powerful techniques for analyzing complexly nested hierarchical systems to flexible procedures for exploratory data analysis.

A fifth and fundamental element is the *purpose* for which an investigation is initiated and pursued. Research may be undertaken for many and varied purposes. One may wish to discover or invent new theoretical understandings of particular educational processes or phenomena. One may seek to develop new methods, techniques, or strategies for solving specific problems. One may wish to acquire a more complete description or accounting of the conditions associated with particular schools, students, or content areas. One may seek to apply previously acquired understandings in the amelioration or improvement of current educational conditions, whether of practice or policy. One may attempt to connect or integrate previously distinct areas of theory, practice, or policy. In some cases, the research is pursued to improve particular forms of practice or to inform specific policies. In other cases, the research seeks to test or extend a theoretical formulation in a related discipline such as psychology or sociolinguistics. Some research is undertaken to evaluate or understand the impact of practice in a particular school or classroom. Other research is directed at the formulation of broad generalizations and principles. And, often, the research is undertaken in the interest of a particular ideology or value system to which the investigators are committed. These examples surely do not exhaust the range of purposes for which educational inquiries are conducted. Different purposes address different priorities and privilege different research strategies.

Nevertheless, whatever their purposes, researchers must be capable of communicating their discoveries to a community of peers in education. Research begins in wonder and curiosity but ends in teaching. The work of the researcher must always lead to a process in which we teach what we have learned to our peers in the education community. Our work is neither meaningful nor consequential until it is understood by others. The process of research is incomplete until the researcher can communicate his or her understandings clearly, persuasively, and effectively.

The forms of educational research are identified by how they address the following five facets of its structure: its core problems and topics, the settings in which investigations are conducted, the backgrounds and experience of the investigators who conducted its studies, the methods of inquiry they used, and the purposes for which the research was pursued. As these combinations have changed over the past century, the study of education has evolved. Most important, the determination of which kinds of questions or methods are legitimate is not under the jurisdiction of a Supreme Court or other formal authority. The loosely defined "community of scholars and practitioners" in education is continuously at work accommodating to some new influences while resisting others.

Since the focus of this book is on research methods, I will devote most of my attention in this chapter to that topic. But, as we shall soon see, questions of method are often difficult to disentangle from the web of relationships in which they are embedded. And the elements of that web include the features designated earlier.

On Method

Few works in the English language are as rich as Shakespeare's *Hamlet*. One phrase is of particular interest. Hamlet is in deep grief and despair over the recent death of his father, the king of Denmark. In his melancholy, he has been acting rather strangely, and many have called him mad. Yet, Polonius observes of Hamlet, "Though this be madness, yet there is method in it." What does Shakespeare wish to convey with this phrase? How can the apparent lack of coherence or sanity of Hamlet's behavior be characterized by method? To assert that something has method is to claim that there is an order, a regularity, obscure though it may be, that underlies an apparent disorder, thus rendering it meaningful. Method is the attribute that distinguishes research activity from mere observation and speculation.

When adversaries argue about the nature of the world or the best approach to some particular human endeavor, we typically find ourselves evaluating their respective claims by examining the methods they used to reach their conclusions. There are few subjects that generate as much passion among scientists as arguments over method. This is not surprising, since scholars who agree on matters of method can pursue research questions in a parallel fashion and then argue over the results of their respective investigations. However, if they do not agree even on some matters of research method, then their findings are likely to be incommensurable. There will be no way to properly compare one inquiry with the other. It is for this reason that major controversies in educational research so frequently focus on problems of research method. What is the role of research methodology in educational research? How can we tell proper from improper uses of research methods? To answer these questions, we must turn to a central concept in educational research methodology: disciplined inquiry.

Method and Disciplined Inquiry

Educational researchers typically are eager to distinguish their work from other forms of discourse that, for them, cannot lay claim to being research. Take, for example, the following statement from the preface of Lawrence

Cremin's (1961) prize-winning history of American progressive education, *The Transformation of the School*:

> There is currently afoot a simple story of the rise of progressive education, one that has fed mercilessly on the fears of anxious parents and the hostilities of suspicious conservatives. In it John Dewey, somewhat in the fashion of Abou Ben Adhem, awakes one night with a new vision of the American school: the vision is progressive education. Over the years, with the help of a dedicated group of crafty professional lieutenants at Teachers College, Columbia University, he is able to foist the vision on an unsuspecting American people. The story usually ends with a plea for the exorcising of this devil from our midst and a return to the ways of the fathers. This kind of morality play has always been an influential brand of American political rhetoric, used by reformers and conservatives alike. But it should never be confused with history! (p. vii)

Cremin forcefully draws the distinction between doing history and engaging in political rhetoric. Clearly, he claims, the results of the two forms of discourse must be treated with different degrees of respect and credibility. "Real history" should be given far greater credence than mere political rhetoric. How is one to distinguish between the two? I would suggest that, while not entirely a matter of method, historians would distinguish their work from that of rhetoricians by the ways observations are collected, evidence is marshaled, arguments are drawn, and opportunities are afforded for replication, verification, and refutation.

When we speak of research, we speak of a family of methods that share the characteristics of disciplined inquiry. Cronbach and Suppes (1969) attempted to define disciplined inquiry a number of years ago in a monograph prepared with the collaboration of their colleagues in the National Academy of Education. The following are some of the definitions of disciplined inquiry they suggest:

> Disciplined inquiry has a quality that distinguishes it from other sources of opinion and belief. The disciplined inquiry is conducted and reported in such a way that the argument can be painstakingly examined. The report does not depend for its appeal on the eloquence of the writer or on any surface plausibility. (p. 15)

> Whatever the character of a study, if it is disciplined the investigator has anticipated the traditional questions that are pertinent. He institutes control at each step of information collection and reasoning to avoid the sources of error to which these questions refer. If the errors cannot be eliminated he takes them into account by discussing the margin for error in his conclusions. Thus, the report of a disciplined inquiry has a texture that displays the raw materials entering the argument and the logical processes by which they were compressed and rearranged to make the conclusion credible. (pp. 15–16)

The preceding definition of disciplined inquiry could be misconstrued to imply that the appropriate application of research methods in education always leads to a sterile, ritualized, and narrowly conceived form of investigation. This is not the case. As Cronbach and Suppes observe subsequently:

> Disciplined inquiry does not necessarily follow well established, formal procedures. Some of the most excellent inquiry is free-ranging and speculative in its initial stages, trying what might seem to be bizarre combinations of ideas and procedures, or restlessly casting about for ideas. (p. 16)

What is important about disciplined inquiry is that its data, arguments, and reasoning be capable of withstanding careful scrutiny by another member of the scientific community.

If it is clear what constitutes disciplined inquiry and there is little disagreement regarding the need for research methods to be consistent with the standards of disciplined inquiries, why should this field be so filled with controversy? There are several reasons.

First, scientific inquiries cannot involve mere recitation of the "facts of the case." Indeed, inquiry demands the selection of a particular set of observations or facts from among the nearly infinite universe of conceivable observations. Just as in a court of law, the legal adversaries may disagree profoundly about the relevance of a piece of evidence or the warrant to be given to the conclusions drawn from each other's reasoning; thus, in disciplined inquiry in education, there is often lack of consensus about the grounds, the starting points, for chains of reasoning.

There is another, even more serious source of disagreements about method. Disciplined inquiry not only refers to the ordered, regular, or principled nature of investigation; it also refers to the disciplines themselves, which serve as the sources for the principles of regularity or canons of evidence used by the investigator. What distinguishes disciplines from one another is the manner in which they formulate their questions, how they define the content of their domains and organize that content conceptually, and the principles of discovery and verification that constitute the ground rules for creating and testing knowledge in their fields. These principles are different in the different disciplines.

A major reason why research methodology in education is such an exciting area is that education is not itself a discipline. Indeed, education is a field of study, a locus containing phenomena, events, institutions, problems, persons, and processes that themselves constitute the raw material for inquiries of many kinds. The perspectives and procedures of many disciplines can be brought to bear on the questions arising from and inherent in education as a field of study. As each of these disciplinary perspectives is brought to bear on the field of education, it brings with it its own set of concepts, methods, and procedures, often modifying them to fit the phenomena or problems of education. Such modifications, however, can rarely violate the principles defining those disciplines from which the methods were drawn.

Applications of Research Methods: Some Examples

Differences in method are not merely alternative ways of reaching the same end or answering the same questions. What distinguishes methods from one another, usually by virtue of their contrasting disciplinary roots, is not only the procedures they use but the very types of questions they tend to raise. This point might best be understood if I take an area of educational inquiry and describe how questions would be asked and studies conducted from the perspectives of different forms of disciplined inquiry in that field of study. Each of the examples I draw will be credible pieces of research, that is, forms of disciplined inquiry. This exercise will illustrate the variety of forms of research method that can be used in a disciplined manner in the same domain of inquiry.

One of the most important areas of educational research is the study of reading. Millions of dollars and the efforts of many individual investigators are invested in research to help us understand more about the teaching and learning of reading. What do we wish to know? What kinds of questions ought we to ask about language, reading, and learning? What kinds of reading research are possible, and what can we learn from each?

One reasonable question is, "What makes some people successful readers and others unsuccessful?" How can you predict which sorts of people are going to have difficulty learning to read, in order, perhaps, to institute preventive measures before serious damage has been done? In this sort of research, one would collect a variety of measures on individuals, including measures of their performance on a number of tasks, their demographic or personal characteristics, aspects of their backgrounds, and anything else that could conceivably assist in accurate prediction of the likelihood of reading difficulty or success. An investigator would then use the techniques of correlation and regression to investigate the relationships between those predictors and sets of useful outcome measures of reading performance for students of various ages. Correlation as a statistical procedure could be used to determine how two variables are related or how much they are related. The approach would be quantitative and would involve no intervention or manipulation other than that required to administer the instruments needed to collect the necessary data. In general, correlational research attempts to describe the relationships among naturally occurring variables or phenomena without attempting to change them.

Another investigator might now say, "I'm not really interested in predicting reading failure or success. I want to identify the best possible methods for teaching reading to all youngsters, irrespective of their backgrounds or aptitudes." Such an individual is unlikely to be satisfied with research methods that correlate attributes of individuals with concurrent or subsequent reading performance. This individual will be inclined to design experimental studies. Individuals or groups would be assigned systematically to contrasting methods of reading instruction. The effects of these contrasting methods then would be compared by testing the reading performances of those who have been taught. This approach involves experimental methods that contrast strikingly with those of correlational research. Naturally, there are times when the degree of control over the assignment of individuals or groups to treatments is not as great as may be theoretically desirable. We may, for example, wish to contrast two schools that are using very different reading programs. Since pupils were not originally assigned to those schools at random, this cannot be considered a "true" experiment. In such cases, we see researchers use other methods that attempt to identify which treatment was best without the benefits of random assignment. These often are called "quasi-experimental" procedures.

Yet another investigator may say that neither predicting reading performance nor identifying the best methods of teaching reading constitutes the question of interest for her. Instead, she may ask, "What is the general level of reading performance across different age, sex, social, or ethnic groups in the population?" "Where do the most significant areas of reading success and failure occur?" and "What are the reading habits of particular groups in the general population?" This investigation will be conducted best by using a variety of survey techniques measuring reading performance or questioning reading practices. The work of the National Assessment of Educational Progress or of the International Education Association studies of cross-national achievement exemplifies this approach. Once again, different procedures are used to ask different questions and to solve different problems for different purposes.

In the cases I have described thus far, the significant questions concern how well or how much reading ability has been gained or developed. Thus, there are comparisons between alternative methods of teaching reading or among different individuals or cohorts of students learning to read. Quite another sort of question can be asked about reading. There are many times when we wish to know not how many or how well but simply how. How is reading instruction carried out? What are the experiences and perceptions of teachers and students as they engage in the teaching and learning of reading? What is the underlying or explicit system of rules by which this complex activity is accomplished?

Although at first blush this might seem a much less powerful form of question than the quantitative questions preceding it, this is not necessarily the case. Some of the most important and influential investigations in the history of social science have been of that form. Perhaps an example can illustrate that point. When Binet and Simon were asked to develop a better method for identifying the children in the public schools of Paris who could profit from special education programs, they responded by creating the individual intelligence test. The goal of their research and development was to improve the precision with which one could measure differences in intellectual ability among persons.

Nearly 20 years later, a young Swiss associate of Simon, Jean Piaget, became intrigued with a very different sort of question about human intelligence. He asked, "What does intelligence look like, and how does it develop?" He was most concerned with the common elements characterizing the intellectual performance of all individuals at a given stage of development rather than the levels of performance that distinguished among them. He was attempting to answer questions about shared regularities rather than measuring systematic differences.

By way of analogy, one individual interested in investigating the game of golf may decide to focus on differences in performance among golfers. What distinguishes good golfers from poor golfers? The study can be conducted experimentally, by contrasting alternative methods of training golfers. It can be accomplished correlationally by examining the attributes of poor- and well-scoring golfers through use of everything from videotape analyses to measures of age, experience, and social characteristics. But a very different question would be "How does one play the game of golf?" What are the functional rules of the game? In this case, another investigator is interested in understanding the common elements or regularities shared by all golfers, whether they are national champions or weekend duffers.

To continue the examples about reading, there are investigators attempting to understand how reading instruction is accomplished in the classroom in general. They tend to use the methods of case study as they document or portray the everyday experiences of teachers and students in the teaching and learning of reading. In much case-study work, there is a general assumption that American public schools are very similar to one another as institutions. Therefore, individual experiences of learning to read will not differ enormously from one setting to another. In other case-study work, the assumption may be that "average" reading development is irrelevant. These researchers wish to document the dramatic diversity among individuals in the rate, sequence, and character of their development of reading competence.

These studies are likely to focus on only one classroom or school or, at most, a small number. Depending on the orientation of the researcher, the portrayals could emphasize the social character of learning to read in a classroom group, the intellectual and emotional experiences of individual children struggling to master the intricacies of reading, or even the manner in which individual children acquire the implicit rules for turn taking and status attainment in the classroom. Data gathering can include compiling detailed prose descriptions written longhand on yellow legal pads; videotaping classroom episodes and analyzing their contents exhaustively; interviewing teachers and students to discover their reactions, perceptions, or expectations in classrooms; and collecting examples of work produced by teachers and students for careful review and interpretation.

The disciplines from which these methods draw their rules of discovery and verification typically are anthropology, ethology, linguistics, or particular subfields of sociology, such as symbolic interaction. More recently, humanistic disciplines like aesthetics and the hermeneutic methods of philosophy fruitfully have been added to the tool kit. These contrast sharply with the disciplinary roots of the more traditional approaches, predominantly psychology, agriculture, genetics, and quantitative sociology, including demography.

A philosopher approaching the problem of research in reading might raise yet another set of questions. He or she might examine the kinds of inquiry just described and observe that the concept of reading has not been adequately defined. What does it mean to be able to read? Do we denote by the term *reading* the ability to recognize the correspondence between visible symbols and sounds in isolation, mere word identification? Do we imply the ability to comprehend written prose, and, if so, at what level of sophistication or subtlety? For example, does someone who knows how to read have the ability to detect the difference between assertion and irony in a prose passage? Analysis of the meaning of the reading process affects the kinds of tests and measurements of reading achievement that are constructed. What we choose to define as reading will be important whether we are pursuing predictive studies of reading failure or success, experimental studies of reading instruction methods, or general surveys of reading performance. A philosopher would conduct inquiries into the nature of the reading process that would entail quite different research procedures from those of other investigators. These analytic procedures would be disciplined by the rules of evidence proper to philosophy.

Similarly, questions of what distinguishes readers from nonreaders can be approached as historical research. As soon as someone attempts to answer the question "What proportion of the U.S. population is illiterate?" the ambiguity of the definition of "literacy" becomes apparent. How well must a person read and write to be considered literate? How has that definition changed for societies with contrasting economic systems, religious orientations, sex-role prescriptions, or social-class hierarchies? A careful historical analysis can help account for both the conditions that foster increased literacy among members of a society and the possible consequences of illiteracy for those members.

I have attempted in the examples just presented to illustrate the variety of ways in which complementary types of research methods can be applied to a topic of inquiry in education: reading instruction. Moreover, I have tried to indicate that the alternative methods not only approach the doing of research differently but, by and large, ask different questions and hence generate quite different answers. This is hardly surprising and surely not disturbing. The need for a multiplicity of methods was recognized centuries ago, perhaps most eloquently by Aristotle, who, in the introduction to his treatise *De Anima* (On the Soul), observes:

> It might be supposed that there was some single method of inquiry applicable to all objects whose essential nature we are endeavoring to ascertain . . . in that case what we should seek for would be this unique method. But if there is no single and general method for solving the question of essence, our task becomes still more difficult; in the case of each different subject we have to determine the appropriate process of investigation. (1947a, pp. 145–146)

Generalizability of Research

However different the objects of investigation and the goals of inquiry, there are certain problems shared by all research methods, including the generalizability of findings: the degree to which findings derived from one context or under one set of conditions may be assumed to apply in other settings or under other conditions. Although there may be disclaimers from some research practitioners, all researchers strive for some degree of generalizability for their results. They are rarely content to have the research they have conducted generate understanding that is relevant only to the particular cases that were observed. There are several forms of generalization. The most frequently discussed is generalization from the particular sample of individuals who are tested, taught, or observed in a given study to some larger population of individuals or groups of which they are said to be representative. For example, if we conduct a study of reading comprehension with third graders in Philadelphia, can we generalize our results to third graders all over the country? Or must we limit our generalizations to children of certain social and economic backgrounds, ability levels, and the like?

A second form of generalization is from the particular tasks or settings in which a piece of work is conducted to that population of tasks or settings that the research situation is claimed to represent. For example, one may compare phonics and whole-language approaches with reading instruction using two particular sets of books or methods. If one finds one approach consistently superior, can one generalize these findings to all phonics and whole-language methods? Or must one limit one's generalizations to those particular teaching materials alone?

Although both types of generalizability are important, much more has been written about the first kind, generalizability across people, than about the second, generalizability across situations. We shall see that the two have certain elements in common. In classical statistics, the argument was made that if one samples randomly from a population in making certain measurements or conducting certain experiments, inferences then can be drawn properly to the entire population from which the random sample was taken. Unfortunately, it is rarely the case that investigators truly sample randomly from a total population to which they might ultimately wish to generalize. A truly random sample is one in which each individual in the population has an equal chance of appearing and in which selection of one individual is independent of the selection of any other. In a now-classic article, Cornfield and Tukey (1956) argued that this is never the case. Indeed, we sample as best we can and then make a case for the subsequent claims of generalizability. To use their metaphor, we must then build an inferential bridge between the particular groups of people we studied directly in our research and those other groups to whom we wish to generalize. We do so by documenting as comprehensively as possible the characteristics of the individuals we have studied and the procedures we have used. Then the reader can examine our documentation and critically evaluate whether our claims of generalizability are warranted. More specifically, the reader must judge whether the findings we report for the individuals we have studied should be considered applicable to any other group of individuals regarding whom our reader might be interested.

Cornfield and Tukey's concept of bridge building extends fruitfully to other aspects of generalization as well. When we report on a setting or a task, we must be equally careful to document in detail its characteristics so that readers who are as concerned about the generalizability of our task characteristics as they are about the generalizability of our sample can make the appropriate inferences.

Finally, we can now see that those who perform case studies are confronted with a problem of generalizability that is not different in kind from that confronted by their quantitative colleagues. To claim that one is conducting a case study requires that an answer be provided to the question "What is this a case of?" Not every description is a case study. It may be a description of a singular individual or event. To claim that something is a case study is to assert that it is a member of a family of situations or events of which it is in some sense representative. In much the same way that the reader of a quantitative study must build his Cornfield-Tukey bridge to evaluate whether the results of that study are relevant to certain other settings, so the critical reader of a case study must examine whether an inferential bridge can be built between this case and other cases of interest to the reader.

Controversy Over Method: Experimental Versus Correlational

One of the best-known examples of a controversy over method was explicated by Cronbach (1957) in his now-classic article, "The Two Disciplines of Scientific Psychology." Cronbach observed that the field of psychology had divided early into two major streams: the correlational and the experimental. Both of these streams share what Cronbach calls the "job of science," which is to ask questions of nature. A discipline, he observes, is a method of asking questions and testing answers to determine whether those answers are sound. Correlational psychology is not a form of research that uses only one statistical technique, namely, correlation. Those researchers who are deemed correlationists are interested in studying the natural covariations occurring in nature. They are committed to understanding the functional relationships between variations in one set of events or characteristics and variations in another. Thus, they may ask about the relationship between income and achievement, or between the number of physicians per thousand population and infant mortality, or between phases of the moon and the behavior of tides on earth. They see nature as presenting itself for inspection and the role of the scientist as that of identifying which of the variations that nature presents are associated with other processes or outcomes.

In contrast, experimentalists are interested, as Cronbach observes, only in the variation they themselves create. The experimental method is one in which scientists change conditions in order to observe the consequences of those changes. They are interested in understanding how nature is put together, not by inspecting nature as it is but by introducing modifications or changes in nature in order to better understand the consequences of those changes for subsequent states. They argue that only through the systematic study of planned modifications can we distinguish causal relationships between events or characteristics from mere chance co-occurrences. Thus, for example, foot size and vocabulary are correlated in the general population, but that does not mean that large feet cause larger word knowledge (or vice versa). It merely reflects the larger vocabulary size of older (and, hence, bigger) people relative to children.

All too frequently ignored is the intersection of research methods with the underlying theoretical, political, or social purposes of the research being conducted. As I indicated earlier in this chapter, research methods are not merely different ways of achieving the same end. They carry with them different questions, different ways of asking questions, and often different commitments to educational and social ideologies. We can observe this intersection of ideology and method in considering the historical roots of correlational and experimental approaches.

In the scientific world of late-19th-century England, the work of Charles Darwin on the origin of the species commanded special attention. Central to his evolutionary theory was the principle of natural selection: Nature selects those species or subspecies for ultimate survival that are best adapted to the conditions confronting them. "Survival of the fittest" is a phrase used to describe the process by which individuals and species adapt to variations in environmental conditions in order to survive. The "struggle for life" favors those whose structure and behavior are adaptive to the challenges of their environment and thus are more likely to produce offspring who flourish.

This view of human evolution as a struggle for survival had a substantial impact on prevailing views of society. Buttressed by the centrality of competition and the free market to the economic thinking of 19th-century England, a movement called "social Darwinism" developed. Social Darwinists viewed members of a society as struggling for rewards and undergoing "selection" based on their talents or merits.

Francis Galton, a cousin of Darwin, observed that it was important to study those variations in human abilities and performance contributing most significantly to successful adaptation. He thus began systematically studying those human attributes contributing most to social effectiveness. He assumed that those characteristics were enduring traits unlikely to undergo change. His research was broad indeed, ranging from studies of what he viewed as hereditary genius to investigation of the efficacy of prayer. His research was characteristic of what we now call correlational studies. He developed early forms of the statistical methods that currently underlie correlational research.

Galton's work is historically linked to the brand of social theory that came to be known as conservative Darwinism (Cremin, 1961). Conservative Darwinists attempted to develop better means for identifying those members of the society who were most likely to adapt successfully and to provide opportunities to those individuals, whatever their social class or family background, to receive education and other perquisites from the society. They constituted the forerunners of the modern testing movement, which can be seen as a way of applying correlational psychology to the problem of identifying the fittest in the society and thereby providing them opportunities for social mobility and leadership.

The testing movement thus began as an attempt to divorce the ability of individuals from their social backgrounds by basing economic and social mobility on performance rather than on patrimony. Ironically, those who now oppose the testing movement base their opposition on the argument that tests merely support and amplify existing social class and ethnic differences.

Opposition to this application of Darwinism to social research developed quickly. Scientists and social reformers questioned the assumption that existing individual or group differences were durable or necessary by nature. Indeed, they claimed that such differences were typically historical or social artifacts created by political inequalities. The role of the educator, they asserted, was not merely to develop better ways of identifying the variations already occurring in nature in order to select individuals who are most competent. The responsibility of educators was to identify those interventions in nature that would lead to more successful adaptation and survival for the largest number of human beings. Thus, while survival of the fittest remained the watchword, the responsibility of the educator was to increase the proportion of individuals in the world who are fit, and the responsibility of the educational researcher was to experiment with alternative methods of rendering individuals more fit, more adaptable, than they might otherwise have become. This group was known historically as reform Darwinists, and their political philosophy is implicit in many applications of experimental methods to educational research.

The goal of the correlationist thus became to understand and exploit the natural and, presumably, enduring variations among individuals, while that of the experimentalist was to create conditions to reduce those variations.

This example of how the two major streams in scientific psychology are ultimately rooted in distinctive political or social commitments is not meant to leave the impression that these two alternatives must always remain sharply contrasted and never integrated. Indeed, many researchers have devoted their careers to identifying research methods capable of transcending the contrast between experimental and correlational methods. These investigators may ask, "For which kinds of learners do which kinds of teaching methods, school reforms, or other interventions work best?" That is a topic, however, that goes far beyond the proper subject of this discussion.

Thus, although Hippocrates was correlating and Galileo experimenting centuries before Darwin, these two strategies of research took on distinctly new ideological implications in the hands of competing Darwinists. In our day, the values commitment implicit in the choice of method is often unrecognized, even by the investigators themselves. This makes it even more dangerous to treat methodological issues without an understanding or concern for the specific substantive questions being asked. One of the enduring problems in research methodology has been the tendency to treat selection of method as primarily a technical question not associated with the underlying theoretical or substantive rationale of the research to be conducted.

Selecting the method most appropriate for a particular disciplined inquiry is one of the most important, and difficult, responsibilities of a researcher. The choice requires an act of judgment grounded in knowledge both of methodology and of the substantive area of the investigation.

Quantitative and Qualitative Methods

In looking at the differences between quantitative research methods and those typically dubbed qualitative, such as case study methods or ethnographic methods, we find another type of political or social contrast that is of interest. Quantitative methods, whether correlational or experimental, require relatively large and carefully selected samples of individuals. Quantitative approaches generally include sampling of both individuals and situations in ways that attempt to maximize the generalizability of the findings to the widest possible population. As noted earlier, correlational researchers sample from individuals and settings as they are rather than as they might be. And in much experimental research, choices of treatment sample conditions that tend to be within the realm of common experience.

In contrast, it is intriguing to examine the types of settings frequently studied by qualitative researchers. For example, studies of open classrooms, free schools, or other radical educational innovations are often conducted through case studies or ethnographic methods. In these studies, the researcher is attempting to portray the workings of circumstances that differ dramatically from what typically presents itself in the "natural" functioning of our society and our educational systems. It is as if the researcher is attempting to document, with vivid characterizations, that nature need not be the way it typically is. The researcher is attempting to communicate that we can create settings far different from those we may discover through random sampling. Moreover, disciplined inquiry carries the implicit message that those settings can be both sensible and rule governed.

Often qualitative researchers studying unusual educational settings accuse quantitative researchers attempting to characterize education, more generally, as committed to maintaining the educational status quo. Qualitative researchers, in contrast, often espouse a commitment to demonstrating the viability of truly alternative educational approaches.

I do not want to create these contrasts too starkly. Obviously, many studies of broader educational questions are conducted with qualitative methods, such as some of the more striking investigations of school desegregation or evaluations of special programs. Conversely, many quantitative studies of educational change, such as those conducted in the National Follow-Through experiment, are attempts to introduce significant new approaches to the practices of contemporary education. Here again, however, I have been trying to draw attention to the intricate ways in which the multiplicity of methods we have available in educational research presents us not merely with an enormous technical challenge but with the opportunity to investigate an impressive variety of questions from a rich set of alternative social and political perspectives.

Newer Forms of Inquiry: Dewey's Influence

This volume is filled with examples and discussions of both time-honored and relatively new developments in educational research methodology. I find it particularly interesting to examine more recent developments and their implications for the work of educational scholars. Although I could choose from many alternatives, there are two newer forms of educational inquiry that I will highlight to exemplify the kinds of changes that are under way in educational research. These examples merely are representative and are far from exhaustive. Other chapters in this volume beautifully exemplify additional contemporary approaches, such as those characterized by building on the methods and concepts of the arts and humanities. I will now, however, examine forms of teacher research and the concept of the design experiment. Each of these can be understood as a reflection of educational research returning to the traditions and principles first proposed by John Dewey at the beginning of this century.

To appreciate how much change is being introduced into educational research, we must acknowledge a rebirth of interest in John Dewey's thinking, not only as a philosopher of education but, indeed, as an educational leader with significant views regarding the conduct of educational scholarship. When

Dewey pioneered in the creation of the Department of Pedagogy, Philosophy, and Psychology at the then-new University of Chicago in the late 1890s, he brought with him a radical conception of educational research. He also introduced the concept of a "laboratory school" as part of a research university and contrasted that institution with the "demonstration schools" that were prevalent among the normal schools of that era.

The historian Ellen Lagemann (1988) has provided particularly important insights into Dewey's thinking at that time. She argues that Dewey held several key principles regarding research in education. Dewey's first principle was that educational research is essentially experimental and that these experiments must be carried out within the naturalistic settings of schools qua laboratories. This commitment to experimentation and intervention set him in clear opposition to the conservative Darwinists. The claim that educational research is both experimental and naturalistic subsequently became unpopular with educational researchers during most of this century. Real research occurred in laboratories, they would claim, not in nature. Only when natural processes could be manipulated under strictly controlled conditions could the power of scientific methods be realized. Nevertheless, Dewey claimed that educational research could and should combine both the experimental and the natural.

A second principle was that educational research should serve as a testing ground of the link between scientific and social innovation. Lagemann quotes Dewey's claim that a laboratory school's special function was to "create new standards and ideals and thus to lead to a gradual change in conditions" (1988, p. 197). Thus, the laboratory school does not serve solely as a setting for testing research hypotheses and discovering psychological principles, although that is a significant role. The laboratory school also is a site for "existence proofs." If we can create and sustain a particular instructional innovation in a real school, we have demonstrated the possibility that it can exist. Once its existence has been demonstrated, we can study its characteristics and the conditions that either foster or inhibit its development. Thus, the laboratory qua school and school qua laboratory become settings for creating and documenting visions of the possible.

In these senses, Dewey's vision was of a field of educational research that was inseparable from developmental efforts in curriculum design and school reform. One studied, for example, the learning and teaching of school subjects through the development of innovative curriculum in a radically redesigned school context. The notion that one could achieve understanding of the principles of school learning in settings far removed from schools and their curriculum materials was absurd for Dewey.

Teacher Research

One of the most dramatic examples of this kind of inquiry in our own day is the creation of forms of "teacher research," such as those exemplified by the work of Magdalene Lampert. In these studies, the investigators are themselves teachers who are both subjects and objects of research. The teacher-scholars in question not only investigate teaching; they are the teachers under investigation. Not since the earliest days of modern psychology, when Hermann Ebbinghaus (1885/1913) used himself as a subject in his own laboratory experiments on memory, have scholars made themselves the objects of study. Even then, the conditions of the research were far more controlled and artificial, and the function under investigation—memory of a list of nonsense syllables—was hardly an arena for special expertise. The research on classroom mathematics teaching of Magdalene Lampert serves as a bridge between the psychological study of the learning and teaching of school subjects and the long-neglected tenets of the Dewey school: to study education by designing new practices of teaching and learning school subjects and examining the conditions and consequences of their implementation.

For a number of years, Magdalene Lampert has taught the mathematics curriculum to a fifth-grade class in a Michigan public elementary school. She would assume responsibility for math teaching from the classroom's full-time teacher and would teach the mathematics lessons for each day, collect abundant examples of student work, videotape many of the classroom interactions, maintain detailed journals recounting and reflecting on her own practice, periodically examine the children using both standardized and custom-designed assessments, plan the next day's lessons, and then begin the process anew. Using her own thinking, acting, and reflecting as the database, she analyzed the practice of teaching and learning mathematics. She attempted to document her plans, goals, and strategies; to reconstruct the recurring dilemmas and decisions she faced; and to analyze and classify those dilemmas and decisions in systematic terms. Here was reflective teaching in nearly prototypical form.

In her published papers, Lampert attempted to characterize the routine dilemmas of mathematics teaching, employing extensive case materials from her own practice to support her arguments. She asked what it meant to teach and learn mathematics with understanding and used detailed descriptions of her interactions with students to illustrate her points. Reading Lampert's articles, one begins to develop a clearer sense of the complexities of teachers' thinking, judgments, and decisions, as well as their actions and their consequences, when they actively pursue the goals of higher order mathematical thinking with their students. In this work, Lampert exemplified several aspects of a new approach to research in education. She exemplified most specifically an emphasis on analysis of the nature of mathematical learning and knowing among students and the development of a research methodology for teachers conducting reflective case studies of their own practice.

In Lampert's work, we encounter a research method that substantially erodes the time-honored distinction between subject and object, between the researcher and the researched. Lampert is in fact a university professor who spends part of each day in classrooms, but teacher research is not limited to university-based scholars. We are also witnessing an upsurge in the study of teaching by full-time classroom teachers (Cochran-Smith & Lytle, 1993). I anticipate that this development will grow sufficiently in strength to provide yet another new paradigm for educational research in which teachers organize efforts to investigate their own practice, to document and analyze student learning and motivation, and to pursue other inquiries best undertaken by educators who maintain an ongoing and continuous relationship with life in schools and classrooms because they are full-time inhabitants of those settings rather than episodic visitors.

Let no one be deceived regarding the complexity of such work and the demands it places on its practitioners. Lampert and her like-minded colleagues are quite unusual scholar-practitioners. They are not only experienced classroom teachers with the skills and dispositions to conduct disciplined inquiries into their own practice; they are also deeply knowledgeable about their subject matter and the principles of its pedagogy. The admonition that researchers must be well versed in the substance of the subject matters whose pedagogy they study is not limited to university personnel. If teacher researchers wish to pursue investigations of the psychology and/or pedagogy of particular school subjects, they will need the kind of substantive sophistication displayed by Lampert. Equally important, Lampert and her colleagues have solid grounding in the canons of disciplined inquiry and its documentation. The legitimacy of being "insiders" and speaking with the "teacher's voice" does not, in itself, establish a warrant for the claims of teacher research.

Teachers as Collaborators and Investigators

The work of Lampert and her colleagues is likely to signal the entry of many more teachers into the world of school-based research. Once we privilege the natural classroom and school site as a proper setting for research on the psychology of school subjects and proceed to relax our methodological orthodoxies and offer legitimacy to such forms of inquiry as case studies and investigations of one's own practice, we invite classroom teachers to join us as investigators. Interestingly, John Dewey argued that the teachers in the Laboratory School should be co-investigators with the professors and graduate students. When Lagemann (1988) characterized the relationship that Dewey and his close colleague George Herbert Mead had with the remarkable Jane Addams, she observed that Addams's "most characteristic medium was the anecdote and . . . [Dewey and Mead's] was the theoretical hypothesis" (p. 195). Narrative may be a much more natural form of discourse for schoolteachers than are the more paradigmatic forms favored by social scientists. The new language of a collaborative form of inquiry may well evolve into a kind of narrative-paradigmatic pidgin.

However, there is always a danger that any study undertaken by a practitioner is treated with deference and any investigation pursued by an outside investigator is greeted with suspicion. The "worry over warrant" should never wane (Phillips, 1986). The identity, role, experience, and skill of the investigator is an important aspect of a work's validity, especially in those research methods (such as ethnography) in which separation of the method from the investigator is difficult. Nevertheless, judgments of validity can never be reduced to reading the resumé of the investigator, whether in teacher research or in any other form of inquiry.

If teacher research represents one new strategy of educational inquiry, another is the development of "design experiments." These strategies can be seen as attempts to wed the systematic design and intervention impulses of the classical experiment with the natural classroom-based adaptiveness of real teachers teaching real children.

Design Experiments

Alan Collins (1992) and Ann Brown (1992) have begun to advocate a new form of theory-oriented action research in classrooms that they call "design experiments." These are curriculum-specific interventions in classrooms that are theoretically driven, collaboratively designed and progressively adapted with classroom teachers, and documented and assessed via combinations of quantitative and qualitative methods (conjunctions of ethnography and measurement); such interventions willfully confound multiple independent variables in ways that would make most traditional methodologists blanch. Consistent with Dewey's principles, they are both experimental and naturalistic. If it is necessary to work within a natural classroom learning environment to study real school learning in a generalizable manner, then we may have no choice but to pursue much of educational research in such settings. Brown insists that there remain good reasons to explore some psychological processes under more pristine and controlled laboratory conditions, and I certainly have no cause to disagree. The alternation between natural sites and highly controlled settings may characterize the future dance steps of educational research. And the other needed form of flexibility may well be a methodological versatility that will include much more vigorous uses of field research methods and case studies in the pursuit of understanding. Along with their design characteristics, another feature of these approaches is the frequency with which the investigators either do their own teaching or, more frequently, collaborate actively and interactively with classroom teachers, who participate as partners in both the design and adaptation of the interventions studied.

Design experiments in natural settings conducted collaboratively with practitioners produce a set of research methods unimagined by the educational researcher of the 1940s and 1950s, not to mention a set of approaches that makes many contemporary educational researchers profoundly uncomfortable. Pretest and posttest measures are regularly used (along with midcourse monitoring) to establish the direction and degree of changes in students' knowledge, understandings, and attitudes. These measures include multiple-choice examinations, essays, project reports, and analyses of discourse during lessons. Ethnographers, videographers, and discourse analysts collect data in many forms to document the patterns of interaction and engagement, of self-regulation and conversation, characteristic of teachers and students in the classroom under different circumstances. Teacher journals are compared with the participant observer's notes, and student portfolios provide evidence of how the students made sense of the instruction. The control group, that most ubiquitous of signs that the "scientific method" is in use, typically disappears in a design experiment. Since this is not an experiment in which a single variable is manipulated while all else remains constant, it is unclear what one would control. An entire program or curriculum is the treatment, and that treatment is redesigned and adapted as needed. The logic of the classic control group thus becomes moot. Control must be introduced, needless to say, but through systematic documentation and frequent, precise measurement.

In addition to serving as a manifestation of Dewey's conception of educational research that is both experimental and naturalistic, the design experiment also represents an attempt to bridge the gap between new versions of the "two disciplines" of educational scholarship. If, in Cronbach's day, the tension was between the interventionism of experimentation and the naturalism of correlation, both of which are quantitative forms of psychological inquiry usually carried out under laboratory or carefully instrumented conditions, the contemporary tension might be characterized as one between the classroom-based experimental program and the naturalistic documentation and analysis of classroom life. That is, the two disciplines of today could be viewed as broad-scale, systematic, classroom-based experimentation on the one hand and rich, ethnographic descriptions and analyses of classroom life on the other hand. A design experiment is typically a marriage of experiment and ethnography, of adaptive experimentation and thick ethnographic description.

Choosing Among Methods

For many years, the most frequently used educational research methods, and therefore those with the greatest legitimacy, have been the quantitative methods of experimental, correlational, quasi-experimental, and survey research. Their disciplinary roots are in agriculture, genetics and other studies of heredity, psychology, and actuarial studies of life expectancies conducted two centuries ago in the service of insurance companies. They not only share fairly long traditions in education but also carry with them the prestige of quantifiable precision. Through the application of modern statistical methods, researchers can more precisely estimate the likelihood and size of errors in estimates of the state of nature than is usually possible in approaches deriving from anthropology, history, the arts, or philosophy. Should we tend to use the more traditional methods because we understand them better and they have a longer track record? John Stuart Mill argued:

> If there are some subjects on which the results obtained have finally received the unanimous assent of all who have attended to the proof, and others which . . . have never succeeded in establishing any considerable body of truths, so as to be beyond denial or doubt; it is by generalizing the methods successfully followed by the former enquiries and adapting them to the latter, that we may hope to remove this blot on the face of science.

Yet, an equally brilliant British philosopher of the next century, Alfred North Whitehead, was far less certain that well-developed and understood methods were always likely to be superior. He observed: "Some of the major disasters of mankind have been produced by the narrowness of men with a good methodology . . . to set limits to speculation is treason to the future."

If we are not always well advised to choose the methods that have been used the longest and that we understand best, what of choosing methods on the grounds of precision, on the grounds that some methods provide us a much better base for knowing exactly how much we know and how much is likely to be error? Here again, we are advised to focus first on our problem and its characteristics before we rush to select the appropriate method. We can again hark back to Aristotle, who made this famous point about precision in *Ethics*:

> Our discussion will be adequate if it has as much clearness as the subject matter admits of, for precision is not to be sought for alike in all discussions, any more than in all the products of crafts. . . . For it is the mark of an educated man to look for precision in each class of things just so far as the nature of the subject admits; it is evidently equally foolish to accept probable reasoning from a mathematician and to demand from a rhetorician scientific proofs. (1947b, pp. 309–310)

We must avoid becoming educational researchers slavishly committed to a particular method. The image of the little boy who has just received a hammer for a birthday present and suddenly finds that the entire world looks to him like a variety of nails is too painfully familiar to be tolerated. We must first understand our problem and decide what questions we are asking, and then we must select the mode of disciplined inquiry most appropriate to those questions. If the proper methods are highly quantitative and objective, fine. If they are more subjective or qualitative, we can use them responsibly as well.

The anthropologist Geertz (1973) probably put it best:

> I have never been impressed by the argument that, as complete objectivity is impossible in these matters (as, of course, it is) one might as well let one's sentiments run loose. As Robert Solow has remarked, that is like saying that as a perfectly aseptic environment is impossible, one might as well conduct surgery in a sewer. (p. 30)

Geertz also observed, as cited in Wolcott's discussion of ethnographic research method in this volume, "You don't have to know everything to understand something."

Summary

I shall now summarize the important points I have tried to make in this introductory discussion of research methodology. What distinguishes research from other forms of human discourse is the application of research methods. When we conduct educational research, we make the claim that there is method to our madness. Educational research methods are forms of disciplined inquiry. They are disciplined in that they follow sets of rules and principles for pursuing investigations. They are also disciplined in another sense. They have emerged from underlying social or natural science disciplines that have well-developed canons of discovery and verification for making and testing truth claims in their fields. Education itself is not a single discipline but, rather, a field of study on which we bring to bear the various forms of disciplined inquiry discussed here.

Each of these forms of inquiry asks different questions. I have tried to illustrate some of the questions characteristic of several forms of educational research methodology. I also have tried to indicate the ways in which the selection of research method is frequently related to theoretical or ideological commitments of the investigator (for a particularly instructive example of this principle in the history of education, see Tyack, 1976). (Parenthetically, the possibilities of doing certain kinds of social research change as the political and social mood of a society evolves. For example, the notion of randomly assigning individuals to contrasting experimental treatment groups may seem far less acceptable a research strategy in these days of legislation requiring informed consent and protection of human subjects. Can we continue to practice experimental social and educational research and still abide by the law of the land that requires informed consent of all participants in research?)

Finally, each of the examples of research methodology discussed must in some fashion deal with questions of precision and generalizability, although the standards and criteria will vary from one form of disciplined inquiry to another.

The neophyte educational researcher, when confronted with this imposing array of alternative research methodologies, may be tempted to throw up his or her hands in despair and say, "What can I possibly do to become competent in this field?" I can suggest several answers. First, attempt to become skilled and experienced in at least two forms of research methodology. Facility in only one strikes me as somewhat dangerous, the equivalent of a methodological "Johnny One-Note." Second, be fully aware of the full, rich variety of methods that constitute the family of disciplined inquiry in educational research. Recognize that the most effective programs of educational research are likely to be characterized by what Merton (1975), the distinguished sociologist, and Schwab (1969), the eminent philosopher of education, have called applications of "disciplined eclectic." The best research programs will reflect intelligent deployment of a diversity of research methods applied to their appropriate research questions. Finally, do not limit your education to methodology alone; only by combining substantive knowledge and methodological competence will you become a well-rounded, effective educational researcher. Here, once again, an insight of Aristotle's is relevant.

> Now each man judges well the things he knows, and of these he is a good judge. And so the man who has been educated in a subject is a good judge of that subject, and the man who has received an all-round education is a good judge in general. (1947b, p. 310)

Selection of appropriate methods is an act of judgment that may be undertaken privately but must be justified and explained publicly.

Epilogue: Method Revisited

Ernest Boyer made a simple claim in his influential monograph *Scholarship Reconsidered*. He stated that the work of the scholar "becomes consequential only as it is understood by others" (p. 23). While Boyer placed that sentence thoughtfully and strategically in his introduction to the notion of the scholarship of teaching, clearly the claim applies equally well to all forms of scholarship. That is, scholarship in all of its forms becomes consequential only as it is understood by others—others who are engaged in related processes of discovery, invention, and investigation—and thus it becomes consequential as it stimulates, builds upon, critiques, or otherwise contributes to any community of scholars who depend on one another's discoveries, critical reviews, and inventive applications to move the work of the field ahead.

In that connection, it may be useful to recall that the root meaning of the word *method* did not originally refer to a technique for collecting or analyzing data. The "method" used by scholars was traditionally the form of argument, the chain of reasoning in which they organized their premises, their evidence, and their logical moves to create a cogent, persuasive argument that would enlighten their students and peers. Thus, a scholar's method referred to the manner in which he or she organized and taught what was discovered to others. Even today, although we ordinarily distinguish clearly between methods of teaching and methods of research, both are based on the same underlying notion: the organization and application of a coherent, well-reasoned, and persuasive argument that can enlighten and shape the understandings of others. One's method combines the ways one organizes one's ideas, the cogency with which one presents them in a reasoned argument, and the routines one uses to conduct one's disciplined inquiries. To understand research methods properly, therefore, we must understand the function of method within the larger operation of scholarly work and scholarly communities. In the final analysis, a shared sense of research method holds a scholarly community together and permits it to operate communally and collaboratively.

The Community of Scholars and Scholarship as Community Property

To engage in the processes of inquiry, to become a scholar of and in education, is not only to take on the mantle of method and the rigor of discipline. It entails becoming an active member of a community of scholars and a community of educators. We must pursue and publish our research in ways that reflect the moral obligations of community membership. These obligations are entailed when we recognize that this is a community whose members are interdependent; each of us depends on the trust we can place in the work of other members of the community, because an intellectual and scholarly community rests on the assumption that its members can build on each other's work. We offer our findings, our new knowledge, to one another as community property. (Think of the trust we place in the purity of the food we eat, the preparation and training of the pilots in whose planes we fly, or the physicians in whose hands we entrust our bodies.)

It is no accident that the most grievous sins that a scholar can commit are not the sins of intellectual error. That is, if you do a piece of research and report your findings honestly in a manner consistent with the technical and ethical standards of "method," and subsequently other scholars conclude that your argument was flawed or your data do not hold up, you remain an honorable and respected member of the scholarly community. You are like the judge on a lower court whose decision is reversed by a higher one. All good scholars can point to examples of their own published papers whose claims did not hold up over time because of the critical scrutiny of their research community. Indeed, that is the way the system is designed to work.

The unforgivable sins, however, are plagiarism, appropriating the work of others without attribution, and fraud, the willful misrepresentation of one's data and methods. That is, if a researcher uses the words and work of another scholar (especially taking his or her very words verbatim) without acknowledgment of the source, he or she has committed an act of plagiary. So important is the trust we place in the care with which other scholars have conducted their studies and the accuracy with which they have reported their work that we have developed a system of citations, references, and bibliographic acknowledgments to document our use of their ideas and the extent to which we are building on their findings. Thus, if a scholar makes a claim and cites another scholar's work in conjunction with that claim, the presence of the reference is judged to strengthen the warrant of the claim.

If an investigator knowingly misrepresents findings or procedures of analysis, he or she is guilty of fraud. If a researcher reports having conducted an analysis following certain rules or principles, and it turns out that he or she did not, that scholar has violated so fundamental a tenet of the scholarly community that he or she risks severe public censure or even expulsion by its members. Simply put, no individual scholar working alone can possibly discover or integrate the knowledge he or she needs. We depend on the trust we can place on the methodological integrity of our peers to support and advance one another's work.

How is knowledge as community property different from other forms of property? For scholars, research is community property because it can be used again and again in the building and rebuilding of knowledge. The same findings, the same cases, the same criticisms and analyses can be used in the construction of many arguments and chains of narrative. A work of research does not get used up. It is not like a brick, a board, or any other piece of normal building material. If anything, a piece of research becomes more robust and sturdy the more often it is used by its author and by others to support new arguments and to undergird new claims.

So, what is the most fundamental obligation of the disciplined inquirer, the responsibility from which all of the canons of method derive? I will never forget a conversation I had with my former teacher, Benjamin Bloom of the University of Chicago, while serving as his research assistant. He had just conducted an unconventional (to my youthful eyes) statistical analysis on a set of data we had discovered in a 60-year-old archival source. "Are you permitted to do that?" I asked suspiciously. Bloom smiled at me indulgently and replied, "You are permitted to do anything you please as long as you honestly and completely report what you did, how you did it, and your reasons for doing it so that your colleagues are fully informed. They are then in a position to judge whether or not they are prepared to accept the warrant for your claims and to be persuaded by your findings." As the physicist Percy Bridgeman once asserted (doubtless having heard these lines from his own teachers), "Scientific method is doing one's damnedest with one's mind, no holds barred." As long, I would add, as you fully reveal to your readers exactly which "holds" you employed.

Every researcher must ask of his or her investigation, "What is this a case of?" whether the study is a design experiment, a school-reform ethnography, a classical regression analysis, or a singular piece of teacher research. The claim to generalizability for any study, whether to a population of persons or of situations, must be established through exhaustive reporting of one's settings, data, and methods, along with a carefully reasoned argument. Most often, the argument must be rooted in a combination of theory and careful documentation of conditions. Technique alone can never warrant generalizability.

The well-known adage "publish or perish" is typically understood as a commentary on the academic profession and its vicissitudes. It has a deeper meaning, however. Scholars must recognize that their obligation is not only to learn but to teach. If scholars do not publish important discoveries, integrations, or applications for their peers, their ideas will perish, their insights will wither and die.

Research Methods and Their Disciplines

Taken together, the observations I have made lead to the conclusion that the research methods of education have undergone a radical change in recent years. There has been a decided qualitative turn reflecting the influence of cognitive science, anthropology, the arts, and linguistics. Interpretive, aesthetic, and hermeneutic approaches have become more widespread. This turn has been further amplified by an interest in everyday school and classroom life as a basis for both disciplinary and interdisciplinary investigation. Nevertheless, formal experiments and the increasingly inventive methods of inferential statistics remain quite central to our enterprise, and appropriately so. In fact, the norm for educational research has become an eclectic combining of approaches that were once considered noncommensurable. Design experiments are a lovely example of that combination.

A variety of methods comprise educational research: historical, philosophical, case studies, ethnographic field studies, hermeneutics, experiments, quasi-experiments, aesthetic criticisms, surveys. Each is demanding and rigorous and follows disciplined rules or procedures. Taken together, these approaches build a methodological mosaic that is the most exciting current field of applied social research: the study of education.

References

Aristotle. (1947a). De anima [On the soul]. In R. McKeon (Ed.), *Introduction to Aristotle* (pp. 135–245). New York: Modern Library.

Aristotle. (1947b). Nicomachean ethics. In R. McKeon (Ed.), *Introduction to Aristotle* (pp. 308–543). New York: Modern Library.

Boyer, E. L. (1990). *Scholarship reconsidered: Priorities of the professoriate*. Princeton, NJ: The Carnegie Foundation for the Advancement of Teaching.

Brown, A. L. (1992). Design experiments: Theoretical and methodological challenges in creating complex interventions in classroom settings. *Journal of the Learning Sciences, 2*(2), 141–178.

Cochran-Smith, M., & Lytle, S. L. (1993). *Inside-outside: Teacher research and knowledge.* New York: Teachers College Press.

Collins, A. (1992). Toward a design science of education. In E. Scanlon & T. O'Shea (Eds.), *New Directions in Educational Technology.* New York: Springer.

Cornfield, J., & Tukey, J. W. (1956). Average values of mean squares in factorials. *Annals of Mathematical Statistics, 27*, 907–959.

Cremin, L. A. (1961). *The transformation of the school.* New York: Vintage Books.

Cronbach, L. J. (1957). The two disciplines of scientific psychology. *American Psychologist, 12*, 671–684.

Cronbach, L. J., & Suppes, P. (Eds.). (1969). *Research for tomorrow's schools: Disciplined inquiry for education.* New York: Macmillan.

Ebbinghaus, H. (1913). *Memory: A contribution to experimental psychology.* New York: Teachers College Press. (Original work published 1883)

Geertz, C. (1973). Thick description. In C. Geertz (Ed.), *The interpretation of cultures* (pp. 3–30). New York: Basic Books.

Lagemann, E. (1988). The plural worlds of educational research. *History of Education Quarterly, 29*(2), 184–214.

Merton, R. K. (1975). Structural analysis in sociology. In P. Blau (Ed.), *Approaches to the study of social structure.* New York: Free Press.

Phillips, D. C. (1987). Validity in qualitative research: Why the worry about warrant will not wane. *Education and Urban Society, 20*(1), 9–24.

Schwab, J. J. (1969). The practical: A language for curriculum. *School Review, 78*, 1–23.

Tyack, D. (1976). Ways of seeing: An essay on the history of compulsory schooling. *Harvard Educational Review, 46*, 355–389.

Suggestions for Further Reading

Following are some suggested readings on research methods and the impact of disciplined inquiry in education; each will broaden and deepen your insights on how research on education is conducted and how it shapes the field.

Cronbach, L. J., & Suppes, P. (Eds.). (1969). *Research for tomorrow's schools: Disciplined inquiry for education.* New York: MacMillan.   This is a report of a special committee of the National Academy of Education. It includes a detailed discussion of disciplined inquiry, a number of historical case studies of educational research programs, and a set of policy recommendations.

Denzin, N. K. (1978). *The research act: A theoretical introduction to sociological methods* (2nd ed.). New York: McGraw-Hill.   A sound introduction to the "qualitative" approaches to social research.

Erickson, F. (1986). Qualitative methods in research on teaching. In M.C. Wittrock (Ed.). *Handbook of research on teaching.* New York: MacMillan, pp. 119–161.

Geertz, C. (1973). Thick description. In C. Geertz, *The interpretation of cultures.* New York: Basic Books.   A most eloquent and influential account of the sorts of description practiced by the cultural anthropologist.

Kerlinger, F. N. (1973). *Foundations of behavioral research* (2nd ed.). New York: Holt, Rinehart and Winston.   A now-classic statement of the rationale and methods for quantitative studies in the social sciences and education.

Schwab, J. J. (1979). *Science, curriculum & liberal education.* Chicago: University of Chicago Press.   In this volume of collected papers, Schwab's essays "What do scientists do?" and his series of three contributions on "The practical" are most germane to the present topics.

Suppes, P. (Ed.). (1978). *Impact of research on education: Some case studies.* Washington, DC: National Academy of Education.   A set of historical case studies involving areas as diverse as vocabulary and word-frequency research, intelligence testing, and the influences of Freud, Skinner, and Piaget. A paperback edition of the case study summaries is also available.

Study Questions

1. Think of a specific example of controversy involving competing claims for educational approaches, e.g., the fairness of intelligence tests, admissions standards for professional schools, free schools vs. traditional education, modern math vs. traditional math, etc. How would you study the problem in a *disciplined inquiry?* What examples of non-disciplined inquiry can you recall or construct as applied to that same problem?

2. How would you apply each of the methods described in this paper to (a) reading research, and (b) other fields of study in education?

3. Outline a program of research on reading that effectively *combines* several of the methods described in this chapter as distinct alternatives, e.g., experimental, correlational, case study, historical.

4. In your own words, what does it mean to generalize from a sample of individuals to some larger population? From a particular research task to a larger domain of tasks? Give an example of each in the following areas of research: ability testing, effectiveness of instructional methods, and development of computational skills.

5. "Some of the major disasters of mankind have been produced by the narrowness of men with a good methodology." What do you think Whitehead meant by that observation? Do you agree? Can you think of any examples? What can we do to prevent the disasters attributable to narrowness about methodology, however good?

6. What are the principal features that distinguish disciplined inquiry methods from other ways of asserting truth or plausibility?

7. Two types of generalizability are discussed in this paper—generalizing from a sample of persons to a population of persons, and generalizing from a research context to a population of contexts. Do these two types of generalizability present problems of similar difficulty? In the methods of inquiry familiar to you, do researchers handle these two types of generalizability similarly?

8. Quantitative and qualitative inquiry methods are obviously distinguished by their relative emphasis on numerical data. Is this the principal difference between them? What other features distinguish quantitative from qualitative modes of inquiry?

9. If you had a specific research problem in mind, what factors would you consider in choosing a method of disciplined inquiry to apply to the problem? If you had a general area of research in mind, but not a specific problem, do you think that choice of an inquiry method would influence your selection of a research problem? Why or why not?

10. You are advised in this paper to "become familiar with more than one method of disciplined inquiry." Why is this a good suggestion? What might you gain from becoming skilled in several methods? What might you lose if you have skills in only one method?

Reading

Introduction
Ways of Seeing, Ways of Knowing

Lee S. Shulman

Ways of Seeing is a paper that must be read at several levels, for it carries multiple messages. It is, first, an essay on the history of compulsory schooling in America. But it is an uncommon essay, for it does not array its data in accordance with a single explanation for the phenomena described. Indeed, it is not only a piece of history, but an essay in historiography, that branch of knowledge that deals with the methods of historical investigation and inference. In it, Tyack attempts to make transparent the most important stage of historical research, which is not the collection of evidence but the offering of explanation. Historical facts become historical evidence only when placed in a framework of explanation, a way of seeing without which facts are mute, incapable of "speaking for themselves."

This aspect of Tyack's essay makes it the ideal companion for our opening paper, "Disciplines of Inquiry in Education." The messages are parallel, even congruent. Tyack argues for the insufficiency of any single perspective in providing explanations for historical data. Similarly, I state that educational research must necessarily draw upon multiple disciplinary perspectives in its efforts to understand and improve educational practice.

Why does historiography present such a lovely analog for the world of educational research *writ large*? History, more than most other disciplines, is a hybrid, a methodological home for a wide variety of approaches, techniques, and modes of inquiry. Among all the disciplines, it has resisted categorization. Some consider history part of the social sciences; others count it among the humanities. Some historians focus their efforts on the conflicts among nations; others attend to the domestic battles within a family or a particular school. Some historians count, measure, and analyze the resulting numbers; others describe, narrate, and interpret personal meanings. Most able historians do some of each, counting and describing, measuring and interpreting. We find in history, as we do in educational research, a methodological mosaic.

Tyack begins his essay with a telling quote from Kenneth Burke who observed that "a way of seeing is always a way of not seeing." He informs us that historians, like scholars in most other fields, typically make their reputations through adherence to a single line of argument. Nevertheless, he suggests, "it seems useful to entertain alternative modes of explanation as a way of avoiding the reductionism that selects evidence to fit a particular thesis. Using different lenses to view the same phenomenon may seem irresponsibly playful to a true believer in any one interpretation, but at least it offers the possibility of self-correction. . . ."

Tyack proceeds to illustrate his point with a presentation of the basic data on changes in compulsory attendance legislation in the United States during the 19th and 20th centuries and associated statistics on school attendance during those same periods. The "facts" are apparently clear. But what do they mean? Why did state after state pass such legislation? Why were more and more youngsters attending public schools? If the answer seems obvious to many of us (it certainly did to me before reading the essay), it is only because we have failed to consider alternative explanations.

Tyack then shows how at least five different kinds of explanation can be advanced to account for the phenomenon of compulsory schooling. They are not mutually exclusive, but they are certainly distinctive. Each accounts for the facts, more or less. None accounts for all. Each emerges from a different disciplinary or ideological framework. These frameworks call for contrasting definitions of the problem, of the units of analysis, and of the adequacy of an explanation.

Tyack's analysis thus calls our attention to the significance of both units of analysis and universe of discourse as essential elements in any attempt to use educational research as the basis for description, explanation, planning, or prediction. What should be described? What are the "natural units"?

It may be useful to think of an analogy from biology. One can argue that the natural starting point for biological inquiry and explanation is the individual cell, for it is the building block of all other forms of life or biological structures. To explain any biological phenomenon, therefore, should require that the biologist relate structures and functions to their underlying cellular components. To understand how living systems function, therefore, is to explain how cells aggregate to form organs, organ systems, and organisms. Thus biological explanation draws from below, from biochemistry, biophysics, and the like.

Alternatively, it can be asserted that the organism itself, that entity capable of independent existence and functioning—whether composed of one cell or millions—is the proper unit of analysis. Starting from the organism, one would then seek explanations of how individual organs function to enable the organism's activities, how they are organized into systems, and how equilibrium among and within those systems is maintained. Biological explanation would focus on asking how the parts of intact organisms are themselves organized into functioning wholes.

Finally, though by no means exhaustively, one could argue that neither cells nor organisms are adequate as units of inquiry, for each is no more than a part of an even larger natural whole, which is the community or ecosystem. It is as impossible to understand the workings of any individual organism independent of its ecosystem as it is impossible to define the functions of a cell independent of the organized system of organs to which it contributes.

In a similar fashion, Tyack notes on page 68, historians differ over the units of inquiry and the forms of explanation.

> Those arguing for the political construction of education emphasize the role of the state. . . .The ethnocultural interpretation posits religious-ethnic differences as a motive force. . . .The organizational synthesis stresses the role of the new middle class. . . .Human capital theorists focus on the family as a decision unit in calculating the costs and benefits. . . .Marxists see class struggle as the source of the dialectic that produces historical change. Each interpretation, in turn, directs attention to certain kinds of evidence which can confirm or disprove its assertions of causation. . . .
>
> The models deal with social reality on quite different levels: the individual or the family, the ethnocultural group, the large organization, and the structure of political or economic power in the society as a whole.

"Ways of Seeing" illustrates with great clarity the manner in which these alternative frameworks are brought to bear on a given body of data. While advocating the use of multiple perspectives by individual scholars, Tyack also warns against the dangers of unbridled eclecticism, in which every imaginable explanation is thrown together. Research in education requires judgment and selectivity grounded in broad understanding, certainly broader than can be provided by any single explanatory perspective. Ways of seeing are ways of knowing and of not knowing. And knowing well is knowing in more than a single way.

Ways of Seeing: An Essay on the History of Compulsory Schooling

DAVID B. TYACK
Stanford University

In this essay the author describes the rise of compulsory schooling in the United States and then views this phenomenon through five different explanatory models. The first two are largely political, revealing compulsory schooling as a form of political construction and as an outgrowth of ethnocultural conflict. Noting the rise of educational bureaucracies, the author next offers an organizational interpretation as a third way of viewing compulsory schooling. The last two models are largely economic: one depicts the growth in schooling as an investment in human capital, and the other, using a Marxian approach, shows compulsory schooling to be a means of reproducing the class structure of American society. In conclusion, Professor Tyack observes that alternative ways of seeing not only draw on different kinds of evidence, but also depict different levels of social reality and so aid us in gaining a wider and more accurate perception of the past.

I should warn you that what you are about to read is not a bulletproof, airtight, unsinkable monograph. It is an *essay* in the root sense of the word: a trial of some ideas. Kenneth Burke wrote that "a way of seeing is always a way of not seeing."[1] In our specialized age people are taught and paid to have tunnel vision—and such specialization has many benefits. Socialization within the academic disciplines focuses inquiry: economists explain events in economic terms, sociologists in sociological ways, psychologists by their own theories. Splintering even occurs within

---

[1] Kenneth Burke, *Permanence and Change* (New York: New Republic, 1935), p. 70.

Harvard Educational Review   Vol. 46   No. 3   August 1976

fields; Freudians and behaviorists, for example, see the world through quite different lenses.[2]

Historians tend to be eclectic more often than people in other disciplines, but they often make their reputations by developing a single line of argument. The frontier was the major shaping force in American history, Turner tells us. Status anxiety is the key to the progressive leaders, Hofstadter argues. Economic interests are the figure in the historical carpet, Beard claims. Other historians make their reputations by attacking Turner, Hofstadter, or Beard.[3] And so it goes.

Historiography normally is retrospective, telling us in what diverse ways scholars have explained events like the American Civil War. What I propose to do here is a kind of prospective historiography. I am impressed with the value of explicitly stated theories of interpretation but also struck by the value of discovering anomalies which any one theory does not explain. Thus, it seems useful to entertain alternative modes of explanation as a way of avoiding the reductionism that selects evidence to fit a particular thesis. Using different lenses to view the same phenomenon may seem irresponsibly playful to a true believer in any one interpretation, but at least it offers the possibility of self-correction without undue damage to an author's self-esteem.[4]

The topic of compulsory schooling lends itself to sharply different valuations, as the cartoons in figures 1 and 2 suggest. Earlier students of compulsion, like Forest Ensign and Ellwood Cubberley, regarded universal attendance as necessary for social progress and portrayed the passage and implementation of compulsory laws as the product of noble leaders playing their role in a long evolution of democracy.[5] Standing firmly on "the structure of civilization," as in figure 1, leaders used the mechanism of schooling to raise "American Social and Economic Life." In recent years radical critics have offered a quite different view of compulsory schooling. Figure 2 visually represents some of the elements of this revised interpretation. The school offers different and unequal treatments based on the race, sex, and class of incoming students. Compartmentalized internally, it produces a segmented labor force incapable of perceiving common interest. Rather than liberating the individual, the school programs him or her so as to guarantee the profits of the invisible rulers of the system. The school is thus an imposition that

[2] Everett C. Hughes, *Men and Their Work* (Glencoe, Ill.: Free Press, 1958).
[3] Herbert Bass, ed., *The State of American History* (Chicago: Quadrangle Books, 1970).
[4] Edward N. Saveth, ed., *American History and the Social Sciences* (New York: Free Press, 1964).
[5] Forest C. Ensign, *Compulsory School Attendance and Child Labor* (Iowa City, Iowa: Athens Press, 1921); Ellwood P. Cubberley, *Changing Conceptions of Education* (Boston: Houghton Mifflin, 1909).

FIGURE 1

Source: Edgar Mendenhall, *The City School Board Member and His Task* (Pittsburgh, Kans.: College Inn Books, 1929), frontispiece.

FIGURE 2

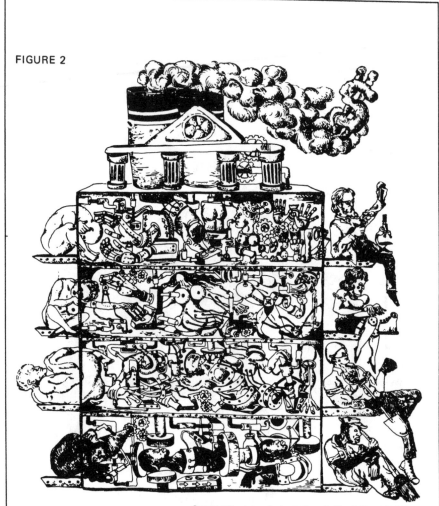

Source: Diane Lasch, *Leviathan*, 1, No. 3 (June 1969), 12.

dehumanizes the student and perpetuates social stratification.[6] Such differing valuations as these necessarily influence explanatory frameworks and policy discussion.

In this intentionally open-ended essay, I first sketch what I take to be the phe-

[6] A sampling of radical views can be found in writings of Paul Goodman, Ivan Illich, Michael Katz, and Samuel Bowles and Herbert Gintis (the last two are discussed below in the "Marxian Analysis" section).

nomena of compulsory schooling that the theories should explain. Then I examine two sets of interpretations, political and economic, which I find initially plausible. Some of the explanations are complementary, some contradictory; some explain certain events well but not others. Although each discussion is brief, I have tried to state the theories fairly, believing it not very useful to shoot down interpretations like ducks in a shooting gallery, only to bring out the *right* one (mine) at the end. But naturally I have interpretive preferences. Therefore, I intend to indicate what I see as flaws in the theories and anomalies they may not explain. In my conclusion, I do not attempt to reconcile the various interpretations in any definitive way, but instead suggest what we can learn from such comparative explorations.

What Needs to Be Explained?

At this point in my reading, I see two major phases in the history of compulsory school attendance in the United States. During the first, which lasted from mid-nineteenth century to about 1890, Americans built a broad base of elementary schooling which attracted ever-growing numbers of children. Most states passed compulsory-attendance legislation during these years, but generally these laws were unenforced and probably unenforceable. The notion of compulsion appears to have aroused ideological dispute at this time, but few persons paid serious attention to the organizational apparatus necessary to compel students into classrooms. Therefore, this phase might be called the *symbolic* stage. The second phase, beginning shortly before the turn of the twentieth century, might be called the *bureaucratic* stage. During this era of American education, school systems grew in size and complexity, new techniques of bureaucratic control emerged, ideological conflict over compulsion diminished, strong laws were passed, and school officials developed sophisticated techniques to bring truants into schools. By the 1920s and 1930s increasing numbers of states were requiring youth to attend high school, and by the 1950s secondary-school attendance had become so customary that school-leavers were routinely seen as "dropouts."[7]

Even before the common-school crusade of the mid-nineteenth century and before any compulsory laws, Americans were probably in the vanguard in literacy and mass schooling among the peoples of the world. Although methods of support and control of schools were heterogeneous in most communities before 1830, enrollment rates and literacy were very high—at least among whites. Public-school

---

[7] For a more detailed explication of this phasing, see my study *The One Best System: A History of American Urban Education* (Cambridge, Mass.: Harvard Univ. Press, 1974).

TABLE 1

Selected Educational Statistics for the United States, 1840–1890

	1840	1850	1860	1870	1880	1890
Enrollment rates of persons aged 5–19, in percentage (a)	37	42	49	60	58	64
Percentage of enrolled pupils attending daily (b)	–	–	–	59	62	64
Average length of school term, in days (b)	–	–	–	132	130	134
Percentage of population 10 years and older illiterate (c)	25–30	23	20	20	17	13

Sources: a) John K. Folger and Charles B. Nam, *Education of the American Population* (Washington, D.C.: GPO, 1967), chs. 1,4.

b) W. Vance Grant and C. George Lind, *Digest of Educational Statistics,* 1974 ed. (Washington, D.C.: GPO, 1975), p. 34.

c) Folger and Nam, *Education,* pp. 113-114.

advocates persuaded Americans to translate their generalized faith in education into support of a particular institution, the common school. Between 1850 and 1890 public expenditures for schools jumped from about $7 million to $147 million. Funds spent on public schools increased from 47 percent of total educational expenditures to 79 percent during those years.[8] Table 1 indicates both the high initial commitment to schooling and the gradual increase in attendance and decline in illiteracy.[9]

Educational statistics and data on literacy during the nineteenth century are notoriously unreliable, but table 1 at least suggests the magnitude of change. The aggregated national data, however, mask very important variations in attendance and literacy by region (the South lagged far behind the rest of the nation); by ethnicity (commonly forbidden to read under slavery, Blacks were about 90 percent illiterate in 1870; and foreign-born adult whites were considerably less liter-

[8] Albert Fishlow, "Levels of Nineteenth-Century Investment in Education," *Journal of Economic History,* 26 (1966), 418–24; Albert Fishlow, "The American Common School Revival: Fact or Fancy?" in *Industrialism in Two Systems: Essays in Honor of Alexander Gerschenkron,* ed. Henry Rosovsky (New York: Wiley, 1966), pp. 40–67.

[9] John K. Folger and Charles B. Nam, *Education of the American Population* (Washington, D.C.: GPO, 1967), chs. 1, 4; W. Vance Grant and C. George Lind, *Digest of Educational Statistics,* 1974 ed. (Washington, D.C.: GPO, 1975).

ate than native-born); and by other factors such as social class and urban or rural residence. Furthermore, the use of the broad age range of five to nineteen (common for both census and Office of Education statistics) hides variations in attendance at different age levels in different kinds of communities. In the industrial states, for example, children tended to start school earlier and to leave earlier than in farm states. In a census sample of both kinds of states, however, eight or nine out of ten children attended school from ten to fourteen. Finally, the percentages obscured the magnitude of the sevenfold absolute growth in enrollment from 1840 to 1890; in the latter year, over fourteen million children were in school. By the close of the nineteenth century the typical child could expect to attend school for five years, according to United States Commissioner of Education William T. Harris; Harris and many others regarded this as a triumph, and indeed by then the United States led the world in its provision for mass education.[10]

These changes in attendance and literacy before roughly 1890 took place with minimal coercion by the states—despite the fact that by then twenty-seven legislatures had passed compulsory-attendance laws. A survey in 1889 revealed that in all but a handful of states and individual cities the laws were dead letters. Indeed, in several cases state superintendents of education said that responsible local officials did not even know that there was such legislation.[11] Educators were often ambivalent about enforcement of compulsory-attendance laws. Often they did not want the unwilling pupils whom coercion would bring into classrooms. In many communities, especially big cities, schools did not have enough seats even for children who wanted to go to school. And many citizens regarded compulsion as an un-American invasion of parental rights. Except in a few states like Connecticut and Massachusetts, provisions for enforcement were quite inadequate.[12]

Phase two of the history of compulsory schooling, the bureaucratic stage, built on the base of achievement laid down during the symbolic stage. The basically simple structure of the common school became much more elaborate, however, and mass education came to encompass the secondary school as well, as indicated by table 2.

Public attitudes toward compulsory schooling appeared to become more positive in the years after 1890. This was true even in the South, which had previously

10 Folger and Nam, pp. 25, 3, 211–68; William T. Harris, "Elementary Education," in *Monographs on Education in the United States*, ed. Nicholas M. Butler (Albany, N.Y.: J. B. Lyon, 1900), pp. 79–139.

11 United States Commissioner of Education, "Compulsory Attendance Laws in the United States," *Report for 1888–1889*, I (Washington, D.C.: GPO, 1889), ch. 18, pp. 470–531.

12 Mary J. Herrick, *The Chicago Schools: A Social and Political History* (Beverly Hills, Calif.: Sage, 1971), p. 58; John D. Philbrick, *City School Systems in the United States*, U.S. Bureau of Education, Circular of Information, No. 1 (Washington, D.C.: GPO, 1885), pp. 154–55.

TABLE 2

Selected Educational Statistics for the United States, 1900–1950

	1900	1910	1920	1930	1940	1950
Enrollment rates of persons aged 5–19, in percentage (a)	72	74	78	82	84	83
Percentage of enrolled pupils attending daily (a)	69	72	75	83	87	89
Percentage of total enrollment in high schools (a)	3	5	10	17	26	23
High School graduates as percentage of population 17 years old (b)	6	9	17	29	51	59
Percentage of population 10 years and older illiterate (c)	11	8	6	4	3	3
Estimates of educational attainment, in years (d)	–	8.1	8.2	8.4	8.6	9.3

Sources: a) W. Vance Grant and C. George Lind, *Digest of Educational Statistics*, 1974 ed. (Washington, D.C.: GPO, 1975), p. 34.
b) United States Bureau of the Census, *Historical Statistics of the United States: Colonial Times to 1957* (Washington, D.C.: GPO, 1960), p. 207.
c) John K. Folger and Charles B. Nam, *Education of the American Population* (Washington, D.C.: GPO, 1967), p. 114.
d) Folger and Nam, *Education*, p. 132.

resisted such legislation. States passed new laws with provisions for effective enforcement, including requirements for censuses to determine how many children there were, attendance officers, elaborate "pupil accounting," and often state financing of schools in proportion to average daily attendance. Age limits were gradually extended upwards, especially under the impact of the labor surplus in the Depression, until by the mid-1930s youths were typically required to attend school until age sixteen.

Early in the century the great majority of teenagers in school were lumped in the upper grades of the elementary school as a result of the frequent practice of forcing children to repeat grades. In the 1920s and 1930s, however, the practice of "social promotion"—that is, keeping age groups together—took hold, and the percentage of teenagers in high schools increased sharply. The increasing numbers of children compelled to attend schools, in turn, helped to transform the structure and curriculum of schooling. Of course, there were still many children who escaped the net of the truant officer, many who were denied equality of educational opportunity: an estimated two million children aged six to fifteen were not in any school in 1940. But during the twentieth century universal elementary and secondary schooling gradually was accepted as a common goal and approached a common reality.[13]

Over the long perspective of the last century and a half, both phases of compulsory school attendance may be seen as part of significant shifts in the functions of families and the status of children and youth. Households in American industrial cities became more like units of consumption than of production. Indeed, Frank Musgrove contends that the passage of compulsory-school legislation in England "finally signalized the triumph of public over private influences as formative in social life and individual development; in particular, it tardily recognized the obsolescence of the educative family, its inadequacy in modern society in child care and training."[14] Advocates of compulsory schooling often argued that families—or at least some families, like those of the poor or foreign-born—were failing to carry out their traditional functions of moral and vocational training. Immigrant children in crowded cities, reformers complained, were leading disorderly lives, schooled by the street and their peers more than by Christian nurture in the home. Much of the drive for compulsory schooling reflected an animus against parents considered incompetent to train their children. Often combining fear of social unrest with humanitarian zeal, reformers used the powers of the state to intervene in families and to create alternative institutions of socialization.

Laws compelling school attendance were only part of an elaborate and massive transformation in the legal and social rules governing children.[15] Children and youth came to be seen as individuals with categorical needs: as patients requiring specialized medical care; as "delinquents" needing particular treatment in the courts; and as students deserving elaborately differentiated schooling. Specific adults came to be designated as responsible for aiding parents in the complex tasks of child care: teachers, truant officers, counselors, scout leaders, and pediatricians, for example—not to mention Captain Kangaroo. Formerly regarded as a central

13 United States Bureau of the Census, *Historical Statistics of the United States: Colonial Times to 1957* (Washington, D.C.: GPO, 1960), pp. 207, 215; John K. Norton and Eugene S. Lawler, *Unfinished Business in American Education: An Inventory of Public School Expenditures in the United States* (Washington, D.C.: American Council on Education, 1946); Newton Edwards, *Equal Educational Opportunity for Youth* (Washington, D.C.: American Council on Education, 1939), p. 152.

14 Frank Musgrove, "The Decline of the Educative Family," *Universities Quarterly*, 14 (1960), p. 377.

15 John W. Meyer and Joane P. Nagel, "The Changing Status of Childhood," paper presented at the Annual Meeting of the Society for the Study of Social Problems, San Francisco, Calif., 1975.

function of the family, education came finally to be regarded as synonymous with schooling. The common query "Why aren't you in school?" signified that attendance in school had become the normal career of the young.[16]

Political Dimensions of Compulsory Attendance

Only government can compel parents to send their children to school. In legally compelling school attendance, the democratic state not only coerces behavior but also legitimizes majority values, as Michael S. Katz has argued.[17] Thus, sooner or later, any historian investigating compulsory school attendance logically needs to attend to political processes.

In recent years, however, few historians of American education have paid close attention either to the politics of control of schools or to the nature of political socialization in schools. Echoing Horace Mann's concern for social cohesion as well as social justice, R. Freeman Butts has suggested that both radical historians (stressing imposition by economic elites) and "culturist" historians (broadening the definition of education to include all "habitats of knowledge") have somewhat neglected the political functions of public schooling in both national and international contexts—what he calls civism.[18] Such neglect did not characterize much of the earlier work in the history of education, which like writings in other branches of history, had a marked political and indeed nationalistic flavor. Among political sociologists, the emergence of new nations has also aroused interest in the political construction of education.

I begin, then, with an examination of a broad interpretive framework which stresses education as a means of incorporating people into a nation-state and legitimizing the status of "citizen" and "leader." After noting difficulties in relating these notions to the loosely organized political system of the United States, I proceed to a rather different form of analysis—namely, one which seeks to interpret the passage of compulsory-schooling laws as a species of ethnocultural conflict. This explanation appears to fit phase one far better than phase two. To interpret phase two I draw upon what one historian has called "the organizational synthesis," an approach that seeks to explain political and social changes during the progressive era in terms of the growing importance of large-scale bureaucratic organizations and the attempt to resolve political issues by administrative means.

[16] Robert H. Bremner, ed., *Children and Youth in America: A Documentary History*, I–II (Cambridge, Mass.: Harvard Univ. Press, 1970–71).
[17] Michael S. Katz, "The Concepts of Compulsory Education and Compulsory Schooling: A Philosophical Inquiry," Diss. Stanford Univ., Palo Alto, Calif., 1974.
[18] R. Freeman Butts, "Public Education and Political Community," *History of Education Quarterly*, 14 (1974), 165–83.

The Political Construction of Education

It is natural in the Watergate era to agree with Dr. Johnson that "patriotism is the last refuge of the scoundrel" and to suspect that nationalistic rhetoric about schooling disguises real motives. Yet I am struck by the range of ideology and class among persons in the United States who justified compulsory public education on explicitly political grounds. If the patriots were scoundrels, there were many of them in assorted walks of life. Moreover, nationalism has been associated with compulsory attendance not in the United States alone but also in European nations during the nineteenth century and in scores of developing nations today. In 1951 UNESCO sponsored a series of monographs on compulsory education around the globe; the organization assumed that all United Nations members agreed on "the general principle of the necessity of instituting systems of compulsory, free and universal education in all countries."[19]

How can one construe the political construction of education? Why does schooling seem so important to the modern state? In their essay, "Education and Political Development," John W. Meyer and Richard Rubinson have argued that modern national educational systems in effect create and legitimate citizens. New nations are commonly composed of families and individuals who identify with regions, religions, ethnic groups, tribes, or interest groups. Such persons rarely think of themselves as either participants in or subjects of the state. Indeed, the whole notion of universal citizenship might seem to them fanciful and implausible. Meyer and Rubinson argue that the central political purpose of universal education is precisely to create citizens and legitimize the state. Families in potentially divisive subgroups turn over their children to state schools to learn a common language, a national history, and an ideology that incorporates them as citizens into the broader entity called the state. The point is not that this new compulsory political socialization is actually successful in accomplishing its cognitive or affective tasks, but simply that the institutional process is designed to create a new category of personnel—citizens. Similarly, advanced education may create and legitimate elites. People who formerly ruled by hereditary right or other kinds of ascriptive privilege may still wield power, but the rituals of higher state education turn them into legitimate "civil servants." As states expand their control over new sectors of society, state schooling gives an apparently rational and modern justification for new social rules that replace the older ones based on regional, ethnic, religious, or family loyalties. By these means, education helps to institutionalize the authority of the state.[20]

[19] Australian National Commission for UNESCO, *Compulsory Education in Australia* (Paris: UNESCO, 1951), preface.

[20] John W. Meyer and Richard Rubinson, "Education and Political Development," in *Review of Research in Education*, III, ed. Fred Kerlinger (Itasca, Ill.: F. E. Peacock, 1975), 134–62.

It is a complicated argument. Let me illustrate with historical examples from American, French, and Prussian experience. After the American Revolution, numerous theorists like Thomas Jefferson, Benjamin Rush, and Noah Webster argued that without a transformed educational system the old pre-Revolutionary attitudes and relationships would prevail in the new nation. Rush said that a new, uniform state system should turn children into "republican machines." Webster called for an "Association of American Patriots for the Formation of an American Character," strove to promote uniformity of language, and wrote a "Federal Catechism" to teach republican principles to school children. Jefferson wanted to create state primary schools to make loyal citizens of the young. In addition, many early theorists wanted a national university to prepare and legitimate elites for leadership.[21] Similarly, French writers on education after the 1789 Revolution advocated a universal state system that would teach all French citizens to read and would give them pride in their country's history and political institutions. In both cases education was regarded as an instrument deliberately used to create a new status, to turn people with diverse loyalties into citizens of a new entity—the republican state.

The use of schooling as a means of incorporating people into the nation-state was not limited to liberal regimes, however. Compulsory schooling also served militant nationalism in conservative Prussia during the nineteenth century by attaching people to the centralized and corporate state. Victor Cousin observed in his report on Prussian education that the parental duty to send children to school "is so national, so rooted in all the legal and moral habits of the country, that it is expressed by a single word, *Schulpflichtigkeit* [school duty, or school obligation]. It corresponds to another word, similarly formed and similarly sanctioned by public opinion, *Dienstpflichtigkeit* [service obligation, that is military service]."[22]

To some degree the political construction of education I have sketched here does fit the development of compulsory schooling in the United States. As mentioned above, post-revolutionary writers on education stressed the need to use schools to transform colonials into citizens. Repeating their arguments, Horace Mann contended that common schools would imbue the rising generation with traits of character and loyalties required for self-government. Waves of immigration intensified concern over the incorporation of new groups into the polity. For a time the federal government took an active interest in schooling ex-slaves so that they,

[21] David Tyack, *Turning Points in American Educational History* (Waltham, Mass.: Blaisdell, 1967), pp. 83–119.

[22] Cousins, as quoted in Edward Reisner, *Nationalism and Education Since 1789: A Social and Political History of Modern Education* (New York: Macmillan, 1922), p. 134; ch. 2.

too, might become proper citizens like their foreign-born fellow compatriots.[23] The national government even used schooling as a way to shape people conquered in war into the predetermined mold of republican citizenship: witness the fate of Native American children torn from their parents and sent to boarding schools, the dispatch of American teachers to Puerto Rico and the Philippines after the Spanish-American war, and the attempts to democratize Germany and Japan after World War II.[24] Even the Japanese-Americans "relocated" during World War II were subjected to deliberate resocialization in the camps' public schools.[25]

Clearly, Americans had enormous faith in the power of schooling to transform all kinds of people—even "enemies"—into citizens. The process of entry into the status of citizenship was rather like baptism; like the sprinkling of water on the head of a child in an approved church, schooling was a ritual process that acquired political significance because people believed in it. Characteristically, Americans intensified their attempts at political socialization in schools whenever they perceived a weakening of loyalties (as in World War I), or an infusion of strangers (as in peak times of immigration), or a spreading of subversive ideas (whether by Jesuits or Wobblies or Communists). Interest in compulsory attendance seems to correlate well with such periods of concern.[26]

There are problems, however, with applying this conception of the political construction of education to the United States. The ideas of the revolutionary theorists were not put into practice in their lifetime, for example. One could argue that early Americans learned to be citizens by participating in public life rather than by schooling and indeed, that they had in effect been American "citizens" even before the Revolution. Before the common-school crusade, educational institutions tended to reflect differences of religion, ethnicity, and social class—precisely the sorts of competing loyalties presumably detrimental to national unification. Furthermore, in the federated network of local, state, and national governments, it was by no means clear what "the state" really was. Although many advocates of compulsion turned to Prussia for evidence on how the state could incorporate

23 William Edward Burghardt DuBois, *Black Reconstruction in America, an Essay toward a History of the Part which Black Folk Played in the Attempt to Reconstruct Democracy in America, 1860–1880* (Cleveland, Ohio: World Pub., 1964), pp. 637–69.

24 John Morgan Oates, *Schoolbooks and Krags: The United States Army in the Philippines, 1898–1902* (Westport, Conn.: Greenwood Press, 1973).

25 Charles Wollenberg, *All Deliberate Speed: Segregation and Exclusion in California Schools, 1855–1975* (Berkeley: Univ. of California Press, forthcoming), ch. 3.

26 Howard K. Beale, *A History of Freedom of Teaching in American Schools* (New York: Charles Scribner's Sons, 1941); John W. Meyer, "Theories of the Effects of Education on Civil Participation in Developing Societies," unpublished paper, Dept. of Sociology, Stanford Univ., Palo Alto, Calif., May 1972.

the young into schools for the public good, opposition to centralization of state power was strong throughout the nineteenth century. The ritualized patriotism of Fourth-of-July orations and school textbooks was popular, but actual attempts to coerce parents to send their children to school were often seen as un-American and no business of the state. Prussian concepts of duty to the state sharply contrasted with nineteenth-century American beliefs in individualism and laissez-faire government. Different groups in American society tended to express different points of view about using the state to reinforce certain values and to sanction others.[27] I will explore this point in the next section on ethnocultural politics.

During most of the nineteenth century, the apparatus of federal and state control of education was exceedingly weak. Although leaders from Horace Mann forward talked of the virtues of centralization and standardization in state systems, state departments of education were miniscule and had few powers. In 1890 the median size of state departments of education, including the superintendent, was two persons. At that time there was one state education official in the United States for every one hundred thousand pupils. One pedagogical czar with effective sanctions and rewards might have controlled such masses, but state departments of education prior to the turn of the twentieth century rarely had strong or even clear-cut powers.[28] Federal control was even weaker, although some reformers dreamed of massive federal aid and extended powers for the Office of Education. In effect, the United States Commissioner of Education was a glorified collector of statistics—and often ineffectual even in that role. An individual like Henry Barnard or William T. Harris might lend intellectual authority to the position, but the Office itself probably had trivial influence on American schools.[29] De facto, most control of schools lay with local school boards.

So the theory of the political construction of education is powerfully suggestive, but the American historical experience raises certain anomalies. Most Americans during the early national period apparently felt no need to legitimize citizenship through formal state schooling, although that idea began to take hold by mid-nineteenth century. Until the end of the century there was considerable opposition to centralized state power, both in theory and in practice. Thus it is difficult to envisage *the state* during either period as legitimizing individuals as citizens through education or effectively extending its jurisdiction into other parts of society like the family.

Much of this changed in the era beginning roughly in 1890, as the notion of the

[27] Merle Curti, *The Roots of American Loyalty* (New York: Columbia Univ. Press, 1946).

[28] Department of Superintendence, NEA, *Educational Leadership: Progress and Possibilities* (Washington, D.C.: NEA, 1933), p. 246, ch. 11.

[29] Donald Warren, *To Enforce Education: A History of the Founding Years of the United States Office of Education* (Detroit: Wayne State Univ. Press, 1974).

state as an agency of social and economic reform and control took hold and an "organizational revolution" began. Thus it seems useful to supplement the broad theory of the political construction of education with two other interpretations that give a more focused perspective on the two phases of compulsion.

Ethnocultural Politics in Compulsory-School Legislation during the Nineteenth Century

During the nineteenth century Americans differed significantly in their views of citizenship and the legitimate domain of state action, including compulsory-attendance legislation. A number of interpreters of the political contests of the period have argued that these cleavages followed ethnic and religious lines. In a perceptive essay on this ethnocultural school of interpretation, James Wright notes that these historians dissent from both the economic class-conflict model of Charles Beard and the consensus model that emerged after World War II. The ethnocultural historians, he says, do not argue

> . . . a simplistic model in which ward heelers appeal to ethnic, religious, or racial prejudices and loyalties in order to divert attention from "real" economic issues. Rather, the real issues of politics have been those most significant relative to life style and values: prohibition, public funding or control of sectarian schools, sabbatarian laws, woman suffrage, and efforts to hasten or retard ethnic assimilation.[30]

Richard Jensen points out that religious congregations, often divided along ethnic lines, were very important in shaping political attitudes and behavior in the Midwest. Such sectarian groups provided not only contrasting world views but also face-to-face communities that reinforced them. Like Paul Kleppner, Jensen has identified two primary religious persuasions that directly influenced political expression. One was represented by the *pietistic* sects—groups like the Baptists and Methodists that had experienced great growth as a result of the evangelical awakenings of the century—which tended to reject church hierarchy and ritual and insist that right belief should result in upright behavior. Seeing sin in the world, as represented by breaking the Sabbath or drinking alcohol, for example, the pietists sought to change society and thereby, as Kleppner explains, "to *conserve* their value system and to restore the norms it preserved." The *liturgicals*, by contrast, believed that salvation came from right belief and from the preservation of the particular orthodoxies represented in the creeds and sacraments of the church. Liturgicals like Roman Catholics and Lutherans of certain synods tended to see morality as the preserve not of the state but of the church, the family, and the

[30] James Wright, "The Ethnocultural Model of Voting: A Behavioral and Historical Critique," *American Behavioral Scientist*, 16 (1973), p. 655.

parochial school. According to both Kleppner and Jensen, the Republican Party tended to attract the pietists, the Democratic Party the liturgicals. By and large, the Republicans supported a "crusading moralism" for a single standard of behavior, while the Democrats spoke for a "counter-crusading pluralism."[31]

These politically important religious distinctions cut across ethnic lines. Although old-stock Americans tended to be pietistic and Republican, the Irish Catholics to be liturgical and Democratic, for example, other ethnic groups, like the Germans, split into different camps. *The* immigrant vote was a fiction based on nativistic fear; canny politicians knew better. Furthermore, this kind of status-group politics needs to be distinguished from the theory of the politics of status anxiety or status discrepancy that was advanced by political scientists and by Richard Hofstadter in the 1950s. Status groups asserting themselves through the political process during the nineteenth century rarely saw themselves on the skids socially. Rather than regarding ethnocultural politics as in some sense pathological, it is quite as accurate to describe it as the positive assertion of groups that believed in their own values and life styles and sought to extend their group boundaries and influence.[32]

The politics of "crusading moralism" and "counter-crusading pluralism" often focused on issues like temperance or Sabbath observance and frequently resulted in blue laws, which, like dead-letter compulsory-attendance legislation, were often more symbolic assertions than implementable decisions. Republican politicians often winked at breaches of the laws where it was politically astute to do so. It was one thing to enforce prohibition in a town where the only public drinker was the town Democrat, and quite another to do so in German wards of Milwaukee. Laws which stamped the pietistic foot and said "Be like me" might satisfy symbolically without alienating dissenters by active enforcement.[33]

Were nineteenth-century compulsory-school-attendance laws of that character largely passed by Republican pietists? I don't know, but the hypothesis seems worth testing by evidence; perhaps by the political composition of the state legislatures that passed such laws and by values expressed in textbooks. For now, the interpretation seems plausible. Evangelical ministers were at the forefront of the common-school crusade as the frontier moved westward, and ministers like Josiah Strong saw the school as a bulwark of the evangelical campaign to save the cities.

[31] Richard Jensen, *The Winning of the Midwest: Social and Political Conflict, 1888–1896* (Chicago: Univ. of Chicago Press, 1971), pp. 63–66, xv; Paul Kleppner, *The Cross of Culture: A Social Analysis of Midwestern Politics, 1850–1900* (New York: Free Press, 1970), pp. 71–74.

[32] John W. Meyer and James G. Roth, "A Reinterpretation of American Status Politics," *Pacific Sociological Review*, 13 (1970), 95–102; Joseph R. Gusfield, *Symbolic Crusade: Status Politics and the American Temperance Movement* (Urbana, Ill.: Univ. of Illinois Press, 1963), chs. 1, 6, 7.

[33] Jensen, p. 122.

Public schooling was widely publicized as the creation of "our Puritan, New England forefathers." Pietists saw themselves not as an interest group but as representatives of true American values. People who wanted compulsory-attendance laws were presumably already sending their children to school; by branding the nonconforming parent as illegal or deviant, they thereby strengthened the norms of their own group (the explanation follows what can be called the tongue-clucking theory of the function of crime).[34]

Much of the rhetoric of compulsory schooling lends itself to this ethnocultural interpretation and further refines the theory of the political construction of education. In 1891 superintendents in the National Education Association (NEA) passed a resolution favoring compulsory education. The resolution's preamble stated that "in our free Republic the State is merely the expression of the people's will, and not an external governmental force." The NEA statement sounds quite different than the notion of a strong central state creating citizens through schooling, as in the view explored above. Why then, did the state have to compel citizens to send their children to school? Because compulsion created liberty.[35]

The assumptions behind this Orwellian paradox become more clear when one reads accounts of the discussions of compulsion which took place that year in the National Council of Education, the prestigious think tank of the NEA. A committee had just reported to the Council that the idle and vicious were filling the jails of the nation, corrupt men were getting the ballot, and "foreign influence has begun a system of colonization with a purpose of preserving foreign languages and traditions and proportionately of destroying distinctive Americanism. It has made alliance with religion. . . ." The committee was really saying that there were two classes of citizens, us and them. Said an educator in the audience: "The report assumes that when the people established this government they had a certain standard of intelligence and morality; and that an intelligent and moral people will conform to the requirements of good citizenship." Things have changed, he observed: "People have come here who are not entitled to freedom in the same sense as those who established this government." The question was whether to raise these inferior newcomers to the standards of the Anglo-Saxon forefathers or to "lower this idea of intelligence and morality to the standard of that class" of new immigrants from southern and eastern Europe. Republican liberty depended on a homogeneity of virtue and knowledge that only compulsion could create in

34 Timothy L. Smith, "Protestant Schooling and American Nationality," *Journal of American History*, 53 (1967), 679–95; David B. Tyack, "Onward Christian Soldiers: Religion in the American Common School," in *History and Education*, ed. Paul Nash (New York: Random House, 1970), pp. 212–55.

35 J. K. Richards, *Compulsory Education in Ohio: Brief for Defendent in Error in the Supreme Court of Ohio, Patrick F. Quigley v. The State of Ohio* (Columbus, Ohio: Westbote, 1892), p. 23.

the new generation. Almost without exception native-born and Protestant, NEA leaders in the nineteenth century took naturally to the notion that real citizens were those who fit the pietist mold.[36]

In 1871, in a speech on the "New Departure of the Republican Party," Republican Senator Henry Wilson linked compulsory schooling to nativist and Protestant principles. Pointing out that the Fifteenth Amendment had expanded suffrage to include Blacks and that unrestricted immigration was flooding the nation with millions "from Europe with all the disqualifications of their early training," he argued for an educational system that would transform "the emigrant, the freedman, and the operative" into proper citizens in accord with the "desirable traits of New England and the American character."[37] An editorial in the *Catholic World* promptly attacked Wilson for wanting compulsory schooling to mold all "into one homogeneous people, after what may be called the New England Evangelical type. Neither his politics nor his philanthropy can tolerate any diversity of ranks, conditions, race, belief, or worship."[38]

Evidence of ethnic and religious bias abounds in the arguments about compulsory schooling throughout the nineteenth century. In the 1920s bias surfaced again in Oregon when the Ku Klux Klan and its allies passed a law that sought to outlaw private schooling. Two compulsory-schooling laws in Illinois and in Wisconsin in 1889 aroused fierce opposition from liturgical groups, especially German Catholics and Lutherans, because of their provisions that private schools teach in the English language and that they be approved by boards of public education. In both states Democrats derided the laws as instances of Republican paternalism and hostility to pluralism; defeated Republicans learned to disavow spokesmen who believed that extremism in defense of virtue is no vice. After the disastrous votes in 1892, one Republican wrote to a friend that "defeat was inevitable. The school law did it—a silly, sentimental and damned useless abstraction, foisted upon us by a self-righteous demagogue."[39] Both Kleppner and Jensen see these contests over compulsory instruction in English as classic examples of ethnocultural politics.[40]

These Illinois and Wisconsin conflicts may, however, be exceptional cases; other states passed similar laws requiring English-language instruction and state ac-

[36] National Education Association, *Journal of Addresses and Proceedings, 1891* (Topeka: Kansas Pub. House, 1891), pp. 295, 298, 393–403.
[37] Henry Wilson, "New Departure of the Republican Party," *Atlantic Monthly*, 27 (1871), 11–14.
[38] Editorial, *Catholic World*, 13 (1871), 3–4; John Whitney Evans, "Catholics and the Blair Education Bill," *Catholic Historical Review*, 46 (1960), 273–98.
[39] Jensen, pp. 122, 129.
[40] Kleppner, pp. 169–70.

creditation without such contests erupting. It is possible that there was bipartisan support for the ineffectual state laws passed before 1890 and that widespread belief in public education made consensus politics the wisest course. The South, which lagged in compulsory legislation, had few immigrants and few Catholics; its population was native-born and evangelical with a vengeance. How well does an ethno-cultural hypothesis fit the South? Is the educational politics of race substantially different from white ethnocultural politics? Only careful state-by-state analysis can test the theory that ethnocultural politics was a key factor in compulsory-attendance legislation during the nineteenth century. But where there is the smoke of ethnocultural rhetoric it is plausible to seek political fires.[41]

In any case, the high point of ethnocultural politics of compulsory education was probably the nineteenth century. The assumption persisted into the twentieth century that there were *real* citizens—those with the right heredity and principles —who needed to shape others to their own image. But at the turn of the century attention shifted to efficient organizational means for compelling school attendance.

From Politics to Administration:
An Organizational Interpretation

Despite some notable exceptions, open ethnocultural strife in school politics appears to have subsided during phase two of compulsory attendance. Many of the decisions that once had been made in the give-and-take of pluralistic politics now shifted to administrators within the system. At the turn of the century a powerful and largely successful movement centralized control of city schools in small boards of education elected at large rather than by ward. Furthermore, state departments of education grew in size and influence and led in the consolidation of rural schools and the enforcement of uniform educational standards. Advocates of these new forms of governance argued that education should be taken out of politics and that most decisions were best made by experts. Government by administrative experts was, of course, a form of politics under another name: decisions about who got what in the public allocation of scarce resources were simply shifted to a new arena. The line between public and private organizations became blurred as proponents of centralization urged that school systems adopt the corporate model of governance. As decision-making power shifted to superintendents and their staffs, the number of specialists and administrators ballooned. School systems grew in size, added tiers of officials, and became segmented into functional divisions:

[41] Horace Mann Bond has given us a brilliant analysis of how the politics of race mixed with the politics of competing economic groups in his *Negro Education in Alabama: A Study in Cotton and Steel* (Washington, D.C.: Associated Pub., 1939).

elementary, junior high, and high schools; vocational programs of several kinds; classes for the handicapped; counseling services; research and testing bureaus; and many other departments.[42]

The new provisions for compulsory schooling reflected these bureaucratic technologies. In city schools, in particular, large attendance departments were divided into supervisors, field workers, and clerks. Attendance experts developed the school census, elaborate forms for reporting attendance, manuals on "child accounting," and civil-service requirements for employment. By 1911 attendance officers were numerous and self-conscious enough to start their own national professional organization. Schools developed not only new ways of finding children and getting them into school, but also new institutions or programs to cope with the unwilling students whom truant officers brought to their doors: parental schools, day-long truant schools, disciplinary classes, ungraded classes, and a host of specialized curricular tracks. Local officials gathered data by the file full to aid in planning a rational expansion and functional specialization of the schools. Doctoral dissertations and other "scientific" studies analyzed existing patterns of attendance and promoted the new methods.[43]

Surely one can find examples of these new techniques and institutional adaptations prior to phase two, but what I find striking is the very rapid increase in the machinery of compulsion and the structural differentiation of the schools in the years after 1890. A new method of inquiry called "educational science" helped educators to gather and process information so that they could not only describe quantitatively what was going on in schools, but also forecast and plan. In national organizations these new functional specialists shared ideas and strategies of change. Older local perspectives gradually gave way to more cosmopolitan ways of thinking. The new hierarchical, differentiated bureaucracies seemed to many to be a superb instrument for continuous adaptation of the schools to diverse social conditions and needs. Theoretically at least, issues of religion or ethnicity were irrelevant to decision making in such bureaucracies, as were parochial tastes or local prejudices.[44]

Samuel Hays sees the rise of large-scale organizations and functional groups as characteristic of many sectors of American society during the twentieth century. He points out that the new technical systems defined what were problems and used

[42] Marvin Lazerson, *Origins of the Urban Public School: Public Education in Massachusetts, 1870–1915* (Cambridge, Mass.: Harvard Univ. Press, 1971), chs. 5–9; Joseph M. Cronin, *The Control of Urban Schools: Perspectives on the Power of Educational Reformers* (New York: Free Press, 1973).

[43] Frank V. Bermejo, *The School Attendance Service in American Cities* (Menasha, Wis.: George Banta Pub., 1924).

[44] Tyack, *One Best System,* part 4.

particular means for solving them. "Reason, science, and technology are not inert processes by which men discover, communicate, and apply facts disinterestedly and without passion, but means through which, through systems, some men organize and control the lives of other men according to their particular conceptions as to what is preferable." He argues that the rapid growth of empirical inquiry—normally called "science"—has enabled people in organizations to plan future courses of action. This differentiates these new technical systems from earlier bureaucracies. Not only did these new methods change decision making within organizations, but functional specialists like educators, engineers, or doctors banded together in organizations to influence the larger environment collectively as interest groups.[45]

How does this vision of organizational change help explain the enactment and implementation of compulsory schooling? John Higham has observed that "the distinctive feature of the period from 1898 to 1918 is not the preeminence of democratic ideals or of bureaucratic techniques, but rather a fertile amalgamation of the two. An extraordinary quickening of ideology occurred in the very midst of a dazzling elaboration of technical systems."[46] Robert Wiebe, likewise, sees the essence of progressivism as "the ambition of the new middle class to fulfill its destiny through bureaucratic means."[47] Thus one might interpret the passage of child-labor legislation and effective compulsory-attendance laws as the work of functional groups and national reform associations that combined ideological commitment with bureaucratic sophistication. These groups knew how to create enforcement systems that would actually work, and they followed up on their results. Active in this way were such groups as educators (who increasingly came to the forefront in compulsory-schooling campaigns), labor unions, the National Child Labor Committee, and elite educational associations (like the Philadelphia Public Education Association) with cosmopolitan connections and outlooks.[48]

In his essay, "The Emerging Organizational Synthesis in Modern American History," Louis Galambos says that historians of this persuasion believe

> . . . that some of the most (if not the single most) important changes which have taken place in modern America have centered about a shift from small-scale, informal, locally or regionally oriented groups to large-scale, national, formal or-

[45] Samuel Hays, "The New Organizational Society," in *Building the Organizational Society: Essays on Associational Activity in Modern America,* ed. Jerry Israel (New York: Free Press, 1972), pp. 2–3, 6–8.

[46] John Higham, "Hanging Together: Divergent Unities in American History," *Journal of American History,* 61 (1974), p. 24.

[47] Robert Wiebe, *The Search for Order, 1877–1920* (New York: Hill & Wang, 1967), p. 166.

[48] Walter Trattner, *Crusade for the Children: A History of the National Child Labor Committee and Child Labor Reform in America* (Chicago: Quadrangle Books, 1970).

ganizations . . . characterized by a bureaucratic structure of authority. This shift in organization cuts across the traditional boundaries of political, economic, and social history.[49]

This interpretation has called attention to the fact that large-scale organizations deeply influence the lives of most Americans, and to a degree it has explained how. There is somewhat less agreement among historians as to *why* this shift has taken place or how to assess the human consequences. Most historians would agree that the rise of complex organizations relates in some fashion to new technology, new forms of empirical inquiry, and institutional innovations designed to cope with size and scope of functions. Economic historians like Thomas Cochran, Alfred Chandler, and Fritz Redlich have described how business firms changed from small, local enterprises (often owned and run by a single family) to vast and diversified multi-tier bureaucracies in order to cope with problems of growth of markets, complexity of production, and widening spans of control.[50] Raymond Callahan and others have shown how educational administrators consciously emulated these new business corporations.[51]

Although the new organizational approach in history may provide a useful focus for the study of compulsory attendance, especially in the years after 1890, the interpretation is not without flaws. It may not be sound to generalize urban experience to the educational system as a whole; bureaucratization was probably neither rapid nor systemic throughout American schools, but gradual and spreading from certain centers like drops of gas on water. The conceptualization of an organizational revolution is also somewhat rudimentary at this point, leading to the same dangers of misplaced concreteness one finds in the use of concepts like "modernization" and "urbanization." It is very important not to portray this kind of organizational change as an inevitable process. Some people helped to plan the changes and benefited from them, others did not; some results were intended, others were not. Schools are rarely so politically neutral as they portray themselves. One virtue of the economic interpretations to which we now turn is that they provide models of behavior that help to explain the interests or motivations of people who acted collectively in organizations.[52]

[49] Louis Galambos, "The Emerging Organizational Synthesis in Modern American History," *Business History Review*, 44 (1970), p. 280.

[50] Thomas C. Cochran, *Business in American Life: A History* (New York: McGraw-Hill, 1972), chs. 9, 16; Alfred D. Chandler, Jr., and Fritz Redlich, "Recent Developments in American Business Administration and Their Conceptualization," *Business History Review*, 35 (1961), 1–31.

[51] Raymond E. Callahan, *Education and the Cult of Efficiency* (Chicago: Univ. of Chicago Press, 1962).

[52] For some of these criticisms of the "organizational synthesis" I am indebted to Wayne Hobson's unpublished manuscript, "Social Change and the Organizational Society," Stanford Univ., Palo Alto, Calif., 1975.

Two Economic Interpretations of School Attendance

It is misleading, of course, to attempt to separate economic interpretations too sharply from political ones. In the three variants of political models sketched above, issues of economic class are present even where, as in ethnocultural conflict, they may not be salient. Both of the economic interpretations I examine also involve political action. Not surprisingly, however, economic historians tend to focus on economic variables, and it is useful to see how far this kind of analysis carries us in interpreting school attendance.

Two contrasting views seem most relevant: human-capital theory and a Marxian model. Both have precursors in nineteenth-century educational thought, but both have received closest scholarly attention during the last generation. Both are related to political interpretations in the broad sense in which Thomas Cochran says that the economic order shaped the political order: "On the fundamental level the goals and values of a business-oriented culture established the rules of the game: how men were expected to act, what they strove for, and what qualities or achievements were rewarded."[53] Naturally, economic interpretations may differ in what they take to be the basic driving forces in historical events, and such is the case in the two models I explore.

Human-Capital Theory and School Attendance

Mary Jean Bowman has described the notion of investment in human beings "as something of a revolution in economic thought." The notion of investigating the connection between resources spent on increasing the competence of workers and increased productivity and earnings was not entirely new, of course, but experience after World War II showed that "physical capital worked its miracles only in lands where there were many qualified men who knew how to use it (the Marshall Plan countries and Japan)." Economists interested in economic growth then began to analyze the effects of "human capital" on development and discovered that education appeared to have considerable explanatory power.[54]

Work on investment in human beings moved from general studies of the contribution of schooling to economic growth in whole societies to analyses of the rates of return of formal education to individuals. Economists treated the micro-decision making of individuals or families about schooling as a form of rational cost-benefit analysis. They developed increasingly sophisticated ways to estimate rates of return on investment in education by including not only the direct costs of schooling

53 Cochran, p. 304.

54 Mary Jean Bowman, "The Human Investment Revolution in Economic Thought," *Sociology of Education*, 39 (1966), 113, 117; Berry R. Chiswick, "Minimum Schooling Legislation and the Cross-Sectional Distribution of Income," *Economic Journal*, 315 (1969), 495–507.

but also the value of foregone earnings and the costs of maintaining students as dependents. Albert Fishlow, for example, has calculated that during the nineteenth century the "opportunity costs" paid by parents about equalled the sums paid by the public to support all levels of the educational system. Despite disagreements over specific rates of return, most economists agree that schooling does have significant impact on growth and earnings.[55]

Although economists have only recently honed the theory of human investment, similar notions have been current in educational circles for a long time. An idea circulating among educators for over a century has been that schooling created economic benefits for the society as a whole through greater productivity and for individuals through greater earnings. The first influential advocate of this view in the United States was Horace Mann, Secretary of the Board of Education of Massachusetts, who devoted his *Fifth Annual Report* in 1842 chiefly to this theme. In his report Mann presented an economic justification for greater investment in schooling, but his arguments were soon picked up as justification for compulsory school attendance. As Maris Vinovskis has observed, Mann actually preferred to advocate education by noneconomic arguments—the role of schools in moral or civic development, for example. But in his fifth year as Secretary, when his work was under political attack in the legislature and when a depression was forcing government to retrench, Mann decided that the time had come to show thrifty Yankees that education was a good investment. He argued that education not only produced good character and multiplied knowledge "but that it is also the most prolific parent of material riches." As proof he adduced the replies of businessmen to his questionnaire asking about the differences between educated and uneducated workers. What his study lacked in objectivity and scientific rigor it made up in evangelical enthusiasm; Mann concluded that money spent on primary schooling gave an aggregate rate of return to society of about 50 percent. He claimed that education enabled people to become rational decision makers by "comprehending the connections of a long train of events and seeing the end from the beginning." In addition to instilling this orientation toward the future—perhaps of most benefit to entrepreneurs—schooling made workers punctual, industrious, frugal, and too rational to cause trouble for their employers.[56]

Although Mann's evidence was largely impressionistic, his questionnaire highly biased, and his conclusions suspect for those reasons, his report was welcome ammunition to school reformers across the country. The New York legislature printed

[55] Bowman, 118-19; Fishlow, "Levels of Investment," p. 426; Marc Blaug, *An Introduction to the Economics of Education* (London: Penguin, 1972), chs. 1-3.
[56] Maris Vinovskis, "Horace Mann on the Economic Productivity of Education," *New England Quarterly*, 43 (1970), 562, 550-71.

and distributed eighteen thousand copies; Boston businessmen applauded him for proving that the common school was not only "a nursery of souls, but a mine of riches"; and a leading educator said in 1863 that Mann's report probably did "more than all other publications written within the past twenty-five years to convince capitalists of the value of elementary instruction as a means of increasing the value of labor."[57] In 1870 the United States Commissioner of Education surveyed employers and workingmen and reported results similar to those of Mann.[58] A committee of the United States Senate which took testimony on "the relations between labor and capital" in the mid-1880s found that businessmen and employees across the nation tended to agree that schooling increases the productivity and predictability of workers.[59] So fixed had this view become by the twentieth century—reflecting dozens of rate-of-return studies at the turn of the century—that a high school debaters' manual on compulsory schooling listed these as standard arguments for the affirmative:

> Education is the only guarantee of the prosperity of every individual in the State. Education will pay in dollars and cents.
> The education of the State and the wealth of the State bear a constant ratio, one increasing with the other.[60]

As human-capital theory has developed in recent years, economists have applied models of decision theory to the development of compulsory schooling in the nineteenth century. Generally they have focused upon individuals or their families and assumed that they make rational calculations of their presumed future benefits. For example, in their essay "Compulsory Schooling Legislation: An Economic Analysis of Law and Social Change in the Nineteenth Century," William Landes and Lewis Solmon adopted as their "theory of the determinants of schooling levels" the model that an individual "would maximize his wealth by investing in schooling until the marginal rate of return equaled marginal cost (expressed as an interest rate)."[61] They found that in 1880 there was a higher investment in schooling in states that had compulsory-attendance laws than in those that did not.

---

57 Vinovskis, p. 570.
58 United States Commissioner of Education, *Report for 1870* (Washington, D.C.: GPO, 1870), pp. 447–67.
59 United States Senate, *Report of the Committee of the Senate upon the Relations between Labor and Capital and Testimony Taken by the Committee* (Washington, D.C.: GPO, 1885), II, 789–90, 795–96, and IV, 504–5, 729–30.
60 John S. Patton, ed., "Selected Arguments, Bibliographies, Etc., for the Use of the Virginia High School and Athletic League," *University of Virginia Record, Extension Series,* I (1915), 103–104.
61 William Landes and Lewis Solmon, "Compulsory Schooling Legislation: An Economic Analysis of Law and Social Change in the Nineteenth Century," *Journal of Economic History,* 32 (1972), 58–59.

But by also examining levels of schooling in 1870, when only two states had laws, they discovered that the states which passed laws during the 1870s had already achieved high levels of investment in public education prior to enactment of compulsory legislation. They concluded that compulsory-education laws did not much influence the supply and demand curves and were

> . . . not the cause of the higher schooling levels observed in 1880 in states with laws. Instead, these laws appear merely to have formalized what was already an observed fact; namely, that the vast majority of school-age persons had already been obtaining a level of schooling equal to or greater than what was to be later specified by statute.[62]

In other words, the legislation merely applauded the decisions of families who had concluded that schooling paid off for their children. But this does not explain why parents had to be forced by law to send children to school. In another article, Solmon admits that variation in state support for schooling "might reflect politics rather than individual market decisions, but even these are worked out in the 'political market place' and presumably reflect the tastes of the 'typical' individual."[63]

Why, then, pass the laws? Landes and Solmon argue that on the demand side, educators wanted "legislation that compels persons to purchase their product" (the laws did appear to increase the number of days the schools were open); and law may have had external benefits "to members of the community since it is a way of giving formal recognition to the community's achievement in committing more resources to schooling."[64] With regard to supply, since schooling was already widely available and most parents were sending their children anyway, the cost of passing the laws was minimal in light of the presumed gains.

Albert Fishlow reaches similar conclusions in his study of investment in education during the nineteenth century. He notes a rapid rise of spending on human capital in the industrialized nations of the United States, England, France, and Germany. But in contrast with the key role of the central state in Europe, Fishlow says, American investment arose from a local consensus on the value of education: "Under such circumstances, the educational commitment was a matter of course from parents to children rather than from community to schools."[65] Most parents, he argues, made the calculation that education was worth the price, both in public outlays and in private opportunity costs. But there were some families that did

---

[62] Landes and Solmon, 77–78.

[63] Lewis Solmon, "Opportunity Costs and Models of Schooling in the Nineteenth Century," *Southern Economic Journal,* 37 (1970), 72.

[64] Landes and Solmon, pp. 87–88.

[65] Fishlow, "Levels of Investment," pp. 435–36.

not make this decision, and Fishlow argues that "the entire history of compulsory-schooling legislation and of child-labor legislation is usefully viewed as social intervention to prevent present opportunity costs from having weight in the educational decision."[66]

The actual opportunity costs differed sharply between rural and urban communities and between richer and poorer families. Schools in farm areas could adjust the academic calendar to match the need for child labor in agriculture, thus nearly eliminating the need to forego the earnings of children. In cities, by contrast, work opportunities were generally not seasonal, and compulsory attendance effectively barred children from adding substantially to family income. In addition, the poor did not have the same opportunity to invest in their children as did middle- and upper-income families, since they could not generally borrow capital against their children's presumed higher future income. Thus the very large private contribution to schooling through the opportunity costs was a source of major educational inequality—one recognized, incidentally, by truant officers, judges, and other officials who confronted the problems of compulsory attendance firsthand.[67]

How convincing is the human-investment paradigm in explaining the history of school attendance? On the surface it appears to require quite a stretch of the imagination to envisage families actually making the complex calculations of future benefit embodied in some of the models of economists. But, as Mary Jean Bowman writes, "the economist is not concerned, as is the psychologist, with explaining individual behavior per se. If people behave *as if* they were economically rational, that is quite enough, provided we are dealing with multiple decision units."[68] The decision-making model is of course a conscious simplification, omitting factors of public welfare or intrinsic pleasure that probably do affect choice. If one defines as voluntary that school attendance which is unconstrained by law (in the absence of law, or beyond legally required years, or in communities where laws were unpublicized or unenforced), it does appear that voluntary attendance was influenced in part by the prospect of future economic advantage, for families always had competing demands on their incomes. And the evidence is quite convincing that compulsory laws were passed in states where most citizens were already investing in schooling up to the point required by law. A powerful recurring argument for compulsion was that taxpayers could realize the full return on their large investment only if free schooling reached all the children; the presumption was that children who were out of school needed education the most and would

66 Fishlow, p. 427.
67 Fishlow, p. 426; Solmon, 68–72.
68 Bowman, p. 120.

become an economic burden to the community if left uneducated. Hence there was a social benefit in investing in all children as human capital. Thus far the human-capital theory seems fruitful.

The kind of decision making assumed by this theory requires, I believe, at least some awareness of the economic benefits of education. Did nineteenth-century Americans, in fact, link schooling with economic success? In this century we have become accustomed to thinking of schools as sorters, as institutions that help to determine the occupational destiny of students. Increasingly, not only the professions but many other jobs as well have come to require educational credentials or prescribed levels of schooling even for entry-level positions.[69] Not only is this screening function of schools embodied in specific institutional arrangements, like high-school counseling programs, but it has also become common knowledge in the population at large. In 1973, 76 percent of respondents in a Gallup poll said they thought education was "extremely important" to "one's future success."[70]

There is little evidence, however, that citizens in the nineteenth century thought this way about schooling. Rhetoric about the purposes of education emphasized socialization for civic responsibility and moral character far more than as an investment in personal economic advancement. Indeed, there is some counter-evidence that businessmen, for one group, were actually hostile to the notion of education beyond the confines of the common school.[71] The arguments of Horace Mann and his early successors stressed not so much *individual* earnings as *aggregate* productivity and the workmanlike traits such as reliability and punctuality. The most influential spokesmen for nineteenth-century educators—people like William T. Harris—did stress a general socialization for work, but they tended to see success as the result of later behavior in the marketplace. Harris estimated that as late as 1898, the average person attended school for only five years. Out of one hundred students in all levels of education, ninety-five were in elementary, four were in secondary, and only one was in higher education.[72] Furthermore, family incomes were much lower in the nineteenth century than in mid-twentieth, and the structure of the labor force was far different. The percentage of the population engaged in agriculture dropped from 37.5 in 1900 to 6.3 in 1960, while the

[69] Ivar E. Berg, *Education and Jobs: The Great Training Robbery* (New York: Praeger, 1970).

[70] Stanley Elam, ed., *The Gallup Polls of Attitudes towards Education, 1969–1973* (Bloomington, Ind.: Phi Delta Kappa, 1973), p. 169.

[71] Irwin Wyllie, *The Self-made Man in America* (New Brunswick, N.J.: Rutgers Univ. Press, 1954), ch. 3; Cochran, pp. 174–76.

[72] Harris, 3–4, 54; Selwyn Troen, *The Public and the Schools: Shaping the St. Louis System, 1838–1920* (Columbia: Univ. of Missouri Press, 1975), ch. 6.

percentage in white-collar occupations rose from 17.6 to 43.5 in those years.[73] It is likely, then, that motives other than future rate of return on educational investments in individuals were more significant during the nineteenth century than in the twentieth. The micro-decision-making paradigm of human capital better explains our more recent history, when disposable family income has substantially risen, when parents are better educated and more capable of calculating future benefits, and when schooling has become far more important in sorting people into occupational niches.[74]

A Marxian Analysis

"We are led to reject the individual choice model as the basis for a theory of the supply of educational services," Samuel Bowles and Herbert Gintis have written.

> The model is not wrong—individuals and families do make choices, and may even make educational choices roughly as described by the human capital theorists. We reject the individual choice framework because it is so superficial as to be virtually irrelevant to the task of understanding why we have the kinds of schools and the amount of schooling that we do.[75]

Why superficial? Because the individual choice model provides only a partial interpretation of production, treats the firm "as a black box," and offers no useful insight into the basic question of how the capitalist class structure has been reproduced. The perpetuation of great inequalities of wealth and income over the past century and the development of schools as social institutions have not resulted simply from an aggregation of individual choices, Bowles and Gintis argue; rather, schooling has served to perpetuate the hierarchical social relations of capitalist production. In their view, society is not a marketplace of individuals maximizing their advantages but a class structure in which power is unequally divided. It may appear that the American educational system has developed in accord with "the relatively uncoordinated 'investment' decisions of individuals and groups as mediated by local school boards," but in actuality these "pluralistic" accommodations have taken place in response to changes in production "governed by the pursuit

[73] United States Bureau of the Census, *Historical Statistics of the United States* (Washington, D.C.: GPO, 1960), pp. 67–78.

[74] In "Education and the Corporate Order," *Socialist Revolution*, 2 (1972), p. 51, David K. Cohen and Marvin Lazerson point out that the "tendency to use market criteria in evaluating education flowered around the turn of the century"; for a survey of such studies, see A. Caswell Ellis, "The Money Value of Education," U.S. Bureau of Education, *Bulletin No. 22* (Washington, D.C.: GPO, 1917).

[75] Samuel Bowles and Herbert Gintis, "The Problem with Human Capital Theory—A Marxist Critique," *American Economic Review*, 65 (1975), 78.

of profit and privilege by those elements of the capitalist class which dominate the dynamic sectors of the economy." By setting boundaries of decision—establishing the rules of the game—the capitalist class determines the range of acceptable choice in a manner that strengthens and legitimizes its position.[76]

Bowles and Gintis are primarily interested in the consequences of the system of schooling rather than in the conscious motives of elites or school leaders. The important question is whether the outcomes of formal education have supported capitalism—for example, through differential training of workers and employers in ways that maintain the social division of labor. From this point of view, if Mann were a saint and yet his system of education perpetuated injustice because it supported exploitative relations of production, then the case for radical change would be all the stronger.

In developing their model of economic and educational change, Gintis and Bowles do not treat compulsory attendance in detail, but one can easily extrapolate an interpretation of compulsion from their theory. Their explanation has two major components. First, they account for educational reform periods, which shaped ideology and structure, as accommodations to contradictions engendered by capital accumulation and the incorporation of new groups into the wage-labor force. Second, they seek to demonstrate how the educational system has served capitalist objectives of achieving technical efficiency, control, and legitimacy.

"The capitalist economy and bicycle riding have this in common," they argue: "forward motion is essential to stability." As capital accumulates and new workers are drawn into expanded enterprises, potential conflict arises. Bowles and Gintis say that the contradictions inherent in this process gave rise to the common-school movement during the mid-nineteenth century, a time of labor militancy as the wage-labor force expanded and inequality increased. Such contradictions, they believe, also gave rise to the progressive movement at the turn of the twentieth century—a period of conflict between big business and big labor. Social discord stemmed from the integration of immigrant and rural labor into the industrial system. During these times, they argue, workers demanded more education, and "progressive elements in the capitalist class" acceded to the demands only insofar as they could adapt the school to their own purposes. Bowles and Gintis see educational development, then, "as an outcome of class conflict, not class domination." Workers won schooling for their children, but by controlling decision making in education and "suppressing anti-capitalist alternatives," the ruling class maintained the social relations of production while ameliorating conditions and dampening conflict. In this view, schooling has been a crucial tool for perpetuat-

[76] Bowles and Gintis, p. 75.

ing the capitalist system amid rapid economic change. Periodically, when the schools ceased to correspond with the structure of production, major shifts in the scope and structure of education took place, dominated in the final analysis by the class that set the agendas of decision.[77]

How did schools meet the capitalist objectives of technical efficiency, control, and legitimacy? Gintis and Bowles claim that the social relations of the school closely matched the needs of the hierarchical relations of production. The school prepared individuals differentially—in skills, traits of personality, credentials, self-concepts, and behavior—for performance in different roles in the economic hierarchy. This differentiation was congruent with social definitions of race, sex, and class. Thus, for example, when structures of production were relatively simple, schools concentrated on such qualities as punctuality, obedience to authority, and willingness to work for extrinsic rewards—all of which were useful in shaping a disciplined labor force for industry or commerce. As economic organizations became larger and more complex and the labor force increasingly segmented in level and function, schooling in turn grew more differentiated. This segmentation, coupled with differential treatment based on race and sex, helped to splinter employees into separate groups and to blind them to their common interest as workers. Schooling increasingly selected those who would get the good jobs; the rhetoric of equality of opportunity through education rationalized unequal incomes and status and legitimized the system. "The predominant economic function of schools," Bowles and Gintis observe, was "not the production or identification of cognitive abilities but the accreditation of future workers as well as the selection and generation of noncognitive personality attributes rewarded by the economic system."[78] As the work of different classes differed, so did the pattern of socialization in schools.

Just as Mann prefigured some of the human-capital theory, earlier Marxian theorists anticipated some of the Bowles–Gintis model, but they tended to see the laboring class as a more continuously active agent in educational change and capitalists as more hostile to public education. In 1883, for example, Adolph Douai, as a representative of the Socialistic Labor Party of the United States, presented a Marxist perspective on schooling to the United States Senate committee on the

---

[77] Samuel Bowles and Herbert Gintis, "Capitalism and Education in the United States," *Socialist Revolution*, 5 (1975), 111, 116–18.

[78] Samuel Bowles and Herbert Gintis, "The Contradictions of Liberal Educational Reform," in *Work, Technology, and Education*, ed. Walter Feinberg and Henry Rosemont, Jr. (Urbana, Ill.: Univ. of Illinois Press, 1975), pp. 124, 133; I have cited these essays by Bowles and Gintis because the more complete version of their analysis was not available at the time of writing. Now, see *Schooling in Capitalist America: Educational Reform and the Contradictions of Economic Life* (New York: Basic Books, 1976), esp. chs. 2, 4, 5, 7, and 9.

relations between labor and capital.[79] Half a century later, in the midst of the Great Depression, Rex David wrote a Marxian pamphlet on *Schools and the Crisis*.[80] Both strongly urged the creation of free and compulsory education for all young people; both stressed the opposition of capitalists to expanded educational opportunity; both saw teachers and other intellectual workers mostly as servants of vested interests but believed that educators could become an important means of spreading the light for socialism. For them as for a number of progressive labor historians, the working class was normally the dominant part of the coalition pushing for equality, and the ruling class was frequently hostile.

The interpretation of these earlier Marxists differs in emphasis from but does not directly contradict the Bowles-Gintis theory of educational change. Bowles and Gintis develop a more explicit model of how an apparently liberal educational system played a crucial part in reproducing unequal distribution of wealth and hierarchical relations of production. They further argue that owners and employers were not part of an undifferentiated group of capitalists but that the schooling reforms were engineered by those who controlled the leading sectors of the economy—exemplified by the corporate leaders at the turn of the century who sought to stabilize and rationalize the economy and supporting social institutions.[81]

Bowles and Gintis offer a general model of capitalist education rather than a specific interpretation of compulsory attendance. Thus what follows is my own extrapolation from their writing. Since they say that the "impetus for educational reform and expansion was provided by the growing class consciousness and political militancy of working people," presumably worker groups were advocates of universal attendance, perhaps aided by "progressive elements in the capitalist class." According to the theory that entry of new groups into the wage-labor force prompted demands for education, one might predict that the compulsory-education laws would appear first where the wage-labor force was growing most rapidly. At the same time, the ineffectiveness of these laws during the nineteenth century might be interpreted in part as a sign of ambivalence toward universal education among capitalists themselves (some might have preferred cheap child labor to the labor of schooled youth or adults, for example). On the other hand, phase two, the period of effective laws and increasing bureaucratization, might reflect growing capitalist consensus on the value of differentiated schooling in producing a segmented labor force for increasingly complex social relations of production. Indeed, the correspondence of the structure and processes of the schools with those

---

[79] Douai's testimony is in United States Senate, *Report on Labor and Capital*, II, 702–43.
[80] Rex David, *Schools and the Crisis* (New York: Labor Research Assoc., 1934).
[81] Bowles and Gintis, "Contradictions."

of the work place is precisely the point of the analysis; changes in the latter drive the former.[82]

The Marxian model sketched here is to a degree congruent with both the general theory of the political construction of education and the organizational snythesis. It suggests, however, that the capitalist class, as the ruling class, defines the production of citizens through education according to its own interests in the political economy. It adds to the organizational synthesis an explanation of why the large organization became dominant: capitalists had concentrated their ownership and power. It does not deny the choice model of human-capital theory, but it declares that the choices have been set within a capitalist zone of tolerance; further, it adds the notions of class conflict and reproduction of social structure.

The Bowles-Gintis analysis addresses important questions and poses a clear, explicit model. In my view, however, this kind of class analysis does not sufficiently explain the motive force of religious and ethnic differences in political and social life, especially within the working class. It tends to downplay important variations among employers' attitudes toward child labor and the different forms of education. The older Marxist view here has some substance; as Thomas Cochran and others have documented, many businessmen were opposed to extension of educational opportunity. The wage-labor hypothesis does not help us to understand widespread provision of schooling and numerous compulsory-schooling laws in communities and states in which the family farm was the predominant mode of production. As class analysis becomes further refined, however, it promises to add much to our understanding of both the continuities in social structure and the dynamics of economic and educational change.[83]

Conclusion

So what does one learn from exploring alternative ways of seeing compulsory schooling? Should one simply add them all together, like the observations of the blind men feeling an elephant, and say that the reality is in fact accessible only through multiple modes of analysis, that each mode is helpful but partial? Do some explanations fit only a particular time or place? To what degree are the interpretations mutually exclusive, and to what degree do they overlap? How might

82 Bowles and Gintis, "Capitalism," pp. 118, 126–33.

83 On ethnic and religious dimensions to school politics see Troen, chs. 2–4; Diane Ravitch, *The Great School Wars, New York City, 1805–1973: A History of the Public Schools as Battlefield of Social Change* (New York: Basic Books, 1974), chs. 3–7. As Solmon and Fishlow indicate (see references in footnote 67 above), enrollments in rural schools in many parts of the nation were higher than in industrialized areas; almost two-thirds of the states that passed compulsory-schooling legislation prior to 1890 were overwhelmingly rural in the distribution of population.

one test the assumptions and assertions of each by empirical investigation? Would any kind of factual testing be likely to change the mind of a person committed to a particular way of seeing or to a particular purpose?

The different kinds of interpretations do call attention to different actors, motives, and evidence, and in this sense one could say that the historian interested in all the phenomena of compulsory schooling might simply add together the various sets of observations. Those arguing for the political construction of education emphasize the role of the state and stress the importance of incorporating a heterogeneous populace into a unified state citizenry. The ethnocultural interpretation posits religious-ethnic differences as a motive force in political actions. The organizational synthesis stresses the role of the new middle class in changing the nature of American life through the creation of large organizations that dominate political and economic activities. Human-capital theorists focus on the family as a decision unit in calculating the costs and benefits of schooling. Finally, the Marxists see class struggle as the source of the dialectic that produces historical change. Each interpretation, in turn, directs attention to certain kinds of evidence which can confirm or disprove its assertions of causation: growth of new state rules and apparatus, religious differences expressed in political conflict, the rise of large organizations and related ideologies, the individual and social rates of return on schooling, and changes in the social relations of production and of schooling.[84]

There are problems with simple additive eclecticism, however. Some interpretations do fit certain times and places better than others, as we have seen. More fundamentally, the models deal with social reality on quite different levels: the individual or the family, the ethnocultural group, the large organization, and the structure of political or economic power in the society as a whole. Scholars advancing such interpretations often have quite different conceptions of what drives social change and hence quite different notions of appropriate policy. Some may concentrate on changing the individual, others on improving the functioning of organizations, and still others on radically restructuring the society. Ultimately, one is likely to adopt a framework of interpretation that matches one's perception of reality and purpose in writing, and thus simple eclecticism may lead to blurring of vision and confusion of purpose.

To argue that one should not mix interpretations promiscuously does not mean that it is unwise to confront alternative conceptualizations or to attempt to integrate them into a more complex understanding of social reality. This, in turn, may make historians more conscious of the ways in which theories and empirical re-

[84] Charles M. Dollar and Richard J. Jensen, *Historian's Guide to Statistics* (New York: Holt, Rinehart and Winston, 1971), chs. 1–2.

search interact with one another, so that an anomalous piece of evidence may call a theory into question and a new mode of explanation may be generated.[85] One of my purposes in this essay has been to extend the boundaries of discussion about the history of American education. I have become convinced that much of the recent work in the field—my own included—has used causal models too implicitly. It has also tended to constrict the range of value judgments. Was schooling "imposed" by elites on an unwilling working class, for example, or was John Dewey a servant of corporate capitalism? Entertaining explicit alternative models and probing their value assumptions may help historians to gain a more complex and accurate perception of the past and a greater awareness of the ambiguous relationship between outcome and intent—both of the actors in history and of the historians who attempt to recreate their lives.[86]

[85] Martin Rein, *Social Science and Public Policy* (London: Penguin, 1976); Henry Levin, "Education, Life Chances, and the Courts: The Role of Social Science Evidence," *Law and Contemporary Problems*, 39 (1975), 217–40.

[86] Robert K. Merton, "The Bearing of Sociological Theory on Empirical Research," and "The Bearing of Empirical Research on Sociological Theory," in *Readings in the Philosophy of the Social Sciences*, ed. May Brodbeck (New York: Macmillan, 1968), pp. 465–85.

Section II
Arts-Based Educational Research

Arts-Based Educational Research

Tom Barone
Arizona State University

Elliot Eisner
Stanford University

From the birth of the field of educational research until rather recently, engaging in research has generally meant doing social science. Within the past decade or two, however, growing numbers of educational scholars and researchers have begun to explore approaches to inquiry that are more artistic than scientific in character. In this chapter we report on the intellectual yield from those explorations.

We begin with an attempt to clarify terms. What does it mean to say that an approach to educational research is arts based? Arts-based research is defined by the presence of certain aesthetic qualities or design elements that infuse the inquiry and its writing. Although these aesthetic elements are in evidence to some degree in all educational research activity, the more pronounced they are, the more the research may be characterized as arts based.

What are these design elements? Although we cannot delineate all of them here, we will attend to several of the most significant in the literary forms of art. Our selection is not because of logocentrism or a failure of belief in the potential usefulness of nonverbal artistic media; it is because we recognize that most arts-based educational inquirers have, at least up to this time, employed words as their medium of expression.

Seven Features of Arts-Based Educational Inquiry

1. The Creation of a Virtual Reality

Good art possesses a capacity to pull the person who experiences it into an alternative reality. Objects of art are, as the aesthetician Suzanne Langer (1957) put it, "virtual entities." In a work of art such as a dance, she argued, actual physical realities such as place, gravity, and muscular control disappear as the viewer apprehends elements such as "the moving forces of the dance, the apparent centers of power and their emanations, their conflicts and resolutions, lift and decline, their rhythmic life" (Langer, 1957, p. 6). These are the virtual realities of the "semblance, the composed apparition" that is the dance. They are elements of a dynamic image that is not physically given but created by the dancer.

Similarly, Iser (1974) has talked about the creation of a *virtual world* by a literary author. This virtual world can also be located through the particular physical realities it evokes. These realities are most apparent in the literary genre of social realism. In this kind of literary work especially (although by no means exclusively), the author acutely observes and documents the telling details of human activity. The examples are innumerable, from the empirical particulars of the heart attack experienced by the fictional character Harry Angstrom in John Updike's (1990) *Rabbit at Rest*, to the historical events in the life of Lee Harvey Oswald in Don Delillo's (1988) *Libra*. Inside the field of education they can be identified in the work of Paley (1981, 1986) or in works such as Lightfoot's (1983) *The Good High School* and Freedman's (1990) *Small Victories*. The authors of each of these books locate often subtle but significant human activities within a recognizable sociohistorical context and bestow *verisimilitude* upon the virtual world of the story (Bruner, 1987). In a text with verisimilitude, the reader recognizes some of the portrayed qualities from his or her own experiences and is thereby able to believe in the possibility—the credibility—of the virtual world as an analogue to the "real" one.

But as with the experiences of performing and watching a dance, the focus in writing and reading a piece of literature is not so much on the individual, particular physical realities as it is on a "composed apparition," a virtual whole. This is true whether the credible virtual world created by the author and recreated by the reader of a literary work is fictional or nonfictional. In either case, it serves the same purpose in the same way. Readers of a good story may sense that they are moving away from the everyday, "real" world and temporarily leaving it to enter one with which they are less familiar. But they may find that the apparition of the storied world itself becomes a kind of heuristic device that speaks directly to familiar, nearby concerns as it raises questions about them. For example, readers of Kidder's (1989) *Among Schoolchildren* or other literary journalism may realize that they are at the same time vicariously participating in the experiences of a distant fifth-grade classroom and making judgments about the rightness of certain of their own educational practices as well as the conditions that tend to foster them. Kidder's story may provide a new perspective on (among other things) the limits of a teacher's caring and dedication in a hostile institutional setting.

The journey away from one's own lived-world into the realm of the literary text may thus be likened to that of an astronaut's voyage from Earth to moon and back again. In each case, the traveler visits a location near enough to a previously experienced object to recognize it but far enough to place it in a revealing (sometimes startling) new context. A new set of meanings and values suddenly adheres to objects and practices previously taken for granted. Back on Earth, the voyager is a changed person. Old ways of seeing are negated in favor of a fresh outlook, perspective, paradigm, and ideology.

2. The Presence of Ambiguity

A second feature of texts of arts-based educational inquiry is the presence of an ambiguous quality. Iser (1974) has noted that good writers of literature invite their readers into the reconstruction of the virtual world of the text by carefully positioned *blanks* or *gaps* in the text. These gaps are "the unwritten part of the text" (Iser 1974, p. 58) that must be filled in by active readers with personal meaning from their own experiences outside the text. Readers cannot merely inspect the text more closely to ascertain greater meaning, but they must, as Maitre (1983, p. 38) put it, "create additional material by a further imaginative act." The aim of the literary artist is not to prompt a single, closed, convergent reading but rather to persuade readers to contribute answers to the dilemmas posed within the text. In this sense, the literary text exhibits what Maitre (1983) has called *indeterminacy*. It is this indeterminacy, a state of being indefinite, that distinguishes literary activity from propaganda and other didacticisms.

Bakhtin (1981) uses the term *novelness* to describe the type of writing that inspires some readers to enter into a dialogue with it. Often found in literature but not exclusively in novels, novelness is a characteristic of writing that encourages a multiplicity of readings and a variety of interpretations of phenomena (Holquist, 1990, p. 84). Bakhtin contrasts the quality of novelness with that of *epicness*. Epic texts are meant to impart the final word, to shut out other voices, to close down interpretive options. Epic writing is devoid of gaps to be filled in by the reader. Epic writing produces the kind of declarative texts (Belsey, 1980) that aim to reduce uncertainty and includes many texts of science and philosophy. But even texts that exhibit some other literary characteristics may be declarative and epic, like didactic tales meant to instruct the reader about absolute moral virtues or final truths. An example of epic educational storytelling is the kind imagined by Berliner (1992). Berliner suggested that stories be written in which teachers and students explicate and illustrate findings that were derived and legitimated through research strategies based on social science.

3. The Use of Expressive Language

A third characteristic of arts-based inquiry involves the use of certain rhetorical strategies and devices, especially the kind of language used. Writers of literature use language that is metaphorical and evocative. Literary language is designed to call forth imaginative faculties, inviting the reader to fill gaps in the text with personal meaning. In literature the language choices are expressive and connotative rather than direct and denotative. They are designed to enhance meaning in a roundabout way. Dewey (1934) put it this way: Whereas scientists aim to *state* meaning, artists aim to *express* meaning.

> A statement sets forth the conditions under which the experience of an object or situation may be had. It is a good, that is, effective, statement in the degree in which these conditions are stated in such a way that they can be used as directions by which one may arrive at an experience.
>
> The poetic as distinct from the prosaic, esthetic art as distinct from scientific, expression as distinct from statement, does something different from leading to an experience. It constitutes one. (p. 84)

This notion reverberates in Langer's (1942) distinction between *representational symbols* and *presentational symbols*. The former, found in propositional discourse, point to the intended meanings of their referents. That is, the reader is prompted to move directly from the words to those referents. But presentational, or artistic, symbols are metaphors. Metaphors re-create experiences through the form they take, never signifying a closed, literal meaning but enabling the reader to experience that which they express (Eisner, 1991).

One example of metaphorical usage in arts-based educational research can be found in Barone's (1983) literary case study of a North Carolina high school arts program. Before introducing the character of the art teacher, Don Forrister, the author describes the Appalachian landscape in which Forrister lives and works. The reader is brought to experience certain qualities within the setting and within Appalachian life. Then Barone locates these qualities within Forrister's teaching. In an extended metaphor, Barone compares nature's slow, careful, patient shaping of the Appalachian mountains with the art teacher's effect on many of his students.

4. The Use of Contextualized and Vernacular Language

Another characteristic of artistic language is its contextualized nature.

Closely observed descriptions of particular human phenomena are prized not only by novelists, biographers, art critics, and other literary types, but also by writers such as ethnographers who employ some textual design features favored by social scientists. "Thick" literary description grounds the writing in a particular context so that the complexities adhering to a unique event, character, and/or setting may be adequately rendered.

In that regard, arts-based inquirers do not rely primarily on theoretical argot, as scientists and philosophers do, but they depend on nontechnical, everyday, vernacular forms of speech that are more directly associated with lived experiences. Speech that is theoretical tends to be abstract, one step removed from the primary qualities confronted in everyday events. Moreover, theory tends to be fashioned from within a preselected framework, one that is identified with a particular specialized field, or research subcommunity. The grammar and vocabulary of theory are elements of what Toulmin (1953) called the *participant languages* of those who toil in specialized fields. Such language, he argued, is designed quite well for technical purposes. It is highly denotative and conventional language that participants in a particular field can use with precision to communicate knowledge and information to other participants who have been initiated into that particular field.

Less constrictive of meaning is language that is not as parochial and specialized. Typically this sort of language is used in the transdisciplinary activities of ordinary commerce by laypeople (onlookers, in Toulmin's [1953] term). Such language is vernacular language. Vernacular forms of speech are more likely to be useful in expressing the meanings of school experiences than are theoretical forms of discourse. Consider the following passage from Kotlowitz's (1991) *There Are No Children Here*. It is a description of the activities of a black second-grader who finds refuge from the dangerous world outside in his schoolwork:

> When he got bored or had nothing better to do, he practiced his penmanship. His teachers noted that he had an unusually neat and delicate handwriting for some-

one so young. But Pharoah worked at it, usually writing his name over and over on a piece of paper, so that by the time he had finished, his name appeared maybe two dozen times, leaping in all directions. The P's would stand out in their grace and dominance over the other letters; he would even loop the letter's stem to give it a more pronounced presence. Sometimes, if he got carried away, his name would angle upward, with curls adorning the other letters, too, as if his name were a fanciful spaceship about to rocket off the edge of the paper. (p. 62)

How is the language in this excerpt characteristic of arts-based inquiry? First, it is expressive: Note the metaphorical allusion to the sense of power that Pharoah may derive from his obsession with writing. Second, it is "thickly" descriptive of what may be called the "dailiness" of school life. And finally, the writing is highly accessible to nonresearcher readers (or "onlookers") who can easily participate in making meaning from the text.

5. The Promotion of Empathy

Contextualized, expressive, and vernacular language contributes to another important dimension of arts-based educational inquiry—its facility for promoting empathic understanding. The ability to understand empathically is the ability to participate vicariously in another form of life. Within the arts and humanities, empathic understanding is the result of an inquirer's achievement of intersubjectivity. The inquirer's use of contextualized, expressive, and vernacular language motivates the readers to reconstruct the subjects' perspective within themselves. Second, empathic understanding is the inquirer's ability to promote the reconstruction of that perspective within her or his readers.

Rorty (1989) emphasized the capacity of literature to produce powerful descriptions of the perspectives of certain kinds of people—people with whom it is difficult to feel a sense of human solidarity, those looked upon as aliens who live, said Rorty, "outside of the range of 'us'." For example, the technocratic superstructure of the educational institutions ensures that inhabitants of those institutions are included in this list of existential foreigners. Following Rorty's view, relating vivid depictions of their ways of viewing the world may reduce this alienation among schoolpeople and with those outside the school.

Contextualized, expressive, and vernacular language is uniquely qualified to produce those vivid depictions. Literary language allows re-creation of the mental atmosphere, thoughts, feelings, and motivations of the characters in a story, drama, or essay. Through it, readers are brought to vicariously experience events from a different perspective.

6. Personal Signature of the Researcher/Writer

Of course, the perspectives of its various characters are not all that is advanced within a piece of literature. The characters are, after all, only elements within a virtual world that is the creation of a writer (and re-creation of readers). The author shapes the reality in accordance with his or her own particular thesis, or controlling insight, which the text is composed to suggest. The thesis is a pervasive quality in the text that serves to structure the various components of the work. This tentative personal statement of the author also serves as a mediator for choosing what to include or exclude from the text.

Because a literary thesis is a personal statement arising out of the negotiations between an author and the phenomena under scrutiny, no two will ever be quite the same. This is true even when two nonfictional case studies are about the same person, cultural setting, or event. The reader is encouraged to participate in a variety of perspectives and not to arrive at a single, correct version of reality. Each work of arts-based literary inquiry, therefore, embodies the unique vision of its author. In that sense, each displays that author's personal signature.

7. The Presence of Aesthetic Form

The uniqueness of a work of literature is evident in the composition of both formal and substantive elements that are arranged to further the thesis of the work. One important formal element is the format, or manner and style of arranging the content of the text. The features of traditional quantitative research texts tend to be standardized. They generally include (in this order) a statement about the problem and its background, definitions of relevant terminology, a review of related literature, a description of the methodology and design, a presentation and analysis of the data secured, and a summary and discussion of the findings, which includes implications for further research. Unlike those of traditional quantitative research texts, the formats of arts-based research texts tend not to be standardized. There are some broad similarities among some arts-based educational research texts, typically in the story format.

Stories—at least those that honor the Western, Aristotelian tradition—are formed within a basic pattern that includes three phases. At the outset, there is the framing of a dilemma, a problematic situation affecting the main character. This dilemma produces tension, drama, significance, and interest: The reader of an effective story will be drawn into this dilemma that is the beginning of the story's plot. In the middle phase of the story, complications ensue, and the plot thickens. Finally there is a resolution—not necessarily a tidy summation, or definitive *solution* to the dilemma, but a sense that the character has changed or grown as a result of the detailed events. (Because of the ambiguous character of literature mentioned above, the reader is often left to make personal judgments about the rightness of the resolution.)

By the end of a story—or other kind of arts-based educational inquiry text—its format and contents will serve to create a new vision of certain educational phenomena. When readers re-create that vision, they may find that new meanings are constructed, and old values and outlooks are challenged, even negated. When that occurs, the purposes of art have been served.

The Spectrum of Educational Inquiry

The foregoing descriptions constitute a few of the elements of design that adhere to arts-based forms of educational inquiry. There are surely others. Moreover, it should not be assumed that all arts-based inquiry will exhibit every one of these features. Generally speaking, the more a text exhibits these design elements, the more artistic it is in character.

Finally, it should be noted that recently many qualitative forms of social science have taken on several of these characteristics—for example, thick description and the personalization of textual form. The result has been what Geertz (1988) has called *genre blurring*, a phenomenon that makes it difficult to categorize and label authors and their works. Indeed, we prefer not to encourage sorting of educational research texts into two separate containers labeled "artistic" and "scientific" or into corresponding containers labeled "qualitative" and "quantitative." Instead, we suggest a continuum that ranges from those texts that exhibit many artistic characteristics to those that exhibit few.

Texts reporting the results of experiments will reside at one end of this continuum. Poetic and storied texts will occupy the other. In between can be found a rich and wondrous spectrum of writings, some primarily quantitative in nature, others scientifically qualitative (from grounded theory research to ethnography), and still others more narrative and personal in style. Our point is that until very recently only a relatively small part of that spectrum had been considered a legitimate field on which an educational inquirer was allowed to play. Because we hope to expand the playing field, we are focusing here on more artistic forms of research.

What are some kinds of texts located near the arts-based end of the educational inquiry continuum? The two arts-based genres that have gained most prominence and acceptance among credentialed educational researchers—and the ones highlighted here—are educational criticism and narrative storytelling. These are not the only literary forms of educational research; others include literary case studies, literary history, literary ethnography, life histories, teacher lore, and student lore. Also, many novels and short stories with themes related to schooling or education have, over the years, been written by professional writers, most of whom are not educationist academics.

Before exploring the origins of literary-style educational research texts written by educationists, we make three important points. First, because of the tendency to blur genres (Geertz, 1988), it is often difficult, sometimes impossible, to classify particular texts within distinct categories. For example, is Donmoyer's (1983) portrait of a high school principal an educational biography, literary case study, educational criticism, or all of the above? Second, more written discourse *about* arts-based educational research currently exists than do actual examples of it. This is understandable to us because theoretical justifications are often required to legitimate nontraditional research modes. Moreover, we sense that the ratio of theoretical justification to exemplar is diminishing as the academic educational community gives these modes wider acceptance. Third, as suggested above, many literary-style texts (especially works of fiction) inquiring into educational phenomena have originated from outside that academic community. Barone (1992a) has detailed how a particular view of educational researchers as professional social scientists has meant the abandonment of storytelling about schoolpeople to noneducationists, especially popular novelists and journalists. With the growth of acceptance by educationists of researcher-artists, the line between academy-based and lay-produced texts about educational matters has begun to fade. Arts-based texts, exhibiting the kind of expressive, vernacular language described above, are often more accessible to lay audiences than are technically oriented texts.

Educational Criticism

One important kind of educational inquiry that draws its sustenance from the arts is called *educational criticism*. Educational criticism is the brainchild of Elliot Eisner. Over the last two decades Eisner (1976, 1977, 1979, 1991) has written extensively on the nature of this arts-based approach to educational research and evaluation. Several of his students have joined him in this effort, elaborating theoretically on the concept of educational criticism and contributing critiques of various sorts of educational phenomena (Barone, 1987; Donmoyer, 1980; Flinders, 1995; McCutcheon, 1976; Vallance, 1977).

Educational criticism demands that the inquirer attend to the subtleties and nuances of educational materials, settings, and events. The educational critic perceives and appreciates the important qualities of these educational artifacts and discloses them through the evocative and expressive language of an art critic. Eisner (1985, p. 223) quoted Dewey's (1934, p. 324) description of the aim of art criticism: "the reeducation of the perception of the work of art." *Educational* critics aim to reeducate readers' perception of educational phenomena. Upon what kinds of educational phenomena does the educational critic focus? They range from school architecture and physical environment, to the curriculum materials used in classrooms, to the performances of teachers teaching, to the evaluation of school programs, to critical essays about the lives individual schoolchildren lead. Indeed, no educational phenomenon is, in principle, outside of the purview of the educational critic.

Eisner (1991) has identified and discussed four important dimensions in the structure of educational criticism that serve to reeducate readers' perceptions of educational matters. These dimensions are *description, interpretation, evaluation*, and *thematics*. Of course, educational criticisms are rarely divided into neat segments in accordance with these dimensions; instead one finds these elements interwoven throughout a criticism, with description preceding interpretation and then giving way again to description, which flows into evaluation and back to interpretation, and so on. Moreover, the dimensions are not totally independent of each other. Because language is involved, for example, pure, evaluation-free descriptions or interpretations are impossibilities. Still, naming and describing these dimensions can offer insight into the complex structure of the educational critique.

Of the four dimensions of criticism, *description* is one of the most arts-related. Descriptions help readers to visualize what educational phenomena are like. To grant readers access to these phenomena, critics describe in language that is "literary"; that is, it is expressive and vernacular (see above). This use of language provides access to a virtual reality and promotes vicarious participation in (i.e., empathic understanding of) a previously alien form of life.

Interpretation performs a different service than that performed by description. It moves beyond the realm of a literary writer to the realm of discursive critic: Interpretive text *explains* meaning. It does so in order to make obvious the import of events and situations. For Eisner (1991), interpretation can involve the use of theories—even social science theories—that put particular qualities into meaningful contexts. The purpose of employing theory in educational criticism, however, is not to predict or control events. It is, rather, to edify—to identify the factors that bear upon a particular educational practice, and to shed light on potential consequences of that practice.

The third structural element of educational criticism is *evaluation*, the making of explicit assessments of the goodness of the educational events and situations described and interpreted. Educational critics are not relativists. They see education as a value-laden enterprise—some schooling experiences are more growth inducing, more *educational*, than others. A critic, therefore, renders judgments—not opinions—about the quality of the phenomena under investigation. A judgment differs from an opinion in that the latter is a bald, terse, and often uninteresting, statement of personal taste, but the former is suspended within an elaboration of reasons for the critic's conclusions about matters at hand.

A final dimension in educational criticism is one that is common to all literary writings. It is the dimension of *thematics*. A critic, like a playwright, storyteller, or novelist, will develop a work around a particular controlling insight or issue. As described above, a theme will serve as a means for mediating between phenomena that are competing for inclusion in an account. Particulars that address the central issue (and subissues in elaborate works) are likely to be folded into the text. The theme is a pervasive quality in the text; it resurfaces throughout, and provides coherence and unity in the essay, critique, or piece of literary fiction. There is one important distinction to be made between the theme of a critique and that of a work of art. In the latter, the theme is never made explicit, rather it lurks beneath the surface of the text, subtly guiding the reading while remaining out of sight. In works of educational criticism, however, the theme is often made explicit, the central insight or insights are pronounced and explained in the critical analysis. The theme also contributes to the process of generalizing from a work of criticism, a notion to be more fully explored in a later section of this chapter.

Through this description of the important structural elements of educational criticism, it becomes clear that this kind of inquiry is not itself art, although it evidences many of the facets of literature discussed earlier in this chapter. Moreover, because educational criticism was the first form of arts-based inquiry seriously and persistently advanced in the literature on educational research methodology, it has served an important legitimating function. In addition to its own intrinsic worth as a qualitative research approach for disclosing important information about educational events and situations, it has opened the door to the acceptance of many forms of arts-based inquiry that are even more artistic in nature. The work done in the articulation of the nature and purposes of educational criticism has indeed changed the face of educational research.

Narrative Storytelling

A second branch of arts-based educational research includes various forms of storytelling about educational characters and events. Educational storytelling has a long history, of course. Untold numbers of short stories, biographies, autobiographies, novels, and even plays have been written over the years, albeit without an official imprimatur as educational research. Stories written by nonuniversity-based writers about the lives of schoolpeople—especially teachers—serve as examples of narrative texts often not thought of as "real research" (Armstrong, 1980; Calkins, 1983; Dennison, 1969; Freedman, 1990; Natkins, 1986; Paley, 1981, 1986).

Recently, however, many educationists have been pressing for academic legitimation of storytelling genres. These scholars see the "personal accounts" (Lancy, 1993) generated within these narrative forms of inquiry as useful and important texts for improving education. Evidence of their impact comes in the numerous articles and books on the topics of narrative and storytelling in the field of education, the special issues of important educational journals (e.g., *International Journal of Qualitative Studies in Education,* 1995) devoted to this kind of inquiry, and the number of papers about narrative presented at professional conferences such as those of the American Educational Research Association.

The history of the movement toward storytelling as educational inquiry is more complex than that of educational criticism. Interest in this discursive form began brewing in fields outside of education. The "narrative turn" in human studies and social sciences was largely the result of the ascendance of literary theory to a place of great prominence in the intellectual world (Booth, 1961, 1979; Kermode, 1967; Polkinghorn, 1988; Ricoeur, 1984, 1985, 1988; Scholes & Kellogg, 1966). Indeed, a "literary turn" in the fields of anthropology and sociology soon had inquirers in those fields characterized as storytellers (Geertz, 1988; Van Maanen, 1988) and poets (Clifford & Marcus, 1986).

Inside the field of education (and the field of curriculum, in particular) the origins of the fascination with storytelling lie partly in the reconceptualist movement inspired by William F. Pinar and Madeleine Grumet (Grumet, 1987, 1990; Pinar, 1975, 1980; Pinar & Grumet, 1976). Theorists in this movement have encouraged using written and oral biographies and autobiographies for the study of educational experiences. The aim in these studies is to entice the reader to reconceptualize the educational process through intimate disclosures from the lives of individual educators and students (see Willis 1978). Another stream of educational storytelling flowed out of the research on teacher knowledge. Elbaz (1991) described this research as looking at teaching "'from the inside,' focusing on teacher thinking (Clark and Peterson, 1986), the culture of teaching (Feiman-Nemser and Floden, 1986), and the personal, practical knowledge of teachers (Connelly and Clandinin, 1985; Elbaz, 1983)."

Today, variations on the theme of story as research abound. The researching of biography and life history has been advanced by Goodson (1992) and

Goodson and Walker (1991) as a source of valuable episodes in educational research. Indeed, stories about the lives of teachers researched and written by university-based scholars have burgeoned. Some important examples include works by Bullough (1989), Jackson (1968), Miller (1990), Ryan (1970), and Yonemura (1986). Schubert and Ayers (1992) also attend to the "local detail and everyday life of teaching," (p. v) or what they prefer to call "teacher lore." Berk (1980) was among the first educational researchers to focus on the biographies of students. Pagano (1992) and Barone (1992b) have each proposed a place for fictional accounts at the research table; Sellito (1991) and Ross (1986), authors of educational novels as dissertations, have already dined at that table. Barone (1980) has also explored the parallels between storytelling and accounts of literary journalism. Essays and books by Carol Witherell and Nel Noddings (Witherell & Noddings, 1981), Janet Miller (1990), Daniel McLaughlin and William Tierney (1993), and Kathy Carter (1993) are among the many that have contributed to the literature on the nature of the personal and professional knowledge that accumulates as a result of episodes in the storied lives of schoolpeople.

But perhaps no educational writers have advanced the cause of educational storytelling with greater persistence than F. Michael Connelly and D. Jean Clandinin. For Clandinin and Connelly (1987; 1988; see also Connelly & Clandinin, 1990), stories represent the structured quality of experience that is studied by narrative researchers: "Thus we say that people by nature lead storied lives and tell stories of them, whereas narrative researchers describe such lives, collect and tell stories of them, write narratives of experience" (Connelly & Clandinin, 1990, p. 2). The narrative stories that Connelly and Clandinin favor exhibit several of the arts-based features described above, especially the jargon-scarce, vernacular prose, the perspectival nature of the text, and the promotion of empathic understanding of the lives of educational practitioners. But in their seminal work, Connelly and Clandinin (1985), like most other narrative theorists, did not emphasize the traditional formal qualities of storytelling, including expressive forms of language and the aesthetic story form.

Indeed, for many narrativists the aesthetic format of storytelling is downplayed, dismissed, or sacrificed to other concerns. Narrativist authors who collaborate with practitioners in their research often choose to place autobiographical content in a theoretical envelope, enfolding it within commentary from a critical science or other analytical perspective (e.g., Britzman, 1990; McLaren, 1993). Others, reacting to the form fetishes of modernist literary critics, find outdated, and even dangerous, the notion of a text that lures the reader into the problematic situation of its characters only to present a tidy resolution to the problem. Still others suggest that the format of problem setting, complication, and resolution is a white, Anglo-American characteristic of story (Nespor & Barylske, 1991).

Barone (1995), on the other hand, has noted the value of some educational stories that—at least momentarily, prior to ultimate analysis by critics and theorists—deserve their own textual breathing space. Citing major works of literature, he argues that the story format is best suited to promoting *epiphanic moments* (Denzin, 1989) in its readers. These are major transactional moments that disrupt the ordinary flow of life by questioning the usual definitions of important facets of one's world. This power of story derives from its capacity to entice the reader into a powerful vicarious experience (see above). Although usually not as potent as a peak experience in "real life," the story occurs in a space where vividly drawn, imaginary problematic life-situations can spotlight the reader's own. The results can be alterations to the meanings given to the reader's life projects, changes in the life story being plotted outside of the illusion of the text.

Some (although by no means all) stories may even attempt to do artfully what critical theorists have done through direct argument, namely highlight and critique unfortunate maldistributions of power within societies and institutions. The challenge for such texts (called *critical stories* by Barone [1992c] or *narratives of struggle* by hooks [1991]) is to describe and explain cruel conditions within our social institutions and the larger cultural forces that maintain them, while avoiding the pitfalls of polemicism and propaganda. In other words, these stories must maintain a delicate balance by striving to be socially conscientious while retaining the necessary ambiguity that is a hallmark of good art.

The Current State of Play

The approach that we have described has not had easy sailing in the educational research community. The very concept of artistically based research is regarded as an oxymoron by more than a few members of the community. To them, research is a concept that is embedded in a scientific conception of method. The idea that something as personal and as subjective as art can perform a research function does not fit comfortably into their traditional views of research method. What scholars worry about is the difficulty of replicating findings that depend on individual talents and personal perceptions. How can a dependable body of knowledge be constructed, they ask, if there is no public method through which others can validate the research claims? Indeed, can we speak of a method at all when the tactics employed are in large measure idiosyncratic, opportunistic, and unique to the investigator?

Furthermore, matters of generalizability are fundamental in the conduct of science. Scientific work is not concerned with *that* cat, but with cats. Case studies, which are almost always the focus of artistically based inquiry, address particular circumstances and do not necessarily represent the features of any particular population. And even if they do, it would not be possible under the approach described in this chapter to know if they do. Thus, matters of replicability, validity and generalization—three pillars upon which social science research rest—are at best shaky in so-called artistically based research, or they don't exist at all.

Other sources of resistance, we believe, are rooted in the difficulties that people normally have with the emergence of paradigms that appear to challenge or threaten the ones that they hold dear. Thomas Kuhn (1962) has written extensively about these matters in the natural sciences. Kuhn points out that revolutionary science, that form of scientific inquiry in which radically new theories are generated and pursued, is often rejected by those who have the greatest investment in the more traditional theories. One cannot help but observe that this may be due, at least in part, to matters of power and politics. Competence and skill in a domain can afford those who possess them with positions of stature. With positions of stature also come opportunities to exercise power. One doesn't have to look far within the university setting to recognize that those who judge the adequacy of research proposals and the competence of dissertation writers are in enormously influential positions. When the rules of what constitutes acceptable inquiry change, so too do the criteria for appraising not only the quality of the work to be judged but also the competence of the judges.

We point this out not to complain, but to describe what we believe to exist: It is a human characteristic to question approaches that seem to violate the canons with which one has become comfortable.

Just how does someone doing artistically based research address questions of reliability, validity, and generalization? In the first place, it should be recognized that the very terms that we have just used are themselves a part of the stock-in-trade of conventional research methods. Bruner (1990) described these terms as being closer to the paradigmatic than to narrative. To ask about matters of validity, a term rooted in statistical research procedures, is to begin the inquiry by using assumptions that may be inappropriate. Nevertheless, we will provide here as adequate a response as we can to the concerns underlying the questions that we have identified.

We start with validity. The primary aim of all research is to further human understanding. The aim of *educational* research is to further human understanding so that the quality of educational practice can be improved. The achievement of such an aim, in turn, increases the probability that students will be able to lead an enhanced quality of life. In short, educational research serves its most important function when it enhances people's lives. Given this view, validity is related to the instrumental utility of the research that was undertaken to achieve such aims. Artistically grounded research that furthers understanding and that enables a reader to notice what had not been seen before, to understand what had not been understood, to secure a firmer grasp and deeper appreciation of complex situations contributes to the end to which educational research is committed. Our conception of validity is rooted in the ways arts-based research helps us notice, understand, and appraise.

The question remains, of course, as to what constitutes understanding. If a pragmatic test is applied, understanding is furthered when more effective educational policy or practice occurs as a result. Validation, in a narrower sense, occurs when the observations that are made through artistically grounded qualitative research are acknowledged and valued by a competent, critical community. The terms *competent* and *critical community* are important. Competent refers to a level of discernment that not all individuals possess: The appreciation of great works of art requires great audiences. No less is true for artistically grounded research, or for research of a scientific character. To offer a tautology, those who are not competent to judge are in no position to judge the merits of a set of procedures or observations.

The second term, *critical community*, refers to the fact that work in education like work in other fields is a part of an intellectual network. "Validation" depends upon the acknowledgment of the work by members of that community. The community is defined by social and intellectual networks, by meetings of learned societies, by books, and by academic journals. Validation is inevitably a social affair. The same is true in the scientific community. Scientific research conclusions also need to be acknowledged by such a community. Validation, therefore, is the acknowledgment of the value of the research by a competent, critical community. However, the ultimate test of validity is the extent to which it facilitates the formation of effective educational policy or the improvement of some aspect of educational practice.

With respect to generalization, our view is that although artistically grounded research pays incredibly subtle attention to the particulars of the case it addresses, there are always likely to be thematic outcomes of such attention, outcomes that pertain to far more than the case itself. This observation is demonstrated in the extent to which artistic characterizations form powerful prototypes: Schema theory is relevant here. Schemas represent perceptual and cognitive structures through which we make sense of a complex world. The theoretical paradigms of science are, in a sense, echoed in the thematic structures of artistically generated research. Once having recognized some aspect of, say, teaching or schooling through the vivid portrayal of an individual circumstance, a reader is in a position to locate similar features in other situations when they exist. Artistically grounded research provides canonical images, often through storied narratives, that give us frames through which a clear focus can be secured.

Are there limitations to the approach that we have described? Of course there are. There are limitations to any approach to the study of the world. That is why multivocality is so important. Different frameworks provide different pictures. Different pictures make different kinds of understanding possible. When one is using quantitative techniques, there is a particular kind of precision and reliability possible that is virtually impossible to achieve in the approach that we are describing. Nevertheless, the use of quantitative procedures restrict what it is that can be addressed. Quantification is, after all, a particular descriptive process. Describing a loved one through numbers is hardly likely to reveal those special qualities for which one's love has been given. Not everything can be described with anything. The limits of quantification are not the limits of our world.

The foregoing should not be interpreted to mean that artistically based approaches to educational research should never employ number. There are aspects of the educational world that are best described by number, given the purposes of the inquirer. When those purposes emerge within an artistically based approach to educational research, numbers ought to be used; it's the intelligent thing to do. However, if the dominant feature of the research is quantitative, if the data are statistically treated, if correlational and experimental methods are emphasized, the research is not likely to have the kind of artistic character that we are describing here. This does not mean that there are not artistic features to social science inquiry. There are. In a curious sense, art has no monopoly on art.

We have already discussed the way in which matters of validity and generalizability are addressed within the context of artistically grounded approaches to educational research. Another issue that emerges pertains to matters of truth. Truth has been a fundamental concept in Western philosophical thought. In the main, for educational researchers, the concept has rested upon a notion of correspondence. What is believed to correspond are the facts of the world (whether or not they are as we believe them) and an investigator's claims about those facts. In traditional philosophical circles, truth is achieved to the degree to which claims about reality correspond to reality.

For reasons that have been discussed by many philosophers, we find it impossible to entertain a correspondence theory of truth because to know whether one's claims about reality correspond to reality would require that someone know the reality to which one's claims correspond. If someone knew reality, the need for claims about it would be superfluous.

Our conception of truth has to do with the inevitably tentative judgments of a critical community concerning a state of affairs. We regard beliefs about any state of affairs as fallible and tentative. Beliefs about what is true change, as the history of science so eloquently attests. The best we can do is to construe the world as best we can—that is, to try to make sense of it—and to offer our conjectures about its features to a critical community for purposes of refutation. We work with the ideas that we find attractive and credible until other ideas are found more serviceable, more elegant, or more persuasive. Artistically grounded approaches to educational research yield products that enable us to organize our comprehension. They are intended to satisfy our rationality—and so too do scientific theories. Thus, our view of truth is a view that requires some form of critical acceptance. It is well to note that acceptance, in many cases, does not come immediately. The work that both artists and scientists generate often has to wait decades until it finds an accepting critical public.

This view of truth gives the notion a dynamic quality. Truth is not something that one can fix, package, label, and ship across the land. It is a living quality of mind that requires the active reflection of an interested party. As such, it is modified by every knower: No two people have the same conception of a state of affairs.

The potential limitation of such a view is that it seems to undermine the very foundations that many of us find so attractive for purposes of our own cognitive security. What shall we do when we cannot find that slab of granite upon which we can securely stand? One of the strengths of the view we have advanced is that it liberates us from blind authority and the dogmas and doctrines of institutions that close the questions and cease the inquiry. In the view that we are describing, everyone has the opportunity to function as a creator of his or her own understanding. We believe that such a view is far more promising despite its uncertainties than the aspiration to come to a single, closed consensus about the way the world is.

Related to the notions we have just advanced is the concern that scholars have expressed about artistically grounded work being subjective. The polarities "subjective" and "objective" are well entrenched in our language. They reflect certain deep-seated assumptions about differences between the world and ourselves. The dichotomy between what is subjective and what is objective is not only built into our language, but it is also built into our thought processes by the ways in which we have been acculturated. Objective knowledge is supposed to be about the world out there. Subjectivity pertains to the "world" within us. Historically, the aim of epistemology, the Greek term which refers to true and certain knowledge, was to provide an objective and true description of an objectively known world. Science, since the Enlightenment at least, was believed to employ procedures that made it increasingly difficult for a subjective self to enter into an objectively described—that is a scientifically described—world.

The language associated with the concept of objectivity is telling—cool, dispassionate, distanced, and impersonal, for example—and the same language is associated with science. But as we have come to learn, it is not possible to uncouple mind from matter. What we take to be a state of affairs is not only a function of the qualities that constitute that state, but it is also a function of what we bring to those qualities. What we bring to those qualities is influenced by the icons and linguistic categories that our culture has provided, by our personal proclivities, by the values that we have assimilated, and by the entire variety of conceptual structures that have become part and parcel of our cognitive life. Given this view, the notion of an objectively known world that is somehow experienced independent of our interior life seems far-fetched. What we have is an interaction between ourselves and the world; indeed it is not possible, in our view, to locate a line between them. We are part of all we see and what we see is a part of us.

There is utility in the fact that our subjectivities differ. It is the differences among us that make possible individually unique perspectives and it is the differences among these individually unique perspectives that feed our culture: We learn most from those who are least like us. Looked at collectively, it is the creation of an array of harmonious subjectivities that makes a culture rich. It is in the diversity and complexity that such harmonious differences create that we as a culture can achieve the highest levels of civilization. Our view, on the one hand, is that the concepts subjective and objective convey unfortunate notions about separations between humans and the experienced world that do not exist. These locutions imply separations that are unreal.

On the other hand, our view is that it is well to recognize that personal experiences among humans differ and that these differences need not be seen as liabilities but as rich sources from which we can learn to experience qualities of the world that we might not otherwise encounter. The utility, validity, or reliability of a writer's portrayal of a social scene is not to be appraised by the extent to which others writing independently about the same scene produce an identical portrayal, but rather by whether the portrayals created by different individuals help us see things we hadn't noticed before. Put another way, unlike traditional conceptions of interjudge reliability in social science methodology, conceptions that seek high interjudge correlations, our test of the utility of artistically grounded research is whether the portrait, narrative, or educational criticism portrays qualities that advance our understanding or enable us to act in more effective ways. Productive idiosyncracy more than replicability or mimesis is the higher good.

This view leads us to observations about the relationship between fact and fiction, between, say, a novel and a work of social science.

In his classic essay "Thick Description," Clifford Geertz (1973) pointed out that the etymology of fiction was "fictio." *Fictio* in Latin refers to the process of making. Geertz pointed out that science itself, certainly ethnography, is something made. From this perspective, the line between fiction and truth is not as clear as some might believe. Genres are blurred, as Geertz (1983) wrote in another essay. For us, the essence of perception is that it is selective. Observations of schools, of classrooms, of teaching are always incomplete— indeed they must be. Nothing would be more confusing than a portrait, rendering, portrayal, or educational criticism that tried to describe everything. As Berliner (1986) says, the effort to see everything is the mark of a novice. Experts know what to neglect.

Selective neglect provides the material for the making of meaning. Meaning is achieved as *portions* of the world are construed and organized, and the representation of that world is composed into a telling document. This document may take liberties with the world as it is seen. In narrative research, for example, composites of individuals might be created in order to make a point more telling. Emphasis may be added to drive home an idea or to sustain interest. No portrait of the world, whether on the stage or in the physics laboratory, is a mirror of reality. Selection and construal always occur. The question that needs to be asked, therefore, is not one pertaining to the mimetic features of the work, but whether the work advances understanding, whether it illuminates important qualities, whether it deepens our comprehension of the factors, forces, and conditions that animate human beings.

Novels may do this much more incisively and effectively than reports that use procedures that provide the utmost in quantitative precision but which, nevertheless, fail to generate insight to the reader. *Schindler's List,* Steven Spielberg's epic film of the Holocaust, is a vivid case in point. In a very significant sense, the film is a fiction. It displays events that did not actually happen in the sequence in which they were rendered. The interiors within which Schindler works are imaginative constructions. The words spoken are inventions of writers. The people portraying the main characters are, we must not forget, actors. Yet, the film makes possible forms of vicarious experience that help us grasp at the deepest level events that we believe have taken place. In fact, the Austrian government felt so strongly about the film's educational benefits for the young that it waived its age restriction so that children under sixteen could see it. Here we have government policy acknowledging the educative virtues of a work of art.

How do we avoid being taken in by propaganda? How do we defend ourselves against advertising? How do we test the validity, the truth, and the accuracy of works like *Schindler's List* or, for that matter, other artistically grounded research studies in education and elsewhere? Works of art, in contrast to propaganda, often generate as many questions as they generate answers. Yet there is no acid test to determine the true value of either art or propaganda. We can be taken in by either. But we hasten to add that we can be taken in by scientific work as well as by works of art. The very categories and procedures that we believe to be legitimate in science may themselves create a profound bias because of what such procedures neglect. We mistakenly take the part for the whole. We forget that the methodology that is used in social science to give us a so-called objective take on the world is itself not only partial but also riddled with values that do not readily surface on first inspection. We would say that work in science and in art need critical scrutiny and that the ability to critically examine such work using criteria appropriate to each is of profound importance. The development of such critical acumen ought to be a part of any program that is designed to prepare students to do research, whether in an artistic or scientific mode.

Throughout this chapter we have discussed artistically based approaches to educational research as if the primary medium through which such reports would be presented would be written prose. It is true that what has been called "storied narratives" and "educational criticism" have employed linguistic material almost exclusively. Scholars write and publishers publish. The coin of the realm is language, written language at that, and we do not see, at least in the short term, these traditions being displaced. Nevertheless, it is important for us to point out that neither language nor number have a monopoly on the means through which humans represent what they have come to know. In fact, one eminent philosopher, Michael Polanyi (1958) makes it plain that "we know more than we can tell." If this is true, and to us it seems unassailable, then it seems to follow that research need not be limited to written reports. Experience in the world is, after all, construed from "multimedia" events and is not limited to what we read or hear. It is fundamentally multisensuous (or at least multisensory) and achieves meaning not only by undergoing a linguistic transformation but also by taking shape in a variety of ways. Visual images, for example, make it possible to formulate meanings that elude linguistic description. Humans invented maps to make plain relationships that would be many times more difficult to describe in words or number. Scientists create models whose synchronic features make it possible to grasp relationships that diachronic media such as language find difficult to portray. We now have virtual reality and telepresence to help us perform medical operations. The means through which we learn about and act upon the world has expanded.

It is clear that humans have invented a variety of forms of representation that are intended to transform and transmit the ideas, the images, and the aspirations that they have formed. From the beginnings of the images put on the walls of the Lascaux caves some 40 thousand years ago to present-day photographs and multimedia, representational forms perform epistemic functions. The most lucid examples are found in popular culture. Television and film, music and dance all make possible both ways of knowing and forms of understanding that will not take the impress of literal language. Indeed, both poetry and literature transcend the limits of literal language. And so, too, does the visual image.

The field of educational research has not yet begun to explore the ways in which, say, film might be used to help people understand what schooling is about, how teaching may proceed, or what students might be learning. Although recent work in what is called "authentic assessment" is, in some ways, related to the use of such forms, it is still far removed from the tough-minded traditions of a research practice that is itself a child of positivist and neopositivist validation criteria. Consider, for example, the matter of research *claims* and warranted *assertability*. Both conditions depend, at least implicitly, on the use of language. To make a claim is to make a statement. To have warrant for an assertion is to have grounds for something that one *says*. Both require the use of language as a basis for validation. Why such limits?

It seems to us that educational research ought to exploit the capacities of mind to process information in a variety of ways. A parochial conception of the vehicles with which we think are legitimate for doing and reporting educational research will certainly limit the varieties of understanding and the forms of meaning that we are able to secure. The medium matters.

It seems self-evident to say that the medium matters, yet that description does not say enough. What also matters is the way in which the medium is treated. It is here that the artistic treatment of a form of representation is important. A form of representation that is inartistically handled is not likely to have the kind of impact or clarity that one hopes to achieve. An inartistic film is feckless. An artless video is likely to have little consequence. An effort to combine music with visual images and with literary language that is handled without sensitivity to aesthetic qualities is likely to contribute little to our understanding. What makes a film like *Schindler's List* powerful is not simply that it is on film, but that its director, its actors, indeed, the entire crew of highly skilled technicians, created a work of art. What we are suggesting here is an expansion of the traditional means through which research has been undertaken as well as an expansion of the media through which the results of research are made available to some public.

As we have already indicated, for some in the educational research community this will appear to be wrong-headed, even blasphemous. It's troublesome enough to talk about the virtues of artistically crafted research in which language is the medium, but to talk about research that is made available through film and video and through music and artistically crafted prose is to create forms that cannot possibly endure analysis or meet the rigors of defensible research standards. We can almost hear the objections in the wings. Are we really creating, as some have claimed, a Tower of Babel?

We think not. We see no reason why tradition should define the limits of our aspirations. It is true that tradition provides a sense of stability, as it did for the fiddler on the roof. But mere stability is not enough. When stability reigns, one does not poke one's nose out of the tent. We need to reconcile two competing aspirations: stability and change. Change makes growth possible, and stability provides the continuity needed for community. Community without change is stagnant. Change without community has no social merit. We need both.

The implications of exploring and exploiting new forms of representation for the conduct and display of educational research are profound. It is beyond the scope of this chapter to discuss those implications in detail, but attention to a few might reveal their import for the education of educational researchers.

Consider what would need to be done to prepare educational researchers to do the kind of research we have been discussing. First, educational researchers have to understand some of the complex philosophical notions concerning the ways in which knowledge and knowing have been described. This would require familiarity with a philosophical literature that addresses standard forms of philosophical realism as well as literature of a phenomenological character. In addition, they would need to understand the relationship between relativism and pluralism and how symbolic forms, particularly those that are artistically treated, become means for advancing human understanding. The works of A.J. Ayer, Maurice Merlieu-Ponty, Ernst Cassirer, John Dewey, Susanne Langer, Nelson Goodman, Richard Rorty, and others would be relevant.

Those using artistically treated forms to conduct research ought to have a firm foundation in the relevant philosophical literature so that the process of doing that work becomes more than a technical achievement. In the broadest of terms we are talking about an understanding of alternative epistemologies.

Along with the foregoing there is, of course, the practical matter of acquiring the skills and sensibilities needed to use alternative forms of representation artistically. This achievement can be said to have two parts. First, there are technical requirements involved in, say, using a camera or a camcorder. One needs to know how things work at the very minimum. Second, and more demanding, is the problem of using the techniques one has acquired artistically. Doing so requires aesthetic judgment, and aesthetic judgment depends on refined sensibilities. Put another way, the creation of art requires artistry. To the extent to which artistically based research approximates those forms we call works of art, the sensibilities necessary to create such work need to be developed.

So researchers will need to develop both technical and artistic skills, and schools of education will need to make both human and material resources available to enable them to do so. Material resources pertain to both equipment and space—studios. Human resources refer to staff members or faculty who themselves are able to help students acquire such skills. Schools now provide such resources, of course, to develop the technical skills of statistics and computers. Computer laboratories are available in which students can refine the skills that they have acquired in their use. We are suggesting an expansion of what learning to do educational research requires.

The development of technical skills and aesthetic sensibilities must, of course, be related to ideas worth creating. If a scholar's initial perceptions lack insight, technical skills and even refined sensibilities are likely to lead to little more than superficial productions, though, at times, glittering ones. The content for artistic creation initiates in ideas that are fed by what is called perceptivity: seeing what most people miss. We need to find out the extent to which perceptivity can be developed.

Associated with perceptivity is the matter of providing a deep interpretation, or, as Geertz (1973) has said, a thick description of the events portrayed. Just what does this episode signify? What is its theoretical import? How does it relate to other matters within the situation? Answers to questions like these demand sophisticated analytic skills and imaginative extrapolation. What a researcher does with what he or she sees is critical. That doing depends upon imaginative extrapolation.

The acquisition of the skills, sensibilities, and interpretative abilities that we have described do not emerge in an initial exploration. Pilot studies are needed if for no other reason than to provide the kind of practice necessary for developing and refining the skills that we have described. Programs that prepare educational researchers will need to provide many occasions through which such pilot work can be undertaken.

Related to matters of research production is the importance of providing group critiques by other researchers and faculty. Such critiques, a common feature in most schools of art and music, not only offer useful feedback to the individual or individuals who have generated the work, but they also edify those who engage in the critique. Group critique is a form of cooperative learning. It fosters a learning community. It is not a time to tear apart a researchers work, but rather to explore its strengths and limitations so that it can become even stronger.

It would also be useful if exhibitions of the research took place during the academic year. Such exhibitions would afford others the opportunity to see what the research looks like, to find out what people do when they create it, and to determine whether it has an attractive pull for viewers. Put another way, the work of educational researchers needs to have a social setting so that it has public visibility. Researchers must now confine their observations to journals and books. We are talking about the creation of alternative arenas within which the work we have described can emerge. Unless alternative arenas are available to showcase new forms of representation, their development is likely to be hampered.

It is worth noting that the American Educational Research Association has become sensitive to the need for new formats and new venues for the display of educational research. Its 1993 Annual meeting, which attracted about 7,000 educational researchers from all over the world, explored various ways in which research could be presented. The creation of these new avenues reflects a tacit awareness by the world's major research organization that the conventional formats for the presentation of educational research have important limitations. We applaud the AERA's continuing efforts to increase diversity in the presentation of educational research.

Finally, faculty in schools of education will need to be appointed who not only have the traditional scholarly skills but also are willing and able to teach writing, film, photography, music, dance, or other artistic pursuits. We foresee the faculty in schools of education consisting of people who know how to create artistically generated educational research. Such appointments would help institutionalize the ideas we have advanced in this chapter. With their presence, the base of educational research will gradually change. We believe this change will significantly further our understanding of schooling and as a result enable us to create wiser educational policy and more effective educational practice.

Suggestions for Further Reading and References

Armstrong, M. (1980). *Closely observed children: Diary of a primary classroom*. London: Writers and Readers in association with Chameleon.

Bakhtin, M. M. (1981). *The dialogic imagination: Four essays*. Austin: University of Texas Press.

Barone, T. (1980). Effectively critiquing the experienced curriculum: Clues from the "new journalism." *Curriculum Inquiry, 10* (1), 29–53.

Barone, T. (1983). Things of use and things of beauty: The Swain County High School Arts Program. *Daedalus, 112* (3), 1–28.

Barone, T. (1987). On equality, visibility, and the fine arts program in a black elementary school: An example of educational criticism. *Curriculum Inquiry, 17* (4), 421–446. Barone, T. (1989). Ways of being at risk: The case of Billy Charles Barnett. *Phi Delta Kappan, 71* (2), 147–151.

Barone, T. (1990). Using the narrative text as an occasion for conspiracy. In E. Eisner & A. Peshkin (Eds.), *Qualitative Inquiry in Education: The Continuing Debate* (pp. 305–326). New York: Teachers College Press.

Barone. T. (1992a). A narrative of enhanced professionalism: Educational researchers and popular storybooks about schoolpeople. *Educational Researcher, 21* (9), 15–24.

Barone, T. (1992b). On the demise of subjectivity in educational inquiry. *Curriculum Inquiry, 22*(1), 25–38.

Barone, T. (1992c). Beyond theory and method: A case of critical storytelling. *Theory into Practice, 31*(2), 142–146.

Barone, T. (1995). Persuasive writings, vigilant readings, and reconstructed characters: The paradox of trust in educational storysharing. *International Journal of Qualitative Studies in Education, 8*(1) 63–74.

Belsey, C. (1980). *Critical practice*. London: Methuen.

Berk, L. (1980). Education in lives: Biographic narrative in the study of educational outcomes. *The Journal of Curriculum Theorizing, 2*(2), 88–154.

Berliner, D. (1986). In pursuit of the expert pedagogue, *Educational Researcher, 15*(7) 5–10.

Berliner, D. (1992). Telling the stories of educational psychology. *Educational Psychologist, 27*, 143–161.

Booth, W. (1961). *The rhetoric of fiction* (2nd ed.). Chicago: University of Chicago Press.

Booth, W. (1979). *Critical understanding*. Chicago: University of Chicago Press.

Britzman, D. (1991). *Practice makes practice: A critical study of learning to teach*. Albany: State University of New York Press.

Bruner, J. (1987). *Actual minds, possible worlds*. Cambridge, MA: Harvard University Press.

Bruner, J. (1990). *Acts of meaning*. Cambridge, MA: Harvard University Press.

Bullough, R. (1989). *First-year teacher: A case study*. New York: Teachers College Press.

Calkins, L. M. (1983). *Lessons from a child: On the teaching and learning of writing*. Melbourne, Australia: Heinemann.

Carter, K. (1993). The place of story in the study of teaching and teacher education. *Educational Researcher, 22*(1), 5–12, 18.

Clandinin, D. J., & Connelly, F. M. (1987). *Narrative, experience, and the study of curriculum.* Washington, DC: The American Association of Colleges for Teacher Education.

Clandinin, D. J., & Connelly, F. M. (1988). Studying teachers' knowledge of classrooms: Collaborative research, ethics and the negotiation of narrative. *The Journal of Educational Thought, 22*(2A), 269–282.

Clark, C. M., & Peterson, L. (1986). Teachers' thought processes. In M. Wittrock (Ed.), *Handbook of research on teaching* (3rd ed.) (pp. 255–295). New York: Macmillan.

Clifford, J., & Marcus, G. E. (Eds.). (1986). *Writing culture: The poetics and politics of ethnography.* Berkeley: University of California Press.

Connelly, F. M., & Clandinin, D. J. (1990). Stories of experience and narrative inquiry. *Educational Researcher, 19*(5), 2–14.

Connelly, F. M., & Clandinin, D. J. (1985). Personal practical knowledge and the modes of knowing: Relevance for teaching and learning. In E. Eisner (Ed.), *Learning and teaching the ways of knowing,* 84th Yearbook, Part 2, of the National Society for the Study of Education. Chicago: University of Chicago Press.

Delillo, D. (1988). *Libra.* New York: Penguin.

Dennison, G. (1969). *The lives of children: The story of the First Street School.* New York: Vantage Books.

Denzin, N. (1989). *Interpretive interactionism.* Newbury Park, CA: Sage.

Dewey, J. (1934/1958). *Art as experience.* New York: Capricorn Books.

Donmoyer, R. (1980). The evaluator as artist. *The Journal of Curriculum Theorizing, 2*(2), 12–26.

Donmoyer, R. (1983). The principal as prime mover. *Daedalus, 112*(3), 81–94.

Eisner, E. W. (1976). Educational connoisseurship and educational criticism: Their forms and functions in educational evaluation. *Journal of Aesthetic Education, Bicentennial Issue, 10*(3–4), 135–150.

Eisner, E. W. (1977). On the uses of educational connoisseurship and educational criticism for evaluating classroom life. *Teachers College Record, 78*(3) 345–358.

Eisner, E. W. (1979). The use of qualitative evaluation. *Journal of Educational Evaluation and Policy Analysis, 1*(6) 11–19.

Eisner, E. W. (1985). *The educational imagination* (2nd ed.). New York: Macmillan.

Eisner, E. W. (1988). The primacy of experience and the politics of method. *Educational Researcher, 17*(5), 23–34.

Eisner, E. W. (1991). *The enlightened eye: Qualitative inquiry and the enhancement of educational practice.* New York: Macmillan.

Eisner, E. W., & Flinders, D. (1994). Educational criticism as a form of qualitative inquiry. *Research in the Teaching of English, 28*(4), 341–357.

Elbaz, F. (1983). *Teacher thinking: A study of practical knowledge.* London: Croom Helm.

Elbaz, F. (1991). Research on teacher's knowledge: The evolution of a discourse. *Journal of Curriculum Studies, 23* (1), 1–19.

Feiman-Nemser, S., & Floden, R. (1986). The cultures of teaching. In M. Wittrock (ed) *Handbook of Research on Teaching* (3rd ed.) (pp. 505–526). New York: Macmillan.

Freedman, S. G. (1990). *Small victories: The real world of a teacher, her students, and their high school.* New York: Harper & Row.

Geertz, C. (1983). *Local knowledge: Further essays in interpretive anthropology.* New York: Basic Books.

Geertz, C. (1988). *Works and lives: The anthropologist as author.* Stanford, CA: Stanford University Press.

Goodson, I. (1992). *Studying teachers' lives.* London: Routledge.

Goodson, I., & Walker, R. (Eds.). (1991). *Biography, identity, and schooling: Episodes in educational research.* New York: Falmer Press.

Grumet, M. (1987). The politics of personal knowledge. *Curriculum Inquiry, 17,* 319–329.

Grumet, M. (1990). On daffodils that come before the swallow dares. In E. Eisner & A. Peshkin (Eds.), *Qualitative inquiry in education: The continuing debate* (pp. 101–120). New York: Teachers College Press.

Holquist, M. (1990). *Dialogism: Bakhtin and his world.* London: Routledge.

Hooks, B. (1991). Narratives of struggle. In P. Mariani (Ed.), *Critical fictions: The politics of imaginative writing* (pp. 53–61). Seattle, WA: Bay Press, 53–61.

Iser, W. (1974). *The implied reader.* Baltimore: Johns Hopkins University Press.

Jackson, P. (1968). *Life in classrooms.* Chicago: Holt, Rinehart & Winston.

Jackson, P. (1992). *Untaught lessons.* New York: Teachers College Press.

Kermode, F. (1967). *The sense of an ending: Studies in the theory of fiction.* London: Oxford University Press.

Kidder, T. (1989). *Among schoolchildren.* Boston: Houghton Mifflin.

Kotlowitz, A. (1991). *There are no children here: The story of two boys growing up in the other America.* New York: Doubleday.

Kozol, J. (1976). *Death at an early age.* New York: Houghton Mifflin.

Kuhn T. (1962). *The structure of scientific revolutions.* Chicago: University of Chicago Press.

Lancy, D. F. (1993). *Qualitative research in education: An introduction to the major traditions.* New York: Longman.

Langer, S. K. (1942/1957). *Problems of art.* New York: Charles Scribner's Sons.

Lightfoot, S. L. (1983). *The good high school: Portraits in character and culture.* New York: Basic Books.

McCutcheon, G. (1976). *The disclosure of classroom life.* Unpublished doctoral dissertation, Stanford University.

McLaren, P. (1993). *Schooling as a ritual performance: Towards a political economy of educational symbols and gestures* (2nd ed.). London: Routledge.

McLaughlin, D., & Tierney, W. G. (Eds.). (1993). *Naming silenced lives: Personal narratives and the process of educational change.* New York: Routledge.

Maitre, D. (1983). *Literature and possible worlds.* London: Pembridge Press.

Miller, J. (1990). *Creating spaces and finding voices: Teachers collaborating for empowerment.* Albany: State University of New York Press.

Natkins, L. G. (1986). *Our last term: A teacher's diary.* Lanham, MD: University Press of America.

Nespor, J., & Barylske, J. (1991). Narrative discourse and teacher knowledge. *American Educational Research Journal, 28*(4), 805–823.

Pagano, J. (1992). Moral fictions: The dilemma of theory and practice. In C. Witherell & N. Noddings (Eds.), *Stories lives tell: Narrative and dialogue in education* (193–206). New York: Teachers College Press.

Paley, V. G. (1981). *Wally's stories: Conversations in the kindergarten.* Cambridge, MA: Harvard University Press

Paley, V. G. (1986). *Molly is three: Growing up in school.* Chicago: University of Chicago Press.

Pinar, W. (1975). The analysis of educational experience. In W. Pinar (Ed.), *Curriculum theorizing: The reconceptualists* (pp. 384–395). Berkeley: McCutchan.

Pinar, W. (1975). Currere: Toward reconceptualization. In W. Pinar (Ed.), *Curriculum theorizing: The reconceptualists* (pp. 396–414). Berkeley: McCutchan.

Pinar, W. (1975). Search for a method. In W. Pinar (Ed.), *Curriculum theorizing: The reconceptualists* (pp. 415–424). Berkeley: McCutchan.

Pinar, W. (1980). Life history and educational experience. *The Journal of Curriculum Theorizing, 2*(2), 159–211.

Pinar, W., & Grumet, M., Eds. (1976). *Toward a poor curriculum.* Dubuque: Kendall Hunt.

Polkinghorn, D. E. (1988). *Narrative knowing and the human sciences.* New York: State University of New York Press.

Polanyi, M. (1967). *The tacit dimension.* London: Routledge and Kegan Paul.

Ricoeur, P. (1984). *Time and narrative, Vol. I.* Chicago: University of Chicago Press.

Ricoeur, P. (1985). *Time and narrative, Vol. II.* Chicago: University of Chicago Press.

Ricoeur, P. (1988). *Time and narrative, Vol. III.* Chicago: University of Chicago Press.

Rorty, R. (1989). *Contingency, irony, and solidarity.* Cambridge: Cambridge University Press.

Ross, V. J. (1986). *Bite the wall!* Palm Springs, CA: ETC Publications.

Ryan, K. (1970). *Don't smile until Christmas: Accounts of the first year of teaching.* Chicago: University of Chicago Press.

Scholes, R., & Kellogg, R. (1966). *The nature of narrative.* Oxford: Oxford University Press.

Schubert, W., & Ayers, W. C. (Eds.). (1992). *Teacher lore: Learning from our own experience.* New York: Longman.

Schutz, A. (1962). In B. Nathanson (Ed.), *The collected papers, Volume I,* (Vol. 1). The Hague: M. Nijhoff.

Sellito, P. (1991). *Balancing acts: A novel.* Unpublished doctoral dissertation, Hofstra University.

Toulmin, S. (1953). *Philosophy of science.* London: Hutchinson University Library.

Updike, J. (1990). *Rabbit at rest.* New York: Fawcett Crest.

Vallance, E. (1977). The landscape of "The Great Plains Experience": An application of curriculum criticism. *Curriculum Inquiry, 7*(2), 87–106.

Van Maanen, J. (1988). *Tales from the field: On writing ethnography.* Chicago: University of Chicago Press.

Willis, G. (Ed.). (1978). *Qualitative evaluation: Concepts and cases in curriculum criticism.* Berkeley: McCutchan.

Witherell, C., & Noddings, N. (1991). *Stories lives tell: Narrative and dialogue in education.* New York: Teachers College Press.

Yonemura, M. (1986). *A teacher at work: Professional development and the early childhood educator.* New York: Teachers College Press.

Study Questions

1. Why do arts-based inquirers create "virtual worlds"? Can a virtual world be nonfictional? Explain.

2. Explain the difference between stating meaning and expressing meaning. Imagine an original example of each.

3. How does literary-style writing promote empathic understanding? Why is it central to arts-based inquiry?

4. What is meant by the story form? How can a story's formal qualities prompt readers to question their value systems?

5. What is the aim of the educational critic, and what is the range of phenomena upon which that critic focuses?

6. What are four important structural elements of educational criticism? What functions does each serve?

7. What are the historical sources of narrative storytelling as educational research?

8. Can arts-based educational studies be "validated"? Explain.

9. Do arts-based studies pertain only to themselves or do they "generalize"? What role do theme and imagery play in the process of "generalization"?

10. Are arts-based studies "truthful"? In what sense? Are they "subjective," "objective," neither, or both? Explain.

11. What forms of representation besides language may arts-based researchers imply?

12. What knowledge, skills, and sensibilities do arts-based educational researchers need? How can these be acquired?

13. How are scientific studies also artistic in character?

Readings

Introduction
Some Examples of Arts-Based Qualitative Research

Tom Barone and Elliot Eisner

The preceding pages described the assumptions, concepts, and issues pertaining to an artistically grounded approach to educational research. This section presents and examines two exemplars of such research: a complete essay and segments from a larger essay. In the full essay, the author, Tom Barone, portrays the life of an individual student and teases out from that portrayal its implications for American schools. The segments are selected from a larger essay by Phillip W. Jackson. These segments illustrate the way aesthetics influence the use of written language. Note how the author uses allusion and innuendo to transcend the literal.

"Ways of Being at Risk: The Case of Billy Charles Barnett," was written by Tom Barone, one of the authors of this chapter. The review you will read has been written by Elliot Eisner, the chapter's co-author.

What is it that Barone is up to in this piece, and in what sense is his work artistically grounded? These two key questions will keep us occupied.

Before we address these questions, keep in mind that we take the view that all research in the social sciences depends in some degree on artistry for its successful completion. Nevertheless, there is a genre of work, which these selections exemplify, that pay particular attention to forms of perception and disclosure that have aesthetic or artistic features. Our selection of essays by Barone and Jackson represent that class of writing and that genre of research.

To reiterate, we regard the works that follow as a genre of research, not simply a genre of writing. Each of the authors is writing from empirical data. In Jackson's case, the data are recalled from the distant past, and in Barone's, from a recent encounter with Billy Charles Barnett. Both authors attempt to make vivid their experience with their central characters. Even in this age of post-modernism, both are interested in saying what is true about the people and situations about whom they write. Both authors are interested in not only the particulars of each situation but also in the larger educational issues these particulars represent. Put another way, there is a generalizing tendency within each of the essays, and it is for the reader to decide on its "validity," import, or usefulness. Both authors have created works that require, on the one hand, attention to matters of fidelity; they ask "Did I get it right?" And on the other hand, the works require their skill in crafting the language and in constructing theoretical and practical implications. In short, both of these works have things to say about the educational world, and these things are born of reflective attention, analytic insight, and the ability to extrapolate to the world beyond the one they wrote about. We think that what they have to say is worth hearing and that it has the capacity to enlarge human understanding. That, of course, is the function of research.

We return to Barone.

One feature of Barone's work on which all else depends is perception. Barone's refined perception—his skills of educational connoiseurship—provides the qualities of experience that he uses to make vivid what is subtle, yet significant. These important subtleties come strikingly alive in Barone's attention to Billy Charles' "slurps on a straw," to the shock of his own realization that he, Barone, did not know either a culture or a way of life existing only two hours from his home, and even more, that this strange culture possessed values that though different from the mainstream were, nevertheless, of value.

The construction of any telling narrative depends on the writer's ability to read the scene. To do this, the scene needs to be seen. Barone notices what counts. Noticing what counts cannot occur without an ability to appreciate the potential meanings of what has been noticed; indeed, noticing what counts requires some sense of what counts in the first place. Barone's observations about Billy Charles' relationship with his mother, his initiative and ability to pursue his bliss, and his assessment of the utility of his own school experience demand an interpretive frame of reference from the start. Barone, like others who work in this genre, brings a wealth of interpretive frameworks to his work.

It should be noted that Barone did not know what he was going to find when he initiated this study. As a matter of fact, he acknowledges that other people led him to believe that he would encounter a very different Billy Charles than the one he found. Barone needed to abandon prior expectations when he saw that they did not fit the case. The act of constructive interpretation and the assessment of the particulars of the case meanings that matter is a creative event. Meaning is not encountered, it is constructed. Barone constructed meaning from how he construed what he encountered.

But meanings are, at least initially, private affairs. They can live in the dark, in a world of our private personal consciousness. They need not be shared. All of us have fantasies we do not share, images we do not portray, and ideas we do not disclose. For ideas to have social value, they need to have a public presence. Artistry is required for making the transition between the interior life of lived experience and the public presence that representation affords.

Writing is a public affair, at least when it is read by someone other than the writer. To write requires a transformation of ideas into a medium whose content and form can convey those ideas back to both the writer and the reader. Artistry is present here too. Note how Barone sets up his piece: He provides a brief glimpse of Billy Charles, the context in which he lives, and, by way of contrast, a brief sketch of himself as a "middle-aged urban academic who, secure in a tenured university position, will *never* leave school." In one short paragraph Barone tells us about Billy Charles' physical features, the vice principal's expectations for the boy's future, and about the distance between Barone's situation and that of Billy Charles. Is this material artistically crafted? Try to write a more telling introductory paragraph in four sentences.

If a reader looks at what Barone *does* in his essay and not simply at what he *says*, the author's strategies emerge quite clearly. Barone begins with a description of the setting and the major players. He provides this information in the first paragraph. He then moves to other people's expectations of Billy Charles; these negative features did not conform to the boy. Billy Charles was not at all what Barone was led to believe about him. Barone's confession displays candor, and he follows up immediately by providing a vivid example of Billy Charles' mastery "of the fundamentals of a world no longer honored in the dominant culture." This set-up of dashed expectations and the compelling description of "jugging," followed by a "Do you know how to make turtle soup?" provides the introductory theme that will be elaborated and made explicit near the end of the essay; that theme is that Billy Charles knows how to survive in a tough, complex world—but it is not the world of schools. He is at risk all right, but it is a risk *created* by the school, not by the boy himself. Furthermore, the school assigns little or no merit to what the child does know, and the culture of the school does not value his culture. The school creates a mismatch between the student and the teachers and between the student and the administrators. Neither the teachers nor the administrators bother to understand the life that Billy Charles has been forced to lead, which was shaped primarily by an abusive father and a mother who does not appear to have the psychological strength to provide what her son needs.

Barone crafts a narrative that keeps the reader on line. The narrative begins with particulars that are embedded in a story that makes them vivid and which gradually opens up to several broad basic educational issues such as: Just what is educationally basic? What values do schools promulgate, and are they helpful in advancing the student's educational development or are they simply instrumental to vocational adaptation? How can meaning be restored to the experience of schooling, especially perhaps to those students who simply have learned to adapt to external demands they do not really care about? Is being in school necessarily a virtue for all students? Might it not just be possible that given the ways in which most schools function, some students would be better served outside of them?

In the end, Barone refuses to give up on the promise of schooling. The current state of schooling, even as problematic as it is, is a condition to be addressed, not an institution to be abandoned. Barone emerges as an optimist, probably not a bad personal state for someone working in the field of education. After all, education is itself an optimistic enterprise.

The potency of Barone's story depends on his ability to make sense of Billy Charles and his life in and out of school. And it depends upon Barone's ability to transform what he sees, feels, and knows into prose that will convey these qualities of life. His text displays a sensitivity to tempo, employs metaphor without apology, exploits image through vivid writing, possesses voice, utilizes plot to sustain interest, and comes to closure with a coda that presents both a tough challenge to educators and, at the same time, a sense of hope. One comes away with questions about the meaning of "being at risk," and, more pointedly, just who or what that well-worn phrase refers to. These questions help us reexamine basic premises and fundamental assumptions. Not much could be more important as we seek to set an agenda for research that will lead to genuine educational reform.

Ways of Being at Risk:
The Case of Billy Charles Barnett

Tom Barone

We are the representatives of two subcultures, meeting at a McDonald's along an interstate highway in northeastern Tennessee. Sitting across from me is Billy Charles Barnett, a tall lanky boy with dark hair, green eyes, a pug nose, and an infectious grin. He is a member of the rural "disadvantaged," a 15-year-old nominated by the vice principal as the student least likely to remain in Dusty Hollow Middle School. I am a middle-aged urban academic who, secure in a tenured university position, will *never* leave school.

I am inclined to believe the warnings of others like me—teachers and administrators at Billy Charles' school—that this teenager from the hills will be "slow" and "hard to talk to." I am, therefore, surprised to discover almost immediately a keen intelligence and an eagerness to share his knowledge about his world. Even more jolting is a sudden realization of my vast ignorance about the ways of people who live within a two-hour drive of my home and about the fundamentals of a world no longer honored in the dominant culture.

Between slurps on a straw, Billy Charles speaks:

> You don't know what jugging is? When you go jugging, first you take a jug that bleach comes in. You rinse it out and tighten the lid and get some soft but strong nylon string. Then you need to get a two-inch turtlehook, real strong . . . and a three- or four-foot line. The best bait is a bluegill, cut in half. You know, you really should use the head part. It's better than the tail, because turtles always go for the head of the fish first. But you can [also] catch catfish, bass, like this. I caught me a 7-and-a-half-pound bass once, jugging. The jug just hangs in the water and nothing can get off the line unless they break it. I can catch a mess of turtles [this way], and then I make turtle soup. Do you know how to make turtle soup?

I find myself squirming in my seat. But why? Why should I be the one feeling inadequate and defensive? No, I didn't know—until Billy Charles told me—that the market was bearish on coonskins this year, and that I could expect no more than $40 for a flawless one of average size. The topic had simply never come up in any graduate course on curriculum theory. Moreover, E. D. Hirsch and his co-authors had included no such items in their *Dictionary of Cultural Literacy: What Every American Needs to Know*. So I take comfort: Not only am I the better educated, but also apparently the better *American* of the two strangers chomping on their cheeseburgers on this unseasonably balmy January afternoon.

Although I know nothing about the price of coonskins, I am better informed about Billy Charles than he is about me. For example, I know that Billy Charles is spending a second year in the seventh grade. I know that he has expressed on numerous occasions his intentions to drop out of school as soon as he can. And I know that, on occasion, he has entertained fantasies of dropping out of life, as well.

The last item is, of course, the most troublesome. *Specific suicidal ideations* is the phrase used by the school psychologist to characterize Billy Charles's morbid fantasies. Having ventured forth from my cozy, book-lined office to conduct a case study of what I thought would be a typical at-risk student, I would soon be forced to rethink my tired notions about such fundamentals as, oh, the meaning of life, the purposes of schooling, and the various ways in which an adolescent can be at risk of not being educated. To explain what I mean, let me tell you my own short version of Billy Charles's life story.

Billy Charles Barnett was born in the hills of northern Tennessee on 28 March 1974. When Billy Charles was 2, his parents were divorced, and his mother received custody of him. His father moved to another part of the state, where he remarried and divorced several times, never receiving custody of any of the children from those marriages. When Billy Charles was 8, his father returned to live near Dusty Hollow. Billy Charles began to visit his father a few times a year. At age 13, in the seventh grade, he began to spend more and more time with a dad who passionately loved to hunt and fish and trap. Billy Charles decided to move into his father's house, located in (he still insists, even today) "paradise": a densely wooded area, thoroughly distanced from the world of convenience stores, gas stations, and book-lined classrooms.

What had begun to stir in Billy Charles is easily remembered by most former 13-year-olds. Billy Charles was beginning to think about who he was: the son, the grandson, the great-grandson, and maybe the great-great-grandson of frontiersmen in the upper South who remained in that region as the frontier moved on. Perhaps the sons of each succeeding generation felt what Billy Charles has hinted to me: violated and abandoned, as "civilization" barged in to distort the shape of their lives. But even today the allure of the woods remains intoxicating to many of the menfolk, who have traditionally been charged with providing their families with the necessities of life.

Some of these men (Billy Charles's stepfather among them) have managed to relegate outdoor activities to the margins of their lives, taking to their shotguns and fishing gear only on weekends. But not Billy Charles. At least not since he started to become a man. Billy Charles has always loved the outdoors, but what his mother calls his "obsession" with hunting, fishing, and trapping, began a couple of years ago and accounts (she insists) for his initial desire to live with his father.

That was a glorious time, according to Billy Charles. He was ecstatic to finally have for his very own a father to connect him to the past that lived within him, a male parent versed in the ways of the wilderness to guide him into his own Appalachian manhood.

Almost daily Billy Charles and his father went out in the wilds, the two of them together, teacher and apprentice. Billy Charles was joyously receiving an education in the *real* basics, eagerly learning the time-honored skills of survival (as opposed to such pale school-honored imitations such as how to write a check or how to fill out a job application). He was absorbed in the fundamentals of the world around him. Almost daily for more than a year, rain or shine, this wilderness school was in session. Even after the master turned on his eager pupil. Even, at least for a while, after the beatings began.

The friction started early in the summer when Billy Charles's father introduced some female strangers into the household: a new wife and a 9-year-old stepdaughter. Billy Charles's version is that he was now burdened with cooking for four instead of for two. ("It was a lot more work and all she [the stepmother] ever did was eat ice cream and watch TV.") The resentment probably runs even deeper, rooted in the slight Billy Charles must have felt as his father's attention was divided and shared with others. Whatever the cause, tensions rose, and the beatings increased in frequency and in severity, reaching a peak when his father attacked him with a horsewhip.

So a father turns viciously on a son, who, in a time of delicate adolescent need, is reluctant to leave—until the final incident of abuse when the new family decides to vacation in Florida.

While in Florida, Billy Charles wrote a letter to his mother, describing his increasingly unhappy life. His father somehow managed to read the letter, and Billy Charles awoke, he says, to the pain of being pulled from the couch by his hair and slammed across the room. Not even the memory of the exciting encounter with a hammerhead shark on a previous day's deep-sea expedition could prevent a second change of custody. Not even the image of his father's face that, as Billy Charles poignantly admitted to me, now makes him depressed when it appears before him unbeckoned. So, on the verge of manhood, Billy Charles went back to Mama, back to a place strewn with so many obstacles to his escape.

Billy Charles has always resisted any encroachment of the school world on his freedom outside. Rarely, for example, has he deigned to do his homework. But he is frequently reminded of his sins of omission, as his mother and three sisters collaborate on school assignments in the crowded kitchen. So he retreats further inward, into a bedroom shared with two young men in their early twenties—his cousin, Carl, and Teddy, a friend of Carl's. (Only temporary boarders, says Billy Charles's stepdad, only until Carl's parents "work things out.") What does he do there all night? Billy Charles corroborated what one of his teachers told me: "I asked him and he said, 'I crawl into bed. And I die.' That's what he said, 'I just die.'"

If Billy Charles feels cramped, is he ever tempted to create some artificial space for himself through the use of drugs? His mother once caught him using an amphetamine. He was promptly hauled off to the police station, and this experience, his mother believes, was sufficiently traumatic for him to swear off any further drug use. Maybe so. But an earlier, much more stunning incident seems to have produced a deeper fear, at least of harder drugs. Several years ago, as Billy Charles tells it, a good friend, while sitting right beside him, had injected himself with an overdose. Just a couple of 9-year-olds in northern Tennessee, one watching the other die, 1980s style. Recently the memory was revived when Teddy's girlfriend died in an identical manner. This, too, has depressed Billy Charles. I have wondered (but have lacked the courage to ask) about the possible relationship between these morbid memories and his own "specific suicidal ideations."

Billy Charles's imagination is his only source of escape during his self-described "imprisonment" by day. The school bus deposits him at Dusty Hollow Middle School at 8:15 every morning, and by second period—math, the period when the cage seems the smallest—Billy Charles is gone. He leaves through his mind—but always on foot. "I am walking in the hills," he says, recalling the leaves and the ground and the foxes and the possums. "I love to walk." Before meeting Billy Charles I had never known a 15-year-old without the slightest desire to drive a car. But driving is simply not of interest to him. Says Billy Charles, "I can walk to wherever I want to go."

Although Billy Charles is rarely present in spirit at school, he drifts less often out of his social studies and reading classes. The social studies class is taught by Billy Charles's favorite teacher, a bright, inventive young man who attempts to inject some liveliness into classroom activities with various simulation games, films, and student-centered projects.

Billy Charles's interest in reading class may be surprising, for Billy Charles has never been an avid reader. There is an encyclopedia in his house, and there are dictionaries. But there are few books and no daily newspaper. Billy Charles has not been raised in a home in which reading is seen as a delicious way to spend idle time. Perhaps his relative success in reading class is due to the special attention that is afforded him there. Billy Charles scores fairly well on most standardized tests, but he was placed in a "special education" reading class because he had been "disruptive" in other classes and was considered more "manageable" in smaller groups. He is reportedly less abusive and obnoxious to the reading teacher.

For the most part, though, school and the world of Billy Charles do not overlap. On weekdays, he is locked in his school's embrace, but he is often dreaming of another time, another place, imagining that he is free, his own man in a future when every day is Saturday. His is a vision awash in nostalgia, adamantly culling out for celebration only the pleasant features of the past—the thrill of the catch, the pan-fired trout, and the time spent under his father's benign tutelage—while screening out the unbearable: his father's scowl, his friend's limp body, or anything (like, say, a car or a classroom) invented since the Industrial Revolution. But the selectivity of Billy Charles's memory is understandable, and it represents, I believe, a hopeful sign. For it is only when his defenses break down and the grim ghosts of episodes past invade his psyche that Billy Charles seems most seriously at risk of abandoning more than just a formal education.

Does his vision of the future include earning a living? Billy Charles is utterly convinced that his own talents at tapping the bounty of nature will be sufficient to provide the necessities of life. As if to seal his argument, he points to his father, who works at odd jobs (currently selling bait out of a small store) to supplement his "natural" income. Others in the area are skeptical about the possibility of living only off the land these days, pointing to stringent enforcement of the legal limitations regarding season and size of catches.

And is Billy Charles foreseeing the possibility of a future family whose hungry mouths demand more than he can provide? Odds are that Billy Charles will once again find his hours divided into time lived and time served, as the time clock replaces the clock on the classroom wall. Still, his expectations are so robustly romantic, so close to those that even members of my branch of our frontier culture were so recently forced to abandon, that I have found myself hoping along with him: Maybe there is a way. What if, for example, he changed his mind about the ethics of teaching for a living? Billy Charles recently forked over $100 for a weekend of instruction in a "trapping school." He found it rather useless (as would any advanced student in a remedial class). "But," I asked, "have you ever thought of opening a school of your own or becoming a guide to earn your own money?"

Grinning, Billy Charles answered, "Oh no, I don't believe that it's right to sell just words, to sell what you know, to make a living."

When I pointed out to him that words are precisely what his teachers sell, his reply was another grin. But Billy Charles is young, so we may hope for future compromises of his rigorous ethical standards. Getting paid for opening up his treasure chest of backwoods wisdom to weekend sportsmen still seems to me both pragmatic and honorable.

Of course, Billy Charles wouldn't need any more formal schooling for such an occupation. On the contrary, if this were his goal, school might then be precisely what he already believes it to be: an unwarranted roadblock on the path to the "good life." This is an unsettling notion to those of us who work devotedly toward fulfilling those goals of universal mandatory schooling. But what are those goals? By the time such academically disinclined students such as Billy Charles reach the middle grades, we think we see their future just ahead. To paraphrase the vice principal at his school, Billy Charles will, at best, become a common laborer like his stepfather, perhaps working nights operating within a forklift. And seldom, if ever, will he read a newspaper or a novel or a book of poetry.

So we abandon any lingering hopes for Billy Charles's conversion to a world of erudition and instead focus on *our* version of the basics. Teenagers unlikely ever to attend college must, we assume, be equipped with the mental skills appropriate to a working class life: minimal competence in the basics; maybe an additional dash of content from the dominant culture (what *every* American needs to know); the basic skills of a trade, which we hope will be acquired in a high school vocational track; and, certainly, the employee's attitude, a demeanor tacitly encouraged by the organizational structure of the school and composed of a nexus of behavioral norms (such a perseverance, promptness, diligence, and intellectual docility) needed for the industrial workplace. If the noncollege-bound acquire these learnings, we the taxpayers are placed at lower risk of having to fork over welfare money, and prospective employers are placed at lower risk of having to provide remedial education for candidates for employment.

But, I ask myself again, what of students such as Billy Charles who have equipped themselves to eke out a living (maybe even legally) within the cracks of the modern global economy? Billy Charles is not illiterate (and perhaps no more aliterate than the average citizen), and he possesses much more than the minimal knowledge needed for his own way of life. Could it be that Billy Charles's economic well-being is jeopardized only by our persistent attempts to inculcate values and behaviors that are, in fact, counterproductive to the successful conduct of his line of work? What use, after all, are passivity and punctuality to denizens of the forest?

Stated flatly, is Billy Charles at risk only if he stays in school? On those moments when I forget about the purposes of schooling that transcend the narrow focus on careers, my answer is yes. Then I am visited by Maria Montessori's vivid metaphor of students in rigid rows of desks as butterflies pinned to a display case. I confess to entertaining, at those moments, the impossible fantasy of pulling the pin and setting Billy Charles free.

How many other Billy Charleses are there—potential dropouts with the wits and wherewithal to survive financially in a world that worships the high school diploma? The conventional wisdom—the wisdom of my subculture, the legitimated wisdom—says "not many." There are other exceptions to the rule, of course, including the future stars of stage, screen, or playing field, the youthful heirs of family fortunes, or even the honest entrepreneurs-to-be. But I am incapable of imagining many stories like that of Billy Charles.

Nevertheless, I am reluctant to abandon the promises of schooling, even for such an exceptional case as Billy Charles. Indeed, his very exceptionality invites us to look beyond the narrowly pragmatic, utilitarian objectives of schooling to recollect a more substantial notion of the purposes of education. His case revives our fading dreams of a broader sort of empowerment that schools once hoped to provide for *all* American children, regardless of their economic or social backgrounds. This included the power to use the disciplines for penetrating more deeply into one's own past and present world, the power to imagine a wide range of alternative worlds in other times and places, and the power to express these understandings by employing many forms of literacy—verbal, visual, musical, kinesthetic, and so on.

This is where the exceptionality of Billy Charles ends and his commonality begins. For these are powers of thought and expression so often denied not only to the Billy Charleses among us but also to the many respectable students for whom schooling is merely endured for the payoff of financial security and social standing. Them I have known much longer, those classroom drones who remain (like Billy Charles) seriously at risk of never becoming truly educated. They may pass their courses, but they are just as inevitably failed by their schools.

The institution of the school has also failed to facilitate mutual acquaintance among the people who inhabit it. I will not document the obstacles that have kept teachers and administrators from seeing Billy Charles as I have been privileged to see him. I leave it to other essays to explore the kind of restructuring that is needed before schoolpeople can pay closer attention to the life histories of other students like Billy Charles. His relatively benign experiences in a less crowded reading class and in a livelier social studies class only hint at the directions of that restructuring.

But even educators like Billy Charles's reading and social studies teachers will usually need help in acquiring the kind of knowledge that I lacked when I first met that scruffy stranger under McDonald's golden arches. Cocooned in the world of the middle-class educator, we are insulated from unfamiliar norms and ways of life. We have lost—indeed, we have been systematically encouraged to lose—the ability to reach out to honor the places (whether the barrio, the ghetto, the reservation, the Appalachian holler, or simply the peaks and pits of adolescence) where our students live.

Of course, a restructuring that gives teachers the time, the resources, and the motivation to learn about the individual worlds of their students will be only a beginning. Empathy alone is not enough. It is merely a necessary condition for a second element crucial to good teaching: the development of educational activities that can broaden students' horizons. Teachers in a school with a Billy Charles Barnett will not only need to understand the importance of making turtle soup, but they will also need to entice students to study cuisines from other cultures. Math teachers will need the curricular finesse to lead students outward from field-and-stream economics to numeracy in other contexts. However, as John Dewey wisely noted long ago, one cannot effectively lead students outward without starting from the place where they currently reside.

Empowering teachers (and students) in this way may require more resources than our society is willing to provide. We will need to reeducate teachers, to reduce their workload, and to purchase material resources to link the local community with the larger one. Thus far, we have lacked the vision and the will to commit the resources necessary to this effort. Instead, we have sometimes resorted to gimmicks to lure our children back to school. In some Florida schools, pizza is offered as an incentive to attend classes. In one Kentucky district, a snazzy car is raffled off as a door prize for students with good attendance records. But should such bribery succeed in filling classrooms with warm bodies, will this no longer be a nation at risk of losing the hearts and wasting the minds of its young people? I think not.

I venture to suggest the heresy that we would not necessarily be better off were the dropout rate to decrease dramatically tomorrow. We conveniently forget the role of the traditional American school in perpetuating a seriously impoverished notion of what constitutes an education. Before we could say that a lower dropout rate is good news, we would need to know whether the reasons for not leaving school are valid ones. Are students remaining because we have become serious about introducing meaning into the life of the classroom? Are they staying because we have equipped our teachers with the means for knowing and respecting their students' pasts even as they attempt to open up their futures? And why would we need to know whether these things are occurring? Because Billy Charles Barnett has reminded us that doing anything less is still a very risky business.

Another Example of Arts-Based Research

Tom Barone and Elliot Eisner

Following are the first two pages of Phillip Jackson's "B[e]aring the Traces: Reflections on a Sense of Being Indebted to a Teacher" (Jackson, 1992). We have selected this piece because we believe it exemplifies one of the ways in which sensitivity, insight, and imagination can be combined to create an apparition. Jackson uses this apparition as the basis of a powerful examination of skepticism: How is it possible to know the world as it really is, thus avoiding the debilitating effects of skepticism regarding our ability to understand or know?

In this chapter, Jackson is primarily concerned with a deep philosophic issue: Can we know what exists? When he writes the word "know," he means *knowledge* of reality, not simply *beliefs* about reality. Knowledge, everyone seems to believe, requires scientific justification, "hard data." He concludes at the end of his examination of this issue—which because of space we cannot include here— that he cannot really know his teacher's effects upon him in the sense in which scientific knowledge is conceived of, but he can act as if they were as important as he believes them to be. By so acting, he can escape the grip of debilitating skepticism or, even worse, cynicism. Certainty and TRUTH are beyond the pale. But we need not despair. Our lives are given meaning by what we do, not by achieving a certainty that is unattainable.

Now this argument which most of his essay addresses is built upon an artistically crafted illustration. The illustration is the one that appears here: reflections on a former teacher. Without the vividness, the suspense, the humor, and the impact he was able to create, the case that follows would have a weak foundation. Mrs. Henzie, recollected by a middle-aged academic, provides the conditions his philosophic inquiry is intended, in part, to illustrate.

The illustration itself is a mix between his uncertainty about what Mrs. Henzie taught him and a vivid portrait of a teacher and her classroom. We are not likely soon to forget Mrs. Henzie's thick ankles, her sensible shoes, her shorter than average dumpy appearance. But especially, we will not forget "Keep your wits about you!" and her octagonal glasses flashing like twin mirrors with reflected light. Most of us can also recall how it felt to be called upon by a teacher who seemed to have eyes in the back of her head!

Jackson's ability to put us there again is critical for helping us understand the lack of clarity, the uncertainty, of what it was that she really taught him or that he learned from her. Yet, at the same time, he has no doubt that it was something important.

What we have here is a study of empirical data transformed in tranquility by a deep and thoughtful scholar. Jackson's is a philosophic study—a kind of narrative research—of his past that is used as a foundation for the study of his present uncertainties.

B(e)aring the Traces:
Reflections on a Sense of
Being Indebted to a Former Teacher

Phillip W. Jackson

Mrs. Theresa Henzi was my high school algebra teacher in Vineland, New Jersey, in 1942, my freshman year. She was a heavyset woman, shorter than average, almost dumpy in appearance, and somewhat dowdy in attire—nondescript dresses with hems at mid-calf, modest cameo brooch pinned to the collar, and "sensible" shoes with low heels and laces. Her ankles were thick and she wore rimless, octagonal glasses whose lenses reflected light much of the time, making it difficult to read the look in her eyes. She had a pleasant, round face framed by warm brown hair, streaked with gray. I would guess she must have been in her mid to late fifties during the year I had her as my teacher.

What I remember most vividly about my early morning classes in Mrs. Henzi's room was the way she handled our homework assignments. Three or four students at a time would be sent to the blackboard at the front of the room to work out one of the problems that had been assigned the day before. These were usually textbook exercises consisting of equations to be simplified and solved for x. Mrs. Henzi, standing at the side of the room opposite the windows, her glasses flashing with reflected light, would read the problem aloud for the students at the board to copy and solve while the rest of us looked on. As each student finished his calculations, he would turn and face the front of the room, moving slightly to one side as he did in order to make his board work visible. Mrs. Henzi would inspect each solution carefully (as would everyone who was seated), noting not only the answer but each of the steps taken to reach it. (All of the calculations had to be displayed in detail on the board.) If everything was correct, she would send the student back to his seat with a word of praise and a curt nod. If the student had made an error she would have him take a close look at his work to see if he could find his mistake. "There is something wrong there, Robert," she would say, "Take another look." If after a few seconds of scrutiny Robert was unable to detect his error, Mrs. Henzi would ask for volunteers (of which there were usually plenty) to point out where their hapless classmate had gone wrong.

The most memorable part of this daily routine usually took place in the midst of each round of blackboard calculations before even the quickest student had finished his work. It was then that Mrs. Henzi would bark a command whose occurrence became routine. Its precise timing was always unexpected, however, and she delivered it in a voice whose volume made the whole class react with a start. "KEEP YOUR WITS ABOUT YOU!" she would thunder. One was seldom sure at first to whom these words were directed, if to anyone in particular. Often they sounded as though they were meant for all of us. But at other times the direction of Mrs. Henzi's gaze made it apparent that she had detected an error in the making and was warning its would-be perpetrator that he or she was about to go wrong and was headed for an algebraic waterloo. Because it was not always clear which of these was so, the effect of each outburst, in addition to startling everyone, was to make those of us in our seats scrutinize the board work with renewed fervor, searching for the error that Mrs. Henzi with her x-ray eyes seemed to have caught almost before it happened.

The students at the board did not always gain in alertness in response to these admonitions. Sometimes one or more of them, each convinced that he or she was the target of Mrs. Henzi's outburst, would go back to check on calculations already completed and in the process become so flustered that they would wind up adding mistakes where there had been none. Even if they could find no errors in their previous work, they would sometimes persist in their search for quite some time before moving on from where they had left off, having wasted a goodly amount of time in the process. On the whole, however, Mrs. Henzi's command had a positive effect. With every refrain of "KEEP YOUR WITS ABOUT YOU!" the class as a whole grew more attentive.

The remainder of what took place during that year in Mrs. Henzi's algebra class is mostly a blur to me now. I recall doing a fair amount of seatwork and I think we were given weekly quizzes on Fridays, but that's about it insofar as my memory of specific events is concerned. Oddly enough, I do not retain any visual memory of Mrs. Henzi in the act of what today is sometimes referred to as "frontal teaching," which is to say, standing in the front of the room, chalk in hand, giving direct instruction about how to do this or that. I try to picture her in that posture, which I am sure she must have adopted on countless occasions, but all I come up with is the image of her standing at the side of the room supervising our daily review of homework, her octagonal eyeglasses flashing like twin mirrors with reflected light.

Conclusion

Tom Barone and Elliot Eisner

The examples of arts-based educational research by Barone and Jackson are two examples among a profusion of such research texts. Their status as legitimate educational research is more secure today than even a decade ago. Still, it is not uncommon to confront skeptics who find such texts entertaining and informative but wonder whether they are *really* research. In return, the authors of this chapter have wondered why the careful scrutinizing of the world by artists of all sorts would be considered any less worthy of being called research than the scrutinizing done by scientists. Do good dramatists not thoroughly investigate the fashions and dialects of particular times and places when writing a play? Do accomplished visual artists not often explore in depth the chemistry and durability of materials with which they aim to work? Are talented novelists not wont to engage—often over the course of a lifetime—in careful, even tedious, study of their own and other cultures to ensure the credibility of their texts? Likewise, do good educational storytellers and educational critics not engage in more than intuition when they *search the world again* (and again and again . . .) for significant empirical details that can serve as basic materials for composing a plausible and edifying critique or story?

When engaged in properly, this artistic research process, like the composition of the story text, is a rigorous undertaking. The result can be a useful product, one that should not be demeaned and marginalized as "merely" creative. The fact that in some quarters such useful nonscience-based texts are still not regarded as research attests to the conservative nature of our academic culture. Still, times change, and academic fields shift. Or more accurately, fields are shifted—they are moved slowly but inevitably by those in the field who imagine new possibilities and who persuade colleagues of their utility. For example, the early educational ethnographers crafted new lenses for viewing previously unnoticed educational phenomena, "data" unable to be captured and displayed within a numerical symbol system. They gradually persuaded their colleagues of the usefulness of these lenses. Think of the response that ethnographic texts were accorded two decades ago by the powerful community of quantitative researchers, and then count the number of ethnography-based presentations at last year's Annual Meeting of the AERA.

It is clear from the increasing attention that arts-based educational inquiry is being accorded in the field that many have already been persuaded of its utility. We hope to convince others through this chapter. To that end we have aimed to introduce those unfamiliar with this kind of research to its essential characteristics, its forms, its history, and some exemplars. Most important, we have attempted to illustrate how the genre of arts-based inquiry, like its predecessors in the educational research arena, will expand possibilities, enabling educators to see more of the things that need to be seen in order to improve educational policy and practice.

Section III
Historical Methods in Educational Research

Recent Methodological Developments in the History of American Education

Carl F. Kaestle
University of Chicago

Historians often observe that their discipline is both science and art. When they say that history is a science, they mean that historians follow certain common procedures of investigation and argument, a fact that allows them to agree on some generalizations about the past even though individual historians' values and their understanding of human nature may differ. In many cases they can agree simply because the evidence is ample and clear, and because they agree on the ground rules. Factual statements like "Horace Mann was born in 1796" cause little debate as long as we are talking about the same Horace Mann and as long as the surviving records are not contradictory. More complex statements can also be verified and may attract wide agreement among historians. Examples are such statements as the following: "The average white fertility rate declined in America between 1800 and 1860," or "Most leading American educators in 1840 believed that public schooling would reduce crime."

However, the rules of investigation and analysis help us less and less as we attempt to make broader generalizations about the past, or make judgments about its relation to the present, and this is part of what we mean when we say that history is also an art. Consider such statements as: "Slavery destroyed the black family," or "Schooling was a major avenue for the social mobility of immigrants." These claims are immensely difficult to study because the relevant facts are complicated and because they involve problems of definition and value judgments. The process of making such historical generalizations is not merely inductive; one cannot simply add up all the little facts and make them into statements about larger structures and processes. Generalization remains an act of creative interpretation, involving the historian's values, interests, and training. Although the evidence establishes some limits, writing history remains subjective to a considerable degree.

The history of education shares the methodological problems of the field of history in general. There is no single, definable method of inquiry, and important historical generalizations are rarely beyond dispute. Rather generalizations are the result of interactions between fragmentary evidence and the values and experiences of the historian. History is a challenging and creative interaction, part science, part art.

It is important for educators to understand this problematic nature of historical methodology because historical statements about education abound far beyond textbooks or required history courses in schools of education. Beliefs about the historical role of schooling in America are encountered every day in arguments for educational policies. For example, in the great debates about urban school decentralization in the 1960s, advocates of decentralization argued that centralization was a device by which social elites in the early 20th century had gained control of urban education, protected the social structure, and tried to impose their particular values on public school children. The decentralizers argued that centralization had been an undemocratic means of social control, and therefore it deserved to be reversed. Opponents of decentralization claimed that it would lead to inefficiency and corruption. Besides, they said, a common, uniform school system had been a successful tool in creating a cohesive, democratic society in America. They too cited history as their authority. Behind these contending positions was a mass of complex evidence and conflicting values. The historian has no magic formula to tell you which analysis is correct.

The uncertain nature of historical generalization has been particularly apparent in the history of American education during the past 25 or 30 years. During this period the traditional methods and assumptions of historians of American education have come increasingly under attack. The controversy has led to fresh insights, new questions and, more than ever, a heightened sense of the precariousness of historical generalizations.

The Traditional Framework

Current methodological issues in the history of American education are best understood in the light of the assumptions and conclusions of traditional American educational historians. Until the 1950s most writers of educational history shared two basic assumptions: first, that the history of education was concerned centrally, indeed, almost exclusively, with the history of public school systems; and second, that state-regulated, free, tax-supported, universal schooling was a good thing. These assumptions were rarely questioned, partly because many of these writers performed a dual role, as educational administrators or professors of education as well as educational historians. Therefore they had a vested interest in seeing public schooling in a good light. But also there was widespread popular agreement that public schooling was an unquestionably positive American institution.

There were several unstated corollaries to these assumptions, and they provided the framework—what some might call the paradigm—for research in educational history. Four elements in this paradigm helped determine methodology and occasioned later criticism. The first has to do with the focus on schooling. Because they tended to equate education with schooling, traditional historians rated the educational well-being and enlightenment of earlier societies by assessing how much formal schooling there was and to what extent it was organized under state control. Because their view of historical development was dominated by their present conception of desirable educational policy, they spent much effort trying to explain the lack of enthusiasm for state-regulated schooling prior to the 1830s, and they underestimated the importance of the family, the workplace, the churches, and other educational agencies in preindustrial society.

Related to this problem of focus is the problem of intent, the second element. Traditional historians of education saw those who favored state-regulated school systems as enlightened leaders working for the common good; they portrayed people who opposed educational reform as ignorant, misled, or selfish. The attribution of human motivation is a very difficult methodological problem in historical writing; it involves careful comparison of public and private statements, if they are available; it requires the historian to distinguish as clearly as possible between the intent and the consequences of actions; and it requires us to separate, if we can, our attempt to determine the historical actor's personal motivation from our own moral judgments about the effects of an event or a policy. Moral judgments may be timeless, but the historical actor's motivation must be understood in the context of the social values and scientific knowledge of the day. The value bias of most traditional educational historians prejudiced them against recognizing self-interest on the part of school reformers or legitimate, principled objection on the part of the opponents. On the other hand, some so-called revisionist historians have simply reversed the bias, making school reformers the villains and their opponents the heroes. Either value bias tends to collapse the complexity of educational history and to side-step methodological problems in determining intent.

A third corollary of the assumption that state schooling was a good thing is the equating of growth with progress. Methodologically this prompted historians to glory in numerical growth, often without controlling for parallel population growth or monetary inflation, and without taking seriously the differential educational opportunities of different groups. The tendency to equate growth with progress is also evident in the traditional history of Roman Catholic schooling in America, which is largely a chronicle of increasing schools, children, and budgets.

A fourth corollary of the goodness theme is the focus on leadership and organization rather than on the educational behavior and attitudes of ordinary people. The methodological implication of this focus on the governors rather than on the clients of schooling is to give central attention to public records created by elites rather than attempting to tease out of scanty evidence some inkling of the educational lives of the inarticulate, as recent social historians of education have been attempting to do.

Most books and doctoral dissertations written prior to 1950 in the field of the history of American education adhered to the paradigm that focuses on the progressive and beneficial evolution of public school systems. There were some notable exceptions, and even within the paradigm many excellent legal, institutional, and intellectual studies were written. Nevertheless, the traditional framework had outlived its usefulness by the late 1950s and early 1960s, when it came under attack.

Two Strands of Revision

The two main strands of revision in the history of American education resulted from distinct critiques of the major tenets of the traditional paradigm: that the history of education is essentially the history of schooling, and that state-regulated schooling was benign and desirable. The first critique broadened the focus of educational history to look at various agencies of instruction other than schools; it has yielded its finest fruits in the works of Bernard Bailyn and Lawrence Cremin on the colonial period of American history, when schooling was much less important in the transmission of knowledge than it is today. However, merely broadening our definition of education to include every aspect of socialization would leave the historian of education hopelessly adrift; each historian must therefore decide what definition of education is implicit in his or her work. The definition depends upon what questions are being asked. If the historian is asking questions about how children acquire skills and beliefs in a society, then the definition of education must be quite broad indeed. If the questions concern the origins of state policy toward education, the historian can legitimately focus on schooling, because past policymakers, like past historians, have equated education with schooling. Society as a whole educates in many ways, but the *state* educates through schools.

A second, quite different, strand of revision in recent educational history has caused considerable commotion among educators. Some revisionists have questioned the assumptions that state-regulated schooling has been generated by democratic and humanitarian impulses and that it has resulted in democratic opportunity. Their work has emphasized variously the exploitative nature of capitalism and how schools relate to it, the culturally abusive nature of mainstream values asserted by the schools, and the negative aspects of increasingly bureaucratic school systems. This reversal of ideological perspective on the development of school systems has not always resulted in methodologically sophisticated work, although as a whole the works labeled "radical revisionism" have raised important questions about the gloomier aspects of our educational system and have made some persuasive statements about our educational failures. Since this chapter is about methodology, not ideology, this is not the place to argue the merits of the radical view of school history.

Quantitative Methods

A small number of educational historians of diverse ideological persuasions pursued a more methodological sort of revision in the 1970s and 1980s. Their methods and their subject matter helped to answer some of the questions the radicals raised. Their work responds to two aspects of the inadequate traditional framework summarized above: a naive use of numerical data and a focus on the leaders rather than on the clients of educational institutions. Recent social historians of education have taken these problems as their starting point. They have adopted techniques from sociology and statistics to map out in some detail patterns of school attendance, years of schooling, school expenditures, voter characteristics on school issues, and other educational variables, correlating them with family and community characteristics and trying to chart changes over time. Much of this work would have been impossible 30 years ago. It was made possible by the development of computer programs for social scientists and by the availability of microfilmed sources of information, such as the manuscript federal censuses of the 19th century. The inspiration and the models have been provided by European historical demographers and by other American social historians, who have been charting changing family structures, mobility patterns, wealth distribution, and other phenomena that affect common people. The new emphasis on parents and children in educational history also parallels similar emphases in other fields of educational research: Sociologists are studying outcomes of schooling, lawyers are studying students' rights, and philosophers are studying the ethics of child-adult relations.

The complex description provided by quantitative historical studies has helped us learn about educational supply and demand in the past, about the role of schooling in different types of communities, and about the different school experiences of different social groups. The great virtue of quantitative educational history is that it got us in touch with some of the realities of schooling in the past; it gave us a way to start doing history from the bottom up and a way to compare popular behavioral patterns with the opinions and policies of educational leaders. However, the quantitative social historian of education also faced problems, some so numerous and frustrating that they caused some researchers to shun the techniques altogether. Others felt compelled by questions that demanded quantitative answers, and they groped toward a more adequate descriptive social history of American education, and toward theories that would help explain the patterns they were discovering.

Here is a short list of some of the problems they encountered: First, statistics and data analysis are unfamiliar to many historians. Even for those who learn the techniques, the work is still very time consuming and expensive. Experts are constantly devising improved and more arcane statistical techniques. Social historians have trailed along behind sociologists and economists, picking and choosing the techniques that seem most appropriate. Some have moved from simple cross-tabulations and graphs into multiple regression and its various offspring. For example, a two-way cross-tabulation might display geographical regions (Northeast, Southeast, Midwest, etc.) in the left column and average years of school completed (0 to 4, 5 to 8, 9 to 11, high school grad, etc.) from left to right. This would be an appropriate and straightforward way to compare the regions' average school attainment rates. However, before speculating about the causes of differences among the regions, we would want to look at such factors as per capita income, occupational structure, and degree of urbanization. Multiple regression is a mathematical procedure that allows one to assess the relative predictive association of several selected factors on one variable, such as school attainment. Multiple regression is, however, complex and time consuming, and it still leaves us the problem of interpreting the observed patterns of association. If a social historian can solve the problems of time, money, and expertise involved in quantitative work, he or she will then have to worry about the audience for whom the work is intended. Most readers of history balk at simple tables; but statistical adequacy demands detailed documentation and detailed presentation of results. This creates problems of style. Methodological sophistication is not worth much if you cannot reach the audience you wish to reach, and it is difficult to serve both a technical audience and a general audience in the same work.

As serious as these matters of training and style are, there are more substantive methodological problems in quantitative educational history. First, the data are crude and incomplete. Often the available school records and population censuses are ambiguous on crucial matters. Often they failed to ask the questions that interest us most now. Most of the data are cross-sectional; they provide only a snapshot of a group at a given moment. But education is a process, and many important questions about educational careers, or the influence of education on people's lives, can be answered only by data that trace individuals over time. Similarly, questions about the role of education in economic development require comparable aggregate data over time. Some historians have taken up this challenge and have developed longitudinal files by linking data from different sources, but that task is prodigious, and the attrition rate in studies of individuals (the cases lost by geographical mobility, death, and the ambiguity of common names) is so great as to render many conclusions dubious. More commonly, historians have tried to infer process from cross-sectional data. For example, they have estimated the average years of schooling completed among different social groups by calculating the average school entry and school leaving ages of the different groups in a single sample year; or they have made inferences about the impact of industrialization on communities' educational practices by comparing communities at different stages of industrialization in a given year. Although the questions in these cases are about processes, in neither case do the data trace individual children or communities over time. The logical and methodological problems of inferring processes from static information are serious, and they constitute an important problem in quantitative history today.

Even within legitimate cross-sectional analysis—that is, in pursuing questions about a population at a given moment—there can be a conflict between statistical adequacy and conceptual adequacy. Because research funds are limited and historical data are sparse, historians often work with small samples. Statisticians tell us that we need fairly large samples in order to be confident that the relationships we observe are not just random variation. If the results are not statistically significant, we cannot generalize from our sample to a larger population. In order to attain statistically significant results, we are sometimes tempted to collapse categories that should remain distinct. For example, if we are trying to relate ethnic background and teenage school attendance while controlling for parental occupation, we may decide to combine immigrant groups with quite different cultural and economic features, in order to achieve statistically significant comparisons between children of immigrants and nonimmigrants. But we risk misunderstanding the experience of distinct groups if we lump Poles, Italians, and Irish together, for example. The best solution to this dilemma is to provide the reader with the significant statistics for the grossly aggregated categories, as well as the descriptively useful information about the smaller subcategories, and then ponder the meaning of both sorts of analysis. Here again there are problems of space limits and the risk of presenting a tedious amount of information.

There are many other problems in this new area of research in educational history. For instance, it is difficult to know how conscientiously the data were reported in the first place or what individual and institutional biases may have affected the results. Caution on this matter is reinforced when we find substantial contradictions between different sources that claim to measure the same variable in the same population. It is also difficult to create time series on educational variables like attendance, teachers' salaries, educational expenditures, or length of school year because often the items were defined differently in different periods or omitted altogether. Even when ample and reliable quantitative information is available, it generally tells us about behavior and structure—numbers of children in school, the size of institutions, data on expenditures, votes on educational issues, and similar matters. The challenge for social historians in the coming decades is to find data, methods, and concepts that will link up behavior with belief, structure with ideas.

Despite these many problems, however, some impressive work that is beginning to emerge helps to locate the history of American education more solidly in the context of social structure and economic development. It is hardly a time for methodological self-congratulation, but neither is it a time for despair. One of the important by-products of quantitative work in educational history has been to sustain the methodological self-consciousness that began with the critiques of the traditional paradigm nearly 30 years ago. When the historian does not take methodology for granted, and when his or her methodology is critically scrutinized by other researchers, and when historians are constantly searching for new sources of evidence and techniques of analysis, then better work will result.

Not all questions are linked to quantitative research, nor is the history of education now subsumed as a branch of social history. It is important to remember that history of education is still vitally concerned with the history of educational ideas. Much good work remains to be done on leadership and on curriculum, on the intellectual and institutional history of education in America. The excitement of the past 30 years has not resulted in a new single methodology, or in a new, broadly accepted interpretation of educational history. However, the collapse of the old consensus has caused educational historians to explore new questions, discard old assumptions, try new techniques, and attempt to meet more rigorous standards of evidence and argument.

Theory and History

Many notable social theorists, including Karl Marx, Max Weber, Emile Durkheim, Ferdinand Tönnies, and Talcott Parsons, wrote about history.

Contemporary theorists from disciplines as diverse as sociology, linguistics, anthropology, philosophy, and statistics also do work that is relevant to historical study. Historians, however, differ in the amount of importance they give to theory, about whether they should attempt to test general theories with historical data, or about whether historians should get involved with theories at all.

Historians should read about theory and think about its relationship to their work for several reasons. Because historical writing is selective and interpretive, it is necessarily guided by the individual historian's sense of what is important, where to find meaning, and how social change and human motivation work. The answers arise partly from the materials, of course. Although history is not *merely* inductive, it is *partly* inductive. The answers also lie in an individual historian's temperament, convictions, hunches, and theories, whether explicit or implicit. By paying attention to the best theoretical work in related disciplines, historians can better identify their informal, personal theories. More important, they can shape their understanding of human experience by learning from other disciplines. Finally, historical work can reflect in important ways on social theories, confirming, refuting, or modifying various theoretical statements.

A historian need not adopt an entire theoretical system in order to profit from theoretical work in other disciplines. Some excellent work has been done from rigorous and systematic theoretical viewpoints, but most historians use theory incidentally and selectively. An excellent example of an educational historian using theories in an eclectic but explicit way is David Tyack's essay "Ways of Seeing," which is reprinted in Section I of this volume.

Theory has many implications for historical methodology, too numerous to cover in this chapter. Theories may influence what sort of evidence we look for, what sort of evidence we will accept, and what sort of arguments we will make from the evidence. For example, if one accepts the Marxist theorem that an individual's relationship to the means of production is crucial to his experience, one will make a concentrated effort to determine historical actors' class status and class consciousness, and one will make class a prominent part of the explanation of historical events. If one accepts anthropologist Clifford Geertz's theory that ritualistic or even apparently trivial everyday behavior can symbolize the deeper meaning of a culture, one will devote much attention to developing an interpretation that moves from observed behavior to cultural meaning. Whether a historian accepts a large theoretical system, uses theory incidentally, or resists the mixing of theory and historical writing, each should be conversant with major theoretical positions in related disciplines and self-conscious about their possible relevance for historical methodology.

Conclusion: Some Fundamental Methodological Concerns

This chapter closes with four key problems to watch for when assessing arguments about the history of education. These problems have been highlighted by work in the social history of education but which are also pertinent to other approaches.

The first problem, the confusion of correlations and causes, is particularly salient in quantitative work but is certainly not unique to it. To demonstrate that two phenomena occur together systematically is not to prove that one causes the other, of course, but historians as well as social scientists are constantly tempted into this kind of argument. For example, Irish families in 19th-century urban America sent their children to school less often and for fewer years, on the average, than many other groups. This finding does not demonstrate that "Irishness" (whatever that is) caused low school attendance. To ascertain a cause, we must ask first whether Irish immigrants also tended to be poor, because it might be poverty that caused low attendance. Then we would need to control for family structures, religion, and other factors. If we satisfied ourselves that controlling for all the factors we could measure, Irish status was independently associated with low school attendance, we still would not yet have established a causal relationship. We would have to investigate, and speculate, on *why* and *how* being Irish affected school attendance. Correlations are just concerned with proximate occurrence; causality is about how things *work*, and correlations don't tell us much about how things work. Because human motivation is often multiple and vague and because society is not very much like a clock, historians must exercise great caution in moving from systematic statistical associations to assertions of causality.

The second problem to which critical readers must give close attention is the definition of key terms. We can subdivide the problem of definition into two common pitfalls: vagueness and presentism. As an example of vagueness, the notion that industrialization caused educational reform is a commonplace in educational history. However, the statement has almost no analytical value until we specify what is meant by the umbrella terms "industrialization" and "educational reform." In contrast, consider this statement: "The expansion of wage labor in 19th-century communities or regions was followed by an expansion of annual school enrollment." This is much more precise, it has important causal implications, and we can investigate it empirically.

By "presentism" we mean assuming that terms had their present-day connotations in the past and applying to past developments present-day terms that did not exist or meant something else at the time. A classic example in educational history involves the use of the word "public." In the 18th century a "public" educational institution was one in which children learned collectively, in contrast with private tutorial education, and it was one devoted to education for the public good, as opposed to mere selfish gain. Thus, the colonial colleges, which were controlled by self-perpetuating trustees and financed mainly by tuition, were thoroughly "public" and were called so at the time. In today's terminology they would be called "private," but calling them "private" in historical work greatly muddies our understanding of 18th-century society. Avoiding presentism requires paying close attention to the etymology of key terms.

The necessity of guarding against presentist terms and concepts, however, does not mean that we can insulate our historical work from our present-day concerns and perceptions, nor should we want to, as long as we are aware of what we are doing. For example, during the 20 years following the Supreme Court's desegregation decision in *Brown v. Board of Education* (1954), most historians who wrote about segregated schools emphasized the injustice of discrimination and the inferior resources of the schools for African Americans. Recently, in the face of much disillusionment with integration, however, some historians have focused instead on the value of late-nineteenth and early twentieth-century segregated schools as community-based and supportive institutions. These two quite different perceptions are largely compatible with each other and respectful of the evidence. Together they can give us a more rounded view of historically segregated schools. There is no purely "objective" view in historical work, of course, but puncturing the myth of objectivity does not give historians license to distort the evidence or merely indulge their ideological inclinations.

A third problem that critical consumers of educational history should keep in mind is the distinction between evidence that provides ideas about how people *should* behave and evidence of how ordinary people *in fact* behaved. Too often we lack evidence of actual behavior and let prescriptive evidence stand in its place; that is, we assume that people did as they were told.

The methodological dilemma is posed by the following problem: If the legislative bodies of a society constantly passed rules requiring school attendance, is it evidence that people of that society valued schooling highly, expressing this value in their legislation, or is it evidence that people in that society did not value school very much, thus alarming its leaders into coercive efforts? To answer the question we need to know something about who makes the rules and about school attendance patterns by different groups. Here is a more specific example to show the lag between elite opinion and popular behavior. There was widespread agreement among professional educators and physicians beginning in the late 1830s in the northeastern part of the United States that school attendance by very young children was unwise, even dangerous to their health, as well as being a nuisance to teachers. Parents were constantly urged to keep their children under 5 or 6 at home. This campaign continued throughout the 1840s and 1850s. To infer from this that children normally began school at age 5 or 6 during these decades, however, would be incorrect. Parents resisted the conventional expertise. As we now know from analysis of manuscript censuses and statistical school reports, they persisted in sending 3- and 4-year-old children to school, for reasons we can only guess, until they were coerced into keeping them home by local regulations on age of school entry in the 1850s and 1860s. Only then did the average age of entry rise substantially. Child-rearing manuals may not cause or even reflect actual child-rearing practices, and exhortations about educational policies often fall on deaf ears.

The fourth and final problem has to do with the distinction between intent and consequences. No matter how wise our educational leaders have been, their powers of foresight have rarely equaled the historians' powers of hindsight. We know how things turned out, which is an inherent advantage in historical analysis, but it is also a problem. The problem lies in the danger of assuming that the historical actors could have (and *should* have) foreseen the full consequences of their ideas and of the institutions they shaped. It is undoubtedly true that many of the consequences of educational leadership have been precisely as the leaders intended; it does not follow, however, that we can infer intent from consequences. The fact that large bureaucracies are effective instruments of racial discrimination does not necessarily mean that their creators had a racist intent. The fact that schooling has done an unimpressive job in reducing crime does not mean that school reformers who touted it for that purpose were hypocrites. We cannot infer intent from consequences. We need direct evidence of intent at the time an act occurred.

No historian can completely transcend or resolve the four problems, but each must recognize the problems and the associated methodological challenges when trying to make meaningful generalizations about our educational past and to sort out the tremendous array of diverse and conflicting views that are presently circulating. Historians have always been scavengers. Because history involves all human experience and thought, historians have constantly raided other disciplines for new techniques of analysis and for new insights into society and human nature. This interdisciplinary approach helps explain why there is no single methodology in history and why historians love their craft so much: because it is so complex and so all-encompassing. Recent trends in the history of American education—the effort to see education as broader than schooling, the effort to see school systems in the context of social and economic development, and the effort to study popular attitudes and behavior as well as the history of elite intentions and actions—have greatly accelerated the borrowing process in this historical subfield. Historians of education have reached out and become involved in the history of the family, of childhood, and of reform institutions, for example, in addition to deepening their traditional commitment to economic and political history as a context for educational development. They have also explored recent work in sociology, anthropology, psychology, and statistics for new techniques and helpful theories.

Because this period of exploration and revision has resulted in diverse eclectic methodologies and because no new methodological or ideological consensus has emerged—in short, because there is no successful paradigm in educational history today—it is all the more important that each reader of educational history be critically alert and independent.

Suggestions for Further Reading

Methodology and Historiography

Bailyn, B. (1960). *Education in the forming of American society*. Chapel Hill: University of North Carolina Press.

Berkhofer, R. F. (1969). *A behavioral approach to historical analysis*. New York: Macmillan.

Butterfield, H. (1931). *The Whig interpretation of history*. London: Bell.

Cremin, L. A. (1965). *The wonderful world of Ellwood Patterson Cubberley: An essay on the historiography of American education*. New York: Teachers College Bureau of Publications.

Graff, H. (1977). The new math: Quantification, the new history, and the history of education. *Urban Education, 2*, 403–439.

Hughes, H. S. (1964). *History as science and art*. New York: Harper & Row.

Kaestle, C. F. (1992). Standards of evidence in educational history: How do we know when we know? *History of Education Quarterly, 32*, 361–366.

Kaestle, C. F. (1992). Theory in comparative educational history: A middle ground. In R. Goodenow and W. Marsden (Eds.), *The city and education in four nations* (pp. 195–204). Cambridge: Cambridge University Press.

Novick, P. (1988). *That noble dream: The "objectivity question" and the American historical profession*. Cambridge: Cambridge University Press.

Rury, J. (1993). Methods of historical research in education. In D. Lancey (Ed.), *Research in education* (pp. 247–269). New York: Longman.

Warren, D. R. (Ed.). (1978). *History, education, and public policy*. Berkeley: McCutchan.

Contrasting Interpretations of American Educational History

Anderson, J. D. (1988). *The education of blacks in the South, 1860–1935*. Chapel Hill: University of North Carolina Press.

Cremin, L. A. (1964). *The transformation of the school: Progressivism in American education*. New York: Alfred Knopf.

Cremin, L. A. (1970). *American education: The colonial experience, 1607–1783*. New York: Harper & Row.

Cubberley, E. P. (1934). *Public education in the United States* (rev. ed.). Boston: Houghton-Mifflin.

Kaestle, C. F. (1983). *Pillars of the republic: Common schools and American society: 1780–1860*. New York: Hill & Wang.

Kaestle, C. F., & Vinovskis, M. A. (1980). *Education and social change in nineteenth-century Massachusetts*. New York: Cambridge University Press.

Katz, M. B. (1968). *The irony of early school reform: Educational innovation in mid-nineteenth century Massachusetts*. Cambridge: Harvard University Press.

Ravitch, D. (1974). *The great school wars: New York City, 1800–1968*. New York: Basic Books.

Spring, J. H. (1972). *Education and the rise of the corporate state.* Boston: Beacon Press.

Tyack, D. B. (1974). *The one best system: A history of American urban education.* Cambridge: Harvard University Press.

Vinovskis, M. A. (1985). *The origins of public high schools: A reexamination of the Beverly high school controversy.* Madison: University of Wisconsin Press.

Study Questions

1. What is meant by the statement, "Any history of education is partly art and partly science"?

2. Is the history of American education the same thing as the history of schooling in the United States?

3. In reporting history, must a historian necessarily impose his or her moral values, or can history be totally objective?

4. Give an example of how present-day concerns or terminology can distort our understanding of the past. Give an example of how they can lead to a better understanding of the past.

5. Describe the "problem of intent" in historical approach.

6. Give examples of research questions that would: (a) properly allow an educational historian to focus only on the schools, and (b) require that education be examined both in and out of schools.

7. Do quantitative research methods, including statistical analyses, have any role in historical research? Why or why not?

8. Is there a single methodology of historical inquiry in education, or are there many different methods? Support your conclusion with examples.

9. Describe the "correlation problem" that is present in both historical and quasi-experimental research.

10. Can historical actions usually be inferred from historical statements of intent? Give examples to support your conclusion.

11. Can conclusions about intent safely be inferred from historical evidence that demonstrates outcomes or consequences? Give an example.

Exercise for Class Discussion:
The History of Education Game

Introduction

Below you will find two historical scenarios with some fragmentary evidence. The scenarios are fictional, but they are similar to situations historians have tried to analyze recently. One is deliberately arranged to be more ambiguous than the other. The game is to decide: what generalizations might I make on the issues posed, and how would I argue these generalizations from the evidence? Second, what questions can I not answer with any confidence from the evidence presented, and what kinds of further evidence would I need before I could answer them? (You might wish to poke around local school archives or research libraries to find out whether such evidence does in fact exist.) The game does not recreate what a historian actually does, but for discussion purposes it should raise some of the same issues historians have faced in similar situations.

The Scenarios

A. Roman Catholics and the Public Schools in Metropolis

Metropolis in 1840 was a large eastern seaport with a high percentage of Roman Catholic immigrants in its population. We are interested in the attitudes of its Catholic citizens toward schooling, and in particular, whether they preferred Catholic parish schools over public schools and, if there were no Catholic schools in their vicinity of the city, whether they preferred public schools to none.

Item 1. The bishop of Metropolis diocese argued repeatedly that Catholic parents could not and would not send their children to the godless public schools. In the absence of sufficient parish schools, he said, large numbers of Catholic children were roaming the streets.

Item 2. Protestant charity workers often commented that street kids and delinquents were disproportionately Catholic and immigrant.

Item 3. The local Catholic newspaper, which sometimes took positions opposed to the clergy, argued that immigrant Catholic parents should send their children to public schools to learn English and become good Americans.

Item 4. Ward school reports, complaining of the bad effects of newly created Catholic parish schools, often reported attendance figures comparing the enrollments at public schools before and after the opening of Catholic schools. Typical of such reports is the following:

TABLE 1. *Metropolis public schools attendance figures: Ward 3, School No. 15*

Time	Boys	Girls	Total
Before St. Mary's School opened	186	170	356
After St. Mary's School opened	120	110	230

Item 5. In arguments with the public school officials, Catholic spokesmen documented numerous instances of derogatory attitudes toward Roman Catholicism in public school textbooks.

If we take these items to be typical, what can you conclude about Catholics' attitudes about having their children attend public and parochial schools? How sure can you be? What other information would be most valuable?

B. The High School Controversy in Milltown

Milltown was a small textile manufacturing town in the middle-Atlantic states. For some time in the 1840s the local school board had been saying that the community needed a public high school, to be located in the center of town, instead of relying on private academies or sending children to the high schools of larger neighboring towns. In 1851 the issue came to a townwide vote, the results of which were recorded in the town meeting minutes.

Item 1. For years the school board had been criticizing wealthy people who sent their children to private schools, saying that they harmed the public school system and withheld their support for greater public school expenditures.

Item 2. The *Milltown Working Man's Advocate* urged all working-class voters to support the high school, arguing that public schooling was one of the crucial avenues of opportunity in America.

Item 3. At a town meeting, however, a factory worker complained that the new school would burden him with taxes even though his children, who needed to work in their teenage years, would not be able to use it.

Item 4. The voting lists, summarized by ward and occupational group, were as follows:

TABLE 2. *Milltown high school vote*

Occupation group	Center ward Total vote	Yes n	Yes %	Outer ward A Total vote	Yes n	Yes %	Outer ward B Total vote	Yes n	Yes %	All wards combined Total vote	Yes n	Yes %
Merchants and manufacturers	78	47	60	22	10	45	11	5	48	111	62	56
Lower white-collar workers	55	39	71	10	6	60	8	3	63	73	48	66
Skilled workers	110	69	63	32	17	54	27	14	52	169	100	59
Unskilled workers	275	124	45	120	50	42	67	27	40	462	201	44
Farmers	15	12	80	87	36	41	108	42	39	210	88	42
Totals	533	289	54	271	119	44	221	91	41	1025	499	49

From these items, what can you say about why the high school vote lost? Does the occupational information given in Item 4 suggest that social class was the crucial factor? What other factors might have been involved?

Discuss your answers before turning to my brief comments on the scenarios.

Comments on the Scenarios

A. Roman Catholics in Metropolis

The bishop was expressing the church's point of view, that public school attendance threatened the faith of Catholic children (Item 1). This belief may have been shared by many Catholic parents, but more evidence would be needed than is cited here. Protestant charity workers and various officials (Item 2) often commented on the high rate of delinquency and crime among immigrants and/or Catholics. Some prejudice may be involved in these opinions, but statistics not cited here tend to support them. However, high rates of crime and delinquency may have resulted from immigrant Catholics' low income status and poor housing. It does not tell us much about parent" attitudes toward the schooling of young children, although it may suggest what the alternatives were for some older children. The advocacy of public schooling by the Catholic newspaper (Item 3) is interesting, because it shows a diversity of opinion among Catholics whose views have been recorded. Parents were faced with conflicting advice. Those who decided to ignore the bishop's advice and send their kids to public schools could find some support for their decision. The statistical information in Item 4 supports this possibility. To the extent that the attendance report is typical, one can conclude that substantial numbers of Catholic parents preferred Catholic schools to public schools, but that lacking Catholic schools they preferred public schools to none at all. Of course, the real bias of the public schools against Catholics (Item 5), as well as the clergy's opposition to public schooling, was probably troubling to many Catholics and probably acted as a deterrent to attendance by some children, as well as creating enthusiasm for the creation of Catholic schools. Still, the quantitative evidence suggests that many Catholic parents wanted schooling for their children, even if it was public schooling.

B. Milltown High School

The evidence here is more ambiguous. Item 1 suggests that wealthy people may have opposed the public high school because they sent their children to private schools, but the evidence is not direct. Two possibilities are suggested about working families lower in the social scale: that they supported the high school as a possible avenue of advancement for their children (Item 2), or that they opposed it because they would have to pay for it while more privileged people's kids used it (Item 3). In fact, there is considerable evidence that both of these attitudes existed among mid-19th-century workingmen. The statistics on the vote (Item 4) do not completely clarify the class issue, even if we use occupational status as an indicator of social class. Looking at the totals by occupational groups for all wards combined, we see that the greatest support came from lower white-collar workers, a small "middle-class" group, and the next greatest support came from skilled workers, also a middling occupational status. But the merchants and manufacturers were not far behind, and among unskilled laborers and farmers a substantial minority also voted for the high school. One could conclude that the middling occupational groups were the most enthusiastic about the high school and that opposition among unskilled workers and farmers accounted for its downfall, perhaps for the reason suggested in Item 3. When we look at the statistics by ward, however, another factor—distance from the town center—becomes clear. Among all occupational groups, residents of the outer wards were more opposed to the high school than residents of the center ward. Farmers, heavily concentrated in the outer wards, voted heavily against the high school, even though that category included men of quite different income levels. Distance still mattered in the mid-19th century. The outer wards may have had strong traditions of neighborhood control, and may have been resentful of townwide institutions. Also, within a given occupation, those with higher incomes and those who were more receptive to educational innovations may have tended to live in the center ward. More evidence would be necessary to make such arguments, however. The evidence in this scenario is more ambiguous than in Scenario A.

In both cases, you surely found many issues to discuss beyond the few raised here. I hope the scenarios have suggested that historical reasoning is not only difficult, but worth the challenge.

Reading

Introduction
A Historiographical Turning Point: Bernard Bailyn's
Education in the Forming of American Society

Carl F. Kaestle

In 1956 a group of scholars convened at Chatham, Massachusetts, to consider "The Role of Education in American History." They concluded that much historical writing about education had been done by authors trained outside of academic history departments, often professors at schools of education committed to a positive judgment on public schooling and a narrowly institutional definition of their subject matter. The committee concluded that history of education as a field should become more involved in the methods and concerns of American historians in general. One member of the group, Bernard Bailyn, soon had an occasion to implement this point of view. A colonial historian trained in the Harvard History Department, Bailyn was at the time teaching the history of American education at Harvard's Graduate School of Education. He was thus ideally situated to assess the relationship between existing histories of education and historical scholarship more generally. This assessment became a book when the Institute for Early American History and Culture at Williamsburg asked Bailyn to write an extended essay on needs and opportunities for study in the history of education in early America. The result was *Education in the Forming of American Society*, which appeared in 1960. The book included two essays. The first, entitled "An Interpretation," included a historiographical critique of the field as well as a hypothetical essay demonstrating the explanatory power of a broader definition of education. The second part of the book was a bibliographical essay that sketched out a broader subject matter for educational historians to ponder.

In the excerpt that follows, from the first essay, Bailyn considers the shared educational functions of family, church, school, and workplace, the impact of the colonial environment on these institutions, and how they changed over time. Defining education not just as schooling but as "the entire process by which a culture transmits itself across the generations," Bailyn explored the central educational roles of the family, the church, and the apprenticeship.

Readers may profitably contemplate how such a perspective could be applied to 20th-century developments. What new institutions and settings have loomed important in the range of children's educational experiences? How has the configuration of educational institutions changed during the 20th century? What tensions have contributed to such shifts, or resulted from them? Also, consider the problem that Bailyn's very broad definition of education poses for students of education in a culturally diverse, technological society.

Bailyn announced that his interpretive essay was hypothetical and warned that it "may well prove to be wrong or misleading." In the subsequent years of exciting research on the colonial family, much of which was stimulated by Bailyn's book, scholars have revised his emphasis on a shift from an extended English family to a nuclear colonial American family. The nuclear family, it seems, was more often the norm in both the premigration English situation and in the colonial settlements. Although the new world environment had not transformed the structure of the family, however, colonial American conditions did change its functions. Bailyn's concept of education as a "configuration of educational processes" has been a major contribution to the field. Furthermore, his insight that in the face of social change people gradually transferred educational functions from one institution to another broadened the analytical framework for understanding schooling and society. Beyond his impact on educational historians as specialists, Bailyn's essay contains a subtle model of social change, one that has withstood the test of time and further research. In Bailyn's explanation, people make unintended and temporary changes in traditional institutions and assumptions when they are confronted with a changed environment or a new set of social relations; only later do these temporary adjustments become rationalized and worked into new institutional configurations.

Although Bailyn's essay is not methodological in a technical sense, it still stands today as the most concise and original statement of a point of view that turned the history of education in new directions. With its broader definition and scope, it prompted subsequent scholars to ask new questions, seek new methods, and gain new insights.

An Interpretation

WHEN THE SPONSORS of this conference invited me to prepare a paper on the needs and opportunities for study in the early history of American education, they hoped that I would be able to present in some coherent form a survey of the writing that now exists in that area and a number of recommendations for further work, including a list of specific topics for papers, monographs, and surveys. At least that is what I understood them to have in mind and what in fact my predecessors in these Institute Conferences have done with excellent results. But when I attempted to follow these directions I found myself confronted with a peculiar problem. The field of study with which I was concerned, unlike the history of science, law, or Indian-white relations, has not suffered from neglect, which firm direction and energetic

Bailyn, Bernard. *Education in the Forming of American Society: Needs and Opportunity for Study*. New York, W.W. Norton, 1960, pp. 3–49. Reproduced by permission.

research might repair, but from the opposite, from an excess of writing along certain lines and an almost undue clarity of direction. The number of books and articles on the schools and colleges of the colonial period, on methods of teaching, on the curriculum, school books, and teachers is astonishingly large; and since at least the end of the nineteenth century the lines of interpretation and the framework of ideas have been unmistakable. And yet, for all of this, the role of education in American history is obscure. We have almost no historical leverage on the problems of American education. The facts, or at least a great quantity of them, are there, but they lie inert; they form no significant pattern.

What is needed, it seems to me, is not so much a projecting of new studies as a critique of the old and, more important, an attempt to bring the available facts into relation with a general understanding of the course of American development. I would like, therefore, to depart somewhat from the usual procedure of this Needs and Opportunities series and approach the subject of education in a round-about way. I would like to start backwards, and begin by tracing back to its origins the path that led to the present interpretation and to consider certain implications of that view. I would like then to suggest an alternative approach and follow it out as far as I am able towards a general statement of the place of education in the forming of American society. It will be a statement at least two of whose limitations can be known in advance. It will not be comprehensive in the sense of touching on all aspects of education in early American history. It will, instead, deal with one theme only, though a theme of preeminent importance, basic, I believe, to an understanding of the larger history. Further, since it will not fall into the familiar categories it will of necessity be based on scattered and incompletely assembled evidence. It will be a hypothesis, in other words, an essay in hypothetical history. Like all such projections it may well prove to be wrong or misleading. But if so, its purpose will nevertheless have been served by eliciting the contrary proof, which, too, will tell a different and I think a more useful kind of story about education than those we are accustomed to hear.

It is only when this much has been accomplished, when the knot of our present entanglements in the history of education has been at least loosened and when the lines of a different interpretation have been suggested, that I wish to turn to the specific needs and opportunities for study in the early history of American education. For I would like to center that discussion, which will be found in a separate bibliographical essay, on the themes stated in the general interpretation.

I

It is not a difficult task to trace back to its origins the present interpretation of education in American history, for its leading characteristic is its separateness as a branch of history, its detachment from the main stream of historical research, writing, and teaching. It is a distinct tributary, and it leads directly back to a particular juncture at the end of the nineteenth century. The turning point may be marked by the completion in 1900 of two notable books. Edward Eggleston's *Transit of Civilization* is a remarkably imaginative effort to analyze "the original investment from which has developed Anglo-Saxon culture in America" by probing "the complex states of knowing and thinking, of feeling and passion of the seventeenth-century colonists." The opening words of the book make clear the central position of education in the ambitious sweep of this history:

What are loosely spoken of as national characteristics are probably a result not so much of heredity as of controlling traditions. Seminal ideas received in childhood, standards of feeling and thinking and living handed down from one overlapping generation to another, make the man English or French or German in the rudimentary outfit of his mind.

All the major topics—"mental outfit," medical notions, language, folklore, literature, "weights and measures of conduct," and land and labor—are conceived as phases in the transmission of a civilization. The longest chapter is entitled "The Tradition of Education." The entire book is, in fact, a study in the history of education; for all the crudities of its construction and imbalances of interpretation, it is one of the subtlest and most original books ever written on the subject.

It should have been a seminal work. It should have led to a highly imaginative treatment of the theme of education in American history. But it did not. It was laid aside as an oddity, for it was irrelevant to the interests of the group then firmly shaping the historical study of American education.

For them, the seminal book, marking "an epoch in the conception of educational history in English," was *A History of Education,* written by that "knight-errant of the intellectual life," as his devoted friend William James called him, the exuberant polymath and free-lance educator, Thomas Davidson. His too was a remarkable book, if only for its scope. Davidson starts with "The Rise of Intelligence" when "man first rose above the brute." Then he trots briskly through "ancient Turanian," Semitic, and Aryan education, picks up speed on "civic education" in Judaea, Greece, and Rome, gallops swiftly across Hellenistic, Alexandrian, Patristic, and Muslim education; leaps magnificently over the thorny barriers of scholasticism, the medieval universities, the Renaissance, Reformation, and Counter-Reformation; and then plunges wildly through the remaining five centuries in sixty-four pages flat.

But it was less the range than the purpose and argument of this book that distinguished it in the eyes of an influential group of writers. Its purpose was to dignify a newly self-conscious profession, education, and its argument, a heady distillation of Social Darwinism, was that modern education was a cosmic force leading mankind to a full realization of itself. A few sentences from Davidson's Preface will make clearer than any explanation could the origins of a distinct school of historical writing. "My endeavor," Davidson wrote,

. . . has been to present education as the last and highest form of evolution. . . . By placing education in relation to the whole process of evolution, as its highest form, I have hoped to impart to it a dignity which it could hardly otherwise receive or claim. From many points of view, the educator's profession seems mean and profitless enough, compared with those that make more noise in the world; but when it is recognized to be the highest phase of the world-process, and the teacher to be the chief agent in that process, both it and he assume a very different aspect. Then teaching is seen to be the noblest of professions, and that which ought to call for the highest devotion and enthusiasm.

For Davidson, as for a whole generation of passionate crusaders for professionalism in education, history was not simply the study of the past. It was an arcane science that revealed the intimate relationship between their hitherto despised profession and the destiny of man. The purpose of his *Textbook in the History of Education* (1906), wrote Paul Monroe, Professor of the History of Education at Teachers College, was not merely to supply information and vicarious experience to the student of education, but, more important, to furnish him with "a conception of the meaning, nature, process, and purpose of education that will lift him above the narrow prejudices, the restricted outlook, the foibles, and the petty trials of the average schoolroom, and afford him the fundamentals of an everlasting faith as broad as human nature and as deep as the life of the race."

A subject that could give the neophyte an everlasting faith in his profession clearly deserved a central position in the curriculum. And such a position it duly received. The History of Education came to be taught as an introductory course, a form of initiation, in every normal school, department of education, and teachers college in the country. A subject of such importance could not be left to random development; the story had to be got straight. And so a few of the more imaginative of that energetic and able group of men concerned with mapping the over-all progress of "scientific" education, though not otherwise historians, took over the management of the historical work in education. With great virtuosity they drew up what became the patristic literature of a powerful academic ecclesia.

The development of this historical field took place, consequently, in a special atmosphere of professional purpose.

It grew in almost total isolation from the major influences and shaping minds of twentieth-century historiography; and its isolation proved to be self-intensifying: the more parochial the subject became, the less capable it was of attracting the kinds of scholars who could give it broad relevance and bring it back into the public domain. It soon displayed the exaggeration of weakness and extravagance of emphasis that are the typical results of sustained inbreeding.

The main emphasis and ultimately the main weakness of the history written by the educational missionaries of the turn of the century derived directly from their professional interests. Seeking to demonstrate the immemorial importance and the evolution of theories and procedures of the work in which they were engaged, they directed their attention almost exclusively to the part of the educational process carried on in formal institutions of instruction. They spoke of schools as self-contained entities whose development had followed an inner logic and an innate propulsion. From their own professional work they knew enough of the elaborate involvement of school and society to relate instruction somehow to the environment, but by limiting education to formal instruction they lost the capacity to see it in its full context and hence to assess the variety and magnitude of the burdens it had borne and to judge its historical importance.

But there is more to it than that. The willingness to restrict the history of education to formal instruction reflects not merely the professional concerns of the writers but also certain assumptions about the nature of history itself. To these writers the past was simply the present writ small. It differed from the present in the magnitudes and arrangement of its elements, not in their character. The ingredients of past and present were the same; and they took their task to be the tracing of the careers of the institutions, ideas, or practices they knew so well. They had no capacity for surprise. They lacked the belief, the historian's instinct, that the elements of their world might not have existed at all for others, might in fact have been inconceivable to them, and that the real task is to describe the dawning of ideas and the creation of forms—surprising, strange, and awkward then, however familiar they may have become since—in response to the changing demands of circumstance.

Distortions and short-circuiting of thought inevitably resulted. Persisting in their search for familiarity in an unfamiliar past, they had no choice but to accept crude facsimiles, deceptive cognates. "Public" was perhaps the most important. In their own time it was the "public" aspect of education that most involved their energies and that framed their vision: "public" *vs.* "private," the state as equalizer and guarantor, assuring through tax-supported, free, publicly maintained and publicly controlled schools the level of education that made democracy effective. Men like Ellwood Cubberley, whose formative professional experience was gained as superintendent of public schools in San Francisco and whose major field as an educator of educators was not history but public administration, saw as the main theme in the history of American education the development of public school systems. Cubberley and the others told a dramatic story, of how the delicate seeds of the idea and institutions of "public" education had lived precariously amid religious and other old-fashioned forms of education until nineteenth-century reformers, fighting bigotry and ignorance, cleared the way for their full flowering. The seeds were there at the beginning—though where, exactly, was a matter of considerable controversy. There is no more revealing historical debate than that between George H. Martin, Agent for the Massachusetts State Board of Education, and Andrew S. Draper, New York State Superintendent of Public Instruction, a debate that ran to six articles in leading educational journals between 1891 and 1893. The question they disputed was whether the appearance of public education in seventeenth-century America should be attributed to the Puritans in Massachusetts or the Dutch in New York. Considering the historical materials available at the time, it was an informed discussion. But it missed the point. Public education as it was in the late nineteenth century, and is now, had not grown from known seventeenth-century seeds; it was a new and unexpected genus whose ultimate character could not have been predicted and whose emergence had troubled well-disposed, high-minded people. The modern conception of public education, the very idea of a clean line of separation between "private" and "public," was unknown before the end of the eighteenth century. Its origins are part of a complex story, involving changes in the role of the state as well as in the general institutional character of society. It is elaborately woven into the fabric of early modern history.

Other, similar anachronisms resulted from reading present issues and definitions back into the past. In the telescoping and foreshortening of history that resulted, the past could be differentiated from the present mainly by its primitivism, the rudimentary character of the institutions and ideas whose ultimate development the writers were privileged to know so well. There was about their writing, consequently, a condescension toward the past that exaggerated the quaintness and unreality of the objects they described. The story became serious only when these antiquities, sufficiently displayed, were left behind and the immediate background of present problems was approached. By their failure to see the past as essentially different and to allow apparent similarities to blend naturally into the unfamiliarities of a distant setting, they lost the understanding of origins and of growth which history alone can provide.

How much they lost, how great was the sacrifice of intellectual leverage that resulted from the concentration on formal institutions and from the search for recognizable antecedents, may be seen in their treatment of the colonial and Revolutionary periods. How were they to make sense of this era? Though it comprised two-thirds of the American past, its pedagogical institutions were so few and so evidently pitiful, so bound down by religion and other antiquated concerns, that it was hard to know what to say about them except that they demonstrated by comparison the extent of subsequent progress. Some authors were quite ingenious. One, R. G. Boone, Professor of Pedagogy at Indiana University, suggested as an "interesting historical study" of the colonial period "the abuse of the principle" of free schools. Not that they wasted much time on the subject. Of the fifteen chapters in Cubberley's exceedingly influential text (over 100,000 copies of it have been sold since its publication in 1919), exactly one is devoted to the first two centuries of American history. But at least Cubberley gave his readers fair warning. He called his book *Public Education in the United States,* and since there was neither public education nor the United States before 1776 he was free in effect to ignore everything that happened before and to assume without explanation that political independence is a logical starting point for the history of educational institutions.

Imbalance, quaintness, and jagged discontinuities mark these brief treatments of the colonial period. Mountains were made of religion in the Puritan laws of the 1640's, of the Symmes and Eaton bequests, of hornbooks, dame schools, Corlet, and Cheever. New England carried the burden, with assists from the Quakers, the Society for the Propagation of the Gospel, and "well-to-do planters." Over it all was the "dominance of the religious purpose," properly illustrated by the *Primer's* alphabetical catechism: "In Adam's Fall/We sinned all." The eighteenth century, lacking even Puritans and the Dutch, was a particular embarrassment, and it was quickly disposed of with remarks about the "waning of the old religious interest," mention of the "rise of the district system," and a few words about some new colleges and an academy. The story lurched and bumped along without apparent purpose or direction. Organization, so clear a reflection of understanding, was primitive when it existed at all. Three "type attitudes" framed Cubberley's colonial material: "compulsory maintenance attitude" (Massachusetts), "parochial-school attitude" (Pennsylvania), and "the pauper school non-state-interference attitude" (Virginia).

It is this casual, inconsequential treatment of the colonial period that is the best measure of the limitations of the history these professional educators wrote and of the school of interpretation, still flourishing, which they founded. Restricting their inquiry to the problems and institutions they knew, they did not recognize, they had no way of understanding, the first, and in some ways the most important, transformation that has overtaken education in America.

This fundamental change, completed before the end of the colonial period and underlying the entire subsequent history of American education, may be seen only when the premises and concerns of the turn-of-the-century educators are laid aside and when one assumes a broader definition of education and a different notion of historical relevance. It becomes apparent when one thinks of education not only as formal pedagogy but as the entire process by which a culture transmits itself across the generations; when one is prepared to see great variations in the role of formal institutions of instruction, to see schools and universities fade into relative insignificance next to other social agencies; when one sees education in its elaborate, intricate involvements with the rest of society, and notes its shifting functions, meanings, and purposes. And it becomes evident also only when one assumes that the past was not incidentally but essentially different from the present; when one seeks as the points of greatest relevance those critical passages of history where elements of our familiar present, still part of an unfamiliar past, begin to disentangle themselves, begin to emerge amid confusion and uncertainty. For these soft, ambiguous moments where the words we use and the institutions we know are notably present but are still enmeshed in older meanings and different purposes—these are the moments of true origination. They reveal in purest form essential features which subsequent events complicate and modify but never completely transform.

The change I have in mind was not unique to America, but like much else of the modern world it appeared here first. It was part of the rapid breakdown of traditional European society in its wilderness setting. In the course of adjustment to a new environment, the pattern of education was destroyed: the elements survived, but their meaning had changed and their functions had been altered. By 1800 education in America was a radically different process from what anyone in the early seventeenth century would have expected. On almost every major point the expectations of the first generation of settlers had been frustrated. These expectations form a necessary background for understanding the transformation of education in colonial America; and therefore before attempting a detailed description of the change I have in mind, I would like to turn to those assumptions, experiences, and ways of thinking of late sixteenth- and early seventeenth-century Englishmen, stressing those features that would be most affected by the American environment.

2

The forms of education assumed by the first generation of settlers in America were a direct inheritance from the medieval past. Serving the needs of a homogeneous, slowly changing rural society, they were largely instinctive and traditional, little articulated and little formalized. The most important agency in the transfer of culture was not formal institutions of instruction or public instruments of communication, but the family; and the character of family life in late sixteenth- and early seventeenth-century England is critical for understanding the history of education in colonial America.

The family familiar to the early colonists was a patrilineal group of extended kinship gathered into a single household. By modern standards it was large. Besides children, who often remained in the home well into maturity, it included a wide range of other dependents: nieces and nephews, cousins, and, except for families at the lowest rung of society, servants in filial discipline. In the Elizabethan family the conjugal unit was only the nucleus of a broad kinship community whose outer edges merged almost imperceptibly into the society at large.

The organization of this group reflected and reinforced the general structure of social authority. Control rested with the male head to whom all others were subordinate. His sanctions were powerful; they were rooted deep in the cultural soil. They rested upon tradition that went back beyond the memory of man; on the instinctive sense of order as hierarchy, whether in the cosmic chain of being or in human society; on the processes of law that reduced the female to perpetual dependency and calibrated a detailed scale of male subordination and servitude; and, above all, on the restrictions of the economy, which made the establishment of independent households a difficult enterprise.

It was these patriarchal kinship communities that shouldered most of the burden of education. They were, in the first place, the primary agencies in the socialization of the child. Not only did the family introduce him to the basic forms of civilized living, but it shaped his attitudes, formed his patterns of behavior, endowed him with manners and morals. It introduced him to the world; and in so doing reinforced the structure of its authority. For the world to the child was an intricate, mysterious contrivance in controlling which untutored skills, raw nature, mere vigor counted for less than knowledge and experience. The child's dependence on his elders was not an arbitrary decree of fate; it was not only biologically but socially functional.

But the family's educational role was not restricted to

elementary socialization. Within these kinship groupings, skills that provided at least the first step in vocational training were taught and practiced. In a great many cases, as among the agricultural laboring population and small tradesmen who together comprised the overwhelming majority of the population, all the vocational instruction necessary for mature life was provided by the family.

The family's role in vocational training was extended and formalized in a most important institution of education, apprenticeship. Apprenticeship was the contractual exchange of vocational training in an atmosphere of family nurture for absolute personal service over a stated period of years. Like other forms of bonded servitude, it was a condition of dependency, a childlike state of legal incompetence, in which the master's role, and responsibilities, was indistinguishable from the father's, and the servant's obligations were as total, as moral, and as personal as the son's. Servants of almost every degree were included within the family, and it was the family's discipline that most directly enforced the condition of bondage. The master's parental concern for his servants, and especially for apprentices, included care for their moral welfare as well as for their material condition. He was expected and required by law to bring them up in good Christian cultivation, and to see to their proper deportment.

What the family left undone by way of informal education the local community most often completed. It did so in entirely natural ways, for so elaborate was the architecture of family organization and so deeply founded was it in the soil of stable, slowly changing village and town communities in which intermarriage among the same groups had taken place generation after generation, that it was at times difficult for the child to know where the family left off and the greater society began. The external community, comprising with the family a continuous world, naturally extended instruction and discipline in work and in the conduct of life. And it introduced the youth in a most significant way to a further discipline, that of government and the state. So extensive and intricate were the community's involvements with the family and yet so important was its function as a public agency that the youth moved naturally and gradually across the border line that separates the personal from the impersonal world of authority.

More explicit in its educational function than either family or community was the church. Aside from its role as formal educator exercised through institutions of pedagogy which it supported and staffed, in its primary purpose of serving the spiritual welfare and guarding the morals of the community it performed other less obvious but not less important educational functions. It furthered the introduction of the child to society by instructing him in the system of thought and imagery which underlay the culture's values and aims. It provided the highest sanctions for the accepted forms of behavior, and brought the child into close relationship with the intangible loyalties, the ethos and highest principles, of the society in which he lived. In this educational role, organized religion had a powerfully unifying influence. Indistinguishable at the parish level from the local community, agent and ward of the state, it served as a mechanism of social integration. In all its functions, and especially in those that may be called educational, its force was centripetal.

Family, community, and church together accounted for

the greater part of the mechanism by which English culture transferred itself across the generations. The instruments of deliberate pedagogy, of explicit, literate education, accounted for a smaller, though indispensable, portion of the process. For all the interest in formal instruction shown in the century after the Reformation in England, and for all the extension of explicitly educational agencies, the span of pedagogy in the entire spectrum of education remained small. The cultural burdens it bore were relatively slight. Formal instruction in elementary and grammar schools, and in the university, was highly utilitarian. Its avowed purpose was the training of the individual for specific social roles. Of the love of letters, knowledge, and science for their own sakes in Elizabethan and Stuart England there was, needless to say, no lack; but the justification for formal education was not phrased in terms of the enrichment of the personality and the satisfactions of knowledge. Literacy had its uses required for the daily tasks of an increasing part of the population. Latin grammar and classical literature, far from being then the cultural ornaments they have since become, were practical subjects of instruction: as necessary for the physician as for the architect, as useful to the local functionary as to the statesman. Even the middle classes, for whom classical education had acquired a special meaning as a symbol of social ascent, justified their interest in grammar school training by reference to its moral and social utility. And the universities' function as professional schools had not been transformed by the influx of sons of gentle and noble families; it had merely been broadened to include training for public responsibility.

The sense of utility that dominated formal education was

related in a significant way to the occupational structure of the society. Despite a considerable amount of occupational mobility, the normal expectation was that the child would develop along familiar lines, that the divergence of his career from that of his parents' and grandparents' would be limited, and that he could proceed with confidence and security along a well-worn path whose turnings and inclines had long been known and could be dealt with by measures specified by tradition.

Whatever their limitations by modern standards, formal institutions of instruction occupied a strategic place in English life, and they therefore fell within the concern of the state. But the role of the state in formal education, though forceful, was indirect. It was exhortatory, empowering, supervisory, regulatory; it was, with rare exceptions, neither initiating nor sustaining. Support for schools and universities was almost universally from private benefaction, usually in the form of land endowments; public taxation was rare and where it existed, local and temporary. The reliable support from endowment funds gave educational institutions above the elementary level a measure of autonomy, an independence from passing influences which allowed them to function conservatively, retarding rather than furthering change in their freedom from all but the most urgent pressures.

Of these characteristics of education as it existed in late sixteenth- and early seventeenth-century England prospective emigrants to America would hardly have been aware, and not simply because they were not habituated to think in such terms. They had little cause to probe the assumptions and circumstances that underlay their culture's self-perpetuation. The rapid expansion of instruc-

tional facilities of which they were witness had not sprung
from dissatisfaction with the traditional modes of education, but from the opposite, from confidence, from satisfaction, and from the desire and the capacity to deal more
fully, in familiar ways, with familiar social needs. The basis
of education lay secure within the continuing traditions
of an integrated, unified culture. The future might be uncertain, but the uncertainties were limited. Nothing disturbed the confident expectation that the world of the
child's maturity would be the same as that of the parents'
youth, and that the past would continue to be an effective
guide to the future.

3

None of the early settlers in English America, not even
those who hoped to create in the New World a utopian
improvement on the Old, contemplated changes in this
configuration of educational processes, this cluster of assumptions, traditions, and institutions. Yet by the end of
the colonial period it had been radically transformed. Education had been dislodged from its ancient position in the
social order, wrenched loose from the automatic, instinctive workings of society, and cast as a matter for deliber-
ation into the forefront of consciousness. Its functionings
had become problematic and controversial. Many were
transferred from informal to formal institutions, from agencies to whose major purpose they had been incidental to
those, for the most part schools, to which they were primary. Schools and formal schooling had acquired a new
importance. They had assumed cultural burdens they had
not borne before. Where there had been deeply ingrained

habits, unquestioned tradition, automatic responses, security, and confidence there was now awareness, doubt, formality, will, and decision. The whole range of education had become an instrument of deliberate social purpose.

In many ways the most important changes, and certainly the most dramatic, were those that overtook the family in colonial America. In the course of these changes the family's traditional role as the primary agency of cultural transfer was jeopardized, reduced, and partly superseded.

Disruption and transplantation in alien soil transformed the character of traditional English family life. Severe pressures were felt from the first. Normal procedures were upset by the long and acute discomforts of travel; regular functions were necessarily set aside; the ancient discipline slackened. But once re-established in permanent settlements the colonists moved toward recreating the essential institution in its usual form. In this, despite heroic efforts, they failed. At first they laid their failure to moral disorder; but in time they came to recognize its true source in the intractable circumstances of material life.

To all of the settlers the wilderness was strange and forbidding, full of unexpected problems and enervating hardships. To none was there available reliable lore or reserves of knowledge and experience to draw upon in gaining control over the environment: parents no less than children faced the world afresh. In terms of mere effectiveness, in fact, the young—less bound by prescriptive memories, more adaptable, more vigorous—stood often at advantage. Learning faster, they came to see the world more familiarly, to concede more readily to unexpected necessities, to sense more accurately the phasing of a new life. They and not their parents became the effective guides to a new world, and they thereby gained a strange, anomalous authority difficult to accommodate within the ancient structure of family life.

Other circumstances compounded the disorder. Parental prestige was humbled by involvement in the menial labor necessary for survival; it faded altogether when means of support failed in the terrible "starving periods" and large households were forced to sub-divide and re-form in smaller, self-sufficient units. Desperate efforts to enforce a failing authority by law came to little where the law was vaguely known, where courts were rude and irregular, and where means of enforcement were unreliable when they existed at all. And the ultimate sanction of a restrictive economy failed them: where land was abundant and labor at a premium it took little more to create a household than to maintain one. Material independence was sooner or later available to every energetic adult white male, and few failed to break away when they could. Dependent kin, servants, and sons left the patriarchal household, setting up their own reduced establishments which would never grow to the old proportions.

The response was extraordinary. There is no more poignant, dramatic reading than the seventeenth-century laws and admonitions relating to family life. Those of Massachusetts are deservedly best known: they are most profuse and charged with intense Old Testament passion. But they are not different in kind from the others. Within a decade of their founding all of the colonies passed laws demanding obedience from children and specifying penalties for contempt and abuse. Nothing less than capital punishment, it was ruled in Connecticut and Massachusetts, was the fitting punishment for filial disobedience. Relaxation of discipline was universally condemned, and parents and masters were again and again ordered to fulfill their duties as guardians of civil order. But as the laws and pleas elaborated so too did the problems. If guardians failed, it was finally asked, who would guard the guardians? The famous Massachusetts law of 1679 creating tithingmen as censors extraordinary logically concluded the efforts of two generations to recreate the family as the ordered, hierarchical foundation of an ordered, hierarchical society. By the end of the century the surviving elders of the first generation cried out in fearful contemplation of the future. Knowing no other form than the traditional, they could look forward only to the complete dissolution of the family as the primary element of social order. When that happened, when "the rude son should strike the father dead," they knew the elemental chaos that would result:

> What plagues and what portents, what mutiny,
> What raging of the sea, shaking of earth,
> Commotion in the winds, frights changes horrors,
> Divert and crack, rend and deracinate
> The unity and married calm of states
> Quite from their fixure. Oh, when degree is shak'd,
> Which is the ladder to all high designs,
> The enterprise is sick.

Degree was shak'd, order within the family badly disturbed; but the conclusion was not chaos. It was a different ordering and a different functioning of the basic social grouping than had been known before.

By the middle of the eighteenth century the classic lineaments of the American family as modern sociologists describe them—the "isolation of the conjugal unit," the "maximum of dispersion of the lines of descent," partible inheritances, and multilineal growth—had appeared. The consequences can hardly be exaggerated. Fundamental aspects of social life were affected. In the reduced, nuclear family, thrown back upon itself, traditional gradations in status tended to fall to the level of necessity. Relationships tended more toward achievement than ascription. The status of women rose; marriage, even in the eyes of the law, tended to become a contract between equals. Above all, the development of the child was affected.

What is perhaps the most fundamental consequence to the development of the child, reaching into his personality and his relations with the world, is the most difficult to establish and interpret. It concerns the process of the child's entry into society. As the family contracted towards a nuclear core, as settlement and re-settlement, especially on the frontier, destroyed what remained of stable community relations, and constant mobility and instability kept new ties from strengthening rapidly, the once elaborate interpenetration of family and community dissolved. The border line between them grew sharper; and the passage of the child from family to society lost its ease, its naturalness, and became abrupt, deliberate, and decisive: open to question, concern, and decision. As a consequence of such a translation into the world, the individual acquired an insulation of consciousness which kept him from naked contact and immediate involvement with the social world about him: it heightened his sense of separateness. It shifted the perspective in which he viewed society: he saw it from without rather than from within; from an unfixed position not organically or unalterably secured. The community, and particularly the embodiment of its coercive power, the state, tended to be seen as external, factitious. It did not command his automatic involvement.

There were other, more evident and more easily established consequences of the pressures exerted on the family during these years. Within a remarkably short time after the beginnings of settlement it was realized that the family was failing in its more obvious educational functions. In the early 1640's both Virginia and Massachusetts officially stated their dissatisfactions in the passage of what have since become known as the first American laws concerning education. The famous Massachusetts statute of 1642, prefaced by its sharp condemnation of "the great neglect of many parents and masters in training up their children in learning and labor," was one of a series of expedients aimed at shoring up the weakening structure of family discipline. It not only reminded parents and masters of their duty to provide for the "calling and implyment of their children" and threatened punishment for irresponsibility, but added to this familiar obligation the extraordinary provision that they see also to the children's "ability to read and understand the principles of religion and the capitall lawes of this country." Virginia's exactly contemporaneous law ordering county officials to "take up" children whose parents "are disabled to maintaine and educate them" reflected the same concern, as did the Duke's Laws of New York in 1665.

Such laws, expressing a sudden awareness, a heightened consciousness of what the family had meant in education, of how much of the burden of imparting civilization to the young it had borne, and of what its loss might mean, were only the first of a century-long series of adjustments. Responses to the fear of a brutish decline, to the threat of a permanent disruption of the family's educational mechanisms, and to the rising self-consciousness in education varied according to local circumstance. In New England a high cultural level, an intense Biblicism, concentrated settlements, and thriving town institutions led to a rapid enhancement of the role of formal schooling. The famous succession of laws passed in Massachusetts and Connecticut after 1647 ordering all towns to maintain teaching institutions, fining recalcitrants, stating and restating the urgencies of the situation, expressed more than a traditional concern with schooling, and more even than a Puritan need for literacy. It flowed from the fear of the imminent loss of cultural standards, of the possibility that civilization itself would be "buried in the grave of our fathers." The Puritans quite deliberately transferred the maimed functions of the family to formal instructional institutions, and in so doing not only endowed schools with a new importance but expanded their purpose beyond pragmatic vocationalism toward vaguer but more basic cultural goals.

In the context of the age the stress placed by the Puritans on formal schooling is astonishing. In the end it proved too great to be evenly sustained. The broad stream of enforcing legislation that flows through the statute books of the seventeenth century thinned out in the eighteenth century as isolated rural communities, out of contact, save for some of their Harvard- and Yale-trained ministers, with the high moral and intellectual concerns of the settling generation, allowed the level to sink to local requirement. But the tradition of the early years was never completely lost, and New England carried into the national period a faith in the benefits of formal schooling and a willingness to perpetuate and enrich it that has not yet been dissipated.

In the south the awareness that only by conscious, deliberate effort would the standards of inherited culture be transmitted into the future was hardly less acute, but there the environment and the pattern of settlement presented more difficult problems than in the north. Lacking the reinforcement of effective town and church institutions, the family in the south was even less resistant to pressures and sustained even greater shocks. The response on the part of the settlers, however much lower their intellectual demands may have been than the Puritans', was equally intense. The seventeenth-century records abound with efforts to rescue the children from an incipient savagery. They took many forms: the importation of servant-teachers, the attempt to establish parish or other local schools, repeated injunctions to parents and masters; but the most common were parental bequests in wills providing for the particular education of the surviving child or children. These are often fascinating, luminous documents. Susan English of York, for example, who could not sign her name, left each of her children one heifer, the male issue of which was to be devoted to the child's education. Samuel Fenn ordered his executors to devote the entire increase of his stock of cattle to the "utmost education" which could be found for his children in Virginia, and John Custis left the labor of fourteen slaves for the preliminary education of his grandson in Virginia, adding a special provision for paying for its completion in England.

The extravagance and often the impracticality of such efforts in Virginia suggest a veritable frenzy of parental concern lest they and their children succumb to the savage environment. All their fearfulness for the consequences of transplantation, their awareness of the strangeness of the present and the perils of the future, seems to have become concentrated in the issue of education. Their efforts in the seventeenth century came to little; the frustrations multiplied. But the impetus was never entirely lost. The transforming effect of the early years carried over into the education of later, more benign times. When in the eighteenth century the re-emergence in the south of approximate replicas of Old World family organizations and of stable if scattered communities furnished a new basis for formal education, something of the same broad cultural emphasis notable in New England became noticeable also in these southern institutions.

This whole cluster of developments—the heightening of sensitivity to educational processes as the family's traditional effectiveness declined, the consequent increase in attention to formal education and in the cultural burdens placed upon it—was not confined to the boundaries of the original seventeenth-century settlements. It was a pattern woven of the necessities of life in the colonies, and it repeated itself in every region as the threat of the environment to inherited culture made itself felt.

4

There was beyond this group of developments another area of education affected by changes in family life. Apprenticeship, sharing the fate of other forms of legal servitude but particularly involved with the fortunes of the family, was significantly altered.

Bonded servitude had fallen under severe pressures in the seventeenth century. With labor scarce and the recruitment of servants difficult when possible, the lines of dependency weakened and became confused. Amid a universal outcry against rampaging insubordination, servants, in far stronger bargaining positions than ever before, reduced their obligations by negotiation, by force, or by fraud, and gained their independence with startling speed and in startling numbers. By the eighteenth century, despite valiant efforts by the leaders of society to maintain the ancient forms of subordination, bonded servitude, with its carefully calibrated degrees of dependency, was rapidly being eliminated, drained off at one end into freedom and independent wage labor, and at the other into the new, debased status of chattel slavery. Between them there remained only the involuntary but yet terminal servitude of the children of indigent parents, common only in a few urban centers, and a reduced system of voluntary indenture by which impoverished immigrants repaid the cost of their transportation and native boys learned the rudiments of trade.

These were remnants, but yet vital remnants. Apprenticeship was still a significant institution for the transmission of skills. But the evidence of its decline was as clear in changes in its internal characteristics as it was in its quantitative decrease.

The tendency to reduce the once extensive network of mutual obligations to a few simple strands and to transfer the burden of all but strict vocational training to external, formal agencies of education increased through the years. Officially, legally, the assumption continued that the master stood *in loco parentis*, that his duties included all those of an upright father, and that the obligations of apprentices remained, as sanctified in law and tradition, filial in scope and character. But both sets of obligations were increasingly neglected as both sides responded to the pressures of the situation.

Masters, pressed for workers, increasingly inclined to look upon apprenticeship as a badly needed source of labor, treated it with increasingly pragmatic simplicity. Moral indoctrination, Christian training, and instruction in literacy seemed encumbrances upon a contractual arrangement of limited purpose. Furthermore, the ancient demands appeared increasingly anomalous and burdensome in families where the entire apparatus of authority had been weakened and where the servants involved were often of necessity incompatible outlanders: Germans, Scots, and Irish. The masters did provide the required occupational training, but with increasing frequency they provided little else.

Nor were they commonly urged by the servants to do more. In a situation where full entrance into crafts, trades, and even professions was open to anyone with a modicum of capital, enterprise, and ingenuity, it was for instruction in specific skills, and only for that, that apprentices were in fact dependent upon their masters. To the apprentices too the old obligations were felt to be archaic entanglements: impediments in the path to independence.

The seventeenth-century statutes reveal extravagant efforts made not merely to retain the broad scope of apprenticeship obligations within the structure of the family, but to extend it, to include within it cultural matters dislodged from other areas and threatened with extinction. But the evidences of failure and the displacement of functions are manifest in the records of successive generations. They are voiced in the increasingly shrill laws and legislative pronouncements of the seventeenth century demanding the proper discharge of broad obligations, exhorting, and threatening punishment for failure. One group of masters—those in charge of public wards—was subjected to particular scrutiny and their performance officially deplored. In the colonies as in England children of the poor or of those otherwise considered incompetent were taken up as potential threats to the community and sold to masters pledged to care for them, body and soul, and equip them with a trade before the age of twenty-one. That such masters should have been required by law to look upon their charges as public dependents and provide them with the full range of parental care and training is hardly surprising. But that law after law should have been necessary to remind them of their duties, to spell out the extent of their responsibilities, and to threaten punishment for neglect is not merely evidence of human greed; it is an indication also of the change that had overtaken the entire institution of apprenticeship.

It might be said, however, that apprenticeship of the poor, being involuntary, was unrepresentative of the institution as a whole. But the direction of change in this form of apprenticeship was characteristic of the others. In all, there took place a reduction in the personal, non-vocational obligations that bound master and servant and a transfer of general educational functions to external agencies. With increasing frequency masters assigned their apprentices to teachers for instruction in rudimentary literacy and in whatever other non-vocational matters they had contracted to teach. The process did not stop there. The transfer was institutionalized by the introduction of evening schools which were originally started, Professor Bridenbaugh explains, "to instruct apprentices whose indentures stipulated a certain amount of reading, writing, and ciphering." The ultimate conclusion was the specific provision in the contracts of apprenticeship not simply that the master provide for the education of his charge but that he send him to school for a particular period of each year. Seybolt found 108 indentures in the province of New York alone that contained such provisions. The common wording was that the apprentice be sent "One Quarter of a Year in Each Year of said Term to a good Evening School in Order to be well instructed in reading, writing Accounting and the like."

The number of such schools in the eighteenth century is remarkable. Exactly how many were started is not known, but Seybolt published as "typical evening school curricula" a list of subjects taught in 100 such institutions between 1723 and 1770. Such numbers cannot be accounted for by the educational needs of apprentices alone. Serving all those "confined in Business in the Day-Time," welcoming all the "emulous sons of industry," as one eighteenth-century advertisement put it, the evening schools satisfied other needs as well, and they thereby take on a special importance in the early history of education in America.

What these needs were is perhaps best seen in the educational work of Benjamin Franklin. For in organizing his famous Junto of printers, scriveners, shoemakers, and joiners this ex-apprentice and tradesman was acting upon the same impulse that led others to turn to the evening schools. At first glance it seems incredible that he could have succeeded in interesting these workmen in the artificially elevated, self-consciously high-brow questions he proposed to them in meeting after meeting. They shared, perhaps, the broad Enlightenment concern with improving the condition of mankind by rethinking and attempting to reshape institutions, and they may have shared also a genuine delight in literature. But no group of people, not even Franklin and his hard-working colleagues in self-improvement, is motivated solely by such elevated and aesthetic impulses. Their interest was a practical, realistic response to the problems they faced in adjusting to the conditions of an altered society.

Franklin, whose whole life, Carl Van Doren remarked, was "the Junto . . . enlarged and extended," knew well what these problems were. Like Henry Adams, and for similar reasons, he saw his entire career as a series of problems in education; indeed, with at least as much justification as Adams he might have called his apologia *The Education* . . . . The similarities between the two autobiographers is, in fact, striking. Both were immensely aware and intelligent egotists, skilled writers, who could not possibly withstand the temptation to spread the record of their lives before the world, skillfully editing as they went along to emphasize their apparently opposite conclusions: while Adams ironically sought his justification by proving that he had failed, Franklin, here as always blandly playing life straight, found his by making an object lesson of his success. But however they chose to interpret it, both told essentially the same story. Defeated or triumphant, both had fought the same battle of locating themselves in an unfamiliar world, a world for which by early training and normal expectation they had not been prepared. Both early in life had realized that the past no longer held the key to the present or future, that the knowledge, traditions, and responses of their parents would not suffice for their needs, that they would have to undertake their own education into careers whose patterns were not only indistinct but nonexistent, mere possibilities whose shape they would themselves determine.

It was this sense of an open-ended universe that lies behind everything Franklin wrote about education and hence about the conduct of life. The purpose of schooling was to provide in systematic form what he had extemporized, haphazardly feeling his way. Convinced that the proper aims of education were to train and equip the young for just such a tour of surprises as he had known, he sketched the plans for a revolution in formal instruction. But it was a subtle revolution, too often interpreted as somehow peculiarly "utilitarian." Indeed, he did expect education to be useful, as who did not; but his revolution consisted in the kind of utility he had in mind. He wanted subjects and instruction that trained not for limited goals, not for close-bound, predetermined careers, but for the broadest possible range of enterprise. He had no argument with the classics as such. What he objected to was their monopoly of the higher branches of education which denied the breadth of preparation needed for the open world he saw. He stated his whole philosophy of education in the single sentence with which he concluded his *Idea of the English School*: "Thus instructed youth will come out of this school fitted for learning any business, calling, or profession."

Any business, *any* calling, *any* profession! This was too much of a new thing even for eighteenth-century America, as Franklin himself discovered when he tried to put his ideas into practice. But if traditional, formal institutions had a resistant force of their own, informal ones did not. What Franklin failed to implant upon the curriculum of the Academy and College in Philadelphia, he and many others, responding in lesser degrees, perhaps, and with more limited understanding but with equal spontaneity to the movement of society around them, accepted as the goals of mutual aid and self-instruction. What lay behind the interest in mutual instruction, in informal education of all sorts, and in extemporized institutions like evening schools was the recognition that one's role in life had not been fully cast, that the immediate inheritance did not set the final limits, that opportunities beyond the expectation of birth lay all about and could be reached by effort.

The juntos and the evening schools, the self-improvement efforts of the eighteenth-century tradesmen, were not a passing phenomenon. They reflect the beginnings of a permanent motion within American society by which the continuity between generations was to be repeatedly broken. The automatic transfer of occupational and social role from generation to generation, with all that this means for the confidence, ease, and security with which the child locates himself in society—this transfer of life patterns had already by Franklin's time been so generally disrupted that the exception was becoming the rule. The increasingly common experience was departure from rather than adherence to the inherited pattern. The result was not only heightened expectations but new uncertainties. Responses were no longer automatic but deliberate, not insensibly acquired in childhood as part of the natural order of things, but learned, usually late, as part of a self-conscious quest for appropriate forms of behavior. Learning—the purposeful acquisition not merely of technical skills but of new ways of thinking and behaving—was essential. It was a necessary part of social and vocational as well as purely intellectual life, and if it could not be acquired through existing institutions it would be otherwise found, by adapting what lay at hand, by creating new devices for self-improvement and education.

5

In these ways, as part of alterations in family life, in the nature of servitude, and in the opportunities for careers, major elements in the traditional pattern of education were transformed. Other changes, associated with other adjustments in society, contributed still further to the recasting of education. Organized religion and the forms of group life were directly involved.

Though poorly informed on the details of living in wilderness communities, the planners of settlement in the early seventeenth century made one obvious but far-reaching assumption that involved them directly in a new educational enterprise. They assumed that society in the colonies would be the opposite of homogeneous, that it would contain disparate and probably conflicting groups, and that the differences would center on matters of religion. It was, consequently, as a Christian duty and the high moral justification for their colonizing ventures that they undertook the task of reconciling the differences by converting the native Indians to civilized Christian living. Doubting neither their power nor the necessity to recreate the familiar unity of social life, they launched the first campaign of missionary education in British America.

In view of the later history of Indian-white relations, it is natural to slight the seriousness of their concern with the fate of the natives and to see in it only a bland piety and hypocrisy. But their sincerity is attested by the extent of the efforts they made in the face of continuous discouragement. In Virginia, Maryland, and especially in Massachusetts, the first and most carefully planned efforts in education were directed not at the settlers but at the Indians. The planning of Henrico College and the East India Company School in Virginia, the Indian College at Harvard, and John Eliot's celebrated missionary efforts culminating in the founding of Natick as the first of the "Praying Indian" towns, were only the most notable episodes in a long and eventful series. While the initial impulse lasted, thousands of pounds and immeasurable amounts of effort were expended on attempts to educate the Indians. And even afterwards, when the major responsibility came to rest not with overseas entrepreneurs but with land-hungry settlers, and when as a consequence aggressive hostility succeeded the early missionary zeal, and partial annihilation became the usual first step in the process of conversion, there remained not merely the rhetoric of earlier days but effective pockets of continuing missionary activity among the colonists.

Epic and farce, high tragedy and low comedy, the education and conversion of the Indians was a drama of endless frustration. The English settlers, insensitive, inflexible, and righteous, poured into bewildered savage minds a mysterious brew of theology, morals, and lore. They were atrocious anthropologists, and they failed almost entirely in their efforts to convert the Indians and to lead them in harmony into a unified society.

The original missionary fervor faded in the eighteenth century as the expanding frontier removed the natives from direct contact with the centers of white population, and commercial and military considerations came to dominate relations between the races. But it had left an ineradicable mark on American life. It had introduced the problem of group relations in a society of divergent cultures, and with it a form of action that gave a new dimension to the social role of education. For the self-conscious, deliberate, aggressive use of education, first seen in an improvised but confident missionary campaign, spread throughout an increasingly heterogeneous society and came to be accepted as a normal form of educational effort.

The drift of missionary education away from its extemporized and optimistic beginnings may be seen first in the variety of its applications by the dominant English elements in the population to the problems presented by the smaller, subordinate groups that appeared by the early eighteenth century. For to the English, a remarkably ethnocentric people, the similarities among others often outweighed the differences, and the hopes once held and the methods devised for converting and civilizing the American aborigenes were easily transferred to imported Africans and to a variety of infidels, from "Papists" to Pietists, and even to settlers of English ancestry: defiant sectarians or backsliders into savagery on the wild frontier. By the 1740's it was a natural response of one like Franklin, struck by the strangeness and integrity of the German communities in Pennsylvania, by their lack of familiarity with English liberties and English government, and fearful of alien domination, to turn to missionary education, and to help in organizing the Society for the Propagation of the Gospel to the Germans in America.

But what gave this dynamic use of education its greatest importance and its characteristic form was its position in the emerging pattern of American denominationalism.

In the unstable, highly mobile, and heterogeneous society of eighteenth-century America, sectarian religion became the most important determinant of group life. It was religion under peculiar pressures and influences. So universal and so numerous had sectarian groups become by the eve of the Revolution that not only was an enforced state orthodoxy almost nowhere to be found but it was often impossible to say which groups represented orthodoxy and which groups dissent. All of them, even the established churches, lacked the full sanction of public authority by which to compel allegiance, and all of them faced an equal threat of erosion among those elements of their membership, especially the young, that were infirm in faith and vulnerable to temptation. Persuasion and nurture would have to do what compulsion could more easily have done. Furthermore, in such voluntary religious groupings "Christianity itself," Professor Mead comments, "tends to be conceived primarily as an activity, a movement, which the group is engaged in promoting." It takes a "promotional and propagandistic" attitude to its confession: the "sense of mission forms the center of a denomination's self-conscious life." Schools and colleges were therefore essential: schools to train the young in purity and loyalty; colleges to educate the educators, to produce a proper ministry and mission, and to provide benefits which otherwise would be sought by the ambitious young from proselytizing rivals. Sectarian groups, without regard to the intellectual complexity of their doctrine or to their views on the value of learning to religion, became dynamic elements in the spread of education, spawning schools of all sorts, continuously, competitively, in all their settlements; carrying education into the most remote frontiers. Even their weaknesses contributed: schism, surging upward from uncontrollable sources of division, multiplied their effect.

But their goals in education, always clear, were always limited. Their aims in education were not served by a neutral pedagogy that might develop according to its own inner impulses and the drift of intellectual currents. The education they desired and created was an instrument of deliberate group action. It bore the burden of defining the group, of justifying its existence by promoting the view that its peculiar interpretations and practices conformed more closely "to those of the early Church as pictured in the New Testament than the views and policies of its rivals." And it was by carefully controlled education above all else that denominational leaders hoped to perpetuate the group into future generations.

The members of such groups participated in a continuous enterprise of indoctrination and persuasion, an enterprise aimed no longer at unifying society but only at aiding one group to survive in a world of differing groups. To them the transmission of culture was problematic in the extreme, surrounded by pitfalls, doubts, and difficulties. Education, so central to their purposes, was deliberate, self-conscious, and explicit. The once-automatic process of transfer would continue to operate only by dint of sustained effort. Education was an act of will.

6

Such a view and use of education, dynamic, aggressive, and disputatious, rested upon the assumption that the control of education would remain in the hands of the group itself, that education, once launched, would not attain an institutional autonomy, an independence, that would free it from the initiating purposes. That this assumption proved workable, that the multiplying units of denominational education adhered to the goals of their founders, was to a considerable extent the result of the forms of institutional financing and control that emerged in the course of the seventeenth century.

In these matters as in so many others, there had been no desire on the part of the settlers to alter the traditional forms. Everywhere the original reliance was on private benefaction, and everywhere, in the very first years, donations for schools were made in the familiar manner. In the Massachusetts Bay area, for example, private donations accounted for the founding of schools in nine towns, and the Hopkins bequest, which in England would have been indistinguishable from hundreds of other private gifts for education, underwrote the creation of three grammar schools in Connecticut and western Massachusetts. But it quickly became apparent that such benefactions would not satisfy the needs. Sufficient funds were not forthcoming, and those that appeared failed to produce the expected yield.

To a large extent these difficulties resulted simply from the lack of surplus wealth. But they were compounded by the peculiar problems encountered in the creation of endowments. For even if the funds were available, how were they to be invested so as to provide a steady and reliable income? In real estate, in land, was the obvious answer; and indeed the profitable endowments that did exist in the seventeenth century were largely investments in real estate. But more often than not land endowments failed to produce the traditional revenues, for their yield was expected to flow from tenancy, which, where unclaimed land was the one abundant commodity, failed to develop to any significant extent. Untenanted land could be, and often was, given as endowment, but its profits, if any, obviously lay in the future. When, as in the case of the Company land set aside for Virginia's Henrico College, tenants were deliberately imported and planted on endowment land, they left at the first opportunity and could be replaced only with the greatest difficulty. Even, as in the more highly populated areas of the north, when rents were forthcoming they were often unreliable. Their value fluctuated sharply as continuous crises—gluts and famines, devastations by wind, weather, the seas, and the Indians—shook the fragile economy. Furthermore, a chronic shortage of specie and the necessity to accept payments in kind involved the recipient in an exchange of goods and hence the risks of trade. Finally, inflation in the eighteenth century, especially in New England, reduced the value of all long-term investments.

Strenuous efforts were made to find new and more reliable forms of investment: public utilities, primarily mills and ferries, short-term personal loans, shipping, even commercial ventures were all tried with varying success. In the end none were reliable enough, nor was the capital available for such endowments sufficient, to finance the education desired by the colonists. Other sources of support were clearly necessary.

They were found only in direct and repeated contributions by the community. There was, at first, not only an understandable reluctance to venture beyond the familiar forms of financing but also considerable confusion as to what procedures were proper once such steps were contemplated. In Massachusetts, for example, the pledge of community property for education became common only after laws were passed compelling individuals of supposed wealth to volunteer more generously; and when it was apparent that not even the grant of common town land would be sufficient and that direct taxation would have to be resorted to, the yield from school rates most often was considered to be only temporary supplements to the more familiar endowments and tuition payments.

The solution that emerged by mid-century in New England—the pooling of community resources in the form of general taxation—did not, of course, appear everywhere. But for all the differences, the various forms that developed shared with taxation one all-important characteristic. Everywhere—in the middle colonies and in the south as well as in New England—the support for schools and even colleges came not from the automatic yield from secure investments but from repeated acts of current donation, whether in the form of taxes, or of individual, family, or community gifts. The autonomy that comes from an independent, reliable, self-perpetuating income was everywhere lacking. The economic basis of self-direction in education failed to develop.

It is this common characteristic which taxation shares with the other modes of colonial school financing, and not its "public" aspects, that gives it great importance in the history of American education. Dependent for support upon annual or even less regular gifts, education at all levels during the early formative years came within the direct control, not of those responsible for instruction, but of those who had created and maintained the institutions. When in the eighteenth century a measure of economic maturity made it possible to revert to other, older forms, the tradition of external control was well established. That it remained so, and that consequently American education at all levels, and especially at the highest, has continued to be sensitive to community pressure, delicately reflecting the shifting interests and needs of the founding and sustaining groups—particularly the denominational, but ethnic and geographic as well—is a consequence of the utility of this tradition in the emerging pattern of American group life.

7

All of these elements in the transformation of education, turning on the great axles of society—family, church, community, and the economy—had become clear before the end of the colonial period. Like all else of those early years that form part of the continuity of American history, they passed through the toils of revolution. They were not unaffected by that event. But the effect of the Revolution on education was typical of its generally limited impress upon social institutions. For the Revolution was a social movement only in a special sense. It did not flow from deep sources of social discontent, and its aims were not to recast the ordering of the society that had developed in the earlier years. In education as in so many other spheres of social action, its effects were to free the trends of the colonial period from legal and institutional encumbrances and to confirm them, to formalize them, to give them the sanction of law in a framework of enlightened political thought.

Much more at first had been expected by the leaders of the Revolution. Most of the major statesmen had sweeping schemes for national systems of education and national universities, or other programs by which the new nationalism and its republican spirit might properly be expressed. But the efforts to realize these plans came to nothing. They rose too far above the needs and interests of the scattered, variegated, semi-autonomous communities that comprised the new nation; they placed too concrete a meaning on national life and a national society. The forces shaping education had never been closely related to the higher political organizations; they had, if anything, grown up in deliberate opposition to them. They owed little to political independence.

But they found a fuller meaning and a more secure status as a consequence of the Revolution. The spontaneity of local impulses, the variety of educational forms, and the immediacy of popular control survived the war and political changes and were actively confirmed. The central question was that of the survival of denominational influence, and the issue was never in doubt. Wherever schemes for state systems of education threatened the influence of sectarian groups they were defeated or fell under the control of the denominations. It took Jefferson forty years to create the University of Virginia, and when it opened in 1825 it had acquired religious attributes he had struggled to eliminate. His famous plan for an elaborate system of public schools in Virginia was wrecked on the shoals of apathy and sectarian opposition and never enacted.

Elsewhere it was the same. Typical and particularly important in itself was the fate of the College of Philadelphia. Like another Anglican institution, King's College, it was seized by the state in 1776, its charter confiscated, and its Board of Trustees eliminated. A new state institution was formed by the legislature in its place. But this act of confiscation threatened essential powers of the denominations —all denominations as it was ultimately realized—as well as the stability of business organizations, and it was therefore repeatedly challenged in its legality, at first by the former Provost, William Smith, and his Trustees, later by others in sympathy with them. Struggling before the legislature, the courts, and the Council of Censors to regain their rights, the defenders of the old charter elaborated the implications of the case until they merged with those of another great political and constitutional issue in Pennsylvania, the seizure by the legislature of the charter of the Bank of North America. Both seizures had been made in the name of the People and as part of an effort to eliminate enclaves of special, state-protected privilege. But who were the People? A handful of legislators? Not bankers, not educators whose enterprise would advance the general good? To eliminate all privilege from private groups was, it would seem, tantamount to giving it all to the State. But what was the State in a republican government? Should it have powers against the people themselves? Was not the answer the multiplication rather than the elimination of privilege?

The debate on these questions in the 1780's was one of the most significant of the entire Revolutionary period. Centering on the nature of privilege and the rights of voluntary groups before the state, it probed the meaning of Revolutionary thought and its bearing on American society. The verdict, the first of a series in several states that culminated in the decision of the Supreme Court in the Dartmouth College case thirty years later, in effect restored the old charter of the College and endorsed the right of initiating groups to control what they had created, to gain from the state equal privileges with all other groups and to retain them even against the state itself.

8

Confirmed rather than disturbed by the Revolution, American education passed on into the nineteenth century as it had developed in the colonial period. On almost every major point the original inheritance had been called into question, challenged by circumstance, altered or discarded. A process whose origins lay in the half-instinctive workings of a homogeneous, integrated society was transformed in the jarring multiplicity, the raw economy, and the barren environment of America. No longer instinctive, no longer safe and reliable, the transfer of culture, the whole enterprise of education, had become controversial, conscious, constructed: a matter of decision, will, and effort.

But education not only reflects and adjusts to society; once formed, it turns back upon it and acts upon it. The consequences of this central transformation of education have significantly shaped the development of American society. Two kinds of results have been perhaps most important. First, education in this form has proved in itself to be an agency of rapid social change, a powerful internal accelerator. By responding sensitively to the immediate pressures of society it has released rather than impeded the restless energies and ambitions of groups and individuals. And the fact that so much of the acquisition of culture has taken place away from the direct influence of family elders and so much of it gained either directly from the environment, from the child's contemporaries, or from formal institutions themselves sensitive to social pressures, has helped create a situation where, as Margaret Mead puts it, "children of five have already incorporated into their everyday thinking ideas that most elders will never fully assimilate."

Second, education as it emerged from the colonial period has distinctively shaped the American personality; it has contributed much to the forming of national character. Crèvecoeur's "American, this new man," was not simply the result of "the government, climate, mode of husbandry, customs, and peculiarity of circumstance," nor of the mixture of peoples and the material abundance which the American Farmer also discussed. What was recognized even before the Revolution as typical American individualism, optimism, and enterprise resulted also from the processes of education which tended to isolate the individual, to propel him away from the simple acceptance of a predetermined social role, and to nourish his distrust of authority.

The transformation of education that took place in the colonial period was irreversible. We live with its consequences still.

Section IV
Philosophic Inquiry
Methods in Education

A Philosopher Looks at Qualitative Research

Maxine Greene
Teachers College, Columbia University

Qualitative researchers ask themselves questions about the meaning of what is happening in some field of human action. They are concerned with making sense of what seems to lack coherence and with putting it into a form that will permit others to enter a "mutual tuning-in relationship" (Schutz, 1964, p. 173) with the actors on the scene. The search is for understanding rather than explanation; the researchers are striving for adequacy of interpretation rather than prediction and control. If quantitative research may be defined by its pursuit of technical or theoretical knowledge, qualitative research may be thought of in terms of an orientation to practical knowledge, or what Aristotle called "phronesis" (Gadamer, 1979, pp. 74–85). Not only is this orientation to practical knowledge related to a form of ethical reasoning, but it connects as well with the modes of interpretation and application called hermeneutics. Hans-George Gadamer wrote the following:

> I think, then, that the chief task of philosophy is to justify this way of reason and to defend practical and political reason against the domination of technology based on science. This is the point of philosophical hermeneutics. It corrects the peculiar falsehood of modern consciousness: the idolatry of scientific methods and of the anonymous authority of the sciences, and it vindicates again the noblest task of the citizen—decision-making according to one's own responsibility—instead of conceding that task to the "expert." (1975, p. 312).

Viewing an urban classroom as a kind of text, the qualitative researcher works to make sense of what appears to be a confused swirl of bodies and voices, scrawlings on the blackboard, and a teacher leaning forward trying to elicit answers from attentive students, those apparently willing to learn. The meanings of what is happening in the space of that classroom exist *for* the students and the teacher in the room, each one attending from her/his own vantage point as a member of the class. The inquirer or researcher must recognize that she/he is also looking from a situated vantage point, affected not only by her/his training or the methodology in use, but by personal history, gender, color, beliefs, and values. John Dewey once explained that "the self is not something ready-made, but something in continuing formation through choice of action . . ." (1916, p. 408). There is, he said, a connection between interest and "the quality of selfhood which exists" (p. 408). In some dimension, the researcher's self is in formation through her/his choice of action with regard to the field of study. The nature of her/his interests generates whatever responsibility she/he takes for interpreting patterns of action, verbal interchanges, and facial expressions for the sake of her/his own understanding and the self-understanding of those who have become the objects of her/his research. Both the inquirer and those being studied must be aware that the study under way is perspectival, situated, in no way abstract or disembodied.

Of course, quantitative approaches are needed at times: It is important to have some record of measured achievement when it comes to school knowledge and to take factual account of the multiple literacies in which youngsters may be involved, the diverse cultures to which they may belong, and the equity (or lack of equity) with which resources are distributed in accord with the differences. Also, it is necessary to have information about children's health, their home situations, the strains on them, the disadvantages from which they may suffer, the special privileges they may enjoy. But this is a framework. To build upon it, we are not bound to idolatry of the scientific method or any other method, even as we strive to direct the several sciences to humane ends. Nor are we required to celebrate the increasing linkages between science and the new technologies. Most important of all, we do not need to submit to what Gadamer called an "anonymous authority" separate from human intention. Qualitative thinkers resist the conception of science as a body of finished propositions derived from empirical research or a set of formulations to be applied as technical rationality to the shifting, induplicable situations in which people live. When scientific inquiries are founded in self-reflectiveness, they lose the anonymity that troubled Gadamer so much. For Jurgen Habermas, for instance, self-reflection "is at once intuition and emancipation, comprehension, and liberation from dogmatic dependence" (1971, p. 208). Self-reflectiveness, he points out, makes us conscious of *why* we think what we do. It helps us discover those factors in our own self-formation that determine our approach to practice as well as the way we work in the world. Inquiries grounded in self-reflectiveness, also, are not likely to be subsumed under what is called "instrumental rationality" or rationality directed toward mainly technical ends (Habermas, 1973, p. 268), meeting the criteria of "an effective control of reality" (Habermas, 1970, p. 92).

For Habermas and many others, the point of knowing should not be primarily the establishment of controls. Rather, it should be the enabling of persons, understood to be acting *subjects*, to engage in free communicative interactions. Only when free communication becomes possible will merely technical rules give way to shared communal values and norms. If this occurs, practical judgments may give rise to ethical reasoning. A concern of this kind is fundamental to the qualitative project and to the effort of qualitative researchers to prevent the objectification of people who are conscious subjects into items or mere things.

Either through personal experience or encounters with African American literature and feminist texts, we are familiar with what it means for living persons to be treated as objects. For Jean-Paul Sartre, this is the same as confusing people with phenomena characterized by what he called "being-in-itself." That is, chairs, tables, and other material phenomena which are what they are and not in a process of becoming. They are what is marked by "being-in-itself." In contrast, what we think of as the self is identified with "being-for-itself," or "the being of possibilities" (Sartre, 1956, p. 95). The human being (the "for-itself") evokes images of growth, of change, even of expansion. She/he experiences new beginnings that are almost impossible to predict or even to capture in calculative terms.

Chairs and tables, for all their apparently objective existence, also transcend the limits of definition, particularly when viewed perspectively. Most of us realize that our perceptions are always incomplete; because, looking out from a specific location (in a room, on a street, in an open field), we can see only aspects or profiles of bookshelves, tables, front yards, treetops, windmills, barns. Each one becomes variously meaningful, depending on context or the point of view from which they are perceived. Because they do not possess consciousness, however, the meanings ascribed to them are not meanings *for* them, but only for those who perceive. Asking ourselves about the difference between knowing about or gaining information about the physical facilities in a school and making sense of what is happening in the hallways and classrooms, we must make clear distinctions between phenomena lacking consciousness (marked by "being-in-itself") and live human beings (marked by "being-for-itself") with consciousness thrusting into the world.

It should be remembered that things produced by human activity take on the character of "a condition of human existence," as Hannah Arendt wrote. They become part of the world's reality as it surrounds us, and their impact on human existence "is felt and received as a conditioning force. The objectivity of the world—its object- or thing-character—and the human condition supplement each other; because human existence is conditioned existence, it would be impossible without things, and things would be a heap of unrelated articles, a non-world, if they were not the conditioners of human existence" (1958, p. 9). This connection between the human condition and the world's objectivity may remind us of the importance of recognizing that what presumes to be an objectively existing world is actually a non-world when not consciously experienced. It should remind us, too, that the ancient separations of consciousness and world, or subject and object, have been held up to question for more than a century, even in the face of stubborn defenses of objectivism.

Although objectivism takes many forms, it may be described as a belief in the independent existence of what is described as reality. Whatever is justified as a truth claim in this connection must correspond to something that existed before human inquiry began. Those acquainted with religious world views recognize the comfort to be gained from relying on a fixed authority when it comes to comprehending what is real. Current conceptions, which have developed notions of reality contingent on vantage points and particular ways of knowing, embody what Clifford Geertz calls an unprecedented "diversity of modern thought" (1983, p. 152). He goes on to describe the uneasiness to which it gives rise—"an uneasiness expressed in a number of not altogether discordant ways: as a fear of particularism, a fear of subjectivism, a fear of idealism, and, of course, summing them all into a kind of intellectualist *Grand Peur,* the fear of relativism. If thought is so much out in the world as this, what is to guarantee its generality, its objectivity, its efficacy, its truth?" (p. 153). What Geertz calls uneasiness underlies to a considerable degree some of the questions now being asked by educational researchers.

The inescapable diversity in so many schools enhances that uneasiness. There are unprecedented numbers of newcomers in public schools—children from countries many of which are unknown to their teachers. Languages, value systems, background traditions vary as never before; and more and more teachers are being asked to develop multicultural curricula in order to take into account the multiplicity of cultural symbol systems affecting what their students know and learn. That very multiplicity and the demand that differences be respected make it increasingly difficult for teachers to counteract the erosion of shared values and what is often described as the collapse of community. Even as they turn their attention to instituting dialogues across the many differences, teachers are being challenged to pay heed to the long-silenced voices of submerged minorities, oppressed women, and displaced children as well. There is, inevitably, greater and greater difficulty facing the teacher committed to understanding how classroom situations mean to all those involved. Similarly, the researcher finds herself/himself having to deal with all kinds of challenges to fixed frameworks and firm definitions, and to the capacity to predict what any given classroom can achieve.

The more particulars and more details that qualitative inquiries amass, the more desire there appears to be to return to some golden age of large, generalized shapes and representations. Lacking that, there is a tendency to invent a new kind of "metanarrative" for our time. For Jean-François Lyotard, a metanarrative implies a "philosophy of history" used to "legitimate knowledge" (1984, p. 16). It is, most often, a large-scale theoretical interpretation supposedly with universal application. Examples might be the idea that an age of reason will lead to universal peace and that a free market society all over the world will guarantee universal human rights. Dominant today is the metanarrative that points to a brilliant technocratic future discoverable in cyberspace. All such narratives deal in totalities and universals; they overlook particularities, differences, contradictions. Lyotard has written about the presumption made by decision-makers about the commensurability of a great range of beliefs and languages as they take for granted the determinability of the whole. "They allocate our lives for the growth of power. In matters of social justice and scientific truth alike, the legitimation of that power is based on its optimizing the system's performance—efficiency" (1984, p. 17). He was talking about "a logic of maximum performance," which is a way of bypassing heterogeneity and contingency, as well as justice. The "logic" he spoke of exists apart from human construction (like Gadamer's "anonymous authority"); it allows for the taken-for-granted objectivity of whatever system exists. Like many of our dreams of the past, Lyotard's is a conceptualization of completion and totality, which is wholly at odds with his own postmodern views and with the values and concerns of qualitative inquiry. What he described is another form of objectivism: the system presents itself as self-existent and separated from human wonder and human inquiry. (We might be tempted to go back to the philosopher Søren Kierkegaard's statement that nothing must be included in the construction of a logical system that *exists* or has existed. "Nothing must then be incorporated in a logical system that has any relation to existence, that is not indifferent to existence" [1947, p. 196]).

Questions having to do with problems of being (ontological problems) and problems of knowing (epistemological problems) underlie all such points of view. For different reasons, both exclude the role of the experiential and the subjective, of that which derives from different (and contingent) minds. Ontological and epistemological questions both, perhaps strangely, evoke a philosophic drama that has been unfolding since classical times. How do we know what we know? How can truth and certainty be attained by fallible creatures in the midst of life? Is knowledge of the Good and the True only within reach of the peculiarly privileged, of the "philosopher-kings"? Are the others to be left to imposed formulations, to intuitions, to superstitions, to sound-bytes, to mere information?

In ancient Greece, when philosophers began pondering such matters, some of them instructed ordinary beings to look upon what they saw with their eyes and heard with their ears as illusions, (shadows cast upon a prison wall, as Socrates explained in Plato's Myth of the Cave [Plato, 1968, p. 269]). What was apprehended through experience or perception had nothing to do with either the true or the good. If individuals were to enter into the realm of pure knowledge and free their souls to turn toward the Idea of the Good, they had not only to struggle out of the cave and learn to stand in the blinding light of the sun but they also had to give up their involvement in everyday affairs and relationships and break with the illusion of coming to know in the routine situations of daily life. Those burdened with the obligations of ordinary living and those preoccupied with the necessities of life could not be expected to look upwards toward the higher realm of pure Forms and Ideas. Later, these pure Forms and Ideas would be regarded as the concepts necessary for ordering experience in the quest for meaning. It was originally believed, however, that they could be grasped or envisaged by the faculty of reason itself, by intuition, or by the "eyes of the mind." *Paideia*, Plato's idea of culture, was symbolized by the sun. The highest aim of *paideia* was the knowledge of Good, "the supreme measure, the measure of all measures." From the point of view of humanity, wrote Werner Jaeger, the image of the cave treats *paideia* "as the transformation and enlightenment of the soul till it reaches the point when it can see the vision of the supreme reality" (1943, p. 294). Again, it must be stressed that this is accomplished by the work of abstract rationality straining to transcend the experienced world.

Beginning with the stirrings of empirical science in the 16th century, scholars could no longer deny the importance of experience and of the kind of knowledge that might expand controls over the exigencies of life. Philosopher after philosopher, beginning with René Descartes (1968), responded by seeking some "ultimate context for thought" (Rorty, 1979, pp. 5–6) that would make philosophy a foundational study. In the dualist Cartesian philosophy, which rests on a separation between mind and body, there was an emphasis on detachment and "clear and distinct ideas" like those existing in the mind of God (Descartes, 1968). The "ultimate context" became one of rejection when it came to the partial and the perspectival; in the interests of purity and clarity of vision, the priority of reason was affirmed once again. This affirmation of reason fed a conviction that a systematic philosophical methodology could unveil the fundamental nature of things in an objectively existent world. Reason, transcending all individual and cultural differences, would disclose what was universally true. If predefined rules and norms were complied with, rational frameworks could be constructed in which conflicts among ideas and values would be resolved. Once that happened, philosophy could be relied upon as a "mirror of nature" (Rorty, 1979), a reflection or a representation of the real.

This approach helped generate much of the thinking in the Enlightenment of the 18th century. Along with the discoveries of so-called natural science, it helped to break the hold of myth, old religions, and superstition. Science was thought to be the exclusive producer of truth; and it was believed that the structure of scientific knowledge demanded that distinctions be made between subject and object, or the mind and the natural world. Language was viewed as a largely neutral medium that mediated between that disembodied mind and allowed for true representations. Not surprisingly, a new metanarrative began to take shape. It had to do with the connections between the rise of science and human progress and between progress and the increasing human capacity to exert control over both society and the physical world.

Many of the rationales for objectivist research derived from this account of things. If reason and the rules of reason governed inductive thinking, for example, they would allow for the construction of theories or explanatory propositions applicable to social as well as natural phenomena. Logics and languages were available that purported to make value-free inquiries conceivable. The vocabularies being invented were said not only to correspond to external realities as normally described, but they also were thought to describe what those realities actually were. Subjectivity, point of view, and emotion were to be set aside; the point of science was to achieve generalizations as pure and reliable as those attained by mathematics.

This particular orientation maintained the Cartesian split between the thinking subject and the substance of things. Immanuel Kant, at the start of the nineteenth century, delivered a blow to such dualism with his emphasis on the human capacity to order and make sense of the sensory materials forever bombarding the human mind. This was done by means of definable rational categories, by means of which such relations as cause and effect, time and space, and the rest could be effected (Kant, 1940, p. 42). Without the ability to use concepts in that fashion, perceptions and sensations would mean nothing. But without the ability to perceive and to sense, conceptions would be wholly abstract and empty. To Kant, such categories and concepts were universal; they did not differ from person to person or from culture to culture. He also regarded moral intuitions and laws and the awareness of free will as universal. Writing that each living being conceives his own existence as an end in itself, he spelled out as a practical imperative the charge, "So act as to treat humanity, whether in thine own person or in that of any other, in every case as an end withal, never as a means" (1929, p. 309). What remains important, along with the recognition of the dependence of what is thought to be real on human construction, is the insistence that people (whoever they are) are not to be treated as means to others' ends. When we ponder ethical reasoning in our own time and in connection with qualitative research, this should remain at the core of our thought.

The interrelations of consciousness and the world had already interested poets like Blake, Wordsworth, and Coleridge and romantic painters like Constable and Turner. Blake raged against the mechanized world being pictured by the Enlightenment thinkers and poets. For him, an objectively existent world could not simply be represented or imitated in painting or poetry; what was perceived and felt had to be transformed by vision and imagination. For Wordsworth and Coleridge, the capacity of imagination allowed human beings to perceive the general in the particular, to find symbolic meanings in the particular, and to bring images into being in the absence of the actual and the observed. Writing in "Tintern Abbey," (1988) the poet Wordsworth anticipated the transactions that give rise to qualitative inquiries. There must be a mingling of perception and imagination if any scene is to be adequately presented, Wordsworth wrote: ". . . of all the mighty world / Of eye and ear, both what they half-create / And what perceive" (1962, p. 419). This approach is at the furthest remove from the depersonalized "spectator" approaches that focused on correspondences with "reality."

G. W. F. Hegel, the German romantic idealist philosopher, becomes important in this context because of his dialectic view of the active human being working toward self-comprehension in relation to history. He placed great emphasis on the role of human thought in producing what is thought to be the world and developed a great spiritual system through which human beings moved, by means of contradictions and resolutions, away from individual spontaneity and toward self-knowledge as part of a world process, a mode of participation in the World Spirit or the Absolute Mind (1949). What remains important is the generative power of his view of dialectical changes and transformation, as humankind developed through continual conflicts between theses and antitheses to syntheses on higher and higher levels of historical change. When the philosopher Kierkegaard rejected the system Hegel created as nothing more than "speculative philosophy in the abstract" (1947, p. 202), he was opening the way still further to the modern interest in the role of the human mind (always in transaction with what surrounds) in the construction of what was believed to be real.

Philosophy in the abstract was explicitly challenged by Karl Marx (1967, 1973) and Friedrich Engels, who adapted the dialectic method to an effort to understand human conflicts, human labor, and other interactions with the changing material world. Building a political economy, they connected cognition and consciousness to their approach to practice in the midst of social life. Activity or practice, when consciously undertaken and reflected upon, was conceived of as *praxis*, something very different from habitual or routinized behavior responsive to unknown forces without. The Marxist idea of consciousness projecting into the concreteness of the world rather than existing as an essence in the brain fed emerging notions that interpretations can come from more than one dominant vantage point. Networks of values, beliefs, and doctrines, or what came to be thought of as ideologies, always played a role in shaping attitudes toward the world. The domination by ideologies and the mystifications occasioned by them (the deceptive views that served the interests of those in power) could, however, be overcome by critical thinking along with cultural action. Human consciousness, viewed in relation to class structures and political arrangements, came to be viewed as the locus of emancipation, if people could be brought to understand the efforts made by others to condition and to mystify. The impressive rational frameworks inherited from the past, along with the metanarratives having to do with the inevitability of human freedom and social justice, were being more and more seriously shaken throughout the 19th century. This was partly due to the advances of industry and capitalism, which began to seem uncontrollable, and partly to the growing visibility of masses of people who had been exploited and silenced for centuries. Not only were many of them empowered to name what worked upon and dominated them; through their naming and their self-reflection, they were able to reconceive their relations to power and their responsibility for transforming their lived worlds.

Changes of this order on the European and American scenes provided themes and subplots for the philosophic drama unfolding in the 20th century. It was a drama having to do with the erosion of ancient fixities and pieties and with questioning about such modern certainties as those having to do with the natural and applied sciences. The turbulent years at the turn of the century saw a laying of the groundwork for the shifts and changes in the relation between qualitative and quantitative inquiry and research. More and more scholars, for instance, began raising sometimes uneasy questions about the dominance of positivism in many of its guises, like the logical positivism in the so-called Vienna Circle (Hempel, 1965). For the philosophers in that circle, the methods of the natural sciences were clearly applicable to the sciences of man. All investigation, including that carried on with respect to social life, was to aim at the attainment of so-called law-like generalizations, permitting predictions through the use of deductive arguments. For them, scientific inquiry had to be, by its very nature, value free, and the relation of theory to practice had to be mainly technical. If general laws could be discovered, the production of desirable states of affairs could be guaranteed so long as the knowledge gained was testable. This was one dimension, of course, of renewed studies in logics and languages, which may have reached a climax (from a contemporary point of view) in Ludwig Wittgenstein's later work, *Philosophical Investigations* (1968), where he moved from a discussion of ordinary language to a discussion of "language games" and their connection to "forms of life." The multiplicity of rule-governed games relates to what is being said today about the illegitimacy of universally valid knowledge and the need to pay attention to heterogeneity and pluralism. In fact, it now appears that the Wittgensteinian approach to language has helped in our understanding of social life. The same may be said with respect to educational research at a moment of multiculturalism and unprecedented diversity.

The drama went on, revealing new themes and plot lines that gradually merged, if only to diverge again. A climax was reached at the close of the 19th century when Wilhelm Dilthey began working toward a hermeneutic approach to social science by objecting to the application of natural science methods to the study of human beings (Palmer, 1969, pp. 98–99). Dilthey was mainly concerned with finding a foundation for humanities and social sciences, both of which he thought of as expressions of human beings' inner lives. Believing that concrete, lived experience must be the starting point of any inquiry, he also tried to find ways of objectively validating the interpretations. The preoccupations were contradictory, but what remains important is the view of understanding that went beyond the cognitive. It had to do with human beings grasping the experience of other human beings and individual lives meeting other individual lives. As restiveness with the objectivist methods increased and the limitations of empirical studies became clear, a variety of scholars from different disciplines turned toward hermeneutics to understand other human beings and the ways they made sense of their worlds.

Hermeneutics as a study had begun with the probing of theological texts. Now the very idea of text widened to include patterns of human action; and hermeneutics was no longer intended primarily for the explication of sacred books or others where the meaning was hidden or abstruse. Especially significant for this discussion is the manner in which Gadamer and others related it to social inquiry. Writing suggestively in many fields, Gadamer may have undertaken the most dramatic critique of objectivism and traditional, value-free scientific expertise. Interested in art, the nature of play, and games, he objected to a "radical subjectivisation" of any one of them (1975, p. 39). All beliefs and actions, he wrote, have to be studied in the context of the language games in which they are found. Moreover, they must be studied in the contexts of history and tradition because language and tradition are so closely bound together. He emphasized the pedagogical importance, in consequence, of initiating persons into language communities where language could always be reinterpreted and changed.

In an effort to understand, a researcher or investigator is often called upon to translate from one language to another. Doing so, she/he has to remain conscious of her/his own beliefs and values. Striving to grasp the meanings expressed by those who are different, the investigator or interpreter must be sensitive to the differences between her/his conceptual frame and the frame of those being studied. The foreignness of certain meanings must be confronted even as the interpreter works to bring them into intelligible relation with her/his own life. When an interpretation is successful (with regard to an event in past history or to a stranger's lived life at the present moment), there may be a "fusion of horizons" (Gadamer, 1975) but never a final resolution of questions having to do with truth and validity. There are always new aspects or profiles of things to be perceived, always recognitions of incompleteness. There is a continual reexamination of the prejudgments and prejudices that may affect judgment. There is always the sense of some new possibility of action. Returning to Sartre's linking of "being-for-itself" with "the being of possibilities" (1956, p. 95), we may realize once more that the self is always in process, moving toward its own future. The understanding sought by the qualitative researcher is an understanding opened to a future, to what might be and is not yet.

For such understanding to be gained, the researcher must feel herself/himself to be personally present to the world being lived by those on the social scene under study. The self-reflectiveness mentioned above must be maintained. There must be a recognition that the realm of meanings is never a purely private one, neither for the investigator nor for the actors on the scene. All exist within and transact with complex fabrics of historical and cultural meanings, some of which they share with others, some of which they do not. The philosophy of phenomenology has played a significant role in clarifying such relationships as the 20th century has moved on. It provides a viewpoint that enables us to "see" that of which we are conscious without the mediating and sometimes distorting lenses of conventions and traditional philosophical theories. Edmond Husserl contributed much to that mode of seeing, as he did to the long-standing critique of objectivism. He identified what he called the "natural attitude" with a tacit acceptance of the "world" as objectively real and reliable for most pursuits (1973). The "natural attitude" is what characterizes the naive and unquestioning acceptance of everyday life except at those moments when we become abruptly conscious of our own experience. If such awareness were to continue, it might become the kind of reflective self-awareness that allows persons to break seriously with what they have taken for granted and pose questions they might never have otherwise asked.

Husserl called for a "radical self-investigation" on the part of the scientist, and indeed on the part of all those naively immersed "in the already-given world, whether it be experiencing, or thinking, or valuing or acting" (1973, p. 152). Preoccupied with the clarification of consciousness and the enhancement of awareness, he continually directed attention to the "life-world." Husserl, like the phenomenologists who followed him, did not move into some esoteric realm when he spoke about reflection on experience. He was attending to the ways in which consciousness grasps the appearances of things, or the ways in which human beings grasp what becomes present or visible to them. It is important for educators also to consider what is meant by the transition from the natural or naive attitude to the questioning, wondering attitude in which most kinds of learning begin. Both the doubt and the wonder are important where learning is concerned. Perhaps one of the best descriptions of both was written by Albert Camus in *The Myth of Sisyphus*. The passage begins with an account of the routines of daily life and then describes the lurch into a new mode of awareness or awakeness:

> It happens that the stage sets collapse. Rising, streetcar, four hours in the office or the factory, meal, streetcar, four hours of work, meal, sleep, and Monday Tuesday Wednesday Thursday Friday and Saturday according to the same rhythm—this path is easily followed most of the time. But one day the "why" arises and everything begins in that weariness tinged with amazement. "Begins"—this is important. Weariness comes at the end of the acts of a mechanical life, but at the same time it inaugurates the impulse of consciousness. It awakens consciousness and provokes what follows. What follows is the gradual return into the chain or it is the definitive awakening (1955, pp. 12–13).

This mode of awakening may be necessary for both the qualitative researcher and those with whom she or he is trying to relate for the sake of understanding. If nothing else, such a moment of awakening arouses a person from submergence in the ordinary and the taken for granted. Very often what has been taken for granted is a conventionally described "normal" classroom, a disorderly or undisciplined classroom, sometimes a kind of prison. When an observer suddenly realizes how little she/he has thought about what lies before her or him, how easily she/he has accepted casual (or racist, or hopeless, or defensive) descriptions, there may well come a moment of "weariness tinged with amazement," a moment that may lead to the beginning of questioning. Only at such times are certain students actually attended to or *noticed;* and, when that takes place, a situation may arise in which all those involved come together in a quest for what it means. And this may be the moment when, as Camus wrote, "everything begins."

The "seeing," the insights associated with the phenomenological viewpoint, were to a degree revisioned by Martin Heidegger who began developing a "hermeneutical phenomenology" in the 1920s and 1930s. As he saw it, the understanding of meaning was never an affair of individual cognition; but it was fundamental to each human being's condition, to her/his "being-in-the-world" (1962, p. 88). Richard Palmer wrote that, for Heidegger, understanding was "the power to grasp one's own possibilities for being, within the context of the life-world in which one exists. Understanding is not a special capacity or gift for feeling into the situation of another person. Nor is it the power to grasp the meaning of some 'expression of life' on an unusually deep level. Understanding is not something to be possessed; it is a constituent element of being in the world" (1969, p. 131). From such a vantage point, the inquiring or observing thinker could never be conceived as a distanced or alien spectator. Rather, Heidegger viewed each thinker as enmeshed in an intersubjective fabric of "preunderstanding" (p. 148 ff.). Heidegger was not particularly interested in social inquiry. He wrote that questioning, however, "moves us into the open, provided that, in questioning, it transforms itself . . . and casts a new space over everything and into everything" (1959, pp. 29–30). Such a conception of questioning cannot but be of relevance for qualitative researchers and their views of interpretation. Heidegger also spoke of the "paralysis of all passion for questioning" in a manner that may speak to the heart of what researchers are attempting to comprehend when they engage with and try to understand what happens in the public schools.

It should be clear that such paralysis is what stands in the way of the sense of situatedness or the self-reflectiveness which is at the heart of qualitative research. For the existential phenomenologist Maurice Merleau-Ponty, "All consciousness is at the same time self-consciousness . . . self-consciousness is the very being of the mind in action" (1967, p. 371). Like Sartre, Merleau-Ponty placed great stress on situations as interpreted texts upon which people impose their goals and plans of action. If we were not, say, troubled or blocked by our lack of understanding of a particular classroom situation, we would not be moved to devise a project for making sense of it. There are, as is well known, numerous observers of public schools (within and outside the bureaucracies) who view urban classrooms as not only beyond understanding but also beyond remedial action of any kind. Phenomenologists believe that obstacles become significant only when people name them as obstacles to their own understanding or fulfillment. If someone has no special interest in trying to understand alienated or nonparticipant youngsters in a given classroom, their alienation or nonparticipation is not identified as something standing in the way of understanding; and, not being felt to be an obstacle, it is not confronted as a problem.

Merleau-Ponty was more concerned than many other philosophers about intersubjectivity and the ways in which consciousness opens to the common. Each person, he said, is inextricably entangled with others and with the world (1967, pp. 453–454). He concluded one book with a quotation from St. Exupery: "Man is but a network of relationships, and these alone matter to him" (1967, p. 456). Again, the notion of network is opposed to the subject-object separation that lay at the heart of the old objectivism qualitative research intends to reject.

Alfred Schutz was another significant phenomenologist whose orientation to social theory and the construction of meanings has fed into the stream of thinking that leads to the contemporary concern with qualitative research. A student of and later an assistant to Husserl, Schutz devoted much of his work to an elaboration on the meanings of *natural attitude* and *life-world*. Affected as well by William James, George Herbert Mead, and John Dewey, Schutz focused on experiential or common sense knowledge in the domains of everyday life. Of considerable importance was his inquiry into what he called multiple realities (1967, pp. 227–259). Adapting the idea of a "province of meaning" from James, Schutz explored the ways in which people moved against the backgrounds of their biographical realities from the natural attitude of the common sense world into various domains of meaning. These domains are associated with dreams, play, religion, the arts, the natural and social sciences. He said that each domain or province was marked by a distinctive "cognitive style" and placed a differing degree of weight on the importance of the "objective" and the "subjective." Schutz put great emphasis upon the ways in which human beings live among others and the manifold ways in which they interact with others.

His examination of the concept *verstehen* (defined by Max Weber before him [1949]) certainly had much to do with the way qualitative research is understood today. Attaching importance to the subjective point of view of the actor in any social scene, Schutz wrote that by "social reality" he understood the objects and occurrences within the social world "as experienced by the common-sense thinking of men living their daily lives among their fellow-men, connected with them in manifold relations of interaction" (1967, p. 53). He reminded his readers that the world is always intersubjective, "a world common to all of us either given or potentially accessible to everyone; and this involves intercommunication and language." For educational researchers, Schutz's contention that only through communication can we understand a social scene means that, if we recognize that the reality of classrooms is that which is experienced by teachers, students, and administrators living and talking together, we can begin to engage in meaningful research.

Interpretive and transactional approaches became more common after the Second World War, as more people recognized that damage could be done by efficient, depersonalized techniques. (We have only to recall the bombing of Dresden, the concentration camps, and Hiroshima.) Nevertheless, the "idolatry" of science did not disappear, and rational frameworks were sought on all sides as the capacity increased for technical control. Thinkers in search of order and mastery kept insisting that "mentality should be logical and principled, calculative and unemotional" (Toulmin, 1990, p. 183), but adversarial voices kept breaking through, enlisting heretofore unconcerned people in the humanities as well as the sciences. Many of those who opposed depersonalized techniques spoke from European experiences and memories of an almost inexplicable history. Others were scholars who were still in touch with the classical past or with the Cartesian flight "into the modern universe of purity, clarity, and objectivity" (Bordo, 1987, p. 5). Plagues of violence, ethnic rivalries, defiance of authorities, and refusals of old legitimations, all fostered a hunger for fixed truths, for answers. A troubling skepticism developed about what the bland authorities could offer to a fragmented, polluted world still dominated, it seemed, by thoughtlessness and greed.

In Christa Wolf's novel *Accident*, a German writer ponders the effects of technology on the lives of her children and herself after the accident at Chernobyl. Feeling deeply uncertain, she cannot help admiring the way everything fits together: "the desire of most people for a comfortable life, their tendency to believe the speakers on raised platforms and the men in white coats; the addiction to harmony and the fear of contradiction of the many seemed to correspond to the arrogance and hunger for power, the dedication to profit, unscrupulous inquisitiveness, and self-infatuation of the few" (1989, p. 17). In the United States, at least for a while, that equation seemed to exclude so many people— African Americans, women, gays and lesbians, Latin Americans, and college students—that there was a restiveness with respect to many things long taken for granted. Coupled with this resistance was a demand that unheard voices be heard and long ignored points of view be taken into account. There was a slow recovery of an American experiential tradition, perhaps a rediscovery of the ideals of American democracy. It was a tradition oriented to memories of landscape and wilderness at odds with the locomotive and the steamboat, those emblems of industrial progress and national might. Those who created the tradition included Emerson, Thoreau, Mark Twain, Whitman, Melville, Sojourner Truth, W. E .B. DuBois, Frances Wright, and others in the arts and public life. Romantic and transcendental, the tradition was founded in the significance of the personal voice and the personal will, but it reached toward a view of communion that would be distinctive in a country marked by strangers meeting in empty spaces, by contradictory ambitions, and by contesting energies. As time went on, oppressive practices alternated more and more with liberating acts; and immigration brought more and more diversity. It became increasingly difficult to speak in terms of a total fabric, of the wholly commensurable, or of a seamless whole.

The focus on experience, groundedness, and the particular became very evident in the work of pragmatists like William James and George Herbert Mead, who made crucial contributions to the stream of thought leading to an interest in the qualitative and the hermeneutic. Objecting to "rationalist propensities" and an overly technical treatment of "common sense categories," (1958, p. 425), James went on to insist that truth was a leading process, going toward useful concepts and "flowing human intercourse." True ideas, he wrote, "lead away from eccentricity and isolation, from foiled and barren thinking" (p. 435). Instead of conceiving of validation or verification in the usual senses, he chose to think of experience and ascertainments of truths as mutable, always in process. To him, everything depended on the consequences for life, not on agreement with preexisting principles. Mead's studies of what it signified to be a social self through membership in a community and by means of symbolic interaction in language (1934) also fed into conceptions of transaction and intersubjectivity rather than the old views of subject-object separation and the objectivism that followed in its wake.

John Dewey's transactional view of knowing and his concern for philosophy as a guide to reflective *praxis* clearly had an effect in undermining the old correspondence theories of knowing. His regard for what he described as the scientific method stemmed from a period before the wedding of science and advanced technology and ought not to be criticized as positivistic or value free. Mind, for Dewey, was not isolated from the world of human value and human action; there was a "necessary connection," he wrote, "with the objects and events, past, present, and future, of the environment with which responsive activities are inherently connected" (1931, pp. 263–264). Richard Rorty has linked Dewey's work to that of Wittgenstein and Heidegger, who are, for Rorty, "peripheral, pragmatic philosophers" who are skeptical about "systematic philosophy, about the whole project of universal commensuration" (1979, p. 368).

Commensuration implies that all opinions or contributions to a discussion can be translated into one another because they all exist upon a common ground of rationality. For Rorty and others who have expressed interest in hermeneutics rather than in epistemology, people are not so much united in their desires to achieve a common rational agreement as they are as "persons whose paths through life have fallen together, united by civility rather than by a common goal, much less than by a common ground" (p. 318). Rorty links the philosophers he has in mind through their mockery of classical descriptions of human beings and their rejection of the idea that language holds a mirror to nature or to the real. He points to their edifying concern for "continuing a conversation rather than . . . discovering Truth" (p. 373). Surely, this has a connection to contemporary views of qualitative research, which seems to appeal to persons whose paths "have fallen together" rather than persons who consult the same abstract principles or share a common ground. Rorty understandably objects to any idea of a single truth or a monological description of phenomena. To become conscious that there is no single truth may be to become conscious of the interpretive and constructive capacities of one's mind. Such a consciousness may lead to a continual questioning of technical and specialized outside authorities, all claiming a kind of anonymity, as it may lead to a continual redefining of the self.

It may be possible to identify the quantitative-qualitative debate with the tension between epistemology and hermeneutics that is so central in the philosophical conversation today. There are still those preoccupied with neutrality and lack of bias in educational as well as social scientific research in general. To stress vantage point and perspective, as hermeneutic researchers do, seems to those who hold fast to natural science paradigms to sacrifice precision and to give way to a harmful relativism. Richard Bernstein (1976) has traced the history of the effort to discover "empirical explanatory theories of human behavior" along with the growing critiques of mainstream science. He writes about the efforts to find "basic invariants, structures, or laws that can serve as a foundation for theoretical explanations" (p. 227). He goes on to say: "It has been projected that the social sciences, as they mature, will discover well-tested bodies of empirical theory which will eventually coalesce in ever more adequate and comprehensive theories. Yet if we judge the results to date of the endeavor to discover such theories, there is no hard evidence that this expectation is being fulfilled" (p. 227). There remain possibilities of common ground, so long as mainstream or quantitative research is infused with critique. The critique, as Bernstein and others see it, must be linked to the self-reflectiveness and the concern for language we have associated with qualitative research.

It is also likely that the interest in qualitative research will merge increasingly with interest in feminist research, with its emphasis on contextualism, standpoint, relationality, and narrative (Nicholson, 1990). As more and more biographical and autobiographical materials are explored, increasing numbers of qualitative researchers consult them and refine their perspectives still further. Ethnographic and anthropological paradigms are also increasingly consulted. In his introduction to *Writing Culture,* James Clifford remarked with respect to the historical and conceptual shifts that have made it so hard to represent those thought of as others: "There is no longer any place of overview (mountaintop) from which to map human ways of life, no Archimedian point from which to represent the world. Mountains are in constant motion. So are islands: for one cannot occupy, unambiguously, a bounded cultural world from which to journey out and analyze other cultures. Human ways of life increasingly influence, dominate, parody, translate, and subvert one another" (1986, p. 22). He was seeking, as many educators are seeking, new kinds of inventiveness and subtlety from a fully reflexive ethnography. Classrooms may not be the bound cultures to which Clifford referred; but there are challenges to translation in those classrooms and challenges to interpretations as well. There may be descriptions of varying degrees of thickness; there may be dialogical modes of bringing translation about; and there may be the singling out of rituals and a manipulation of dominant symbols. There may be, at the end, a difficult task of communicating what was discovered in the research process. Again, there must be an attempt at a fusing of horizons and of "tuning in" to those being studied in the hope that they will be stimulated to tune in themselves.

There are other perspectives to be looked through, of course, such as those derived from a variety of art criticisms, called educational connoisseurship, after Elliot Eisner's work (1991), and those informed by the imaginative capacity, as proposed by G. B. Madison (1988) and Cynthia Ozick (1989). In most cases, distinctions are made between theory making and the devising of constructs that may or may not make understanding more likely. One problem has to do with the connection between what Charles Taylor calls "intersubjective meanings" or ways of "experiencing action in society which are expressed in the language and descriptions constitutive of institutions and practices" (1977, p. 121) and what he calls "common meanings" (p. 122). He is saying that an intersubjective social reality (like the reality of a classroom, for all the "brute data" existing there) has to be largely defined in terms of meanings; they are not necessarily subjective beliefs, but they do constitute the social reality of that classroom. When he comes to common meanings, he says that sharing them is a collective act, but "sharing is something we do each on his own, as it were, even if each of us is influenced by the others" (p. 122). Meanings are not simply shared, however; they become part of a common reference world. And then: "Common meanings are the basis of community. Intersubjective meaning gives people a common language to talk about social reality and a common understanding of certain norms, but only with common meanings does this common reference world contain significant common actions, celebrations, and feelings. These are objects in the world that everybody shares. This is what makes community" (p. 122).

Taylor, like many others, is well aware that his interest in the kind of hermeneutic understanding that allows researchers to tap the life of meaning is at odds with scientific tradition, as presently understood. He knows as well that it is extraordinarily difficult ever to verify what is discovered, even as it is nearly inconceivable to expect predictions from the hermeneutic "sciences" or inquiries. Our capacity—or our incapacity—to understand is rooted in our own self-definitions. Or, as Taylor writes in another place, ". . . we are only selves insofar as we move in a certain space of questions, as we seek and find an orientation to the good" (1989, p. 14). This approach to selves, in turn, evokes one of Richard Rorty's discussions of the "blind impress," which is the determinism under which so many of us live, the importance of giving names, and the importance of reweaving the web of relations within which we continually try to create ourselves. He writes of how necessary it is for the poet (probably any one of us who is strong enough) to *demonstrate* that he is not a copy or replica and says that is merely a special form of an unconscious need everyone has: "the need to come to terms with the blind impress which chance has given him, to make a self for himself by redescribing that impress in terms which are, if only marginally, his own" (1989, p. 43).

There may, then, be continuities between the researcher's struggle to understand the meanings of a confused social scene and her or his forever incomplete struggles to create a self in a space of questioning. There may be continuities, too, between the practical judgment, the *phronesis* asked of the qualitative researcher and her or his orientation to the good. Taylor writes of norms, standards, and ideas of the good when he explains what makes community. We have spoken about the conversation to be released when attention is paid, of the voices to be heard, and of the differences to be explored. There can be no final resolution of either our uncertainties or our moral conflicts; but there can be naming, caring about qualities, and affirmations of the meaning of being in the world. The quest has been going on for at least three centuries. Inconclusive, still, but ardent and full of wonder, the search for the qualitative goes on—a search for selves, for spaces, for community.

References

Arendt, H. (1958). *The human condition.* Chicago: University of Chicago Press.

Bernstein, R. (1976). *The restructuring of social and political theory.* New York: Harcourt Brace Jovanovich.

Bordo, S. (1987). *Flight to objectivity.* Albany: SUNY Press.

Camus, A. (1955). *The myth of Sisyphus.* New York: Alfred A. Knopf.

Clifford, J. (1986). Introduction: Partial truths. In J. Clifford & G. E. Marcus (Eds.), *Writing culture.* Berkeley: University of California Press.

Descartes, R. (1968). *Discourse on method.* Baltimore: Penguin Books.

Dewey, J. (1931). *Art as experience.* New York: Minton, Balch.

Eisner, E. (1991). *The enlightened eye.* New York: Macmillan.

Gadamer, H-G. (1975). Hermeneutics and social science. *Cultural Hermeneutics, 2,* 307–316.

Gadamer, H-G. (1979). Practical philosophy as a model of the human sciences. *Research in Phenomenology, 9,* 74–85.

Geertz, C. (1983). *Local knowledge.* New York: Basic Books.

Habermas, J. (1970). *Towards a rational society.* Boston: Beacon Press.

Habermas, J. (1973). *Theory and practice.* Boston: Beacon Press.

Hegel, G. W. F. (1949). *The phenomenology of mind.* New York: Macmillan.

Heidegger, M. (1959). *Introduction to metaphysics.* New Haven: Yale University Press.

Heidegger, M. (1962). *Being and time.* New York: Harper and Bros.

Hempel, C. G. (1965). *Aspects of scientific explanation.* New York: Free Press.

Husserl, E. (1973). *Cartesian meditations.* The Hague: Martinus Nijhoff.

Jaeger, W. (1943). *Paidaeia,* Vol. III. New York: Oxford University Press.

James, W. (1968). Pragmatism's conception of truth. In J. J. McDermott (Ed.), *The writings of William James* (pp. 449–452). New York: The Modern Library.

Kant, I. (1940). Critique of pure reason. In J. Benda (Ed.), *The living thoughts of Kant* (pp. 41–109). Philadelphia: David McKay Company.

Kant, I. (1929). Theory of ethics. In T. M. Greene (Ed.), *Kant* (Selections) (pp. 311–315). New York: Charles Scribner's Sons.

Kierkegaard, S. (1947). Concluding unscientific postscript. In R. Bretall (Ed.), *Kierkegaard* (pp. 190–258). Princeton: Princeton University Press.

Lyotard, J. F. (1984). *The postmodern condition.* Minneapolis, University of Minneapolis Press.

Madison, G. B. (1988). *The hermeneutics of postmodernity.* Bloomington: Indiana University Press.

Marx, K. (1947). *Writings of the young Marx on philosophy and society.* New York: Anchor Books.

Marx, K. (1973). *Grundrisse.* New York: Vintage Books.

Mead, G. H. (1934). *Mind, self, and society.* Chicago: University of Chicago Press.

Merleau-Ponty, M. (1964). *The primacy of perception.* Evanston, IL: Northwestern University Press.

Merleau-Ponty, M. (1967). *Phenomenology of perception.* New York: Humanities Press.

Nicholson, L. (Ed.) (1990). *Feminism/postmodernism.* New York: Routledge.

Ozick, C. (1989). *Metaphor & memory.* New York: Alfred A. Knopf.

Palmer, R. (1969). *Hermeneutics.* Evanston, IL: Northwestern University Press.

Plato. (1968). The republic. In B. Jowett (Ed.), *The works of Plato, Vol. 2* (pp. 1–416). New York: Tudor Publishing Company.

Rorty, R. (1989). *Contingency, irony, and solidarity.* New York: Cambridge University Press.

Rorty, R. (1979). *Philosophy and the mirror of nature.* Princeton: Princeton University Press.

Sartre, J-P. (1956). *Being and nothingness.* New York: Philosophical Library.

Schutz, A. (1967). Concept and theory formation. In M. Natanson (Ed.), *The problem of social reality* (pp. 48–66). The Hague: Martinus Nijhoff.

Schutz, A. (1964). Making music together. In A. Broderson (Ed.), *Studies in social theory* (pp. 139–178). The Hague: Martinus Nijhoff.

Schutz, A. (1967). On multiple realities. In M. Natanson (Ed.), *The problem of social reality* (pp. 207–259). The Hague: Martinus Nijhoff.

Taylor, C. (1977). Interpretation and the sciences of man. In F. R. Dallmayr & T. A. McCarthy (Eds.), *Understanding and social inquiry* (pp. 101–131). South Bend, IN: Notre Dame University Press.

Taylor, C. (1989). *Sources of the self.* Cambridge: Harvard University Press.

Toulmin, S. (1990). *Cosmopolis: The hidden agenda of modernity.* New York: Free Press.

Weber, M. (1949). *The methodology of the social sciences.* New York: Free Press.

Wittgenstein, L. (1968). *Philosophical investigations.* New York: Macmillan.

Wolf, C. (1989). *Accident: A Day's News.* New York: Farrar, Strauss and Giroux.

Wordsworth, W. (1962). *The Prelude.* New York: Holt, Rinehart, & Winston.

Wordsworth, W. (1988). Tintern Abbey. In S. Heaney (Ed.), *Selected poems of William Wordsworth.* New York: Echo Press.

Suggestions for Further Reading

Dewey, J. (1931). Qualitative thought. In *Philosophy and Civilization* (pp. 93–116). New York: Minton, Balch and Co.

Dewey writes that the qualitative character of the world has often been ignored. He goes on to discuss the role of thought in determining the subject matter of knowledge and the importance of situation when it comes to determining the terms of thought. "Thought," he concludes, "which denies the existential reality of qualitative things is . . . bound to end in self-contradiction. . . ."

Gadamer, H-G. (1977). *Philosophical Hermeneutics.* Tr. and ed., D. E. Linge.

A selection of essays on the nature of hermeneutical reflection and the relation between existential philosophy, phenomenology, and hermeneutics. There is an overview of the philosophical foundations of the 20th century, and there is an account of the rise of phenomenology. The last three essays tell of Heidegger's contribution.

Geertz, C. (1973). Thick Description: Towards an Interpretive Theory of Culture. In *The Interpretation of Cultures* (pp. 3–30). New York: Basic Books.

A clear explanation of what is involved in describing another culture or a social scene. Geertz speaks about cultural analysis as "guessing at meanings, assessing the guesses, and drawing explanatory conclusions from the better guesses. . . ." His language is different, but what he says applies to qualitative research, especially when he warns his reader not to lose touch with the "hard surfaces of life."

Harding, S. (1986). From Feminist Empiricism to Feminist Standpoint Epistemologies (pp. 136–162). In *The Science Question in Feminism*. Ithaca: Cornell University Press.

An account of feminist views of research, with a particularly illuminating discussion of the role of "standpoint" in certain epistemologies.

Rorty, R. (1991). *Part I: Objectivity, Relativism, and Truth* (pp. 21–110). New York: Cambridge University Press.

Affected by Deweyan pragmatism and post-modernism, the six essays in Part I spell out in lively fashion the arguments against objectivity. Rorty then presents some contemporary treatments of science and concludes with a clear account of what he calls "anti-dualist" interpretation.

For an introductory anthology, see *Qualitative Inquiry in Education: The Continuing Debate*. Eds. E.W. Eisner and A. Peshkin. New York: Teachers College Press, 1990.

A varied, readable group of essays drawing from sociology, ethnography, art criticism, feminism, and philosophical ethics.

Study Questions

1. This chapter is entitled "A Philosopher Looks at Qualitative Research"; and it must be said that there are a number of ways of looking at philosophy. Some view it as a mode of thinking about one's own thinking, a way of reflecting on the concepts used to structure or account for what is "real." Others view it, as Ludwig Wittgenstein did, as a way of countering "bewilderment" due to a confused use of language, or (as he put it) "a battle against the bewitchment of our intelligence by means of language." Still others conceive it as a critical awareness of one's own experience of being in the world. Using all or one of the above descriptions, explain how you think this approach differs from that of the anthropologist, the ethnographer, the psychologist, the administrator, or the school board member, anyone of whom might be called upon to express an opinion about qualitative research.

2. How would you now relate the qualitative to the quantitative where educational research is concerned? What is the crucial difference between them? If one is intended to increase understanding, the other to gain verifiable knowledge, how does this affect your conception?

3. How do you understand the notion of interpretation, and why has it taken on such importance to many qualitative researchers?

4. What is the significance of the rejection of objectivism over the years? of the challenges to what was thought of as a subject/object separation?

5. Why do qualitative researchers put so much emphasis on vantage point, point of view, lived perspective? How does this affect their efforts to claim validity for their descriptions or interpretations of lives in classrooms?

6. What is meant by "practical judgment"? In what way does it involve qualitative researchers with questions of what is ethical, what is good and right? How can practical judgments play a part in school improvement or reform? How would you compare the application of such judgments to the empirical statements and generalizations attentive social scientists (using quantitative methods) are able to make?

7. Imagine yourself being asked to serve as observer or "critical friend" in an urban school where achievement rates have been low for a considerable time, where teacher as well as student turnover is great. How would you go about choosing your research methods? Do you necessarily confront an either/or?

8. How do you explain the current interest in narrative, autobiography, journals? In what way do they belong to the category of "qualitative research"? Does the use of them exclude attention to "theory," quantitative measures, what is called "instrumental rationality"?

Readings

Introduction to Readings

Maxine Greene
Teachers College, Columbia University

The philosopher's look at qualitative research that follows focuses on interpretation—or sense-making—with regard to some aspect of the social world. That signifies an exploration of the play of meanings in various educational spaces, an exploration that takes place from the vantage point of particular situations. Each one offers a perspective much affected by the inquirer's own life experience, location, gender, class, and research purposes. It follows that the research undertaken can never be wholly neutral, distanced, or complete, as it might be if it were undertaken from some remote tower or, as some writers say, "from nowhere" (meaning without acknowledged point of view).

Richard Rorty's rejection of the traditional idea that the language of philosophy serves as a "mirror" of an objective reality beyond sustains what might be called our transactional view. Instead of thinking in terms of a subject and object separated from one another, we are treating (as Rorty, Dewey, and Taylor clearly do) the subject (the inquirer, the questioner, the living self-reflective person) as engaged in ongoing transactions with what surrounds. Rorty, conceiving the human being within webs of relationships, does not see her/him identifying herself/himself with regard to some independently existing reality (supernatural or natural). Identity is achieved, as meaning is achieved, through engagement in an ongoing interpretive conversation. Turning to Gadamer, as we have, Rorty concludes *Philosophy and the Mirror of Nature* by acknowledging the importance of the hermeneutic approach and the quest for meaning rather than for validity and final truths.

John Dewey, who exerted a considerable influence on Rorty, is well known for his criticisms of dualism and the subject/object separation. In *Experience and Nature,* he warned of the return of the kind of objectivism "which ignores initiating and reorganizing desire and imagination" to such a degree that it might lead people to become so subjectivist that they withdraw into their own inward landscapes. As Dewey saw it, "philosophical dualism is but a formulated recognition of an impasse in life: an impotence in interaction. . . ." (p. 241) We have, in the following chapter, attempted to point the way to the overcoming of such impasses and to a full acknowledgment of the multiplicity of meanings that go far beyond the matter of truth.

Charles Taylor, in his essay "Interpretation and the Sciences of Man," makes even more specific the concern for meaning on the part of the interpretive scholar; but he also makes clear the relevance of interpretation for the sciences of man. Exact prediction and accurate verification are not to be expected; but it is necessary, Taylor writes, to go "beyond the bounds of a science based on verification to one which would study the intersubjective and common meanings embedded in social reality." The data for the researcher would be the readings of the intersubjective meanings and "the common meanings embedded in social reality" (p. 125). This has been one of the major concerns of our chapter: to find ways of understanding the constructed realities in schoolrooms and schools, to be open to the play of diverse meanings, to find starting places for improvement and reform.

Philosophy Without Mirrors

1. HERMENEUTICS AND EDIFICATION

Our present notions of what it is to be a philosopher are so tied up with the Kantian attempt to render all knowledge-claims commensurable that it is difficult to imagine what philosophy without epistemology could be. More generally, it is difficult to imagine that any activity would be entitled to bear the name "philosophy" if it had nothing to do with knowledge—if it were not in some sense a theory of knowledge, or a method for getting knowledge, or at least a hint as to where some supremely important kind of knowledge might be found. The difficulty stems from a notion shared by Platonists, Kantians, and positivists: that man has an essence—namely, to discover essences. The notion that our chief task is to mirror accurately, in our own Glassy Essence, the universe around us is the complement of the notion, common to Democritus and Descartes, that the universe is made up of very simple, clearly and distinctly knowable things, knowledge of whose essences provides the master-vocabulary which permits commensuration of all discourses.

This classic picture of human beings must be set aside before epistemologically centered philosophy can be set aside. "Hermeneutics," as a polemical term in contemporary philosophy, is a name for the attempt to do so. The use of the term for this purpose is largely due to one book—Gadamer's *Truth and Method*. Gadamer there makes clear that hermeneutics is not a "method for attaining truth" which fits into the classic picture of man: "The hermeneutic phenomenon is basically not a problem of method at all."[1] Rather, Gadamer is asking, roughly, what conclusions might be drawn from the fact that we have to practice hermeneutics—from the "hermeneutic phenomenon" as a fact about people which the epistemological tradition has tried to shunt aside. "The hermeneutics developed here," he says, "is not . . . a methodology of the human sciences, but an attempt to understand what the human sciences truly are, beyond their methodological self-consciousness, and what connects them with the totality of our experience of the world."[2] His book is a redescription of man which tries to place the classic picture within a larger one, and thus to "distance" the standard philosophical problematic rather than offer a set of solutions to it.

For my present purposes, the importance of Gadamer's book is that he manages to separate off one of the three strands—the romantic notion of man as self-creative—in the philosophical notion of "spirit" from the other two strands with which it became entangled. Gadamer (like Heidegger, to whom some of his work is indebted) makes no concessions either to Cartesian dualism or to the notion of "transcendental constitution" (in any sense which could be given an idealistic interpretation).[3] He thus helps reconcile the "naturalistic" point I tried to make in the previous chapter —that the "irreducibility of the *Geisteswissenschaften*" is not a matter of a metaphysical dualism—with our "existentialist" intuition that redescribing ourselves is the most

[1] Hans-Georg Gadamer, *Truth and Method* (New York, 1975), p. xi. Indeed, it would be reasonable to call Gadamer's book a tract against the very idea of method, where this is conceived of as an attempt at commensuration. It is instructive to note the parallels between this book and Paul Feyerabend's *Against Method*. My treatment of Gadamer is indebted to Alasdair MacIntyre; see his "Contexts of Interpretation," *Boston University Journal* 24 (1976), 41-46.

[2] Gadamer, *Truth and Method*, p. xiii.

[3] Cf. ibid., p. 15. "But we may recognize that *Bildung* is an element of spirit without being tied to Hegel's philosophy of absolute spirit, just as the insight into the historicity of consciousness is not tied to his philosophy of world history."

important thing we can do. He does this by substituting the notion of *Bildung* (education, self-formation) for that of "knowledge" as the goal of thinking. To say that we become different people, that we "remake" ourselves as we read more, talk more, and write more, is simply a dramatic way of saying that the sentences which become true of us by virtue of such activities are often more important to us than the sentences which become true of us when we drink more, earn more, and so on. The events which make us able to say new and interesting things about ourselves are, in this nonmetaphysical sense, more "essential" to us (at least to us relatively leisured intellectuals, inhabiting a stable and prosperous part of the world) than the events which change our shapes or our standards of living ("remaking" us in less "spiritual" ways). Gadamer develops his notion of *wirkungsgeschichtliches Bewusstsein* (the sort of consciousness of the past which changes us) to characterize an attitude interested not so much in what is out there in the world, or in what happened in history, as in what we can get out of nature and history for our own uses. In this attitude, getting the facts right (about atoms and the void, or about the history of Europe) is merely propaedeutic to finding a new and more interesting way of expressing ourselves, and thus of coping with the world. From the educational, as opposed to the epistemological or the technological, point of view, the way things are said is more important than the possession of truths.[4]

---

[4] The contrast here is the same as that involved in the traditional quarrel between "classical" education and "scientific" education, mentioned by Gadamer in his opening section on "The Significance of the Humanist Tradition." More generally, it can be seen as an aspect of the quarrel between poetry (which cannot be omitted from the former sort of education) and philosophy (which, when conceiving of itself as super-science, would like to become foundational to the latter sort of education). Yeats asked the spirits (whom, he believed, were dictating *A Vision* to him through his wife's mediumship) why they had come. The spirits replied, "To bring you metaphors for poetry." A philosopher might have expected some hard facts about what it was like on the other side, but Yeats was not disappointed.

Since "education" sounds a bit too flat, and *Bildung* a bit too foreign, I shall use "edification" to stand for this project of finding new, better, more interesting, more fruitful ways of speaking. The attempt to edify (ourselves or others) may consist in the hermeneutic activity of making connections between our own culture and some exotic culture or historical period, or between our own discipline and another discipline which seems to pursue incommensurable aims in an incommensurable vocabulary. But it may instead consist in the "poetic" activity of thinking up such new aims, new words, or new disciplines, followed by, so to speak, the inverse of hermeneutics: the attempt to reinterpret our familiar surroundings in the unfamiliar terms of our new inventions. In either case, the activity is (despite the etymological relation between the two words) edifying without being constructive—at least if "constructive" means the sort of cooperation in the accomplishment of research programs which takes place in normal discourse. For edifying discourse is *supposed* to be abnormal, to take us out of our old selves by the power of strangeness, to aid us in becoming new beings.

The contrast between the desire for edification and the desire for truth is, for Gadamer, not an expression of a tension which needs to be resolved or compromised. If there is a conflict, it is between the Platonic-Aristotelian view that the *only* way to be edified is to know what is out there (to reflect the facts accurately—to realize our essence by knowing essences) and the view that the quest for truth is just one among many ways in which we might be edified. Gadamer rightly gives Heidegger the credit for working out a way of seeing the search for objective knowledge (first developed by the Greeks, using mathematics as a model) as one human project among others.[5] The point is, however, more vivid

[5] See the section called "The Overcoming of the Epistemological Problem . . ." in *Truth and Method*, pp. 214ff., and compare Martin Heidegger, *Being and Time*, trans. John Macquarrie and Edward Robinson (New York, 1962), sec. 32.

in Sartre, who sees the attempt to gain an objective knowledge of the world, and thus of oneself, as an attempt to avoid the responsibility for choosing one's project.[6] For Sartre, to say this is not to say that the desire for objective knowledge of nature, history, or anything else is bound to be unsuccessful, or even bound to be self-deceptive. It is merely to say that it presents a temptation to self-deception insofar as we think that, by knowing which descriptions within a given set of normal discourses apply to us, we thereby know ourselves. For Heidegger, Sartre, and Gadamer, objective inquiry is perfectly possible and frequently actual—the only thing to be said against it is that it provides only some, among many, ways of describing ourselves, and that some of these can hinder the process of edification.

To sum up this "existentialist" view of objectivity, then: objectivity should be seen as conformity to the norms of justification (for assertions and for actions) we find about us. Such conformity becomes dubious and self-deceptive only when seen as something more than this—namely, as a way of obtaining access to something which "grounds" current practices of justification in something else. Such a "ground" is thought to need no justification, because it has become so clearly and distinctly perceived as to count as a "philosophical foundation." This is self-deceptive not simply because of the general absurdity of ultimate justification's reposing upon the unjustifiable, but because of the more concrete absurdity of thinking that the vocabulary used by present science, morality, or whatever has some privileged attachment to reality which makes it *more* than just a further set of descriptions. Agreeing with the naturalists that redescription is not "change of essence" needs to be followed up by abandoning the notion of "essence" altogether.[7]

[6] See Jean-Paul Sartre, *Being and Nothingness*, trans. Hazel Barnes (New York, 1956), pt. two, chap. 3, sec. 5, and the "Conclusion" of the book.

[7] It would have been fortunate if Sartre had followed up his remark that man is the being whose essence is to have no essence by saying

But the standard philosophical strategy of most naturalisms is to find some way of showing that our own culture has indeed got hold of the essence of man—thus making all new and incommensurable vocabularies merely "noncognitive" ornamentation.[8] The utility of the "existentialist" view is that, by proclaiming that we have no essence, it permits us to see the descriptions of ourselves we find in one of (or in the unity of) the *Naturwissenschaften* as on a par with the various alternative descriptions offered by poets, novelists, depth psychologists, sculptors, anthropologists, and mystics. The former are not privileged representations in virtue of the fact that (at the moment) there is more consensus in the sciences than in the arts. They are simply among the repertoire of self-descriptions at our disposal.

This point can also be put as an extrapolation from the commonplace that one cannot be counted as educated—*gebildet*—if one knows *only* the results of the normal *Naturwissenschaften* of the day. Gadamer begins *Truth and Method* with a discussion of the role of the humanist tradition in giving sense to the notion of *Bildung* as something having "no goals outside itself."[9] To give sense to such a notion we need a sense of the relativity of descriptive vocabularies to periods, traditions, and historical accidents. This is what the humanist tradition in education does, and what training in the results of the natural sciences cannot do. Given that sense of relativity, we cannot take the notion of "essence"

---

that this went for all other beings also. Unless this addition is made, Sartre will appear to be insisting on the good old metaphysical distinction between spirit and nature in other terms, rather than simply making the point that man is always free to choose new descriptions (for, among other things, himself).

   [8] Dewey, it seems to me, is the one author usually classified as a "naturalist" who did not have this reductive attitude, despite his incessant talk about "scientific method." Dewey's peculiar achievement was to have remained sufficiently Hegelian not to think of natural science as having an inside track on the essences of things, while becoming sufficiently naturalistic to think of human beings in Darwinian terms.

   [9] Gadamer, *Truth and Method*, p. 12.

seriously, nor the notion of man's task as the accurate representation of essences. The natural sciences, by themselves, leave us convinced that we know both what we are and what we can be—not just how to predict and control our behavior, but the limits of that behavior (and, in particular, the limits of our significant speech). Gadamer's attempt to fend off the demand (common to Mill and Carnap) for "objectivity" in the *Geisteswissenschaften* is the attempt to prevent education from being reduced to instruction in the results of normal inquiry. More broadly, it is the attempt to prevent abnormal inquiry from being viewed as suspicious solely because of its abnormality.

This "existentialist" attempt to place objectivity, rationality, and normal inquiry within the larger picture of our need to be educated and edified is often countered by the "positivist" attempt to distinguish learning facts from acquiring values. From the positivist point of view, Gadamer's exposition of *wirkungsgeschichtliche Bewusstsein* may seem little more than reiteration of the commonplace that even when we know all the objectively true descriptions of ourselves, we still may not know what to do with ourselves. From this point of view, *Truth and Method* (and chapters six and seven above) are just overblown dramatizations of the fact that entire complaince with all the demands for justification offered by normal inquiry would still leave us free to draw our own morals from the assertions so justified. But from the viewpoints of Gadamer, Heidegger, and Sartre, the trouble with the fact-value distinction is that it is contrived precisely to blur the fact that alternative descriptions are possible in addition to those offered by the results of normal inquiries.[10] It suggests that once "all the facts are in" nothing remains except "noncognitive" adoption of an attitude—a choice which is not rationally discussable. It disguises the fact that to use

[10] See Heidegger's discussion of "values" in *Being and Time*, p. 133, and Sartre's in *Being and Nothingness*, pt. two, chap. 1, sec. 4. Compare Gadamer's remarks on Weber (*Truth and Method*, pp. 461ff.).

one set of true sentences to describe ourselves is already to choose an attitude toward ourselves, whereas to use another set of true sentences is to adopt a contrary attitude. Only if we assume that there is a value-free vocabulary which renders these sets of "factual" statements commensurable can the positivist distinction between facts and values, beliefs and attitudes, look plausible. But the philosophical fiction that such a vocabulary is on the tips of our tongues is, from an educational point of view, disastrous. It forces us to pretend that we can split ourselves up into knowers of true sentences on the one hand and choosers of lives or actions or works of art on the other. These artificial diremptions make it impossible to get the notion of edification into focus. Or, more exactly, they tempt us to think of edification as having nothing to do with the rational faculties which are employed in normal discourse.

So Gadamer's effort to get rid of the classic picture of man-as-essentially-knower-of-essences is, among other things, an effort to get rid of the distinction between fact and value, and thus to let us think of "discovering the facts" as one project of edification among others. This is why Gadamer devotes so much time to breaking down the distinctions which Kant made among cognition, morality, and aesthetic judgment.[11] There is no way, as far as I can see, in which to *argue* the issue of whether to keep the Kantian "grid" in place or set it aside. There is no "normal" philosophical discourse which provides common commensurating ground for those who see science and edification as, respectively, "rational" and "irrational," and those who see the quest for objectivity as one possibility among others to be taken account of in *wirkungsgeschichtliche Bewusstsein*. If there is no such common ground, all we can do is to show how the other side

[11] See Gadamer's polemic against "the subjectivization of the aesthetic" in Kant's Third Critique (*Truth and Method*, p. 87) and compare Heidegger's remarks in "Letter on Humanism" on Aristotle's distinctions among physics, logic, and ethics (Heidegger, *Basic Writings*, ed. Krell [New York, 1976], p. 232).

looks from our own point of view. That is, all we can do is be hermeneutic about the opposition—trying to show how the odd or paradoxical or offensive things they say hang together with the rest of what they want to say, and how what they say looks when put in our own alternative idiom. This sort of hermeneutics with polemical intent is common to Heidegger's and Derrida's attempts to deconstruct the tradition.

2. SYSTEMATIC PHILOSOPHY AND EDIFYING PHILOSOPHY

The hermeneutic point of view, from which the acquisition of truth dwindles in importance, and is seen as a component of education, is possible only if we once stood at another point of view. Education has to start from acculturation. So the search for objectivity and the self-conscious awareness of the social practices in which objectivity consists are necessary first steps in becoming *gebildet*. We must first see ourselves as *en-soi*—as described by those statements which are objectively true in the judgment of our peers—before there is any point in seeing ourselves as *pour-soi*. Similarly, we cannot be educated without finding out a lot about the descriptions of the world offered by our culture (e.g., by learning the results of the natural sciences). Later perhaps, we may put less value on "being in touch with reality" but we can afford that only after having passed through stages of implicit, and then explicit and self-conscious, conformity to the norms of the discourses going on around us.

I raise this banal point that education—even the education of the revolutionary or the prophet—needs to begin with acculturation and conformity merely to provide a cautionary complement to the "existentialist" claim that normal participation in normal discourse is merely one project, one way of being in the world. The caution amounts to saying that abnormal and "existential" discourse is always parasitic upon normal discourse, that the possibility of hermeneutics is always parasitic upon the possibility (and perhaps upon the actuality) of epistemology, and that edification always employs materials provided by the culture of the day. To attempt abnormal discourse *de novo*, without being able to recognize our own abnormality, is madness in the most literal and terrible sense. To insist on being hermeneutic where epistemology would do —to make ourselves unable to view normal discourse in terms of its own motives, and able to view it only from within our own abnormal discourse—is not mad, but it does show a lack of education. To adopt the "existentialist" attitude toward objectivity and rationality common to Sartre, Heidegger, and Gadamer makes sense only if we do so in a conscious departure from a well-understood norm. "Existentialism" is an *intrinsically reactive* movement of thought, one which has point only in opposition to the tradition. I want now to generalize this contrast between philosophers whose work is essentially constructive and those whose work is essentially reactive. I shall thereby develop a contrast between philosophy which centers in epistemology and the sort of philosophy which takes its point of departure from suspicion about the pretensions of epistemology. This is the contrast between "systematic" and "edifying" philosophies.

In every sufficiently reflective culture, there are those who single out one area, one set of practices, and see it as the paradigm human activity. They then try to show how the rest of culture can profit from this example. In the mainstream of the Western philosophical tradition, this paradigm has been *knowing*—possessing justified true beliefs, or, better yet, beliefs so intrinsically persuasive as to make justification unnecessary. Successive philosophical revolutions within this mainstream have been produced by philosophers excited by new cognitive feats—e.g., the rediscovery of Aristotle, Galilean mechanics, the development of self-conscious historiography in the nineteenth century, Darwinian biology, mathematical logic. Thomas's use of

Aristotle to conciliate the Fathers, Descartes's and Hobbes's criticisms of scholasticism, the Enlightenment's notion that reading Newton leads naturally to the downfall of tyrants, Spencer's evolutionism, Carnap's attempt to overcome metaphysics through logic, are so many attempts to refashion the rest of culture on the model of the latest cognitive achievements. A "mainstream" Western philosopher typically says: Now that such-and-such a line of inquiry has had such a stunning success, let us reshape all inquiry, and all of culture, on its model, thereby permitting objectivity and rationality to prevail in areas previously obscured by convention, superstition, and the lack of a proper epistemological understanding of man's ability accurately to represent nature.

On the periphery of the history of modern philosophy, one finds figures who, without forming a "tradition," resemble each other in their distrust of the notion that man's essence is to be a knower of essences. Goethe, Kierkegaard, Santayana, William James, Dewey, the later Wittgenstein, the later Heidegger, are figures of this sort. They are often accused of relativism or cynicism. They are often dubious about progress, and especially about the latest claim that such-and-such a discipline has at last made the nature of human knowledge so clear that reason will now spread throughout the rest of human activity. These writers have kept alive the suggestion that, even when we have justified true belief about everything we want to know, we may have no more than conformity to the norms of the day. They have kept alive the historicist sense that this century's "superstition" was the last century's triumph of reason, as well as the relativist sense that the latest vocabulary, borrowed from the latest scientific achievement, may not express privileged representations of essences, but be just another of the potential infinity of vocabularies in which the world can be described.

The mainstream philosophers are the philosophers I shall call "systematic," and the peripheral ones are those I shall call "edifying." These peripheral, pragmatic philosophers are skeptical primarily *about systematic philosophy*, about the whole project of universal commensuration.[12] In our time, Dewey, Wittgenstein, and Heidegger are the great edifying, peripheral, thinkers. All three make it as difficult as possible to take their thought as expressing views on traditional philosophical problems, or as making constructive proposals for philosophy as a cooperative and progressive discipline.[13] They make fun of the classic picture of man, the picture which contains systematic philosophy, the search for universal commensuration in a final vocabulary. They hammer away at the holistic point that words take their meanings from other words rather than by virtue of their representative character, and the corollary that vocabularies acquire their privileges from the men who use them rather than from their transparency to the real.[14]

[12] Consider the passage from Anatole France's "Garden of Epicurus" which Jacques Derrida cites at the beginning of his "La Mythologie Blanche" (in *Marges de la Philosophie* [Paris, 1972], p. 250):

. . . the metaphysicians, when they make up a new language, are like knife-grinders who grind coins and medals against their stone instead of knives and scissors. They rub out the relief, the inscriptions, the portraits, and when one can no longer see on the coins Victoria, or Wilhelm, or the French Republic, they explain: these coins now have nothing specifically English or German or French about them, for we have taken them out of time and space; they now are no longer worth, say, five francs, but rather have an inestimable value, and the area in which they are a medium of exchange has been infinitely extended.

[13] See Karl-Otto Apel's comparison of Wittgenstein and Heidegger as having both "called into question Western metaphysics as a theoretical discipline" (*Transformation der Philosophie* [Frankfurt, 1973], vol. 1, p. 228). I have not offered interpretations of Dewey, Wittgenstein, and Heidegger in support of what I have been saying about them, but I have tried to do so in a piece on Wittgenstein called "Keeping Philosophy Pure" (*Yale Review* [Spring 1976], pp. 336-356), in "Overcoming the Tradition: Heidegger and Dewey" (*Review of Metaphysics* 30 [1976], 280-305), and in "Dewey's Metaphysics" in *New Studies in the Philosophy of John Dewey*, ed. Steven M. Cahn (Hanover, N.H., 1977).

[14] This Heideggerean point about language is spelled out at length

The distinction between systematic and edifying philosophers is not the same as the distinction between normal philosophers and revolutionary philosophers. The latter distinction puts Husserl, Russell, the later Wittgenstein, and the later Heidegger all on the same ("revolutionary") side of a line. For my purposes, what matters is a distinction between two kinds of revolutionary philosophers. On the one hand, there are revolutionary philosophers—those who found new schools within which normal, professionalized philosophy can be practiced—who see the incommensurability of their new vocabulary with the old as a temporary inconvenience, to be blamed on the shortcomings of their predecessors and to be overcome by the institutionalization of their own vocabulary. On the other hand, there are great philosophers who dread the thought that their vocabulary should ever be institutionalized, or that their writing might be seen as commensurable with the tradition. Husserl and Russell (like Descartes and Kant) are of the former sort. The later Wittgenstein and the later Heidegger (like Kierkegaard and Nietzsche) are of the latter sort.[15] Great systematic philosophers are constructive and offer arguments. Great edifying philosophers are reactive and offer satires, parodies, aphorisms. They know their work loses its point when the period they were reacting against is over. They are *intentionally* peripheral. Great systematic philosophers, like great scientists, build for eternity. Great edifying philosophers destroy for the sake of their own generation. Systematic philosophers want to put their subject on the

---

and didactically by Derrida in *La Voix et le Phénomène*, translated as *Speech and Phenomenon* by David Allison (Evanston, 1973). See Newton Garver's comparison of Derrida and Wittgenstein in his "Introduction" to this translation.

[15] The permanent fascination of the man who dreamed up the whole idea of Western philosophy—Plato—is that we still do not know which sort of philosopher he was. Even if the *Seventh Letter* is set aside as spurious, the fact that after millenniums of commentary nobody knows which passages in the dialogues are jokes keeps the puzzle fresh.

secure path of a science. Edifying philosophers want to keep space open for the sense of wonder which poets can sometimes cause—wonder that there is something new under the sun, something which is *not* an accurate representation of what was already there, something which (at least for the moment) cannot be explained and can barely be described.

The notion of an edifying philosopher is, however, a paradox. For Plato defined the philosopher by opposition to the poet. The philosopher could give reasons, argue for his views, justify himself. So argumentative systematic philosophers say of Nietzsche and Heidegger that, whatever else they may be, they are not *philosophers*. This "not really a philosopher" ploy is also used, of course, by normal philosophers against revolutionary philosophers. It was used by pragmatists against logical positivists, by positivists against "ordinary language philosophers," and will be used whenever cozy professionalism is in danger. But in that usage it is just a rhetorical gambit which tells one nothing more than that an incommensurable discourse is being proposed. When it is used against edifying philosophers, on the other hand, the accusation has a real bite. The problem for an edifying philosopher is that qua philosopher he is in the business of offering arguments, whereas he would like simply to offer another set of terms, *without* saying that these terms are the new-found accurate representations of essences (e.g., of the essence of "philosophy" itself). He is, so to speak, violating not just the rules of normal philosophy (the philosophy of the schools of his day) but a sort of meta-rule: the rule that one may suggest changing the rules only because one has noticed that the old ones do not fit the subject matter, that they are not adequate to reality, that they impede the solution of the eternal problems. Edifying philosophers, unlike revolutionary systematic philosophers, are those who are abnormal at this meta-level. They refuse to present themselves as having found out any objective truth (about, say, what philosophy is). They present themselves as doing something different from, and more important than, offering accurate representations of how things are. It is more important because, they say, the notion of "accurate representation" itself is not the proper way to think about what philosophy does. But, they then go on to say, this is not because "a search for accurate representations of . . . (e.g., 'the most general traits of reality' or 'the nature of man')" is an *in*accurate representation of philosophy.

Whereas less pretentious revolutionaries can afford to have views on lots of things which their predecessors had views on, edifying philosophers have to decry the very notion of having a view, while avoiding having a view about having views.[16] This is an awkward, but not impossible, position. Wittgenstein and Heidegger manage it fairly well. One reason they manage it as well as they do is that they do not think that when we say something we must necessarily be expressing a view about a subject. We might just be *saying something*—participating in a conversation rather than contributing to an inquiry. Perhaps saying things is not always saying how things are. Perhaps saying *that* is itself not a case of saying how things are. Both men suggest we see people as saying things, better or worse things, without seeing them as externalizing inner representations of reality. But this is only their entering wedge, for then we must cease to see ourselves as *seeing* this, without beginning to see ourselves as seeing something else. We must get the visual, and in particular the mirroring, metaphors out of our speech altogether.[17] To do that we have to understand speech not only as not the externalizing of inner representations, but as not a representation at all. We have to drop the notion of correspondence for sentences as well as for

[16] Heidegger's *"Die Zeit des Weltbildes"* (translated as "The Age of the World-View" by Marjorie Grene in *Boundary II* [1976]) is the best discussion of this difficulty I have come across.

[17] Derrida's recent writings are meditations on how to avoid these metaphors. Like Heidegger in "Aus einem Gespräch von der Sprache zwischen einem Japaner und einem Fragenden" (in *Unterwegs zur Sprache* [Pfullingen, 1959]), Derrida occasionally toys with the notion of the superiority of Oriental languages and of ideographic writing.

thoughts, and see sentences as connected with other sentences rather than with the world. We have to see the term "corresponds to how things are" as an automatic compliment paid to successful normal discourse rather than as a relation to be studied and aspired to throughout the rest of discourse. To attempt to extend this compliment to feats of *ab*normal discourse is like complimenting a judge on his wise decision by leaving him a fat tip: it shows a lack of tact. To think of Wittgenstein and Heidegger as having views about how things are is not to be wrong about how things are, exactly; it is just poor taste. It puts them in a position which they do not want to be in, and in which they look ridiculous.

But perhaps they *should* look ridiculous. How, then, do we know when to adopt a tactful attitude and when to insist on someone's moral obligation to hold a view? This is like asking how we know when someone's refusal to adopt our norms (of, for example, social organization, sexual practices, or conversational manners) is morally outrageous and when it is something which we must (at least provisionally) respect. We do not know such things by reference to general principles. We do not, for instance, know in advance that if a given sentence is uttered, or a given act performed, we shall break off a conversation or a personal relationship, for everything depends on what leads up to it. To see edifying philosophers as conversational partners is an alternative to seeing them as holding views on subjects of common concern. One way of thinking of wisdom as something of which the love is not the same as that of argument, and of which the achievement does not consist in finding the correct vocabulary for representing essence, is to think of it as the practical wisdom necessary to participate in a conversation. One way to see edifying philosophy *as* the love of wisdom is to see it as the attempt to prevent conversation from degenerating into inquiry, into an exchange of views. Edifying philosophers can never end philosophy, but they can help prevent it from attaining the secure path of a science.

3. Edification, Relativism, and Objective Truth

I want now to enlarge this suggestion that edifying philosophy aims at continuing a conversation rather than at discovering truth, by making out of it a reply to the familiar charge of "relativism" leveled at the subordination of truth to edification. I shall be claiming that the difference between conversation and inquiry parallels Sartre's distinction between thinking of oneself as *pour-soi* and as *en-soi*, and thus that the cultural role of the edifying philosopher is to help us avoid the self-deception which comes from believing that we know ourselves by knowing a set of objective facts. In the following section, I shall try to make the converse point. There I shall be saying that the wholehearted behaviorism, naturalism, and physicalism I have been commending in earlier chapters help us avoid the self-deception of thinking that we possess a deep, hidden, metaphysically significant nature which makes us "irreducibly" different from inkwells or atoms.

Philosophers who have doubts about traditional epistemology are often thought to be questioning the notion that at most one of incompatible competing theories can be true. However, it is hard to find anyone who actually does question this. When it is said, for example, that coherentist or pragmatic "theories of truth" allow for the possibility that many incompatible theories would satisfy the conditions set for "the truth," the coherentist or pragmatist usually replies that this merely shows that we should have no grounds for choice among these candidates for "the truth." The moral to draw, they say, is not that they have offered inadequate analyses of "true," but that there are some terms—for example, "the true theory," "the right thing to do"—which are, intuitively and grammatically, singular, but for which no set of necessary and sufficient conditions can be given which will pick out a unique referent. This fact, they say, should not be surprising. Nobody thinks that there are necessary and sufficient conditions which will pick out, for example, the unique referent of "the best thing for her to have done on finding herself in that rather embarrassing situation," though plausible conditions can be given which will shorten a list of competing incompatible candidates. Why should it be different for the referents of "what she should have done in that ghastly moral dilemma" or "the Good Life for man" or "what the world is really made of"?

To see relativism lurking in every attempt to formulate conditions for truth or reality or goodness which does not attempt to provide uniquely individuating conditions we must adopt the "Platonic" notion of the transcendental terms which I discussed above (chapter six, section 6). We must think of the true referents of these terms (the Truth, the Real, Goodness) as conceivably having no connection whatever with the practices of justification which obtain among us. The dilemma created by this Platonic hypostatization is that, on the one hand, the philosopher must attempt to find criteria for picking out these unique referents, whereas, on the other hand, the only hints he has about what these criteria could be are provided by current practice (by, e.g., the best moral and scientific thought of the day). Philosophers thus condemn themselves to a Sisyphean task, for no sooner has an account of a transcendental term been perfected than it is labeled a "naturalistic fallacy," a confusion between essence and accident.[18] I think we get a clue to the cause of this self-defeating obsession from the fact that even philosophers who take the intuitive impossibility of finding conditions for "the one right thing to do" as a reason for repudiating "objective values" are loath to take the impossibility of finding individuating conditions for the one true theory of the world as a reason for denying "objective physical reality." Yet they should, for formally the two notions are on a par. The reasons for and against adopting a "correspondence" approach to moral

18 On this point, see William Frankena's classic "The Naturalistic Fallacy," *Mind* 68 (1939).

truth are the same as those regarding truth about the physical world. The giveaway comes, I think, when we find that the usual excuse for invidious treatment is that we are shoved around by physical reality but not by values.[19] Yet what does being shoved around have to do with objectivity, accurate representation, or correspondence? Nothing, I think, unless we confuse *contact* with reality (a causal, non-intentional, non-description-relative relation) with *dealing with* reality (describing, explaining, predicting, and modifying it—all of which are things we do under descriptions). The sense in which physical reality is Peircean "Secondness" —unmediated pressure—has nothing to do with the sense in which one among all our ways of describing, or of coping with, physical reality is "the one right" way. Lack of mediation is here being confused with accuracy of mediation. The absence of description is confused with a privilege attaching to a certain description. Only by such a confusion can the inability to offer individuating conditions for the one true description of material things be confused with insensitivity to the things' obduracy.

Sartre helps us explain why this confusion is so frequent and why its results are purveyed with so much moral earnestness. The notion of "one right way of describing and explaining reality" supposedly contained in our "intuition" about the meaning of "true" is, for Sartre, just the notion of having a way of describing and explaining *imposed* on us in that brute way in which stones impinge on our feet. Or, to shift to visual metaphors, it is the notion of having reality unveiled to us, not as in a glass darkly, but with some unimaginable sort of immediacy which would make discourse and description superfluous. If we could convert knowledge from something discursive, something attained by continual adjustments of ideas or words, into something as

[19] What seems to be a sense of being shoved around by values, they reductively say, is just physical reality in disguise (e.g., neural arrangements or glandular secretions programmed by parental conditioning).

ineluctable as being shoved about, or being transfixed by a sight which leaves us speechless, then we should no longer have the responsibility for choice among competing ideas and words, theories and vocabularies. This attempt to slough off responsibility is what Sartre describes as the attempt to turn oneself into a thing—into an *être-en-soi*. In the visions of the epistemologist, this incoherent notion takes the form of seeing the attainment of truth as a matter of *necessity*, either the "logical" necessity of the transcendentalist or the "physical" necessity of the evolutionary "naturalizing" epistemologist. From Sartre's point of view, the urge to find such necessities is the urge to be rid of one's freedom to erect yet another alternative theory or vocabulary. Thus the edifying philosopher who points out the incoherence of the urge is treated as a "relativist," one who lacks moral seriousness, because he does not join in the common human hope that the burden of choice will pass away. Just as the moral philosopher who sees virtue as Aristotelian self-development is thought to lack concern for his fellow man, so the epistemologist who is merely behaviorist is treated as one who does not share the universal human aspiration toward objective truth.

Sartre adds to our understanding of the visual imagery which has set the problems of Western philosophy by helping us see why this imagery is always trying to transcend itself. The notion of an unclouded Mirror of Nature is the notion of a mirror which would be indistinguishable from what was mirrored, and thus would not be a mirror at all. The notion of a human being whose mind is such an unclouded mirror, and who *knows* this, is the image, as Sartre says, of God. Such a being does *not* confront something alien which makes it necessary for him to choose an attitude toward, or a description of, it. He would have no need and no ability to choose actions or descriptions. He can be called "God" if we think of the advantages of this situation, or a "mere machine" if we think of the disadvantages. From this point of view, to look for commensuration rather than simply continued conversation—to look for a way of making further redescription unnecessary by finding a way of reducing all *possible* descriptions to one—is to attempt escape from humanity. To abandon the notion that philosophy must show all possible discourse naturally converging to a consensus, just as normal inquiry does, would be to abandon the hope of being anything more than merely human. It would thus be to abandon the Platonic notions of Truth and Reality and Goodness as entities which may not be even dimly mirrored by present practices and beliefs, and to settle back into the "relativism" which assumes that our only useful notions of "true" and "real" and "good" are extrapolations from those practices and beliefs.

Here, finally, I come around to the suggestion with which I ended the last section—that the point of edifying philosophy is to keep the conversation going rather than to find objective truth. Such truth, in the view I am advocating, is the normal result of normal discourse. Edifying philosophy is not only abnormal but reactive, having sense only as a protest against attempts to close off conversation by proposals for universal commensuration through the hypostatization of some privileged set of descriptions. The danger which edifying discourse tries to avert is that some given vocabulary, some way in which people might come to think of themselves, will deceive them into thinking that from now on all discourse could be, or should be, normal discourse. The resulting freezing-over of culture would be, in the eyes of edifying philosophers, the dehumanization of human beings. The edifying philosophers are thus agreeing with Lessing's choice of the infinite *striving for* truth over "all of Truth."[20] For the edifying philosopher the very idea of being presented with "all of Truth" is absurd, because the Platonic notion of Truth itself is absurd. It is absurd

[20] Kierkegaard made this choice the prototype of his own choice of "subjectivity" over "system." Cf. *Concluding Unscientific Postscript,* trans. David Swenson and Walter Lowrie (Princeton, 1941), p. 97.

either as the notion of truth about reality which is not about reality-under-a-certain-description, or as the notion of truth about reality under some privileged description which makes all other descriptions unnecessary because it is commensurable with each of them.

To see keeping a conversation going as a sufficient aim of philosophy, to see wisdom as consisting in the ability to sustain a conversation, is to see human beings as generators of new descriptions rather than beings one hopes to be able to describe accurately. To see the aim of philosophy as truth—namely, the truth about the terms which provide ultimate commensuration for all human inquiries and activities—is to see human beings as objects rather than subjects, as existing *en-soi* rather than as both *pour-soi* and *en-soi*, as both described objects and describing subjects. To think that philosophy will permit us to see the describing subject as itself one sort of described object is to think that all possible descriptions can be rendered commensurable with the aid of a single descriptive vocabulary—that of philosophy itself. For only if we had such a notion of a universal description could we identify human-beings-under-a-given-description with man's "essence." Only with such a notion would that of a man's *having* an essence make sense, whether or not that essence is conceived of as the knowing of essences. So not even by saying that man is subject as well as object, *pour-soi* as well as *en-soi*, are we grasping our essence. We do not escape from Platonism by saying that "our essence is to have no essence" if we then try to use this insight as the basis for a constructive and systematic attempt to find out further truths about human beings.

That is why "existentialism"—and, more generally, edifying philosophy—can be *only* reactive, why it falls into self-deception whenever it tries to do more than send the conversation off in new directions. Such new directions may, perhaps, engender new normal discourses, new sciences, new philosophical research programs, and thus new objective truths. But they are not the point of edifying philosophy, only accidental byproducts. The point is always the same—to perform the social function which Dewey called "breaking the crust of convention," preventing man from deluding himself with the notion that he knows himself, or anything else, except under optional descriptions.

4. EDIFICATION AND NATURALISM

I argued in chapter seven that it would be a good idea to get rid of the spirit-nature distinction, conceived as a division between human beings and other things, or between two parts of human beings, corresponding to the distinction between hermeneutics and epistemology. I want now to take up this topic again, in order to underline the point that the "existentialist" doctrines I have been discussing are compatible with the behaviorism and materialism I advocated in earlier chapters. Philosophers who would like to be simultaneously systematic and edifying have often seen them as incompatible, and have therefore suggested how our sense of ourselves as *pour-soi*, as capable of reflection, as choosers of alternative vocabularies, might itself be turned into a philosophical subject matter.

Much recent philosophy—under the aegis of "phenomenology" or of "hermeneutics," or both—has toyed with this unfortunate idea. For example, Habermas and Apel have suggested ways in which we might create a new sort of transcendental standpoint, enabling us to do something like what Kant tried to do, but without falling into either scientism or historicism. Again, most philosophers who see Marx, Freud, or both as figures who need to be drawn into "mainstream" philosophy have tried to develop quasi-epistemological systems which center around the phenomenon which both Marx and Freud throw into relief—the change in behavior which results from change in self-description. Such philosophers see traditional epistemology as committed to "objectivizing" human beings, and they hope for a successor subject to epistemology which will do for "reflection" what the tradition did for "objectivizing knowledge."

I have been insisting that we should not try to have a successor subject to epistemology, but rather try to free ourselves from the notion that philosophy must center around the discovery of a permanent framework for inquiry. In particular, we should free ourselves from the notion that philosophy can explain what science leaves unexplained. From my point of view, the attempt to develop a "universal pragmatics" or a "transcendental hermeneutics" is very suspicious. For it seems to promise just what Sartre tells us we are not going to have—a way of seeing freedom as nature (or, less cryptically, a way of seeing our creation of, and choice between, vocabularies in the same "normal" way as we see ourselves *within* one of those vocabularies). Such attempts start out by viewing the search for objective knowledge through normal discourse in the way I have suggested it should be viewed—as one element in edification. But they then often go on to more ambitious claims. The following passage from Habermas is an example:

> . . . the functions knowledge has in universal contexts of practical life can only be successfully analyzed in the framework of a reformulated transcendental philosophy. This, incidentally, does not entail an empiricist critique of the claim to absolute truth. As long as cognitive interests can be identified and analyzed through reflection upon the logic of inquiry in the natural and cultural sciences, they can legitimately claim a "transcendental" status. They assume an "empirical" status as soon as they are analyzed as the result of natural history—analyzed, as it were, in terms of cultural anthropology.[21]

21 Jürgen Habermas, "Nachwort" to the second edition of *Erkenntnis und Interesse* (Frankfurt: Surkamp, 1973), p. 410; translated as "A Postscript to *Knowledge and Human Interests*," by Christian Lenhardt in *Philosophy of the Social Sciences* 3 (1973), 181. For a criticism of the line Habermas takes here—a criticism paralleling my own—see

I want to claim, on the contrary, that there is no point in trying to find a general synoptic way of "analyzing" the "functions knowledge has in universal contexts of practical life," and that cultural anthropology (in a large sense which includes intellectual history) is all we need.

Habermas and other authors who are impelled by the same motives see the suggestion that empirical inquiry suffices as incorporating an "objectivistic illusion." They tend to see Deweyan pragmatism, and the "scientific realism" of Sellars and Feyerabend, as the products of an inadequate epistemology. In my view, the great virtue of Dewey, Sellars, and Feyerabend is that they point the way toward, and partially exemplify, a nonepistemological sort of philosophy, and thus one which gives up any hope of the "transcendental." Habermas says that for a theory to "ground itself transcendentally" is for it to

> become familiar with the range of inevitable subjective conditions which both make the theory possible *and* place limits on it, for this kind of transcendental corroboration tends always to criticize an overly self-confident self-understanding of itself.[22]

Specifically, this overconfidence consists in thinking that

> there can be such a thing as truthfulness to reality in the sense postulated by philosophical realism. Correspondence-theories of truth tend to hypostatize facts as entities in the world. It is the intention and inner logic of an epistemology reflecting upon the conditions of possible experience as such to uncover the objectivistic illusions of such a view. Every form of transcendental philosophy claims to identify the conditions of the objectivity of ex-

Michael Theunissen, *Gesellschaft und Geschichte: Zur Kritik der Kritischen Theorie* (Berlin, 1969), pp. 20ff. (I owe the reference to Theunissen to Raymond Geuss.)

22 Habermas, "Nachwort," p. 411; English translation, p. 182.

perience by analyzing the categorical structure of objects of possible experience.[23]

But Dewey, Wittgenstein, Sellars, Kuhn, and the other heroes of this book all have their own ways of debunking "truthfulness to reality in the sense postulated by philosophical realism," and none of them think that this is to be done by "analyzing the categorical structure of objects of possible experience."

The notion that we can get around overconfident philosophical realism and positivistic reductions only by adopting something like Kant's transcendental standpoint seems to me the basic mistake in programs like that of Habermas (as well as in Husserl's notion of a "phenomenology of the life-world" which will describe people in some way "prior" to that offered by science). What is required to accomplish these laudable purposes is not Kant's "epistemological" distinction between the transcendental and the empirical standpoints, but rather his "existentialist" distinction between people as empirical selves and as moral agents.[24] Normal scientific discourse can always be seen in two different ways—as the successful search for objective truth, or as one discourse among others, one among many projects we engage in. The former point of view falls in with the normal practice of normal science. There questions of moral choice or of edification do not arise, since they have already been preempted by the tacit and "self-confident" commitment to the search for objective truth on the subject in question. The latter point of view is one from which we

[23] Ibid., pp. 408-409; English translation, p. 180.

[24] Wilfrid Sellars uses this latter Kantian distinction to good effect in his insistence that personhood is a matter of "being one of us," of falling within the scope of practical imperatives of the form "Would that we all . . . ," rather than a feature of certain organisms to be isolated by empirical means. I have invoked this claim several times in this book, particularly in chapter four, section 4. For Sellars's own use of it, see *Science and Metaphysics* (London and New York, 1968), chap. 7, and the essay "Science and Ethics" in his *Philosophical Perspectives* (Springfield, Ill., 1967).

ask such questions as "What is the point?" "What moral is to be drawn from our knowledge of how we, and the rest of nature, work?" or "What are we to do with ourselves now that we know the laws of our own behavior?"

The primal error of systematic philosophy has always been the notion that such questions are to be answered by some new ("metaphysical" or "transcendental") descriptive or explanatory discourse (dealing with, e.g., "man," "spirit," or "language"). This attempt to answer questions of justification by discovering new objective truths, to answer the moral agent's request for justifications with descriptions of a privileged domain, is the philosopher's special form of bad faith—his special way of substituting pseudo-cognition for moral choice. Kant's greatness was to have seen through the "metaphysical" form of this attempt, and to have destroyed the traditional conception of reason to make room for moral faith. Kant gave us a way of seeing scientific truth as something which could never supply an answer to our demand for a point, a justification, a way of claiming that our moral decision about what to do is based on *knowledge* of the nature of the world. Unfortunately, Kant put his diagnosis of science in terms of the discovery of "inevitable subjective conditions," to be revealed by reflection upon scientific inquiry. Equally unfortunately, he thought that there really was a decision procedure for moral dilemmas (though not based on *knowledge*, since our grasp of the categorical imperative is not a *cognition*).[25] So he created new forms of philosophical bad faith—substituting "transcendental" attempts to find one's true self for "metaphysical" attempts to find a world elsewhere. By tacitly identifying the moral agent with the constituting transcendental self, he left the road

[25] See Kant's distinction between knowledge and necessary belief at *K.d.r.V.*, A824–B852ff., and especially his use of *Unternehmung* as a synonym for the latter. This section of the First Critique seems to me the one which gives most sense to the famous passage about denying reason to make room for faith at Bxxx. At many other points, however, Kant inconsistently speaks of practical reason as supplying an enlargement of our *knowledge*.

open to ever more complicated post-Kantian attempts to reduce freedom to nature, choice to knowledge, the *pour-soi* to the *en-soi*. This is the road I have been trying to block by recasting ahistorical and permanent distinctions between nature and spirit, "objectivizing science" and reflection, epistemology and hermeneutics, in terms of historical and temporary distinctions between the familiar and the unfamiliar, the normal and the abnormal. For this way of treating these distinctions lets us see them not as dividing two areas of inquiry but as the distinction between inquiry and something which is *not* inquiry, but is rather the inchoate questioning out of which inquiries—new normal discourses—may (or may not) emerge.

To put this claim in another way, which may help bring out its connections with naturalism, I am saying that the positivists were absolutely right in thinking it imperative to extirpate metaphysics, when "metaphysics" means the attempt to give knowledge of what science cannot know. For this is the attempt to find a discourse which combines the advantages of normality with those of abnormality—the intersubjective security of objective truth combined with the edifying character of an unjustifiable but unconditional moral claim. The urge to set philosophy on the secure path of a science is the urge to combine Plato's project of moral choice as ticking off the objective truths about a special sort of object (the Idea of the Good) with the sort of intersubjective and democratic agreement about objects found in normal science.[26] Philosophy which was utterly unedifying, utterly irrelevant to such moral choices as whether or not to believe in God would count not as *philosophy*, but only as some special sort of science. So as soon as a program to put philosophy on the secure path of science succeeds, it simply

[26] The positivists themselves quickly succumbed to this urge. Even while insisting that moral questions were noncognitive they thought to give quasi-scientific status to their moralistic attacks on traditional philosophy—thus making themselves subject to self-referential criticisms concerning their "emotive" use of "noncognitive."

converts philosophy into a boring academic specialty. Systematic philosophy exists by perpetually straddling the gap between description and justification, cognition and choice, getting the facts right and telling us how to live.

Once this point is seen, we can see more clearly why epistemology emerged as the essence of systematic philosophy. For epistemology is the attempt to see the patterns of justification within normal discourse as *more* than just such patterns. It is the attempt to see them as hooked on to something which demands moral commitment—Reality, Truth, Objectivity, Reason. To be behaviorist in epistemology, on the contrary, is to look at the normal scientific discourse of our day bifocally, both as patterns adopted for various historical reasons and as the achievement of objective truth, where "objective truth" is no more and no less than the best idea we currently have about how to explain what is going on. From the point of view of epistemological behaviorism, the only truth in Habermas's claim that scientific inquiry is made possible, and limited, by "inevitable subjective conditions" is that such inquiry is made possible by the adoption of practices of justification, and that such practices have possible alternatives. But these "subjective conditions" are in no sense "inevitable" ones discoverable by "reflection upon the logic of inquiry." They are just the facts about what a given society, or profession, or other group, takes to be good ground for assertions of a certain sort. Such disciplinary matrices are studied by the usual empirical-cum-hermeneutic methods of "cultural anthropology." From the point of view of the group in question these subjective conditions are a combination of commonsensical practical imperatives (e.g., tribal taboos, Mill's Methods) with the standard current theory about the subject. From the point of view of the historian of ideas or the anthropologist they are the empirical facts about the beliefs, desires, and practices of a certain group of human beings. These are incompatible points of view, in the sense that we cannot be at both viewpoints simultaneously. But there is no reason and no need to subsume the two in a higher synthesis. The group in question may itself shift from the one point of view to the other (thus "objectivizing" their past selves through a process of "reflection" and making new sentences true of their present selves). But this is not a mysterious process which demands a new understanding of human knowledge. It is the commonplace fact that people may develop doubts about what they are doing, and thereupon begin to discourse in ways incommensurable with those they used previously.

This goes also for the most spectacular and disturbing new discourses. When such edifying philosophers as Marx, Freud, and Sartre offer new explanations of our usual patterns of justifying our actions and assertions, and when these explanations are taken up and integrated into our lives, we have striking examples of the phenomenon of reflection's changing vocabulary and behavior. But as I argued in chapter seven, this phenomenon does not require any new understanding of theory-construction or theory-confirmation. To say that we have changed ourselves by internalizing a new self-description (using terms like "bourgeois intellectual" or "self-destructive" or "self-deceiving") is true enough. But this is no more startling than the fact that men changed the data of botany by hybridization, which was in turn made possible by botanical theory, or that they changed their own lives by inventing bombs and vaccines. Meditation on the possibility of such changes, like reading science fiction, does help us overcome the self-confidence of "philosophical realism." But such meditation does not need to be supplemented by a transcendental account of the nature of reflection. All that is necessary is the edifying invocation of the fact or possibility of abnormal discourses, undermining our reliance upon the knowledge we have gained through normal discourses. The objectionable self-confidence in question is simply the tendency of normal discourse to block the flow of conversation by presenting itself as offering the canonical vocabulary for dis-

cussion of a given topic—and, more particularly, the tendency of normal epistemologically centered philosophy to
block the road by putting itself forward as the final commensurating vocabulary for all *possible* rational discourse.
Self-confidence of the former, limited sort is overthrown
by edifying philosophers who put the very idea of universal commensuration, and of systematic philosophy, in
doubt.

Risking intolerable repetitiveness, I want to insist again
that the distinction between normal and abnormal discourse does not coincide with any distinction of subject
matter (e.g., nature versus history, or facts versus values),
method (e.g., objectivation versus reflection), faculty (e.g.,
reason versus imagination), or any of the other distinctions
which systematic philosophy has used to make the sense of
the world consist in the objective truth about some previously unnoticed portion or feature of the world. *Anything*
can be discoursed of abnormally, just as anything can become edifying and anything can be systematized. I have been
discussing the relation between natural science and other
disciplines simply because, since the period of Descartes
and Hobbes, the assumption that scientific discourse was
normal discourse and that all other discourse needed to be
modeled upon it has been the standard motive for philosophizing. Once we set this assumption aside, however, we
can also set aside the various anti-naturalisms about which
I have been complaining. More specifically, we can assert
all of the following:

Every speech, thought, theory, poem, composition, and
philosophy will turn out to be completely predictable in
purely naturalistic terms. Some atoms-and-the-void account
of micro-processes within individual human beings will permit the prediction of every sound or inscription which will
ever be uttered. There are no ghosts.

Nobody will be able to predict his own actions, thoughts,
theories, poems, etc., before deciding upon them or inventing them. (This is not an interesting remark about the

odd nature of human beings, but rather a trivial consequence of what it means to "decide" or "invent.") So no
hope (or danger) exists that cognition of oneself as *en-soi*
will cause one to cease to exist *pour-soi*.

The complete set of laws which enable these predictions
to be made, plus complete descriptions (in atoms-and-the-
void terms) of all human beings, would not yet be the
whole "objective truth" about human beings, nor the
whole set of true predictions about them. There would remain as many other distinct sets of such objective truths
(some useful for prediction, some not) as there were incommensurable vocabularies within which normal inquiry
about human beings could be conducted (e.g., all those vocabularies within which we attribute beliefs and desires,
virtues and beauty).

Incommensurability entails irreducibility but not incompatibility, so the failure to "reduce" these various vocabularies to that of "bottom-level" atoms-and-the-void science
casts no doubt upon their cognitive status or upon the
metaphysical status of their objects. (This goes as much
for the aesthetic worth of poems as for the beliefs of persons, as much for virtues as for volitions.)

The assemblage, *per impossible*, of all these objective
truths would still not necessarily be edifying. It might be
the picture of a world without a sense, without a moral.
Whether it seemed to point a moral to an individual would
depend upon that individual. It would be true or false that
it so seemed, or did not seem, to him. But it would not be
objectively true or false that it "really did," or did not, have
a sense or a moral. Whether his knowledge of the world
leaves him with a sense of what to do with or in the world
is itself predictable, but whether it *should* is not.

The fear of science, of "scientism," of "naturalism," of
self-objectivation, of being turned by too much knowledge
into a thing rather than a person, is the fear that all discourse
will become normal discourse. That is, it is the fear that
there will be objectively true or false answers to every ques-

tion we ask, so that human worth will consist in knowing truths, and human virtue will be merely justified true belief. This is frightening because it cuts off the possibility of something new under the sun, of human life as poetic rather than merely contemplative.

But the dangers to abnormal discourse do not come from science or naturalistic philosophy. They come from the scarcity of food and from the secret police. Given leisure and libraries, the conversation which Plato began will not end in self-objectivation—not because aspects of the world, or of human beings, escape being objects of scientific inquiry, but simply because free and leisured conversation generates abnormal discourse as the sparks fly upward.

5. PHILOSOPHY IN THE CONVERSATION OF MANKIND

I end this book with an allusion to Oakeshott's famous title,[27] because it catches the tone in which, I think, philosophy should be discussed. Much of what I have said about epistemology and its possible successors is an attempt to draw some corollaries from Sellars's doctrine that

> in characterizing an episode or a state as that of *knowing*, we are not giving an empirical description of that episode or state; we are placing it in the logical space of reasons, of justifying and being able to justify what one says.[28]

If we see knowing not as having an essence, to be described by scientists or philosophers, but rather as a right, by current standards, to believe, then we are well on the way to seeing *conversation* as the ultimate context within which knowledge is to be understood. Our focus shifts from the relation between human beings and the objects of their inquiry to the relation between alternative standards of

27 Cf. Michael Oakeshott, "The Voice of Poetry in the Conversation of Mankind," in his *Rationalism and Politics* (New York, 1975).

28 Wilfrid Sellars, *Science, Perception and Reality* (London and New York, 1963), p. 169.

justification, and from there to the actual changes in those standards which make up intellectual history. This brings us to appreciate Sellars's own description of his mythical hero Jones, the man who invented the Mirror of Nature and thereby made modern philosophy possible:

> Does the reader not recognize Jones as Man himself in the middle of his journey from the grunts and groans of the cave to the subtle and polydimensional discourse of the drawing room, the laboratory, and the study, the language of Henry and William James, of Einstein and of the philosophers who, in their efforts to break out of discourse to an ἀρχή beyond discourse, have provided the most curious dimension of all? (p. 196)

In this book I have offered a sort of prolegomenon to a history of epistemology-centered philosophy as an episode in the history of European culture. Such philosophy goes back to the Greeks, and goes sideways into all sorts of non-philosophical disciplines which have, at one time or another, proposed themselves as substitutes for epistemology, and thus for philosophy. So the episode in question cannot simply be identified with "modern philosophy," in the sense of the standard textbook sequence of great philosophers from Descartes to Russell and Husserl. But that sequence is, nevertheless, where the search for foundations for knowledge is most explicit. So most of my attempts to deconstruct the image of the Mirror of Nature have concerned these philosophers. I have tried to show how their urge to break out into an ἀρχή beyond discourse is rooted in the urge to see social practices of justification as more than just such practices. I have, however, focused mainly on the expressions of this urge in the recent literature of analytical philosophy. The result is thus no more than a prolegomenon. A proper historical treatment would require both learning and skills which I do not possess. But I would hope that the prolegomenon has been sufficient to let one see contemporary issues in philosophy as events in a certain stage of a conversation—a conversation which once knew nothing of these issues and may know nothing of them again.

The fact that we can continue the conversation Plato began without discussing the topics Plato wanted discussed, illustrates the difference between treating philosophy as a voice in a conversation and treating it as a subject, a *Fach*, a field of professional inquiry. The conversation Plato began has been enlarged by more voices than Plato would have dreamed possible, and thus by topics he knew nothing. of. A "subject"—astrology, physics, classical philosophy, furniture design—may undergo revolutions, but it gets its self-image from its present state, and its history is necessarily written "Whiggishly" as an account of its gradual maturation. This is the most frequent way of writing the history of philosophy, and I cannot claim to have avoided such Whiggery entirely in sketching the sort of history which needs to be written. But I hope that I have shown how we can see the issues with which philosophers are presently concerned, and with which they Whiggishly see philosophy as having always (perhaps unwittingly) been concerned, as results of historical accident, as turns the conversation has taken.[29] It has taken this turn for a long time, but it might

---

[29] Two recent writers—Michel Foucault and Harold Bloom—make this sense of the brute factuality of historical origins central to their work. Cf. Bloom, *A Map of Misreading* (New York, 1975), p. 33: "All continuities possess the paradox of being absolutely arbitrary in their origins and absolutely inescapable in their teleologies. We know this so vividly from what we all of us oxymoronically call our love lives that its literary counterparts need little demonstration." Foucault says that his way of looking at the history of ideas "permits the introduction, into the very roots of thought, of notions of *chance, discontinuity* and *materiality*." ("The Discourse on Language," included in the *Archaeology of Knowledge* [New York, 1972], p. 231) It is hardest of all to see brute contingency in the history of *philosophy*, if only because since Hegel the historiography of philosophy has been "progressive," or (as in Heidegger's inversion of Hegel's account of progress) "retrogressive," but never without a sense of inevitability. If we could once see the desire for a permanent, neutral, ahistorical, commensurating vocabulary as

turn in another direction without human beings thereby losing their reason, or losing touch with "the real problems."

The conversational interest of philosophy as a subject, or of some individual philosopher of genius, has varied and will continue to vary in unpredictable ways depending upon contingencies. These contingencies will range from what happens in physics to what happens in politics. The lines between disciplines will blur and shift, and new disciplines will arise, in the ways illustrated by Galileo's successful attempt to create "purely scientific questions" in the seventeenth century. The notions of "philosophical significance" and of "purely philosophical question," as they are currently used, gained sense only around the time of Kant. Our post-Kantian sense that epistemology or some successor subject is at the center of philosophy (and that moral philosophy, aesthetics, and social philosophy, for example, are somehow derivative) is a reflection of the fact that the professional philosopher's self-image depends upon his professional preoccupation with the image of the Mirror of Nature. Without the Kantian assumption that the philosopher can decide *quaestiones juris* concerning the claims of the rest of culture, this self-image collapses. That assumption depends on the notion that there is such a thing as understanding the essence of knowledge—doing what Sellars tells us we cannot do.

To drop the notion of the philosopher as knowing something about knowing which nobody else knows so well would be to drop the notion that his voice always has an overriding claim on the attention of the other participants in the conversation. It would also be to drop the notion that there is something called "philosophical method" or "philosophical technique" or "the philosophical point of view"

---

itself a historical phenomenon, then perhaps we could write the history of philosophy less dialectically and less sentimentally than has been possible hitherto.

which enables the professional philosopher, *ex officio*, to have interesting views about, say, the respectability of psychoanalysis, the legitimacy of certain dubious laws, the resolution of moral dilemmas, the "soundness" of schools of historiography or literary criticism, and the like. Philosophers often do have interesting views upon such questions, and their professional training as philosophers is often a necessary condition for their having the views they do. But this is not to say that philosophers have a special kind of knowledge about knowledge (or anything else) from which they draw relevant corollaries. The useful kibitzing they can provide on the various topics I just mentioned is made possible by their familiarity with the historical background of arguments on similar topics, and, most importantly, by the fact that arguments on such topics are punctuated by stale philosophical clichés which the other participants have stumbled across in their reading, but about which professional philosophers know the pros and cons by heart.

The neo-Kantian image of philosophy as a profession, then, is involved with the image of the "mind" or "language" as mirroring nature. So it might seem that epistemological behaviorism and the consequent rejection of mirror-imagery entail the claim that there can or should be no such profession. But this does not follow. Professions can survive the paradigms which gave them birth. In any case, the need for teachers who have read the great dead philosophers is quite enough to insure that there will be philosophy departments as long as there are universities. The actual result of a widespread loss of faith in mirror-imagery would be merely an "encapsulation" of the problems created by this imagery within a historical period. I do not know whether we are in fact at the end of an era. This will depend, I suspect, on whether Dewey, Wittgenstein, and Heidegger are taken to heart. It may be that mirror-imagery and "mainstream," systematic philosophy will be revitalized once again by some revolutionary of genius. Or it may be that the image of the philosopher which Kant offered is about to go the way of the medieval image of the priest. If that happens, even the philosophers themselves will no longer take seriously the notion of philosophy as providing "foundations" or "justifications" for the rest of culture, or as adjudicating *quaestiones juris* about the proper domains of other disciplines.

Whichever happens, however, there is no danger of philosophy's "coming to an end." Religion did not come to an end in the Enlightenment, nor painting in Impressionism. Even if the period from Plato to Nietzsche is encapsulated and "distanced" in the way Heidegger suggests, and even if twentieth-century philosophy comes to seem a stage of awkward transitional backing and filling (as sixteenth-century philosophy now seems to us), there will be something called "philosophy" on the other side of the transition. For even if problems about representation look as obsolete to our descendants as problems about hylomorphism look to us, people will still read Plato, Aristotle, Descartes, Kant, Hegel, Wittgenstein, and Heidegger. What roles these men will play in our descendants' conversation, no one knows. Whether the distinction between systematic and edifying philosophy will carry over, no one knows either. Perhaps philosophy will become purely edifying, so that one's self-identification as a philosopher will be purely in terms of the books one reads and discusses, rather than in terms of the problems one wishes to solve. Perhaps a new form of systematic philosophy will be found which has nothing whatever to do with epistemology but which nevertheless makes normal philosophical inquiry possible. These speculations are idle, and nothing I have been saying makes one more plausible than another. The only point on which I would insist is that philosophers' moral concern should be with continuing the conversation of the West, rather than with insisting upon a place for the traditional problems of modern philosophy within that conversation.

CHAPTER ONE

EXPERIENCE AND PHILOSOPHIC METHOD

The title of this volume, Experience and Nature, is intended to signify that the philosophy here presented may be termed either empirical naturalism or naturalistic empiricism, or, taking "experience" in its usual signification, naturalistic humanism.

To many the associating of the two words will seem like talking of a round square, so engrained is the notion of the separation of man and experience from nature. Experience, they say, is important for those beings who have it, but is too casual and sporadic in its occurrence to carry with it any important implications regarding the nature of Nature. Nature, on the other hand, is said to be complete apart from experience. Indeed, according to some thinkers the case is even in worse plight: Experience to them is not only something extraneous which is occasionally superimposed upon nature, but it forms a veil or screen which shuts us off from nature, unless in some way it can be "transcended." So something non-natural by way of reason or intuition is introduced, something supra-empirical. According to an opposite school experience fares as badly, nature being thought to signify something wholly material and mechanistic; to frame a theory of experience in naturalistic terms is, accordingly, to degrade and deny the noble and ideal values that characterize experience.

I know of no route by which dialectical argument can answer such objections. They arise from associations with words and cannot be dealt with argumentatively. One can

Dewey, John. (1958). Experience and the philosophic method. In *Experience and Nature* (Chapter 1, pp. 1a–39). Mineola, NY: Dover. Reproduced with permission.

only hope in the course of the whole discussion to disclose the meanings which are attached to "experience" and "nature," and thus insensibly produce, if one is fortunate, a change in the significations previously attached to them. This process of change may be hastened by calling attention to another context in which nature and experience get on harmoniously together—wherein experience presents itself as the method, and the only method, for getting at nature, penetrating its secrets, and wherein nature empirically disclosed (by the use of empirical method in natural science) deepens, enriches and directs the further development of experience.

In the natural sciences there is a union of experience and nature which is not greeted as a monstrosity; on the contrary, the inquirer must use empirical method if his findings are to be treated as genuinely scientific. The investigator assumes as a matter of course that experience, controlled in specifiable ways, is the avenue that leads to the facts and laws of nature. He uses reason and calculation freely; he could not get along without them. But he sees to it that ventures of this theoretical sort start from and terminate in directly experienced subject-matter. Theory may intervene in a long course of reasoning, many portions of which are remote from what is directly experienced. But the vine of pendant theory is attached at both ends to the pillars of observed subject-matter. And this experienced material is the same for the scientific man and the man in the street. The latter cannot follow the intervening reasoning without special preparation. But stars, rocks, trees, and creeping things are the same material of experience for both.

These commonplaces take on significance when the relation of experience to the formation of a philosophic theory of nature is in question. They indicate that experience, if scientific inquiry is justified, is no infinitesimally thin layer or foreground of nature, but that it penetrates into it, reaching down into its depths, and in such a way that its grasp is capable of expansion; it tunnels in all directions and in so doing brings to the surface things at first hidden—as miners pile high on the surface of the earth treasures brought from below. Unless we are prepared to deny all validity to scientific inquiry, these facts have a value that cannot be ignored for the general theory of the relation of nature and experience.

It is sometimes contended, for example, that since experience is a late comer in the history of our solar system and planet, and since these occupy a trivial place in the wide areas of celestial space, experience is at most a slight and insignificant incident in nature. No one with an honest respect for scientific conclusions can deny that experience as an existence is something that occurs only under highly specialized conditions, such as are found in a highly organized creature which in turn requires a specialized environment. There is no evidence that experience occurs everywhere and everywhen. But candid regard for scientific inquiry also compels the recognition that when experience does occur, no matter at what limited portion of time and space, it enters into possession of some portion of nature and in such a manner as to render other of its precincts accessible.

A geologist living in 1928 tells us about events that happened not only before he was born but millions of years before any human being came into existence on this earth. He does so by starting from things that are now the material of experience. Lyell revolutionized geology by perceiving that the sort of thing that can be experienced now in the operations of fire, water, pressure, is the sort of thing by which the earth took on its present structural forms. Visiting a natural history museum, one beholds a mass of rock and, reading a label, finds that it comes from a tree that grew, so it is affirmed, five million years ago. The geologist did not leap from the thing he can see and touch to some event in by-gone ages; he collated this observed thing with many others, of different kinds, found all over the globe; the results of his comparisons he then compared with data of other experiences, say, the astronomer's. He translates, that is, observed coexistences into non-observed, inferred sequences. Finally he dates his object, placing it in an order of events. By the same sort of method he predicts that at certain places some things not yet experienced will be observed, and then he takes pains to bring them within the scope of experience. The scientific conscience is, moreover, so sensitive with respect to the necessity of experience that when it reconstructs the past it is not fully satisfied with inferences drawn from even a large and cumulative mass of uncontradicted evidence; it sets to work to institute conditions of heat and pressure and moisture, etc., so as actually to reproduce in experiment that which he has inferred.

These commonplaces prove that experience is *of* as well as *in* nature. It is not experience which is experienced, but nature—stones, plants, animals, diseases, health, temperature, electricity, and so on. Things interacting in certain ways *are* experience; they are what is experienced. Linked in certain other ways with another natural object —the human organism—they are *how* things are experienced as well. Experience thus reaches down into nature; it has depth. It also has breadth and to an indefinitely elastic extent. It stretches. That stretch constitutes inference.

Dialectical difficulties, perplexities due to definitions given to the concepts that enter into the discussion, may be raised. It is said to be absurd that what is only a tiny part of nature should be competent to incorporate vast reaches of nature within itself. But even were it logically absurd one would be bound to cleave to it as a fact. Logic, however, is not put under a strain. The fact that something is an occurrence does not decide what kind of an occurrence it is; that can be found out only by examination. To argue from an experience "being an experience" to what it is of and about is warranted by no logic, even though modern thought has attempted it a thousand times. A bare event is no event at all; *something* happens. What that something is, is found out by actual study. This applies to seeing a flash of lightning and holds of the longer event called experience. The very existence of science is evidence that experience is such an occurrence that it penetrates into nature and expands without limit through it.

These remarks are not supposed to prove anything about experience and nature for philosophical doctrine; they are not supposed to settle anything about the worth of empirical naturalism. But they do show that in the case of natural science we habitually treat experience as starting-point, and as method for dealing with nature, and as the goal in which nature is disclosed for what it is. To realize this fact is at least to weaken those verbal associations which stand in the way of apprehending the force of empirical method in philosophy.

The same considerations apply to the other objection that was suggested: namely, that to view experience naturalistically is to reduce it to something materialistic, depriving it of all ideal significance. If experience actually presents esthetic and moral traits, then these traits may also be supposed to reach down into nature, and to testify to something that belongs to nature as truly as does the mechanical structure attributed to it in physical science. To rule out that possibility by some general reasoning is to forget that the very meaning and purport of empirical method is that things are to be studied on their own account, so as to find out what is revealed when they are experienced. The traits possessed by the subject-matters of experience are as genuine as the characteristics of sun and electron. They are *found*, experienced, and are not to be shoved out of being by some trick of logic. When found, their ideal qualities are as relevant to the philosophic theory of nature as are the traits found by physical inquiry.

To discover some of these general features of experienced things and to interpret their significance for a philosophic theory of the universe in which we live is the aim of this volume. From the point of view adopted, the theory of empirical method in philosophy does for experienced subject-matter on a liberal scale what it does for special sciences on a technical scale. It is this aspect of method with which we are especially concerned in the present chapter.

If the empirical method were universally or even generally adopted in philosophizing, there would be no need of referring to experience. The scientific inquirer talks and writes about particular observed events and qualities, about specific calculations and reasonings. He makes no allusion to experience; one would probably have to search a long time through reports of special researches in order to find the word. The reason is that everything designated by the word "experience" is so adequately incorporated into scientific procedures and subject-matter that to mention experience would be only to duplicate in a general term what is already covered in definite terms.

Yet this was not always so. Before the technique of empirical method was developed and generally adopted, it was necessary to dwell explicitly upon the importance of "experience" as a starting point and terminal point, as setting problems and as testing proposed solutions. We need not be content with the conventional allusion to Roger Bacon and Francis Bacon. The followers of Newton and the followers of the Cartesian school carried on a definite controversy as to the place occupied by experience and experiment in science as compared with intuitive concepts and with reasoning from them. The Cartesian school relegated experience to a secondary and almost accidental place, and only when the Galilean-Newtonian method had wholly triumphed did it cease to be necessary to mention the importance of experience. We may, if sufficiently hopeful, anticipate a similar outcome in philosophy. But the date does not appear to be close at hand; we are nearer in philosophic theory to the time of Roger Bacon than to that of Newton.

In short, it is the contrast of empirical method with other methods employed in philosophizing, together with the striking dissimilarity of results yielded by an empirical method and professed non-empirical methods that make the discussion of the methodological import of "experience" for philosophy pertinent and indeed indispensable.

This consideration of method may suitably begin with the contrast between gross, macroscopic, crude subject-matters in primary experience and the refined, derived objects of reflection. The distinction is one between what is experienced as the result of a minimum of incidental reflection and what is experienced in consequence of continued and regulated reflective inquiry. For derived and refined products are experienced only because of the intervention of systematic thinking. The objects of both science and philosophy obviously belong chiefly to the secondary and refined system. But at this point we come to a marked divergence between science and philosophy. For the natural sciences not only draw their material from primary experience, but they refer it back again for test. Darwin began with the pigeons, cattle and plants of breeders and gardeners. Some of the conclusions he reached were so contrary to accepted beliefs that they were condemned as absurd, contrary to commonsense, etc. But scientific men, whether they accepted his theories or not, employed his hypotheses as directive ideas for making new observations and experiments among the things of raw experience—just as the metallurgist who extracts refined metal from crude ore makes tools that are then set to work to control and use other crude materials. An Einstein working by highly elaborate methods of reflection, calculates theoretically certain results in the deflection of light by the presence of the sun. A technically equipped expedition is sent to South Africa so that by means of experiencing a thing—an eclipse—in crude, primary, experience, observations can be secured to compare with, and test the theory implied in, the calculated result.

The facts are familiar enough. They are cited in order to invite attention to the relationship between the objects of primary and of secondary or reflective experience. That the subject-matter of primary experience sets the problems and furnishes the first data of the reflection which constructs the secondary objects is evident; it is also obvious that test and verification of the latter is secured only by return to things of crude or macroscopic experience—the sun, earth, plants and animals of common, every-day life. But just what rôle do the objects attained in reflection play? Where do they come in? They *explain* the primary objects, they enable us to grasp them with *understanding*, instead of just having sense-contact with them. But how?

Well, they define or lay out a path by which return to experienced things is of such a sort that the meaning, the significant content, of what is experienced gains an enriched and expanded force because of the path or method by which it was reached. Directly, in immediate contact it may be just what it was before—hard, colored, odorous, etc. But when the secondary objects, the refined objects, are employed as a method or road for coming at them, these qualities cease to be isolated details; they get the meaning contained in a whole system of related objects; they are rendered continuous with the rest of nature and take on the import of the things they are now seen to be continuous with. The phenomena observed in the eclipse tested and, as far as they went, confirmed Einstein's theory of deflection of light by mass. But that is far from being the whole story. The phenomena themselves got a far-reaching significance they did not previously have. Perhaps they would not even have been noticed if the theory had not been employed as a guide or road to observation of them. But even if they had been noticed, they would have been dismissed as of no importance, just as we daily drop from attention hundreds of perceived details for which we have no intellectual use. But approached by means of theory these lines of slight deflection take on a significance as large as that of the revolutionary theory that lead to their being experienced.

This empirical method I shall call the *denotative* method. That philosophy is a mode of reflection, often of a subtle and penetrating sort, goes without saying. The charge that is brought against the non-empirical method of philosophizing is not that it depends upon theorizing, but that it fails to use refined, secondary products as a path pointing and leading back to something in primary experience. The resulting failure is three-fold.

First, there is no verification, no effort even to test and check. What is even worse, secondly, is that the things of ordinary experience do not get enlargement and enrichment of meaning as they do when approached through the medium of scientific principles and reasonings. This lack of function reacts, in the third place, back upon the philosophic subject-matter in itself. Not tested by being employed to see what it leads to in ordinary experience and what new meanings it contributes, this subject-matter becomes arbitrary, aloof—what is called "abstract" when that word is used in a bad sense to designate something which exclusively occupies a realm of its own without contact with the things of ordinary experience.

As the net outcome of these three evils, we find that extraordinary phenomenon which accounts for the revulsion of many cultivated persons from any form of philosophy. The objects of reflection in philosophy, being reached by methods that seem to those who employ them rationally mandatory are taken to be "real" in and of themselves—and supremely real. Then it becomes an insoluble problem why the things of gross, primary experience, should be what they are, or indeed why they should be at all. The refined objects of reflection in the natural sciences, however, never end by rendering the subject-matter from which they are derived a problem; rather, when used to describe a path by which some goal in primary experience is designated or denoted, they solve perplexities to which that crude material gives rise but which it cannot resolve of itself. They become means of control, of enlarged use and enjoyment of ordinary things. They may generate new problems, but these are problems of the same sort, to be dealt with by further use of the same methods of inquiry and experimentation. The problems to which empirical method gives rise afford, in a word, opportunities for more investigations yielding fruit in new and enriched experiences. But the problems to which non-empirical method gives rise in philosophy are blocks to inquiry, blind alleys; they are puzzles rather than problems, solved only by calling the original material of primary experience, "phenomenal," mere appearance, mere impressions, or by some other disparaging name.

Thus there is here supplied, I think, a first-rate test of the value of any philosophy which is offered us: Does it end in conclusions which, when they are referred back to ordinary life-experiences and their predicaments, render them more significant, more luminous to us, and make our dealings with them more fruitful? Or does it terminate in rendering the things of ordinary experience more opaque than they were before, and in depriving them of having in "reality" even the significance they had previously seemed to have? Does it yield the enrichment and increase of power of ordinary things which the results of physical science afford when applied in every-day affairs? Or does it become a mystery that these ordinary things should be what they are; and are philosophic concepts left to dwell in separation in some technical realm of their own? It is the fact, I repeat, that so many philosophies terminate in conclusions that make it necessary to disparage and condemn primary experience, leading those who hold them to measure the sublimity of their "realities" as philosophically defined by remoteness from the concerns of daily life, which leads cultivated common-sense to look askance at philosophy.

These general statements must be made more definite. We must illustrate the meaning of empirical method by seeing some of its results in contrast with those to which non-empirical philosophies conduct us. We begin by noting that "experience" is what James called a double-barrelled word.[1] Like its congeners, life and history, it includes *what* men do and suffer, *what* they strive for, love, believe and endure, and also *how* men act and are acted upon, the ways in which they do and suffer, desire and enjoy, see, believe, imagine—in short, processes of *experiencing.* "Experience" denotes the planted field, the sowed seeds, the reaped harvests, the changes of night and day, spring and autumn, wet and dry, heat and cold, that are observed, feared, longed for; it also denotes the one who plants and reaps, who works and rejoices, hopes, fears, plans, invokes magic or chemistry to aid him, who is downcast or triumphant. It is "double-barrelled" in that it recognizes in its primary integrity no division between act and material, subject and object, but contains them both in an unanalyzed totality. "Thing" and "thought," as James says in the same connection, are single-barrelled; they refer to products discriminated by reflection out of primary experience.[2]

It is significant that "life" and "history" have the same

[1] Essays in Radical Empiricism. p. 10.
[2] It is not intended, however, to attribute to James precisely the interpretation given in the text.

fullness of undivided meaning. Life denotes a function, a comprehensive activity, in which organism and environment are included. Only upon reflective analysis does it break up into external conditions—air breathed, food taken, ground walked upon—and internal structures—lungs respiring, stomach digesting, legs walking. The scope of "history" is notorious: it is the deeds enacted, the tragedies undergone; and it is the human comment, record, and interpretation that inevitably follow. Objectively, history takes in rivers, mountains, fields and forests, laws and institutions; subjectively it includes the purposes and plans, the desires and emotions, through which these things are administered and transformed.

Now empirical method is the only method which can do justice to this inclusive integrity of "experience." It alone takes this integrated unity as the starting point for philosophic thought. Other methods begin with results of a reflection that has already torn in two the subject-matter experienced and the operations and states of experiencing. The problem is then to get together again what has been sundered—which is as if the king's men started with the fragments of the egg and tried to construct the whole egg out of them. For empirical method the problem is nothing so impossible of solution. Its problem is to note how and why the whole is distinguished into subject and object, nature and mental operations. Having done this, it is in a position to see *to what effect* the distinction is made: how the distinguished factors function in the further control and enrichment of the subject-matters of crude but total experience. Non-empirical method starts with a reflective product as if it were primary, as if it were the originally "given." To non-empirical method, therefore, object and subject, mind and matter (or whatever words and ideas are used) are separate and independent. Therefore it has upon its hands the problem of how it is possible to know at all; how an outer world can affect an inner mind; how the acts of mind can reach out and lay hold of objects defined in antithesis to them. Naturally it is at a loss for an answer, since its premises make the fact of knowledge both unnatural and unempirical. One thinker turns metaphysical materialist and denies reality to the mental; another turns psychological idealist, and holds that matter and force are merely disguised psychical events. Solutions are given up as a hopeless task, or else different schools pile one intellectual complication on another only to arrive by a long and tortuous course at that which naïve experience already has in its own possession.

The first and perhaps the greatest difference made in philosophy by adoption respectively of empirical or non-empirical method is, thus, the difference made in what is selected as original material. To a truly naturalistic empiricism, the moot problem of the relation of subject and object is the problem of what consequences follow in and for primary experience from the distinction of the physical and the psychological or mental from each other. The answer is not far to seek. To distinguish in reflection the physical and to hold it in temporary detachment is to be set upon the road that conducts to tools and technologies, to construction of mechanisms, to the arts that ensue in the wake of the sciences. That these constructions make possible a better regulation of the affairs of primary experience is evident. Engineering and medicine, all the utilities that make for expansion of life, are the answer. There is better administration of old familiar things, and there is invention of new objects and satisfactions. Along with this added ability in regulation goes enriched meaning and value in things, clarification, increased depth and continuity—a result even more precious than is the added power of control.

The history of the development of the physical sciences is the story of the enlarging possession by mankind of more efficacious instrumentalities for dealing witth the conditions of life and action. But when one neglects the connection of these scientific objects with the affairs of primary experience, the result is a picture of a world of things indifferent to human interests because it is wholly apart from experience. It is more than merely isolated, for it is set in opposition. Hence when it is viewed as fixed and final in itself it is a source of oppression to the heart and paralysis to imagination. Since this picture of the physical universe and philosophy of the character of physical objects is contradicted by every engineering project and every intelligent measure of public hygiene, it would seem to be time to examine the foundations upon which it rests, and find out how and why such conclusions are come to.

When objects are isolated from the experience through which they are reached and in which they function, experience itself becomes reduced to the mere process of experiencing, and experiencing is therefore treated as if it were also complete in itself. We get the absurdity of an experiencing which experiences only itself, states and processes of consciousness, instead of the things of nature. Since the seventeenth century this conception of experience as the equivalent of subjective private consciousness set over against nature, which consists wholly of physical objects, has wrought havoc in philosophy. It is responsible for the feeling mentioned at the outset that "nature" and "experience" are names for things which have nothing to do with each other.

Let us inquire how the matter stands when these mental and psychical objects are looked at in their connection with experience in its primary and vital modes. As has been suggested, these objects are not original, isolated and self-sufficient. They represent the discriminated analysis of the process of experiencing from subject-matter experienced. Although breathing is in fact a function that includes both air and the operations of the lungs, we may detach the latter for study, even though we cannot separate it in fact. So while we always know, love, act for and against *things*, instead of experiencing ideas, emotions and mental intents, the attitudes themselves may be made a special object of attention, and thus come to form a distinctive subject-matter of reflective, although not of primary, experience.

We primarily observe things, not observations. But the *act* of observation may be inquired into and form a subject of study and become thereby a refined object; so may the acts of thinking, desire, purposing, the state of affection, reverie, etc. Now just as long as these attitudes are not distinguished and abstracted, they are incorporated into subject-matter. It is a notorious fact that the one who hates finds the one hated an obnoxious and despicable character; to the lover his adored one is full of intrinsically delightful and wonderful qualities. The connection between such facts and the fact of animism is direct.

The natural and original bias of man is all toward the objective; whatever is experienced is taken to be there independent of the attitude and act of the self. Its "thereness," its independence of emotion and volition, render the properties of things, whatever they are, cosmic. Only when vanity, prestige, rights of possession are involved does an individual tend to separate off from the environment and the group in which he, quite literally, lives, some things as being peculiarly himself. It is obvious that a total, un-analyzed world does not lend itself to control; that, on the contrary it is equivalent to the subjection of man to whatever occurs, as if to fate. Until some acts and their consequences are discriminatingly referred to the human organism and other energies and effects are referred to other bodies, there is no leverage, no purchase, with which to regulate the course of experience. The abstraction of certain qualities of things as due to human acts and states is the *pou sto* of ability in control. There can be do doubt that the long periods of human arrest at a low level of culture was largely the result of failure to select the human being and his acts as a special kind of object, having his own characteristic activities that condition specifiable consequences.

In this sense, the recognition of "subjects" as centres of experience together with the development of "subjectivism" marks a great advance. It is equivalent to the emergence of agencies equipped with special powers of observation and experiment, and with emotions and desires that are efficacious for production of chosen modifications of nature. For otherwise the agencies are submerged in nature and produce qualities of things which must be accepted and submitted to. It is no mere play on words to say that recognition of subjective minds having a special equipment of psychological abilities is a necessary factor in subjecting the energies of nature to use as instrumentalities for ends.

Out of the indefinite number of possible illustrations of the consequences of reflective analysis yielding personal or "subjective" minds we cite one case. It concerns the influence of habitual beliefs and expectations in their social generation upon *what* is experienced. The things of primary experience are so arresting and engrossing that we tend to accept them just as they are—the flat earth, the march of the sun from east to west and its sinking under the earth. Current beliefs in morals, religion and politics similarly reflect the social conditions which present themselves. Only analysis shows that the *ways* in which we believe and expect have a tremendous affect upon *what* we believe and expect. We have discovered at last that these ways are set, almost abjectly so, by social factors, by tradition and the influence of education. Thus we discover that we believe many things not because the things are so, but because we have become habituated through the weight of authority, by imitation, prestige, instruction, the unconscious effect of language, etc. We learn, in short, that qualities which we attribute to objects ought to be imputed to our own ways of experiencing them, and that these in turn are due to the force of intercourse and custom. This discovery marks an emancipation; it purifies and remakes the objects of our direct or primary experience. The power of custom and tradition in scientific as well as in moral beliefs never suffered a serious check until analysis revealed the effect of personal ways of believing upon things believed, and the extent to which these ways are unwittingly fixed by social custom and tradition. In spite of the acute and penetrating powers of observation among the Greeks, their "science" is a monument of the extent to which the effects of acquired social habits as well as of organic constitution were attributed directly to natural events. The de-personalizing and de-socializing of some objects, to be henceforth the objects of physical science, was a necessary precondition of ability to regulate experience by directing the attitudes and objects that enter into it.

This great emancipation was coincident with the rise of "individualism," which was in effect identical with the reflective discovery of the part played in experience by concrete selves, with their ways of acting, thinking and desiring. The results would have been all to the good if they had been interpreted by empirical method. For this would have kept the eye of thinkers constantly upon the origin of the "subjective" out of primary experience, and then directed it to the function of discriminating what is usable in the management of experienced objects. But for lack of such a method, because of isolation from empirical origin and instrumental use, the results of psychological inquiry were conceived to form a separate and isolated mental world in and of itself, self-sufficient and self-enclosed. Since the psychological movement necessarily coincided with that which set up physical objects as correspondingly complete and self-enclosed, there resulted that dualism of mind and matter, of a physical and a psychical world, which from the day of Descartes to the present dominates the formulation of philosophical problems.

With the dualism we are not here concerned, beyond pointing out that it is the inevitable result, logically, of the abandoning of acknowledgment of the primacy and ultimacy of gross experience—primary as it is given in an uncontrolled form, ultimate as it is given in a more regulated and significant form—a form made possible by the methods and results of reflective experience. But what we are directly concerned with at this stage of discussion is the result of the discovery of subjective objects upon philosophy in creation of wholesale subjectivism. The outcome was, that while in actual life the discovery of personal attitudes and their consequences was a great liberating instrument, psychology became for philosophy, as Santayana has well put it, "malicious." That is, mental attitudes, *ways* of experiencing, were treated as self-sufficient and complete in themselves, as that which is primarily *given*, the sole original and therefore indubitable data. Thus the traits of genuine primary experience, in which natural things are the determining factors in production of all change, were regarded either as not-given dubious things that could be reached only by endowing the only certain thing, the mental, with some miraculous power, or else were denied all existence save as complexes of mental states, of impressions, sensations, feelings.[1]

One illustration out of the multitude available follows. It is taken almost at random, because it is both simple and typical. To illustrate the nature of experience, what experience really is, an author writes: "When I look at a chair, I say I experience it. But what I actually experience is only a very few of the elements that go to make up a chair, namely the color that belongs to the chair under these particular conditions of light, the shape which the chair displays when viewed from this angle, etc." Two points are involved in any such statement. One is that "experience" is reduced to the traits connected with the

---

[1] Because of this identification of the mental as the sole "given" in a primary, original way, appeal to experience by a philosopher is treated by many as necessarily committing one to subjectivism. It accounts for the alleged antithesis between nature and experience mentioned in the opening paragraph. It has become so deeply engrained that the empirical method employed in this volume has been taken by critics to be simply a re-statement of a purely subjective philosophy, although in fact it is wholly contrary to such a philosophy.

act of experiencing, in this case the act of seeing. Certain patches of color, for example, assume a certain shape or form in connection with qualities connected with the muscular strains and adjustments of seeing. These qualities, which define the act of seeing when it is made an object of reflective inquiry, *over against what is seen,* thus become the chair itself for immediate or direct experience. Logically, the chair disappears and is replaced by certain qualities of sense attending the act of vision. There is no longer any other object, much less the chair which was bought, that is placed in a room and that is used to sit in, etc. If we ever get back to this total chair, it will not be the chair of direct experience, of use and enjoyment, a thing with its own independent origin, history and career; it will be only a complex of directly "given" sense qualities as a core, plus a surrounding cluster of other qualities revived imaginatively as "ideas."

The other point is that, even in such a brief statement as that just quoted, there is compelled recognition of an *object* of experience which is infinitely other and more than what is asserted to be alone experienced. There is the *chair* which is looked at; the *chair displaying* certain colors, the *light* in which they are displayed; the angle of vision implying reference to an organism that possesses an optical apparatus. Reference to these *things* is compulsory, because otherwise there would be no meaning assignable to the sense qualities—which are, nevertheless, affirmed to be the sole data experienced. It would be hard to find a more complete recognition, although an unavowed one, of the fact that in reality the account given concerns only a selected portion of the actual experience, namely that part which defines the act of experiencing, to the deliberate omission, *for the purpose of the inquiry in hand,* of *what* is experienced.

The instance cited is typical of all "subjectivism" as a philosophic position. Reflective analysis of one element in actual experience is undertaken; its result is then taken to be primary; as a consequence the subject-matter of actual experience from which the analytic result was derived is rendered dubious and problematic, although it is assumed at every step of the analysis. Genuine empirical method sets out from the actual subject-matter of primary experience, recognizes that reflection discriminates a new factor in it, the *act* of seeing, makes an object of that, and then uses that new object, the organic response to light, to regulate, when needed, further experiences of the subject-matter already contained in primary experience.

The topics just dealt with, segregation of physical and mental objects, will receive extended attention in the body of this volume.[1] As respects *method*, however, it is pertinent at this point to summarize our results. Reference to the primacy and ultimacy of the material of ordinary experience protects us, in the first place, from creating artificial problems which deflect the energy and attention of philosophers from the real problems that arise out of actual subject-matter. In the second place, it provides a check or test for the conclusions of philosophic inquiry; it is a constant reminder that we must replace them, as secondary reflective products, in the experience out of which they arose, so that they may be confirmed or modified by the new order and clarity they introduce into it, and the new significantly experienced objects for which they furnish a method. In the third place, in seeing how they thus function in further experiences, the philosophical re-

[1] Chapters IV and VI.

sults themselves acquire empirical value; they are what they contribute to the common experience of man, instead of being curiosities to be deposited, with appropriate labels, in a metaphysical museum.

There is another important result for philosophy of the use of empirical method which, when it is developed, introduces our next topic. Philosophy, like all forms of reflective analysis, takes us away, for the time being, from the things had in primary experience as they directly act and are acted upon, used and enjoyed. Now the standing temptation of philosophy, as its course abundantly demonstrates, is to regard the results of reflection as having, in and of themselves, a reality superior to that of the material of any other mode of experience. The commonest assumption of philosophies, common even to philosophies very different from one another, is the assumption of the identity of objects of knowledge and ultimately real objects. The assumption is so deep that it is usually not expressed; it is taken for granted as something so fundamental that it does not need to be stated. A technical example of the view is found in the contention of the Cartesian school—including Spinoza—that emotion as well as sense is but confused thought which when it becomes clear and definite or reaches its goal is *cognition*. That esthetic and moral experience reveal traits of real things as truly as does intellectual experience, that poetry may have a metaphysical import as well as science, is rarely affirmed, and when it is asserted, the statement is likely to be meant in some mystical or esoteric sense rather than in a straightforward everyday sense.

Suppose however that we start with no presuppositions save that what is experienced, since it is a manifestation of nature, may, and indeed, must be used as testimony of the characteristics of natural events. Upon this basis, reverie and desire are pertinent for a philosophic theory of the true nature of things; the possibilities present in imagination that are not found in observation, are something to be taken into account. The features of objects reached by scientific or reflective experiencing are important, but so are all the phenomena of magic, myth, politics, painting, and penitentiaries. The phenomena of social life are as relevant to the problem of the relation of the individual and universal as are those of logic; the existence in political organization of boundaries and barriers, of centralization, of interaction across boundaries, of expansion and absorption, will be quite as important for metaphysical theories of the discrete and the continuous as is anything derived from chemical analysis. The existence of ignorance as well as of wisdom, of error and even insanity as well as of truth will be taken into account.

That is to say, nature is construed in such a way that all these things, since they are actual, are naturally possible; they are not explained away into mere "appearance" in contrast with reality. Illusions are illusions, but the occurrence of illusions is not an illusion, but a genuine reality. What is really "in" experience extends much further than that which at any time is *known*. From the standpoint of knowledge, objects must be distinct; their traits must be explicit; the vague and unrevealed is a limitation. Hence whenever the habit of identifying reality with the object of knowledge as such prevails, the obscure and vague are explained away. It is important for philosophic theory to be aware that the distinct and evident are prized and why they are. But it is equally important to note that the dark and twilight abound. For in any object of primary experience there are always potentialities which are not explicit; any object that is overt is charged with possible consequences that are hidden; the most overt act has factors which are not explicit. Strain thought as far as we may and not all consequences can be foreseen or made an express or known part of reflection and decision. In the face of such empirical facts, the assumption that nature in itself is all of the same kind, all distinct, explicit and evident, having no hidden possibilities, no novelties or obscurities, is possible only on the basis of a philosophy which at some point draws an arbitrary line between nature and experience.

In the assertion (implied here) that the great vice of philosophy is an arbitrary "intellectualism," there is no slight cast upon intelligence and reason. By "intellectualism" as an indictment is meant the theory that all experiencing is a mode of knowing, and that all subject-matter, all nature, is, in principle, to be reduced and transformed till it is defined in terms identical with the characteristics presented by refined objects of science as such. The assumption of "intellectualism" goes contrary to the facts of what is primarily experienced. For things are objects to be treated, used, acted upon and with, enjoyed and endured, even more than things to be known. They are things *had* before they are things cognized.

The isolation of traits characteristic of objects known, and then defined as the sole ultimate realities, accounts for the denial to nature of the characters which make things lovable and contemptible, beautiful and ugly, adorable and awful. It accounts for the belief that nature is an indifferent, dead mechanism; it explains why characteristics that are the valuable and valued traits of objects in actual experience are thought to create a fundamentally troublesome philosophical problem. Recognition of their genuine and primary reality does not signify that no thought and knowledge enter in when things are loved, desired and striven for; it signifies that the former are subordinate, so that the genuine problem is how and why, to what effect, things thus experienced are transformed into objects in which cognized traits are supreme and affectional and volitional traits incidental and subsidiary.

"Intellectualism" as a sovereign method of philosophy is so foreign to the facts of primary experience that it not only compels recourse to non-empirical method, but it ends in making knowledge, conceived as ubiquitous, itself inexplicable. If we start from primary experience, occurring as it does chiefly in modes of action and undergoing, it is easy to see what knowledge contributes—namely, the possibility of intelligent administration of the elements of doing and suffering. ,We are about something, and it is well to know what we are about, as the common phrase has it. To be intelligent in action and in suffering (enjoyment too) yields satisfaction even when conditions cannot be controlled. But when there is possibility of control, knowledge is the sole agency of its realization. Given this element of knowledge in primary experience, it is not difficult to understand how it may develop from a subdued and subsidiary factor into a dominant character. Doing and suffering, experimenting and putting ourselves in the way of having our sense and nervous system acted upon in ways that yield material for reflection, may reverse the original situation in which knowing and thinking were subservient to action-undergoing. And when we trace the genesis of knowing along this line, we also see that knowledge has a function and office in bettering and enriching the subject-matters of crude experience. We are prepared to understand what we are about on a grander scale, and to understand what happens even when we seem to be the hapless puppets of uncontrollable fate. But knowledge that is ubiquitous, all-inclusive and all-monopolizing, ceases to have meaning in losing all context; that it does not appear to do so when made supreme and self-sufficient is because it is literally impossible to exclude that context of non-cognitive but experienced subject-matter which gives what is *known* its import.

While this matter is dealt with at some length in further chapters of this volume, there is one point worth mentioning here. When intellectual experience and its material are taken to be primary, the cord that binds experience and nature is cut. That the physiological organism with its structures, whether in man or in the lower animals, is concerned with making adaptations and uses of material in the interest of maintenance of the life-process, cannot be denied. The brain and nervous system are primarily organs of action-undergoing; biologically, it can be asserted without contravention that primary experience is of a corresponding type. Hence, unless there is breach of historic and natural continuity, cognitive experience must originate within that of a non-cognitive sort. And unless we start from knowing as a factor in action and undergoing we are inevitably committed to the intrusion of an extra-natural, if not a supernatural, agency and principle. That professed non-supernaturalists so readily endow the organism with powers that have no basis in natural events is a fact so peculiar that it would be inexplicable were it not for the inertia of the traditional schools. Otherwise it would be evident that the only way to maintain the doctrine of natural continuity is to recognize the secondary and derived character aspects of experience of the intellectual or cognitive. But so deeply grounded is the opposite position in the entire philosophic tradition, that it is probably not surprising that philosophers are loath to admit a fact which when admitted compels an extensive reconstruction in form and content.

We have spoken of the difference which acceptance of empirical method in philosophy makes in the problem of subject-object and in that of the alleged all-inclusiveness of cognitive experience.[1] There is an intimate connection between these two problems. When real objects are identified, point for point, with knowledge-objects, all affectional and volitional objects are inevitably excluded from the "real" world, and are compelled to find refuge in the privacy of an experiencing subject or mind. Thus the notion of the ubiquity of all comprehensive cognitive experience results by a necessary logic in setting up a hard and fast wall between the experiencing subject and that nature which is experienced. The self becomes not merely a pilgrim but an unnaturalized and unnaturalizable alien in the world. The only way to avoid a sharp separation between the mind which is the centre of the processes of experiencing and the natural world which is experienced is to acknowledge that all modes of experiencing are ways in which some genuine traits of nature come to manifest realization.

The favoring of cognitive objects and their characteris-

[1] To avoid misapprehension, it may be well to add a statement on the latter point. It is not denied that any experienced subject-matter whatever may *become* an object of reflection and cognitive inspection. But the emphasis is upon "become"; the cognitive never *is* all-inclusive: that is, when the material of a prior non-cognitive experience is the object of knowledge, it and the act of knowing are themselves included within a new and and wider non-cognitive experience—and *this* situation can never be transcended. It is only when the temporal character of experienced things is forgotten that the idea of the total "transcendence" of knowledge is asserted.

tics at the expense of traits that excite desire, command action and produce passion, is a special instance of a principle of selective emphasis which introduces partiality and partisanship into philosophy. Selective emphasis, with accompanying omission and rejection, is the heart-beat of mental life. To object to the operation is to discard all thinking. But in ordinary matters and in scientific inquiries, we always retain the sense that the material chosen is selected for a purpose; there is no idea of denying what is left out, for what is omitted is merely that which is not relevant to the particular problem and purpose in hand.

But in philosophies, this limiting condition is often wholly ignored. It is not noted and remembered that the favored subject-matter is chosen for a purpose and that what is left out is just as real and important in its own characteristic context. It tends to be assumed that because qualities that figure in poetical discourse and those that are central in friendship do not figure in scientific inquiry, they have no reality, at least not the kind of unquestionable reality attributed to the mathematical, mechanical or magneto-electric properties that constitute matter. It is natural to men to take that which is of chief value to them at the time as *the* real. Reality and superior value are equated. In ordinary experience this fact does no particular harm; it is at once compensated for by turning to other things which since they also present value are equally real. But philosophy often exhibits a cataleptic rigidity in attachment to that phase of the total objects of experience which has become especially dear to a philosopher. *It* is real at all hazards and only it; other things are real only in some secondary and Pickwickian sense.

For example, certainty, assurance, is immensely valuable in a world as full of uncertainty and peril as that in which we live. As a result whatever is capable of certainty is assumed to constitute ultimate Being, and everything else is said to be merely phenomenal, or, in extreme cases, illusory. The arbitrary character of the "reality" that emerges is seen in the fact that very different objects are selected by different philosophers. These may be mathematical entities, states of consciousness, or sense data. That is, whatever strikes a philosopher from the angle of the particular problem that presses on him as being self-evident and hence completely assured, is selected by him to constitute reality. The honorable and dignified have ranked with the mundanely certain in determining philosophic definitions of the real. Scholasticism considered that the True and the Good, along with Unity, were the marks of Being as such. In the face of a problem, thought always seeks to unify things otherwise fragmentary and discrepant. Deliberately action strives to attain the good; knowledge is reached when truth is grasped. Then the goals of our efforts, the things that afford satisfaction and peace under conditions of tension and unrest, are converted into that which alone is ultimate real Being. Ulterior functions are treated as original properties.

Another aspect of the same erection of objects of selective preference into exclusive realities is seen in the addiction of philosophers to what is simple, their love for "elements." Gross experience is loaded with the tangled and complex; hence philosophy hurries away from it to search out something so simple that the mind can rest trustfully in it, knowing that it has no surprises in store, that it will not spring anything to make trouble, that it will stay put, having no potentialities in reserve. There is again the predilection for mathematical objects; there is Spinoza with his assurance that a true idea carries truth intrinsic in its bosom; Locke with his "simple idea"; Hume with his "impression"; the English neo-realist with his ultimate atomic data; the American neo-realist with his ready-made essences.

Another striking example of the fallacy of selective emphasis is found in the hypnotic influence exercised by the conception of the eternal. The permanent enables us to rest, it gives peace; the variable, the changing, is a constant challenge. Where things change something is hanging over us. It is a threat of trouble. Even when change is marked by hope of better things to come, that hope tends to project its object as something to stay once for all when it arrives. Moreover we can deal with the variable and precarious only by means of the stable and constant; "invariants"—for the time being—are as much a necessity in practice for bringing something to pass as they are in mathematical functions. The permanent answers genuine emotional, practical and intellectual requirements. But the demand and the response which meets it are empirically always found in a special context; they arise because of a particular need and in order to effect specifiable consequences. Philosophy, thinking at large, allows itself to be diverted into absurd search for an intellectual philosopher's stone of absolutely wholesale generalizations, thus isolating that which is permanent in a function and for a purpose, and converting it into the intrinsically eternal, conceived either (as Aristotle conceived it) as that which is the same at all times, or as that which is indifferent to time, out of time.

This bias toward treating objects selected because of their value in some special context as the "real," in a superior and invidious sense, testifies to an empirical fact of importance. Philosophical simplifications are due to choice, and choice marks an interest *moral* in the broad sense of concern for what is good. Our constant and unescapable concern is with prosperity and adversity, success and failure, achievement and frustration, good and bad. Since we are creatures with lives to live, and find ourselves within an uncertain environment, we are constructed to note and judge in terms of bearing upon weal and woe—upon value. Acknowledgment of this fact is a very different thing, however, from the transformation effected by philosophers of the traits they find good (simplicity, certainty, nobility, permanence, etc.) into fixed traits of real Being. The former presents something *to be accomplished,* to be brought about by the *actions* in which choice is manifested and made genuine. The latter ignores the need of action to effect the better and to prove the honesty of choice; it converts what is desired into antecedent and final features of a reality which is supposed to need only logical warrant in order to be contemplatively enjoyed as true Being.

For reflection the eventual is always better or worse than the given. But since it would also be better if the eventual good were now given, the philosopher, belonging by status to a leisure class relieved from the urgent necessity of dealing with conditions, converts the eventual into some kind of Being, something which *is*, even if it does not *exist*. Permanence, real essence, totality, order, unity, rationality, the *unum, verum et bonum* of the classic tradition, are eulogistic predicates. When we find such terms used to describe the foundations and proper conclusions of a philosophic system, there is ground for suspecting that an artificial simplification of existence has been performed. Reflection determining preference for an eventual good has dialectically wrought a miracle of transubstantiation.

Selective emphasis, choice, is inevitable whenever reflection occurs. This is not an evil. Deception comes only when the presence and operation of choice is concealed, disguised, denied. Empirical method finds and points to the operation of choice as it does to any other event. Thus it protects us from conversion of eventual functions into antecedent existence: a conversion that may be said to be *the* philosophic fallacy, whether it be performed in behalf of mathematical subsistences, esthetic essences, the purely physical order of nature, or God. The present writer does not profess any greater candor of intent than animates fellow philosophers. But the pursuance of an empirical method, is, he submits, the only way to secure execution of candid intent. Whatever enters into choice, determining its need and giving it guidance, an empirical method frankly indicates what it is for; and the fact of choice, with its workings and consequences, an empirical method points out with equal openness.

The adoption of an empirical method is no guarantee that all the things relevant to any particular conclusion will actually be found, or that when found they will be correctly shown and communicated. But empirical method points out when and where and how things of a designated description have been arrived at. It places before others a map of the road that has been travelled; they may accordingly, if they will, re-travel the road to inspect the landscape for themselves. Thus the findings of one may be rectified and extended by the findings of others, with as much assurance as is humanly possible of confirmation, extension and rectification. The adoption of empirical method thus procures for philosophic reflection something of that cooperative tendency toward consensus which marks inquiry in the natural sciences. The scientific investigator convinces others not by the plausibility of his definitions and the cogency of his dialectic, but by placing before them the specified course of searchings, doings and arrivals, in consequence of which certain things have been found. His appeal is for others to traverse a similar course, so as to see how what they find corresponds with his report.

Honest empirical method will state when and where and why the act of selection took place, and thus enable others to repeat it and test its worth. Selective choice, denoted as an empirical event, reveals the basis and bearing of intellectual simplifications; they then cease to be of such a self-enclosed nature as to be affairs only of opinion and argument, admitting no alternatives save complete acceptance or rejection. Choice that is disguised or denied is the source of those astounding differences of philosophic belief that startle the beginner and that become the plaything of the expert. Choice that is avowed is an experiment to be tried on its merits and tested by its results. Under all the captions that are called immediate knowledge, or self-sufficient certitude of belief, whether logical, esthetic or epistemological, there is something selected for a purpose, and hence not simple, not self-evident and not intrinsically eulogizable. State the purpose so that it may be re-experienced, and its value and the pertinency of selection undertaken in its behalf may be tested. The purport of thinking, scientific and philosophic, is not to eliminate choice but to render it less arbitrary and more significant. It loses its arbitrary character when its quality and consequences are such as to commend themselves to the reflection of others after they have betaken themselves to the situations indicated; it becomes significant when reason for the choice is found to be weighty and its consequences momentous. When choice is avowed, others can repeat the course of the experience; it is an experiment to be tried, not an automatic safety device.

This particular affair is referred to here not so much as matter of doctrine as to afford an illustration of the nature of empirical method. Truth or falsity depends upon what men find when they warily perform the experiment of observing reflective events. An empirical finding is refuted not by denial that one finds things to be thus and so, but by giving directions for a course of experience that results in finding its opposite to be the case. To convince of error as well as to lead to truth is to assist another to see and find something which he hitherto has failed to find and recognize. All of the wit and subtlety of reflection and logic find scope in the elaboration and conveying of directions that intelligibly point out a course to be followed. Every system of philosophy presents the consequences of some such experiment. As experiments, each has contributed something of worth to our observation of the events and qualities of experienceable objects. Some harsh criticisms of traditional philosophy have already been suggested; others will doubtless follow. But the criticism is not directed at the experiments; it is aimed at the denial to them by the philosophic tradition of selective experimental quality, a denial which has isolated them from their actual context and function, and has thereby converted potential illuminations into arbitrary assertions.

This discussion of empirical method has had a double content. On one hand, it has tried to make clear, from the analogy of empirical method in scientific inquiry, what the method signifies (and does *not* signify) for philosophy.

Such a discussion would, however, have little definite import unless the *difference* that is made in philosophy by the adoption of empirical method is pointed out. For that reason, we have considered some typical ways and important places in which traditional philosophies have gone astray through failure to connect their reflective results with the affairs of every-day primary experience. Three sources of large fallacies have been mentioned, each containing within itself many more sub-varieties than have been hinted at. The three are the complete separation of subject and object, (of *what* is experienced from *how* it is experienced); the exaggeration of the features of known objects at the expense of the qualities of objects of enjoyment and trouble, friendship and human association, art and industry; and the exclusive isolation of the results of various types of selective simplification which are undertaken for diverse unavowed purposes.

It does not follow that the products of these philosophies which have taken the wrong, because non-empirical, method are of no value or little worth for a philosophy that pursues a strictly empirical method. The contrary is the case, for no philosopher can get away from experience even if he wants to. The most fantastic views ever entertained by superstitious people had some basis in experienced fact; they can be explained by one who knows enough about them and about the conditions under which they were formed. And philosophers have been not more but less superstitious than their fellows; they have been, as a class, unusually reflective and inquiring. If some of their products have been fantasies, it was not because they did not, even unwittingly, start from empirical method; it was not wholly because they substituted unchecked imagination for thought. No, the trouble has been that they have failed to note the empirical needs that generate their problems, and have failed to return the refined products back to the context of actual experience, there to receive their check, inherit their full content of meaning, and give illumination and guidance in the immediate perplexities which originally occasioned reflection.

The chapters which follow make no pretence, accordingly, of starting to philosophize afresh as if there were no philosophies already in existence, or as if their conclusions were empirically worthless. Rather the subsequent discussions rely, perhaps excessively so, upon the main results of great philosophic systems, endeavoring to point out their elements of strength and of weakness when their conclusions are employed (as the refined objects of all reflection must be employed) as guides back to the subject-matter of crude, everyday experience.

Our primary experience as it comes is of little value for purposes of analysis and control, crammed as it is with things that need analysis and control. The very existence of reflection is proof of its deficiencies. Just as ancient astronomy and physics were of little scientific worth, because, owing to the lack of apparatus and techniques of experimental analysis, they had to take the things of primary observation at their face value, so "common-sense" philosophy usually repeats current conventionalities. What is averred to be implicit reliance upon what is given in common experience is likely to be merely an appeal to prejudice to gain support for some fanaticism or defence for some relic of conservative tradition which is beginning to be questioned.

The trouble, then, with the conclusions of philosophy is not in the least that they are results of reflection and theorizing. It is rather that philosophers have borrowed from various sources the conclusions of special analyses, particularly of some ruling science of the day, and imported them direct into philosophy, with no check by either the empirical objects from which they arose or those to which the conclusions in question point. Thus Plato trafficked with the Pythagoreans and imported mathematical concepts; Descartes and Spinoza took over the presuppositions of geometrical reasoning; Locke imported into the theory of mind the Newtonian physical corpuscles, converting them into given "simple ideas"; Hegel borrowed and generalized without limit the rising historical method of his day; contemporary English philosophy has imported from mathematics the notion of primitive indefinable propositions, and given them a content from Locke's simple ideas, which had in the meantime become part of the stock in trade of psychological science.

Well, why not, as long as what is borrowed has a sound scientific status? Because in scientific inquiry, refined methods justify themselves by opening up new fields of subject-matter for exploration; they create new techniques of observation and experimentation. Thus when the Michelson-Moley experiment disclosed, as a matter of gross experience, facts which did not agree with the results of accepted physical laws, physicists did not think for a moment of denying the validity of what was found in that experience, even though it rendered questionable an elaborate intellectual apparatus and system. The coincidence of the bands of the interferometer was accepted at its face value in spite of its incompatibility with Newtonian physics. Because scientific inquirers accepted it at its face value they at once set to work to reconstruct their theories; they questioned their reflective premisses, not the full "reality" of what they saw. This task of re-adjustment compelled not only new reasonings and calculations in the development of a more comprehensive theory, but opened up new ways of inquiry into experienced subject-matter. Not for a moment did they think of explaining away the features of an object in gross experience because it was not in logical harmony with theory—as philosophers have so often done. Had they done so, they would have stultified science and shut themselves off from new problems and new findings in subject-matter. In short, the material of refined scientific method is continuous with that of the actual world as it is concretely experienced.

But when philosophers transfer into their theories bodily and as finalities the refined conclusions they borrow from the sciences, whether logic, mathematics or physics, these results are not employed to reveal new subject-matters and illuminate old ones of gross experience; they are employed to cast discredit on the latter and to generate new and artificial problems regarding the reality and validity of the things of gross experience. Thus the discoveries of psychologies taken out of their own empirical context are in philosophy employed to cast doubt upon the reality of things external to mind and to selves, things and properties that are perhaps the most salient characteristics of ordinary experience. Similarly, the discoveries and methods of physical science, the concepts of mass, space, motion, have been adopted wholesale in isolation by philosophers in such a way as to make dubious and even incredible the reality of the affections, purposes and enjoyments of concrete experience. The objects of mathematics, symbols of relations having no explicit reference to actual existence, efficacious in the territory to which mathematical technique applies, have been employed in philosophy to determine the priority of essences to existence, and to create the insoluble problem of why pure essence ever descends into the tangles and tortuosities of existence.

What empirical method exacts of philosophy is two things: First, that refined methods and products be traced back to their origin in primary experience, in all its heterogeneity and fullness; so that the needs and problems out of which they arise and which they have to satisfy be acknowledged. Secondly, that the secondary methods and conclusions be brought back to the things of ordinary experience, in all their coarseness and crudity, for verification. In this way, the methods of analytic reflection yield material which form the ingredients of a method of designation, denotation, in philosophy. A scientific work in physics or astronomy gives a record of calculations and deductions that were derived from past observations and experiments. But it is more than a record; it is also an indication, an assignment, of further observations and experiments to be performed. No scientific report would get a hearing if it did not describe the apparatus by means of which experiments were carried on and results obtained; not that apparatus is worshipped, but because this procedure tells other inquirers how they are to go to work to get results which will agree or disagree in their experience with those previously arrived at, and thus confirm, modify and rectify the latter. The recorded scientific result is in effect a *designation* of a method to be followed and a *prediction* of what will be found when specified observations are set on foot. That is all a philosophy can be or do. In the chapters that follow I have undertaken a revision and reconstruction of the conclusions, the reports, of a number of historic philosophic systems, in order that they may be usable methods by which one may go to his own experience, and, discerning what is found by use of the method, come to understand better what is already within the common experience of mankind.

There is a special service which the study of philosophy may render. Empirically pursued it will not be a study of philosophy but a study, by means of philosophy, of life-experience. But this experience is already overlaid and saturated with the products of the reflection of past generations and by-gone ages. It is filled with interpretations, classifications, due to sophisticated thought, which have become incorporated into what seems to be fresh, naïve empirical material. It would take more wisdom than is possessed by the wisest historic scholar to track all of these absorbed borrowings to their original sources. If we may for the moment call these materials prejudices (even if they are true, as long as their source and authority is unknown), then philosophy is a critique of prejudices. These incorporated results of past reflection, welded into the genuine materials of first-hand experience, may become organs of enrichment if they are detected and reflected upon. If they are not detected, they often obfuscate and distort. Clarification and emancipation follow when they are detected and cast out; and one great object of philosophy is to accomplish this task.

An empirical philosophy is in any case a kind of intellectual disrobing. We cannot permanently divest ourselves of the intellectual habits we take on and wear when we assimilate the culture of our own time and place. But intelligent furthering of culture demands that we take some of them off, that we inspect them critically to see what they are made of and what wearing them does to us. We cannot achieve recovery of primitive naïveté. But there is attainable a cultivated naïveté of eye, ear and thought, one that can be acquired only through the discipline of severe thought. If the chapters which follow contribute to an artful innocence and simplicity they will have served their purpose.

I am loath to conclude without reference to the larger liberal humane value of philosophy when pursued with empirical method. The most serious indictment to be brought against non-empirical philosophies is that they have cast a cloud over the things of ordinary experience. They have not been content to rectify them. They have discredited them at large. In casting aspersion upon the things of everyday experience, the things of action and affection and social intercourse, they have done something worse than fail to give these affairs the intelligent direction they so much need. It would not matter much if philosophy had been reserved as a luxury of only a few thinkers. We endure many luxuries. The serious matter is that philosophies have denied that common experience is capable of developing from within itself methods which will secure direction for itself and will create inherent standards of judgment and value. No one knows how many of the evils and deficiencies that are pointed to as reasons for flight from experience are themselves due to the disregard of experience shown by those peculiarly reflective. To Waste of time and energy, to disillusionment with life that attends every deviation from concrete experience must be added the tragic failure to realize the value that intelligent search could reveal and mature among the things of ordinary experience. I cannot calculate how much of current cynicism, indifference and pessimism is due to these causes in the deflection of intelligence they have brought about. It has even become in many circles a sign of lack of sophistication to imagine that life is or can be a fountain of cheer and happiness. Philosophies no more than religions can be acquitted of responsibility for bringing this result to pass. The transcendental philosopher has probably done more than the professed sensualist and materialist to obscure the potentialities of daily experience for joy and for self-regulation. If what is written in these pages has no other result than creating and promoting a respect for concrete human experience and its potentialities, I shall be content.

Interpretation and the Sciences of Man

CHARLES TAYLOR

I

i

IS THERE A SENSE IN WHICH INTERPRETATION IS ESSENTIAL TO explanation in the sciences of man? The view that it is, that there is an unavoidably "hermeneutical" component in the sciences of man, goes back to Dilthey. But recently the question has come again to the fore, for instance, in the work of Gadamer,[1] in Ricoeur's interpretation of Freud,[2] and in the writings of Habermas.[3]

Interpretation, in the sense relevant to hermeneutics, is an attempt to make clear, to make sense of an object of study. This object must, therefore, be a text, or a text-analogue, which in some way is confused, incomplete, cloudy, seemingly contradictory—in one way or another, unclear. The interpretation aims to bring to light an underlying coherence or sense.

This means that any science which can be called "hermeneutical," even in an extended sense, must be dealing with one or another of the confusingly interrelated forms of meaning. Let us try to see a little more clearly what this involves.

1) We need, first, an object or field of objects, about which we can speak in terms of coherence or its absence, of making sense or nonsense.

2) Second, we need to be able to make a distinction, even if only a relative one, between the sense or coherence made, and its embodiment in a particular field of carriers or signifiers. For otherwise, the task of making clear what is fragmentary or confused would be radically impossible. No sense could be given to this idea. We have to be able to make for our interpretations claims of

Charles Taylor, "Interpretation and the Sciences of Man," *Review of Metaphysics* 25 (1971): 3–34, 45–51.

Originally published in the *Review of Metaphysics*, Volume 25 (1971), reprinted with permission.

the order: the meaning confusedly present in this text or text-analogue is clearly expressed here. The meaning, in other words, is one which admits of more than one expression, and, in this sense, a distinction must be possible between meaning and expression.

The point of the above qualification, that this distinction may be only relative, is that there are cases where no clear, unambiguous, nonarbitrary line can be drawn between what is said and its expression. It can be plausibly argued (I think convincingly although there isn't space to go into it here) that this is the normal and fundamental condition of meaningful expression, that exact synonymy, or equivalence of meaning, is a rare and localized achievement of specialized languages or uses of civilization. But this, if true (and I think it is), doesn't do away with the distinction between meaning and expression. Even if there is an important sense in which a meaning re-expressed in a new medium can not be declared identical, this by no means entails that we can give no sense to the project of expressing a meaning in a new way. It does of course raise an interesting and difficult question about what can be meant by expressing it in a clearer way: what is the "it" which is clarified if equivalence is denied? I hope to return to this in examining interpretation in the sciences of man.

Hence the object of a science of interpretation must be describable in terms of sense and nonsense, coherence and its absence; and must admit of a distinction between meaning and its expression.

3) There is also a third condition it must meet. We can speak of sense or coherence, and of their different embodiments, in connection with such phenomena as gestalts, or patterns in rock formations, or snow crystals, where the notion of expression has no real warrant. What is lacking here is the notion of a subject for whom these meanings are. Without such a subject, the choice of criteria of sameness and difference, the choice among the different forms of coherence which can be identified in a given pattern, among the different conceptual fields in which it can be seen, is arbitrary.

In a text or text-analogue, on the other hand, we are trying to make explicit the meaning expressed, and this means expressed by or for a subject or subjects. The notion of expression refers us to that of a subject. The identification of the subject is by no means necessarily unproblematical, as we shall see further on; it may be one of the most difficult problems, an area in which prevailing epistemological prejudice may blind us to the nature of our object of study. I think this has been the case, as I will show below. And moreover, the identification of a subject does not assure us of a clear and absolute distinction between meaning and expression as we saw above. But any such distinction, even a relative one, is without any anchor at all, is totally arbitrary, without appeal to a subject.

The object of a science of interpretation must thus have: sense, distinguishable from its expression, which is for or by a subject.

ii

Before going on to see in what way, if any, these conditions are realized in the sciences of man, I think it would be useful to set out more clearly what rides on this question, why it matters whether or not we think of the sciences of man as hermeneutical, what the issue is at stake here.

The issue here is at root an epistemological one. But it is inextricable from an ontological one, and, hence, cannot but be relevant to our notions of science and of the proper conduct of inquiry. We might say that it is an ontological issue which has been argued ever since the seventeenth century in terms of epistemological considerations which have appeared to some to be unanswerable.

The case could be put in these terms: what are the criteria of judgment in a hermeneutical science? A successful interpretation is one which makes clear the meaning originally present in a confused, fragmentary, cloudy form. But how does one know that this interpretation is correct? Presumably because it makes sense of the original text: what is strange, mystifying, puzzling, contradictory is no longer so, is accounted for. The interpretation appeals throughout to our understanding of the "language" of expression, which understanding allows us to see that this expression is puzzling, that it is in contradiction to that other, etc., and that these difficulties are cleared up when the meaning is expressed in a new way.

But this appeal to our understanding seems to be crucially inadequate. What if someone does not "see" the adequacy of our interpretation, does not accept our reading? We try to show him how it makes sense of the original non- or partial sense. But for him to follow us he must read the original language as we do, he must recognize these expressions as puzzling in a certain way, and hence be looking for a solution to our problem. If he does not, what can we do? The answer, it would seem, can only be more of the same. We have to show him through the reading of other expressions why this expression must be read in the way we propose. But success here requires that he follow us in these other readings, and so on, it would seem, potentially forever. We cannot escape an ultimate appeal to a common understanding of the expressions, of the "language" involved. This is one way of trying to express what has been called the "hermeneutical circle." What we are trying to establish is a certain reading of text or expressions, and what we appeal to as our grounds for this reading can only be other readings. The circle can also be put in terms of part-whole relations: we are trying to establish a reading for the whole text, and for this we appeal to readings of its partial expressions; and yet because we are dealing with meaning, with making sense, where expressions only make sense or not in relation to others, the readings of partial expressions depend on those of others, and ultimately of the whole.

Put in forensic terms, as we started to do above, we can only convince an interlocutor if at some point he shares our understanding of the language concerned. If he does not, there is no further step to take in rational argument; we can try to awaken these intuitions in him, or we can simply give up; argument will advance us no further. But of course the forensic predicament can be transferred into my own judging: if I am this ill-equipped to convince a stubborn interlocutor, how can I convince myself? how can I be sure? Maybe my intuitions are wrong or distorted, maybe I am locked into a circle of illusion.

Now one, and perhaps the only sane response to this would be to say that such uncertainty is an ineradicable part of our epistemological predicament. That even to characterize it as "uncertainty" is to adopt an absurdly severe criterion of "certainty," which deprives the concept of any sensible use. But this has not been the only or even the main response of our philosophical tradition. And it is another response which has had an important and far-reaching effect on the sciences of man. The demand has been for a level of certainty which can only be attained by breaking beyond the circle.

There are two ways in which this break-out has been envisaged. The first might be called the "rationalist" one and could be thought to reach a culmination in Hegel. It does not involve a negation of intuition, or of our understanding of meaning, but rather aspires to attainment of an understanding of such clarity that it would carry with it the certainty of the undeniable. In Hegel's case, for instance, our full understanding of the whole in "thought" carries with it a grasp of its inner necessity, such that we see how it could not be otherwise. No higher grade of certainty is conceivable. For this aspiration the word "break-out" is badly chosen; the aim is rather to bring understanding to an inner clarity which is absolute.

The other way, which we can call "empiricist," is a genuine attempt to go beyond the circle of our own interpretations, to get beyond subjectivity. The attempt is to reconstruct knowledge in such a way that there is no need to make final appeal to readings or judgments which can not be checked further. That is why the basic building block of knowledge on this view is the impression, or sense-datum, a unit of information which is not the deliverance of a judgment, which has by definition no element in it of reading or interpretation, which is a brute datum. The highest ambition would be to build our knowledge from such building blocks by judgments which could be anchored in a certainty beyond subjective intuition. This is what underlies the attraction of the notion of the association of ideas, or if the same procedure is viewed as a method, induction. If the original acquisition of the units of information is not the fruit of judgment or interpretation, then the constatation that two such elements occur together need not either be the fruit of interpretation, of a reading or intuition which cannot be checked. For if the occurrence of a single element is a brute datum, then so is the co-occurrence of two such elements. The path to true knowledge would then repose crucially on the correct recording of such co-occurrences.

This is what lies behind an ideal of verification which is central to an important tradition in the philosophy of science, whose main contemporary protagonists are the logical empiricists. Verification must be grounded ultimately in the acquisition of brute data. By "brute data," I mean here and throughout data whose validity cannot be questioned by offering another interpretation or reading, data whose credibility cannot be confounded or undermined by further reasoning.[4] If such a difference of interpretation can arise over given data, then it must be possible to structure the argument so as to distinguish the basic, brute data from the inferences made on the basis of them.

The inferences themselves, of course, to be valid must similarly be beyond the challenge of a rival interpretation. Here the logical empiricists added to the rival interpretation. Here the logical empiricists added to the armory of traditional empiricism which set great store by the method of induction, the whole domain of logical and mathematical inference which had been central to the rationalist position (with Leibniz at least, although not with Hegel), and which offered another brand of unquestionable certainty.

Of course, mathematical inference and empirical verification were combined in such a way that two theories or more could be verified of the same domain of facts. But this was a consequence to which logical empiricism was willing to accommodate itself. As for the surplus meaning in a theory which could not be rigorously co-ordinated with brute data, it was considered to be quite outside the logic of verification.

As a theory of perception, this epistemology gave rise to all sorts of problems, not least of which was the perpetual threat of skepticism and solipsism inseparable from a conception of the basic data of knowledge as brute data, beyond investigation. As a theory of perception, however, it seems largely a thing of the past, in spite of a surprising recrudescence in the Anglo-Saxon world in the 'thirties and 'forties. But there is no doubt that it goes marching on, among other places, as a theory of how the human mind and human knowledge actually function.

In a sense, the contemporary period has seen a better, more rigorous statement of what this epistemology is about in the form of computer-influenced theories of intelligence. These try to model intelligence as consisting of operations on machine-recognizable input which could themselves be matched by programs which could be run on machines. The machine criterion provides us with our assurance against an appeal to intuition or interpretations which cannot be understood by fully explicit procedures operating on brute data—the input.[5]

The progress of natural science has lent great credibility to this epistemology, since it can be plausibly reconstructed on this model, as for instance has been done by the logical empiricists. And, of course, the temptation has been overwhelming to reconstruct the sciences of man on the same model; or rather to launch them in lines of inquiry that fit this paradigm, since they are constantly said to be in their "infancy." Psychology, where an earlier vogue of behaviorism is being replaced by a boom of computer-based models, is far from the only case.

The form this epistemological bias—one might say obsession—takes is different for different sciences. Later I would like to look at a particular case, the study of politics, where the issue can be followed out. But in general, the empiricist orientation must be hostile to a conduct of inquiry which is based on interpretation, and which encounters the hermeneutical circle as this was characterized above. This cannot meet the requirements of intersubjective, non-arbitrary verification which it considers essential to science. And along with the epistemological stance goes the ontological belief that reality must be susceptible to understanding and explanation by science so understood. From this follows a certain set of notions of what the sciences of man must be.

On the other hand, many, including myself, would like to argue that these notions about the sciences of man are sterile, that we cannot come to understand important dimensions of human life within the bounds set by this epistemological orientation. This dispute is of course familiar to all in at least some of its ramifications. What I want to claim is that the issue can be fruitfully posed in terms of the notion of interpretation as I began to outline it above.

I think this way of putting the question is useful because it allows us at once to bring to the surface the powerful epistemological beliefs which underlie the orthodox view of the sciences of man in our academy, and to make explicit the notion of our epistemological predicament implicit in the opposing thesis. This is in fact rather more way-out and shocking to the tradition of scientific thought than is often admitted or realized by the opponents of narrow scientism. It may not strengthen the case of the opposition to bring out fully what is involved in a hermeneutical science as far as convincing waverers is concerned, but a gain in clarity is surely worth a thinning of the ranks—at least in philosophy.

iii

Before going on to look at the case of political science, it might be worth asking another question: why should we even pose the question whether the sciences of man are hermeneutical? What gives us the idea in the first place that men and their actions constitute an object or a series of objects which meet the conditions outlined above?

The answer is that on the phenomenological level or that of ordinary speech (and the two converge for the purposes of this argument) a certain notion of meaning has an essential place in the characterization of human behavior. This is the sense in which we speak of a situation, an action, a demand, a prospect having a certain meaning for a person.

Now it is frequently thought that "meaning" is used here in a sense which is a kind of illegitimate extension from the notion of linguistic meaning. Whether it can be considered an extension or not is another matter; it certainly differs from linguistic meaning. But it would be very hard to argue that it is an illegitimate use of the term.

When we speak of the "meaning" of a given predicament, we are using a concept which has the following articulation. a) Meaning is for a subject: it is not the meaning of the situation *in vacuo*, but its meaning for a subject, a specific subject, a group of subjects, or perhaps what its meaning is for the human subject as such (even though particular humans might be reproached with not admitting or realizing this). b) Meaning is of something; that is, we can distinguish between a given element—situation, action, or whatever—and its meaning. But this is not to say that they are physically separable. Rather we are dealing with two descriptions of the element, in one of which it is characterized in terms of its meaning for the subject. But the relations between the two descriptions are not symmetrical. For, on the one hand, the description in terms of meaning cannot be unless descriptions of the other kind apply as well; or put differently, there can be no meaning without a substrate. But on the other hand, it may be that the same meaning may be borne by another substrate—e.g., a situation with the same meaning may be realized in different physical conditions. There is a necessary role for a potentially substitutable substrate; or all meanings are of something.

And thirdly, c) things only have meaning in a field, that is, in relation to the meanings of other things. This means that there is no such thing as a single, unrelated meaningful element; and it means that changes in the other meanings in the field can involve changes in the given element. Meanings can't be identified except in relation to others, and in this way resemble words. The meaning of a word depends, for instance, on those words with which it contrasts, on those which define its place in the language (e.g., those defining "determinable" dimensions, like color, shape), on those which define the activity or "language game" it figures in (describing, invoking, establishing communion), and so on. The relations between meanings in this sense are like those between concepts in a semantic field.

Just as our color concepts are given their meaning by the field of contrast they set up together, so that the introduction of new concepts will alter the boundaries of others, so the various meanings that a subordinate's demeanor can have for us, as deferential, respectful, cringing, mildly mocking, ironical, insolent, provoking, downright rude, are established by a field of contrast; and as with finer discrimination on our part, or a more sophisticated culture, new possibilities are born, so other terms of this range are altered. And as the meaning of our terms "red," "blue," "green" is fixed by the definition of a field of contrast through the determinable term "color," so all these alternative demeanors are only available in a society which has, among other types, hierarchical relations of power and command. And corresponding to the underlying language game of designating colored objects is the set of social practices which sustain these hierarchical structures and are fulfilled in them.

Meaning in this sense—let us call it experiential meaning—thus is for a subject, of something, in a field. This distinguishes it from linguistic meaning which has a four and not three-dimensional structure. Linguistic meaning is for subjects and in a field, but it is the meaning of signifiers and it is about a world of referents. Once we are clear about the likenesses and differences, there should be little doubt that the term "meaning" is not a misnomer, the product of an illegitimate extension into this context of experience and behavior.

There is thus a quite legitimate notion of meaning which we use when we speak of the meaning of a situation for an agent. And that this concept has a place is integral to our ordinary consciousness and hence speech about our actions. Our actions are ordinarily characterized by the purpose sought and explained by desires, feelings, emotions. But the language by which we describe our goals, feelings, desires is also a definition of the meaning things have for us. The vocabulary defining meaning—words like "terrifying," "attractive"—is linked with that describing feeling—"fear," "desire"—and that describing goals—"safety," "possession."

Moreover, our understanding of these terms moves inescapably in a hermeneutical circle. An emotion term like "shame," for instance, essentially refers us to a certain kind of situation, the "shameful," or "humiliating," and a certain mode of response, that of hiding oneself, of covering up, or else "wiping out" the blot. That is, it is essential to this feeling's being identified as shame that it be related to this situation and give rise to this type of disposition. But this situation in its turn can only be identified in relation to the feelings which it provokes; and the disposition is to a goal which can similarly not be understood without reference to the feelings experienced: the "hiding" in question is one which will cover up my shame; it is not the same as hiding from an armed pursuer; we can only understand what is meant by "hiding" here if we understand what kind of feeling and situation is being talked about. We have to be within the circle.

An emotion term like "shame" can only be explained by reference to other concepts which in turn cannot be understood without reference to shame. To understand these concepts we have to be in on a certain experience, we have to understand a certain language, not just of words, but also a certain language of mutual action and communication, by which we blame, exhort, admire, esteem each other. In the end we are in on this because we grow up in the ambit of certain common meanings. But we can often experience what it is like to be on the outside when we encounter the feeling, action, and experiential meaning language of another civilization. Here there is no translation, no way of explaining in other, more accessible concepts. We can only catch on by getting somehow into their way of life, if only in imagination. Thus if we look at human behavior as action done out of a background of desire, feeling, emotion, then we are looking at a reality which must be characterized in terms of meaning. But does this mean that it can be the object of a hermeneutical science as this was outlined above?

There are, to remind ourselves, three characteristics that the object of a science of interpretation has: it must have sense or coherence; this must be distinguishable from its expression, and this sense must be for a subject.

Now insofar as we are talking about behavior as action, hence in terms of meaning, the category of sense or coherence must apply to it. This is not to say that all behavior must "make sense," if we mean by this be rational, avoid contradiction, confusion of purpose, and the like. Plainly a great deal of our action falls short of this goal. But in another sense, even contradictory, irrational action is "made sense of," when we understand why it was engaged in. We make sense of action when there is a coherence between the actions of the agent and the meaning of his situation for him. We find his action puzzling until we find such a coherence. It may not be bad to repeat that this coherence in no way implies that the action is rational: the meaning of a situation for an agent may be full of confusion and contradiction; but the adequate depiction of this contradiction makes sense of it.

Making sense in this way through coherence of meaning and action, the meanings of action and situation cannot but move in a hermeneutical circle. Our conviction that the account makes sense is contingent on our reading of action and situation. But these readings cannot be explained or justified except by reference to other such readings, and their relation to the whole. If an interlocutor does not understand this kind of reading, or will not accept it as valid, there is nowhere else the argument can go. Ultimately, a good explanation is one which makes sense of the behavior; but then to appreciate a good explanation, one has to agree on what makes good sense; what makes good sense is a function of one's readings; and these in turn are based on the kind of sense one understands.

But how about the second characteristic, that sense should be distinguishable from its embodiment? This is necessary for a science of interpretation because interpretation lays a claim to make a confused meaning clearer; hence there must be some sense in which the "same" meaning is expressed, but differently.

This immediately raises a difficulty. In talking of experiential meaning above, I mentioned that we can distinguish between a given element and its meaning, between meaning and substrate. This carried the claim that a given meaning *may* be realized in another substrate. But does this mean that we can *always* embody the same meaning in another situation? Perhaps there are some situations, standing before death, for instance, which have a meaning which can't be embodied otherwise.

But fortunately this difficult question is irrelevant for our purposes. For here we have a case in which the analogy between text and behavior implicit in the notion of a hermeneutical science of man only applies with important modifications. The text is replaced in the interpretation by another text, one which is clearer. The text-analogue of behavior is not replaced by another such text analogue. When this happens we have revolutionary theatre or terrorist acts designed to make propaganda of the deed, in which the hidden relations of a society are supposedly shown up in a dramatic confrontation. But this is not scientific understanding, even though it may perhaps be based on such understanding, or claim to be.

But in science the text-analogue is replaced by a text, an account. Which might prompt the question, how we can even begin to talk of interpretation here, of expressing the same meaning more clearly, when we have two such utterly different terms of comparison, a text and a tract of behavior? Is the whole thing not just a bad pun?

This question leads us to open up another aspect of experiential meaning which we abstracted from earlier. Experiential meanings are defined in fields of contrast, as words are in semantic fields.

But what was not mentioned above is that these two kinds of definition aren't independent of each other. The range of human desires, feelings, emotions, and hence meanings is bound up with the level and type of culture, which in turn is inseparable from the distinctions and categories marked by the language people speak. The field of meanings in which a given situation can find its place is bound up with the semantic field of the terms characterizing these meanings and the related feelings, desires, predicaments.

But the relationship involved here is not a simple one. There are two simple types of models of relation which could be offered here, but both are inadequate. We could think of the feeling vocabulary as simply describing pre-existing feelings, as marking distinctions which would be there without them. But this is not adequate because we often experience in ourselves or others how achieving, say, a more sophisticated vocabulary of the emotions makes our emotional life more sophisticated and not just our descriptions of it. Reading a good, powerful novel may give me the picture of an emotion which I had not previously been aware of. But we can't draw a neat line between an increased ability to identify and an altered ability to feel emotions which this enables.

The other simple inadequate model of the relationship is to jump from the above to the conclusion that thinking makes it so. But this clearly won't do either, since not just any new definition can be forced on us, nor can we force it on ourselves; and some which we do gladly take up can be judged inauthentic, or in bad faith, or just wrong-headed by others. These judgments may be wrong, but they are not in principle illicit. Rather we make an effort to be lucid about ourselves and our feelings, and admire a man who achieves this.

Thus, neither the simple correspondence view is correct, nor the view that thinking makes it so. But both have prima facie warrant. There is such a thing as self-lucidity, which points us to a correspondence view; but the achievement of such lucidity means moral change, that is, it changes the object known. At the same time, error about oneself is not just an absence of correspondence; it is also in some form inauthenticity, bad faith, self-delusion, repression of one's human feelings, or something of the kind; it is a matter of the quality of what is felt just as much as what is known about this, just as self-knowledge is.

If this is so, then we have to think of man as a self-interpreting animal. He is necessarily so, for there is no such thing as the structure of meanings for him independently of his interpretation of them; for one is woven into the other. But then the text of our interpretation is not that heterogeneous from what is interpreted; for what is interpreted is itself an interpretation; a self-interpretation which is embedded in a stream of action. It is an interpretation of experiential meaning which contributes to the constitution of this meaning. Or to put it another way: that of which we are trying to find the coherence is itself partly constituted by self-interpretation.

Our aim is to replace this confused, incomplete, partly erroneous self-interpretation by a correct one. And in doing this we look not only to the self-interpretation but to the stream of behavior in which it is set; just as in interpreting a historical document we have to place it in the stream of events which it relates to. But of course the analogy is not exact, for here we are interpreting the interpretation and the stream of behavior in which it is set together, and not just one or the other.

There is thus no utter heterogeneity of interpretation to what it is about; rather there is a slide in the notion of interpretation. Already to be a living agent is to experience one's situation in terms of certain meanings; and this in a sense can be thought of as a sort of proto-"interpretation." This is in turn interpreted and shaped by the language in which the agent lives these meanings. This whole is then at a third level interpreted by the explanation we proffer of his actions.

In this way the second condition of a hermeneutical science is met. But this account poses in a new light the question mentioned at the beginning whether the interpretation can ever express the same meaning as the interpreted. And in this case, there is clearly a way in which the two will not be congruent. For if the explanation is really clearer than the lived interpretation then it will be such that it would alter in some way the behavior if it came to be internalized by the agent as his self-interpretation. In this way a hermeneutical science which achieves its goal, that is, attains greater clarity than the immediate understanding of agent or observer, must offer us an interpretation which is in this way crucially out of phase with the explicandum.

Thus, human behavior seen as action of agents who desire and are moved, who have goals and aspirations, necessarily offers a purchase for descriptions in terms of meaning—what I have called "experiential meaning." The norm of explanation which it posits is one which "makes sense" of the behavior, which shows a coherence of meaning. This "making sense of" is the proffering of an interpretation; and we have seen that what is interpreted meets the conditions of a science of interpretation: first, that we can speak of its sense or coherence; and second, that this sense can be expressed in another form, so that we can speak of the interpretation as giving clearer expression to what is only implicit in the explicandum. The third condition, that this sense be for a subject, is obviously met in this case, although who this subject is is by no means an unproblematical question as we shall see later on.

This should be enough to show that there is a good prima facie case to the effect that men and their actions are amenable to explanation of a hermeneutical kind. There is, therefore, some reason to raise the issue and challenge the epistemological orientation which would rule interpretation out of the sciences of man. A great deal more must be said to bring out what is involved in the hermeneutical sciences of man. But before getting on to this, it might help to clarify the issue with a couple of examples drawn from a specific field, that of politics.

II

In politics, too, the goal of a verifiable science has led to the concentration on features which can supposedly be identified in abstraction from our understanding or not understanding experiential meaning. These—let us call them brute data identifications—are what supposedly enable us to break out from the hermeneutical circle and found our science four square on a verification procedure which meets the requirements of the empiricist tradition.

But in politics the search for such brute data has not gone to the lengths which it has in psychology, where the object of science has been thought of by many as behavior qua "colorless movement," or as machine-recognizable properties. The tendency in politics has been to stop with something less basic, but—so it is thought—the identification of which cannot be challenged by the offering of another interpretation or reading of the data concerned. . . . This is what is referred to as "behavior" in the rhetoric of political scientists, but it has not the rock bottom quality of its psychological homonym.

Political behavior includes what we would ordinarily call actions, but ones that are supposedly brute data identifiable. How can this be so? Well, actions are usually described by the purpose or end-state realized. But the purposes of some actions can be specified in what might be thought to be brute data terms; some actions, for instance, have physical end-states, like getting the car in the garage or climbing the mountain. Others have end-states which are closely tied by institutional rules to some unmistakable physical movement; thus, when I raise my hand in the meeting at the appropriate time, I am voting for the motion. The only questions we can raise about the corresponding actions, given such movements or the realization of such end-states, are whether the agent was aware of what he was doing, was acting as against simply emitting reflex behavior, knew the institutional significance of his movement, etc. Any worries on this score generally turn out to be pretty artificial in the contexts political scientists are concerned with; and where they do arise they can be checked by relatively simple devices, e.g., asking the subject: did you mean to vote for the motion?

Hence, it would appear that there are actions which can be identified beyond fear of interpretative dispute; and this is what gives the foundation for the category of "political behavior." Thus, there are some acts of obvious political relevance which can be specified thus in physical terms, such as killing, sending tanks into the streets, seizing people and confining them to cells; and there is an immense range of others which can be specified from physical acts by institutional rules, such as voting for instance. These can be the object of a science of politics which can hope to meet the stringent requirements of verification. The latter class particularly has provided matter for study in recent decades—most notably in the case of voting studies.

But of course a science of politics confined to such acts would be much too narrow. For on another level these actions also have meaning for the agents which is not exhausted in the brute data descriptions, and which is often crucial to understanding why they were done. Thus, in voting for the motion I am also saving the honor of my party, or defending the value of free speech, or vindicating public morality, or saving civilization from breakdown. It is in such terms that the agents talk about the motivation of much of their political action, and it is difficult to conceive a science of politics which doesn't come to grips with it.

Behavioral political science comes to grips with it by taking the meanings involved in action as facts about the agent, his beliefs, his affective reactions, his "values," as the term is frequently used. For it can be thought verifiable in the brute data sense that men will agree to subscribe or not to a certain form of words (expressing a belief, say); or express a positive or negative reaction to certain events, or symbols; or agree or not with the proposition that some act is right or wrong. We can thus get at meanings as just another form of brute data by the techniques of the opinion survey and content analysis.

An immediate objection springs to mind. If we are trying to deal with the meanings which inform political action, then surely interpretive acumen is unavoidable. Let us say we are trying to understand the goals and values of a certain group, or grasp their vision of the polity; we might try to probe this by a questionnaire asking them whether they assent or not to a number of propositions, which are meant to express different goals, evaluations, beliefs. But how did we design the questionnaire? How did we pick these propositions? Here we relied on our understanding of the goals, values, vision involved. But then this understanding can be challenged, and hence the significance of our results questioned. Perhaps the finding of our study, the compiling of proportions of assent and dissent to these propositions is irrelevant, is without significance for understanding the agents or the polity concerned. This kind of attack is frequently made by critics of mainstream political science, or for that matter social science in general.

To this proponents of this mainstream reply with a standard move of logical empiricism: distinguishing the process of discovery from the logic of verification. Of course, it is our understanding of these meanings which enables us to draw up the questionnaire which will test people's attitudes in respect to them. And, of course, interpretive dispute about these meanings is potentially endless; there are no brute data at this level, every affirmation can be challenged by a rival interpretation. But this has nothing to do with verifiable science. What is firmly verified is the set of correlations between, say, the assent to certain propositions and certain behavior. We discover, for instance, that people who are active politically (defined by participation in a certain set of institutions) are more likely to consent to certain sets of propositions supposedly expressing the values underlying the system.[6] This finding is a firmly verified correlation no matter what one thinks of the reasoning, or simple hunches, that went into designing the research which established it. Political science as a body of knowledge is made up of such correlations; it does not give a truth value to the background reasoning or hunch. A good interpretive nose may be useful in hitting on the right correlations to test, but science is never called on to arbitrate the disputes between interpretations.

Thus, in addition to those overt acts which can be defined physically or institutionally, the category of political behavior can include assent or dissent to verbal formulae, or the occurrence or not of verbal formulae in speech, or expressions of approval or rejection of certain events or measures as observed in institutionally-defined behavior (for instance, turning out for a demonstration).

Now there are a number of objections which can be made to this notion of political behavior; one might question in all sorts of ways how interpretation-free it is in fact. But I would like to question it from another angle. One of the basic characteristics of this kind of social science is that it reconstructs reality in line with certain categorial principles. These allow for an intersubjective social reality which is made up of brute data, identifiable acts and structures, certain institutions, procedures, actions. It allows for beliefs, affective reactions, evaluations as the psychological properties of individuals. And it allows for correlations between these two orders or reality: e.g., that certain beliefs go along with certain acts, certain values with certain institutions, etc.

To put it another way, what is objectively (intersubjectively) real is brute data identifiable. This is what social reality *is*. Social reality described in terms of its meaning for the actors, such that disputes could arise about interpretation which couldn't be settled by brute data (e.g., are people rioting to get a hearing, or are they rioting to redress humiliation, out of blind anger, because they recover a sense of dignity in insurrection?), this is given subjective reality, that is, there are certain beliefs, affective reactions, evaluations which individuals make or have about or in relation to social reality. These beliefs or reactions can have an effect on this reality; and the fact that such a belief is held is a fact of objective social reality. But the social reality which is the object of these attitudes, beliefs, reactions can only be made up of brute data. Thus any description of reality in terms of meanings which is open to interpretive question is only allowed into this scientific discourse if it is placed, as it were, in quotes and attributed to individuals as their opinion, belief, attitude. That this opinion, belief, etc. is held is thought of as a brute datum, since it is redefined as the respondent's giving a certain answer to the questionnaire.

This aspect of social reality which concerns its meanings for the agents has been taken up in a number of ways, but recently it has been spoken of in terms of political culture. Now the way this is defined and studied illustrates clearly the categorial principles above. For instance, political cultural is referred to by Almond and Powell[7] as the "psychological dimension of the political system" (23). Further on they state: "Political culture is the pattern of individual attitudes and orientations towards politics among the members of a political system. It is the subjective realm which underlies and gives meaning to political actions" (50). The authors then go on to distinguish three different kinds of orientations, cognitive (knowledge and beliefs), affective (feelings), and evaluative (judgments and opinions).

From the point of view of empiricist epistemology, this set of categorial principles leaves nothing out. Both reality and the meanings it has for actors are coped with. But what it in fact cannot allow for are intersubjective meanings, that is, it cannot allow for the validity of descriptions of social reality in terms of meanings, hence not as brute data, which are not in quotation marks and attributed as opinion, attitude, etc. to individual(s). Now it is this exclusion that

I would like to challenge in the name of another set of categorial principles, inspired by a quite other epistemology.

ii

We spoke earlier about the brute data identification of acts by means of institutional rules. Thus, putting a cross beside someone's name on a slip of paper and putting this in a box counts in the right context as voting for that person; leaving the room, saying or writing a certain form of words, counts as breaking off the negotiations; writing one's name on a piece of paper counts as signing the petition, etc. But what is worth looking at is what underlies this set of identifications. These identifications are the application of a language of social life, a language which marks distinctions among different possible social acts, relations, structures. But what underlies this language?

Let us take the example of breaking off negotiations above. The language of our society recognizes states or actions like the following: entering into negotiation, breaking off negotiations, offering to negotiate, negotiating in good (bad) faith, concluding negotiations, making a new offer, etc. In other more jargon-infested language, the semantic "space" of this range of social activity is carved up in a certain way, by a certain set of distinctions which our vocabulary marks; and the shape and nature of these distinctions is the nature of our language in this area. These distinctions are applied in our society with more or less formalism in different contexts.

But of course this is not true of every society. Our whole notion of negotiation is bound up for instance with the distinct identity and autonomy of the parties, with the willed nature of their relations; it is a very contractual notion. But other societies have no such conception. It is reported about the traditional Japanese village that the foundation of its social life was a powerful form of consensus, which put a high premium on unanimous decision.[8] Such a consensus would be considered shattered if two clearly articulated parties were to separate out, pursuing opposed aims and attempting either to vote down the opposition or push it into a settlement on the most favorable possible terms for themselves. Discussion there must be, and some kind of adjustment of differences. But our idea of bargaining, with the assumption of distinct autonomous parties in willed relationship, has no place there; nor does a series of distinctions, like entering into and leaving negotiation, or bargaining in good faith (sc. with the genuine intention of seeking agreement).

Now the difference between our society and one of the kind just described could not be well expressed if we said we have a vocabulary to describe negotiation which they lack. We might say, for instance, that we have a vocabulary to describe the heavens that they lack, viz., that of Newtonian mechanics; for here we assume that they live under the same heavens as we do, only understand it differently. But it is not true that they have the same kind of bargaining as we do. The word, or whatever word of their language we translate as "bargaining," must have an entirely different gloss, which is marked by the distinctions their vocabulary allows in contrast to those marked by ours. But this different gloss is not just a difference of vocabulary, but also one of social reality.

But this still may be misleading as a way of putting the difference. For it might imply that there is a social reality which can be discovered in each society and which might exist quite independently of the vocabulary of that society, or indeed of any vocabulary, as the heavens would exist whether men theorized about them or not. And this is not the case; the realities here are practices; and these cannot be identified in abstraction from the language we use to describe th m, or invoke them, or carry them out. That the practice of negotiation allows us to distinguish bargaining in good or bad faith, or entering into or breaking off negotiations, presupposes that our acts and situation have a certain description for us, e.g., that we are distinct parties entering into willed relations. But they cannot have these descriptions for us unless this is somehow expressed in our vocabulary of this practice; if not in our descriptions of the practices (for we may as yet be unconscious of some of the important distinctions) in the appropriate language for carrying them on. (Thus, the language marking a distinction between public and private acts or contexts may exist even where these terms or their equivalents are not part of this language; for the distinction will be marked by the different language which is appropriate in one context and the other, be it perhaps a difference of style, or dialect, even though the distinction is not designated by specific descriptive expressions.)

The situation we have here is one in which the vocabulary of a given social dimension is grounded in the shape of social practice in this dimension; that is, the vocabulary wouldn't make sense, couldn't be applied sensibly, where this range of practices didn't prevail. And yet this range of practices couldn't exist without the prevalence of this or some related vocabulary. There is no simple one-way dependence here. We can speak of mutual dependence if we like, but really what this points up is the artificiality of the distinction between social reality and the language of description of that social reality. The language is constitutive of the reality, is essential to its being the kind of reality it is. To separate the two and distinguish them as we quite rightly distinguish the heavens from our theories about them is forever to miss the point.

This type of relation has been recently explored, e.g., by John Searle, with his concept of a constitutive rule. As Searle points out,[9] we are normally induced to think of rules as applying to behavior which could be available to us whether or not the rule existed. Some rules are like this, they are regulative like commandments: don't take the goods of another. But there are other rules, e.g., that governing the Queen's move in chess, which are not so separable. If one suspends these rules, or imagines a state in which they have not yet been introduced, then the whole range of behavior in question, in this case, chess playing, would not be. There would still, of course, be the activity of pushing a wood piece around on a board made of squares 8 by 8; but this is not chess any longer. Rules of this kind are constitutive rules. By contrast again, there are other rules of chess, such as that one say "j'adoube" when one touches a piece without intending to play it, which are clearly regulative.[10]

I am suggesting that this notion of the constitutive be extended beyond the domain of rule-governed behavior. That is why I suggest the vaguer word 'practice'. Even in an area where there are no clearly defined rules, there are distinctions between different sorts of behavior such that one sort is considered the appropriate form for one action or context, the other for another action or context, e.g., doing or saying certain things amounts to breaking off negotiations, doing or saying other things amounts to making a new offer. But just as there are constitutive rules, i.e., rules such that the behavior they govern could not exist without them, and which are in this sense inseparable from that behavior, so I am suggesting that there are constitutive distinctions, constitutive ranges of language which are similarly inseparable, in that certain practices are not without them.

We can reverse this relationship and say that all the institutions and practices by which we live are constituted by certain distinctions and hence a certain language which is thus essential to them. We can take voting, a practice which is central to large numbers of institutions in a democratic society. What is essential to the practice of voting is that some decision or verdict be delivered (a man elected, a measure passed), through some criterion of preponderance (simple majority, two-thirds majority, or whatever) out of a set of micro-choices (the votes of the citizens, MPs, delegates). If there is not some such significance attached to our behavior, no amount of marking and counting pieces of paper, raising hands, walking out into lobbies amounts to voting. From this it follows that the institution of voting must be such that certain distinctions have application: e.g., that between someone being elected, or a measure passed, and their failing of election, or passage; that between a valid vote and an invalid one which in turn requires a distinction between a real choice and one which is forced or counterfeited. For no matter how far we move from the Rousseauian notion that each man decide in full autonomy, the very institution of the vote requires that in some sense the enfranchised choose. For there to be voting in a sense recognizably like ours, there must be a distinction in men's self-interpretations between autonomy and forced choice.

This is to say that an activity of marking and counting papers has to bear intentional descriptions which fall within a certain range before we can agree to call it voting, just as the intercourse of two men or teams has to bear descriptions of a certain range before we will call it negotiation. Or in other words, that some practice is voting or negotiation has to do in part with the vocabulary established in a society as appropriate for engaging in it or describing it.

Hence implicit in these practices is a certain vision of the agent and his relation to others and to society. We saw in connection with negotiation in our society that it requires a picture of the parties as in some sense autonomous, and as entering into willed relations. And this picture carries with it certain implicit norms, such as that of good faith mentioned above, or a norm of rationality, that agreement correspond to one's goals as far as attainable, or the norm of continued freedom of action as far as attainable. These practices require that one's actions and relations be seen in the light of this picture and the accompanying norms, good faith, autonomy, and rationality. But men do not see themselves in this way in all societies, nor do they understand these norms in all societies. The experience of autonomy as we know it, the sense of rational action and the satisfactions thereof, are unavailable to them. The meaning of these terms is opaque to them because they have a different structure of experiential meaning open to them.

We can think of the difference between our society and the simplified version of the traditional Japanese village as consisting in this, that the range of meaning open to the members of the two societies is very different. But what we are dealing with here is not subjective meaning which can fit into the categorial grid of behavioral political science, but rather intersubjective meanings. It is not just that the people in our society all or mostly have a given set of ideas in their heads and subscribe to a given set of goals. The meanings and norms implicit in these practices are not just in the minds of the actors but are out there in the practices themselves, practices which cannot be conceived as a set of individual actions, but which are essentially modes of social relation, of mutual action.

The actors may have all sorts of beliefs and attitudes which may be rightly thought of as their individual beliefs and attitudes, even if others share them; they may subscribe to certain policy goals or certain forms of theory about the polity, or feel resentment at certain things, and so on. They bring these with them into their negotiations, and strive to satisfy them. But what they do not bring into the negotiations is the set of ideas and norms constitutive of negotiation themselves. These must be the common property of the society before there can be any question of anyone entering into negotiation or not. Hence they are not subjective meanings, the property of one or some individuals, but rather intersubjective meanings, which are constitutive of the social matrix in which individuals find themselves and act.

The intersubjective meanings which are the background to social action are often treated by political scientists under the heading "consensus." By this is meant convergence of beliefs on certain basic matters, or of attitude. But the two are not the same. Whether there is consensus or not, the condition of there being either one or the other is a certain set of common terms of reference. A society in which this was lacking would not be a society in the normal sense of the term, but several. Perhaps some multi-racial or multi-tribal states approach this limit. Some multi-national states are bedevilled by consistent cross-purposes, e.g., my own country. But consensus as a convergence of beliefs or values is not the opposite of this kind of fundamental diversity. Rather the opposite of diversity is a high degree of intersubjective meanings. And this can go along with profound cleavage. Indeed, intersubjective meanings are a condition of a certain kind of very profound cleavage, such as was visible in the Reformation, or the American Civil War, or splits in left wing parties, where the dispute is at fever pitch just because both sides can fully understand the other.

In other words, convergence of belief or attitude or its absence presupposes a common language in which these beliefs can be formulated, and in which these foundations can be opposed. Much of this common language in any society is rooted in its institutions and practices; it is constitutive of these institutions and practices. It is part of the intersubjective meanings. To put the point another way, apart from the question of how much people's beliefs converge is the question of how much they have a common language of social and political reality in which these beliefs are expressed. This second question cannot be reduced to the first; intersubjective meaning is not a matter of converging beliefs or values. When we speak of consensus we speak of beliefs and values which could be the property of a single person, or many, or all; but intersubjective meanings could not be the property of a single person because they are rooted in social practice.

We can perhaps see this if we envisage the situation in which the ideas and norms underlying a practice are the property of single individuals. This is what happens when single individuals from one society interiorize the notions and values of another, e.g., children in missionary schools. Here we have a totally different situation. We *are* really talking now about subjective beliefs and attitudes. The ideas are abstract, they are mere social "ideals." Whereas in the original society, these ideas and norms are rooted in their social relations, and are that on the basis of which they can formulate opinions and ideals.

We can see this in connection with the example we have been using all along, that of negotiations. The vision of a society based on negotiation is coming in for heavy attack by a growing segment of modern youth, as are the attendant norms of rationality and the definition of autonomy. This is a dramatic failure of "consensus." But this cleavage takes place in the ambit of this intersubjective meaning, the social practice of negotiation as it is lived in our society. The rejection wouldn't have the bitter quality it has if what is rejected were not understood in common, because it is part of a social practice which we find it hard to avoid, so pervasive is it in our society. At the same time there is a reaching out for other forms which have still the "abstract" quality of ideals which are subjective in this sense, that is, not rooted in practice; which is what makes the rebellion look so "unreal" to outsiders, and so irrational.

iii

Intersubjective meanings, ways of experiencing action in society which are expressed in the language and descriptions constitutive of institutions and practices, do not fit into the categorial grid of mainstream political science. This allows only for an intersubjective reality which is brute data identifiable. But social practices and institutions which are partly constituted by certain ways of talking about them are not so identifiable. We have to understand the language, the underlying meanings, which constitute them.

We can allow, once we accept a certain set of institutions or practices as our starting point and not as objects of further questioning, that we can easily take as brute data that certain acts are judged to take place or certain states judged to hold within the semantic field of these practices. For instance, that someone has voted Liberal, or signed the petition. We can then go on to correlate certain subjective meanings—beliefs, attitudes, etc.—with this behavior or its lack. But this means that we give up trying to define further just what these practices and institutions are, what the meanings are which they require and hence sustain. For these meanings do not fit into the grid; they are not subjective beliefs or values, but are constitutive of social reality. In order to get at them we have to drop the basic premise that social reality is made up of brute data alone. For any characterization of the meanings underlying these practices is open to question by someone offering an alternative interpretation. The negation of this is what was meant as brute data. We have to admit that intersubjective social reality has to be partly defined in terms of meanings; that meanings as subjective are not just in causal interaction with a social reality made up of brute data, but that as intersubjective they are constitutive of this reality.

We have been talking here of intersubjective meanings. And earlier I was contrasting the question of intersubjective meaning with that of consensus as convergence of opinions. But there is another kind of nonsubjective meaning which is also often inadequately discussed under the head of "consensus." In a society with a strong web of intersubjective meanings, there can be a more or less powerful set of common meanings. By these I mean notions of what is significant which are not just shared in the sense that everyone has them, but are also common in the sense of being in the common reference world. Thus, almost everyone in our society may share a susceptibility to a certain kind of feminine beauty, but this may not be a common meaning. It may be known to no one, except perhaps market researchers, who play on it in their advertisements. But the survival of a national identity as francophones is a common meaning of *Québecois*; for it is not just shared, and not just known to be shared, but its being a common aspiration is one of the common reference points of all debate, communication, and all public life in the society.

We can speak of a shared belief, aspiration, etc. when there is convergence between the subjective beliefs, aspirations, of many individuals. But it is part of the meaning of a common aspiration, belief, celebration, etc. that it be not just shared but part of the common reference world. Or to put it another way, its being shared is a collective act, it is a consciousness which is communally sustained, whereas sharing is something we do each on his own, as it were, even if each of us is influenced by the others.

Common meanings are the basis of community. Intersubjective meaning gives a people a common language to talk about social reality and a common understanding of certain norms, but only with common meanings does this common reference world contain significant common actions, celebrations, and feelings. These are objects in the world that everybody shares. This is what makes community.

Once again, we cannot really understand this phenomenon through the usual definition of consensus as convergence of opinion and value. For what is meant here is something more than convergence. Convergence is what happens when our values are shared. But what is required for common meanings is that this shared value be part of the common world, that this sharing be shared. But we could also say that common meanings are quite other than consensus, for they can subsist with a high degree of cleavage; this is what happens when a common meaning comes to be lived and understood differently by different groups in a society. It remains a common meaning, because there is the reference point which is the common purpose, aspiration, celebration. Such is for example the American Way, or freedom as understood in the USA. But this common meaning is differently articulated by different groups. This is the basis of the bitterest fights in a society, and this we are also seeing in the U.S. today. Perhaps one might say that a common meaning is very often the cause of the most bitter lack of consensus. It thus must not be confused with convergence of opinion, value, attitude.

Of course, common meanings and intersubjective meanings are closely interwoven. There must be a powerful net of intersubjective meanings for there to be common meanings; and the result of powerful common meanings is the development of a greater web of intersubjective meanings as people live in community.

On the other hand, when common meanings wither, which they can do through the kind of deep dissensus we described earlier, the groups tend to grow apart and develop different languages of social reality, hence to share less intersubjective meanings.

Hence, to take our above example again, there has been a powerful common meaning in our civilization around a certain vision of the free society in which bargaining has a central place. This has helped to entrench the social practice of negotiation which makes us participate in this intersubjective meaning. But there is a severe challenge to this common meaning today, as we have seen. Should those who object to it really succeed in building up an alternative society, there would develop a gap between those who remain in the present type of society and those who had founded the new one.

Common meanings, as well as intersubjective ones, fall through the net of mainstream social science. They can find no place in its categories. For they are not simply a converging set of subjective reactions, but part of the common world. What the ontology of mainstream social science lacks is the notion of meaning as not simply for an individual subject; of a subject who can be a "we" as well as an "I." The exclusion of this possibility, of the communal, comes once again from the baleful influence of the epistemological tradition for which all knowledge has to be reconstructed from the impressions imprinted on the individual subject. But if we free ourselves from the hold of these prejudices, this seems a wildly implausible view about the development of human consciousness; we are aware of the world through a "we" before we are through an "I." Hence we need the distinction between what is just shared in the sense that each of us has it in our individual worlds, and that which is in the common world. But the very idea of something which is in the common world in contradistinction to what is in all the individual worlds is totally opaque to empiricist epistemology. Hence it finds no place in mainstream social science.. What this results in must now be seen.

III

Thus, to sum up the last pages: a social science which wishes to fulfill the requirements of the empiricist tradition naturally tries to reconstruct social reality as consisting of brute data alone. These data are the acts of people (behavior) as identified supposedly beyond interpretation either by physical descriptions or by descriptions clearly defined by institutions and practices; and secondly, they include the subjective reality of individuals' beliefs, attitudes, values, as attested by their responses to certain forms of words, or in some cases their overt non-verbal behavior.

What this excludes is a consideration of social reality as characterized by intersubjective and common meanings. It excludes, for instance, an attempt to understand our civilization, in which negotiation plays such a central part both in fact and in justificatory theory, by probing the self-definitions of agent, other and social relatedness which it embodies. Such definitions which deal with the meaning for agents of their own and others' action, and of the social relations in which they stand, do not in any sense record brute data, in the sense that this term is being used in this argument; that is, they are in no sense beyond challenge by those who would quarrel with our interpretations of these meanings.

Thus, I tried to adumbrate above the vision implicit in the practice of negotiation by reference to certain notions of autonomy and rationality. But this reading will undoubtedly be challenged by those who have different fundamental conceptions of man, human motivation, the human condition; or even by those who judge other features of our present predicament to have greater importance. If we wish to avoid these disputes, and have a science grounded in verification as this is understood by the logical empiricists, then we have to avoid this level of study altogether and hope to make do with a correlation of behavior which is brute data identifiable.

A similar point goes for the distinction between common meanings and shared subjective meanings. We can hope to identify the subjective meanings of individuals if we take these in the sense in which there are adequate criteria for them in people's dissent or assent to verbal formulae or their brute data identifiable behavior. But once we allow the distinction between such subjective meanings which are widely shared and genuine common meanings, then we can no longer make do with brute data indentification. We are in a domain where our definitions can be challenged by those with another reading.

The profound option of mainstream social scientists for the empiricist conception of knowledge and science makes it inevitable that they should accept the verification model of political science and the categorial principles that this entails. This means in turn that a study of our civilization in terms of its intersubjective and common meanings is ruled out. Rather this whole level of study is made invisible.

On the mainstream view, therefore, the different practices and institutions of different societies are not seen as related to different clusters of intersubjective or common meanings, rather, we should be able to differentiate them by different clusters of "behavior" and/or subjective meaning. The comparison between societies requires on this view that we elaborate a universal vocabulary of behavior which will allow us to present the different forms and practices of different societies in the same conceptual web.

Now present day political science is contemptuous of the older attempt at comparative politics via a comparison of institutions. An influential school of our day has therefore shifted comparison to certain practices, or very general classes of practices, and proposes to compare societies according to the different ways in which these practices are carried on. Such are the "functions" of the influential "developmental approach."[11] But it is epistemologically crucial that such functions be identified independently of those intersubjective meanings which are different in different societies; for otherwise, they will not be genuinely universal; or will be universal only in the loose and unilluminating sense that the function-name can be given application in every society but with varying, and often widely varying meaning—the same term being "glossed" very differently by different sets of practices and intersubjective meanings. The danger that such universality might not hold is not even suspected by mainstream political scientists since they are unaware that there is such a level of description as that which defines intersubjective meanings and are convinced that functions and the various structures which perform them can be identified in terms of brute data behavior.

But the result of ignoring the difference in intersubjective meanings can be disastrous to a science of comparative politics, viz., that we interpret all other societies in the categories of our own. Ironically, this is what seems to have happened to American political science. Having strongly criticized the old institution-focussed comparative politics for its ethnocentricity (or Western bias), it proposes to understand the politics of all society in terms of such functions, for instance, as "interest articulation" and "interest aggregation" whose definition is strongly influenced by the bargaining culture of our civilization, but which is far from being guaranteed appropriateness elsewhere. The not surprising result is a theory of political development which places the Atlantic-type polity at the summit of human political achievement. . . .

IV

It can be argued then, that mainstream social science is kept within certain limits by its categorial principles which are rooted in the traditional epistemology of empiricism; and secondly, that these restrictions are a severe handicap and prevent us from coming to grips with important problems of our day which should be the object of political science. We need to go beyond the bounds of a science based on verification to one which would study the intersubjective and common meanings embedded in social reality.

But this science would be hermeneutical in the sense that has been developed in this paper. It would not be founded on brute data; its most primitive data would be readings of meanings, and its object would have the three properties mentioned above: the meanings are for a subject in a field or fields; they are moreover meanings which are partially constituted by self-definitions, which are in this sense already interpretations, and which can thus be reexpressed or made explicit by a science of politics. In our case, the subject may be a society or community; but the intersubjective meanings, as we saw, embody a certain self-definition, a vision of the agent and his society, which is that of the society or community.

But then the difficulties which the proponents of the verification model foresee will arise. If we have a science which has no brute data, which relies on readings, then it cannot but move in a hermeneutical circle. A given reading of the intersubjective meanings of a society, or of given institutions or practices, may seem well founded, because it makes sense of these practices or the development of that society. But the conviction that it does make sense of this history itself is founded on futher related readings. Thus, what I said above on the identity-crisis which is generated by our society makes sense and holds together only if one accepts this reading of the intersubjective meanings of our society, and if one accepts this reading of the rebellion against our society by many young people (sc. the reading in terms of identity-crisis). These two readings make sense together, so that in a sense the explanation as a whole reposes on the readings, and the readings in their turn are strengthened by the explanation as a whole.

But if these readings seem implausible, or even more, if they are not understood by our interlocutor, there is no verification procedure which we can fall back on. We can only continue to offer interpretations; we are in an interpretative circle.

But the ideal of a science of verification is to find an appeal beyond differences of interpretation. Insight will always be useful in discovery, but should not have to play any part in establishing the truth of its findings. This ideal can be said to have been met by our natural sciences. But a hermeneutic science cannot but rely on insight. It requires that one have the sensibility and understanding necessary to be able to make and comprehend the readings by which we can explain the reality concerned. In physics we might argue that if someone does not accept a true theory, then either he has not been shown enough (brute data) evidence (perhaps not enough is yet available), or he cannot understand and apply some formalized language. But in the sciences of man conceived as hermeneutical, the nonacceptance of a true or illuminating theory may come from neither of these, indeed is unlikely to be due to either of these, but rather from a failure to grasp the meaning field in question, an inability to make and understand readings of this field.

In other words, in a hermeneutical science, a certain measure of insight is indispensable, and this insight cannot be communicated by the gathering of brute data, or initiation in modes of formal reasoning or some combination of these. It is unformalizable. But this is a scandalous result according to the authoritative conception of science in our tradition, which is shared even by many of those who are highly critical of the approach of mainstream psychology, or sociology, or political science. For its means that this is not a study in which anyone can engage, regardless of their level of insight; that some claims of the form: "if you don't understand, then your intuitions are at fault, are blind or inadequate," some claims of this form will be justified; that some differences will be nonarbitrable by further evidence, but that each side can only make appeal to deeper insight on the part of the other. The superiority of one position over another will thus consist in this, that from the more adequate position one can understand one's own stand and that of one's opponent, but not the other way around. It goes without saying that this argument can only have weight for those in the superior position.

Thus, a hermeneutical science encounters a gap in intuitions, which is the other side, as it were, of the hermeneutical circle. But the situation is graver than this; for this gap is bound up with our divergent options in politics and life.

We speak of a gap when some cannot understand the kind of self-definition which others are proposing as underlying a certain society or set of institutions. Thus some positivistically-minded thinkers will find the language of identity-theory quite opaque; and some thinkers will not recognize any theory which does not fit with the categorial presuppositions of empiricism. But self-definitions are not only important to us as scientists who are trying to understand some, perhaps distant, social reality. As men we are self-defining beings, and we are partly what we are in virtue of the self-definitions which we have accepted, however we have come by them. What self-definitions we understand and what ones we don't understand, is closely linked with the self-definitions which help to constitute what we are. If it is too simple to say that one only understands an "ideology" which one subscribes to, it is nevertheless hard to deny that we have great difficulty grasping definitions whose terms structure the world in ways which are utterly different from, incompatible with our own.

Hence the gap in intuitions doesn't just divide different theoretical positions, it also tends to divide different fundamental options in life. The practical and the theoretical are inextricably joined here. It may not just be that to understand a certain explanation one has to sharpen one's intuitions, it may be that one has to change one's orientation—if not in adopting another orientation, at least in living one's own in a way which allows for greater comprehension of others. Thus, in the sciences of man insofar as they are hermeneutical there can be a valid response to "I don't understand" which takes the form, not only "develop your intuitions," but more radically "change yourself." This puts an end to any aspiration to a value-free or "ideology-free" science of man. A study of the science of man is inseparable from an examination of the options between which men must choose.

This means that we can speak here not only of error, but of illusion. We speak of "illusion" when we are dealing with something of greater substance than error, error which in a sense builds a counterfeit reality of its own. But errors of interpretation of meaning, which are also self-definitions of those who interpret and hence inform their lives, are more than errors in this sense: they are sustained by certain practices of which they are constitutive. It is not implausible to single out as examples two rampant illusions in our present society. One is that of the proponents of the bargaining society who can recognize nothing but either bargaining gambits or madness in those who rebel against this society. Here the error is sustained by the practices of the bargaining culture, and given a semblance of reality by the refusal to treat any protests on other terms; it hence acquires the more substantive reality of illusion. The second example is provided by much "revolutionary" activity in our society which in desperate search for an alternative mode of life purports to see its situation in that of an Andean guerilla or Chinese peasants. Lived out, this passes from the stage of laughable error to tragic illusion. One illusion cannot recognize the possibility of human variation, the other cannot see any limits to man's ability to transform itself. Both make a valid science of man impossible.

In face of all this, we might be so scandalized by the prospect of such a hermeneutical science, that we will want to go back to the verification model. Why can we not take our understanding of meaning as part of the logic of discovery, as the logical empiricists suggest for our unformalizable insights, and still found our science on the exactness of our predictions? Our insightful understanding of the intersubjective meanings of our society will then serve to elaborate fruitful hypotheses, but the proof of these puddings will remain in the degree they enable us to predict.

The answer is that if the epistemological views underlying the science of interpretation are right, such exact prediction is radically impossible. This, for three reasons of ascending order of fundamentalness.

The first is the well-known "open system" predicament, one shared by human life and meteorology, that we cannot shield a certain domain of human events, the psychological, economic, political, from external interference; it is impossible to delineate a closed system.

The second, more fundamental, is that if we are to understand men by a science of interpretation, we cannot achieve the degree of fine exactitude of a science based on brute data. The data of natural science admit of measurement to virtually any degree of exactitude. But different interpretations cannot be judged in this way. At the same time different nuances of interpretation may lead to different predictions in some circumstances, and these different outcomes may eventually create widely varying futures. Hence it is more than easy to be wide of the mark.

But the third and most fundamental reason for the impossibility of hard prediction is that man is a self-defining animal. With changes in his self-definition go changes in what man is, such that he has to be understood in different terms. But the conceptual mutations in human history can and frequently do produce conceptual webs which are incommensurable, that is, where the terms can't be defined in relation to a common stratum of expressions. The entirely different notions of bargaining in our society and in some primitive ones provide an example. Each will be glossed in terms of practices, institutions, ideas in each society which have nothing corresponding to them in the other.

The success of prediction in the natural sciences is bound up with the fact that all states of the system, past and future, can be described in the same range of concepts, as values, say, of the same variables. Hence all future states of the solar system can be characterized, as past ones are, in the language of Newtonian mechanics. This is far from being a sufficient condition of exact prediction, but it is a necessary one in this sense, that only if past and future are brought under the same conceptual net can one understand the states of the latter as some function of the states of the former, and hence predict.

This conceptual unity is vitiated in the sciences of man by the fact of conceptual innovation which in turn alters human reality. The very terms in which the future will have to be characterized if we are to understand it properly are not all available to us at present. Hence we have such radically unpredictable events as the culture of youth today, the Puritan rebellion of the sixteenth and seventeenth centuries, the development of Soviet society, etc.

And thus, it is much easier to understand after the fact than it is to predict. Human science is largely *ex post* understanding. Or often one has the sense of impending change, of some big reorganization, but is powerless to make clear what it will consist in: one lacks the vocabulary. But there is a clear assymetry here, which there is not (or not supposed to be) in natural science, where events are said to be predicted from the theory with exactly the same ease with which one explains past events and by exactly the same process. In human science this will never be the case.

Of course, we strive *ex post* to understand the changes, and to do this we try to develop a language in which we can situate the incommensurable webs of concepts. We see the rise of Puritanism, for instance, as a shift in man's stance to the sacred; and thus, we have a language in which we can express both stances—the earlier mediaeval Catholic one and the Puritan rebellion—as "glosses" on this fundamental term. We thus have a language in which to talk of the transition. But think how we acquired it. This general category of the sacred is acquired not only from our experience of the shift which came in the Reformation, but from the study of human religion in general, including primitive religion, and with the detachment which came with secularization. It would be conceivable, but unthinkable, that a mediaeval Catholic could have this conception—or for that matter a Puritan. These two protagonists only had a language of condemnation for each other: "heretic," "idolator." The place for such a concept was pre-empted by a certain way of living the sacred. After a big change has happened, and the trauma has been resorbed, it is possible to try to understand it, because one now has available the new language, the trans-formed meaning world. But hard prediction before just makes one a laughing stock. Really to be able to predict the future would be to have explicited so clearly the human condition that one would already have pre-empted all cultural innovation and transformation. This is hardly in the bounds of the possible.

Sometimes men show amazing prescience: the myth of Faust, for instance, which is treated several times at the beginning of the modern era. There is a kind of prophesy here, a premonition. But what characterizes these bursts of foresight is that they see through a glass darkly, for they see in terms of the old language: Faust sells his soul to the devil. They are in no sense hard predictions. Human science looks backward. It is inescapably historical.

There are thus good grounds both in epistemological arguments and in their greater fruitfulness for opting for hermeneutical sciences of man. But we cannot hide from ourselves how greatly this option breaks with certain commonly held notions about our scientific tradition. We cannot measure such sciences against the requirements of a science of verification: we cannot judge them by their predictive capacity. We have to accept that they are founded on intuitions which all do not share, and what is worse that these intuitions are closely bound up with our fundamental options. These sciences cannot be "wertfrei"; they are moral sciences in a more radical sense than the eighteenth century understood. Finally, their successful prosecution requires a high degree of self-knowledge, a freedom from illusion, in the sense of error which is rooted and expressed in one's way of life; for our incapacity to understand is rooted in our own self-definitions, hence in what we are. To say this is not to say anything new: Aristotle makes a similar point in Book I of the *Ethics*. But it is still radically shocking and unassimilable to the mainstream of modern science.

NOTES

1. Cf. e.g., H. G. Gadamer, *Wahrheit und Methode*, Tübingen, 1960.
2. Cf. Paul Ricoeur, *De L'interprétation*, Paris, 1965.
3. Cf. e.g., J. Habermas, *Erkenntnis und Interesse*, Frankfurt, 1968.
4. The notion of brute data here has some relation to, but is not at all the same as the "brute facts" discussed by Elizabeth Anscombe, "On Brute Facts," *Analysis*, v. 18, 1957–1958, pp. 69–72, and John Searle, *Speech Acts*, Cambridge, 1969, pp. 50–53. For Anscombe and Searle, brute facts are contrasted to what may be called 'institutional facts', to use Searle's term, i.e., facts which presuppose the existence of certain institutions. Voting would be an example. But, as we shall see below in part II, some institutional facts, such as X's having voted Liberal, can be verified as brute data in the sense used here, and thus find a place in the category of political behavior. What cannot

as easily be described in terms of brute data are the institutions themselves. Cf. the discussion below in part II.

5. Cf. discussion in M. Minsky, *Computation,* Englewood Cliffs, N.J., 1967, pp. 104–107, where Minsky explicitly argues that an effective procedure, which no longer requires intuition or interpretation, is one which can be realized by a machine.

6. Cf. H. McClosky, "Consensus and Ideology in American Politics," *American Political Science Review*, v. 58, 1964, pp. 361–382.

7. Gabriel A. Almond and G. Bingham Powell, *Comparative Politics: A Developmental Approach*, Boston and Toronto, 1966. Page references in my text here and below are to this work.

8. Cf. Thomas C. Smith, *The Agrarian Origins of Modern Japan*. Stanford, 1959, ch. 5. This type of consensus is also found in other traditional societies. Cf. for instance, the *desa* system of the Indonesian village.

9. J. Searle, *Speech Acts: An Essay in the Philosophy of Language,* Cambridge, 1969, pp. 33–42.

10. Cf. the discussion in Stanley Cavell, *Must We Mean What We Say?* New York, 1969, pp. 21–31.

11. Cf. Almond and Powell, *op. cit.*

Section V
Ethnographic Research in Education

Ethnographic Research in Education

Harry F. Wolcott
University of Oregon

Cultural anthropologists conducting ethnographic research describe their activities with a modest phrase: "doing fieldwork." In 1971, about the time anthropologists began writing self-consciously about how they conducted their studies, Rosalie Wax (1971) took that very phrase, "doing fieldwork," for the title of an account of her research experiences and some lessons she wanted to draw for the benefit of future fieldworkers. Until then, it had not been fashionable for anthropologists to devote such singular attention to methodological issues per se. Indeed, it was not unusual for anthropologists to disappear completely from published accounts, seeming to leave "the natives" forever in a pristine precontact state. Today's anthropologists have become more self-conscious, more explicit, and far more reflexive about the works and lives of others and themselves, as is suggested by *Works and Lives*, the title of anthropologist Clifford Geertz's 1988 book, and forthright accounts of fieldwork in edited volumes like *Taboo* (Kulick & Willson, 1995) or *Out in the Field* (Lewin & Leap, 1996).

In recent years, ethnographic research has also been acknowledged, and to some extent welcomed, as an alternative research strategy for inquiring into educational practice. It is even gaining access to hallowed territory once the exclusive domain of educational psychology—learning itself. Neither alone nor in combination with other qualitative approaches—which are sometimes confused for it—is ethnography likely to wring educational research from the iron grip of the statistical methodologists. The numbers involved are too big, the stakes too high, to invoke research results unsupported by measurement data. But it is comforting to note educator receptivity to other ways of asking and

Note: This text was originally drafted in 1978 for a series of one-hour taped lectures, accompanied by a printed supplement, dealing with aspects of qualitative methods. The lecture was revised for publication as a chapter in the 1988 AERA volume *Complementary Methods for Research in Education* and has undergone another major revision for publication here, as well as update after update following interminable delays. For readers of the earlier volume, parts of what follows will be familiar, and other parts will be new. Although many references have been updated, I continue to call attention to earlier works apt to be overlooked in the burgeoning literature on qualitative and ethnographic research. Through these years I have addressed several topics that can be introduced only briefly here; I hope readers will forgive the shameless number of citations I make to my own work. Appreciation is expressed to Professors Richard Jaeger and Geoff Mills for providing feedback from students on the revised material, one of whom concluded that ethnography is a "new vague approach" to educational research.

other ways of looking—the enthusiastic reception to the first edition of this volume is a case in point. Today one often hears educators discussing "ethnography" or the "ethnographic approach," and sessions with either of those magic terms in their title continue to pack 'em in at Annual Meetings of the American Educational Research Association.

Despite that welcome, few educators have a clear sense of how ethnographers conduct their research, whether in schools or out. Furthermore, *educational ethnography* has taken on something of a life of its own. Its practitioners do not necessarily concern themselves with the ways they are alike or different from ethnographers outside education or even from researchers who follow closely related approaches like participant observation studies, field studies, or case studies. Although ethnography may be better understood today than it was a few years ago, I still doubt that anyone, ethnographers included, ever knows *exactly* what kind of a report will result from ethnographic research or *exactly* what to expect when the term *ethnography* is linked with some everyday process such as speaking or reading. To illustrate: When I first began revising this chapter, I came across an announcement for an edited volume titled *The Ethnography of Reading* (Boyarin, 1993). After ordering a copy, I began to wonder and attempted to predict what its contents might include. I did not correctly anticipate a single one of the chapters, although its contents strike me as authentically ethnographic, cover to cover.

Whatever ethnography entails, there's a lot more of it around these days. Today's educators have a far better *general* idea of what to expect from anyone who claims to follow a "qualitative," "descriptive," "naturalistic," or "constructivist" approach to research, even if they cannot always distinguish purebred ethnography from its close cousins. Some of what I discuss here will deal with research in this broad qualitative/descriptive sense. I will also identify what I think is special to ethnography itself, in support of my strongly felt but not universally shared position that ethnography is *not a synonym for qualitative/descriptive research* but is *one particular form* of it (cf. Jessor, Colby, & Shweder, 1996).

Something of a mystique surrounds fieldwork—among the insiders who engage in it as well as outsiders who do not—and I intend to explore the basis for that mystique. I cannot entirely dispel it, but I suggest that the real mystique surrounding ethnography is not in "doing fieldwork" but in doing the mindwork that must occur before, during, and after the fieldwork experience in order to bring the ethnographic process to fruition. (See Wolcott, 1995, Part Three, "Fieldwork as Mindwork.")

Ethnography as Both Process and Product

Ethnography refers both to the research *process* and to the customary *product* of that effort—the written ethnographic account. (See an extended discussion in Sanjek, 1995.) I must limit this discussion to a description of the research techniques anthropologists use in doing fieldwork. That is a sufficient task for a single chapter in a book designed to introduce a number of alternative approaches. It is also the obvious starting point for someone new to this discipline. But it is not sufficient to make a competent ethnographer out of an interested reader.

The necessary next step is to do some in-depth reading in cultural anthropology, giving particular attention to the ethnographic literature. One needs to understand how different ethnographers, working in different traditions, with different agendas, and among different peoples, have conceptualized and written about cultural systems. Although there is a sufficiently large corpus of material to make "educational ethnography" a genre in its own right, I think one must also make an independent effort at reading the works of anthropologists who are not concerned so single-mindedly with what goes on in schools. The references and annotated materials in this section identify a number of such studies.

The word "ethnography" means a picture of the "way of life" of some identifiable group of people. Those people could be any culture-bearing group, in any time or place. In times past, anthropologists usually studied among a group that was a small, intact, essentially self-sufficient social unit, and it was always a group notably "strange" to the observer. An anthropologist's purpose as ethnographer was to learn about, record, and ultimately to portray the culture of that other group in order to deepen our understanding about the different ways human beings have resolved the problems created by being human in the first place.

Anthropologists always study human behavior in terms of cultural context, not because people are preoccupied with culture but because that is the way anthropologists frame their studies. Particular individuals, groups, customs, institutions, or events are the focus of their efforts. They are the building blocks with which anthropologists construct generalizable descriptions of the life-ways of socially interacting sets of people, their "cultures." Yet culture itself is always an abstraction, regardless of whether one is referring to Culture in general or to the culture of a specific social group. Every ethnographer faces the question of balance between individual and group, ranging from an earlier tradition in which no *individuals* appear at all to a recent emphasis on "person-centered" ethnography. Richard Fox summarizes the latter position by describing the ethnographer's task as "writing about the everyday life of persons, not the cultural life of a people" (1991, p. 12). Attending to the everyday life of persons is splendid advice for *initiating* ethnographic inquiry, but there seems little point in embarking on so endless a task without also seeking some deeper level of understanding.

Here, I recognize, would be a great place to offer a crisp definition of culture, but I am hesitant to do so. The arguments concerning the definition of culture, what one anthropologist refers to as "this undifferentiated and diffuse variable," continue to constitute a critical part of the ongoing dialogue among anthropologists. To what extent, for example, does culture consist of what people *actually do*, what they *say they do*, what they *say they should do*, or to *meanings* they assign to such behavior? Does culture make prisoners of us or free us from a mind-boggling number of daily decisions? Does culture emanate from our minds, our hearts, or our stomachs; from our ancestors, our totems, or our deities? And if someone really devised a culture-free test, could we ever find a culture-free individual to take or to interpret it?

In terms of understanding the ethnographer's task, I draw attention to Ward Goodenough's definition of culture, which I have found particularly instructive. In the wake of anthropology's affair with postmodernism, definitions like this have gone out of vogue, but I think they will resurface again, little changed except for gender language:

> The culture of any society is made up of the concepts, beliefs, and principles of action and organization that an ethnographer has found could be attributed successfully to the members of that society in the context of his dealings with them. [Goodenough 1976, p. 5]

The appeal of this definition lies in the verb that describes what ethnographers do: They *attribute* culture to a society. That way of conceptualizing culture underscores a number of critical points. First and foremost, as noted, the ethnographic preoccupation is with culture. Second, as Goodenough notes here (and underscores elsewhere, e.g., Goodenough, 1981, p. 103n), culture is a phenomenon associated with how groups of people interact with each other. It is not to be confused for people themselves but with what people do and say as they go about their everyday affairs. Therefore, we cannot describe people as "belonging" to a culture any more than they can be said to "belong" to a language. Third, culture is implicit. It cannot be observed directly, and ordinarily only an ethnographer would be concerned with making it explicit at all. For everyone else, it is enough to know "how we do things around here," or to recognize how "they" do things in ways that make them distinguishable from us. And finally, the ultimate test of the ethnographic accomplishment in making the culture of a group explicit is the extent to which an ethnographer succeeds in attributing these aspects of culture to the group under study. The satisfactoriness of the explanation is what counts, not the power of the method for deriving it.

If you are an ethnographer or aspire to be one, this is what you will be up to—assuming, if we may, that in the course of *his* lifetime of dealings with them, Goodenough has successfully attributed to ethnographers the concepts, beliefs, and principles of action and organization that capture the essence of what it is that ethnographers do.

Without having to go so far as to try to make their own culture (or cultures, as explained below) explicit, or to try to obtain the comprehensive and "holistic" view the professional ethnographer seeks, *all* human beings are similarly preoccupied with trying to discern and to act appropriately within the cultural systems of the social units in which they hold or seek membership. We all have to figure out and become competent in numerous microcultural systems and in at least one macrocultural system (Goodenough, 1976). Everyone, anthropologist included, does that out of necessity. Ethnographers also do it in fulfillment of their professional responsibility.

Ordinarily an outsider to the group being studied, the ethnographer tries harder to know more about the cultural system he or she is studying than any individual who is a natural participant in it. In that effort, the anthropologist has the advantage of an outsider's broad and analytical perspective, yet by reason of that very detachment, is unlikely ever totally to acquire an insider's point of view. The ethnographer walks a fine line. With too much distance and perspective, one is labeled aloof, remote, insensitive, superficial; with too much familiarity, empathy, or identification, one is suspected of having "gone native." The more successful fieldworkers resolve the tension between involvement and detachment (see Powdermaker, 1966); others go home early.

In my opportunities for ethnographic research—inquiries into the social behavior of particular culture-bearing groups of people—I have most often been in modern, industrial settings and never, anywhere, have I met anyone "primitive." Yet I confess that when I conjure up an image of an ideal ethnographer, I envision someone pulling a canoe onto a beach and stepping into the center of a small group of huts among lightly clad villagers in an exotic tropical setting. This imagery is not entirely a figment of my imagination, for it was in conducting research among often exotic and always "different" peoples that anthropology got its start and anthropologists built their discipline. The self-conscious reflection by anthropologists in examining how their earlier traditions and experiences in exotic and numerically manageable settings have both limited and expanded the range of work they find themselves doing (for an early example, see Messerschmidt, 1981) and in agonizing over their role vis-à-vis The Other (e.g., the whole postmodern era as reflected, for example, in Fox, 1991) is a relatively recent phenomenon.

My old-fashioned image of the ethnographer-at-work evinces still more elements that contribute to a fieldwork mystique and continue to exert an influence in contemporary settings. The exotic continues to have its appeal, not only for the romantic notions involved but also for the fact that one's capabilities for observing, recording, and analyzing everyday behavior—what Malinowski (1922, p. 20) referred to as the "imponderabilia of actual life"—are presumed to be enhanced in unfamiliar settings.

I do not mean to pass over that point too quickly. When we talk about conducting ethnographic research in schools, we face the problem of trying to conduct our studies as though we were in a strange new setting. In fact, most of us have been in more or less continuous contact in schools since about the age of six, first as students, then as teachers and administrators, and finally as academicians or researchers, or both. Educational anthropologists continue to debate whether cross-cultural experience should be prerequisite to conducting ethnographically oriented research in schools. The underlying issue is how to ensure that school researchers intent on attributing "culture" to others have themselves experienced culture in some conscious, comparative way.

Note that I pictured my ideal ethnographer traveling alone. I might have included a spouse or field assistant, but I definitely do not picture a team of researchers or technical assistants. My image also assumes that the anthropologist is there to stay—to become, for awhile, part of the local scenery rather than to remain only long enough to have each resident fill in a questionnaire, submit to a brief interview, or complete a few test items. Tradition even informs the expectation of how long my ideal ethnographer should remain in the field: at least one year, preferably longer.

That is hardly to claim that ethnographic studies are always of 12 months' duration; rather, in the absence of other determinants, one is advised to remain long enough to see a full cycle of activity. In traditional settings, such events were usually played out in the seasons of a calendar year. We are accustomed to thinking of the school "year" the same way. In my study of the elementary school principalship, were it not for the anthropological practice of examining annual cycles, I might easily have overlooked that a principal's annual cycle can better be described in terms of overlapping cycles of about 19 months' duration. Looking at the annual cycle that way helps explain the tension that may arise at the "end" of each school year when teachers are trying desperately to get everything finished up for this year while principals are trying to cajole them into planning for the next one (Wolcott, 1973, pp. 178–191).

Note also that my image of ethnographic research is an image of people: researcher and researched. The ethnographer is the research instrument. That instrument—the anthropologist in person—has been faulted time and time again for being biased, inattentive, ethnocentric, partial, forgetful, overly subject to infection and disease, incapable of attending to everything at once, easily distracted, simultaneously too involved and too detached, and the list goes on and on. Yet, what better instrument could we ever devise for observing and understanding human behavior?

If we could actually step into my vision and inquire of my image ethnographer how she or he planned to carry out fieldwork in a new setting, it might be disconcerting to hear a somewhat ambiguous response posing a number of possible ideas but expressing a certain hesitancy about pursuing any one of them to the exclusion of the others. I doubt that an old-fashioned ethnographer would be the least bit embarrassed to confess that after doing some mapping and a village census, she or he wasn't sure just what would be attended to next. Such tentativeness not only allows the ethnographer to move into settings where one cannot frame hypotheses in advance but also reflects the open style that most ethnographers prefer for initiating fieldwork.

Such tentativeness is not intended to create a mystique. To those comfortable only with hypothesis testing, however, an encounter with someone intrigued by trying to discern *what the hypotheses might be* can prove unsettling. The hardest question for the ethnographer is not so difficult for researchers of other bents: What is it that you look at when you conduct your research? The ethnographer's answer is, of course, "It depends."

What an ethnographer looks at and writes about depends on a number of factors: the nature of the problem that sends the researcher into the field in the first place; the ethnographer's personality; the course of events during fieldwork; the process of sorting, analyzing, and writing that transforms the fieldwork experience into the completed account; and the expectations for the final account, including how and where it is to be circulated and what its intended audiences and purposes are. The mystique surrounding ethnography is associated with being in the field because we all harbor romantic ideas of "going off to spend a year with the natives." It is easy to lose sight of the ethnographer's ultimate responsibility to prepare an account intended to enhance human understanding.

Nonetheless, what anthropologists ordinarily do in the course of fieldwork provides us with a way of looking at ethnographic research in action, regardless of whether the field site is an island in the Pacific or a classroom in the intermediate wing of the local elementary school. I turn next to a point-by-point examination of the customary research techniques of the anthropologist doing fieldwork.

Ethnographic Research Techniques

The most noteworthy thing about ethnographic research techniques is their lack of noteworthiness. No particular research technique is associated exclusively with cultural anthropology, and there is no guarantee that anyone will produce ethnography simply by employing one or more of these techniques. I should make that statement more emphatic: There is no way one could ever hope to produce an ethnography simply by employing many, most, or all of the research techniques that ethnographers use. Ethnography is not a reporting process guided by a specific set of techniques, as Frederick Erickson reminded educational researchers many years ago (1977). It is an inquiry process carried out by human beings and guided by a point of view that derives from experience in the research setting and from the knowledge of prior anthropological research.

Unlike prevailing tradition in educational research, preoccupation with method is not sufficient to validate ethnographic research. Ethnographic significance is derived socially, not statistically, from discerning how ordinary people in their customary settings go about their everyday lives. As Clifford Geertz has observed, "Anthropological interpretations must be tested against the material they are designed to interpret; it is not their origins that recommend them" (1968, p. vii).

None of the field research techniques that I describe below, including the ethnographic mainstay *participant observation*, is all that powerful or special. The full potential of fieldwork is realized through what can also be faulted as its greatest shortcoming: its dependency on firsthand experience and observation.

Just why ethnographic research should be singled out as *particularly* vulnerable because of its dependency on a human observer has always puzzled me. Is there any human endeavor that has achieved independence from the humans who created it or apply it? Fieldworkers try to forestall the criticism, nonetheless. One way is through a somewhat tortured striving for objectivity ("There really is a there out there . . .") leavened with a recognition that ultimately everything is subjective anyway ("but how I report will, of necessity, be filtered through my own perceptions"). Another is through efforts at "triangulation," obtaining information from multiple sources rather than relying solely on one method. Anthropologist Pertti Pelto has described this as the "multi-instrument approach": The anthropologist is the research instrument who, in the process of gathering information, utilizes observations made over extended periods of time, from multiple sources of data, employing multiple techniques. By being on the scene, the ethnographer not only is afforded continual opportunity to ask questions but also seeks constantly to reflect on the best questions to ask.

There is no standard for enumerating even the most commonly employed fieldwork practices. The list of techniques that I present and discuss below was adapted originally from Pertti and Gretel Pelto's text *Anthropological Research: The Structure of Inquiry* (1978) and then tested against the subsequent outpouring of views on ethnographic research and the preparation of ethnographic researchers (see, for example, Plattner, 1989). Many iterations later, my evolving inventory of techniques continues (a) to emphasize the two major strategies in fieldwork, *participant observation* and *interviewing,* (b) to underscore the use ethnographers make of other sources, and (c) to demonstrate how reporting is integral to the research process, not separate from and adjunct to it.

Many anthropologists summarize fieldwork practice by referring only to two terms, *participant observation* and *interviewing.* And some might insist that one term, *participant observation,* says it all. In that sense, participant observation causes confusion. Like the term *ethnography,* it has come to have two meanings. Obviously, it may refer to taking the role of a participant observer, one of the important ways anthropologists obtain information. But it may also refer globally to *all* the techniques employed in fieldwork, thus serving as a synonym for fieldwork itself. Here I use *participant observation* in its more restricted sense—as one particular, and particularly important, approach to fieldwork.

Each of the four basic strategies I identify is illustrated by a familiar set of techniques and could be expanded to include still others. The four strategies include the two critical ones already noted—*participant observation* and *interviewing*—augmented by a third for *making and using records.* In recognition of the absolute necessity to advance fieldwork to the critical deskwork stage, I have now added a category for *reporting the research.* Adhering to a set of categories described more fully elsewhere (Wolcott, 1992), and yielding to the temptations of alliteration, I have assigned to the first three strategies the comprehensive labels "experiencing," "enquiring," and "examining."

Admittedly, approaching the topic of field techniques in this logical, orderly way is better suited to informing others about fieldwork than to pursuing one's own. In the field, matters of sequence and sensitivity in employing different techniques are every bit as important as the choice of them. Problems of gaining entrée and maintaining rapport, coupled with the endless task of note writing, account for a good portion of the fieldworker's attention and energy. In the bush, such everyday concerns as potable water, food purchase and preparation, sanitation, or even a reliable way to receive and send mail may take precedence over all else. Whatever the contemporary equivalents of those seemingly romantic problems, I call attention here to the techniques themselves, not to how and when one uses them or how information acquired through these techniques is subsequently processed. Those facets require one to *think* like an anthropologist, not simply to act like one. Some important contrasts with more conventional approaches will be apparent in this discussion and will provide the opportunity for summary remarks following this overview of techniques.

Experiencing Through Direct Observation

Participant observation is so integral to fieldwork that some anthropologists would never think to include it in a list of explicit techniques. I know that other anthropologists are appalled when colleagues appear to reify the obvious fact that fieldwork assumes one's presence among members of a group being studied, as circumstances permit. There are ambiguities and contradictions aplenty in this seemingly simple solution to pursuing ethnographic research. Anthropologist Russ Bernard cautions that although participant observation is "the foundation of anthropological research," it is best not to regard it as a method at all but as "a *strategy* that facilitates data collection in the field—all kinds of data, both qualitative and quantitative" (Bernard, 1988, p. 148, 150; see also Bernard, 1994, chap. 7).

All humans are participant observers in everything they do, yet they do not claim to be ethnographers. We are ethnographic observers when we attend to the cultural context of the behavior we are engaging in or observing. In doing so, we look for mutually understood sets of expectations and explanations that enable us to provide cultural interpretations about what is occurring and what meanings we may reasonably presume are being attributed by others present.

I think it is fair to ask anyone who claims to have conducted research as a participant observer to provide a fuller description about how each facet—participant, observer, and some workable combination of the two—was played out in the research setting. Each facet becomes intertwined with a host of conditions, many of which are beyond the control of the ethnographer. Even were we to assume that every ethnographer was equally capable of getting as involved as he or she wanted, and of always having an exquisite sense of just how involved that should be, other constraints limit the extent to which one can engage in or observe human social behavior.

Schools, like other formal institutions, impose rather narrow expectations on how anyone—insider or outsider alike—may participate or observe in them. When outsiders come to a school as "observers," it is pretty hard for people in that setting to distinguish among visiting social scientists, professors of education, parents, or teachers from other schools. Schools offer few role options, but one role that is well structured is that of the observer-visitor. Most studies conducted in schools as participant observer research are really observer studies, augmented by an occasional chance to talk briefly with students or teachers. With the "protections" currently imposed by formal clearance procedures, even opportunities for casual conversation have become problematic.

I should point out that there are costs as well as benefits in taking a more active role. In my own initiation to fieldwork (Wolcott, 1967), occupying dual roles as teacher and as a researcher in a cross-cultural classroom made a genuine participant observer study possible but also diverted from my research effort the energy that full-time teaching demands. Richard King (1967, 1974) and Gerry Rosenfeld (1971) are among other early observers who produced ethnographic studies from the teacher's perspective. Anthropologist Sylvia Hart (1982) found that by volunteering as a classroom aide, she achieved an optimum balance between opportunities to participate and to observe in studying the social organization of one school's reading program. A few anthropologists have attempted to take the role of the student in the classroom (e.g., Burnett, 1969; Spindler & Spindler, 1982). It always amuses me to think of my mentor George Spindler, a major contributor to anthropology and education, sitting at his third-grade desk in a village school in Germany. But it is worth noting that of the relatively few early accounts obtained from the perspective of either the teacher or the student as participant observer, the researchers who conducted them represented several disciplinary interests—sociology (e.g., Everhart, 1983; McPherson, 1972), social psychology (e.g., Smith & Geoffrey, 1968), education (e.g., Cusick, 1973)—rather than only anthropology.

The label "participant observation" has become a familiar one among educational researchers, but, as noted, my impression is that most of what is casually passed off as participant observation research is decidedly nonparticipatory. There is no awkwardness in this, for no opprobrium attaches to being a nonparticipant while conducting research in formal education settings; more frequently, researchers are required to assure those in charge that their presence will cause no interruption. Rather than accord the status of "participant observer" to every researcher who so much as enters a school with a note pad, however, I think we might develop more carefully descriptive categories that prompt researchers to think about and to disclose the role they actually assume during their fieldwork.

For field research both in and out of schools, I have found it useful to make a distinction among different degrees of participation, to take into account whether the researcher has (and is able to use) the opportunity to be an *active participant*, is (or eventually becomes) a *privileged, active observer;* or is at best a *passive observer*. Most field-workers in schools are privileged observers rather than active participants. Because the label "ethnography" implies involvement, my hunch is that the extent of genuine participation on the part of researchers is simply *assumed* by readers to be greater than it was. Whatever the actual case, the ethnographic approach invites researchers to become more involved and to experience through several senses rather than remain only an interested onlooker.

Today's applied anthropologists now talk about brief or "spot" observations and employ techniques such as Rapid Rural Appraisal used in development work (also variously referred to as Rapid Anthropological Assessment, Rapid Ethnographic Assessment, or Ethnographic Reconnaissance; see Beebe, 1995; van Willigen & Finan, 1991). To me the terms *rapid* and *ethnographic* do not seem well paired for guiding educational research; hearing them prompts instead a reminder of Ray Rist's caution years ago about conducting "Blitzkrieg

Ethnography" (Rist, 1980). I recognize the need for ethnographers to adapt their skills to new field situations, but I think ethnography can play a more important role by encouraging educational researchers to slow their efforts and widen their gaze. My counsel is for researchers to do less more thoroughly. There are already checklists aplenty for speedy classroom assessment; ethnography invites attention to the very contexts and subtleties that "quick and dirty" research must, of necessity, ignore.

Enquiring: When the Ethnographer Asks

The second major category of fieldwork techniques, *enquiring*, points to all the ways researchers obtain data by *asking*. That includes formal interviewing, of course, but it covers a far broader range of activities. The research techniques themselves are not all that unfamiliar, for they are also used by sociologists, social psychologists, collection agencies, psychiatrists, detectives, journalists, and the CIA. The only distinction ethnographers might wish to draw is that they work with cherished and respected (and sometimes paid) *informants*, but their more investigatively oriented colleagues use (and sometimes pay) *subjects* or *informers*. Today even the term *informant* rests a bit uneasily. In the current climate of congeniality, many ethnographers prefer to regard those among whom they study as *participants*.

As for interviewing itself, one can identify several familiar forms employed by ethnographers. "Casual" interviews are little more than conversations in which the fieldworker inquires into something of interest; systematic interviewing requires an increasing element of structure. Distinctions can be made among life history/life cycle interviews; semistructured, or informal, interviews; structured, or formal, interviews; surveys; household census; questionnaires (written or oral); and projective techniques. Because we are looking at school-related research, we probably need to add a special category for interview data obtained through other measurement techniques, including standardized test results.

The category "Enquiring" covers a broad range of data-gathering techniques. How else can I group together collecting life history data, conducting a structured interview, and administering an IQ test as a common set of activities? I include here anything that the fieldworker does that intrudes upon the natural setting and is done with the conscious intent to obtain information directly and purposefully. Even so-called casual conversation has to be viewed as purposeful when fieldworkers find themselves talking with people they would not be talking with were it not for the fieldwork itself.

In the participant observer role, ethnographers let the field parade before them. In the interviewer role, ethnographers take a critical step in research that can never be reversed—they *ask*. And regardless of whether they ask "How's things?", the sum of nine plus eight, what someone "sees" in a set of inkblots or drawings, or for someone's life story, they have imposed some structure upon the setting. In that sense, ethnographers are like other field researchers. They are also different, in at least two ways. First, they are less likely to put too much faith in any one instrument, set of answers, or techniques. Second, they are more likely to be concerned with the suitability of the technique across different populations. For example, an ethnographer is more likely to prepare a questionnaire *after* coming to know a setting well than to initiate a study using a questionnaire already constructed (or mailed, in lieu of ever visiting at all). Conversely, given a highly standardized instrument like an intelligence test, a skeptical educator-ethnographer might even try "de-standardizing" it, as Richard King (1967) did with Indian pupils in the Yukon Territory, when he set out to see whether his pupils couldn't literally get smarter every week through practice and instruction in how to take standardized tests.

The idea of key-informant interviewing—often associated with the collection of life histories but certainly not limited to them—is probably the most purely "anthropological" of any of the techniques under discussion here. It flies in the face of a prevailing notion in education research that truth resides only in large numbers. Anthropologists are so fond of their special term *informant* that they sometimes seem inclined to refer to all their subjects that way. But the terms *informant* and, especially, *key informant* have a special meaning in field research. An informant is an individual with whom one spends a disproportionate amount of research time because that individual appears to be particularly well-informed, articulate, approachable, or available.

For the anthropological linguist, one key informant is as large a "sample" as one needs in order to work out the basic grammar of an unknown language. Ethnographers do not usually rely on a single informant, but I suspect that, to a far greater extent than their accounts imply, most fieldworkers rely most heavily on only a few individuals. Inscriptions in completed ethnographies attest to the contribution informants have made to the doing of ethnography. (See the accounts in Casagrande, 1960, for an early effort on the part of anthropologists to acknowledge not only the personal experience but also the collaborative effort involved in fieldwork and their special debts owed their key informants.)

Researchers using ethnographic techniques in educational settings have not made extended use of key informants in their studies. (For an exception, see Chang, 1992.) My hunch is that most of us feel so well versed about what goes on in schools that *we become our own key informant in school research.* I have referred to this approach as "ethnography-minus-one" (Wolcott, 1984). The phrase *ethnography-minus-one* serves notice that in school-related studies it is too often the researcher who is telling us what everything means (and perhaps even how things *should* be) rather than trying "to grasp the native's point of view, his relation to life, to realise *his* vision of *his* world," as Malinowski said more than 75 years ago (1922, p. 25). There is probably no single factor that poses a greater threat to realizing the potential of ethnography than this problem of the researcher who already knows, without ever having to ask, what the "native's point of view" is—or ought to be. There are unique problems to be faced in doing ethnographic research in settings already familiar and where our subjects are *us* rather than *them*.

The *life history*, or biographical approach, is uniquely suited to anthropology, although it is not uniquely anthropological. The life history helps to convey how social contexts of such vital interest to ethnographers are played out in the lives of specific individuals. Life history also helps anthropologists get a feeling for how things were before they arrived on the scene and for how people view or choose to portray their own lives (see, for example, Langness & Frank, 1981). Given pervasive anthropological interests in how things change and how they stay the same, attention to life history adds a critical historical dimension to the ethnographic account at the same time that it provides a focus on somebody rather than on everybody.

As I have come to realize the extent to which the personal ambitions of educators exert a driving force in American education, I have been pleased to see more educational researchers adapting a life history approach to help us recognize and examine the impact of personal careers on the dynamics of public education. I think this approach is particularly well suited to dissertation studies (see, for example, Munro, 1991, 1993). Alternatively, looking at the life cycle of educational innovations, projects, fads, or movements provides an opportunity for discerning pervasive "patterns" in educator behavior (e.g., Wolcott, 1977).

I contrast *semistructured interviews* with *structured formal interviews*, the next two techniques to be considered, in order to emphasize that being in the field ordinarily provides the ethnographer unlimited opportunity to talk informally with subjects. Semistructured interviews do not follow a fixed sequence of predetermined questions. They capitalize on the fact that the ethnographer is the research instrument. Ranging as they do from casual conversation to direct questioning, informal interviews usually prove more important than structured interviews in an extended study (see Agar, 1996). Being on the scene allows the researcher to obtain information from people reluctant to submit to a structured interview but willing to talk casually to a neutral but interested listener. I have often found that people will grant a lengthy face-to-face interview yet insist they are too busy to fill out even the briefest questionnaire.

Conducting a *household census* has always been a standard fieldwork practice, but traditional ethnographers otherwise shied away from the impersonal *surveys* and *questionnaires* all too common in educational research. Today, however, the latter two techniques have become standard ethnographic procedures, particularly when working with sophisticated, literate, and busy people from whom some baseline census data might be helpful, warranted, and perhaps all one can hope to get. But I have seen anthropologists register surprise when colleagues claim survey techniques as part of their customary field procedures. Anthropologists might feel pressed to explain *why* they employed such techniques in a particular setting, just as researchers of other orientations might feel the need to explain *why they did not*. In collecting census data or genealogical data, or in following the formal eliciting techniques of the so-called "new" ethnography or "ethnoscience" approaches (see, for example Spradley, 1979, 1980; Spradley & McCurdy, 1988; Werner & Schoepfle, 1987a, 1987b), ethnographers follow procedures that are entirely systematic—but they utilize them in order to discern how humans categorize the world about them, not merely, in David Plath's phrase, to strike a pose for the lens of science (quoted in Smith 1990,

p. 365). (For a well-rounded discussion of systematic approaches to fieldwork, see Bernard, 1994.)

Unlike most research reported by educators or psychologists, the ethnographer never intends to base a study on the findings of only one technique, one instrument, or one brief encounter. Take a look at the appendices anthropologists traditionally have included with their studies. They do not ordinarily provide copies of questionnaires or interview schedules. Instead they provide additional information about their subjects: maps; household composition; glossaries; descriptions of ceremonies, songs, chants, magic; and perhaps a report about the fieldwork experience. They do not include a copy of a mailed questionnaire form and an accompanying cover letter.

I include *projective techniques* here more to record an era in fieldwork than to describe contemporary practice, particularly if the category brings to mind such earlier standbys as the use of Rorschach inkblot cards or pictures from the Thematic Apperception Test. Ever in search of a unifying theory of humankind, anthropologists were intrigued by the psychoanalytic interpretations of the Freudians. In the 1930s and 1940s, it was common for anthropologists not only to employ projective tests and to report observations cast in a psychoanalytic framework but to undergo the personal experience of psychoanalysis before venturing into the field. Those interests permeate much of the ethnography recorded in that period.

I doubt that many ethnographers today could produce a set of Rorschach cards, although anthropologists have always shared interests with psychologists and psychiatrists and have joined forces with others in pioneering work in cognitive studies. Given the diversity that the fieldworker invariably confronts, there is obvious appeal in employing any technique that can be administered to everyone alike. George and Louise Spindler have reported on a number of modified projective techniques they have developed as eliciting techniques in field research. These methods include the drawings used in their Instrumental Activities Inventory (Spindler, 1974a; Spindler & Spindler, 1965, 1982) as well as transcultural sensitization through the use of 35 mm color slides (Spindler, 1974b) and film used as both a record of activity and a stimulus for interviews (Spindler & Spindler, 1987).

The final interview activity to be mentioned here, *other measurement techniques*, includes the standardized tests so prevalent in school settings and serves as a reminder that fieldworkers may use virtually any kind of test to elicit information. In spite of the obvious attractions of obtaining quantifiable data of the sort so familiar among educational researchers, anthropologically oriented fieldworkers are often reluctant to use measurement techniques in their research, and they may object vigorously to being required to administer tests or questionnaires selected or devised by others in large-scale research projects. As educators, we are inclined to forget how intrusive test-taking can be and how different it is to test *in* school, where evaluation is a way of life, and to test in populations *out* of school. Anyone who has listened to an adult describe the trauma associated with having to take a driving test (or even the written examination required to obtain a driver's license) after a period of test-free years is reminded of how tests can frighten and alienate. And more than 50 years ago anthropologists were expressing concern "whether tests can ever be constructed which will reveal the psychological mechanism of intelligence as such, and eliminate the influence of cultural and educational opportunity" (Nadel, 1939, p. 186).

I have not forgotten the experience of a colleague who wished to obtain some systematic data early in the course of his first fieldwork. He began by making a house-to-house census in the village where he was conducting research. While collecting that information, he decided to explore the sociometrics of villager interaction and their perceptions of personal power and influence. Because he was residing in the village, was accepted by the villagers, and had sought their cooperation through both formal and informal channels, they dutifully answered his questions revealing their private and personal judgments. But, once having complied, for the next 3 months no one volunteered further information on *any* topic. Only slowly did he regain the rapport he once had. Questioning can be rude work. Ethnography is not intended to be rude business. Persistent, maybe, but not rude.

Examining: Using and Making Records

To emphasize the importance of historical documents and public records in ethnographic research, I use the term *archives* to refer specifically to one type of written source, and *other written documents,* a broad catch-all term, for everything else. The importance of archival materials in ethnographic research may reflect the close link between colonial administrations and the early development of both British and American anthropology. In any case, it is important to note that anthropologists use many kinds of written records; they do not limit themselves to what is available in libraries.

Like historians, ethnographers find primary documents of all sorts—official records, newspapers, letters, and diaries—of great value. In working with populations that include school-age children, anthropologists have sometimes sponsored essay contests to encourage young people to write about their experiences. I have mentioned fieldwork in which my duties as village teacher seemed to hamper opportunity for interaction. I was so busy keeping school that I often had little idea of what was going on in the village. Eventually, I discovered that the problem had a compensating side. My customary classroom practice of having students write in class every day was providing not only a daily account of village events but also the further insight of the students' views of those events in a privileged communication to the teacher. Furthermore, my young chroniclers were at an age when they moved easily throughout the village, more easily than I could and far more easily than did their circumspect elders. My only hesitancy in relating this episode is that it took me so long to realize how valuable my students' written accounts were in my efforts to learn about village life.

Far too many "data-gathering" procedures in educational research are designed with an overriding concern for obtaining data that are manageable and codable, with breadth too often subsituted for depth. To date, ethnographers seem impressed by what computers can do, but we have yet to see the full impact of the computer on fieldwork except in forcing every researcher to ask the agonizing question of whether everything noted in the field should—must?—be entered into the word processor. Most fieldworkers continue to collect information in a variety of forms, rather than with an eye to the degrees of freedom afforded by a punchcard or software program, but I worry that younger colleagues are beginning to sound more and more like "data freaks." Perhaps that is why some anthropologists continue to express a preference for the term *fieldwork* rather than *data gathering*. Apparently it never occurs to anyone to complain about, as well as to celebrate, our even-increasing capacity to record information. I took notebooks, a portable typewriter, and a 35 mm camera into the field in 1962. I have publicly lamented that inexpensive tape recorders, "faster" film, and videotape were not readily available in those days to help in documentation. In reality, however, it may have been a blessing in disguise not to be swamped with "data" too easy to collect, as today's researchers are inclined to be. I had to work quickly to get the account written before "headnotes" faded from memory to leave me with written notes that captured only part of what I had experienced. (See Ottenberg's discussion about headnotes in the insightful volume *Fieldnotes* edited by Roger Sanjek, 1990.)

It is hard to envision a scene in which colleagues eagerly assemble to see what a quantitatively oriented researcher has brought back to the office after a period of intense data gathering. It is hard to imagine an ethnographer who would not have collected pictures, maps, or examples of local handiwork, even if the field site was a nearby classroom. The wall adornments of anthropologists' offices and homes display the results of compulsive collecting. But the use of nonwritten sources is primarily for examination and illustration, not ornamentation. Linguists with their tapes and ethnographers with their photographs, films, or artifacts, all find primary materials invaluable in analysis and write-up, as well as for subsequently testing the adequacy of their developing descriptions and explanations.

I trust I have provided sufficient examples to make the case for the importance of both using and making *maps, photographs, and audio- or videotapes* in pursuing ethnographic research. In spite of my caution about data overload, the judicious recording of both sight and sound are invaluable aids in fieldwork. The use of photography, particularly in ethnographic filmmaking, has received special attention for many years (J. Collier & M. Collier, 1986; Crawford & Turton, 1992; Hockings, 1995; Rollwagen, 1993) and has been applied effectively in classroom research, especially for studies of nonverbal communication (J. Collier, 1973; M. Collier, 1979; Erickson & Wilson, 1982) and other fine-grained studies of classroom ethnography or "micro-ethnography." Ethnographers have long pointed the way to collecting and using recorded sights and sounds to keep us from restricting the input and output of our inquiries only and always to the printed word.

The subject of mapping brings me full circle to participant observation, for one of the first things the ethnographer is advised to do in a new field setting is to make a map. Think how interesting it might prove to teachers, and how natural an activity for an ethnographer, to prepare a map of a school and school ground, to plot how different categories of people at the school move through its space, and to probe reasons they offer for why various things are used or placed as they are. Whose automobiles are parked in specially marked spaces? Why are all visitors directed to report to the front office, and how is it that schools have "front offices," like factories, rather than, say, reception rooms? Why is the nurse's office so near the front office? Do nurses usually have offices? If the principal is the instructional leader of the school, why is the Instructional Materials Center or Learning Center so far from his or her office? How do new students learn about "territory" in the school? Under what circumstances can certain territory be invaded, and by whom? You see how quickly one thing can lead to another—and how a knowledge of the setting and the people in it helps one get a sense of which questions to ask, of whom, when, and in what manner.

Reporting the Research

As every experienced fieldworker discovers, the mystique of ethnography is in the process of transforming field experience into a completed account, not in the doing of fieldwork itself. (For a "realistic" account of this problem in classroom research, see Larequ, 1996.) Rosalie Wax (1971) wisely counseled wouldbe ethnographers to allow at least as much time for analyzing and writing as they planned to spend in the field. I can only underscore that the time for analyzing and writing should be reckoned in equivalents of "uninterrupted days." Fair warning is hereby given that the time commitment is great in terms of customary expectations for research in education. My own fieldwork-based dissertation added two years to my program of doctoral studies in education and anthropology—one full year of participant observation research and a second year to write it up. At that, it took another 25 years before I could offer the perspective I finally added as an Afterword (Wolcott, 1989).

It is in the write-up, rather than in the fieldwork, that materials become ethnographic. What human beings do and say is not psychological, sociological, anthropological, or what have you. Those disciplinary dimensions come from the structures we impose on what we see and understand. It is in the ethnographer's transformation of data and of the fieldwork experience itself that the material takes ethnographic shape as both a description of what is going on among a particular social group and a cultural interpretation of how that behavior "makes sense" to those involved (see Wolcott, 1987).

As ethnography has "caught on" in educational research, I think astute observers who have produced excellent descriptive accounts have sometimes tacked that term to their work as though it is synonymous with observation itself. Let me repeat, and emphasize, that one might utilize all the field research techniques described here and not come up with ethnography, and an anthropologist might not employ any of the customary field research techniques and still produce an ethnographic account—or at least a satisfactory ethnographic reconstruction.

Admittedly, not every cultural anthropologist cares that much about producing ethnography. Some are more theoretically, philosophically, or even mathematically inclined. As in any field, some anthropologists become preoccupied with issues of method, the analysis of other people's data, or computer solutions to classic anthropological problems. The more action-oriented look for ways to use data already available or apply lessons already learned. One journal in the field of cultural anthropology—the *American Ethnologist*—went so far as specifically to exclude descriptive ethnographic studies from its purview during its early years of publication. Nevertheless, descriptive ethnographic accounts are the building blocks of the discipline of cultural anthropology, just as fieldwork itself has remained the sine qua non of the cultural anthropologist.

As noted, only relatively recently have anthropologists given much explicit attention to "method." Even less attention has been directed to the difficult business of organizing and writing, other than to repeat well-worn maxims that fieldwork amounts to naught if the notes are not transformed into an ethnographic account, to advise neophyte field-workers to begin writing early (preferably to complete a first draft while still in the field), and to acknowledge, more with awe than with instruction, when an occasional ethnographer seems to have made a literary as well as a scholarly contribution.

For the beginning writer of a descriptive account, let me offer a few suggestions I have discussed elsewhere (Wolcott, 1990, 1994. 1995). First, I strongly support the idea of coupling the writing task to ongoing fieldwork; it is splendid indeed if one is able to follow the advice to prepare an initial draft while fieldwork is in progress. In attempting to set down in writing what you understand, you also become acutely aware of what you do not understand. You can identify gaps in the data while you still have opportunity to make further inquiry. If you lack the time, practice, or perspective required for drafting a full account, you nonetheless can begin to "think" in chapters, sections, or expanded outlines, and thus keep tuned to the difficult task sometimes dismissed as simply "writing up one's notes."

Wherever and whenever the task of writing begins, a second bit of advice is to begin at a relatively easy place where you feel well informed and know (or should know!) what you are talking about. One good starting point is to describe your fieldwork approach, although you may be tempted at first to say far more than needed. Describe where you went and what you did *to get the information you are actually going to use in the final account.* Your discussion of your method(s) may subsequently become part of your first chapter, an appendix, or, if it gets out of hand, a separate, publishable paper.

Another starting point is to begin with the descriptive portion of the account, actively resisting as long as possible the temptation to begin making inferences, interpretation, or even the most cautious analysis. Simply get on with telling the story of what happened. Not only will this help to satisfy the anthropological preference for providing a high ratio of information to explanation (Smith, 1964), but it also invites readers to join with you as you subsequently shift to more analytical or interpretive modes. Readers already will have some idea of your database. Description, analysis, and interpretation need not be dramatically separated in the final account, but I think it is a valuable exercise for anyone new to descriptive writing to begin by preparing an account as free as possible from one's own inferences and preferences. (I have elaborated more fully on this description-analysis-interpretation distinction in Wolcott, 1994.)

My next (and favorite) bit of advice might seem to have come from a short course on writing, but I found it among the instructions for assembling a wheelbarrow: Make sure all parts are correctly in place before tightening. Take advantage of the fluidity available in developing an ethnographic account. Both problem and interpretation should remain in flux, and they should influence decisions about what must be included or may be deleted from the descriptive narrative. In that sense, although ethnographic accounts can be finished, they are never really completed. Rather, as Geertz (1983, p. 6) suggests, quoting Paul Valéry, what we do is *abandon* them.

Finally, let me repeat advice I frequently give to students and colleagues: I would not use the term *ethnography* in my title, or claim to be providing ethnography in my written account, unless I was certain that the work needed and warranted that claim. That point goes beyond merely finding an appropriate title. I turn to it next.

"Doing Ethnography" Versus "Borrowing Ethnographic Techniques"

Armed with a list of fieldwork techniques such as those reviewed above, and duly cautioned about the critical complementary tasks involved in subsequent deskwork, is a neophyte researcher ready to start "doing" ethnography? I think not. Let me repeat some cautions already noted and attempt to provide a broad perspective on ethnographic research.

First, none of these fieldwork techniques is exclusive to anthropology. No single one, including participant observation, guarantees that the results will be ethnographic.

Second, although one can be reasonably certain that the ethnographer will use several techniques, there is no magic formula for combining them. Anthropologists conduct their inquiries into human social behavior by observing and by asking. When you think about it, most of us have been doing those two things, and for basically the same reasons—to achieve cultural competence—since we first were able to observe and to ask. Our continued practice in that regard is scant basis for thinking that we will suddenly start producing ethnography instead of simply acting more or less appropriately. At the same time, here is a gentle reminder to all researchers. In becoming active participants in our various "communities of practice" (Lave & Wenger's term, 1991, p. 29ff.), we ourselves have relied on numerous sources, numerous techniques, and ample time for attending to multiple facets in our lives, not just to a few that were easy to understand or that satisfied rigorous statistical tests.

A certain reserve is warranted in educational research when we claim to be "doing ethnography" yet restrict our research to a few weekday hours spent in schools. The anthropologist conducting ethnographic research ordinarily attends to broad cultural contexts. Educational researchers, focused as they are on particular problems, and intent not only to address those problems but to remedy them as well, do not ordinarily want or need to do ethnographies or even "microethnographies." Rather than risk an unwarranted claim, I think educational researchers are better advised to exhibit some reserve in noting how they may at times *avail* themselves of several techniques for getting their information, how their approach may be *influenced* by the characteristic long-term thoroughness of the ethnographer, or how their perspective or analysis may be *informed* by relevant prior work in anthropology. As anthropologist Roger Sanjek has observed, not *everything* that begins in the field needs to be called ethnography (1991, p. 620). I think it useful to distinguish between anthropologically informed researchers who *do ethnography* and a vast majority of educational researchers who sometimes *draw upon ethnographic approaches* in conducting descriptive studies in educational settings.

It is not the techniques employed that make a study ethnographic. Nor is it necessarily what one looks at. The critical element is the perspective through which one interprets what one has seen. In research among pupils in classrooms and in other learning environments—work generated out of ethnographic interests—ethnographically oriented researchers have looked at smaller units of behavior, such as classroom teaching and learning styles, or at the classroom "participant structures" through which teachers arrange opportunities for verbal interaction (Philips, 1972, 1983). They are developing an ever-increasing capacity for examining fine detail—for example, in repeated viewings of filmed or videotaped segments of behavior. Nevertheless, they embed their analysis in cultural context. The greater anthropological contribution to the study of education may lie in helping educators to locate learning in out-of-school contexts and to become more aware of their assumptions about the nature of learning itself, allowing themselves to be co-opted in helping to study (and inevitably to evaluate) what goes on in schools. The work of Jean Lave and her associates into the "quintessentially social character" of learning and of knowledge use is exemplary in this regard (see, for example, Lave, 1985; Lave & Wenger, 1991), most recently posing a challenge as to whether there is any such thing as learning sui generis (Lave, 1993, p. 5).

I am dismayed when I hear educators suggest that we have made no progress toward providing *an* ethnography of schooling, but I become equally concerned when I hear others imply that we will someday complete *the* ethnography of schooling. The task of description, and thus the potential for ethnography, is endless. We know we do not need to describe everything. We seek to identify those dimensions critical to our understanding of human social behavior and then to describe them exceedingly well. With his pithy phrase, "It is not necessary to know everything in order to understand something," anthropologist Geertz (1973, p. 20) reminds us that we may make headway through modest increments.

Ideally, each of us should be able to follow whatever research approach seems best suited for the problem at hand. The reality, of course, is that we usually have our research approach pretty much in mind when we identify our research problems. Our approaches frame our problems. Thus we need to seek out educationally significant problems for which qualitative/descriptive research in general, and ethnographic research in particular, seem best suited. The realistic question for an ethnographically oriented researcher is not "How should this question be addressed?" but "What contribution, if any, can I make by taking an ethnographic approach to this problem?

Ethnography is well suited to answer the question, "What is going on here?" That is, first, a question of behaviors and events, and, second, a question of meanings. It is not a question that educators often ask, for it gets mixed up with a ready answer about what *should* be going on, even if it is not. Ethnography is not well suited to answer the normative question most pressing to education's practitioners, "What should we be doing?" Ethnographers attend instead to complexity, to what those in a setting believe should be the case, to tensions arising from divergent points of view, and to paradoxes between stated objectives and the ways people go about trying to reach them. Such observations, however, may offer little solace to the educator thus informed, for whom the reaction is likely to be, "It's even more complicated than I thought" or "You're only making the obvious obvious."

Genuine ethnographic inquiry proceeds best under conditions where there will be time to find out what is going on, and where there is reason to believe that knowing what things mean to those involved could conceivably make a difference. It also requires some understanding of how—or whether—one particular instance, or event, or case, or individual described in careful detail is not only unique but also shares characteristics in common with other instances or events or cases or individuals. The ethnographer looks for the generic in the specific, following a "natural history" approach that seeks to understand classes of events through the careful examination of specific ones. "Ethnography is always more than description," writes anthropologist James Peacock, carefully adding, "Ethnography reveals the general through the particular, the abstract through the concrete" (1986, p. 83). Thus ethnography is not a license to generalize, it is a mandate to build, and build upon, a solid basis of careful description.

Like other social scientists, ethnographers are concerned with "representativeness" but they approach that problem differently through efforts to contextualize a particular case under study among other cases. The question in anthropological sampling is not "Is this case representative?" but "What is this case representative of?" You conduct your research where you can, with whatever available key informant or classroom or family or village best satisfies your research criteria, and then you undertake to learn how that one is similar to, and different from, others of its type in important systematic ways. In the absence of being able to select their samples, as Margaret Mead explained years ago, anthropologists must attend to where and how the cases they select fit into some larger picture. Any member of a group is a "perfect sample" of that group, she insisted, provided that the member's individual characteristics and position within the group are "properly specified" (1953, p. 648). For feet-of-clay ethnographers like myself, this is the major role for theory to play, not to tell us what we should see, but to *help us make sense of what we have seen* in terms of some broader context or issue. (More on this in Wolcott, 1995.)

The ethnographer's concern is always for context. One's focus moves constantly between figure and ground—like a zoom lens on a camera—to catch the fine detail of what individuals are doing and to keep a perspective on the context of that behavior. To illustrate: An ethnographer assisting in educational program evaluation ought to be looking not only at the program under review but at the underlying ethos of evaluation as well. What meaning does evaluation have for different groups or individuals? How do certain people become evaluators of others? Who, in turn, evaluates them? It is this very issue of evaluation that has prompted me to plead on behalf of regarding ethnographic research not only as an alternative form *of* educational evaluation but also as an alternative *to* educational evaluation. The processes and consequences of educational evaluation warrant ethnographic attention unlikely to spring from those professionally committed to it.

Evaluation is one element worthy of ethnographic attention; there are others. In studying cases of conscious efforts to introduce educational change, for example, ethnographers ought to be looking at the "donors" of change as well as at the recipients or targets of it. Years ago Frederick Erickson posed another question that continues to guide much current ethnographic research in classrooms: What do teachers and children have to know in order to do what they are doing? And renewed interest in issues of culture transmission and acquisition raise tantalizing questions about how culture can be said to be shared when no two individuals ever experience it in exactly the same way (see Wolcott, 1991, 1996).

The Role of Ethnographic Research in Education

Is ethnographic research becoming a more potent force in shaping the course of formal education? I would like to claim that it is, because it is the kind of research that most interests me. But I am pessimistic. I find little evidence that educational research of *any* type has much impact on practice, and our descriptive efforts to portray how things are do not seem likely to capture the imagination of those already impatient and determined to improve them.

In and of themselves, ethnographic accounts do not point the way to policy decisions; they do not give clues to what should be done differently or suggest how best to proceed. Ethnographers' attention tends to focus on *how things are and how they got that way*, but educators are preoccupied with *how things might become*. Educators tend to be action oriented, but ethnography does not point out lessons to be gained or action to be taken. Anyone who takes time to read a ethnographic account will probably realize that it increases the complexity of the setting or problem being addressed rather than decreases it.

Only slowly are we creating a constituency of informed researchers and practitioners who have realistic expectations about how qualitative approaches in general, or ethnographic approaches in particular, fit into some larger research mission. Perhaps as a newcomer to qualitative approaches, you have a role to play in this. Let me conclude with three recommendations for how you might simultaneously benefit from and participate in furthering the use of ethnographic approaches in educational research.

First, as suggested at the beginning of this essay, expand your reading base to include some ethnography, and expand your professional reading to include a broad range of qualitative studies. Like the linguist who can amaze you by explicating rules of your own language that you never knew you knew, ethnographers' accounts of education should have a ring of authenticity, for here you will find yourself one of the "natives" being described. Such studies ought to help you grasp something of ethnographic research itself as well as help you better understand the central processes in which you are engaged both professionally and personally: the transmission and acquisition of culture. If they do not, speak out about how, in your perception, observers are missing the point about what is going on or what teachers are trying to accomplish. Through trying to explicate the difference between what observers see and what teachers try to do, you will begin to understand the important and useful distinction between what we do and what we say we do, between culture as revealed in everyday lives and culture as an idealized system of mutual expectations about what ought to be.

Second, become conscious of and familiar with the variety of field techniques described here. Watch for instances in which a multi-instrument approach would be preferable to relying on only one source of information. You might catch yourself in action as a teacher or administrator and ask whether, in your own professional circumstances, you tend to place too much reliance on too few ways of finding out. It is a ready trap for practitioner and researcher alike. (For an inventory of some other ready traps confronting fieldworkers, see Fine, 1993; Wolcott, 1995.)

Third, take a cue from the ethnographer and develop a keen appreciation for context in educational research. Whether reading research reports or trying to understand a setting in which you yourself are a participant, keep probing for more factors that may be involved. Educators have a tendency (and, realistically, a need) to oversimplify in order to make things manageable, and to glom onto single-issue answers (hot lunch) or explanations (broken home) to complex issues. Ethnographers are not entirely free from this tendency; if they were, they would not set out to reduce accounts of human social behavior to a certain number of printed pages or a reel of film. But ethnographers remain constantly aware of complexity and context.

There are no unwanted findings or extraneous circumstances in ethnographic research. I wonder if it is the inattention to broader contexts, to the "real world" of classroom and school, that has made educational research seem largely irrelevant to its practitioners in the past. If so, the concern for context that ethnography has engendered may be the most important contribution it has to make, not only in the work of ethnographers but also in the influence they have exerted on educational researchers more generally.

References

Agar, M. H. (1996). *The professional stranger: An informal introduction to ethnography* (2nd ed.). New York: Academic Press.

Beebe, J. (1995). Basic concepts and techniques of rapid appraisal. *Human Organization, 54*(1), 42–51.

Bernard, H. R. (1988). *Research methods in cultural anthropology.* Newbury Park, CA: Sage.

Bernard, H. R. (1994). *Research methods in anthropology: Qualitative and quantitative approaches* (2nd ed.). Thousand Oaks, CA: Sage.

Boyarin, J. (Ed.). (1993). *The ethnography of reading.* Berkeley: University of California Press.

Burnett, J. H. (1969). Ceremony, rites, and economy in the student system of an American high school. *Human Organization, 28*(1), 1–9.

Casagrande, J. B. (1960). *In the company of man.* New York: Harper and Brothers.

Chang, H. (1992). *Adolescent life and ethos: An ethnography of a U.S. high school.* Bristol, PA: Falmer Press.

Collier, J., Jr. (1973). *Alaskan Eskimo education: A film analysis of cultural confrontation in the schools.* New York: Holt, Rinehart & Winston.

Collier, J., Jr., & Collier, M. (1986). *Visual anthropology: Photography as a research method.* Albuquerque: University of New Mexico Press.

Collier, M. (1979). *A film study of classrooms in western Alaska.* Fairbanks, AK: Center for Cross-Cultural Studies.

Crawford, P. I., & Turton, D. (1992). *Film as ethnography.* Manchester, UK: Manchester University Press.

Cusick, P. A. (1973). *Inside high school: The student's world.* New York: Holt, Rinehart & Winston.

Erickson, F. (1977). Some approaches to inquiry in school-community ethnography. *Anthropology and Education Quarterly, 8*(2): 58–69.

Erickson, F., & Wilson, J. (1982). *Sights and sounds of life in schools: A resource guide to film and videotape for research and education* (Research Series No. 125). East Lansing: Michigan State University Institute for Research on Teaching.

Everhart, R. B. (1983). *Reading, writing and resistance: Adolescence and labor in a junior high school.* Boston: Routledge and Kegan Paul.

Fine, G. A. (1993). Ten lies of ethnography: Moral dilemmas in field research. *Journal of Contemporary Ethnography, 22*(3), 267–294.

Fox, R. G. (Ed.). (1991). *Recapturing anthropology: Working in the present.* Santa Fe, NM: School of American Research Press.

Geertz, C. (1968). *Islam observed.* Chicago: University of Chicago Press.

Geertz, C. (1973). Thick description. In C. Geertz (Ed.), *The interpretation of cultures* (pp. 3–30). New York: Basic Books.

Geertz, C. (1983). *Local knowledge: Further essays in interpretive anthropology.* New York: Basic Books.

Geertz, C. (1988). *Works and lives: The anthropologist as author.* Stanford, CA: Stanford University Press.

Goodenough, W. H. (1976). Multiculturalism as the normal human experience. *Anthropology and Education Quarterly, 7*(4): 4–7.

Goodenough, W. H. (1981). *Culture, language, and society.* Menlo Park, CA: Benjamin/Cummings.

Hart, S. (1982). Analyzing the social organization for reading in one elementary school. In Spindler, G. (Ed.), *Doing the ethnography of schooling: Educational anthropology in action* (pp. 410–438). New York: Holt, Rinehart & Winston. (Reissued 1988 by Waveland Press, Prospect Heights, IL.)

Hockings, P. (Ed.). (1995). *Principles of visual anthropology* (2nd ed.). Berlin: Mouton de Gruyter.

Jessor, R., Colby, A., & Shweder, R. (Eds.). (1996). *Ethnography and human development.* Chicago: University of Chicago Press.

King, A. R. (1967). *The school at Mopass: A problem of identity.* New York: Holt, Rinehart & Winston.

King. A. R. (1974). The teacher as a participant-observer: A case study. In Spindler, G. D. (Ed.), *Education and cultural process: Toward an anthropology of education.* New York: Holt, Rinehart & Winston.

Kulick, D., & Willson, M. (Eds.). (1995). *Taboo: Sex, identity, and erotic subjectivity in anthropoligical fieldwork.* New York: Routledge.

Langness, L. L., & Frank, G. (1981). *Lives: An anthropological approach to biography.* Novato, CA: Chandler and Sharp.

Lareau, A. (1996). Common problems in field work: A personal essay. In A. Lareau & J. Schultz (Eds.), *Journeys through ethnography: Realistic accounts of fieldwork* (pp. 195–236). Boulder, CO: Westview Press.

Lave, J. (Guest ed.). (1985). The social organization of knowledge and practice: A symposium. *Anthropology and Education Quarterly, 16*(3), 171–213.

Lave, J. (1993). The practice of learning. In S. Chaiklin & J. Lave (Eds.), *Understanding practice* (pp. 3–32). New York: Cambridge University Press.

Lave, J., & Wenger, E. (1991). *Situated learning: legitimate peripheral participation.* New York: Cambridge University Press.

Levin, E., & Leap, W. L. (Eds.). (1996). *Out in the field: Reflections of lesbian and gay anthropologists.* Urbana: University of Illinois Press.

Malinowski, B. (1922). *Argonauts of the western Pacific.* New York: E. P. Dutton.

McPherson, G. H. (1972). *Small town teacher.* Cambridge, MA: Harvard University Press.

Mead, M. (1953). National character. In A. L Kroeber (Ed.), *Anthropology today* (pp. 642–667). Chicago: University of Chicago Press.

Messerschmidt, D. A. (Ed) (1981). *Anthropologists at home in North America: Methods and issues in the study of one's own society.* New York: Cambridge University Press.

Munro, P. (1991). A life of work: Stories women teachers tell. Unpublished doctoral dissertation, University of Oregon.

Munro, P. (1993). Continuing dilemmas of life history research: A reflexive account of feminist qualitative inquiry. In D. Flinders & G. Mills (Eds.), *Theory and concepts in qualitative research* (pp. 163–177). New York: Teachers College Press.

Nadel, S. F. (1939). The application of intelligence tests in the anthropological field. In F. C. Bartlett, M. Ginsberg, E. L. Lindgren, & R. H. Thouless (Eds.), *The study of society* (pp. 184–198). London: Kegan, Paul, Trench, Trubner.

Ottenberg, S. (1960). Thirty years of fieldnotes: Changing relationships to the text. In Roger Sanjek (Ed.), *Fieldnotes* (pp. 139–160). Ithaca, NY: Cornell University Press.

Peacock, J. L. (1986). *The anthropological lens: Harsh light, soft focus.* New York: Cambridge University Press.

Pelto, P. J., & Pelto, G. H. (1978). *Anthropological research: The structure of inquiry* (2nd ed.). New York: Cambridge University Press.

Philips, S. U. (1972). Participant structures and communicative competence: Warm Springs children in community and classroom. In Cazden, C., John, V. P., & Hymes, D. (Eds.), *Functions of language in the classroom* (pp. 370–394). New York: Teachers College Press. (Reissued 1985 by Waveland Press, Prospect Heights, IL.)

Philips, S. U. (1983). *The Invisible Culture: Communication in Classroom and Community on the Warm Springs Indian Reservation.* New York: Longman.

Plattner, S. (1989). Commentary: Ethnographic method. *Anthropology Newsletter, 32*: 30, 21.

Powdermaker, H. (1966). *Stranger and friend: The way of an anthropologist.* New York: Norton.

Rist, Ray C. (1980). Blitzkrieg ethnography: On the transformation of a method into a movement. *Educational Researcher, 9*(2), 8–10.

Rollwagen, J. R. (Ed.). (1993). Anthropological film and video in the 1990s: Case studies in documentary filmmaking and videomaking. Vol. 1. Brockport, NY: The Institute Press.

Rosenfeld, G. (1971). *"Shut those thick lips!": A study of slum school failure.* New York: Holt, Rinehart & Winston.

Sanjek, R. (Ed.). (1990). *Fieldnotes: The makings of anthropology.* Ithaca, NY: Cornell University Press.

Sanjek, R. (1991). The ethnographic present. *Man, 26*(4):609–628.

Sanjek, R. (1995). "Ethnography." In A. Barnard & J. Spencer (Eds.), *Encyclopedic dictionary of social and cultural anthropology.* London: Routledge.

Smith, A. G. (1964). The Dionysian innovation. *American Anthropologist, 66,* 251–265.

Smith, L. M., & Geoffrey, W. (1968). *The complexities of an urban classroom.* New York: Holt, Rinehart & Winston.

Smith, Robert J. (1990). Hearing voices, joining the chorus: Appropriating someone else's fieldnotes. In R. Sanjek (Ed.), *Fieldnotes* (pp. 356–370). Ithaca, NY: Cornell University Press.

Spindler, G. D. (1974a). Schooling in Schönhausen: A study in cultural transmission and instrumental adaptation in an urbanizing German village. In G. D. Spindler (Ed.), *Education and cultural process: Toward an anthropology of education* (pp. 230–277). New York: Holt, Rinehart & Winston.

Spindler, G. D. (1974b). Transcultural sensitization. In G. D. Spindler (Ed.), *Education and cultural process: Toward an anthropology of education* (pp. 449–462). New York: Holt, Rinehart & Winston.

Spindler, G. D., & Spindler, L. (1965). The Instrumental Activities Inventory: A technique for the study of the psychology of acculturation. *Southwestern Journal of Anthropology, 21,* 1–23.

Spindler, G. D., & Spindler, L. (1982). Roger Harker and Schönhausen: From the familiar to the strange and back again. In Spindler, G. (Ed.), *Doing the ethnography of schooling: Educational anthropology in action* (pp. 21–46). New York: Holt, Rinehart & Winston. (Reissued 1988 by Waveland Press, Prospect Heights, IL.)

Spindler, G. D., & Spindler, L. (1987). In prospect for a controlled cross-cultural comparison of schooling: Schoenhausen and Roseville. In G. D. Spindler (Ed.), *Education and cultural process: Anthropological approaches* (2nd ed., pp. 389–400). Prospect Heights, IL: Waveland Press.

Spradley, J. (1979). *The ethnographic interview.* New York: Holt, Rinehart & Winston.

Spradley, J. (1980). *Participant observation.* New York: Holt, Rinehart & Winston.

Spradley, J., & McCurdy, D. (1988). *The cultural experience: Ethnography in complex society.* Prospect Heights, IL: Waveland Press. (Originally published 1972.)

van Willigen, J., & Finan, T. (Eds.). (1991). *Soundings: Rapid and reliable research methods for practicing anthropologists* (NAPA Bulletin #10). Washington, DC: American Anthropological Association.

Wax, R. H. (1971). *Doing fieldwork: Warnings and advice.* Chicago: University of Chicago Press.

Werner, O., Schoepfle, G. M. (1987a). *Foundations of ethnography and interviewing: Vol. 1. Systematic fieldwork.* Newbury Park, CA: Sage.

Werner, O., & Schoepfle, G. M. (1987b). *Ethnographic analysis and data management: Vol. 2. Systematic fieldwork.* Newbury Park, CA: Sage.

Wolcott, H. F. (1967). *A Kwakiutl village and school.* New York: Holt, Rinehart & Winston. (Reissued 1989 by Waveland Press with a new afterword.)

Wolcott, H. F. (1973). *The man in the principal's office: An ethnography.* New York: Holt, Rinehart & Winston. (Reissued 1984 with a new preface by Waveland Press, Prospect Heights, IL.)

Wolcott, H. F. (1977). *Teachers versus technocrats: An educational innovation in anthropological perspective.* Eugene, OR: Center for Educational Policy and Management, University of Oregon.

Wolcott, H. F. (1980). How to look like an anthropologist without being one. *Practicing Anthropology, 3*(1), 6–7, 56–59.

Wolcott, H. F. (1984). Ethnographers sans ethnography: The evaluation compromise. In D. M. Fetterman (Ed.), *Ethnography in educational evaluation* (pp. 177–210). Beverly Hills, CA: Sage.

Wolcott, H. F. (1987). On ethnographic intent. In G. Spindler & L. Spindler (Eds.), *Interpretive ethnography of education: At home and abroad* (pp. 35–57). Hillsdale, NJ: Lawrence Erlbaum.

Wolcott, H. F. (1989). *A Kwakiutl village and school 25 years later* (rev. ed. with new afterword). Prospect Heights, IL: Waveland Press. (Reprinted in Wolcott, H. [1994]. *Transforming qualitative data.* Thousand Oaks, CA: Sage.)

Wolcott, H. F. (1990). *Writing up qualitative research: Vol 20. Sage University Press Series in Qualitative Research.* Newbury Park: CA: Sage.

Wolcott, H. F. (1991). Propriospect and the acquisition of culture. *Anthropology and Education Quarterly, 22*(3), 251–273.

Wolcott, H. F. (1992). Posturing in qualitative inquiry. In M. D. LeCompte, W. L. Millroy, & J. Preissle (Eds.), *Handbook of qualitative research in education* (pp. 3–52). San Diego, CA: Academic Press.

Wolcott, H. F. (1994). *Transforming qualitative data: Description, analysis, and interpretation.* Thousand Oaks, CA: Sage.

Wolcott, H. F. (1995). *The art of fieldwork.* Walnut Creek, CA: AltaMira Press.

Wolcott, H. F. (1996). Peripheral participation and the Kwakiutl potlatch. *Anthropology and Education Quarterly, 27*(4), 467–492.

Suggestions for Further Reading

Ethnographers attend both to what people do and to what people say they do. One can also learn about ethnographic research through either approach—reading ethnographers' accounts or reading what ethnographers say they do and how they tell others to go about doing ethnographic research. The references suggested here for further reading distinguish between reading ethnography and reading *about* ethnography. My advice is to do more of the former, attending to what ethnographers have accomplished rather than getting caught up in endless details and recipes for how to proceed. The following references distinguish between accounts that deal specifically with education and accounts that present ethnography in more traditional settings.

Note: References preceded by an asterisk (*) are available in more than one edition, often including paperbacks. No specific publisher or edition is listed for those references; the date indicates the year of original publication.

I. Reading to Gain an Anthropological Perspective

Every field has its classics. Two "oldies but goodies" in cultural anthropology are Ruth Benedict's *Patterns of Culture* (1934) and Clyde Kluckhohn's *Mirror for Man* (1949). Benedict's book has been faulted for treating culture as "personality writ large," and her Apollonian-Dionysian distinction is long out of fashion, but the cross-cultural and comparative perspective comes through clearly in her exquisite prose. Kluckhohn's book continues to offer an inviting introduction to anthropology, intended, as the author was careful to point out, "for the layman, not for the carping professional" (p. ix.) The title suggests Kluckhohn's perspective on the role he saw for the discipline: "Anthropology holds up a great mirror to man and lets him look at himself in his infinite variety" (p. 11).

In 1973, Clifford Geertz published a collection of his earlier essays in *The Interpretation of Cultures*. He also added an important new one, "Thick Description: Toward an Interpretive Theory of Culture," an essay that set many anthropologists off on a new tack looking for symbols and meanings in lieu of structures and functions. The essay contines to be widely cited and quoted and warrants being read in its entirety.

For those willing to work their way through an introductory textbook, William Haviland's book, now in its 8th edition, Alexander Moore's 1992 rewrite of his earlier (1978) *Cultural Anthropology,* and Paul Bohannan's efforts at a fresh approach in *We, the Alien,* deserve special mention. Roger Keesing's two successive iterations of a text originally authored by his father, Felix Keesing, and published in 1958, remained a standard for years. Ostensibly designed as an undergraduate text, Robert Borofsky's edited Assessing Cultural Anthropology (1994) offers a set of state-of-the-art essays that warrant the attention of all scholars interested in this field.

*Benedict, R. (1934). *Patterns of culture.*

Bohannan, P. (1992). *We, the alien: An introduction to cultural anthropology.* Prospect Heights, IL: Waveland Press.

Borofsky, R. (Ed.). (1994). *Assessing cultural anthropology.* New York: McGraw-Hill.

Geertz, C. (1973). *The interpretation of cultures.* New York: Basic Books.

Haviland, W. (1996). *Cultural anthropology* (8th ed.). Fort Worth, TX: Harcourt Brace.

Keesing, R., & Keesing, F. (1976). *Cultural anthropology: A contemporary perspective.* New York: Holt, Rinehart & Winston.

*Kluckhohn, C. (1949). *Mirror for man.*

Moore, A. (1992). *Cultural anthropology: The field study of human beings.* San Diego: Collegiate Press.

II. Reading Ethnographies

A. The Classics

For readers who prefer a "guided tour" to the classics, rather than simply picking one or two off the shelf, there is a new genre designed just for them. The authors of this genre intend to foster a critical, informed reading without assuming that every *consumer* of ethnography wants also to become a *producer* of ethnography. Two authors who are well-suited to such lead an excursion through the classics are Paul Atkinson and David Jacobson, each with his personal selection of classics identified by way of illustration.

As to my own choices among the classics, I have picked only a handful, hoping that by keeping the number small, I may entice you to read all of them. Because they are frequently quoted or cited in the work of others, let me call particular attention to two. First and foremost is Malinowski's *Argonauts of the Western Pacific.* Whatever its shortcomings, this book probably comes closest to being THE standard ethnography that is most likely to be recommended as a "must read," even if more on the basis that it will be good for you than that you are in for a reading treat. And for a neoclassic, let me suggest Clifford Geertz's "Deep Play: Notes on the Balinese Cockfight," an often-cited essay that demonstrates a markedly different style from the way Malinowski had gone about his research and reporting half a century earlier.

The names of British social anthropologists E. E. Evans-Pritchard and Raymond Firth bring to my mind the two studies closely associated with them that I have included here. Margaret Mead was a prolific author; I cite two of her watershed studies. I do not suggest that her works necessarily serve as models for either the doing or the writing of ethnography, but it is important to have a glimpse of her fine mind at work and to appreciate how consistently she brought the lessons from cross-cultural study to bear as a perspective on understanding our own lives. *Coming of Age in Samoa* was based on her earliest fieldwork and broke with ethnographic tradition because the study was problem-focused from the outset. Ethnographers have argued the pros and cons of that approach ever since. *New Lives for Old*, subtitled *Cultural Transformation—Manus, 1928–1953*, was written after she returned to the site of earlier fieldwork in New Guinea. Educational researchers share with anthropologists an interest in "change," but the 25-year interval in Mead's study raises questions as to whether field studies in education ever allow time for change to occur.

Colin Turnbull wrote quite good ethnography and good not-quite ethnography and was careful to distinguish between them. Readers might enjoy teasing out the difference in two selections identified below; the earlier one (1961) is a popularized and popular account, the later (1965) is a more academic account of fieldwork among the same people.

Atkinson, P. (1992). *Understanding ethnographic texts.* Newbury Park, CA: Sage.
*Evans-Pritchard, E. E. (1940). *The Nuer.*
*Firth, Raymond. (1936). *We, the Tikopia.*
Geertz, C. (1972). Deep play: Notes on the Balinese cockfight. *Daedalus, 101,* 1–37. Reprinted in C. Geertz (Ed.). (1973). *The interpretation of cultures* (pp. 412–453). New York: Basic Books.
Jacobson, D. (1991). *Reading ethnography.* Albany: State University of New York Press.
*Malinowski, B. (1922). *Argonauts of the western Pacific.*
*Mead, M. (1956). *New Lives for Old.*
*Mead, M. (1930). *Growing up in New Guinea.*
*Turnbull, C. (1961). *The forest people: A study of the Pygmies of the Congo.*
Turnbull, C. (1965). *Wayward servants: The two worlds of the African Pygmies.* Garden City, NY: Natural History Press.

B. Contemporary

From here on, I list only a few titles in each category, and in spite of an effort to achieve balance, my choices reflect personal preferences or studies that have been well received by my students. Ortner's work represents a traditional ethnographic setting and careful ethnographic reporting, joined with a symbolic analysis, to describe ritual behavior among the Sherpas of Nepal. Latour and Woolgar examine the cultural system of a scientific laboratory, and Estroff conducts her ethnography among psychiatric outpatients, two settings closer to home. James Spradley's systematic approach to fieldwork is represented by his study of "urban nomads" on Seattle's skid road. Some students find his approach a useful antidote to what they otherwise perceive as a far too casual and unstructured way to conduct research, that "new, vague approach" noted by a student reviewer. A collection that Spradley coedited with David McCurdy offers a helpful introduction that, accompanied by 12 brief case study examples written by undergraduate students, continues to prompt lively critique among others new to ethnographic research.

Estroff, S. (1981). *Making it crazy: An ethnography of psychiatric clients in an American community.* Berkeley: University of California Press. (Reissued in paperback in 1985 with an added epilogue.)
Latour, B., & Woolgar, S. (1986). *Laboratory life: The construction of scientific facts.* Princeton, NJ: Princeton University Press. (Originally published 1979 by Sage.)
Ortner, S. (1978). *Sherpas through their rituals.* New York: Cambridge University Press.

Spradley, J. (1970). *You own yourself a drunk: An ethnography of urban nomads.* Boston: Little, Brown.

Spradley, J., & McCurdy, D. (1988). *The cultural experience.* Prospect Heights, IL: Waveland Press. (Originally published 1972.)

C. Person-centered Ethnography

Questions of the "locus" of culture—the relation of the individual to society and where an anthropologist's interests ought properly to start and stop—are issues over which anthropologists themselves are never likely to come to complete agreement. One asks, "If culture is a group phenomenon, can anthropological inquiry focus on individuals?" And another asks, "Where does culture exist at all if not in the minds of the individuals who make up that group?" Nevertheless, anthropologists often work extensively with key informants and sometimes render accounts through anthropological life histories. I note life histories here in support of my call for more studies of this nature in educational research. I list six such studies. The two by Oscar Lewis won literary acclaim, precipitating rather severe professional scrutiny at the time concerning the unseen hand of the ethnographer as editor.

Crapanzano, V. (1980). *Tuhami: Portrait of a Moroccan.* Chicago: University of Chicago Press.

Lewis, O. (1961). *The children of Sanchez: Autobiography of a Mexican family.* New York: Random House.

Lewis, O. (1965). *La vida: A Puerto Rican family in the culture of poverty—San Juan and New York.* New York: Random House.

Mintz, S. (1974). *Worker in the cane: A Puerto Rican life history.* New York: Norton. (Originally published 1960 by Yale University Press.)

*Shostak, M. (1981). *Nisa: The life and works of a !Kung woman.*

*Simmons, L. (Ed.). (1942). *Sun chief: The autobiography of a Hopi Indian.*

D. Ethnography in Education

Readings suggested in this section reveal the wide range of topics studied during the past three decades. Prior to that, anthropologists were inclined to draw their lessons for educators from work among nonliterate people that was not focused so exclusively on education or schooling (see the early review bibliographies by Burnett and by Rosenstiel).

The citations include a review by George and Louise Spindler of the Case Studies in Education and Culture, a total output of 17 cases inaugurated in 1967 under their editorship. Several of those cases have been reissued by Waveland Press, and anyone interested in learning what is currently available should contact Waveland at P.O. Box 400, Prospect Heights, IL 60070. Also included is an essay by Elizabeth Eddy that reviews the nine volumes of the Anthropology and Education Series from Teachers College Press that appeared between 1965 and 1978 under the editorship of Solon Kimball. As the Spindlers noted in their review, perhaps series like these were ahead of their time. A major new section on anthropology made its first appearance in the second edition of the International Encyclopedia of Education, under the editorial supervision of John Ogbu, more than 20 years after the Spindler series stopped adding new titles.

Britzman, Deborah P. (1991). *Practice makes practice: A critical study of learning to teach.* Albany: State University of New York Press.

Burnett, J. (1974). *Anthropology and education: An annotated bibliographic guide.* New Haven, CT: Human Relations Area Files (HRAF) Press.

Chang, H. (1992). *Adolescent life and ethos: An ethnography of a US high school.* Bristol, PA: Falmer Press.

Cazden, C., John, V., & Hymes, D. (Eds.). (1972). *Functions of language in the classroom.* New York: Teachers College Press. (Reissued 1985 by Waveland Press, Prospect Heights, IL.)

Eddy, E. (1983). Review essay: The "Anthropology and Education" series, Solon T. Kimball, general editor. *Anthropology and Education Quarterly, 14,* 141–147.

Emihovich, C. (Ed.). (1989). *Locating learning: Ethnographic perspectives on classroom research.* Norwood, NJ: Ablex.

Moffatt, M. (1989). *Coming of age in New Jersey: College and American culture.* New Brunswick, NJ: Rutgers University Press.

Ogbu, J. (Section Ed.). (1994). Anthropology of education (Vol. 3). *International encyclopedia of education* (2nd ed.). Oxford, England: Elsevier Science, Ltd.

Rosenstiel, A. (1977). *Education and anthropology: An annotated bibliography.* New York: Garland.

Spindler, G. (Ed.). (1988). *Doing the ethnography of schooling: educational ethnography in action.* Prospect Heights, IL: Waveland Press. (Originally published 1982.)

Spindler, G., & Spindler, L. (1983). Review essay: The *Case studies in education and culture* from cradle to grave. *Anthropology and Education Quarterly, 14,* 73–80.

Spindler, G., & Spindler, L. (Eds.). (1987). *Interpretive ethnography of education: At home and abroad.* Hillsdale, NJ: Lawrence Erlbaum.

Wolcott, H. (1973). *The man in the principal's office: An ethnography.* New York: Holt, Rinehart & Winston. (Reissued 1984 by Waveland Press, Prospect Heights, IL.)

Woods, P. (1996). *Researching the art of teaching: Ethnography for educational use.* London: Routledge.

E. Anthropological Perspectives on Minority Education

Although anthropologists have always attended to cultural differences, a growing awareness about issues of minority education prompts a separate category here. The works listed below suggest the range of materials available as a resource and their changing emphasis over time, from case studies of isolated schools for Indian children (Philips, 1983; Wolcott, 1967) and "urban" minorities (Gibson, 1988; Heath, 1983; Ogbu, 1974), to edited collections (Jacob and Jordan, 1993; Saravia-Shore and Arvizu, 1992), to blueprints for social intervention through what the Spindlers have termed "cultural therapy" (1994), to John Ogbu's sustained efforts in developing a theory of minority education.

Gibson, M. (1988). *Accommodation without assimilation: Sikh immigrants in an American high school.* Ithaca, NY: Cornell University Press.

Heath, S. (1983). *Ways with words: Language, life, and work in communities and classrooms.* New York: Cambridge University Press.

Jacob, E., & Jordan, C. (Eds.). (1993). *Minority education: Anthropological perspectives.* Norwood, NJ: Ablex.

Ogbu, J. (1974). *The next generation: An ethnography of education in an urban neighborhood.* New York: Academic Press.

Philips, S. (1983). *The invisible culture: Communication in classroom and community on the Warm Springs Indian reservation.* New York: Longman.

Saravia-Shore, M., & Arvizu, S. (Eds.). (1992). *Cross-cultural literacy: Ethnographies of communication in multiethnic classrooms.* New York: Garland.

Spindler, G., & Spindler, L. (Eds.). (1994). *Pathways to cultural awareness: Cultural therapy with teachers and students.* Thousand Oaks, CA: Corwin.

Wolcott, H. F. (1967). *A Kwakiutl Village and School.* New York: Holt, Rinehart & Winston. (Reissued 1989 by Waveland Press, Prospect Heights, IL, with a new Afterword.)

V. Reading About Ethnographic Research

A. Early Accounts

Although anthropologists sometimes wrote chapters on specific methodological topics for encyclopedic tomes devoted to portraying their entire field, method itself did not become the focus of their books or articles until the 1960s. Naroll and Cohen's long-awaited *Handbook of Method in Cultural Anthropology*, published in 1970, was the first of its kind, helping anthropologists convince their audiences—and each other—that they really did have "methods." And a new genre of first-person accounts, such as those of Hortense Powdermaker and Rosalie Wax cited here, incorporated those methods into the warnings and advice of autobiographical accounts describing how the methods were played out in individual careers.

Given the dearth of guidelines for conducting ethnographic research, the often-quoted and even more frequently cited introductory chapter Malinowski prepared for *Argonauts of the Western Pacific*, published in 1922, "The Subject, Method and Scope of this Enquiry," served for years as the definitive statement about fieldwork. In that brief description Malinowski makes a strong case for the overall goal "of which an Ethnographer should never lose sight," namely "to grasp the native's point of view, his relation to life, to realise *his* vision of *his* world" (1922, p. 25). Malinowski's words have been subjected to much echoing and interpretation. They continue to provide a useful orientation for fieldworkers, although his directives are not without ambiguity. For example, on page 9 Malinowski warns would-be ethnographers of the need to distinguish between a *preconceived idea* ("pernicious in any scientific work") and a *foreshadowed problem* ("the main endowment of a scientific thinker"). The apparent blessing thus bestowed on foreshadowed problems has been incorporated into many a study, but I have yet to find anyone who can make a convincing distinction between the two. Until I do, I will go on suspecting that a preconceived idea is just a foreshadowed problem that has been better honed. I think Malinowski was warning fieldworkers to approach their topics with an open mind rather than one already made up. Clearly the thing to do is to read his brief essay for yourself.

*Malinowski, B. (1922). The subject, method and scope of this inquiry. Introduction to *Argonauts of the western Pacific.*

Naroll, R., & Cohen, R. (Eds.). (1970). *A handbook of method in cultural anthropology.* New York: Natural History Press.

Powdermaker, H. (1966). *Stranger and friend: The way of an anthropologist.* New York: Norton.

Spindler, G. (Ed). (1970). *Being an anthropologist: Fieldwork in eleven cultures.* New York, Holt, Rinehart & Winston. (Reissued 1987 by Waveland Press, Prospect Heights, IL.)

Wax, R. (1971). *Doing fieldwork: Warnings and advice.* Chicago: University of Chicago Press.

B. Contemporary Sources

I might identify any number of useful sources here. Those selected are texts that students have found helpful. I particularly enjoy Michael Agar's informative, offhand style. I can't imagine how I ever taught classes in ethnographic research without Roger Sanjek's wonderful collection *Fieldnotes: The Makings of Anthropology.* The little monograph by Susan Weller and Kim Romney offers a gentle introduction to systematic fieldwork techniques. I include it as well to call attention to the entire series on qualitative research techniques published by Sage, of which it is now one of more than 40 specialized titles, each devoted to a specific topic (e.g., archival strategies and techniques, conversation analysis, focus groups, gender issues, reliability and validity).

Agar, M. H. (1996). *The professional stranger: An informal introduction to ethnography* (2nd ed.) New York: Academic Press.

Bernard, H. R. (1994). *Research methods in anthropology: Qualitative and quantitative approaches* (2nd ed.). Thousand Oaks, CA: Sage. ("Closet quantifiers" will find comfort in Bernard's emphasis on systematic data collection, but every serious field-oriented researcher ought to have a copy of this excellent book at hand.)

Messerschmidt, D. A. (Ed.). (1981). *Anthropologists at home in North America: Methods and issues in the study of one's own society.* New York: Cambridge University Press.

Sanjek, R. (Ed.). (1990). *Fieldnotes: The makings of anthropology.* Ithaca, NY: Cornell University Press.

Van Maanen, J. (1988). *Tales of the field: On writing ethnography.* Chicago: University of Chicago Press.

Weller, S. C., & Romney, A. K. (1988). *Systematic data collection. Qualitative Research Methods Series, Vol. 10.* Newbury Park, CA: Sage.

C. Person-centered Approaches

Lives, written by L. L. Langness and Gelya Frank, offers an easy introduction to researchers interested in pursuing anthropological life history. It also contains a 50-page bibliography identifying much of the important work done to the time of its publication in 1981. *Interpreting Life Histories* carries the discussion forward in both time (1985) and complexity. Sage Publications has now introduced an interdisciplinary series devoted exclusively to the narrative study of lives co-edited by Ruthellen Josselson.

Anthropologist David Mandelbaum's earlier (1973) essay serves the dual purposes of discussing the life history approach in general and illustrating it with a case study. It should be noted that the subjects of anthropological life histories more typically are "everyday" people rather than individuals of such social and political importance as Mandelbaum's choice of Gandhi for an illustrative case. Such prominent figures usually attract the attention of biographers, whose selections are influenced by their subjects' unusual qualities, gifts, or times.

Langness, L. L., & Frank, G. (1981). *Lives: An anthropological approach to biography.* Novato, CA: Chandler and Sharp.

Mandelbaum, D. G. (1973). The study of life history: Gandhi. *Current Anthropology, 14,* 3, 177–206.

Watson, L. C., & Watson-Franke, M. (1985). *Interpreting life histories: An anthropological inquiry.* New Brunswick, NJ: Rutgers University Press.

D. Ethnographic Research in Formal Education

In my essay "Ethnographic Research in Education," I list extensive references on this topic, so here I mention only a few for emphasis. I have already cited *Doing the Ethnography of Schooling*, which George Spindler edited, as a good source for completed ethnographies; I include it again here because it is also an excellent source on method, with contributors exhibiting a wide range of approaches from microethnography to life history.

Erickson, F. (1984). What makes school ethnography 'ethnographic'? *Anthropology and Education Quarterly, 15,* 51–66.

Spindler, G. (Ed.). (1988). *Doing the ethnography of schooling: Educational anthropology in action.* Prospect Heights, IL: Waveland Press. (Originally published in 1982.)

Wolcott, H. F. (1987). On ethnographic intent. In G. Spindler & L. Spindler (Eds.), *Interpretive ethnography of education* (pp. 37–57). Hillsdale, NJ: Lawrence Erlbaum.

Wolcott, H. F. (1990). Making a study 'more ethnographic.' *Journal of Contemporary Ethnography, 19,* 44–72. (Reissued 1995 in J. Van Maanen [Ed.]. *Representation in Ethnography* [pp. 79–111]. Thousand Oaks, CA: Sage.)

IV. Additional Resources in Qualitative/Descriptive Research

In the preceding essay, and again in this list of further readings, I have taken a deliberately narrow view, treating ethnography as the research approach most closely associated with the work of cultural anthropologists and field-oriented sociologists. Whether or not a study can pass such strict anthropological muster is not necessarily a burning issue for every educational researcher. Numerous resources available today take a broad, interdisciplinary approach, including but not limiting themselves to ethnography, or making no particular effort to treat ethnography as special and different from other closely related qualitative approaches. I call attention to a few particularly noteworthy sources. In the case of my own works and some of the others cited, ethnography's uniqueness is carefully protected, but the audience being addressed is assumed to be that of qualitative/descriptive researchers more generally.

Denzin, N., & Lincoln, Y. (Eds.). (1994). *Handbook of qualitative research.* Thousand Oaks, CA: Sage.

Eisner, E., & Peshkin, A. (Eds.). (1990). *Qualitative inquiry: The continuing debate.* New York: Teachers College Press.

Glesne, C., & Peshkin, A. (1992). *Becoming qualitative researchers: An introduction.* White Plains, NY: Longman.

Hammersley, M., & Atkinson, P. (1983). *Ethnography: Principles in practice.* London: Tavistock.

Lancy, D. F. (1993). *Qualitative research in education: An introduction to the major traditions.* White Plains, NY: Longman.

LeCompte, M., Millroy, W., & Preissle, J. (Eds.). (1992). *Handbook of qualitative research in education.* San Diego, CA: Academic Press.

Maxwell, J. A. (1996). *Qualitative research design: An interactive approach.* Thousand Oaks, CA: Sage.

Miles, M., & Huberman, M. (1994). *Qualitative data analysis: An expanded sourcebook* (2nd ed.). Thousand Oaks, CA: Sage.

Van Maanen, J. (Series ed.). *Qualitative research methods series.* Thousand Oaks, CA: Sage.

Wolcott, H. F. (1990). Writing up qualitative research. *Qualitative Research Methods Series,* Vol. 20. Newbury Park, CA: Sage.

Wolcott, H. F. (1994). *Transforming qualitative data: Description, analysis, and interpretation.* Thousand Oaks, CA: Sage.

Wolcott, H. F. (1995). *The art of fieldwork.* Walnut Creek, CA: AltaMira Press.

V. Journals and Organizations

The resources listed above offer researchers the opportunity to become familiar with ethnography by reading widely among readily available materials. Information is also available from several national organizations whose members include individuals with interests in ethnographic research and whose annual meetings and journals provide a forum for scholarly exchange. Attendance at their meetings or inspection of their journals is an excellent way to learn about current issues, find others who share interest in a specific problem, or begin an active organizational involvement. Details about subscriptions and memberships may be obtained by writing to the addresses listed below:

Anthropology and Education Quarterly. Membership journal of the Council on Anthropology and Education (CAE) of the American Anthropological Association. Subscription and membership information, CAE, c/o American Anthropological Association, 4350 N. Fairfax Drive, Suite 640, Arlington, VA 22203.

Cultural Anthropology Methods (CAM) Journal. Newsletter published three times a year by Editorial Consulting Services, 5246 NW 47th Lane, Gainesville, FL 32606.

Educational Researcher. Membership journal of the American Educational Research Association, 1230 17th Street, NW, Washington, DC 20036-3078. Qualitative approaches are prevalent in Division G, Social Context of Education, and in a Special Interest Group (SIG) on Qualitative Research.

Human Organization. Membership journal of the Society for Applied Anthropology (SfAA), P.O. Box 24083, Oklahoma City, OK 73124-0083. Members also receive a career-oriented publication, *Practicing Anthropology.*

Journal of Contemporary Ethnography. Subscription journal published by Sage Publications, 2455 Teller Road, Thousand Oaks, CA 91320.

Qualitative Inquiry. Subscription journal published by Sage Publications, 2455 Teller Road, Thousand Oaks, CA 91320.

QSE: International Journal of Qualitative Studies in Education. Subscription journal published by Taylor and Francis, 242 Cherry St. Philadelphia, PA 19106-1906.

Study Questions

1. Ethnographers themselves are divided about whether participant observation or interviewing is more important in fieldwork. What are some important differences in the kinds of data obtained by grounding a study in one approach or the other? Is it more informative to know what people *say* or what they *do*, or is that really the issue?

2. If you wished to develop an ethnographic account of a third-grade class over a period of an entire school year, what roles might allow you to be a genuine *participant* observer? What are some possible advantages and limitations of each role?

3. Teachers sometimes argue about whether they should look at student records before meeting a new class at the beginning of the term or form their own impressions first. Similarly, ethnographers ponder whether to consult what others have written before initiating fieldwork in an unfamiliar setting. What arguments can you muster on behalf of both sides of the argument, consulting or not consulting other ethnographers' work prior to initiating one's own? On which side do you feel the stronger case can be made?

4. Quantitatively oriented colleagues sometimes allow that ethnographic approaches are all right for exploratory research as long as the "real" work that follows is quantitative. Of course such a "throw-'em-a-fish" approach makes ethnographically oriented researchers unhappy, but is there merit in the argument? Can, and should, ethnography be more than exploratory?

5. Should ethnographers try to be more objective in their field research, or should they try to convince their audiences that ultimately everything is subjective anyway? Are the two positions necessarily in opposition?

6. What are some important differences between a biography and an anthropological life history? For researching educators' lives, what might be the advantages and drawbacks of pursuing one alternative or the other?

7. The author of this chapter expresses a personal reservation about the impact of educational research on classroom practice. How might that issue be posed as a research question to be studied ethnographically? Is this a topic that ultimately would need to be explored quantitatively?

8. Should an ethnographer ever use standardized tests in gathering information about a group of students? If so, would the ethnographer be likely to use tests the same way they are used by a school system's director of testing?

9. The author is on record as recommending not only that fieldworkers write an early draft of a study while the research is in progress but also to consider the possibility of writing a draft of the study *before doing any fieldwork at all*. Are there aspects of formal education about which you are so familiar that this idea

may not be as far-fetched as it may seem? Propose a topic or two on which you could start writing immediately, and discuss how such early writing (or "prewriting") might make your research more effective.

10. "Triangulation" seems an obvious strategy and safeguard when presented in a seminar on research. In the field, however, it can pose real dilemmas for the researcher. Can you identify some ways that it might backfire? What precautions might a researcher take to prevent that from happening? And how many different ways of triangulating can you come up with?

11. Can one generalize from the kind of case study produced by an ethnographer? If so, to what extent? If not, why bother with case studies at all?

12. Educator subculture itself warrants anthropological scrutiny. Why, for example, are you now learning to do something you do not know how to do and may never have done—conduct research—when presumably you have come "back to school" in order to become a better educator?

13. How wide a range of topics can you identify that might be appropriate for an edited collection to be titled *The Ethnography of Reading*? If you were editing such a volume, what kinds of submissions would you expect to receive from educational researchers interested in the topic? Of those, which type would you include? What guidelines would you use to assess the "ethnographicness" of contributed articles so that the volume warrants its claim as *ethnography* rather than simply research on reading?

14. In his introduction to the illustrative reading that follows, the author poses the question of whether the example he selected warrants the label "research" at all. He also cites reservations expressed by colleagues who have questioned whether the article is a suitable model for students being introduced to educational research. What is the function of a model? Do you consider the article to be "real" research? What criteria define educational research? Do the same criteria apply to research in general?

Reading

Introduction
A Case Study Using an Ethnographic Approach

Harry F. Wolcott

Doctoral students invited to read the original draft of the preceding material and familiar with my strongly held and frequently stated position about the quantum jump between *borrowing a fieldwork technique or two* and *doing ethnography* asked why I devoted my attention almost exclusively to explicating those techniques.

I explained that in spite of my insistence that fieldwork techniques do not lead directly to ethnography, it was probably the techniques themselves that were of greatest interest to an audience of educational researchers. Furthermore, techniques are especially amenable to a discussion like this. They can be described with some specificity, they can be organized into lists convenient for orderly presentation, and they can be grouped into manageable clusters that convey the basic fieldwork strategies (participant observation and interviewing) without losing sight of the importance of multiple ways of, and plenty of time for, finding out.

With techniques adequately in tow, and fieldwork properly demystified, I felt that I could then move on and make what is for me (but not necessarily for my readers) the major point of all this. *The essence of ethnography derives from its anthropological concern for cultural interpretation rather than for how one looks or what one looks at.*

I do not take ethnographic research *techniques*, in and of themselves, to be all that important. (For an excellent and comprehensive techniques-oriented discussion, see Bernard 1994. My position is spelled out in detail in Wolcott, 1995.) However, they do provide a convenient and, for educational researchers, a familiar way to approach an unfamiliar approach. Therefore, I introduced the topic of ethnographic research by describing fieldwork techniques.

In selecting a case to *illustrate* ethnographic research in education, I hope I lend support to my position that description, analysis, and interpretation—rather than a preoccupation with techniques—are the core of the ethnographic enterprise. In the self-contained case study that follows, with the exception of brief mention of "months of informal conversations and many hours of formal interviews" and the ethnographer's admission of working with heavy hand in excerpting and reorganizing the material around several dominant themes, there is no mention at all of fieldwork. The case consists of a great deal of description, much of it in a key informant's own words as he chose to relate it, coupled with a conscious and explicit effort on my part as ethnographer to examine the account in terms of a particular issue and framed in an anthropological perspective.

A *cross-cultural* perspective, on the other hand, may seem conspicuous by its absence in the example selected. If that is not quite by design, at least it allows me to make an important point about cultural interpretation. Pushing serendipity to its limits, the ethnographer of this study—myself—was working literally as well as figuratively in his own backyard. I had not sought out my informant, nor had he sought me out. Like all humans, however, he had a story to tell, and I became interested in hearing and, subsequently, in recording it. We each had personal and complex motives but achieved some common purposes in the telling and listening. The cultural perspective for the interpretation draws on the distinction that anthropologists (and sometimes others) make between *schooling* and *education*, with both processes, in turn, seen in the even broader context of *enculturation*, how each of us acquires the basic cultural orientation that will influence a lifetime of thought and action.

I encourage my students to direct their first formal attempts at ethnographic interviewing—if, indeed, there really is something properly called an ethnographic interview, rather than an ethnographic interpretation of one—toward people of cultural backgrounds markedly different from their own. I recognize that eventually most of them will draw on their own cultural perspective for unveiling patterns of social behavior among others rather like themselves. The cultural perspective so critical to ethnography derives in large measure from insight gained in cross-cultural settings, but every setting invites a cultural perspective if one chooses to take it. That is what I endeavor to do in the case study that follows: to employ a cultural perspective. I might also note a point frequently overlooked by educational researchers: The mere fact of being in a cross-cultural setting does not perforce mean that research conducted there will reveal dimensions of culture.

Another reason for selecting this particular piece for illustration is to show what one researcher can do through extended interviewing with one informant, subsequently organizing the material for a journal-length article in terms of its relevance to one particular issue. The case reflects an anthropological life history approach, a particular form of ethnography in which attention is drawn more toward an individual than toward an interactive group.

The article was originally commissioned as a think-piece intended to bring an anthropological perspective to the problem of defining educational adequacy (so that, American style, we could attach a dollar amount to the concept of adequacy and determine how well school districts and states "measure up"). I reinterpreted the original assignment to create an opportunity to collect and use case study material to examine the notion of educational adequacy itself. From the beginning, the research was problem-focused and highly specific—a partial life history of one young man—but the context was broad (holistic), the perspective cultural.

The heavy reliance on interview data in the completed account is another conscious element in my placing it before you as something of a model. Whenever we conduct our research in settings familiar to us, or where we see only a portion of the lives of the people we are studying—two conditions that usually obtain in research in schools—we are well advised to let informants speak for themselves before we impose our interpretations on them.

At the risk of presenting too much data (and sometimes being accused of offering too little interpretation), I attempt always to provide sufficient information not only to illustrate the basis for my interpretation but also to give readers an adequate basis for reaching their own interpretations. Long after I submit a final draft for a report or publication, I continue to mull over my interpretations, realizing, in what Clifford Geertz (1973, p. 29) characterizes as a chronic problem in ethnography, that I still haven't quite gotten it right. Readers willing to engage with data collected by someone else ought to have sufficient information at hand to warrant such engagement. Toward that end, ethnographers need to remain aware of the difference between trying to be convincing with their interpretations and trying to prove them. The ethnographer's goal is interpretation, not proof; by its very choice of subject matter, ethnography is necessarily ambiguous, just as it is necessarily incomplete.

I should note of this case study that nothing I had written had ever prompted more response from early readers anxious to "jump in," either to quarrel with my interpretation, to extend it, or to suggest an altogether different definition of the problem or different perspective on what "society" ought to do about it. To be able to provoke that response made me feel I had performed the descriptive task well, even while I continue to this day to wrestle with the interpretation.

Pointing the way to responsible social action, however, is quite another responsibility, one that goes beyond ethnography. To go even as far as I do here in raising policy issues in my concluding remarks, I must switch roles so that the educator and reformer in me can question what might be done differently or "better." Ethnographers are not denied the right to offer judgments, opinions, and advice, but they should leave no doubt as to their having stepped out of their researcher role before rendering such judgments. You will have to discern for yourself whether the boundaries between description and interpretation, or between *what is* and *what might be done about it*, seem adequately marked.

Finally, I selected this particular example because it demonstrates ethnographers' concerns for what Clifford Geertz (1973) calls "complex specificness" even in addressing a topic as global as educational adequacy. That "specificness" is achieved through the natural history approach described in the essay. The approach seeks to understand classes of events through the careful examination of specific ones. Through the vehicle of an abbreviated life history related by one 20-year-old, I have tried to provide an account that brings a perspective to issues of broad social significance, including academic achievement, school dropouts, youth unemployment, provision of welfare services, delinquency, and educative opportunity and responsibility beyond formal schooling. But those are abstractions employed by social scientists, policy makers, and educators. The case relates the specific form in which such abstractions revealed themselves in everyday reality as one American youth experienced and perceived it.

Like this revised edition, the first edition of *Complementary Methods* was forever in the making. When contributors were asked to select illustrative "readings" to accompany their essays, the case study had just been published. I welcomed the opportunity to present the material and the questions it posed to a broader audience of educators. As for my intent to convey ethnographic research as an approach that is not preoccupied with method per se, I felt that the conspicuous absence of attention to method might help relay an implicit message about process as well.

I felt I had been successful on the latter score until an overseas colleague begged me not to share this case with her beginning graduate students to guide forays of their own into qualitative study. "It isn't really research," she stated succinctly. What she meant, she hastened to explain, was that the case did not offer a proper model: It lacked a statement of the problem, a review of relevant literature, a researchable hypothesis, clearly specified procedures, and nice, neat "findings." Prior to that moment, I don't think I had ever been fully aware of how very lockstep we have made educational research and reporting, at least as we transmit it to students being inducted into it: Introduction, Hypotheses, Method, Results, Discussion. I now recognize that this case, which I had singled out as a model *of* and *for* qualitative work in education, may have served quite the opposite purpose, to illustrate that qualitative research isn't really research at all! As noted in the set of study questions accompanying this section, that seems a question worthy of serious discussion.

The original interviewing was completed in the fall of 1981, my report submitted in 1982, and the article rewritten for publication in the *Anthropology and Education Quarterly* in 1983. I also wrote something of a sequel to this account. That piece, first published in 1987, is far more conjectural than the one that appears here. I call attention to it for anyone interested in pursuing the personal dimensions of the Brad story, but I do not commend it as a model for neophyte fieldworkers who need to demonstrate their capacity for thick-but-relevant description. During this period there has also been an expanding literature on issues related to homelessness (see, for example, Snow & Anderson, 1993; Wright, 1989) and the use of life history among the unemployed (e.g., Angrosino, 1994).

Subsequent events prompted still more writing (1990), taking the case far beyond its original focus on schooling, and the article that appears here has now become the first part of a trilogy. The three parts appeared together for the first time in *Transforming Qualitative Data* (Wolcott, 1994), each piece illustrating one of three emphases that form the structure and argument of that book: description, analysis, interpretation. But that, as they say, is another story. Sufficient here to invite you to read how an ethnographically oriented researcher, working with one informant, and reporting within the space limitations of a journal-length article, set out to show what might be learned through that approach. Not proved, mind you, but seen in a different perspective, perhaps to be understood just a bit better.

References

Angrosino, M. V. (1994). On the bus with Vonnie Lee: Explorations in life history and metaphor. *Journal of Contemporary Ethnography 23*, 14–28.

Bernard, H. R. (1994). *Research methods in anthropology: Qualitative and quantitative approaches* (2nd ed.). Thousand Oaks, CA: Sage.

Geertz, C. (1973). Thick description. In C. Geertz (Ed.), *The interpretation of cultures* (pp. 1–30). New York: Basic Books.

Snow, D. A., & Anderson, L. (1993). *Down on their luck: A study of homeless street people*. Berkeley, CA: University of California Press.

Wolcott, H. F. (1983). Adequate schools and inadequate education: The life history of a sneaky kid. *Anthropology and Education Quarterly, 14*, 3–32.

Wolcott, H. F. (1987). Life's not working: Cultural alternatives to career alternatives. In G. W. Noblit & W. T. Pink (Eds.), *Schooling in social context: Qualitative studies* (pp. 303–325). Norwood, NJ: Ablex.

Wolcott, H. F. (1990). On seeking—and rejecting—validity in qualitative research. In E. W. Eisner & A. Peshkin (Eds.), *Qualitative inquiry in education: The continuing debate* (pp. 121–152). New York: Teachers College Press.

Wolcott, H. F. (1994). *Transforming qualitative data: Description, analysis, and interpretation*. Thousand Oaks, CA: Sage.

Wolcott, H. F. (1995). *The art of fieldwork*. Walnut Creek, CA: AltaMira Press.

Wright, J. D. (1989). *Address unknown: The homeless in America*. Hawthorne, NY: Aldine de Gruyter.

Adequate Schools and Inadequate Education: The Life History of a Sneaky Kid

Harry F. Wolcott

"I guess if you're going to be here, I need to know something about you, where you're from, and what kind of trouble you are in," I said to the lad, trying not to reveal my uncertainty, surprise, and dismay at his uninvited presence until I could learn more about his circumstances. It wasn't much of an introduction, but it marked the beginning of a dialogue that lasted almost 2 years from that moment. Brad (a pseudonym, although as he noted, using his real name wouldn't really matter, because "no one knows who I am anyway") tersely stated his full name, the fact that his parents had "split up" and his mother was remarried and living in southern California, the local address of his father, and that he was not at present in any trouble because he wasn't "that stupid." He also volunteered that he had spent time in the state's correctional facility for boys, but quickly added, "It wasn't really my fault."

It was not our meeting itself that was a surprise; it was that Brad had been living at this remote corner of my steep and heavily wooded 20-acre homesite on the outskirts of town for almost 5 weeks. In that time he had managed to build a 10-foot-by-12-foot cabin made of newly cut sapling logs and roofed with plywood paneling. A couple of weeks earlier, I had stumbled across his original campsite, but I assumed it had been made by some youngster enjoying a bivouac en route to hiking a nearby ridge that afforded a fine view, a popular day hike for townspeople, and occasional overnight adventure for kids. I also found a saw, but I thought it had been left by a recent surveying party. Brad had been watching me at the time and later admitted cursing to himself for being careless in leaving tools about.

I did not realize I now had both a new cabin and an unofficial tenant until a neighbor reported that his 8-year-old son claimed not only to have seen but also to have spoken to a "hobo" while wandering through my woods. The "hobo" turned out to be the then 19-year-old, of medium build and slightly stoop-shouldered, standing opposite me. And it is his story that I am about to relate.

As intrigued and involved as I eventually became with Brad and his story, my purpose in providing this account transcends the individual case, although I will tie my remarks closely to it. That purpose is related to my professional interest in anthropology and education and, particularly, in cultural acquisition, drawing upon anthropology both for approach and for perspective in looking at educational issues (see Wolcott, 1982). There is no shortage of case study materials about alienated youth.[1] Attention here will be drawn particularly to educationally relevant aspects of this case. Brad's story underscores and dramatizes the critical distinction that anthropologists make between schooling and education and raises questions about our efforts at education for young people beyond the purview of the schools.[2] Adequate schools may be necessary, but they are not sufficient to insure an adequate education.

At first impression, Brad's strategy for coping with his life seemed as bold, resourceful, and even romantic as was his building of a cabin. Faced with jobs he did not want to do (he abhors dishwashing, yet that seemed to be the only work he felt he could get, because "those jobs are always open") and expenses he could not afford (renting an apartment, buying and operating a motorcycle), he had chosen to change his lifestyle radically by reducing his cash needs to a minimum. What he could not afford, he would try to do without.

Never before had he done the things he now set out to do. He had never lived in the woods (though he had gone camping), never built a log house (though he had occasionally helped his father in light construction), and never thought about a personal inventory of essential items. He had identified the cabin site, which was hidden from view but had a commanding view of its own, during one of his endless and solitary explorations of streets, roads, and paths in and around the city. The location was near a section of the city where he once lived as a child. He went deep into a densely wooded area, entering from the east and failing to realize how close he had come to my house on the county road around the west side of the ridge. But he knew he had to be near town. He needed to be where, one way or another, he could pick up the things essential to his anticipated lifestyle. He did not need much, but what he did need—hammer, saw, nails, sleeping bag, stove, cooking utensils, flashlight and lantern, pants and shoes, containers for carrying and storing water—he scrounged, stole, or, occasionally and reluctantly, purchased.

Brad displayed few qualities that would earn him the title of outdoorsman. His tools and equipment often were mislaid or neglected. He proved terrible at tying knots. He cut trees unnecessarily and turned his own trails into slippery troughs of mud. In spite of occasional references to himself as "Jungle Boy," he was basically a city boy making whatever accommodation was necessary to survive inexpensively. His fuel and food came from town; he was totally dependent on the city even though he could not afford to live in it. If his menu gradually became more like that of the woodsman (potatoes, onions, pancakes, melted cheese sandwiches, eggs, soup, canned tuna, powdered milk, and powdered orange juice), it was because he realized that these items could almost stretch $70-worth of food stamps into a month's ration of food. He washed and dried his clothes in coin-operated machines at night at a nearby apartment house complex. His battery-operated radio played almost constantly, and he became even more cabin-bound watching a small battery-operated TV set his mother purchased for him during a brief visit, their first in over 2 years.

It was not Brad's habit to take leisurely walks in the woods, spend time enjoying sunsets, or listen to bird calls. He brought what he could find (and carry up steep, narrow trails) of his urban environment with him. Though not very sociable, he calculatingly mismanaged his purchases so that on many days he "had to" bicycle 2 miles each way to his favorite store to get a pack of cigarettes and perhaps buy a can of beer or "smoke a joint" in a nearby park. The only direction he traveled was to town. Yet almost without exception he returned to his cabin each evening, usually before darkness made the trip hazardous on an unlit bike. The security of having literally created a place all his own lent a critical element of stability to his life. He was proud of what he had built, even though he acknowledged that his cabin would be "bigger and better in every way" were he starting over. His dreams for improving it never ceased.

For awhile he envisioned building a tree house high in a giant Douglas fir nearby. A fearless tree climber, he attached a high pulley and cable swing so he could trim branches and hoist construction materials. The tree house idea occupied his thoughts for weeks. During that time, few improvements were made on the cabin. The idea of being virtually inaccessible high in a tree proved more appealing than practical, however, and eventually he gave it up, brought his tools back to the cabin, and began work in earnest on improvements that included cutting out a section of wall and adding a lean-to bunk bed. The cable was removed from the tree house site and found its permanent place as a hillside swing with a breathtaking arc among the treetops on the slope below. Swinging was a literal as well as figurative high for him; pausing to rest between turns at the strenuous exercise, he volunteered the only positive comment I ever heard him make regarding the future: "I'll still swing like this when I'm 60."

In brief glimpses, other people's lives often appear idyllic. Brad's "Robinson Crusoe" life had many appealing qualities. He seemed to have freed himself of the trappings of the Establishment, which he saw as a curiously roundabout and unappealing system that required him to take a job he hated in order to earn enough to provide transportation to and from work and money for the rent of some cheap place where he would rather not live. He had seen his father work hard, dream even harder, and yet, in Brad's opinion, "get nowhere." Brad was trying to figure out for himself what he wanted in life and whether it was really worth the effort.

I found it hard to argue on behalf of what some menial job would get him. I heard quite well his argument that, lacking in skill or experience, he would probably have to do work at once physically harder and lower paying than most jobs today. He could be an indefatigable worker, but I think he felt some anxiety about being able to "keep up" on jobs requiring hours of continuous hard physical labor. An earlier and short-lived job as a tree planter had convinced him that hard work does not insure success.

A glimpse into Brad's daily life does not dispel the romantic view of his existence. He arose when he wanted and retired when he wanted (although, with the cold, dark, and perennial dampness of the Northwest's winters, and with little to do, he spent so much time "in the sack" that getting to sleep became a constantly compounding problem). He could eat when he chose and cook or not as mood—and a rather sparse cupboard—dictated. Food and cigarette needs dominated his schedule of trips to town. A trip to the store, or to see about food stamps (in effect he had no address, so he went to the Welfare Office in person) or to secure other supplies (a tire for the bicycle, fuel for lanterns or the stove, hardware items for the cabin) occurred once or twice a week. And if there was no needed trip, he was free to decide—quite consciously, though rather impulsively, I think—how to spend the day.

Although the cabin was sometimes untidy and Brad seldom washed utensils before they were to be used again, he kept his person and his clothes clean. He brushed his teeth regularly. He never went to town without "showering" or at least washing his face and hair. In warm weather he underscored the nymphlike nature of his existence by remaining almost, or totally, unclad in the seclusion of his immediate cabin area, though he was excruciatingly self-conscious in public settings. His preference for privacy was highlighted by recollections of his distress at regimented public showering "on procedures" at reform school, and such experience had made options like joining the armed services something he insisted he would only do if he had to. Brad was, at first glance, a free spirit. He regarded himself that way, too: "I do what I want."

The Cultural Context of a Free Spirit

There is no absolute set of things to be wanted or ways to fill one's days and dreams, just as there is no absolute set of things to be learned (see Wallace, 1961b, 38). What people learn or want or do or dream about is embedded in particular macro- and microcultural systems.

Brad was aware of many things in his "culture" that he felt he could do without, including—up to a point—seeking much involvement within his society, seeming to heed its expectations, or depending on its resources. But he was accustomed to technological innovations and had been reared in a society where other people appeared, at least to him, to have everything they needed. Although he saw himself as living figuratively, as well as literally, at the edge of society, he was still society's child. He was free to insist, "I do what I want" but he was not free to do what he wanted. What he had learned to want was a function of his culture, and he drew narrowly and rather predictably from the cultural repertoire of the very society from which he believed he was extricating himself.

Brad needed to cook. An open fire is slow and quite impractical on a rainy day. One needs a camp stove in order to cook inside a cabin. And fuel. And then a better stove. Cold water is all right for washing hands, but it can be a bit too bracing for washing one's hair or torso, especially outside with the wind blowing. One needs a bigger pan to heat water for bathing. Soap and shampoo. A towel. A new razor. A mirror. A bigger mirror. Foam rubber mattress. A chair. A chaise lounge.

One needs something to look at and listen to. Magazines are a brief diversion, but rock music is essential. One needs a radio. Flashlight batteries are expensive for continual radio listening; a radio operated by an automobile battery would be a better source—and could power a better radio. An automobile battery needs to be recharged. Carrying a battery to town is awkward, and constantly having to pay for battery charges is expensive. As well as access to a power supply (in my carport), one needs a battery charger. No, this one is rated too low; a bigger one is needed. Luckily not a harsh winter, but a wet one. The dirt floor gets muddy; a wood floor would be better. The roof leaks; a heavier grade of plywood and stronger tarpaulin to place over it are required. The sleeping bag rips where it got wet; a replacement is necessary. Shoes wear out from constant use on the trails; clothes get worn or torn. Flashlights and batteries wear out. Cigarettes (or tobacco), matches, eggs, bread, Tang, Crisco, pancake flour, syrup—supplies get low. An occasional steak helps vary the austere diet.

One needs transportation. A bicycle is essential, as are spare parts to keep it in repair. Now a minor accident: the bicycle is wrecked. No money to buy a new one. Brad "hypes" himself up and sets out to find a replacement. Buy one? "When they're so easy to get? No way!"

The Life History of a Sneaky Kid

Here is the place to let Brad relate something of his life and how he had tried to make sense of, and come to grips with, the world about him.

Ideally, in relating a life history through an ethnographic autobiography, informants tell their stories almost entirely in their own words (e.g., classics such as Leo Simmons's *Sun Chief* [1942], or Oscar Lewis's *Children of Sanchez* [1961]; see also Brandes [1982]). There should be a high ratio of information to explanation in a life story; sometimes there is no explanation or explicit interpretation at all. Time, space, and purpose require me to proceed more directly. I have worked with a heavy hand in reorganizing material and selecting the most cogent excerpts from months of informal conversations and many hours of formal interviews that Brad volunteered for this purpose.[3]

I have given particular attention to aspects of Brad's story that illustrate the two major points of this paper: that education consists of more than schooling, and that we give little systematic attention to the course of a young person's education once out of school. For these purposes I have dwelt more on social concerns than on personal or psychological ones. Brad had some personal "hang-ups" focused largely on his acceptance of his body and a preoccupation with sexual fantasy as yet unfulfilled, *Portnoy's Complaint* personified. In time, I realized he had some deep-seated emotional hang-ups as well (or, more candidly, not quite in time, because he sank unexpectedly into a mood of utter despair and abruptly announced he was "hitting the road" because he saw no future where he was), but my concern in this paper is with Brad as a social rather than a psychological being, and thus with personality-in-culture rather than with personality per se.

"In the Chute"

A speaker at the American Correctional Association meetings in 1981 was reported in the national press to have used the phrase "in the chute" to describe individuals whose lives seem headed for prison even though they have not yet arrived there: "People who are in the chute, so to speak, and heading toward us, are beginning that movement down in infancy."

Brad was not yet "in the chute." It is not inevitable that he end up in trouble, but he could. Excerpts from his life story suggest how things point that way. Here he recalls a chain of events that started at age 10 with what proved a traumatic event in his life, his parents' divorce.

On the Loose. "After my parents got divorced, I was living with my dad. I had quite a bit of freedom. My dad wasn't around. If I didn't want to go to school, I just didn't go. Everybody who knows me now says, "That guy had the world's record for ditching school." My dad was at work all day and there was no one to watch me. I was pretty wild. My dad took me to a counseling center at the university; they told me I was "winning the battles but losing the war."

"After my dad got remarried, I had no freedom any more. I had a new mother to watch me. I got mad at her a couple of times, so I moved in with her parents. I went to seventh grade for awhile and got pretty good grades. Then I went to southern California to visit my mother. When my dad said he'd have to "make some arrangements" before I could return, I just stayed there. But I got into a hassle with my stepdad, and I ditched some classes, and suddenly I was on a bus back to Oregon.

"My father had separated again and I moved into some little apartment with him. He wanted me to go to another school, but I said, "Forget it, man, I'm not going to another school. I'm tired of school." So I'd just lay around the house, stay up all night, sleep all day.

"Finally I told my mom I'd be a "good boy," and she let me move back to southern California. But I got in another hassle with my stepdad. I ran out of the house and stayed with some friends for a few months, but then the police got in a hassle with me and they said I'd have to go back with my dad or they were going to send me to a correctional institution. The next thing you know, I was back on the bus."

Getting Busted. "By then my dad had remarried again. I wasn't ready for another family. I stayed about 2 days, then I left. I figured any place was better than living there. But they got pissed at me because I kept coming back [breaking into the house] for food, so they called the cops on me. Running away from them, I broke my foot and had to go to the hospital. Then I got sent to reform school. They had a charge against me [contraband], but I think the real reason was that I didn't have any place to go. I was in reform school for 8 months."

Second-Rate Jobs and Second-Rate Apartments. "I finally played their "baby game" and got out of reform school. Then they sent me to a halfway house in Portland. I got a job, made some money, got a motorcycle, moved to another place, then that job ended. I got another job with a church-going plumber for awhile, but I got fired. Then I came back and worked for my dad, but there wasn't nothing to do, and I got in some family hassles, so I got a few jobs and lived in some cheap apartments.

"For awhile I was a bum down at the Mission. I'd get something to eat, then I'd go sleep under a truck. My sleeping bag was all I had. I knew winter was coming and I'd have to do something. I saw a guy I knew and he said 'Hey, I've got a place if you'd like to crash out until you get something going.' So I went there and got a job for about four months washing dishes. Then my mom came up from California to visit and found me an apartment. God, how I hated that place, with people right on the other side of those thin walls who know you're all alone and never have any visitors or anything. I quit washing dishes; they cut me down to such low hours I wasn't making any money anyway. So I just hibernated for the winter."

A New Life. "When the rent ran out, I picked up my sleeping bag and the stuff I had and headed for the hills at the edge of town. I found a place that looked like no one had been there for awhile, and I set up a tarp for shelter. I decided to take my time and build a place for myself, because I wasn't doing anything anyway. I just kept working on it. I've been here a year and a half now. I've done some odd jobs, but mostly I live on food stamps.

"I used to think about doing something like this when I lived in Portland. I read a book called *How to Live in the Woods on Pennies a Day*. I even tried staying out in the woods a couple of times, but I didn't know exactly what to do. I wasn't thinking about a cabin then. All I knew was that I needed some place to get out of the wind and some place to keep dry. I saw this piece of level ground and knew that if I had tools and nails I could probably put up some walls. As I went along I just figured out what I would need.

"I put up four posts and started dragging logs around till the walls were built. There were plenty of trees around. It took about a week to get the walls. I slept in a wet sleeping bag for a couple of nights, 'cause I didn't have a roof. The first roof was some pieces of paneling that I carried up from some kids' tree fort. I had a dirt floor but I knew I'd have to have a wood floor some day. I knew about plaster because I had worked with it before, so I smeared some on the walls. All that I really needed at first was nails. I got other stuff I needed from new houses being built nearby."

"Picking Up" What Was Needed. "I got around town quite a bit. Any place where there might be something, I'd take a look. If I found anything that I needed, I'd pick it up and take it home. I just started a collection: sleeping bag, radio, plywood for the roof, windows, a stove, lanterns, tools, clothes, water containers, boots. If you took away everything that's stolen, there wouldn't be much left here. Like the saw. I just walked into a store, grabbed it, put a piece of cloth around it to hide it, and walked out.

"Before I got food stamps, I'd go to the store with my backpack, fill it with steaks and expensive canned food, and just walk out. If anybody saw me, I'd wave at them and keep walking. I didn't have much to lose, I figured. The closest I ever got to being stopped, I had two six-packs of beer and some cooked chicken. The guy in the store had seen me there before. I just waved, but he said, 'Stop right there.' I ran out and grabbed my bike, but he was right behind me. I knew the only thing I could do was drop the merchandise and get out of there with my skin and my bike, and that's what I did. He didn't chase me; he just picked up the bag and shook his head at me."

The Bicycle Thief. "We lived in the country for about 3 years while I was growing up. Moving back into town was kinda different. I went pretty wild after moving to town. Me and another kid did a lot of crazy stuff, getting into places and taking things. I'd stay out all night just looking in people's garages. I'd get lots of stuff. My room had all kinds of junk in it. That's when I was living with my dad, and he didn't really notice. He still has an electric pencil sharpener I stole out of a church. He never knew where I got it.

"Instead of going to school, I'd stay home and work on bikes. We used to steal bikes all the time. We'd get cool frames and put all the hot parts on them. I've stolen lots of bikes—maybe around 50. But I probably shouldn't have never stolen about half of them, they were such junk. I just needed them for transportation."

Being Sneaky. "I've always been kind of sneaky, I guess. That's just the way I am. I can't say why. My mom says that when I was a small kid I was always doing something sneaky. Not always—but I could be that way. I guess I'm still that way, but it's not exactly the same. It's just the way you think about things.

"I don't like to be sneaky about something I could get in trouble for. But I like to walk quietly so no one will see me. I could get in trouble for something like sneaking in somebody's backyard and taking a rototiller. I did that once. I sold the engine.

"I guess being sneaky means I always try to get away with something. There doesn't have to be any big reason. I used to tell the kid I was hanging around with, 'I don't steal stuff because I need it. I just like to do it for some excitement.'

"Last year I went 'jockey-boxing' with some guys who hang around at the park. That's when you get into people's glove compartments. It was a pretty dead night. One guy wanted a car stereo. He had his tools and everything. So we all took off on bicycles, five of us. I was sort of tagging along and watching them—I didn't really do it. They got into a couple of cars. They got a battery vacuum cleaner and a couple of little things. You go to apartment houses where there's lots of cars and you find the unlocked ones and everybody grabs a car and jumps in and starts scrounging through.

"I've gone through glove compartments before and I probably will again some day if I see a car sitting somewhere just abandoned. But I'm not into it for fun anymore, and it doesn't pay unless you do a lot. Mostly young guys do it.

"I'm still mostly the same, though. I'll take a roll of tape or something from the supermarket. Just stick it in my pants. Or if I saw a knife that was easy to take. That's about it. Oh, I sneak into some nearby apartments to wash my clothes. I pay for the machines, but they are really for the tenants, not for me. And I'll sneak through the woods with a piece of plywood for the cabin."

I Don't Have to Steal, But. . . "I'm not what you'd call a super thief, but I will steal. A super thief makes his living at it; I just get by. I don't have to steal, but it sure makes life a hell of a lot easier. I've always known people who steal stuff. It's no big deal. If you really want something, you have to go around looking for it. I guess I could teach you how to break into your neighbor's house, if you want to. There's lots of ways—just look for a way to get in. It's not that hard to do. I don't know what you'd call it. Risky? Crazy?

"I can be honest. Being honest means that you don't do anything to people that you don't know. I don't like to totally screw somebody. But I'll screw 'em a little bit. You could walk into somebody's garage and take everything they have—maybe $5,000 worth of stuff. Or you could just walk in and grab a chain saw. It's not my main hobby to go around looking for stuff to steal. I might see something, but I wouldn't go out of my way for it."

Breaking and Entering. "I remember busting into my second-grade classroom. I went back to the schoolground on the weekend with another kid. We were just looking around outside and I said, 'Hey, look at that fire escape door—you could pull it open with a knife.' We pulled it open and I went in and I took some money and three or four little cars and a couple of pens. There wasn't anything of value, but the guy with me stocked up on all the pens he could find. We got in trouble for it. That was the first time I broke in anywhere. I don't know why I did it. Maybe too many television shows. I just did it because I could see that you could do it.

"And I've gotten into churches and stores. I've broken into apartment house recreation rooms a lot, crawling through the windows. And I've broken into a house before.

"I went in one house through the garage door, got inside, and scrounged around the whole house. God, there was so much stuff in that house. I munched a cake, took some liquor, took some cameras. Another time I thought there was nobody home at one house, and I went around to the bathroom window, punched in the screen, and made a really good jump to the inside. I walked in the house real quietly. Then I heard somebody walk out the front door, so I split. I didn't have nothin' then; I was looking for anything I could find. I just wanted to go scrounging through drawers to find some money.

"If I ever needed something that bad again and it was total chaos [i.e., desperation], I could do it, and I would. It's not my way of life, but I'd steal before I'd ever beg."

Inching Closer to the Chute. "Just before I started living at the cabin, I kept having it on my mind that I needed some money and could rob a store. It seemed like a pretty easy way to get some cash, but I guess it wasn't a very good idea. I had a B-B gun. I could have walked in there like a little Mafia, shot the gun a few times, and said, 'If you don't want those in your face, better give me the money.' There were a couple of stores I was thinking of doing it to.

"I was standing outside one store for about 2 hours. I just kept thinking about going in there. All of a sudden this cop pulls into the parking lot and kinda checks me out. I thought, 'Oh, fuck, if that cop came over here and searched me and found this gun, I'd be shit.' So as soon as he split, I left. And after thinking about it for so long.

"But another time, I really did it. I went into one of those little fast-food stores. I had this hood over my head with a little mouth hole. I said to the clerk, 'Open the register.' And she said, 'What! Are you serious?' I knew she wasn't going to open it, and she knew I wasn't about to shoot her. So then I started pushing all the buttons on the cash register, but I didn't know which ones to push. And she came up and pulled the key. Then someone pulled up in front of the store and the signal bell went 'ding, ding.' So I booked.

"Another time I thought about going into a store and telling this cashier to grab the cash tray and pull it out and hand it to me. Or else I was going to wait till near closing time when they go by with a full tray of 20-dollar bills and grab it. Or go into a restaurant right after closing time, like on a Saturday night or something, and just take the whole till. I was going to buy a motorcycle with that. All I needed was $400 to get one.

"If I was ever that hurting, I could probably do it if I had to. It's still a possibility, and it would sure be nice to have some cash. But you wouldn't get much from a little store anyway. I'd be more likely just to walk in and grab a case of beer."

I'm Not Going to Get Caught. "I can't straighten out my old bike after that little accident I had the other day, and that means I need another bike. I'll try to find one to steal—that's the easiest way to get one. I should be able to find one for free, and very soon, instead of having to work and spend all that money, money that would be better off spent other places, like reinstating my driver's license.

"The way I do it, I go out in nice neighborhoods and walk around on people's streets and look for open garages, like maybe they just went to the store or to work and didn't close the door. I walk on streets that aren't main streets. Someone might spot me looking around at all these bikes, but even if somebody says something, they can't do anything to you. The cops might come up and question me, but nothing could happen.

"Now, if I was caught on a hot bike . . . but that's almost impossible. If I was caught, they'd probably take me downtown and I'd sit there awhile until I went to court, and who knows what they'd do. Maybe give me six months. They'd keep me right there at the jail. But it's worth the risk, because I'm not going to get caught. I did it too many times. I know it's easy.

"Even if I worked, the only thing I'd be able to buy is an old Schwinn 10-speed. The bike I'm going to get will be brand new. Maybe a Peugeot or a

Raleigh. A $400 bike at least. It might not be brand new, but if I could find a way, I'd get a $600 bike, the best one I could find. And I'll do whatever I have to, so no one will recognize it."

Home Is the Hunter. "I think this will be the last 'bike hunting trip' I'll ever go on . . . probably. I said it *might* be the last one. I could probably do one more. When I get to be 24 or 25, I doubt that I'll be walking around looking for bikes. But, if I was 25 and I saw a nice bike and I was in bad shape and really needed it, I'd get it. I'm not going to steal anything I don't need, unless it's just sitting there and I can't help it, it's so easy. I'm not really corrupt, but I'm not 'innocent' any more. I can be trusted, to some people." ["Can I trust you?" I asked.] "Yeah. Pretty much. I dunno. When it comes to small stuff. . ."

Growing Up. "When I was growing up, I was always doing something, but it wasn't that bad. My parents never did take any privileges away or give me another chance. Anytime I did something in California, my mother and step-dad just said, 'Back to Oregon.' They didn't threaten, they just did it. My mom could have figured out something better than sending me back to Oregon all the time. She could have taken away privileges or made me work around the house. And in Oregon, my dad could have figured a better way than throwing me out of the house. Bad times for me were getting in a hassle with my parents. Then I wouldn't have no place to go, no money or nothin'. That happened with all of them at different times."

[By my count, Brad was reared in six families, including a time when he lived with his mother at her sister's home and when he lived with one stepmother's parents for awhile. That fact seemed not particularly disconcerting to him, but the abruptness of being dispatched among them was.]

"The last time I got kicked out in California, I moved back to Oregon, but I only stayed in the house a couple of days. My stepmom and my dad started telling me I wasn't going to smoke pot any more, I would have to go to school, I was going to have to stop smoking cigarettes, and other shit like that. And I didn't like anything about that fucking house. Another reason is that my dad said I couldn't have a motorcycle. So I split. I just hung around town, sleeping anywhere I could find. I ripped off a quilt and slept out on a baseball field for awhile. I stayed in different places for a couple of weeks. Then I got busted, got sent to reform school, then I got some work and the first thing I did was buy a motorcycle. I was riding without a license or insurance for awhile. Even after I got a license, I kept getting tickets, so finally my license got suspended, and my dad took the motorcycle and sold it to pay for the tickets.

"If I had kids, I would just be a closer family. I would be with them more and show that you love them. You could talk to your kids more. And if they do something wrong, you don't go crazy and lose your temper or something."

Getting Paid for Dropping Out. "I've earned some money at odd jobs since I came here, but mostly I live on food stamps. I knew that if I wasn't working and was out of money, food stamps were there. I've been doing it for quite awhile. When I was at the Mission, I had food stamps. A guy I worked with once told me, all I had to do was go down there and tell 'em you're broke, that's what it's there for. I haven't really tried looking for a job. Food stamps are a lot easier. And I'd just be taking a job away from someone who needs it more. Now that I've figured out the kinds of things to buy, I can just about get by each month on $70 for food. If I couldn't get food stamps, I'd get a job. I guess food stamps are society's way of paying me to drop out."

Hiding Out From Life. "So now I've got this cabin fixed up, and it really works good for me. This is better than any apartment I've ever had.

"I guess by living up here I'm sorta hiding out from life. At least I'm hiding from the life I had before I came up here. That's for sure. The life of a dumpy apartment and a cut-rate job. This is a different way of life.

"This place works a lot for me. What would I have been doing for the year and a half in town compared to a year and a half up here? Like, all the work I've done here, none of it has gone for some landlord's pocketbook. I should be able to stay here until I get a good job.

"I like living like this. I think I'd like to be able to know how to live, away from electricity and all that."

The romantic Robinson Crusoe aspects of a young man carving out a life in the wilderness, what his mother referred to as "living on a mountaintop in Oregon," is diminished by this fuller account of Brad's lifestyle. Brad would work if he "had to," but he had found that for awhile—measured perhaps in years rather than weeks—he did not have to. If he was not hiding out from life, he had at least broken out of what he saw as the futility of holding a cut-rate job in order to live a cut-rate existence.

Brad kept a low profile that served double duty. He had a strong aversion to being "looked at" in settings where he felt he did not "blend in," and his somewhat remote cabin protected him from the eyes of all strangers—including the law. His cabin became his fortress; he expressed concern that he himself might be "ripped off." On sunny weekends, with the likelihood of hikers passing through the woods, he tended to stay near the cabin, with an eye to protecting his motley, but nonetheless precious, collection of tools and utensils, bicycles and parts, and personal belongings. He sometimes padlocked the cabin (though it easily could have been broken into) and always locked his bike when in town if he was going to be any distance from it. Had he been ripped off, he would hardly have called the police to help recover his stolen items; few were his in the first place.

Technically he was not in trouble with the law. To some extent the law exerted a constraining influence on him. In his view, to get caught was the worst thing that could happen to him and would have been "stupid" on his part. That tended to circumscribe both the frequency and extent of the illicit activities in which he engaged. But the law also menaced him as a down-and-outer and as a relatively powerless kid, a kid without resources. The law works on a cash basis. Working for me, Brad earned and saved enough money to purchase an engine for his bicycle in order to circumvent his earlier problems with the motorcycle, only to discover via a traffic violation of over $300 (reduced to $90 with the conventional plea, "Guilty, with explanation") that a bicycle with an engine on it is deemed a motorized vehicle. He was required by law to have a valid operator's license (his was still suspended), a license for the vehicle, and insurance. To make himself "legal" he needed about $175 and would continue to face high semiannual insurance premiums. In his way of thinking, that expense got him "nothing"; he preferred to take his chances. Traffic fines were actually a major budget item for him, but his argument remained the same, "I won't get caught again.'

Margaret Mead once commented that most Americans would agree the "worst" thing a child can do is to steal (in MacNeil & Glover, 1959). As a "sneaky kid" Brad had already been stealing stuff—little stuff, mostly—for more than half his lifetime. He seemed to me to be approaching the moment when he would have to decide whether to dismiss his stealing as a phase of growing up and doing "crazy things" (jockey-boxing, breaking into the classroom on weekends, petty shoplifting, stealing bicycles) or to step into the "chute" by joining the big leagues. With mask and gun, he had already faced the chute head-on. That event might have ended otherwise, had not someone called his bluff. With the occurrence of repeated traffic fines, the courts themselves could conceivably precipitate for him a desperate need for quick and easy money.

World View: "Getting My Life Together"

The material presented thus far lends ample support to Brad's depiction of himself as a "sneaky kid" with a number of antisocial and unsociable traits. In the past 10 of his 20 years, Brad's antics often had resulted in trouble ("hassles") and had paved the way for more trouble than actually had befallen him. (In that regard, it is ironic that being sent to reform school, though on the technically serious charge of "supplying contraband" coupled with "harassment" was, in his opinion, more a consequence of having "nowhere else to go" than of the offenses themselves.) From mainstream society's point of view, Brad's story would seem to reflect the enculturation process going awry, a young person growing apart from, rather than a part of, the appropriate social system. Brad did not behave "properly" on certain critical dimensions (e.g., respect for other people's property, earning his way), and therefore his almost exemplary behavior on other dimensions (his lack of pretense, his cleanliness, and, particularly, his resourcefulness and self-reliance) was apt to be overlooked. He was not a social asset, and he seemed destined for trouble.

Yet in both word and deed (and here is the advantage of knowing him for 2 years, rather than depending solely on formal interviews), Brad repeatedly demonstrated how he was more "insider" than "outsider" to the society he felt was paying him to drop out. In numerous ways he revealed a personal world view not so far out of step with society after all. Adrift though he may have been, he was not without social bearings. The odds may have been against him, but they were not stacked. This was neither a "minority" kid fighting the immediate peril of the ghetto, nor a weak kid, nor a dumb kid, nor an unattractive kid, nor a kid who had not, at some time in his life, felt the security of family. Indeed, somewhere along the way he learned to value security so highly that his pursuit of it provided him an overriding sense of purpose.

Both Brad's parents had worked all their adult lives and, judging from statements I heard them make, took pride in their efforts. If they were "not really rich," as Brad sized it up, they were at least comfortable. Perhaps from Brad's point of view they had paid too high a price for what they had, or had given up too much to attain it, but they are the embodiment of the American working class. As Brad expressed it, "My dad's worked all his life so he can sit at a desk and not hold a screwdriver any more. But he just works! He never seems to have any fun."

Absolutely no one, including anthropologists who devote careers to the task, ever learns the totality of a culture; conversely, no one, including the most marginal or socially isolated of humans, ever escapes the deep imprint of macro- and microcultural systems in which he or she is reared as a member of a family, a community, and a nation. Evidence of that cultural imprinting abounds in Brad's words and actions. I have combed his words and found evidence that in examining his world view one can find glimmers of hope, if only he does not "get caught doing something stupid" or in some unexpected way get revisited by his past. Though he occasionally makes some deliberate, unsanctioned responses, Brad appears well aware of the "cultural meanings" of his behavior (see Wallace 1961a, p. 135).

If Brad does "make it" it will be largely because of the cultural imprinting of values instilled at some time in that same past. Let me here make the point to which I will return in conclusion: There was no constructive force working effectively on Brad's behalf to guide, direct, encourage, or assist him. He had no sponsor, no support system, virtually no social network. The agencies poised to respond to him will act when and if he makes a mistake and gets caught. He cannot get help without first getting into trouble. The only social agency that exerted a positive educative influence on him was an indirect consequence of the mixed blessing of food stamps that kept him from having to steal groceries but made it unnecessary for him to work. He had learned to spend his allotment wisely in order to make it last the month.

The following excerpts, selected topically, suggest the extent to which Brad already had acquired a sense of middle-class morality and an ethos of working to achieve material success. They point, as well, to loose strands that remain someday to be woven together if he is to be bound more securely to the Establishment.

A Job—That's All That Makes You Middle Class. "A job is all that makes you middle class. If I'm going to have a job, I've got to have a bike that works,

I've got to have a roof, I've got to have my clothes washed. And I'd probably need rain gear, too. You can't go into any job in clothes that look like you just came out of a mud hut.

"Even though I've worked for a while at lots of different things, I guess you could say that I've never really held a job. I've worked for my dad a while—altogether about a year, off and on. I helped him wire houses and do other things in light construction. I scraped paint for a while for one company. I worked for a graveyard for about 8 months, for a plumber a while, and I planted trees for a while.

"I wouldn't want to have to put up with a lot of people on a job that didn't make me much money. Like at a check-out counter—that's too many people. I don't want to be in front of that many people. I don't want to be a known part of the community. I don't mind having a job, but I don't like a job where everyone sees you do it. Working with a small crew would be best—the same gang every day. I'd like a job where I'm out and moving. Anything that's not cleaning up after somebody else, where you're not locked up and doing the same thing over and over, and where you can use your head a little, as well as your back.

"My mother said, 'If you had a little job right now, you'd be in heaven.' Yeah, some cash wouldn't hurt, but then I'd have to subtract the $70 I wouldn't get in food stamps, and there might not be a whole hell of a lot left. So I'm living in the hills and I'm not workin'. No car, either. So no girl friend right now. No big deal.

"If I did have a job, the hardest thing about it would be showing up on time and getting home. Living out here makes a long way to go for any job I might get.

"If you get your life together, it means you don't have to worry so much. You have a little more security. That's what everybody wants. Money—a regular job. A car. You can't have your life together without those two things.

"My life is far better than it was. I've got a place to live and no big problems or worries. I don't worry about where I'm going to sleep or about food. I've got a bike. Got some pot—my home-grown plants are enough now, so I don't have to worry about it, even though it's not very high class. But you've got to have a car to get to work in the morning and to get home. I can go on living this way, but I can't have a car if I'm going to do it.

"Sometimes my mom sends me clothes, or shampoo, or stuff like that. But if I had a job, I wouldn't need that. She'd help me with a car someday, if she ever thinks I'm financially responsible."

Building My Own Life. "I'm not in a big hurry with my life. If I can't do super-good, I'll do good enough. I don't think I'll have any big career.

"Maybe in a way I'll always be kind of a survivalist. But I would like to be prepared for when I get to be 50 or 60—if I make it that far—so that I wouldn't need Social Security. I get my food stamps, so I guess I'd have to say I'm part of The Establishment. A job would get me more into it.

"Over a period of time I've learned what food to buy and what food not to buy, how to live inexpensively. I get powdered milk, eggs, dry foods in bulk, and stuff like that. Food costs me about $80 per month. I could live on $100 a month for food, cigarettes, fuel, and a few little extras, but not very many, like buying nails, or a window, or parts for a bike. But I don't really need anything. I've got just about everything I need. Except there is a few things more.

"I might stay here a couple of years, unless something drastically comes up. Like, if a beautiful woman says she has a house in town, that would do it, but if not for that, it isn't very likely. I'll have to build my own life.

"I wouldn't mind working. I wouldn't mind driving a street-sweeper or something like that, or to buy a $30,000 or $60,000 piece of equipment, and just make money doing stuff for people. You see people all over who have cool jobs. Maybe they just do something around the house like take out washing machines, or they own something or know how to do something that's not really hard labor but it's skilled labor.

"But living this way is a good start for me. I don't have to work my life away just to survive. I can work a little bit, and survive, and do something else."

Being by Myself. "At this time of my life it's not really too good to team up with somebody. I've got to get my life together before I can worry about just going out and having a beer or a good time.

"Being by myself doesn't make all that much difference. I guess that I'm sorta a loner. Maybe people say I'm a hermit, but it's not like I live 20 miles out in nowhere.

"I don't want to be alone all my life. I'd like to go camping with somebody on the weekend. Have a car and a cooler of beer and a raft or something. It's nice to have friends to do that with. If I had a car and stuff, I'm sure I could get a few people to go. Without a car, man, shit . . .

Friends. "A friend is someone you could trust, I suppose. I've had close friends, but I don't have any now. But I have some 'medium' friends. I guess that's anybody who'd smoke a joint with me. And you see some people walking down the street or going to a store or to a pay phone. You just say, 'Hi, what's going on?'

"I know lots of people. Especially from reform school. I've already seen some. They're not friends, though; they're just people you might see to say hello and ask them what they've been up to and ask them how long they did in jail.

"The first time I met one guy I know now, I was pushing my bike and I had my backpack and some beer and I was drinking a beer. I'd never seen him before. He said, 'Hey, wanna smoke a joint?' I said, 'Sure.' So I gave him a couple of beers and we smoked some pot and started talking. I told him I lived up in the hills. I see him around every now and then. He's known me for a year and I talk to him sometimes and joke around. He's sort of a friend.

"I had a few friends in southern California, but by the time I left there I wasn't too happy with them. I guess my best friend was Tom. I used to ride skateboard with him all day. His older brother used to get pot for us. That's when I think I learned to ride the very best. We always used to try to beat each other out in whatever we did. I was better than him in some things and after a while he got better than me in a couple of things. But I think I was always a little bit more crazier than he was—a little bit wilder on the board."

I've Been More Places and Done More Things. "I've lived in a lot of different places. Like going to California. Living out in the country. Living different places in town. Dealing with people. Living at the reform school. Living in Portland. Living here.

"I've definitely had more experiences than some of the people I went to school with, and I've had my ears opened more than they have. In some things, I'm wiser than other kids my age.

"I saw a guy a few weeks ago who is the same age as me. He lived in a house behind us when I was in fifth grade. He still lives with his parents in the same place. I think about what he's been doing the last 9 years and what I've been doing the last 9 years and it's a big difference. He went to high school. Now he works in a gas station, has a motorcycle, and works on his truck. I guess that's all right for him, so long as he's mellow with his parents. That way he can afford a motorcycle.

"But you've got what you've got. It doesn't make any difference what anybody else has. You can't wish you're somebody else. There's no point in it."

Some Personal Standards. "In the summer I clean up every day. When it starts cooling down, I dunno; sometimes if it's cold, I just wash my head and under my arms. Last winter I'd get a really good shower at least every three days and get by otherwise. But I always wash up before going to town if I'm dirty. I don't want to look like I live in a cabin.

"I don't really care what people on the street think of me. But somebody who knows me, I wouldn't want them to dislike me for any reason.

"And I wouldn't steal from anybody that knew me, if they knew that I took something or had any idea that I might have took it, whether I liked them or not. I wouldn't steal from anybody I liked, or I thought they were pretty cool. I only steal from people I don't know.

"I don't like stealing from somebody you would really hurt. But anybody that owns a house and three cars and a boat—they're not hurtin'. It's the Law of the Jungle—occasionally people get burned. A lot of people don't, though. As long as they've got fences and they keep all their stuff locked up and don't leave anything laying around, they're all right. The way I see it, 'If you snooze, you lose.'

"If you say you'll do something, you should do it. That's the way people should operate. It pisses me off when somebody doesn't do it. Like, you tell somebody you're going to meet them somewhere, and they don't show up. But giving my word depends on how big of a deal it is; if it's pretty small, it would be no big deal.

"Sure, stealing is immoral. I don't like to screw somebody up for no good reason. But my morals can drop whenever I want.

"I went to Sunday School for awhile and to a church kindergarten. I guess I heard all the big lessons—you get the felt board and they pin all the stuff on 'em and cut out all the paper figures: Jesus, Moses. But our family doesn't really think about religion a whole lot. They're moral to a point but they're not fanatics. It's too much to ask. I'd rather go to hell. But any little kid knows what's right and wrong."

Moderation: Getting Close Enough, Going 'Medium' Fast. "One of my friend's older brothers in southern California was a crazy fucker. He'd get these really potent peyote buttons and grind them up and put them in chocolate milkshakes. One time they decided to go out to the runways where the jets were coming in, cause they knew somebody who did it before. Planes were coming in continually on that runway. They'd go out there laying right underneath the skid marks, just right under the planes. I never would get that close. Just being out there, after jumping the fence and walking clear out to the runway, is close enough. I never did lie on the runway . . .

"On the skateboard, I just go medium fast . . .

"The fun part of skiing is knowing when to slow down . . .

"When those guys went 'jockey-boxing,' I didn't actually do it with them. I just was tagging along . . .

"Robbing a store seemed like a pretty easy way to get some cash, but I guess it wasn't a very good idea. . .

"I don't know why I didn't get into drugs more. I smoke pot, but I've never really cared to take downers and uppers or to shoot up. I don't really need that much . . .

"I like to smoke pot, but I don't think of myself as a pothead. A pothead is somebody who is totally stoned all day long on really good pot, really burned out all the time. I smoke a joint, then smoke a cigarette, and I get high. I just like to catch a buzz . . .

"If you really get burnt out, your brain's dead. You can get burned out on anything if you do it too much. I don't do it enough to make it a problem. If you take acid, you never know who's made it or exactly what's in it. I've taken it before and gotten pretty fried. I don't know if it was bad acid, but it wasn't a very good experience. . .

"Sometimes when I want to be mellow, I just don't say anything. I just shut up. Or somebody can mellow out after a day at work—you come home, smoke a joint, drink a beer—you just sort of melt . . ."

Putting It All Together. "Anything you've ever heard, you just remember and put it all together the best you can. That's good enough for me."

Formal Schooling

I knew little of Brad's schooling when I began systematically to collect life history data from him. By his account he had often been "slow" or "behind the rest of the class." He could read, but he faltered on "big words." He could write, but his spelling and punctuation were not very good. He had trouble recalling number sequences and basic arithmetic facts. ("Lack of practice," he insisted.) In one junior high school he had been placed in "an EH [educationally handicapped] class with the other stonies." As he recalled, "I don't know if I felt I was special or not, but I didn't like those big classes."

Measures of IQ or scholastic achievement did not really matter any more. Brad was well aware of his capacities and limitations. How far he was once "below average" or "behind" in his schoolwork had become, as it always had been, purely academic. Schooling for him was over; he was out.

Formal schooling aside, for practical purposes Brad could read, he could write, he could do simple arithmetic. The only book he "requisitioned" for his cabin was a dictionary. That alone was incredible; even more incredibly, he occasionally labored through it to find a word—no easy task when the alphabet had to be recited aloud in order to locate an entry.

Schooling had played a part in Brad's life, but not the vital part educators like it to play. In 10 years he had been enrolled in eight schools in two states, ranging from early years at a small country school to a final 8 months at a state reformatory, and including attendance at urban elementary, junior high, and senior high schools. I traced his attendance record where he boasted having "the world's record for ditching school." Perhaps it was not the world's record, but following his midyear enrollment in grade 5 he maintained 77 percent attendance for that year and 46 percent attendance in grade 6 the year following. He changed schools during the academic year at least once in grades 4, 5, and 6, as well as beginning the term in a new school four different years: "I guess I was in school a lot, but I was always in a different school."

In Brad's assessment, school "did what it's supposed to do . . . You gotta learn to read." He laid no blame, noting only that "Maybe school could of did better." He acknowledged that he might have done better, too:

"I was just never that interested in school. If I knew I had to do something, I'd try a little bit. I could probably have tried harder."

The earliest school experience he could recall was in a church-sponsored kindergarten. Hearing Brad use objectionable language, the teacher threatened to wash his mouth with soap. At the next occasion when the children were washing their hands, he stuck a bar of soap in his mouth: "I showed the kids around me, 'Hey, no big deal, having soap in your mouth.'"

He recalled first grade as a time when "I learned my ABCs and everything. It was kind of neat." Apparently his enthusiasm for schooling stopped there. He could think of no particular class or teacher that he especially liked. His recollection of events associated with subsequent grades involved changes of schools, getting into trouble for his classroom behavior, or skipping school altogether. As early as fourth grade he remembered difficulty "keeping up" with classmates.

By his own assessment Brad did "OK" in school, but he recalled excelling only once, an art project in clay that was put on display and that his mother still kept. During grade 7 his attendance improved and, for one brief term, so did his grades, but he was not really engaged with what was going on and he felt lost in the large classes:

"In those big classes, like, you sit around in a big horseshoe, and you've got a seat four rows back, with just one teacher. Like English class, I'd get there at 9:00 in the morning and put my head down and I'd sleep through the whole class. It was boring, man.

"Another class they tried to get me in was typing. I tried for a little while, but I wasn't even getting close to passing, so I just gave up."

Brad's public schooling ended in southern California. When he got shunted back to Oregon, he did not enroll in school again, although after being "busted," schooling was his principal activity during 8 months in reform school. He felt that he had attended "a couple of pretty good schools" in southern California during grades 8, 9, and, briefly, 10, but, as usual, the times he remembered were times spent out of class, not in it:

"By the end of school, I was cutting out a lot. Like, I didn't need PE. Look at this kid—he's been riding bicycles and skateboards all day all his life. I didn't need no PE. I don't need to go out in the sun and play games. I wasn't interested in sports. So I'd go get stoned. I'd take a walk during that class, go kick back in an orange grove, maybe eat an orange, get high, smoke a cigarette, and by the time I'd walk back, it was time for another class. I did it for a long time and never got caught. Anyhow, then I switched schools."

Brad felt that his lack of academic progress cost him extra time in reform school, "So I started to speed up and do the stuff and then I got out." In his assessment, "I was doing 9th-grade work. I probably did some 10th- and 11th grade stuff, but not a lot."

Although young people seldom return to public schools after serving "time," I asked Brad to identify the grade levels to which he might have been assigned had he gone back to school:

"For math, if I went back, I'd just be getting into 10th grade. In reading, I'd be a senior or better. Spelling would be about 8th grade. I can spell good enough. Handwriting, well, you just write the way you write. My writing isn't that bad if I work on it. I don't worry about that much."

On the other hand, he did recognize limitations in his command of basic school skills. He had "kind of forgotten" the multiplication facts, and he was pretty rusty on subtracting and recalling the alphabet. To be a good speller, he once mused, you've got to "do it a lot" but at reform school he did only "a little bit." His awareness of these limitations is revealed in a letter intended for his mother but later abandoned in favor of a cheerier style:

Hi
if I sit hear and stair
at this pieac of paper
eny longer ill go crazy
I dont think im scaird
of witing just dont like
to remind myself I
need improvment. its
raining alot
past few days but its warm
'n dry inside. . . .

Reading was the school skill at which Brad felt most proficient, and his confidence was not shaken by the fact that some words were difficult for him. He said he did not enjoy reading, but he spent hours poring over instruction manuals. My impression was that although his oral reading was halting, he had good reading comprehension. That was also his assessment. When, at his father's insistence, he briefly entertained the idea of joining the Army, Brad had first to take the G.E.D. exam (for his high school General Educational Development certificate) and then take a test for the Army. He felt he passed "pretty high" on the Army test and he felt he did "super, super good" on some parts of the G.E.D., "like reading and a couple of other ones."

Brad once observed philosophically, "The people in college today are probably the ones who didn't sleep when I was in English class." At the same time, school was a closed chapter in his life. Other than to acknowledge that he "might have tried harder," however, he expressed no regrets over school as an opportunity missed. Anticipating that his lack of school skills would prove a barrier to enrollment in any technical training program, he could not imagine ever returning to the classroom. And, like most school leavers, he could not think of anything that might have been done that would have kept him in school.[4]

Adequate Schools and Inadequate Education: An Interpretation

It might be socially "desirable" if Brad could read better, write better, do better, and spell better. With better spelling skills, he would "stare" rather than "stair" at a blank page and perhaps feel less self-conscious about needing "improvment." Considering that he devoted some attention (although certainly not exclusive attention) to schooling for 10 of his 20 years, he does not perform these skills very well.

On the other hand, that he can do them as well as he does might also be a tribute to the public schools. Brad's level of school achievement may be disappointing, but it is not inadequate. He is literate. He did get "something" out of school. True, his performance at the 3 Rs could be more polished, but the importance of his proficiency with such amenities pales before problems of greater social consequence. Brad's schooling has stopped, but his learning continues apace. Exerting some positive, constructive influence on that learning as it pertains to Brad's enculturation into society presents society's current challenge. That challenge has not been taken up.

Schools can affect the rate and level of academic achievement, but they do not set the course of students' lives. They do not and cannot "reach" everyone, even though they may ever so briefly touch each person. Schooling is not everyone's cup of tea. As Brad put it, "I've always liked learning. I just didn't like school."

Learning—in the broad enculturative sense of coming to understand what one needs to know to be competent in the roles one may expect to fulfill in society, rather than in the narrow sense of learning-done-at-school—is an ongoing process in which each person engages throughout a lifetime. In Brad's case, the direction that process was taking seemed to reflect all too well what he felt society expected of him: nothing. He was left largely to his own resources to make sense of his world and create his own life (cf. Mann, 1982, 343). He endeavored quite self-consciously to "figure things out," but his resolutions often put him at odds with society; what appeared as inevitable conclusions to him were neither inevitable nor necessarily appropriate in terms of community norms.

Maybe we cannot reach him; surely we cannot reach everyone like him. But I was astounded to realize that no systematic, constructive effort was being exerted to influence the present course of Brad's life. No agency offered help, or direction, or concern, and neither did any of the "institutions" that ordinarily touch our lives: family, school, work, peer group. If it is naive to regard these influences as invariably positive and constructive, our interactions with them do, nonetheless, contribute to our sense of social "self." Brad was, for the most part, out of touch with them all.

If Brad is able to "get his life together," it will have to be almost entirely through his own effort. Perhaps his personal style as a loner helped buffer him from peer influences that seemed to me, as a wary adult, as likely to get him into trouble as to guide him on the straight and narrow; that he could find time and space "on a mountaintop in Oregon" rather than on a beach or under a freeway in southern California seemed to me to give him an advantage over other "street people." His lifestyle was not overly complicated by urban trappings or the quickened pace of city life. He was not crowded or pushed. At the same time, he could neither escape the influence of material wants and creature comforts so prevalent in the society in which he lives nor deny a deeply felt need to connect with someone, somewhere. Seeming loner that he often appeared, even Brad could acknowledge, "There must be a group that I would fit in, somewhere in this town."

He had learned to "hunt and gather" for his necessities in the aisles of supermarkets, in neighborhood garages, and at residential building sites. He conceded that stealing was wrong, but necessity (broadly defined to allow for some luxuries as well) took precedence over conformity among his priorities. He saw "no alternative" for getting the things he felt he needed but could not afford. Still, he took only what he considered necessary, not everything he could get his hands on. He was not a "super thief," and he did not see himself ever becoming one.

I do not see how society can "teach" Brad not to be sneaky, not to shoplift, not to steal. Most families try to do that. His family wasn't entirely successful in its attempts, though more of the message seems to have gotten through than one might at first assume.[5] In that regard I find useful the distinction between deviant *acts* and deviant *persons* as suggested by anthropologist Robert Edgerton (1978). In spite of occasional deviant acts, Brad's statements reveal his underlying enculturation into the prevailing ethos of mainstream American society. He was well aware of the meanings of his acts to others; as he noted, "Any little kid knows what's right and wrong." Although he prided himself on the cunning necessary to survive his "hard life" by whatever means necessary, he staunchly defended his behavior—"I couldn't get by without stealing stuff"—as well as himself: "I am not that rotten of a kid!"

There was a foundation on which to build, but there was no external help, or support, or even a modicum of encouragement shaping that process. Was schooling "an" opportunity in Brad's life, or was it the only directed opportunity he would get? It seems to me there might be and should be a more concerted effort to exert a positive influence to provide him with reasonable and realistic routes of access back into the cultural mainstream. To have any effect, however, such efforts would have to be in the form of increasing the options available to him, rather than trying to "shove" him in some particular direction; he has already heard the lectures about good citizenship.

The community's best strategy would seem to be to assure that *opportunities* exist for a person like Brad to satisfy more of his wants in socially acceptable ways. Fear of getting caught isn't much of a deterrent to someone who thinks he's "too smart" to get caught. Armed robbery is already within the realm of things Brad might do. With an attitude toward behaviors like shoplifting, "ripping things off," burglary, operating a vehicle with a suspended license, or even his preoccupation with obtaining an adequate supply of "pot" that "just about everybody—or at least everybody my age—does it," he can too easily find himself "in the chute" without realizing that everybody isn't there after all. Having gotten out of mainstream society, he does not see a way back in. Nor is he convinced it is worth the effort to try.

It is convenient—and an old American pastime—to place blame on the schools. When directed toward the schools, questions concerning educational adequacy invite that kind of blame-setting by relating the present inadequacies of youth to prior inadequacies of the schools (see Levin, 1983). Employing the anthropologist's distinction between schooling and education encourages us to review the full range of efforts the community makes to exert a positive educative influence on our lives, not only during the school years but in the postschool years as well.[6] The problems Brad now poses for society are not a consequence of inadequate schooling. They dramatize the risk we take by restricting our vision of collective educational responsibility to what can be done in school.

One hears arguments that today's youth vacillate between extremes of taking what they want or expecting everything to be handed to them on a silver platter. One finds a bit of both in Brad's dreams of pulling off a robbery or suddenly finding himself owning and operating a $60,000 piece of machinery, as well as in his reluctance to do work like dishwashing that entails cleaning up after others and where everyone can watch you perform a menial job.

But I wonder if young people like Brad really believe that society "owes" them something? Perhaps that is an expression of frustration at failing to see how to *begin* to accumulate resources of their own comparable to what they perceive "everyone else" already has. A willingness to defer gratification must come more easily to those who not only have agonized during the deferment but also have eventually realized some long-awaited reward. Nothing Brad had ever done had worked out that well—at least prior to his effort to build both a new cabin and a new lifestyle. He had virtually no sense of deferred gratification. With him, everything was now or never.

In a society as materialistic as ours, opportunity is realized essentially with money rather than "school" or "work." To Brad, money represented security and he had limited access to it. That is why food stamps, in an annual amount less than $900, figured so importantly to him. His use of the stamps has left me wondering whether it might be possible to design some governmental agency that would calculatedly confront individuals like Brad in an educative way.

But the educative value of a welfare dole is limited, and, as Brad discovered, the power of the dole-givers and their labyrinth of regulations is ultimate. The stamps made a better consumer of him (buying generic brands, buying large quantities, buying staples), but he realized that the first $70 of any month's takehome pay would be money he would otherwise have received free from the food stamp program. To "earn" his stamps, he had to remain poor.[7] Had he found the second-rate job he so dreaded, part of his earnings would simply have replaced the dole, his other expenses (transportation, clothes, maybe a second-rate apartment) would have increased dramatically, and he would have been trapped in a second-rate life again. Until his food stamps were summarily canceled for 2 months, after he failed to participate in a ritual midwinter job search during a period of staggering recession and regional unemployment, he did not aggressively seek work. When he finally realized he was destitute and began in earnest to look for work, 38 days passed before he even got turned down for a job! He put in many hours at painting and yard clean-up for me (although he refused to equate working for me with "real work") and reverted to "ripping off" items he felt he needed but could not afford.

I invited Brad's thoughts on what might be done to help people like him. Other than a dream of finding "just the right job" (never fully specified) without ever going to look for it, his idea was of a "day work" program wherein anyone who needed money could appear at a given time, do a day's work, and promptly receive a day's pay. I'm sure Brad's thoughts turned to the end of the day when each worker would receive a pay envelope, while I wondered what one would do with a motley pick-up crew that wouldn't inadvertently make mockery of work itself. Yet implicit in his notion are at least two critical points.

First is a notion of a right to work: If (when) one is willing, one should be able to work and, if in dire need, be paid immediately in cash. Brad found no such right in his life. Although he had been able to find—but not hold—a number of jobs in the past, now he heard only "No Help Wanted" and read only "Not Presently Taking Applications." He was not entirely without social conscience when he observed that if he found a job he would only be taking it away from someone who needed it more. Brad did not really need a job. And, as he had begun to "figure out," no one really needed him. Maybe he was right; maybe $70 in food stamps was society's way of paying him to drop out.

Second is a notion of an overly structured wage and hour system that effectively prices most unskilled and inexperienced workers like Brad out of the job market and requires a full-time commitment from the few it accepts. Brad's material needs were slight. He could have preserved the best elements in his carefree lifestyle by working part time. However, the labor market does not ordinarily offer such options except for its own convenience. Either you want a job or you do not want a job. But work for its own sake cast no spell over Brad; he did not look to employment for satisfaction, for meaningful involvement, or for achieving self respect. Money was the only reason one worked.[8]

School provides opportunity and access for some youth; employment provides it for others. Neither school nor work presently exerted an influence on Brad. He was beyond school, and steady employment was beyond him. Without the effective support of family or friends, and without the involvement of school or work, he was left to his own devices. In his own words, he could not see a way to win and he did not have anything to lose. From mainstream society's point of view, we would be better off if he did.

After so carefully making provision for Brad's schooling, society now leaves his continuing education to chance, and we are indeed taking our chances. But educative adequacy in the lives of young people like Brad is not an issue of schooling. Schools provided him one institutional opportunity; they no longer reached him, and no other agency was trying. His next institutional "opportunity," like his last one, may be custodial. If it is, we all lose; Brad will not be the only one who will have to pay.[9]

Summary

"The important thing about the anthropologist's findings" writes Clifford Geertz (1973), one of anthropology's more articulate spokesmen, "is their complex specificness, their circumstantiality" (p. 23). Whatever issue anthropologists address, they characteristically begin an account and look for illustration through real events or cases bounded in time and circumstance. The effective story should be "specific and circumstantial," but its relevance in a broader context should be apparent. The story should make a point that transcends its modest origins. The case must be particular, but the implications broad.

Following that tradition, I have related a specific and circumstantial life story to illustrate the necessity of regarding education as more than just schooling, and of pointing out how little we attend to that broader concern. That may seem a roundabout way to address so complex an issue, but it is a way to bring an anthropological perspective to the problem.

Brad's story is unique, but his is not an isolated case. He is one among thousands of young people who simply "drift away." His uninvited presence on my

20-acre sanctuary, in search of sanctuary for himself, brought me into contact with a type of youth I do not meet in my work as a college professor. He piqued my anthropological interest with a world view that was in many ways strikingly similar to mine but with a set of coping strategies strikingly different. It is easy for people like me to think of people like Brad as someone else's problem, but, for a moment that lingered out to 2 years, he quite literally brought the problem home to me. I do not find ready answers even in his particular case; I am certainly not ready to say what might, can, or must be done in some broader context.

Little is to be gained from laying blame at the feet of Brad's parents or his teachers, and to do so is to ignore indications of repeated, if not necessarily effective, efforts to help and guide him. Though our extended conversations may have been enlightening to Brad, as they surely were to me, my more direct efforts to help seemed to go awry. At the end, he departed almost as unexpectedly as he had arrived. I am not sure what I think "society" can accomplish for an amorphous "them" when my own well-intended efforts with just one youth seemed only to demonstrate to him that I had my life "together" (his term) in a manner virtually unattainable for him. The easiest course is to blame Brad, but to do so is to abandon hope and a sense of collective responsibility.

The only certainty I feel is that it is in our common interest to seek ways to provide opportunities intended to exert a continuing and constructive educational influence on the lives of young people like Brad. I do not know whether Brad can or will allow himself to be reached effectively or in time. I do know that from his perspective he saw neither attractive opportunities nor sources of potential help; by his own assessment, he simply did not matter. He was not free of his society, but he had become disconnected from it. Once adrift, nothing seemed to beckon or guide him back.

Because we tend to equate education with schooling, we are inclined to look to the past and ask where the schools went wrong. Brad's story, in which school played only a minor role, serves as a reminder of the importance of other educative influences in our lives. It also points out how little systematic attention we give to discerning what those influences are or how we might better use them to augment, complement, and otherwise underwrite the massive efforts we direct at youth during their in-school years. In that broad perspective, our efforts at *education* appear woefully inadequate in spite of the remarkable accomplishments of our schools. Until I found Brad living in my backyard, however, the problem remained essentially abstract. Now it has confronted me with the "complex specificness" of one young human life.

Notes

Acknowledgments. A portion of the work on which this article is based was performed pursuant to Contract No. NIE-P-81-0271 of the National Institute of Education dealing with issues of educational adequacy under the School Finance Project. Data collection and interpretation are, however, the responsibility of the author. Appreciation is expressed to W. W. Charters, Jr., Stanley Elam, Barbara Harrison, Bryce Johnson, Malcolm McFee, and Esther O. Tron, as well as to "Brad," for critical reading and helpful suggestions with early drafts of this paper.

1. If I found any surprise in reviewing the literature, it was in discovering some remarkable similarities between Brad's story and the ground-breaking classic first published half a century ago, Clifford Shaw's *The Jack-Roller: A Delinquent Boy's Own Story* (1930).

2. Meyer Fortes, writing in 1938, noted the firmly established axiom that "education in the widest sense is the process by which the cultural heritage is transmitted from generation to generation, and that schooling is therefore only part of it" (p. 5). Melville Herskovits (1948) subsequently introduced the encompassing term *enculturation* for referring to education in Fortes's "widest sense," but he retained the term *education*, suggesting that it be restricted to "its ethnological sense of directed learning" in turn distinct from and more encompassing than *schooling*, defined as "that aspect of education carried out by specialists" (p. 311; see also Wallace, 1961b).

3. I have been careful to observe the few conditions Brad imposed on my use of the information; he, in turn, was paid for time spent interviewing and for later checking the written account, and early drafts were informed by his comments. That is not to imply that he was entirely satisfied with my portrayal or my interpretation, but he was satisfied that what I reported was accurate. If only to please me, he even commented that he hoped his story might "help people understand."

4. See, for example, the *Oregon Early School Leavers Study* (Oregon Department of Education, 1980), in which only one third of the young people interviewed responded that "something might have been done to affect their decision to quit public secondary school" (p. 16).

5. Brad expressed only resentment toward his father, but often mentioned his mother's efforts to provide a positive influence on him. When Brad introduced me to her, after he proudly showed her the cabin during her brief but long-anticipated visit, I asked whether she felt she could exert a guiding influence over him living 1,000 miles away. "We've always been a thousand miles apart" she replied, "even when we were under the same roof."

On a different occasion, responding to Brad's announcement that he needed to "find" another bicycle, I asked, "What would your mother think about you stealing a bike? That it's dumb; that it's smart?"

"Neither," he replied. "She'd just think that I must have needed it. She wouldn't say anything. She doesn't lecture me about things like that. But she used to cut out everything they printed in the paper about 'pot' and put it on my walls and she'd talk about brain damage."

6. Although the distinction between education and schooling is sometimes acknowledged, it is not necessarily regarded as having much significance, at least for understanding contemporary society. To illustrate, note in the following excerpt how educator/economist Henry Levin, addressing the topic *Education and Work* (1982), at once recognizes the distinction between education and schooling but bows to what he describes as the "convention" of equating them:

> Although the term education is sometimes used interchangeably with schooling, it is important to note that schooling is not the only form of education. However, schooling represents such a dominant aspect of education in modern societies that the convention of equating education and schooling in the advanced industrialized societies will also be adopted here. (p. 1)

7. The irony of the implications and consequences when *not* working has become prerequisite to maintaining a steady income is nicely spelled out in Estroff, 1981. See especially Chapter 6, "Subsistence Strategies: Employment, Unemployment, and Professional Disability."

8. Paul Willis (1980) notes in his study of working-class youth that it is this "reign of cash" that precipitates their contact with the world of work (p. 39). As one of his informants explained, "Money is life." Brad's mother expressed a similar view: "Money, not love, makes the world go round."

9. For a grim scenario, including some discomforting parallels and similarities, see Mailer, 1979. The protagonist of Mailer's "true life novel" makes special note of the impact of reform school on his life (Chapter 22). Brad did not reveal the extent of the impact on his own life of the same reform school, but he did include it specifically in his brief inventory of significant "experiences." Similarities noted earlier between Brad's account and Shaw's *The Jack-Roller* (1930) seem less pronounced in a subsequently published follow-up, *The Jack-Roller at Seventy* (Snodgrass, 1982).

References

Brandes, S. (1982). Ethnographic autobiographies in American anthropology. In E. A. Hoebel, R. Currier, & S. Kaiser (Eds.), *Crisis in anthropology: View from Spring Hill, 1980.* New York: Garland Publishing Company.

Edgerton, R. (1978). The study of deviance—Marginal man or everyman? In G. D. Spindler (Ed.), *The making of psychological anthropology* (p. 442–476). Berkeley: University of California Press.

Estroff, S. E. (1981). *Making it crazy: An ethnography of psychiatric clients in an American community.* Berkeley: University of California Press.

Fortes, M. (1938). *Social and psychological aspects of education in Taleland.* Supplement to *Africa, 11*(4), 1–64.

Geertz, C. (1973). *The interpretation of cultures.* New York: Basic Books.

Herskovits, M. J. (1948). *Man and his works: The science of cultural anthropology.* New York: Alfred A. Knopf.

Levin, H. M. (1982). *Education and work.* Program Report No. 82-B8. Palo Alto, CA: Institute for Research on Educational Finance and Governance, Stanford University.

Levin, H. M. (1983). Youth unemployment and its educational consequences. *Educational Evaluation and Policy Analysis, 5*(2), 231–247.

Lewis, O. (1961). *Children of Sanchez: Autobiography of a Mexican family.* New York: Random House.

MacNeil, I., & Glover, G. (Producers). (1959). *Four families* (Film narrated by Ian MacNeil and Margaret Mead). National Film Board of Canada.

Mailer, N. (1979). *The executioner's song.* New York: Warner Books.

Mann, D. (1982). Chasing the American dream: Jobs, schools, and employment training programs in New York State. *Teachers College Record, 83*(3), 341–376.

Oregon Department of Education. (1980). *Oregon early school leavers study.* Salem: Oregon Department of Education.

Shaw, C. R. (1930). *The jack-roller: A delinquent boy's own story.* University of Chicago Press.

Simmons, L. (Ed.). (1942). *Sun Chief. The autobiography of a Hopi Indian.* New Haven: Yale University Press.

Snodgrass, J. (Ed.). (1982). *The jack-roller at seventy: A fifty-year follow-up.* Lexington, MA: D. C. Heath.

Wallace, A. F. C. (1961a). The psychic unity of human groups. In B. Kaplan (Ed.), *Studying personality cross-culturally* Evanston, IL: Row Peterson and Company.

Wallace, A. F. C. (1961b). Schools in revolutionary and conservative societies. In F. C. Gruber (Ed.), *Anthropology and education* (pp. 25–54). Philadelphia: University of Pennsylvania Press.

Willis, P. E. (1980). *Learning to labour: How working class kids get working class jobs.* Hampshire, England: Gower Publishing. (Originally published 1977).

Wolcott, H. F. (1982). The anthropology of learning. *Anthropology and Education Quarterly, 13*(2), 83–108.

Section VI
Case Study Methods in
Educational Research

Case Study Methods in Educational Research: Seeking Sweet Water

Robert E. Stake
University of Illinois

Here is another update of an old warhorse "Seeking Sweet Water." When it first was foaled in the 1970s, case study was seldom considered a proper educational research method. Now case study is one of the most popular, and usually respected, forms for studying educators and educational programs. In that short period—as described by Denzin and Lincoln (1994)—qualitative, naturalistic, and interpretive studies have helped people understand the enormously complex problems of the schools and the society. Case studies have not found the solution for education's problems, but with most research and development efforts proving to be more disappointment than breakthrough, researchers and others have appreciated deep, self-referential probes of problems.

This new dialogue covers much of the same ground and draws upon the same main reference work, Charles Brauner's (1974) "The First Probe," but looks into some of the new questions that puzzle graduate students in the '90s. Through much of the dialogue, I am chatting with a hypothetical graduate student, Devonne Johnson. An English teacher in Chicago, Devonne is beginning doctoral work, figuring after she retires she will need a new way to fight the battles of the inner-city schools. She doesn't plan on being a professor or researcher, but then most of my doctoral students started that way. The account you are about to read is fictitious. The participants are Devonne Johnson, DJ, and me, BS.

DJ: What's so special about case study?

BS: It's special because it's about one thing: one person, one classroom, one curriculum, one case. You learn the intricate complexity of one case. And sometimes you find that what is true of that one case is true about other cases too, things you hadn't noticed before. Sociologists call it the micro-macro problem.

DJ: And you learn by watching?

BS: That is the most common way, but for each case study, several methods are used. People have different notions as to what a case study is. The term "case study" belongs to medicine, social work, urban planning, plant pathology. It belongs to science and to social service. It belongs to the vernacular as much as to technology. It is a popular form of research in many fields. But case study has problems, some of which are not so apparent.

DJ: Like what?

BS: Well, it doesn't have a set routine, which is one way a researcher and other people can tell if the study was done properly. And if you really want to find out what is common across many cases, case study is seldom the best way to do it. But the concern with qualitative case studies is that they are too subjective. Too much rides on the researcher's impressions.

DJ: But you like qualitative methods.

BS: Indeed I do. Sometimes qualitative studies let us peer deeply into the heart of an issue. Somehow, the words "sweet water" come to mind. The first American pioneers found it drier and drier as they trekked west. When they found water fit for humans and livestock, it was a precious discovery. Even green or muddy, they called it "sweet water." I feel a bit the same way when a case unfolds.

DJ: What's an example of "sweet water"?

BS: For educational research, one of the early case studies was an evaluation report by Lou Smith and Paul Pohland called "Educational Technology and the Rural Highlands." Thinking back, Lou told me:

"The computer-assisted instruction program that we studied in the 'Rural Highlands' was a broadly based attempt to change student achievement in arithmetic, hopefully an integration of computer-aided instruction with the classroom work. We looked for relationships between what went on at the terminals and during the regular classroom work. One general observation we made was that the relationships seemed minimal. For instance, reading from my notes, on the 17th of November:

> I made a specific point of checking with two of the [first grade] girls about where they were currently in their math lessons. I wondered then how closely the drills that they were taking corresponded to what they were doing in class. Apparently it is not very close. Ruth told me that the day's classroom lesson was on "writing mathematical sentences." The drills, however, were all simple addition and subtraction problems.

Later in the school year, this issue was examined again. For instance, according to notes, on April 2, I asked Edith about the relationship between the materials she had on the teletype and what they were doing in class. The conversation ran as follows:

> Observer: Are you doing multiplication in class?
> Edith: We're doing fractions.

I also asked Dick.
>   Observer: Is [the drill] anything like what you're doing in class? His answer
>   was a very emphatic, "No!"

We searched our notes and records for factors that seemed to be involved in creating this situation. Several came to mind: (a) the approximately six-week delay in starting the computer-assisted instruction program seemed critical; (b) there were frequent system breakdowns, that is, the physical structure of the system, the teletypes, the telephone lines, the computers, the terminals had difficulties; and (c) few teachers appeared to be aware of or chose to exercise the option of reassigning 'units' to the children. In this sense it was a broadly based, complex, systemic set of causes. (Smith & Pohland, 1974, pp. 5–54)."

DJ: That sounds like the usual screw-up. How could that have been "sweet water"?

BS: In the early '70s, many of us believed that good technology could liberate the teacher from mechanical aspects of instruction and monitoring. We appreciated neither the complexity of the innovation nor what the teacher did. Such studies gave us a clear look at the muddy mess. It was dismaying and it was electrifying. We started to see that large innovations didn't provide simple solutions but often created bottlenecks.

DJ: But this was just one example. How could you conclude that the others would be unworkable?

BS: We may have treated such cases as more typical than we should have. But it was not the particulars that were generalizable but the systematicity. I think we recognized that if only one thing could go wrong, it may not; but if 40 things could go wrong, some surely would. The "sweet water" here was realizing that lots more things could go wrong than we ever dreamed.

And it was not just by chance that we tasted that sweetness. Smith and Pohland designed their case study to help us readers scrutinize the teaching and learning system in that arithmetic class. It wasn't a feature story for the newspaper telling us about "real, lovable human beings," good guys deserving our support or bad guys deserving our indignation. Smith and Pohland were working on a conceptual structure, building up an understanding as an author, perhaps a biographer, would, making interpretations, yet leaving room for readers or listeners to make their own. They worked through tough issues, such as whether or not there was an alignment and cross-structuring of the arithmetic taught by computer and that taught by the teacher.

DJ: Tell me again how this case study is different from a newspaper story.

BS: There are some important similarities. Both are trying to develop an understanding through the description of what, where, how, when, and why. Both use narrative and testimony. The difference is in the use of theme. The reporter tries to tell the story primarily to be interesting to the reader. The case researcher starts out looking for what is meaningful to researchers but simultaneously tries to discover what is meaningful to the case people. Really, the case is precious.

DJ: All cases are precious?

BS: Whoops, hyperbole. I should have said paramount.

DJ: Didn't you tell me that you studied Harper School because you were hired to find out how Chicago school reform was working?

BS: Right. The overriding issue was districtwide school reform. While I was studying Harper, I gave it my full attention. I wanted to understand the school as thoroughly as I could. Some of my issues and later my assertions were drawn from concern about reform. When the case is instrumental to the study of a policy or phenomenon or systemic relationship, I call it an *instrumental* case study. Or if several cases are studied as part of work on a policy, phenomenon, or systemic relationship, I call them a *collective* case study. It is then when we most expect to generalize from case study.

DJ: And what's it called when your interest pretty much begins and ends on the case itself, like when you helped Doug McLeod do a case study of the development of the NCTM Standards?

BS: I call it an *intrinsic* case study.

DJ: And how does the distinction between instrumental and intrinsic affect how you do it?

BS: The methods are pretty much the same while the study is going on. What you do before and after is different, of course. With all case studies, you are trying to understand and interpret the case. Perhaps with intrinsic studies you pay more attention to *emic issues* and *thick description*.

DJ: What are those?

BS: First let me distinguish between emic and etic issues. *Etic issues* are the ones you bring with you as the researcher. Maybe your department head gave them to you, or your funding agent. Maybe you got some from your last research. When you start a project, usually you start with etic issues. The issues you discover from acquaintance with the case, the issues that most deeply affect the case, are emic issues. Thick description is description of the case that reveals the perceptions and values of the people who belong to the case. With intrinsic case study, you probably are a little freer to pursue the emerging concerns. With instrumental case study, even though you are trying to understand the case in all its complexity and across its many contents, you probably stick closer to etic issues, the ones ultimately you are going to interpret regarding other cases beyond this one.

DJ: So the issues you are ultimately going to interpret cannot be the case?

BS: No, issues are not cases. I think of the case as something having personality, place, purpose, and some kind of life. For me, that can include an agency, a curriculum, a program, but not an unconnected group or population or general activity. Lou Smith put it more in physical terms:

"The definition of a case study is certainly not unambiguous. Somehow the term 'bounded system' usually comes to mind—that is, the study of a bounded system. The crux of the definition is having some conception of the unity or totality of a system with some kind of outlines or boundaries.

For instance, take a child with learning disabilities as the bounded system. You have an individual pupil, in a particular circumstance, with a particular problem. There are observable behaviors. There are speculations— sometimes, following Malinowski, I call them foreshadowed problems. What the researcher looks for are the systematic connections among the observable behaviors, speculations, causes, and treatments. What the study covers depends partly on what you are trying to do. The unity of the system depends partly on what you want to find out.

In our work, we've been greatly interested in finding out how systems work over time. But emphasis on time is a sub-issue. The key notion is that you've got some kind of entity, a case, a kind of unity. A part of that unity may be perceived and studied in a case study" (Personal communication).

DJ: I like the boundedness and unity ideas.

BS: So the principal difference between case studies and other research is that the focus of attention is the case, not a sample, not the whole population of cases. In most other scientific studies, the researchers search for an understanding that ignores the uniqueness of individual cases and generalizes beyond particular instances. They search for what is common, pervasive, and lawful. In the case study, there may or may not be an *ultimate* interest in the generalizable. For the time being, the search is for an understanding of the particular case, in its idiosyncrasy, in its complexity, the case.

DJ: I have the impression that case studies read pretty much the same. What do you mean they use different methods?

BS: The principal difference is not one of method. It is true that most case studies in education today use what passes as ethnographic method: watching, asking, and searching through records. The good field-workers make carefully planned observations in natural settings. They use interviews for observations that they cannot make themselves. They go over the records time and time again, interpreting, trying out alternative meanings. In another section of this book, Harry Wolcott, a widely respected case researcher, describes the work of ethnographers. Wolcott's orientation has been found useful, but case study does not require it. It is up to the researcher to decide what will further the understanding of the case.

On almost every campus we find a special kind of statistical case study, an institutional research study. It may show up as an annual report to the board of trustees. The student body is described in terms of age, area of specialization, and hometown or country. The faculty is described in the aggregate, too, in terms of rank, sex, members of minority races, degrees held, and publications authored. The budget and endowment trends are also reported. This statistical description of one institution is a case study although it is seldom named as such. As another example, doctors and social workers keep both statistical and anecdotal case records. Case studies are special because they have a different focus. The case study focuses on a bounded system, whether a single actor, a single classroom, a single institution, or a single national program.

What is being studied is the case. The case is something deemed worthy of close watch. It has character, it has a totality, it has boundaries. It is not something we want to represent by a score. It is not something we want to represent only by an array of scores. It is a complex, dynamic system. We want to understand its complexity. Lou Smith used a fancy name, "bounded system," to indicate that we are going to try to figure out what complex things go on within that system. The case study tells a story about a bounded system.

DJ: Gets you going a bit, doesn't it? But surely there is more than one story that could be told.

BS: There are many different stories to be told. The fact that different case researchers tell different stories is sometimes said to indicate that case-study findings lack validity. But the Taj Mahal does look different in the moonlight. Different researchers have different questions to answer, different conceptualizations of the situation, and set different boundaries for the case. It's the same with qualitative and quantitative research. Your question is very important. Our testimonies are a constructed truth. Not only does the researcher ultimately define the study but regularly enters into the life space of the case in such a vigorous way that the research becomes an interaction between researcher and case.

DJ: Isn't that pretty intrusive? How could it be naturalistic then?

BS: Yes, a compromise is sought. How to get close enough to see, even to take part, and still not cause the episodes to be substantially changed. I think it takes a lot of experience but even the old pros miss. Well, we were talking about which story to tell. Story lines change even during the study. Howard Becker and colleagues, working in the 1950s on what has now become a classic, *Boys in White,* tells of first having a "developmental perspective" as they undertook fieldwork at the University of Kansas School of Medicine, but later shifting to another orientation. Their words:

"We began our study with a concern about what happens to medical students as they move through medical school. This concern receded as we became more and more preoccupied with what went on in the school itself and, particularly with the problem of the level and direction of academic effort of medical students. Nevertheless, there are some things we can say about how medical students change and develop as they go through school.

What happens to students as a result of their schooling? One view is that they are socialized into a professional role. Mary Jean Huntington (1957) has shown that medical students are more likely, with each succeeding year in school, to say that they thought of themselves as a doctor rather than as a student on the occasion of their last contact with a patient. She interprets this to mean that medical students gradually develop a professional self-image in the course of their medical training.

We have not found this framework useful in analyzing our data on the Kansas medical students. We have already seen in earlier chapters that the Kansas students do not take on a professional role while they are students, largely because the system they operate in does not allow them to do so. They are not doctors, and the recurring experiences of being denied responsibility make it perfectly clear to them that they are not. Though they may occasionally, in fantasy, play at being doctors, they never mistake their fantasies for the fact, for they know that until they have graduated and are licensed they will not be allowed to act as doctors." (Becker, Geer, Hughes, & Strauss, 1961, p. 127)

Boys in White is not the story of a medical student or several medical students. It is the story of the preprofessional life of students at one medical school. What happened when the students went home for Christmas or what happened between the dean and the provost was out outside the Becker team's interests. The way I analyzed it, student life was their case, and they recognized certain boundaries around that case. Their study, as all studies, was not going to include everything about the case. And it would include some contexts extending far beyond the case. Therefore, the boundaries of the study and the boundaries for the case will be different. Are you still with me?

DJ: I think so. I have about given up hope that you will tell me how to do one.

BS: Okay. I have a handout I'll give you later. At the start you usually know which case you care about. Sometimes someone else assigns it to you. Sometimes you figure that case is the stepping stone to something more important. But the case is selected. You have to get familiar with it, that is, to figure out its boundaries, to figure out its ordinary routines, its habitat, its other contexts, its significant others. To me that is all part of setting the boundaries.

Then you need some kind of conceptual structure, some thematic foci, to give priority to some things about the case and to rule others out. No matter how important a holistic view is to you, you cannot tell the whole story. For your focus, you develop research questions—including issue questions and information questions. Usually we only gradually come to realize which issue or issues are best to build the inquiry around, and later, which to build the report around.

And then you look for patterns, consistencies, repetitions, and manifestations pertinent to your issues. You know that all researchers are looking for patterns, covariations, and regularities that beg for better interpretation. Case researchers too. They may classify or code some of the different things they are looking for and keep tallies and make frequency distributions and contingency tables. Or they may directly interpret the patterns. Often both. The consistencies are there. Even in unique persons, even in unique curricula, even in unique bond referendum campaigns, there are patterns. Those deeply related to the issues are what the researcher is seeking: "sweet water," refreshing, sustaining, advancing the frontier.

DJ: Here's something I have been thinking about. Would it be a pattern? Whenever the child started to cry, the teacher became busy with the other children.

BS: Sure. Sometimes we think of a code to put on the pattern, such as "negative reinforcement."

DJ: Is this the place I am supposed to say, "What about that report on the architecture students?"

BS: Right. At the end of this chapter is the complete text of an exemplary study in the case study tradition. It is a program evaluation report of a University of British Columbia orientation program written by philosopher Charles Brauner. He called it "The First Probe." Let's interrupt our conversation while you read it. When you finish, let's talk about the case, the issues, and the patterns there.

At this point, it is important that readers read "The First Probe."
Having finished reading "The First Probe" . . .

DJ: Unbelievable!

BS: Meaning what?

DJ: Did that really happen?

BS: A 2-week orientation for UBC incoming freshmen architecture students took place at Defense Island, Port Alberni, and the brick kiln. It rained for 14 days.

DJ: You're saying Brauner may have fictionalized some of it? Or at least embellished?

BS: I know that Charles Brauner likes to write, that he likes to write fiction. But here I think he really saw all that happen. Then, what he wrote down were his unique interpretations.

DJ: That was *his* story. No one else would have told the same story.

BS: Right. That was his story, his research report, his construction of truth.

DJ: He did not seem to worry much about how others saw it.

BS: No.

DJ: But isn't research supposed to be objective, impersonal?

BS: We need to play by the rules. Sometimes the rules call for objectivity. Some case study reports are highly objective accounts with highly conventional interpretations. But sometimes the rules call for subjective interpretation. Good research can be subjective, interpretative, an interaction between the researcher and the phenomena. One of the great questions of research is, Which rules do I use? (What methods? what style? what subjectivity?) That is what this research-methods book is about. The answers depend on the research questions, on the sponsors and prospective readers, and greatly on the researcher. I think this style of reporting worked beautifully for Charles Brauner. So interpretive! So driven by his personal concerns! His rules were almost those of *critical study*. I don't think I could make his style work for me. I pride myself in presenting a much larger core of "incontestable description" and I want to portray the different perceptions of different students, different staff members. Brauner's story was not about the array of experiences of different architecture students. He did not say that all people were affected the same by the orientation but that most of those new students were shaken by an experience that would survive registration, possibly even their professional careers.

DJ: But Brauner said he did not know how they had been affected.

BS: Yes, his evaluation did not include what we might call the ordinary evidence of impact. But in spite of what evaluation specialists propose, deep and enduring impact of programs cannot be captured. Even objective indicators are subjective and debatable. People want to know about impact. Brauner wrote about impact. He was confident of impact, but knew that the real story of impact was beyond his reach, personal, deep, and ineffable.

DJ: Meaning what?

BS: "Ineffable" means beyond words, beyond description.

DJ: So case studies approach the ineffable?

BS: Some do. Case studies have the opportunity to go much further than most research to pursue complex, situational themes to the limits of human under-standing. Brauner's case study is an extraordinary example of interpretative inquiry. Most qualitative, naturalistic, ethnographic case studies will be more descriptive and less interpretative than Brauner's. Some will look for patterns through precise counts, such as tallying acts of aggression at the five sites. You recall that Brauner made a passing allusion to the diminishing acts of aggression during the two weeks. He could have kept track.

DJ: Qualitative case studies can be quantitative?

BS: In qualitative case study, objective measurements are regularly found, and regression analysis and statistical inference are occasionally found. When data are drawn from a large number of elements, such as the case of a college hav-ing a large number of students or the case of a teacher having a large number of lessons, some coding of the elements and quantitative analysis is appropri-ate. Interpreting the statistical indicators in terms of the narrative, situational, particularistic character of the case keeps it a qualitative case study, even with massive quantitative data. In all qualitative studies, the priority on interpreta-tion is high. Attending to statistical patterns, the interpretation is made with tables, comparisons, and contingency coefficients. More commonly, interpre-tations of field-site observations are made directly from the encounter and from study and restudy of narrative accounts of those observations. Case study methods books by Robert Yin (Yin, 1989) and Matthew Miles and Michael Huberman (1994) are among the best quantitatively oriented books to get acquainted with. In "The First Probe," Brauner could have coded and ana-lyzed activities, but he studied them by direct interpretation.

DJ: I know you want to tell me more about validating findings—triangulation, I think you call it. But I want to say I was really impressed with Brauner going off on his own to connect architecture with industrial and social conditions. It seems he wanted to be more explicit about the social responsibility of architects than the orientation planners did. Of course, the faculty had four more years to work the students over. These 2 weeks, I guess, were to get their attention.

BS: Brauner had it easy. He did have to get wet for 2 weeks. But his bad guys could be phantom bad guys. He left many anonymities. He did not have to identify the hoarders or those who botched the brickwork on the flooring repair. He did not have to identify who on the planning committee put teenagers at risk high above the glacier and on Skid Row. Usually in case study we encounter personal and institutional failings—and we rather enjoy exposing them. All the while, we are, to some extent, invading personal spaces, such as classrooms and offices, however public the buildings. We have a difficult time maintaining proper protection for human subjects while digging for deep understanding of the case.

DJ: Did Brauner do that?

BS: I don't know. He didn't illuminate those problems in this account. Often you cannot tell about the ethics of the researcher from the report. Or about the steps taken to triangulate. Brauner gave me the impression of a researcher flying solo. Usually, researchers depend on help from other people, assistance in checking out the design, identifying issues, choosing data sources, interpreting accounts, interviewing to find out what cannot be directly seen, and thinking through how drafts will strike the reader. Most case study researchers can't do all the seeing and thinking themselves. They need to collaborate, to use others' eyes and brains—in identifying issues.

DJ: What were the main issues in "The First Probe?"

BS: You identified one a few moments ago: the responsibility of the professional architect to deal with social problems. Or putting it more in context, will this orientation experience, this shocking and nondirective experience, heighten the social awareness of these architects-to-be? And a second issue, I think, had to do with the concept of the consumer, the client who uses an architect's services. In weighing what consumers ask for, would these people reflect on their own extravagant consumption, their own gluttony? With tom-toms beating, remember:

"And after every mouthful there was wine—heavy, light, dry, sweet, rosé, Chablis, claret, Zinfandel. Hand to mouth and hand to hand; there was no china or silver to be seen. Each person was his own portable larder with supply stations never more than a few steps away. Eating and drinking in Roman Fashion encouraged mobility. When it seemed the dancing could not get wilder or the chorus louder, a Greek bouzouki band struck out. Beginning with their amplified versions of Western songs evocative of the Mediterranean, they worked into their native music, mixing the Greek strings with Turkish woodwinds. In Zorba fashion, the revelers jumped, whirled, stepped, stooped, sprang up, slapped their heels . . . (Brauner, 1974, p. 95)"

Was it too much to expect that come Tuesday morning, the revelers would reflect upon the role of architects fulfilling their clients' fantasies, short-term ends and long-term costs? If consumption was not an issue of his, why would he describe it in such detail?

DJ: He wanted to provide a vicarious experience for the reader. Then they could make, what do you call it, naturalistic generalizations.

BS: Yes, the readers could add this experience to all their other experiences and modify their generalizations, but particularly generalizations involving Brauner's issues. Why all this early attention to the absence of food, shelter, and social order and then the cascade of candy bars, beer, and wine? I think Brauner, with the faculty, wanted to prod the students into considering the society in which they live, in his eyes, a voracious, profligate, and narcissistic society.

DJ: Were these the issues of the architecture faculty or those of the researcher?

BS: Both. The experiences were designed by the faculty. Emphasis on consumption ran through Brauner's description.

DJ: Can you count on the issues of the case and the issues of the researcher coinciding?

BS: No, and there is no reason to want them to. The issues to structure the study will be those that the researcher feels will lead to understanding the case. It will not be unusual for the researcher to focus also on deep concerns of actors within the case. The rules call for the researcher to decide.

DJ: Are the rules the same for dissertation research? It doesn't seem a doctoral student can fly solo? Their committees seem to crack the whip.

BS: Committees vary a great deal in terms of how much freedom they give students. Most of them are conscientious about shaping a dissertation that will help the student get a good career going. They worry less about whether the case is understood or the research question is answered than that the research is managed well. They want data gathering and analysis to be respectable. To most of them, dissertation research is not an exercise in creative knowledge seeking, it is an exercise in moving a career along.

The rules for case study are pretty much the same for yearlong studies as for two week studies. Much more planning, drawing ties to existing research, observing, coding, analyzing, triangulating, and interpreting are expected with long-term studies. Many cases are not important enough to warrant the work or interesting enough to keep a researcher going for a year or more.

Some graduate students design a larger dissertation package by doing multiple case studies, sometimes called collective case study. Such a design diverts the basic thinking away from what is essential about the individual case to what is common across cases. Looking for commonality more than uniqueness is what most of the other methods of this book are about. The strength of case study is its attention to the individuality and complexity of the single case.

DJ: Let's see if I understand the weaknesses or problems of qualitative case study. It is subjective, but that sometimes is an asset. It is a questionable basis for generalization. It doesn't have a set routine or recipe.

BS: All that. Then there are the ethical questions, putting people at risk. But the one that bugs me most of all is cost. Even when case study is small and informal, to do the job that needs to be done takes more time than we expect, lots more.

DJ: And with all that, you still promise "sweet water"?

BS: You know I do. The "sweet water" in "The First Probe" comes from having a unique and important story to tell and getting it told in a thought-provoking way. The architecture faculty devised the experience and the students lived it—but thanks to Charles Brauner, and to Dick Jaeger, our editor, thousands of graduate students in education have lived it vicariously, and have reflected upon it, not only as to the question of "Is this really research?" but the question of "How can a faculty cause its incoming students to search their souls?" This faculty's interpretation of needed opportunity is "sweet water"; the students' complete immersion in the experience is "sweet water"—not because it was good for the faculty or the students, but because it was good for Brauner's readers. Do you agree?

DJ: I'll think about it. I would like to ask you, "Why did you have us talking like this rather than just writing a chapter like the rest of the book?"

BS: "Sweet Water" was first a part of an AERA tape cassette collection. Because a tape is to be heard, a conversation seemed appropriate. When we converted the tapes to the book, *Complementary Methods*, for reasons I don't recall, we kept the same text. Now, in revision, partly because *you* are here, partly because case study so frequently presents dialogue, I kept the format.

DJ: And you wanted me here to make a point about recursion, right? OK. One of the devices of presenting interpretation is to present a dialogue, then stand back and talk about the meaning or technique of that dialogue. Some computer people and some writers call that "recursion." It can be "embedded text," like a play within a play, representing two levels of consciousness. We are into recursion now, the same two people talking about the dialogue we had earlier. And it looked like recursion when Charles Brauner shifted to discussion of method in his final section, "The Mode," although he didn't return to the narrative. Recursion is one of many devices known to writers, playwrights, and biographers, for example, to facilitate reflection and elevation of the level of interpretation.

BS: For example, we could speculate here on the thoughts Dick Jaeger will have when he wonders whether or not to edit out this commentary about recursion.

DJ: Yes that would be another example. So the point is, the narrative and dialogic form often used in case study reporting has a long and sophisticated history. Researchers can use it not only for report writing but also for contemplating the design of the study and considering how the research can dig deeply into the meanings of the case and get those meanings shared with readers.

References

Becker, H. S., Geer, B., Hughes, E., & Strauss, A. (1961). *Boys in white: Student culture in medical school.* Chicago: University of Chicago Press.

Brauner, C. (1974). The first probe. In *Four evaluation examples: Anthropological, economic, narrative, and portrayal, AERA monograph Series on Curriculum Evaluation, 7* (pp. 77–98). Chicago: Rand McNally.

Jaeger, R. M. (Ed.). (1988). *Complementary methods for research in Education.* Washington, DC: American Educational Research Association.

Miles, M. B., & Huberman, A. M. (1994). *Qualitative data analysis: An expandable sourcebook of new methods.* Newbury Park, CA: Sage.

Smith, L., & Pohland, P. (1974). Education, technology, and the rural highlands. In *Four evaluation examples: Anthropological, economic, narrative, and portrayal, AERA Monograph Series on Curriculum Evaluation, 7* (pp. 5–54). Chicago: Rand McNally.

Stake, R. E. (1995). *The art of case study research.* Newbury Park, CA: Sage.

Stake, R. E. (1992). A housing project elementary school. In J. Nowakowski, M. Stewart, & D. W. Quinn (Eds.) *The NCREL/SFA Chicago school reform study project* (pp. 30–54). Oak Brook, IL: North Central Regional Educational Laboratory.

Yin, R. K. (1989). *Case study research: Design and methods.* Newbury Park, CA: Sage.

Suggestions for Further Reading

Anonymity

Mitchell, R. G., Jr. (1993). *Secrecy and fieldwork.* Newbury Park, CA: Sage.

Biographic Method

Smith, L. (1994). Biographical method. In N. Denzin & Y. Lincoln (Eds.), *Handbook of qualitative research* (pp. 286–305). Newbury Park, CA: Sage.

Categorical Analysis

Upton, G. J. G. (1978). *The analysis of cross-tabulated data.* New York: Wiley.

Coding

Miles, M., & Huberman, M. (1994). *Qualitative data analysis: An expanded source book of new methods.* Newbury Park, CA: Sage.

Colleague Help

Yin, R. (1984). *Case study research design: Design and methods.* Applied Social Research Methods Series, Vol 5. Newbury Park, CA: Sage.

Collective Case Study

Stake, R. E. (1995.). *The art of case study research.* Newbury Park, CA: Sage.

Computer Use

Richards, T., & Richards, L. Using computers in qualitative research. In N. Denzin & Y. Lincoln (Eds.), *Handbook of qualitative research* (pp. 445–462). Newbury Park, CA: Sage.

Conceptual Organizers

Merriam, S. B. (1988). *Case study research in education.* San Francisco: Jossey-Bass.

Constructed Truth

Schwandt, T. (1994). Constructivist, interpretist approaches to human inquiry. In N. Denzin & Y. Lincoln (Eds.), *Handbook of qualitative research* (pp. 118–137). Newbury Park, CA: Sage.

Contingencies

Miles, M., & Huberman, M. (1994). *Qualitative data analysis: An expanded sourcebook for new methods.* Newbury Park, CA: Sage.

Critical Study

Carr, W., & Kemmis, S. (1986). *Becoming critical: Education, knowledge and action research.* East Geelong, Victoria: Deakin University Press.

Data Analysis

Miles, M., & Huberman, M. (1994). *Qualitative data analysis: A source book of new methods.* Newbury Park, CA: Sage.

Data Management

Huberman, M., & Miles, M. (1994). Data management and analysis methods. In N. Denzin & Y. Lincoln (Eds.), *Handbook of qualitative research* (pp. 428–444). Newbury Park, CA: Sage.

Deception

Nyberg, D. (1993). *The varnished truth.* Chicago: University of Chicago Press.

Direct Interpretation

Erickson, F. (1986). Qualitative methods in research on teaching. In M. Wittrock (Ed.), *Handbook of research on teaching* (pp. 119–161). New York: Macmillan.

Ethics

Glesne, C., & Peshkin, A. (1992). *Becoming qualitative researchers.* White Plains, NY: Longman.

Ethnographic Research

Wolcott, H. F. (1997). Ethnographic research in education. In R. M. Jaeger (Ed.), *Complementary methods for research in education* (2nd ed.) (pp. 327–353). Washington, DC: American Educational Research Association.

Field Study

Delamont, S. (1992). *Fieldwork in educational settings: Methods, pitfalls and perspectives.* London: Falmer.

Generalizations

Hamilton, D. (1980). Generalizations in the educational sciences: Problems and purposes. In T. Popkowitz & R. Tabaschnick (Eds.), *The study of schooling: Field-based methodologies in educational research* (pp. 227–244). New York: Praeger.

Grounded Theory

Glaser, B. G., & Strauss, A. (1967). *The discovery of grounded theory: Strategies for qualitative research.* Chicago: Aldine Press.

Image Analysis

Harper, D. (1989). Visual sociology: Expanding sociological vision. In G. Blank et al. (Eds.), *New technologies in sociology: Practical applications in research and work* (p. 81–97). New Brunswick, NJ: Transaction.

The Ineffable

Polanyi, M. (1962). *Personal knowledge: Towards a post-critical philosophy.* Chicago: University of Chicago Press.

Instrumental Case Study

Stake, R. E. (in press). *Case study research methods: An intensive study.* Newbury Park, CA: Sage.

Interpretation

Schwandt, T. (1994). Constructivist, interpretist approaches to human inquiry. In N. Denzin & Y. Lincoln (Eds.), *Handbook of qualitative research* (pp. 118–137). Newbury Park, CA: Sage.

Interviewing

Mishler, E. G. (1986). *Research interviewing.* Cambridge: Harvard University Press.

Intrinsic Case Study

Stake, R. E. (1995). *The art of case study research.* Newbury Park, CA: Sage.

Micro-Macro Problem

Hamel, J. (1992). On the status of singularity in sociology. *Current Sociology, 40(1)*, 99–119.

Naturalistic Inquiry

Schatzman, L., & Strauss, A. (1973). *Field research: Strategies for a natural sociology.* Englewood Cliffs, NJ: Prentice Hall.

Naturalistic Generalization

Stake, R. E. (1994). Case Studies. In N. Denzin & Y. Lincoln (Eds.), *Handbook of qualitative research* (pp. 236–247). Newbury Park, CA: Sage.

Objectivity

Scriven, M. (1972). Objectivity and subjectivity in educational research. In H. Dunkel (Ed.), *Philosophical redirection of educational research* (pp. 1–34). Chicago: National Society for the Study of Education.

Patterns

Diesing, P. (1972). *Patterns of discovery in the social sciences.* London: Routledge & Kegan Paul.

Phenomenology

Holstein, J. A., & Gubrium, J. F. (1994). Phenomenology, ethnomethodology, and interpretive practice. In N. Denzin & Y. Lincoln (Eds.), *Handbook of Qualitative Research* (pp. 262–272). Newbury Park, CA: Sage.

Preparation

Janesek, V. J. (1994). The dance of qualitative research design. In N. Denzin & Y. Lincoln (Eds.), *Handbook of Qualitative Research* (pp. 209–219). Newbury Park, CA: Sage.

Qualitative Methods

Denzin, N., & Lincoln, Y. (Eds.). (1994). *Handbook of Qualitative Research.* Newbury Park, CA: Sage.

Readers

Eco, U. (1994). *Six walks in the fictional woods.* Cambridge: Harvard University Press.

Recursion

Hofstadeter, D. R. (1979). *Gödel, Escher, Bach.* New York: Basic Books.

Regression Analysis

Runkel, P. (1990). *Casting nets and testing specimens: Two grand methods of psychology.* New York: Praeger.

Relativism

Bernstein, R. (1988). *Beyond objectivism and realism.* Philadelphia: University of Pennsylvania Press.

Single Versus Multiple Cases

Yin, R. K. (1979). *Case study research: Design and methods.* Newbury Park, CA: Sage.

Singularity

Simons, H. (Ed.). (1980). *Toward a science of the singular.* Norwich, England: University of East Anglia.

Story Telling

Coles, R. (1989). *The call of stories: Teaching and the moral imagination.* New York: Houghton Mifflin.

Subjectivity

Scriven, M. (1972). Objectivity and subjectivity in educational research. In H. Dunkel (Ed.), *Philosophical redirection of educational research* (pp. 1–34). Chicago: National Society for the Study of Education.

Thick Description

Geertz, C. (1973). Thick description: Toward an interpretive theory of culture. In C. Geertz, *Interpretation of culture* (pp. 1–52). New York: Basic Books.

Triangulation

Altheide, D. L., & Johnson, J. M. (1994). Criteria for assessing internal validity in qualitative research. In N. Denzin & Y. Lincoln (Eds.), *Handbook of Qualitative Research* (pp. 485–499). Newbury Park, CA: Sage.

Understanding

von Wright, G. H. (1971). *Explanation and understanding.* Ithaca: Cornell University Press.

Uniqueness

Bradshaw, Y., & Wallace, M. (1991). Informing generality and explaining uniqueness: The place of case studies in comparative research. *International Journal of Comparative Sociology, 32*(1–2), 154–171.

Vicarious Experience

Stake, R. E. (1994) Case studies. In N. Denzin & Y. Lincoln (Eds.), *Handbook of qualitative research* (pp. 236–247). Newbury Park, CA: Sage.

Writing Reports

van Maanen, J. (1988). *Tales of the field: On writing ethnography.* Chicago: University of Chicago Press.

Exemplary Case Studies

Becker, H. S., Geer, B., Hughes, E., & Strauss, A. (1961). *Boys in white: Student culture in medical school.* Chicago: University of Chicago Press.

Blythe, R. (1969). *Akenfield.* Harmondsworth, England: Penguin.

Brauner, C. (1974). The first probe. In *Four evaluation examples: Anthropological, economic, narrative and portrayal. AERA Monograph Series on Curriculum Evaluation, 7,* 77–98. Chicago: Rand McNally.

Edgerton, R. B. (1967). *The cloak of competence.* Berkeley: University of California Press.

Hollingshead, A. D. (1949). *Elmstown's youth: The impact of social classes on adolescence.* New York: Wiley.

Jenkins, D. (1984). Chocolate cream soldiers: Sponsorship, ethnography, and sectarianism. In R. G. Burgess (Ed.), *The research process in educational settings: Ten case studies* (pp. 235–250). London: Falmer.

Kelly-Byrne, D. (1989). *A child's play life.* New York: Teachers College Press.

Kozol, J. (1991). *Savage inequalities: Children in America's schools.* New York: Harper.

Liebow, E. (1967). *Talley's Corner.* Boston: Little, Brown.

Lightfoot, S. L. (1983). *The good high school: Portraits of character and culture.* New York: Basic Books.

Mabry, L. (1991). Nicole, seeking attention. In *Learning to fail: Case studies of students at risk* (pp. 1–24). Bloomington, IN: Phi Delta Kappa.

MacDonald, B., Adelman, C., Kushner, S., & Walker, R. (1982). *Bread and dreams: A case study of bilingual schooling in the USA.* Norwich, England: F. Crowe and Sons.

Peshkin, A. (1978). *Growing up American.* Chicago: University of Chicago Press.

Smith, L., & Geoffrey, W. (1969). *The complexities of an urban classroom.* New York: Holt, Rhinehart & Winston.

Spradley, J. P., & Mann, B. J. (1975). *The cocktail waitress: Woman's work in a man's world.* New York: Wiley.

Stake, R. E., Bresler, L., & Mabry, L. (1991). *Custom and cherishing: The arts in elementary schools.* Urbana: University of Illinois: Council for Research in Music Education.

Whyte, W. F. (1981). *Street corner society.* Chicago: University of Chicago Press.

Study Questions

1. Is case study research used solely in education, or is its use widespread?

2. Is a case study distinguished by the method of research used, or could any of the methods of educational research be used in a case study?

3. What is meant by a "case" in case study research? Almost anything can be called a case but in terms of this chapter, about half the following make good cases for case study research. Can you identify the good cases and explain how they fit the research methods described in this chapter.

a substitute teacher
the work ethic
the first school for the blind
an average student
the 1936 Olympics
cooperative learning
the 2004 Olympics
Rorschach (inkblots) testing
all Catholics
development of the NCTM Math Standards
the last day of school
Advance Placement Calculus
the effects of U.S. budget cuts
the local legal assistance office
professional development policies
the Norwegian Ministry of Education

4. Could a case study report be simply a description of happenings, or does it have to include interpretation? When we call it case study research, does it have to include interpretation?

5. If there are many possible cases and a case is not selected for you, how would you decide which case to study?

6. Does a case need to be clearly typical or representative of other cases to have value? Could a case study be useful if it is highly atypical? Should the researcher have a general responsibility for informing the reader how typical the case is? Could one do a case study if the case had absolutely nothing in common with other cases?

7. Are the boundaries of a case study and the set of issues it addresses always best determined before the study begins? Is it a better idea not to have any issues in mind when beginning a case study?

8. Reliable measures are defined by psychometricians as those which repeatedly come out the same no matter who is doing the measuring. Qualitative case

study reports even of exactly the same case are expected to vary from researcher to researcher. Is this reason enough to conclude that qualitative case studies are unreliable?

9. A case study is completed on one Chicago elementary school. In it, the teachers were found to put a higher priority on children's social development than on academic development, even though citywide school reform programs were emphasizing academic development. On what grounds could a reader generalize that the same probably is true for teachers in most of the city's 470 elementary schools?

10. What is meant by "naturalistic generalization"? How is it different from "formalistic" or "scientific" generalization? Suppose an author provides vicarious experience, but the readers do not change their minds about an issue. How could this process still be "naturalistic generalization"?

11. Considering anyone responsible for case study research, what should be done, if anything, to see that observations are not selected and interpretations made to further the researcher's point of view? Is it an ethical problem? Is there a viable argument that says research should be designed to serve school improvement, not to be its deterrent?

Exercise

In my case study research methods classes, I regularly use field observation as an opening exercise. The rules go like this:

Project A. Observe an event this weekend. In class, one week from now, submit an 800- to 1200-word report. Presume that the report would be used to help sponsors, organizers, or distant readers understand what happened and what the event is accomplishing. Identify several *issues* of potential or actual concern. Discuss these issues with other members of the class as you see fit and anticipate identifying your conceptual organizers in class.

[The same event is specified for everyone so that discussions are based on a common experience. Those who cannot observe that event are asked to select one of their own, such as a wedding, a tournament, an orientation session, or a retreat. In my fall classes, the common event usually has been the local Sweet Corn Festival. It is important that the event have a caselike quality, with boundaries, purposes, and organization, and that it involve a large group of people.]

[The italicized topics in the "Suggestions for Further Reading" above could be used to stimulate reflection on how the project was organized, carried out, and reported.]

Reading

Introduction
Analyzing the Case Study

Robert E. Stake

This section contains the entire text of "The First Probe," a case study written by Charles Brauner. This vivid account of a presession workshop for newly enrolled architecture students at the University of British Columbia is an excellent case study for further analysis.

As you read the article, consider who might find the material useful. The potential audience could include faculty at other schools of architecture, faculty at experimental educational institutions, faculty at traditional educational institutions, students in general, students in architecture, funding agencies, or researchers studying higher education. Are you able to determine from the content, style, or organization of the material which of these audiences might be intended? Try to imagine the points of view of several potential audiences. The outline of the "bounded system" might vary for each audience, yielding a variety of case studies. An important question for any case study researcher is, "Why would they want it?" The answer to this question is critical in shaping the system boundaries. For example, if Brauner had prepared a report for the President of the University of British Columbia, would you expect it to be different? If so, in what ways?

Another consideration is the degree to which the reader believes in the accuracy of the case study report. If the reader is to understand and evaluate the conclusions drawn by the researcher, the report must provide accurate and complete supporting data. It is possible that some readers might find certain aspects of the Brauner report hard to believe. Does it appear that Brauner did any extra work on those less credible parts? If so, how well do you think his efforts succeeded?

As part of the assurance of credibility, many researchers believe that raw data should be presented along with the interpretations, giving readers a chance to make their own interpretations. Brauner's observations are in a narrative format without quotes, and he explicitly states that the account is based on 3-month-old memory unaided by a contemporaneous diary. Do you feel that Brauner provided sufficient uninterpreted observations to back up his conclusions?

Credibility is enhanced when case study researchers confirm the accuracy of their observations. We do not know whether Brauner asked any of the participants to correct misstatements or misinterpretations in this report. Do you spot any findings that probably should have been confirmed by those who were there?

Asking participants for confirmation presents additional dilemmas. There may be large discrepancies between participant and observer perceptions; or a participant may believe that the researcher has no right to report certain information about the participant, even if it is accurate. How do you feel about the desirability of getting confirmation from participants? How should discrepancies in viewpoint be resolved? Who ultimately decides what material can be used and what principles should guide that decision? Which events described in "The First Probe" are most subject to being questioned on these grounds?

The final issue in establishing the credibility of a case study report is that of completeness. Triangulation has been mentioned as an important way of verifying conclusions. As you read "The First Probe," try to decide what more, if anything, you would like to know about the workshop described. How would that additional information be obtained? Would observations be the best way to get that additional information? Why or why not?

3. The First Probe

Charles J. Brauner

University of British Columbia

Rain and mystery opened and closed the presession workshop for students entering architecture at the University of British Columbia. Foul weather and wonder about what was to come provided the only obvious threads linking three weeks of activities that ran from foraging to feast, Spartanism to splendor, privation to saturation. Shrouded in rumors as thick as the clouds overhead, 55 students from all over Canada and several distant countries gathered together for the first time in mid-August on a dock opposite Vancouver's Stanley Park. As college graduates with a common interest in architecture, they had no trouble combining into spontaneous conversation groups.

When the six members of staff arrived, a sense of relief rippled through the crowd as they quieted to hear where they were going. But they were not told. Disappointed, they loaded their camping equipment onto one of the boats and divided into two parties for boarding. All the way out to Horseshoe Bay and up Howe Sound they speculated. After two hours of sailing through thickening fog they no longer knew whether they were traveling north or south. When the boats dropped anchor at a small island a few miles off Britannia Beach they had no idea where they were. Small boats took them to Defense Island in groups of six. Densely forested and guarded by an Indian mask carved in a drift log at the landing, the island was deserted. Three-quarters of a mile long and one-quarter mile wide, with a backbone of rock that ran its length, the island seemed to offer a minimum challenge. By the time the last boat landed, two girls and the main party had a fire going in the opening on the crest. At noon everyone stood around waiting to be fed. Wet, having nothing but what they wore and carried in their

This paper first appeared in the *Architectural Review,* Vol. 146, No. 874, Dec. 1969, pp. 451–56, and was reproduced with minor editing in *Four Evaluation Examples: Anthropological, Economic, Narrative, and Portrayal* (AERA Monograph Series No. 7; Chicago, Rand McNally, 1974, pp. 77–98). It is reproduced here in the latter version, again with permission of the *Architectural Review.*

pockets, but reassured by seeing the staff similarly unequipped, they did not take alarm when the boats sounded their horns and pulled away.

After a half hour of exploration, John Gaitanakis, a codirector, called the students together and explained that the boat would return in 48 hours. Meanwhile, there was no food, no shelter, and no equipment. The time was theirs to use as they saw fit. The first reaction was disbelief. Having found an axe and some nails on a relief tour, a small group insisted other necessities only awaited discovery. The fact that two five-gallon coffee urns of water had been brought ashore from the boats convinced others that food was there for the finding. A general unwillingness to accept the likelihood of deprivation sent everyone on an hour of fruitless searching. Reassembling with nothing new to report, they conjured up their first fears of famine. They all knew that man could do quite well without food so long as he had water, and fresh water was plentiful both from rain and springs. Nevertheless, half a dozen individuals insisted they would succumb to nausea and disability at the very least. Those most fearful set out to forage for edibles. We warned them that a recent red tide had made the shellfish temporarily poisonous; however, the gloom from this blow did not persist. Soon half the group was busy gathering salal berries and toasting sea kelp, the only edibles to be found. By mid-afternoon a dozen self-selected groups were busy building shelters and gathering wood for night fires. By this time, the shelter parties had coalesced into personality groups of three to five, and they remained intact as living units for the rest of the time on the island. Confronted with the basic choice of whether to improve and inhabit existing shelters from half-formed caves to semitunnels formed by overturned trees or to cut and interweave cedar branches, the majority shied away from using the existing natural cover. However, their finished dwellings distinguished them far less than the characteristics that drew them into alliance. To the staff they became known as the hoarders, the sharers, the defilers, the isolates, the raiders, the includers, the excluders, the worriers, the trusters, and the grumblers. Those who found no common cause in personality, location, habitat, or conversation remained around the fire on the crest. Since this cluster-by-default was three times as large as any of the separate living units, their clearing served as a commons ground. A more barren commons would be hard to imagine.

Once fire and rude shelter were assured, the group found absolutely nothing to do but pass time. No game of matchsticks or burning twigs was too trivial. There was not even enough common concern for anyone to do more than note that one of the groups had made off with half the reserve water supply. Efforts to open discussion on why they were there or what they might do proved so fruitless that the dozen who started the talks could not sustain them for half an hour. In the evening a longer chat on "What is architecture" was started. The downpour and darkness were punctuated only by massive tree trunks and widely spaced fires; boredom dictated the effort at conversation. The only thing that sparked interest was the makeup of the staff—two members of the architecture faculty, a visitor from Outward Bound, a specialist in contemporary dance, a sociologist, and an educational philosopher. The thing that seemed to impress the students most was that the staff saw fit to share their discomfort on equal terms, though they had foreknowledge of what was to come. Again, all question about future events went unanswered. When it became clear no profitable discussion would develop, the staff withdrew to the semishelter of a huge cedar tree and bedded down around a fire.

Only four things distinguished the second day: wetter and colder participants, the end of the berries, the building of a raft, the appearance of a boat, and underground fires that threatened to burn the island down. What had been planned as a minimal existence experience turned out to be a "nonexistence." The hope had been that by being freed of cooking, eating, preparation, and clean up—and thus denied the opportunity to lavish time on such mindless occupations—the students might try to make something special of their stay. Instead they spent all their time on the mindless activities left them: buttressing shelters, improving fireplaces, gathering wood. Beyond that, they were determined simply to sit out their time like convicts awaiting parole. Some spent hours just cleaning their fingernails. Even the making of the raft was undertaken with half an eye to floating somewhere to get food. When a boat came in a group tried to signal their need for supplies. Informed that just three weeks before the Provincial Department of Correction had put some hard cases ashore for survival training, those on the boat did not linger. Surviving their fast in good health but low spirits, the groups greeted the last night with huge fires. The fires burned through the ground cover of rotten needles and

428   COMPLEMENTARY METHODS

branches, igniting the dry mulch that coated the ground to a depth
of 12 feet in places. A group in a cave on a rock ledge burned
themselves out entirely when a covering tree went up in flames
and took two more trees with it. Three other groups had runaway
fires during the night, and the *"Lord of the Flies"* bunch who took
the communal water supply had to use more than 40 buckets of
water to damp underground fires that, they insisted, they had
under control at all times. When it was time to leave, the staff
spent three hours doing nothing but uprooting underground fires
that had been left as extinguished. If it had not been for heavy and
continuous rain, the island would have become an inferno.

By far the most interesting thing to be seen during the island
experience was the students' behavior toward food when it arrived. Before taking us off, the captain of the Columbia landed
oranges, apples, and bread. The "marooned" were told that there
was enough for each to have a piece of fruit and two slices of
bread. The *"Lord of the Flies"* group was the first to the food,
followed by several kindred parties. They raided the stores like
seasoned pirates. Half the loaves of bread disappeared inside
jackets, only because pockets were filled to bursting with fruit.
Eight people got more than half the supplies for 61 people. The
pattern of resentment among those who went without was remarkable. No one could be heard blaming the gluttons, though they
were known to most. The captain became the villain for landing so
little provisions, and there was general resentment that they had
not been given a feast. Finally annoyance focused on the staff for
not anticipating the raiders and deterring them. This settled down
to a criticism of a more general nature. Somehow the staff had
failed to make the experience meaningful. What happened with
the food became symbolic of that failure.

When the boat landed everyone at Brittania Beach, there was a
station wagon waiting with enough bread, sliced meat, fruit,
cookies, and candy bars for all—or so it seemed. Again the mighty
eight plundered the stores. They made sandwiches with more
than an inch of meat—not one, but four and six apiece. Even so,
the meat and the bread held out. Everyone, except one girl who
could hardly eat, overate. The raiders took whole packages of 10
chocolate bars or 36 cookies against future uncertainties. Again,
nothing was said. Interesting in itself, what makes it significant is
that, except for the girl, no one had suffered severe hunger past

the slight pangs of the second day. There was a general feeling of having been physically cleansed.

The unanimous overeating and the special greed of a few seemed more a ritual atonement for failure or a common urge to make up for the empty hours by stuffing their bodies. Overeating by both students and staff remained a characteristic of the group throughout the workshop. A mystery in itself, this hangover from the island cloaked an even deeper feeling. Before going on this trip, several students had known the forest on intimate working terms. Others from cities and foreign countries had heard of it in terms of mixed awe and grandeur. Yet the woods-wise had been as unable to face the challenge of the forest island as the forest unfamiliars. Both had been equally helpless against what neither group had expected to encounter—time. Having brought almost nothing ashore, they found themselves stranded with even less than they imagined. Had they been truly marooned, desperation would have given them common cause that would have filled every moment. Denied even that last resort, they encountered themselves as truly useless. Each one was, harrowingly, alone —only for two days, but that mystery became the yeast that leavened all that followed. However slight, all had suffered a common adversity. However profound, all had faced a common humiliation. In just 48 hours the props of a quarter century of customary daily activity had been knocked flat. They were ready for a new beginning. It was, as it turned out, a workshop of beginnings.

Warmed by cooked food and rations of rum, everyone slept that third night half dry in sleeping bags sheltered by stretches of plastic. Dawn broke clear at 5300 feet, revealing snow-caps surrounding the camp in Garibaldi meadow. Grouped in seven-man teams for the stay on the glacier, some bathed and shaved in mountain streams while others packed for the trip to the top. Rain settled in and efforts to keep dry failed. The question became "Will the weather break long enough for a helicopter to drop in and make 18 lifts from the meadow to the broad back of the glacier?" By mid-afternoon the enveloping mist thinned. Heather, high up the hills, showed magenta against wet grass, as if struggling to serve as tiny beacons. From over the ridge the beat of rotors chopped away at the remaining mist. As sky opened the turbo-jet helicopter swung in, trailing a 55-gallon drum of fuel at the end of a long line. It set the drum between two logs as neatly as a woman might place a vase. The lift was on.

In groups of four and with three additional lifts of 20 backpacks hung in a cargo net beneath the machine, the base camp went to the glacier. The flight up became a personal experience from the moment of lift-off. The machine skimmed off the meadow, circled inside the basin, and darted through a gap in the peaks. The lush Alpine meadow dropped away into rock canyon stripped of vegetation. The helicopter came up to the 500-foot face of the glacier at 120 miles an hour, slipping between clouds and ice like a razor parting tissue. Racing across the frozen ridges of snow that spread all around like a still ocean brought the full fascination of speed up through the glass bubble. As if about to topple over a crest that dropped half a mile, the machine floated into a stall and touched to a stop. Set down at an altitude of 6500 feet, each new arrival looked from the rough crown of encircling peaks into the abyss. A mile across the valley trees disappeared into blue-black on the mountainside. Printed in a solid wash, a stone seemed a clear crystal darkened only by the blue air between. Some students took running slides down steep slopes. Others raced away to the highest ledge they could find. Groups held brief skirmishes in the snow. Still others just sat and looked. Andrew Gruft and two friends experienced in climbing took charge. Safety guidelines were set forth and the prearranged groups were set the task of building shelter. A third of the parties chose to use the snow to their advantage. The rest decided to build their camps on the clear outcropping of rock around the main field. With cooking and shelter under way, half the company set out to use the remaining light to climb by. Curving past blue-green crevasses toward a crest two miles away and 2000 feet above, they strung out like ski troops on maneuvers. Those who stayed behind drank, cooked, joked, built fires from mountain driftwood, improved shelters and attended to idle busywork. Though the rain came back, the mood was as opposite from the island as the surroundings. Although most were cold, wet, getting hungry and tired, no one was bored. The new groupings formed around work, chatter, pranks, and meals. The real chance of a thunder storm on the glacier, rumored to be capable of making experienced climbers panic, held no fear. The known difficulty of climbing down through fog that hid all bearings posed no concern beyond the challenge. The outside chance of severe cold at night worried no one. Where 48 hours on the island had seemed interminable, 36 hours on the glacier seemed no time at all.

Where the dense stand of evergreens reaching up out of sight had hemmed everyone in until each became trapped in some barren patch of self, the broad expanse with nothing on all sides and above became truly timeless. Drawn out from the cramped quarters of self, as vapour must expand in a vacuum, their spirits bubbled to the surface. For the first time there was singing. Who could help but sing on the top of the world? There was play. Joy. Reborn on the glacier while chafing under unexpected discipline, they surged back to life. The island—not the want of food, not the gloom of the forest, not the rain, not the self-inflicted isolation, not the division into camps—had made them old. On the island they behaved like retired folks so old all they had left was to await their final departure. On the glacier they became young again. But the growth they found, like the agedness they settled into when most lost, came from psychological depths none had ever plumbed. Indeed, on the glacier and all through the trip, only a few ever sensed that the territory covered during the workshop paralleled the topography of their spirit. Like animals in a maze, they were much too busy reacting to stimuli to analyze or even to formulate their responses. That would come later.

The climb down the glacier and back to base camp was their first small test of physical endurance. Seven miles over the ice field, down the face, into the valley, and up 4000 feet, they were confronted with the task of covering in each hour what they had flown over in a minute. Sixty-pound backpacks and fog thick enough to limit vision to 50 feet made it a challenge. Divided into three teams of 20 joined by a long stretch of rope, they set out over waist-high ridges of soft snow. The experienced climbers led each unit to the face of the glacier. In a running, tumbling, sliding, skidding free-for-all, each person balanced his pack as best he could and slid down the 45-degree slope as best as he could. Once down in the valley on an unmistakable trail, they were left to make their way up and back to the meadow like draft horses free to find the barn. Those who faced it as a show of strength made it in less than three hours. Others who found it an enjoyable, if demanding, stroll took as long as five hours. Saddled with a pack and confronting an unavoidable two-and-a-half-mile climb up a

20-degree slope, each one had to balance energy against endurance, progress against tedium, interest against fatigue.

Eventually they had to settle down to some common denominator for completing the task. In a narrow, special, private and very physical way, each one had to work out his own "one best means." Some rushed and rested every hundred yards. Others plodded. Many forgot they were climbing at all for as much as a half-mile, caught by the change in perspective as they rose above the valley. A few cursed almost every step. One by one they settled into what Jacques Ellul calls a "technique." They came up against what freedom was left them within the rigid limits of physiological ability and physical conditions. For that brief passage each one worked out his personal style under a special condition of stress. That style told volumes. It was a story that did not take long to tell. Although the style of the others was most apparent and without knowing accurately, fully, or coherently *what* he had exposed, each one sensed that he had exposed himself in some important way. The climb back to the meadow made it clear why certain groups had grown spontaneously on the island and why other combinations of people would not naturally occur. The return from the glacier marked the emergence of an awareness of individual techniques for achieving ends and styles-in-means previously unnoticed.

The new awareness came at the best possible time. Plucked from society and comfort and held in contact with nature for five days, the students were plunged back into the system and surrounded with conveniences. Comfort was a modern motel that provided all facilities and good food and the freedom to roam Port Alberni every evening. Twice each day they would tour a different aspect of the lumber industry. Reborn as social beings, they noticed not only the emperor's nakedness but the alleged cut and fabric of his imaginary gown.

A satrapy of MacMillan Bloedel in the middle of Vancouver Island and left over from an earlier century, Port Alberni is a company town with polluted streams, hepatitis, noxious air, odors that would stun a horse, soot, fumes, loud traffic, periodic layoffs, alcoholism, and treeless hills as side effects of having only one major employer. Yet the effects of industrial technique on the lifestyle of the town were trivial compared to their influence on the men at work. In three days the students saw modern industrial technique at work in fire fighting, paper manufacturing, logging, cutting lumber, and plywood production. Everywhere the most modern equipment stood out as the only evidence of the twentieth century. The two surviving Martin Mars were kept ready as water bombers. The largest planes to see active service in World War II, they pick up 6,000 gallons of water in a 22-second sweep across the surface of a lake.

The pulp and paper mill was as fully automated as possible. Gigantic vats collect, grind, soak, stew, and feed a sticky juice into a block-long oven of drums that press, stretch, dry, bake, and roll up finished newsprint. The nattering of powerful chain saws throughout the forest made a sound as though the whole mountain was host to a swarm of mechanical locusts that would eat it bare. Where the crews had left, the mile-square stands made a cut wheatfield look scraggly. Everything was down. At China Lake the water scooters cut logs from the dumping pools more efficiently than a trained quarter-horse culls a herd. In the sawmill, man-high blades made beams from trees in two cuts. The plywood factory had presses three stories high. Everywhere one technique stood out: Enlarge the machine. Each replacement had been more gigantic than its predecessor. Gradually, the attendant technique became apparent: Rationalize the internal steps of each separate process until that stage is automated. Only then did the discontinuity between gigantic machines begin to make sense. Specialists had automated isolated processes separately, and that separation set the task for human labor. Men did not work so much on, as between, machines. Whenever one complex of machinery finished a set of tasks and another assemblage waited to take it another stage, there was a flurry of human activity. Men rushed pell-mell to fill the gap between two independent mechanical processes.

Unique, specialized, temperamental, costly, and irreplaceable, the machines received irreproachable care. Indeed, the machinery was the only thing unique in any of the operations. The company could no more use a $6 million paper dryer to put out forest fires than it could dry paper with the Hawaii Mars. Only the men were standardized, interchangeable, expendable, indistinguishable, and cheap....

Signs posted everywhere announced the daily lifestyle for workers. Like front line troops, they had learned to live with constant danger. The numbers themselves gave a precise arithmetical index of danger, job by job. They announced that the machinery could not be made man-safe. "No matter what you do the machine will get you. It's just a matter of time." "Look, so and so has escaped injury for 283 days." Yet when you are hurt, "It's your fault." "Men *make* accidents." Whenever anyone was asked about the company's concern for the workers, the safety signs were pointed out. After the second day no one asked. Discussion with management provoked hostility. The very thought that unintended psychological and social contaminants might develop as side effects of company policy came as an unpardonable insult. The safety game stood out as symbolic of a fundamental absurdity. Practical businessmen, regarding themselves as deeply involved in the basic struggle to provide necessary commodities, were prisoners of their own fantasies more than the students had been on the island. Practical laborers committed to bread-and-butter wage earning were more lost than they would have been on the glacier when the fog closed in. Worse, both groups believed they were "communicating." Neither suggested its isolation from the other. A huge industrial complex had grown up between them, and yet it remained invisible. . . .

The result of this mutual blindness was Port Alberni, a peculiar but somehow typical wasteland. For all the devastation of physical resources for the production of commercial exports, they came to little by comparison to the degradation of human resources. The forests, the streams, and the air could still replenish themselves. The people had been used beyond any point of return. Having seen how industrial technique devastates a population, the students went on to follow-up that human devastation in a more advanced stage. Their next stop was Skid Row in downtown Vancouver.

Arriving in the usual downpour, everyone checked into the West Hotel at Carrol and Pender Streets just off Chinatown. With two students to a room at $1.50 each per night, they had the next four days to explore eight square blocks. Before turning them loose, Bud Wood, the codirector, gave each one his $5-a-day allotment of cash. Dressed in boots and camping clothes, with beards and untrimmed hair, they had only manners, speech, and curiosity to separate them from the native inhabitants.

The hotel's bar served as base camp, refresher station, rest home, take-off point, runway, rally ground, and seminar room.

Low-slung, huge, noisy, pillared, blue, black-ceilinged, gilded, mirrored, busy, threadbare, and orderly, the bar catered to a cross-section of the population, two beers at a time. That the patrons were not especially bawdy, frantic, violent, boisterous, or hostile came as a surprise. A gravel-voiced citizen entertained each newcomer with the offer of a diamond from the "crown jewels of Czechoslovakia" smuggled on the last plane out of Prague. A few lads lent themselves to the embraces of an Indian girl happy to give them vivid details of her decline and fall. Others received fatherly advice from pensioners about keeping their cash in a side pocket and not flashing anything bigger than a $2 bill. They saw and heard drunks but found the vast majority quite content to drink well within their budget and limit. After buying a few rounds they found themselves treated in return.

Even before they ventured out on the streets they knew a good deal about the community. Most of all, they knew it was a community. The people they had expected to find broken and in a continuous stupor had a spirit and individuality not to be found in Port Alberni. They reflected, without having heard, Camus' dictum in *The Myth of Sisyphus:* "There is no fate that cannot be surmounted by scorn." These survivors of industrial displacement had many battle scars. Yet herded together in a ghetto left over as an omission in city planning, they retained a certain small measure of independence from commercial-industrial technique. By working little, unsteadily, or not at all, they avoided having to stay in anyone's "good grace." They were, in a most limited way, being themselves. The limitation was that by the time they got there, not much of the "self" was left intact. Contrary to expectation, these people had not given up. They laughed, drank, hoped, fought occasionally, talked endlessly, listened, argued, smiled, dreamed, sang, cried, visited, made friends, and worried. The notable difference was that they had no assigned places in which to do these things. They were "at home" on the street or in an alley, in a bar or a temporary room. They were at home in their bodies instead of in some set space, and it soon became clear that this was not a matter of choice but of necessity.

The architecture students soon noted how little space existed to serve the inhabitants. By day and early evening businessmen came in to open shops for customers who came from outside. Only when the outsiders withdrew and the stores and offices were dark and padlocked did the indigenous facilities stand out. There were small restaurants offering cheap food in quantity for every ethnic group—Greek, Polish, Hungarian, Swedish. Cutting across ethnic lines, bars catered to special social tastes. The mixed couples did not mingle with the transvestites. The solitary drinkers stayed away from the party bars. The hotels and rooming houses polarized around still other groupings. The sailors did not register where the salesmen gathered. Though illegal activities went out to wherever demand promised patronage, each had its center of gravity. Prostitution did not interfere with gambling. Dope peddling did not compete with bootlegging. Once it became clear what the boundaries were, it took just six minutes by actual timing to find a "kit" that someone had stashed for mixing, heating, and injecting heroin. A serious customer never had to wait more than a quarter hour to make contact, whatever might be his needs. Service was far better than the checkout line at any supermarket. Yet the traffic was quite small compared to the size of the population.

Gradually the students grasped one of the basic facts of life on Skid Row. The restaurants, the bars, the streets, the alleys, the porches of tenements, and one very small 30- by 40-foot triangular "park" were the only social centers available. Wherever they might go to sleep, they had to come to one of these places to socialize. This was known and accepted. The great majority did not drink to become convivial, they gathered together to relieve each other's boredom, and rather than cast a man out in the rain because he couldn't afford to buy a drink, someone would order him a beer so he could stay. For a group of people who literally lived in their social centers and only slept or recuperated in their rooms, the guarantee of being welcome was essential. Unfortunately, they had to convert with no help the few facilities left them by an unconcerned city. They had to make social centers out of places least amenable to that function, and they did it with nothing but their own depleted personal resources. However limited, warped, undeveloped, starved, or out of kilter, all they had was their own humanity. Because they brought all of it wherever they went, they were, in their own special way, more wholly and fully present, wherever they went, than most men.

They left nothing behind, kept nothing hidden. Carrying the whole of what was left them as selves, these men often enough exhibited facets of self not customarily seen in public, and that, not the people themselves, was the basis for disapproval. The occupants of Skid Row, the students eventually discovered, lived all too public lives. They did in company what the general public regarded as only fit to be done in private. Urinating and making love, vomiting and sleeping, dressing and tending wounds, taking medicine and resting—all was visible, and those who lived in more compartmentalized ways found such a blend offensive. Having just come away from an island and a glacier where such a blend had been a communal and environmental necessity, the students could accept it quite easily. They were surprised to see that the basic pattern of living on Skid Row differed very little from their own style of camping. The trees had given way to high buildings, the icefield had been replaced by pavement, but the ways of coping with a great deal of time and not very much to do remained the same. Like themselves, these folks were the sole occupants of an island. Their little enclosure was threatened by an ever-rising tide of commercial and industrial development that encroached from all sides. Unlike the students, no one had arranged for their departure on a silent morning.

Later, loaded with camping gear, everyone trudged up a mud road through the rain on Sunday afternoon. All they knew was that they had entered the state of Washington and come to Friday Creek, about 20 miles south of Bellingham. From the distance they heard a Gregorian chant coming through the trees. As they turned a bend they came upon what could have been a Roman ruin. Aged, overlaid with 20-foot high trees growing out of the roof, abounding in symmetrical arches, a circular brick building arched up into a perfect dome. From the inside, the abandoned bee-hive brick kiln curved around and around in layers that drew the eye to the hole on top. Moss and moisture filled the dome with a musty incense. A dozen low arches evenly spaced all around opened to the fading daylight as altars of invitation. The deep tones of the Gregorian chant mixed with the candle light to create a mood of reverence.

Moors coming upon a mosque in an alien land could not have been more awestruck. The chant ceased, and silence admitted the sound of a running stream. As eyes grew more accustomed to the dim light, details became more evident. Throughout, the dome bricks of the kiln were set on edge against each other without mortar. Sounds worked across the dome to drop intact at full volume precisely on their nodal points. The scars of intense heat worked up in carbon streaks as shadows of long-extinguished flames, as if to provide the building with memories. One great room was softly lighted so that the glow faded gradually to a deep claret red. Simple, strong, and so boldly clear in design and construction, it bespoke its very nature. It was as natural as the island forest or the glacier snow. It belonged. Only the rubble of broken brick turned up, scattered, and left by thieves in their search for marketable bricks, and mounds of trash showed the hand of men. That dirty smudge had to be erased. In two days the work parties cleared out all the rubble and rebuilt the floor of the kiln with brick taken from the false roof. They stripped all the growth that threatened to crumble the dome, reinforced it by welding the steel bands holding it together, covered it with clear plastic that waterproofed it, and cleared it of rubble and trash inside and out. Equipped with electricity but not lighted by it, the kiln was ready for use. There was a sense of having restored a monument to its original splendor. It came as a shock to find that the kiln was only 10 years old.

The students, delighted to have a task, did the basic renovation in two days and improved it each day thereafter. As it became the social center, fewer people slept inside. Each day a few new members of the architecture staff arrived. The attendant building provided shelter for sleeping and storage. A catering service supplied hot meals, and a barrel of beer went on tap every evening. With five days left to go, the students felt that finally they had about all they wanted. They had no suspicion that work, shelter, food, and drink was the least of the benefits they were to receive.

The cultural program came on slowly. On the evening of the third day at the kiln they all gathered in the dome at dusk. A solo oboist played an hour of modern music before the beer arrived. After refreshments he came back and discussed the notions of sound, space, harmony, rhythm, atonality, improvisation, and composition underlying the works he had played. He gave an impromptu accompaniment to the reading of an original poem, which was followed by the reading of a chapter from a novel that was being written. A bit startled by the exposure, the students set up a couple of Congo drums and beat their way through half the night until the beer was gone.

Another evening a solo cellist played, talked, joked, and worked her way through a night of music appreciation that extended from Brahms to nursery rhymes by way of viola and violin. The second artist established the pattern of the performances beyond their special cultural merits. The students realized that they were encountering people who had spent most of a lifetime mastering some of the most difficult skills ever undertaken by man, but there was something more. By coming to the students and opening themselves to any questions, they were providing an invitation. In a groping way, the questioning began to focus on what they had to give of themselves and find in themselves to rise to the level of artistry.

The impact of the artists began to show in the students' daytime work. A portion of the floor that had been laid down imperfectly was torn up and redone. Damage to the kiln that had not been noticed was repaired. Shelters, walkways around the adjacent buildings, sheds, a crude drinking station called *"The Plastic Pub"* were all repaired. Even personal care improved. The dam down the creek had a waterfall that became a shower. Some shaved. Without being fastidious the students began to restore themselves back from the dishevelment that had gone unchecked from the island through Skid Row. One day an officer from the Immigration Service arrived. He was under the impression that the community was a religious cult. The fact that the students had turned their hand at building "found sculpture" from machine parts laying all around tended to confirm his suspicion. His concern was very specific. In the most courteous way, he inquired whether there were women present. At that point it came as a shock to everyone to realize that sex differences mattered. After assuring himself that the women were not being held by force or the threat of force, he took a considerable interest in the improvements.

One evening a troupe of three actors from Western Washington University put on a one-act performance drawn from a segment of a poem by Koch. After analyzing and reconstructing their moods, they drew several "volunteers" into the center of the dome and went through a verbal charade called "Coil Supreme." Carrying over into a second keg of beer, the drummers and those who worked over the rented piano partied their way into dawn.

By night and by day the groups worked out their special style and technique. Quite at home with themselves and each other, they played as hard as they worked.

The students sought advice from the staff when it suited them and ignored it on the same basis. The spirit first evidenced on the glacier returned in much amplified strength. None of the gloom or

"Lord of the Flies" position so evident on the island reappeared. Midway through their stay at the kiln they found themselves to be a fully developed and emotionally self-sufficient community. Selves that had remained hidden all that time emerged. Discussion, argument, and debate abounded on everything from adultery to Zen. Life histories were revealed, philosophies exposed, attitudes attacked, values endorsed. Without realizing they were doing anything more than restoring an abandoned kiln and having a good time drinking, they began to make unexamined parts of themselves evident. By bringing them out in the open, they took the first step toward building new selves. Their style became fraternal; they took an interest in each other far beyond the usual. When one lad was refused passage on a bus because of long hair and bare feet it hit them all. When another was caught by the Conservation Officer with two 25-pound salmon he had just killed for a barbecue, he had more volunteer "lawyers" than anyone could use.

Their technique became "stumbling Cartesian." Though not fully aware of the extent to which doubt might reach when nothing was taken for granted, they started along the road. The 17 acres they occupied were no longer an abandoned brick kiln on Friday Creek. It became a modern Benedictine Monastery in which work and meditation mixed with an exploration of the arts and, incidentally, beer. Yet the community was in no danger of becoming a cult. Joined in a common though undefined exploration, they gradually became aware of how different they really were. Fortunately they had learned that they did not have to become ostriches to protect the differences. These were the differences that exposure could cultivate just as the performances of the artists contributed to their special uniqueness.

A recital by the University of British Columbia string quartet brought the collaborative dimension of artistic excellence to the fore. For two hours the dome rang with the sound of strings tuned and played in harmony. After the performance they were surprised to find that the local constabulary and several citizens had come to listen. Having known the place as an abandoned ruin good for several loads of brick and having heard all kinds of stories about the weird rites being performed, the local citizens had trouble believing their eyes and ears. Again and again they marvelled at the transformation and remarked that there had never been anything like the performance anywhere in the area before. The word spread that the Canadians were a breed unknown in those parts—hard working, constructive, fun loving, cultured, friendly, open, creative, intelligent, moral, and somehow too good to be true. Alarmed at what seemed to them the decline and decay of their own youth, they showered the visitors with all the virtues they admired but found lacking. So a counter-myth went around as an antidote to the initial accusations.

The following night many citizens returned and brought friends to hear a basso from the San Francisco Opera and watch his wife do interpretive dancing. Their amazement grew. Promises to preserve the kiln and continue to use and improve it abounded. Men swore to protect it against brick thieves and destruction. Local politicos vowed to use all their influence to further what had been started. Regardless of practical limitations that might keep them from accomplishing their ends, the expression of concern was absolutely genuine. A certain hidden passion for improvement had been touched, and though it might be only an emotional outburst, it represented an awakening. And it augmented the same feeling for preservation and continued use of the facilities that living in and around the kiln had stirred in the students. The guests and the host citizenry who had come to find out what was going on were in perfect accord. Having developed a facility entirely for their own use, the students were able to be fully and wholly themselves in a more expanded and complete sense than would ever be possible for anyone on Skid Row. They could open up into the kiln, the grounds, the countryside, the work, the appreciation, and the sharing without keeping parts of themselves compartmentalized.

In just one week they had put together a whole that exceeded the sum of its parts. Without quite knowing what they were doing, they built themselves a vision. The kiln, the brick laying, the artistic performances, the drinking, the communual living, the geographic isolation, and the continuous discussion were only elements of technique for making it possible. However dim or fleeting, vague or contradictory, spotty or insubstantial, they had caught a glimpse. The glimpse, not the activities, had fired their imaginations. In a hermitage of their own making, they had caught the vision of Shangri-la. They had dabbled on the outskirts of Utopia. However soon they might forget it under the press of ordinary affairs, it would not be lost. They had touched on a new dimension.

Preparation for the last night began in a downpour before dawn.

A pit was dug, coals were laid, a spit was built, and a huge leg of beef was started. All through the day plastic was hung to provide shelter for the guests who would arrive at dusk. Wives, girl friends, local citizens, professors, architects, artists, and scientists were invited from half a dozen places between Seattle and Vancouver. Broken brick was dumped into muddy spots down the road so vehicles would not bog down. A fire was built in the dome to dry it out and a cleanup squad brought the interior and the grounds to their peak of cleanliness. Everyone worked full tilt arranging food, lighting, access, extra accommodations, and special effects. Before the staff withdrew, everyone was told to be in the dome, seated and waiting, by six-thirty. As was customary, the students did not know what they would be waiting for. Not prone to let a mystery go unexamined, they gathered.

The staff drove to a residence in Bellingham to put on Restoration period costumes from the University's drama department. The drive back took them through the town of Alger, about two miles from the kiln. Knowing that a dozen local citizens would be in the crossroads bar, they stopped in. The customers saw a Jesuit priest, a Dominican brother, a nun, two squires in velvet great coats, a buccaneer, an Indian woman in a sari, and a girl in a purple page-boy outfit come in. For the first few minutes they were awestruck. All the men had beards. The women were immaculate. Everyone was barefoot or in hiking boots. Looking from the brown wool of the religious costumes to the blue, purple, and butterscotch velvet greatcoats, they gathered their wits. The owner hurried to get a camera. A couple concluded the costuming had to do with the kiln. Toasts and congratulations were offered from all sides, and the group left to meet several dozen guests who were timing their arrival at the property so everyone could enter together. Principal among the guests was Henry Elder, Director of the University of British Columbia School of Architecture, in the full ceremonial dress of a bishop.

Carrying candles and stepping to a chant, the procession strode up the path, through the trees, and into the dome. All attendants and ladies-in-waiting went to the center and stood around the bishop. The staff members in religious and court dress went around the inside edge and stopped at different low arches. For three-quarters of an hour they performed a one-act existential play that had been written the day before. With lines written on anything that could be concealed, the outer ring looked through their openings to describe different worlds. Each report they gave to the bishop was explained and distorted by his chief administrator. The bishop was asked to decide which world would survive. His answer—that none should survive—was relayed back by the administrator. As each one around the outside blew out his candle, the bishop grew more worried. By extinguishing his aide's candle before all were out, he allowed all the others to relight theirs. The play began with a three minute oration of Pericles' funeral speech in Greek, and ended with the priest chanting a Mass in Latin. All the players withdrew as a soprano sang a soft but bright solo. For several minutes no one spoke.

Just as applause began to ring through the dome half a dozen girls appeared wearing shapely togas and carrying bowls of fruit and jars of wine. Two students in loincloths carried a barbecued leg of beef on their shoulders. More serving girls came in with wicker trays. Loaves of bread—light, dark, french, sour dough —were passed around and everyone broke off what he wanted. Large cheeses—hard and soft, sharp and mild, pungent and creamy—were served. Whole roast chickens were broken apart and passed along; a dozen varieties of salami and platters of beef dripping with natural juices passed from hand to hand. Grapes, nuts, oranges, bananas, plums, and apples were offered. And after every mouthful there was wine—heavy, light, dry, sweet, rosé, Chablis, claret, Zinfandel. Hand to mouth and hand to hand; there was no china or silver to be seen. Each person was his own portable larder with supply stations never more than a few steps away. Eating and drinking in Roman fashion encouraged mobility.

Two drummers set up a wild beat on the tom-toms. Chains formed and circled. The dancing began. Shouts of *olé* mixed with toasts and the room began to rock.

When it seemed the dancing could not get wilder or the chorus louder, a Greek bouzouki band struck out. Beginning with their amplified versions of Western songs evocative of the Mediterranean, they worked into their native music, mixing the Greek strings with Turkish woodwinds. In Zorba fashion, the revelers jumped, whirled, stepped, stooped, sprang up, slapped their heels. Joyfully exhausted, they welcomed the chance to sit and watch when a belly dancer appeared. Beginning with the dance of the veils, she introduced a new motion each time she peeled off a layer. Revealed under the last layer of thinnest gauze, she gyrated seemingly in seven separate directions at once, all the while maintaining a thumping beat with her whole midriff that would have done credit to the girls of Bora Bora. As she went into her last number a young architect burst into the dome clad in nothing but a few vines appropriately draped. In a wild duet of Nature Boy and the Snake of Eden they stimulated the audience into a frenzy of gymnastics it had not known it could even attempt.

Quite beyond themselves, the crowd did not notice the next stage until the strobe lights set out a pattern of flashes that resembled the cannon blasts at the seige of Sevastopol. All motion was frozen in a series of disjointed stills, and the roar of artillery came over the powerful amplifier. A rock-and-roll band of amplified guitars and rim-rattling drums opened a light show. On a parachute held up to the curve of the dome, projectors flashed subliminal images in quick succession and overlay. Color blazed through the smoke and splashed along the silk like dry dust cast by a contemporary Jackson Pollock. The blinding flashes of light slowed the gyrations of the dancers into a slow-motion satire of a Chaplin film. And throughout the dome the ear-splitting roar of the band pressed as thick as an invisible fog suddenly turned harder than steel. Frozen in frantic postures by the flashes of bright and black they were held there motionless by noise so stunning it solidified the very blood in their veins. It was the light, the black, the blindness, the deafness, the start, the stop, the roar, the numbness of Creation. And it went on until dawn.

Somewhere in the rain and the mystery of that night of thoughtless noise, the end came. When they saw the debris by daylight, the workshop was already over. The cleanup was silent. They were going home. Or were they? Something seemed to bar the way. A question? A small doubt? Some wonder? They could not stay, but no one was happy to leave. There was a sense of a vision fading, the trace of a ghost. When would there be another night like the last? Beneath that selfish question, another concern began to stir. Somehow it had been more than just another workshop. Defense Island, Garibaldi Glacier, Port Alberni, Skid Row, and the brick kiln at Friday Creek had been stages in a launching. They had broken away from a tight confinement in a narrowly constricted sense of self. If they were not yet free, at least the bonds of a constraining psychological and social gravity had been weakened. Although they might never find a self-sustaining orbit, they had made a good start. They had begun a first probe toward relevance.

THE MODE

Anyone who has had an adventure and told the tale should have no trouble understanding how or why this account was written. Yet a few details might help. Since no diary was kept, *narrative* accuracy rests entirely on memories three months old. Certainly, some latent *personal* reactions must have been made to seem paramount simply through backward projection at the time of writing. Which ones they are will never be known. Most of the *conjectures* about what might have been learned were efforts to expose the potential inherent in such situations. Once the trip was over, no one was asked to give an account of what he learned. *Normative* judgments were made with the firmness and informality of convictions stated in conversation. Much was made of the *positive* features of people, places, and events. The *negative* aspects of industries, slums, and attitudes were set out in sharp relief. Did some things grow in the telling? Undoubtedly. Hence, it is to be expected that some will view these admissions as unforgivable lapses that render the account worthless. Harsh though it may be, such a verdict could be defended and respected for its grounds. It would be a mistake, however, to take these confessions as a sneak-attack on diaries, clinical records, opinion surveys, questionnaires, interviews, or the analysis and justification of normative judgments. What omissions there are resulted from trying to give an account different in kind from any that rely on such techniques. Overall, this other kind of account seeks to fuse the old to the new. For depth it would restore to the discussion of human problems the reflection so often found in the essays of the eighteenth century. For impact it would create the immediacy of today's reportorial fiction. By working within a framework made of man's most important moods held in constant tension, it may be possible to give expression to that vital *core* of human understandings so lacking in the findings of specialists. A diagram of the crucial moods held in steady tension might make it easier to envision how the core could be conceived (see Figure 3.1). In such an

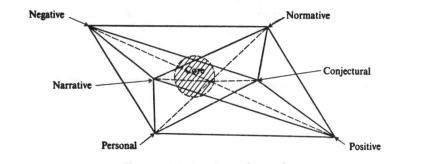

Figure 3.1 Six Crucial Moods

enterprise balance is everything. Yet nowhere can the limits of the moods or the strength of the vectors be stated in advance. To strike the needed balances in the writing, unguided by fixed reference points, is the essence of the literary mode. To find the appropriate posture is to convey an aspect of the human story too often left untold.

Section VII
Survey Methods in Educational Research

Survey Research Methods in Education

Richard M. Jaeger
University of North Carolina at Greensboro

What Is Survey Research?

The purpose of survey research is to describe specific characteristics of a large group of persons, objects, or institutions. For example, a survey researcher might want to know the average length of time all public school teachers in a state had been employed as full-time teachers. Another survey researcher might want information on the attitudes toward school of all high school students in a very large school system. A third researcher might want to investigate the number of dollars spent on the education of each student during the last full school year by the 2,000 largest school systems in the United States. These examples have several characteristics in common: First, the researchers are interested in specific facts that describe a large group. Second, the groups that are of interest are well defined. Third, all the researchers want to know something about the present conditions of a group, rather than something about what would happen if they changed something (such as doubling the tax rate in the 2,000 largest school systems, and then determining the effect of the increased revenues on those school systems' expenditures for public education). Fourth, in each example, the most obvious way to secure the desired information would be to ask the right people.

The researcher who wanted to know the average amount of full-time teaching experience of all public school teachers in a particular state could, at least theoretically, ask every public school teacher in the state how long (s)he had been teaching full time. If all of these teachers provided the desired information, calculating the group's average years of full-time teaching experience would be a simple matter, particularly with a computer. But gathering data from all public school teachers in the state would be a waste of time and money if the researcher just wanted to know the average for the entire group. Even in Delaware (the state with the fewest public school teachers), there are about 6,000 teachers. And in California, the state with the greatest number of public school teachers, there are over 212,000. Instead of asking every teacher, a more sensible approach would be to choose carefully some of the teachers in the state and ask each of them how long they had been teaching full time. The researcher could then calculate the average length of time the chosen teachers had been teaching full time, and use that figure as an estimate of what would have been found if all public school teachers in the state had been asked.

Some Basic Vocabulary

This example illustrates what is usually done in survey research—that is, collecting data from or about some members of the group that is of interest, rather than collecting data from or about all group members. In fact, we can use the example to introduce some of the most important vocabulary of survey research. The group consisting of all public school teachers in the state is an example of a *population*. In general, a population is any group of persons, objects, or institutions that have at least one characteristic in common. In this case, members of the population are public school teachers, and all are employed in the state that the researcher is investigating. The average length of time all members of the population have been employed full time is an example of a *population parameter*. A population parameter is any numerical value that can be calculated using information on all members of a population, such as the average age of all school buildings in the State of New York, or the total number of students enrolled in the public schools of Los Angeles, or the range of heights of the players on all professional basketball teams in the United States.

The smaller group of teachers that was chosen from the population to provide information on the length of time they had been teaching full time is an example of a *sample*. In survey research, a sample is a part of the population of interest; it is the part used for collection of data. If they are to provide information that is useful in estimating population parameters, samples have to be chosen carefully, according to well-defined rules. We will have more to say about the kinds of rules that are used and the appropriate sizes of samples. Samples that are useful in estimating population parameters are said to be *representative* of the population.

With just a few more definitions, you will know the basic vocabulary of survey research, so stick with it. In our example, once the sample of teachers had been selected, the researcher collected data from each sampled teacher and used those data to calculate the average full-time teaching experience of all teachers in the sample. That average is an example of a *sample statistic*. In general, a sample statistic is any numerical value that is calculated using data from members of a sample. Sample statistics are useful not only to describe the sample that provides data to compute them, but also to serve as estimates of corresponding population parameters. In our example, the average full-time teaching experience of sampled teachers was used as an estimate of what would have been found, had all teachers in the population provided data on their full-time teaching experience.

So a survey is a research study in which data are collected from the members of a sample, for the purpose of estimating one or more population parameters. Using simple English rather than the jargon of survey research, we would say that a survey is a research study in which data are collected from part of a group, for the purpose of describing one or more characteristics of the whole group.

So far we have treated the data collection part of survey research as though it were trivially simple: "If you want to know how many years of full-time teaching experience a public school teacher has, just ask." In truth, different ways of asking would yield different answers to this question. If you called teachers on the phone or asked them face to face, you might get one answer. But if you asked teachers by mailing them a form to complete, you might get another. The way the question was phrased could have a great influence on the types of answers you received. The question seems to be straightforward, but if you think about it, you'll see that it is quite ambiguous. What does full-time teaching mean? Is it defined as teaching at least 4 hours per day, or does some other number of hours per day define the minimum? To be counted as full time, must a person teach every weekday during all weeks that school is in session? Should a semester of student teaching be counted as full-time teaching experience? What about teaching in private schools or nursery schools: Do those experiences count toward full-time teaching experience? To secure data that were comparable, every teacher in the sample would have to be given the same set of rules. If data were collected through telephone calls or face-to-face interviews, the rules could be explained to responding teachers, and specific questions could be answered. For a survey conducted through the mail, the questionnaire would have to carry the burden of clearly explaining the rules. Responding teachers would not have the chance to ask for clarification. Writing clear, unambiguous survey questions is a difficult and time-consuming task, about which we will have more to say later.

In a well-designed survey in which data are collected through interviews, all interviewers are given strict instructions on the questions they are to ask, the order in which questions are to be asked, whether or not they can ask follow-up questions or probe for additional clarification when they do not understand a response, and what they are to tell respondents about the purpose of the survey and the organization that is sponsoring it. The instructions for interviewers and the questions they are to ask are contained in a form called an *interview protocol.*

When data are collected through a mail survey, the instrument that contains the survey questions is called a *questionnaire.* The questionnaire must also contain instructions on how to respond; definitions of terms likely to be unclear to respondents; any necessary instructions on questions that are to be answered by those who fall into one category, but skipped by those who fall into another; and instructions on what to do with the questionnaire once it has been completed.

Whether a survey is conducted using mailed questionnaires or through interviews, a critical objective for the survey researcher is to present all respondents with questions that they interpret and understand in exactly the same way. Perhaps this goal can never be accomplished completely, but strict attention to detail and care in phrasing questions, definitions, and instructions will certainly reduce ambiguity and misunderstanding.

Some Familiar Surveys

Two commercial survey organizations, the Gallup Poll and the Harris Poll, conduct hundreds of surveys every year. The topics of these surveys range from specialized marketing studies for business clients to the annual Gallup Poll on citizens' satisfaction with U. S. public education. Often the results of Harris Poll and Gallup Poll surveys of the general population are reported by the major news services, and appear in newspapers throughout the nation. After reading an article reporting the results of one of these surveys, you might have wondered how reliable conclusions could have been reached on the basis of data provided by a relatively small sample of respondents. Surveys of the general population of U.S. adults, a population that numbers about 175 million, often report results based on information secured from a sample of only 1,500. Although every person sampled must represent over 115,000 persons in the population, the reported survey results are quite reliable. Those who are unfamiliar with sampling methods often assume that they must sample a large proportion of a population (say 10% or 25%) in order to represent it well. That is true only if the population is very small. When fairly large populations are sampled (e.g., populations with 10,000 or more members), the reliability of sample estimates depends far more on the actual size of the sample than on the proportion of the population that is sampled. Thus 1,500 well-selected cases would do about as good a job of representing a population of 175 million or a population of 175 thousand. What matters most is the sample size of 1500 and, of course, choosing those 1,500 persons in a way that represents the entire population.

The decennial census of population conducted by the U.S. Bureau of the Census is somewhat like a survey, in that data are compiled from the information reported by individual respondents. However, the census of population is called a census and not a survey, for one important reason. Rather than sampling the population of U.S. residents, the census attempts to collect data from or about everyone in the population. In survey research, a study that involves collection of data from all members of a population is called a *census*, regardless of the nature of the population. The population can be composed of people, institutions, governments, or animals, and the study is still called a census if data are collected for every member of the population.

Exit polls conducted by television news networks during major elections are another kind of survey that might be familiar to you. An exit poll is used to collect information on voters' choices prior to final tabulations of votes, so that election outcomes can be predicted. Exit polls are called *polls* rather than surveys because of the limited amount of information they seek. The questionnaire or interview protocol used in a poll might contain only one or two questions; the instrument used in a survey typically contains many questions on a variety of topics and is far more complex.

Field Studies Versus Experiments

Survey research is part of a larger category of inquiry that social scientists call *field studies*. Another widely used method of social science inquiry is called *experimental research*. Several characteristics distinguish field studies from experimental research, but the defining difference concerns the kinds of actions taken by the researcher. In an experimental study, the researcher *does* something to the subjects or objects of the research, and then attempts to determine the effects of his or her actions. For example, in an experimental study of the effects of curriculum on student achievement, the researcher might assign one group of students to a new, innovative curriculum, and assign another group to a traditional curriculum. The assignment of students would use a process that depended on chance alone in determining which students received which curriculum. At the end of the school year, the researcher would administer the same kind of achievement test to all students, regardless of the curriculum they received, and would regard the groups' average achievement test scores as indicators of the relative effectiveness of the two curricula. In this example the new curriculum was introduced solely to determine its effects on student achievement.

In a field study, the researcher doesn't "do" anything to the objects or subjects of research, except observe them or ask them to provide data. The research consists of collecting data on things or people as they are, without trying to alter anything. In fact, those who conduct field studies often try to be as unobtrusive as possible, to minimize the effect of data collection on the objects or persons being studied. This is certainly the case in survey research. A survey researcher might want to know about teachers' honest attitudes toward their school principals, unaltered by the act of asking. The more intrusive a survey, the lower the chances that it will accurately reflect real conditions.

About the Rest of This Chapter

This chapter has four major sections, including the one you are now reading. In the next section, you will learn about the essential steps in planning and conducting a survey. That section is a general guide to the sorts of things you would have to think about and do if you were to conduct a survey of your own. The third section is a bit less pragmatic and somewhat more analytical than the second. It contains a discussion of the role of generalization in survey research. It also describes the types of conditions and assumptions that must hold if survey results are to generalize to the population of interest. The fourth section is built around a checklist of things to ask and things to look for when you are reviewing a report on a survey. Although surveys can provide trustworthy and accurate information, many do not. The fourth section will give you some hints on separating the wheat from the chaff.

Following this chapter is a guide to additional reading about surveys and survey research. You can use this guide to find helpful books and reports on such specialized issues as questionnaire design or sampling methods, and on more general techniques of survey research. You will also find references to some useful internet sites that provide information on surveys.

How to Plan and Conduct a Survey (A Guide to Tasks and Issues)

At first glance, surveys look simple. Just write some questions, ask some people (either directly or by mailing them a questionnaire), count their answers, and write a report. Like most of life, surveys are decidedly more complex at second glance. If you want survey results you can trust, you'll have to exercise a good bit of care. First, you'll have to plan your study thoughtfully and thoroughly. Then you'll have to test your plan. And finally, you'll have to conduct the survey, using every element of your plan and the results of your testing.

There isn't a formula for ensuring a good survey. But years of study and experience have led to guidelines that greatly increase the chances (cf., Moser & Kalton, 1972; Rossi, Wright & Anderson, 1983). Some of those guidelines will now be described.

Problem Definition

It might be obvious that it pays to figure out what you want to know before you start to gather information. However, many novice survey researchers begin by writing a questionnaire or an interview protocol. They write a few questions that are at the heart of the issue they want to investigate, and then think of other things that would be "nice" to know. Often, the result is a survey instrument that is far from the core of the research problem and laden with trivia that don't address the issues that motivated the survey.

The problem to be investigated must be defined clearly and completely, if the right questions are to be asked and needless questions are to be avoided. The place to start in planning a survey is not with the questions that make up a survey instrument but with basic research questions.

One strategy for defining research questions is to use a hierarchical approach, beginning with the broadest, most general questions, and ending with the most specific. Here's an example.

Suppose you wanted to determine why many public school teachers "burn out" so quickly and leave the profession within a few years. Certainly, many former teachers have reasons for leaving the profession that are personal and situation-specific. But it is also likely that some general factors can be identified. Your survey instrument should be structured around these latter factors.

Without too much thought it is easy to hypothesize several categories of reasons that some teachers leave the profession early. One set of factors might be economic, since teachers are paid very poorly and many have to hold a second job to afford the necessities of life. Other factors might have to do with the conditions of work in the schools. Classes are large, lunch hours are short, and students are often unruly and unappreciative. Yet another set of factors might be teachers' perceived social status. Although teaching was a well-respected profession 20 or 30 years ago, recent surveys have suggested that parents and other citizens have far less regard for public school teachers today.

If these three categories of factors exhausted your interest in the reasons teachers leave the profession early, you might structure your research questions as follows:

I. Do economic factors cause teachers to leave the profession early?
   A. Do teachers leave the profession early because of inadequate yearly income?
      1. Do teachers leave the profession early because their monthly income during the school year is too small?
      2. Do teachers leave the profession early because they are not paid during the summer months?
      3. Do teachers leave the profession early because their salary forces them to hold a second job during the school year?

    4. Do teachers leave the profession early because their lack of income forces them to hold a different job during the summer months?

B. Do teachers leave the profession early because of the structure of their pay scale?

    1. Do teachers leave the profession early because the upper limit on their pay scale is too low?

    2. Do teachers leave the profession early because their rate of progress on the pay scale is too slow?

C. Do teachers leave the profession early because of inadequate fringe benefits?

    1. Do teachers leave the profession early because their health insurance benefits are inadequate?

    2. Do teachers leave the profession early because their life insurance benefits are inadequate?

    3. Do teachers leave the profession early because their retirement benefits are inadequate?

II. Do working conditions cause teachers to leave the profession early?

A. Do teachers leave the profession early because the physical conditions of their work are unacceptable?

    1. Do teachers leave the profession early because of deficiencies in the facilities in which they work?

    2. Do teachers leave the profession early because of inadequate teaching materials?

B. Do teachers leave the profession early because of the amount of time their jobs demand?

    1. Do teachers leave the profession early because their jobs require them to work during the evening?

    2. Do teachers leave the profession early because their jobs require them to work on weekends?

    3. Do teachers leave the profession early because of the total amount of time per week their jobs require?

C. Do teachers leave the profession early because of the attitudes and behavior of their students?

    1. Do teachers leave the profession early because their students are undisciplined?

    2. Do teachers leave the profession early because they perceive their students to be uninterested in learning?

    3. Do teachers leave the profession early because they feel that students threaten their safety?

D. Do teachers leave the profession early because of the attitudes and behaviors of their peers and supervisors?

    1. Do teachers leave the profession early because of unacceptable attitudes of their fellow teachers?

    2. Do teachers leave the profession early because of unacceptable behaviors of their fellow teachers?

        3. Do teachers leave the profession early because of unacceptable attitudes of their principals or other supervisors?

        4. Do teachers leave the profession early because of unacceptable behaviors of their principals or other supervisors?

    E. Do teachers leave the profession early because of the types of activities their jobs demand?

        1. Do teachers leave the profession early because their jobs require excessive custodial work?

        2. Do teachers leave the profession early because their jobs require excessive paper work?

III. Does the perceived social status of teaching cause teachers to leave the profession early?

    A. Do teachers leave the profession early because they perceive teaching to be a low-status occupation?

        1. Do teachers leave the profession early because they regard teaching as a powerless occupation?

        2. Do teachers leave the profession early because they feel socially stigmatized?

    B. Do teachers leave the profession early because they think others view teaching as a low-status occupation?

        1. Do teachers leave the profession early because they feel that society regards them as powerless?

        2. Do teachers leave the profession early because they feel that society does not consider them to be professionals?

Notice that this hierarchical set of research questions helps to identify large categories of issues, and then to suggest increasingly specific issues within those categories. At the third, most specific level within this illustration, the research questions practically define the content of a questionnaire or interview protocol. With a well-structured set of research questions as a guide, it is easy to determine whether or not a proposed questionnaire item is essential to the purposes of a survey. Since a wealth of experience and dozens of research studies have shown that participation in a survey depends directly on the length of the survey's questionnaire or interview protocol (the shorter the better), it is essential to eliminate all superfluous questions.

Identification of the Target Population

The *target population* of a survey is the group of persons, objects, or institutions that defines the object of the investigation. An essential requirement of survey research is the explicit, unequivocal definition of the target population. In fact, the target population must be defined so well that it is possible to state with certainty whether any given person, object, or institution is or is not a member of that population.

In an earlier example the target population was defined as all public school teachers in a given state. Is this definition "explicit and unequivocal?" You might think so at first, but the boundaries of the population are actually quite fuzzy. What is to be done with administrative personnel, such as principals and assistant principals, who hold valid teaching certificates and teach one course per day? What about substitute teachers who are not regularly employed at a given school? Are part-time teachers to be included? And what about school psychologists and guidance counselors who teach part of the day and provide psychological services or counseling during most of their work time? Are student teachers who happen to be in the schools at the time the survey is conducted to be treated as public school teachers? If these questions are not addressed unequivocally, practices are sure to vary across the schools used to collect data. In some schools administrative personnel will be included in the sample of respondents and in others they will be omitted. The result will be a sample that does not accurately represent any definable population, including the target population. When survey data are analyzed, statements about the target population will not be trustworthy.

In many survey research studies, explicit definition of the target population is difficult. In the example cited above, there might be sound arguments for including or excluding administrative personnel. The final decision should be based on careful consideration of the intended uses of survey results and the research issues that motivated the survey. The factors that affect teachers' decisions to leave the profession early might also apply to administrative personnel who teach part time. In that case, the researchers might want to include such personnel in their survey, as long as part-time administrators were clearly identified. Conversely, the resources available to conduct the survey might not be sufficient for collecting data from administrators as well as classroom teachers, in which case the more restrictive definition of the target population should be used. The essential point here is that *some* decision must be made so as to ensure the consistency of survey results.

Literature Review

Surveys that address previously unresearched topics are extremely rare. It is far more likely that the topic of a current survey has been investigated in several earlier studies.

A review of previous research can be very helpful in planning a new survey. The work of others can suggest modifications or additions to research questions, survey instruments, or plans for analysis of data. Building on the work of others is sound research practice. Often, it can save days of needless work spent rediscovering or reinventing appropriate solutions to common problems.

Sometimes a minor change in the wording of a questionnaire item will facilitate comparison of current findings with those of earlier studies. However, such comparisons must be made cautiously because small differences in the wording of a questionnaire item or protocol question can lead to large differences between distributions of responses. It is also the case that responses to individual questions are context-dependent. Respondents' answers to a question depend not only on the wording of that question, but also on the series of questions that preceded it. Identical questions set in different contexts can and do evoke different distributions of response. These facts must be considered when reporting differences between "now" and "then."

There are many good sources of information on past survey research studies. Professional journals in the subject matter of the survey provide an excellent place to begin. With the advent of computerized literature search services, the task of determining what research has been done on a particular topic is far less arduous than in precomputer times. The DIALOG system includes many databases in the social sciences. Both DIALOG and the ERIC system are available at most academic libraries in the United States. ERIC provides computerized listings of titles and abstracts of articles contained in about 800 professional journals, in addition to information on many thousands of papers and reports presented at professional meetings or produced by educational research organizations. It is possible to search the ERIC database for information on precisely delimited topics by specifying unique combinations of key search words. For example, words like PUBLIC SCHOOL, TEACHING, and EMPLOYMENT could be used to request a listing of studies on the employment of public school teachers. DIALOG searches can be organized in much the same way as ERIC searches. Searching the world wide web on similar key words will also yield useful information and reference sources.

Selection of a Survey Method

Three basic methods of collecting data are available to the survey researcher: mail surveys, telephone surveys, and face-to-face interviews. Selection of a data collection method is a critical decision, because all methods have specific advantages and disadvantages. An extensive review of the issues involved in choosing a data collection method can be found in most texts on survey research, such as Moser and Kalton (1972), Warwick and Lininger (1975), or Fowler (1993). We will consider only a few examples here.

Mail surveys have the distinct advantage of economy. Because transportation costs are a major expense in most face-to-face interview surveys, mail surveys are almost always less expensive. Telephone interview surveys also eliminate transportation costs, but phone calls are usually more expensive than distribution of questionnaires through the mail, particularly when the survey sample is widely dispersed. In some survey projects, budget restrictions make mail surveys the only feasible choice.

Apart from their economy, many researchers feel that mail surveys have little to recommend them. Past experience has shown that most interview surveys are far more effective in securing the cooperation of respondents than are mail surveys. Without effective procedures to increase survey participation, it is not unusual to find that half the people surveyed by mail fail to return useful questionnaires. Since one can never be sure that the views and characteristics of survey respondents are like those of people who do not respond, it is dangerous to assume that respondents form a representative sample of the target population.

Mail surveys work best when questionnaires are short and simple, and when the topic of the survey can be addressed through a few easily understood questions. Mail survey questionnaires have to be self-explanatory. Whereas an interviewer can ask for clarification if (s)he doesn't understand a respondent's answer, or if the answer is incomplete, the mail survey researcher must live with the respondent's original answer. It is also possible for a respondent to ask an interviewer to clarify a question or define an unfamiliar term. With a mail survey, respondents are on their own. A survey package sent through the mail must clearly tell respondents why they should bother to complete a questionnaire, how they should furnish their answers, what questions they are to answer, and what to do with their questionnaires once they are finished. Unless the survey population consists of a highly educated group, all of this information must be conveyed in simple, jargon-free terms. The range of topics that lend themselves to simple portrayal and communication is clearly limited. Complex issues can be examined through a mail survey only when the survey population is composed of specialists with a common background and a natural interest in the topic.

Telephone interview surveys usually are far less expensive than face-to-face interview surveys, but they have many of the advantages of face-to-face interview surveys. The opportunity to secure additional information when a respondent's answer is either unclear or off the mark is present in both types of survey. In addition, a telephone interviewer can explain the purpose of the survey, why the respondent should participate, and what information is desired. As is true in face-to-face interview surveys telephone interviews allow questions to be asked one at a time, in the order prescribed by the survey researcher. In a mail survey, the respondent can read through all questions before answering any of them, and can provide answers in any order.

The high costs of transportation often limit the methods that can be used to sample respondents in a face-to-face interview survey. For example, if respondents were widely dispersed throughout the United States, the cost of reaching them could be astronomical. Therefore, it might be necessary to adopt a sampling method that secured clusters of respondents in a few widely dispersed areas. This method of sampling is not as desirable as a scheme that allows each respondent to be selected individually. In a telephone interview survey of national scope, telephone costs are relatively constant, regardless of the geographic distribution of respondents. Thus more attractive sampling methods can be used.

Apart from their costs, face-to-face interview surveys have so many advantages that some survey researchers consider alternative methods to be totally unacceptable. The opportunity to clarify respondents' answers by asking additional questions and to provide information to respondents has already been mentioned. In addition, an interviewer who actually sees the person being interviewed can secure a good bit of information through observation. In social surveys, the type and condition of respondents' housing is often an important factor that can be assessed by looking at neighborhoods and individual dwelling units. By watching body language, an interviewer sometimes can tell whether a respondent understands the question being asked, is willing to respond, and has more to say if encouraged to do so.

Rates of cooperation in face-to-face interview surveys are usually higher than those secured through any other method. It is much easier to hang up the phone or throw a questionnaire in the trash than to refuse to talk to an interviewer who comes to one's home or place of business. A respondent's habits of observing the social conventions of politeness and cooperation are more likely to be followed in face-to-face encounters than in a telephone call or in responding to an unexpected piece of mail.

A distinct advantage of face-to-face interview surveys is the opportunity to identify each person who provides information. In a survey conducted through the mail, it is impossible to tell who completed the questionnaires. For example, a set of questionnaires sent to school principals might well be completed by secretaries, assistant principals, or other school personnel. Even in a telephone interview survey, one cannot be certain that the desired respondents are the persons being interviewed.

All of these factors, in addition to others, must be carefully weighed when a survey method is selected. If the survey budget is tight, questionnaires sent through the mail might be the only feasible method of research. If responses from members of the general population are desired and the research topic is complex or sensitive, a mail survey might be totally inadequate. In such cases, reanalysis of data collected in earlier research studies might be far more informative than gathering new data through a survey.

Securing a Sampling Frame

In order to select a sample of persons, objects, or institutions, one must have a list from which to sample. Such a list is called a *sampling frame*. Sampling frames are critically important in survey research because they define the *operational population* of a survey. A target population specifies the desires of a survey researcher, but a sampling frame defines reality. Let's consider an example.

A survey researcher might specify as a target population all fourth-grade teachers in Los Angeles, California, whether employed full time or part time. To avoid ambiguity, the researcher might define a fourth-grade teacher as anyone who teaches at least one fourth-grader or any child who would, by virtue of age, be in a fourth-grade classroom if (s)he attended a graded school. In most cities, finding a sampling frame that matched this operational definition of a target population would be difficult, or impossible. Although public school systems in most cities could provide a list of all of their teachers with fourth-grade classes, securing a list of fourth-grade teachers in nonpublic schools would probably be very difficult. In a city the size of Los Angeles, there are hundreds of nonpublic schools that are virtually independent. Although public school authorities might have a list of these schools, they would not be likely to have a list of the schools' teachers. In addition, the researcher's operational definition of a fourth-grade teacher would include independent music teachers, art teachers, and dance teachers, plus teachers in weekend religious schools. Since it would be very difficult to assemble a sampling frame that matched the researcher's target population, some compromises would have to be made. The easiest solution would be to redefine the target population as all public school fourth-grade teachers in Los

Angeles. If this was not acceptable, restriction of the target population to fourth-grade teachers affiliated with public and nonpublic day schools in Los Angeles would increase the possibility of assembling a useful sampling frame.

The form in which sampling frames are available is also a major consideration in survey research. A very large list on paper is not nearly as convenient as a list in some computer-readable form, such as a diskette or a magnetic tape. If a computer-readable sampling frame were available, the computer could be used to sample from the list in ways that might be infeasible if a list on paper had to be sampled by hand.

Sometimes the unavailability of an appropriate sampling frame severely limits the kind of sampling methods that can be used. If a researcher wanted to select a sample of sixth-grade students from the entire state of California, no single agency could provide the necessary sampling frame. Since there are over 1,000 school systems in California, assembling lists of sixth-graders from all school systems in the state would be very time consuming and expensive. In fact, the costs would likely be prohibitive. If a different sampling approach were to be used, a sampling frame of California's sixth-graders might not be needed. The State Department of Education in California has a list of all public schools in the state that enroll sixth-grade students. This list could be used to sample schools from throughout the state, and then sixth-grade students could be selected only from sampled schools. Sampling frames of sixth-grade students would still have to be secured from sampled schools, but this would be far less costly than building a list of sixth-graders for the entire state. This sampling method is called *two-stage cluster sampling*. It might require selection of more students than would sampling from a statewide list of California's sixth-graders, but avoiding the costs and time required to assemble one huge sampling frame would be well worth the added data collection burden.

Construct Survey Instruments

All of the careful planning that underlies the development of an effective survey can go for nought if the questions asked—whether in an interview or on a questionnaire that is sent through the mail—are not clear, unambiguous, and appropriate to the survey researcher's purpose. In terms of clarity, the ideal survey question is one that will be interpreted in precisely the same way by every survey respondent. You don't want every respondent to give you the same answer, but you do want every respondent to hear or read the same question.

Although there is no science of question writing, survey developers can take advantage of a well-developed and well-tested art in order to move much closer to the ideal of totally unambiguous and readily understood questions. Excellent suggestions on writing questions and constructing survey instruments can be found in a number of books devoted to the topic in whole or in part, including Babble (1973), Berdie and Anderson (1974), Converse and Presser (1986), Foddy (1993), Moser and Kalton (1972), and Warwick and Lininger (1975). In this brief introduction, only a few principles will be illustrated.

Every survey researcher is faced with the dilemma of what questions to include. Usually the temptation is to ask many questions, since having more information is more appealing than having less. Asking for more than is absolutely needed does have its costs. It is a well-established fact that potential respondents are less willing to participate in a long survey than a short one, whether by interview or by mail. Including questions that aren't essential might cost far more than the extra dollars needed to process the information. To keep your survey free of unnecessary questionnaire items, it is helpful to use the sort of detailed research questions that were illustrated earlier. If an interview question or questionnaire item does not address one or more of the research questions, it should not be asked.

No set of rules will guarantee that your questionnaire items or interview questions will be clear and unambiguous, but several are likely to help. When writing a survey instrument, the people who are to respond to your survey should be kept clearly in mind. If you are surveying the general population, remember that many respondents will have far less education than you do. Keep the vocabulary level of your questions as low as possible, without being insulting. Avoid specialized jargon that is likely to be misunderstood by members of the general population. It is often difficult to remember that the "educationese" used by education professionals (e.g., "tracking," "learning readiness," "achievement motivation," etc.) is a foreign language to many members of the general population. Unless you are preparing a survey for members of the education profession, avoid such terms whenever possible. When there is no alternative to using specialized terms, make sure that they are defined on the survey instrument.

Many authors distinguish between different categories of questions in their guides to survey instrument development. One way of categorizing questions is in terms of the type of information they seek—asking for facts versus asking for opinions or judgments. Questions can also be classified in terms of their format—whether they ask a respondent to construct an answer (an open-ended question such as "How many motion picture films did you see during the last year?"), or to select an answer (a *closed-option* question such as "Did you see any motion pictures last year? ___Yes ___No ___I don't know"). Guides to writing often differ across categories of questions. For example, when writing closed-option questions, one must be certain that all possible answer choices are provided, often including an answer labeled "Other, please specify _____." Use of an answer category that permits a respondent to admit ignorance (e.g., "I don't know") is far better than collecting data that are based on ignorance or, in the case of opinion questions, lack of thought.

When asking questions that require respondents to recall events or other information, it is often helpful to provide reference points or prompts. For example, in a health survey you might want to ask each respondent when they last visited a physician. You might instruct your interviewers to help their respondents recall by asking, "Was it before Christmas or after Christmas?" or "Did you visit a physician the last time you were feeling ill? When was that?" When writing a questionnaire item in which you wanted to know what television programs were watched the previous evening, it would make perfect sense to stimulate recall by listing all of the possibilities, and asking respondents to check those they watched. Resulting data would likely be far more accurate than would responses to the item: "List all television programs you watched last night" with no aids to recall. Listing alterative answers and having respondents choose those that are correct is fine, provided all of the possibilities have been listed. The same rule applies when prompts are given. Listing some possibilities and leaving others out is almost certain to bias the answers you will get. If any possibilities are listed make sure they are exhaustive.

The art of writing questions and developing survey instruments has barely been introduced in this brief section. Perhaps these few illustrations will provide some hints on points to consider when you are judging the quality of a survey instrument, and will inspire you to read some of the suggested references before you construct your own instruments.

Define a Sampling Plan

Since the data collection costs of a survey are likely to be *the* major budget item, anything that reduces the amount of data required, without affecting the quality of the resulting information, should be considered seriously. Choosing the best possible sampling method is one important way of increasing the efficiency of a survey, thus reducing costs without sacrificing quality or precision.

How much difference can selection of the right sampling procedure make? In one example involving estimation of the average achievement of the 1,200 sixth-grade students in a medium-sized school system, Jaeger (1984) compared the sample sizes that would be required by 17 different sampling and estimation procedures. The most efficient procedure (stratified random sampling with optimal allocation) required testing only 25 students, and the least efficient procedure (single-stage cluster sampling with unbiased estimation) required testing 1,041 students. Thus the least efficient sampling and estimation procedure required testing more than 41 times the number of students needed by the most efficient procedure! Such dramatic differences won't be found in every survey application, but differences between the sample sizes required by the most efficient and the least efficient sampling procedures available will usually be noticeable.

An extensive discussion of alternative sampling and estimation procedures is beyond the scope of this introductory chapter, but a few of the possibilities will be mentioned. *Simple random sampling* is the most fundamental *probability sampling procedure.* Two principles define simple random sampling: First, every element in the population has the same chance of being sampled. Second, selection of any one element has no influence on the chance that any other element is selected. There is an inherent fairness in the principles that define simple random sampling, since in a population of persons, everyone would have the same chance of being chosen (either initially or after some selections had been made) regardless of who had been chosen already. Simple random sampling is often used as a benchmark when the efficiencies of other sampling procedures are investigated. Some alterative sampling methods have been found to be more efficient than simple random sampling (in the sense that they require the collection of less data to obtain equivalent estimation precision), and others have been found to be less efficient.

One class of sampling methods that is often more efficient than simple random sampling is termed *stratified sampling*. When stratified sampling is used, the population to be sampled is divided into parts (called *subpopulations* or *strata*), and independent samples are selected from each part (called a stratum). The parameter of interest is estimated separately for each stratum, and these estimates are then combined through a weighted averaging procedure. For example, suppose you wanted to know the average height of the 12-year-old children who were enrolled in a particular school, and you didn't want to measure all of them. You could select a sample of the 12-year-olds, and estimate the average height of the population by using the average height of the children in your sample. One way of selecting a sample would be to number all of the 12-year-old children in the population, and then use a table of random numbers (e.g., Rand Corp., 1969) to select the children to be measured. A table of random numbers contains the same proportion of each of the digits 0, 1, 2, 3, 4, 5, 6, 7, 8, and 9, and the arrangement of the digits is totally random (so each digit follows every other digit equally often). Using a table of random numbers ensures that each of the numbered elements in a sampling frame has the same chance of being selected. In our problem, by using a random number table, each of the children in the population would have the same chance of being sampled, and whether or not one child was chosen would not depend at all on whether any other child was chosen. So use of a random number table would meet the requirements of simple random sampling. But suppose you wanted to sample more efficiently. Instead of selecting a simple random sample of 12-year-olds, you could divide your population into a stratum (subpopulation) of boys and a stratum of girls. Since girls typically reach puberty (and therefore have a growth spurt) before boys do, it would not be unusual to find that the stratum of 12-year-old girls had a larger average height than did the stratum of 12-year-old boys. In any case, you would expect the boys and girls to differ noticeably in average height. Since this is the case, if you wanted to estimate the average height of all 12-year-olds regardless of gender, wouldn't it seem sensible to make sure that your sample was balanced in its representation of girls and boys? You could accomplish this through stratified sampling. Once you had divided the population into a stratum of boys and a stratum of girls, you could use a random number table to select a simple random sample from each stratum. You could then estimate the average height of the stratum of girls and the average height of the stratum of boys, using the data from your two simple random samples. The average height of all 12-year-olds would be found by using a formula that appropriately combined the figures for boys and for girls.

Because stratified sampling would ensure that you couldn't select samples that consisted of all boys (who would, on average, be shorter than the population average), or all girls (who would, on average, be taller than the population average), it would eliminate many samples that would do a bad job of estimating the average height of the entire population. This is why stratified sampling is likely to be more efficient than simple random sampling.

In discussing the development of sampling frames, it was noted that the opportunity to use some sampling methods depends on the types of sampling frames that are available. In many survey applications, it is not possible to obtain or construct a sampling frame of the individuals that are of interest; a sampling frame consisting of groups of individuals must be used. An example of this situation, a survey in which estimates were desired for the entire population of sixth-grade students in the public schools of California, was described earlier. In that case, it was suggested that schools with sixth-grade classes be sampled first, followed by selection of sixth-grade students from each of the sampled schools. Since the California State Department of Education has a list of all public schools in the state with sixth-grade classes, an available sampling frame could be used. This type of sampling procedure is known as *cluster sampling*. The schools with sixth-graders are clusters which would provide the groups of sixth-grade students for sampling and measurement. If, when a school was sampled, all sixth-graders in that school were observed or measured, the procedure would be called *single-stage cluster sampling*. If a sample of sixth-graders was selected from each sampled school, the procedure would be called *two-stage cluster sampling*. At the first stage, schools would be sampled, and at the second, sixth-grade students would be sampled.

Depending on how the clusters are chosen and what type of analysis is applied to the data that are collected, the efficiency of cluster sampling can range from very low to very high. Or to put it another way, if you wanted to estimate a population parameter with a given level of precision (e.g., estimate the average height of 12-year-olds to the nearest half inch), you might have to collect much more data, or much less data, using cluster sampling than you would need using simple random sampling. Several of the sampling books in the bibliography at the end of this chapter contain a more detailed discussion of this point.

In summary, when selecting a sampling method, you should choose one that (a) is easy to apply and (b) lets you estimate the parameters you are interested in as precisely as you want, with the smallest possible sample size. Choosing well can make a big difference in the overall cost of your survey.

Designing Field Procedures

The mechanics of collecting data constitute an important part of an effective survey and are termed *field procedures*. In a mail survey, field procedures include mailout of questionnaires, construction and maintenance of records on the distribution of questionnaires, construction and maintenance of records on the receipt of completed questionnaires, and procedures for making repeated requests to people who have not returned completed questionnaires (called *follow-up procedures*). In an interview survey, field procedures include recruitment, training, deployment, and supervision of interviewers, distribution of survey instruments and a schedule of interviews to interviewers, collection of completed survey instruments from interviewers, and rules for making repeated calls on potential respondents who were not available at the time initial calls were made.

If field procedures are not well defined, the quality of a survey will suffer and, in many cases, survey quality cannot be assessed. For example, without a complete list of persons to whom mail survey instruments have been sent, it is not possible to determine the types and proportions of persons who have and have not responded. As a second example, if no rules had been formulated for making repeated calls on potential respondents who were not at home at the time of initial attempts, interviewers would make up their own rules. Since the rules would vary greatly, depending on the tenacity of each interviewer, it would be unlikely that each interviewer would collect data from a comparable sample of respondents. If more tenacious interviewers were assigned to high-income areas while those less apt to make repeated call-backs were assigned to low-income areas, survey results could be biased.

Reduction and Editing of Data

When survey data are collected on questionnaires or through interviews, they are not typically in a form that permits immediate analysis, either by hand or by using a computer. In addition, some of the data collected are inevitably faulty. Some questionnaires or interview protocols are always incomplete. Responses to some questions are usually contradictory or impossible or highly unlikely (e.g., respondents report that they have 25 children or that they were born in 1855).

Prior to analyzing survey data, they must be placed in a form that permits their summarization and interpretation. Since surveys frequently yield large amounts of data, most analyses are conducted with the aid of a computer. In these cases, the data must be available in a form that a computer can process in a fixed, uniform format, either on magnetic tape, magnetic disk, or CD-ROM.

The process of transforming data to an analyzable form is called *data reduction*. Data reduction is sometimes a manual process (such as having a clerk read each interview protocol, code the responses into numerical values, and then enter the resulting data in a magnetic disk file by using a computer terminal) and sometimes an automated process (such as using an optical mark sense reader to scan specially prepared mail survey questionnaires. The scanner reads sets of circles or boxes that have been darkened with a number-two pencil, just as an automatic test scoring machine does.) If respondents have provided narrative responses to questions, these must be read by hand and transformed into numerical codes prior to entering the data into a computer file. Although the coding process often can be completed by a clerk, defining the rules for coding is a difficult task that requires the judgment of a professional survey researcher. It is necessary to establish a set of detailed decision rules that will unequivocally accommodate every possible response to every survey question. Each response must fit into one (and only one) category, usually including "miscellaneous" and "does not apply" categories. Collectively, the categories must be exhaustive and must not overlap.

Once data have been reduced to an analyzable form, they must be edited so as to detect and resolve the inevitable errors. A scheme for handling missing data must be developed. Sometimes a respondent who does not provide complete data is eliminated from the data set. In other editing plans, a respondent is not included in analyses involving a variable for which (s)he has not provided data, but is included in all other analyses. Another possibility is to replace missing data with the average of values provided by all other respondents. Certain advantages are associated with each procedure, and deciding which to use requires considerable thought.

Other editing tasks include checking to see whether the responses to any question are impossible or very unlikely. For example, responses to a question on age (in years) would probably be eliminated or checked against other data if they were, in the case of a survey of adults, less than 18 or more than 100. Regardless of the age group sampled, reported ages that were negative would be flagged for review. Erroneous data sometimes are reported by respondents who complete questionnaires, or by interviewers who fill out protocols. In other cases, the reported data are correct but coding clerks have made an error when they entered the data in a computer file. In all of these situations, faulty data must be eliminated prior to aggregation and analysis of survey results in order to avoid the contamination of accurate data.

Although most editing of survey data takes place after the data have been reduced and placed into a computer file, some preliminary editing might be done when the data are in their "raw" form, either on questionnaires or interview protocols. Responses to questions that are particularly critical might be verified for completeness and appropriateness as soon as survey documents are received, so that additional inquiries can be made if necessary.

Regardless of the form and extensiveness of data reduction and editing, these procedures must be planned in detail at the time a survey is designed.

Plans for Analysis of Data

Although it is unlikely that all desirable data analyses can be specified prior to collecting survey data, it is advantageous to specify a set of proposed analyses in great detail. The principal benefit of such detailed plans is their usefulness in determining whether the data to be collected will provide answers to the research questions developed as part of the survey plan.

By preparing a document that links each item on the survey instruments to one or more research questions and one or more proposed analyses, a survey researcher can ensure that the data to be collected are, in fact, needed to answer the proposed research questions. In addition, the linking document can be used to determine that every proposed data analysis is needed to answer a research question and that all of the research questions can be answered using the data to be collected.

Although the statistical procedures used to analyze survey data are becoming increasingly sophisticated, many survey analyses require only the construction of simple tables and graphs. Cross-tabulation, a procedure in which a researcher computes the numbers and percents of cases that simultaneously fall into various categories of two or more variables, is used extensively. Table 1 is an example of a cross-tabulation. This table shows the number and percent of a sample of graduate students who are simultaneously (a) enrolled in various graduate degree programs and (b) currently enrolled in various research methodology courses. The percentages shown in Table 1 are called *row percents*. They represent the percentages of students enrolled in a particular degree program who are currently enrolled in a specified research methodology course. It is also possible to compute the percentage of students enrolled in a particular research methodology course (e.g., a statistics course) who are also enrolled in each degree program. These percents would be called *column percents*. For example, since 100 of the 305 students enrolled in statistics courses are also enrolled in an education program, the column percent for the Education/Statistics cell of the table would be 33. Finally, it is possible to compute *cell percents* for a cross-tabulation. A cell percent is the percent of the total sample that falls into a particular cell (row and column combination) of the table. As an example, 100 of the 500 students in the sample are enrolled in an education program and are currently enrolled in a statistics course. Since 100 is 20 percent of the 500 students in the sample, the cell percent in the upper left-hand cell would be 20.

Although cross-tabulations cannot be completed until survey data have been collected, it is possible to define the form of the cross-tabulations that will be used. Tables that have titles, row headings, and column headings—everything but the data—are called *table shells*. Constructing a complete set of proposed table titles, together with representative table shells, is a useful way to construct a plan for analysis of survey data.

Plan for Reporting Survey Results

A plan for reporting the results of a survey might be considered a final piece of insurance on the consistency of survey objectives and survey outcomes. Both the detailed set of research questions and the plans for analysis of data, described earlier, can be used to plan the reports that are to be prepared from survey results. Major research questions can be used to define the chapters of a report, and corresponding table shells can be used to organize the material in the chapters.

TABLE 1. *Number and percent of graduate students, by degree program and type of research methodology course*

| Degree program | Research Methodology Course | | | | | | Total |
| | Statistics | | Ethnography | | Historiography | | |
	n	%	n	%	n	%	
Education	100	50	50	25	50	25	200
Sociology	25	25	50	50	25	25	100
Psychology	180	90	20	10	0	0	200
Total	305	61	120	25	75	15	500

In addition to outlining survey reports, a plan for reporting should describe the intended audiences for the reports, and the methods to be used for distributing the reports.

Pilot Survey

A pilot survey is an essential part of any survey research study. Even expert survey researchers cannot predict accurately the effectiveness of survey instruments, plans for distribution and receipt of survey materials, the proportion of a target sample that will participate in a survey, and the time necessary to complete the survey. A pilot survey is used to collect data on all of these points, and more.

Ideally, a pilot survey is the main survey in miniature. To provide required data on the likely success of the main survey, a pilot survey must be planned in detail. The plan should include most of the elements of the main survey, in addition to elements needed to determine the likely pitfalls of the main survey.

Among other things, respondents to a pilot survey are asked whether the questions proposed for the main survey are clear and understandable, whether the instructions for completing survey instruments and providing data are free of ambiguities, and how long it took them to complete the main survey's instruments. An additional questionnaire or interview protocol will have to be developed to secure these essential data.

You might think of a pilot survey as a "dress rehearsal" for the real thing. As a part of that dress rehearsal, the producer, director, and all of the actors and stage hands are responsible for noting exactly what went on, the time needed to run through each act, what worked, what didn't, and why.

Data from a pilot survey are analyzed, just as in the main survey, but with the purpose of determining what must be changed and what can remain as planned.

Revision and Implementation

Components of the main survey, such as instructions, instruments, field procedures, and budget, are revised in accordance with the data provided by the pilot survey. Just like the bones in a skeleton, all of the elements of a survey are connected. If you change one element, everything else must be changed as well. For example, if a questionnaire or interview protocol is revised, it is no longer clear that all of the previously posed research questions will be answerable. And some of the table shells that make up a plan for analysis will surely have to be changed. So modification of survey materials following a pilot survey must include careful attention to the consistency of all survey parts.

Following revision, the plan for the main survey is put into action, and it is at this point that the many benefits of detailed planning become apparent. It would be misleading, however, to suggest that the main survey will be conducted in complete accordance with the plan. More likely, response rates observed for the main survey will differ somewhat from those predicted from the pilot survey. Even the best planning will not allow you to anticipate every problem that will arise when questionnaires are sent through the mail or interviewers are sent into the field. And the presence of real data in the table shells you so carefully developed will undoubtedly suggest new analyses that can shed light on a variety of research questions, some of which were not anticipated when the survey was planned.

But careful planning is the key to sound survey practice. Specifying *why* you want data, *how* you'll collect it, and *what you'll do with it* once you have it, will go a long way toward ensuring the usefulness of the data you collect and avoiding the disappointment of not satisfying your real research needs.

The Role of Generalization

Generalization of findings is central to all research but is the very essence of survey research. In survey research, one asks a relatively small number of people to answer a relatively small number of questions and, on the basis of the answers given, draws conclusions about the conditions, attitudes, opinions, or status of a population of persons, objects, institutions, governments, or other entities.

Generalizing from the data collected to the conclusions drawn is an act of faith that can be supported by logic, theory, and sound survey practice. Such generalization can be better understood by considering its component parts, and the assumptions that it demands.

Generalization in survey research is partly statistical and partly substantive. We will discuss *statistical generalization* first. Consider a simple, but fictitious, example. Suppose that you were an inveterate coin flipper, and had a burning desire to know what proportion of the pennies held by a local bank on a particular day would land "heads," were you to flip each coin once. The pennies held by the bank on that day constitute a population, and the proportion that would land heads is an example of a *population parameter*. You could *calculate* the value of the population parameter if you were willing to work into the night, giving each of the bank's pennies a healthy flip, recording the face that appeared when it landed, and then counting the number of heads that appeared and the number of flips that you made. An alternative that was less physically demanding (and also less demanding of time) would be to select a sample of pennies from the bank's holdings on the day that was of interest, flip each penny in the sample one time, record the number of heads that appeared in those flips, and divide that value by the number of sampled coins. The resulting sample proportion could be used as an *estimate* of what would have been found, if each of the bank's pennies had been flipped.

Now if you took the more sensible and less demanding route to discovering the propensity of the bank's pennies to land heads up, you would have no assurance that the proportion of heads you observed in your sample of flipped pennies would equal the proportion you would have found, had you flipped every penny in the population. Thus the validity of a generalization from the sample of pennies actually flipped to the population of pennies held by the bank on a particular day would be open to question.

Two kinds of statistical error—bias error and random error—threaten the validity of generalizations from a sample statistic to a population parameter. *Bias error* is a form of systematic error, which means that it is predictable. It occurs when the observed sample does not represent the target population. In the penny-flipping example, bias error could occur if the sample of pennies selected for flipping tended to be different from the pennies in the rest of the population in a way that would affect the proportion of heads or tails that appeared when the pennies were flipped. For example, if the sampled pennies tended to be slightly larger in diameter on the side with a tail, that heavier side would probably tend to fall to the bottom, and more heads would appear when the pennies were flipped. In realistic surveys, bias error can arise in many ways. Although pennies cannot refuse to be flipped, people can refuse to be interviewed or to complete questionnaires. Since the people who respond to surveys are very likely to differ from those who refuse or those who cannot be located, high rates of nonresponse can lead to substantial bias error.

Another frequent cause of bias error in surveys is inappropriate or inadequate sampling. Inappropriate sampling occurs when the sampling procedure is flawed by design. The need to use a probability sampling procedure that affords every member of a population the opportunity to enter the sample has already been discussed. Sampling procedures that systematically exclude some members of the target population inevitably lead to bias error. Examples of such procedures include distribution of questionnaires on the quality of education at a meeting of a school's parent-teacher association, when the target population is all parents of students enrolled in the school; and selection of students from elementary schools that are located closest to a district's central office, when the target population is all elementary school students in the district.

Inadequate sampling can occur with the best of sampling designs if the survey is not conducted in accordance with the design. For example, even though potential respondents to an interview survey were selected through simple random sampling, interviewers could fail to secure responses from a large proportion of persons whose jobs required frequent travel or nonstandard working times. Facts about such persons, or their opinions, might well differ systematically from those of respondents who were more accessible.

The second threat to statistical generalization of survey results is *random error*. Random error is inevitable in surveys, but its magnitude can almost always be controlled. Random error occurs because samples are used, and because respondents differ. Therefore the results obtained from one sample almost always differ from those that would have been obtained from another. With most sampling designs, random error can be reduced by taking a larger sample. When samples are large enough, most sample estimates will be fairly close to their corresponding population parameter and statistical generalization will not be threatened by random error. When samples are too small, many sample estimates will differ substantially from their corresponding population parameter, and generalization will be risky.

Valid *substantive generalization* of survey results depends on the satisfaction of a number of assumptions. These assumptions are shown in Figure 1, together with those that must be satisfied to obtain valid statistical generalization.

Construct validity of the survey questions is the first assumption listed under substantive generalization. Construct validity is a complex concept, and this discussion will barely introduce it. To really learn about construct validity, you

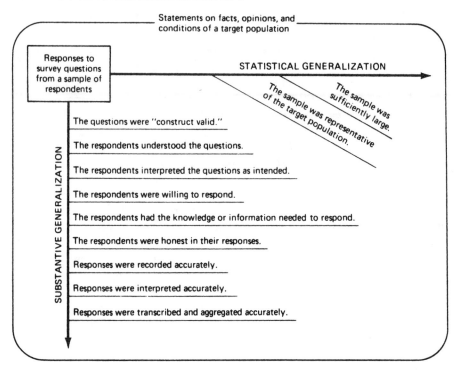

FIGURE 1. *Statistical generalization and substantive generalization in survey research.* *Source:* Jaeger (1984). Reprinted by permission.

should read Cronbach and Meehl (1955) and Cronbach (1971). A *construct* can be described as a "constructed variable" that is unobservable. It is a label that is attached to a consistent set of observable behaviors, People are often described in terms of constructs even though constructs cannot be observed. For example, a recent nationwide survey concluded that teachers have a negative attitude toward their jobs. Unlike the teachers' heights, there is no single yardstick the survey researchers could have used to measure teachers' attitudes. Instead, teachers were asked to respond to a set of 20 statements by selecting options ranging from "Strongly Disagree" to "Strongly Agree." The statements included "If I had the opportunity to start my career again, I would choose to be a teacher;" and "I would recommend that today's college students choose teaching as a career." In drawing their conclusions, the researchers who reported the results of this survey generalized *from* teachers' responses to specific statements to teachers' positions on the construct "job attitude." In doing so, the researchers assumed that the survey questions they asked measured teachers' attitudes appropriately and adequately, and that the questions were consistent with a body of theory that defines the "job attitude" construct.

The researchers scored teachers' responses to each question from 1 to 5, using 1 for "Strongly Disagree," 3 for "Neither Agree nor Disagree," and 5 for "Strongly Agree." They then summed teachers' scores for the 20 questions to produce an overall score that could range from 20 to 100. The issue of construct validity arises when the researchers define the overall score resulting from this process as a measure of "job attitude" and assume that a higher score represents a more positive job attitude than does a lower score. The validity of this form of substantive generalization can never be "proven," but it must be supported through a careful and extensive set of empirical procedures that are based on a theory that includes job attitude. One type of evidence would show that summed scores on the 20 questions were positively correlated with measures of variables that were expected to be positively related to teachers' job attitudes; e.g., the extent of teachers' voluntary participation in their schools' extracurricular activities. Another type of evidence would show that the average summed score on the 20 questions was higher for teachers who, theoretically, would be expected to have more positive job attitudes than for teachers who, theoretically, would be expected to have less positive job attitudes; e.g., teachers in affluent school systems, compared to teachers in very poor school systems.

Two more assumptions underlying valid substantive generalization are (a) that respondents understood the questions that were asked in the survey, and (b) that the respondents' interpretations of the questions were consistent with those intended by the survey researchers. The act of responding, particularly to closed-option questions, is not a guarantee of understanding. In addition, level of understanding is a critical issue. To assure appropriate substantive generalization of survey results, respondents must have understood the questions posed in the survey, and they must have interpreted those questions just as the survey researchers intended. Even questions that seem unambiguous, such as "Where do you live?" admit such diverse, but plausible, responses as "In the South," "100 Main Street," or "In an apartment." These answers clearly indicate that the respondents were answering what were, to them, three different questions. Aggregations of responses such as these will not support interpretable generalizations.

In addition to understanding what was asked, survey respondents must be willing and able to answer the questions posed to them. For the most part, respondents' willingness can be assessed through their overt cooperation, although specific survey questions (perhaps on highly personal or controversial issues) might tax the willingness of generally cooperative respondents. Ability to respond is not so easily assessed, and is certainly not guaranteed just by obtaining answers to the questions that are asked. Having the ability to respond to a question presumes that respondents know the answer or have the information needed to respond available to them. In face-to-face interview surveys, being confronted with an interviewer who expects an answer provides strong motivation to provide an answer, regardless of ability. And in mail surveys that use closed-option questions, it is easy to select an option without any pertinent knowledge or information.

The issue of ability to respond arises not just with "knowledge" questions, but with "opinion" questions as well. Many opinion questions evoke complex feelings that might not be well understood by respondents. Others stimulate conditional responses that might not fit the format of mailed questionnaires or structured interviews. For example, if asked "Do you favor abortion on demand?", a mailed questionnaire with the options "Yes" "No" and "Don't know" might not allow you to express your true opinion. You might favor abortion on demand under some circumstances, but not others. So the format used to pose survey questions and to record responses might limit the accuracy of your response, and thereby threaten valid generalization of findings.

The dependence of substantive generalization on honesty of response is so transparently obvious that further discussion of the point is unnecessary. Even a small proportion of dishonest responses will poison the well of honest ones to an unknown degree and, in doing so, will distort the meaning of aggregated survey results.

Several seemingly mechanical steps in the survey process can, if handed carelessly, undermine the validity of findings. Any systematic errors in recording responses, or in transcribing and analyzing resulting data, can threaten the generalizability of findings. Occasional errors in recording responses, either on the part of respondents who complete a mailed questionnaire, or on the part of interviewers who record respondents' answers on a protocol, will add to random error but not bias error. This statement presumes that such errors are not systematic in nature. As an example of a *systematic error*, interviewers might fail to use a "No opinion" option in recording answers to opinion questions.

When surveys incorporate open-ended questions, respondents' answers must be interpreted before they are converted to numerically codable data. Valid generalization requires that such interpretations be correct; i.e., that they be consistent with the meanings intended by the respondents.

The list of requirements for valid statistical and substantive generalization of survey results portrayed in Figure 1 is extensive, and might appear impossible to achieve. In reality, perfection is unlikely to be realized in any survey. But sound planning followed by careful application of plans can materially increase the validity of generalizations. Rather than viewing the list in Figure 1 as an insurmountable hurdle, you might consider using it as a framework for survey evaluation. That is the topic of the next section of this chapter.

A Short Checklist for Survey Evaluation

So far this chapter has provided a step-by-step guide to conducting surveys and a brief treatise on generalization of survey results. This section contains a short checklist that will help you distinguish between a good survey and a poor one. By using the checklist to review a report of survey procedures and findings, you should be able to answer the essential question, "Should I believe the results?"

Of course you will not find that surveys fall into two clearly distinguishable categories labeled "good" and "bad." Some will be exemplars of good practice in their sampling design or instruments, and then fall short in their field procedures. Others will suffer from basic design flaws but show careful application of that design. Still others will be poorly conceptualized and thereby flawed from the outset; no amount of care in operational planning and implementation will compensate for inadequate or inappropriate specification of research questions. The difficult part of survey evaluation is determining the likely effect of a design or implementation flaw on the validity of survey results. Your evaluation skills will develop as you gain greater experience. In the meantime, be a skeptic and a doubter. Here is a set of evaluative questions you can use to focus your inquiry:

1. Does the report contain a list of specific research questions or issues the survey is intended to address?

2. Do the research questions posed by the investigators appropriately and adequately address the topic of the survey; e.g., in a survey on poverty in the United States, does the research include an examination of poverty as a function of race, level of education, and geographic location?

3. Are the research questions posed by the investigators well organized and well structured?

4. Does the report identify the target population to which generalization was desired?

5. Does the report describe available sampling frames?

6. Does the report indicate a close match between the target population and the operational population?

7. Does the report describe the sampling procedures used? Were probability sampling procedures used?

8. Are nonresponse rates reported for the entire survey and for individual questions?

9. Were nonresponse rates low enough to avoid substantial bias errors?

10. Are any analyses of potential sampling bias reported?

11. Are sample sizes sufficient to avoid substantial random errors? Are standard errors of estimate reported?

12. Is the primary mode of data collection (i.e., mailed questionnaires, telephone interviews, face-to-face interviews) consistent with the objectives, complexity, and operational population of the survey?

13. Are survey instruments provided in the report?

14. Are instructions for completing the survey clear and unambiguous?

15. Are questions on instruments clear and unambiguous?

16. Do questions on instruments encourage respondents' honesty in admitting lack of knowledge or uncertainty?

17. Are questions on instruments free from obvious bias, slanting, or "loading"?

18. Was the survey consistent with ethical research practice; e.g., was the anonymity and/or confidentiality of respondents protected?

19. Does the report contain a description of field procedures?

20. Are field procedures adequate and appropriate? Is it likely that major sources of bias error have been avoided?

21. Are data analyses clearly described?

22. Are data analyses appropriate to the purposes of the survey?

23. Did the survey provide answers to the research questions posed by the investigators?

24. Are the researchers' conclusions sound, or are alternative interpretations of findings equally plausible?

25. Does the survey report contain descriptions of deviations from plans for survey implementation and the likely consequences of such deviations?

26. Does the survey report contain an analysis of the quality of the survey?

Don't expect all (or even most) survey reports to measure up on every one of these points. The list of 26 questions defines an ideal that is rarely realized. If you find a survey that falls short on two, three, or even half a dozen of these questions, you might still find its results to be credible and useful. Think of the checklist as a guide to cautions and thoughtful evaluation, not as an inflexible list of essential criteria.

References

Babble, E. (1973). *Survey research methods.* Belmont, CA: Wadsworth.

Berdie, D., & Anderson, J. (1974). *Questionnaire design and use.* Metuchen, NJ: Scarecrow Press.

Converse, J. M., & Presser, S. (1986). *Survey questions: Handcrafting the standardized questionnaire.* Newbury Park, CA: Sage Publications.

Cronbach, L. (1971). Test validation. In R. L. Throndike (Ed.), *Educational measurement* (2nd ed., pp. 443–507). Washington, DC: American Council on Education.

Cronbach, L., & Meehl, P. (1955). Construct validity in psychological tests. *Psychological Bulletin, 52,* 281–302.

Fowler, F. J. (1993). *Survey research methods* (2nd ed.). Newbury Park, CA: Sage Publications.

Foddy, W. (1993). *Constructing questions for interviews and questionnaires: Theory and practice in social research.* Cambridge, UK: Cambridge University Press.

Jaeger, R. M. (1984). *Sampling in education and the social sciences.* New York: Longman, Inc.

Moser, C., & Kalton, G. (1972). *Survey methods in social investigation* (2nd ed.). New York: Basic Books.

Rand Corporation. (1969). *A million random digits with 100,000 normal deviates.* Glencoe, IL: Free Press.

Rossi, P. H., Wright, J. D., & Anderson, A. B. (1983). *Handbook of survey research.* New York: Academic Press.

Warwick, D., & Lininger, C. (1975). *The sample survey: Theory and practice.* New York: McGraw-Hill.

Suggestions for Further Reading

Since governments have counted people at least from Old Testament days, and the history of social surveys dates back to the late 1700s, the existence of a rich literature on survey methods should not be surprising. You can gain useful insights on effective survey research not only from books on methodology, but from high-quality surveys as well. In addition, substantial information about survey methods and results can now be gained through selective searches on the World Wide Web and the Internet. The following annotated list of sources should help you get started.

Sources on Method

Several books on survey method, although not up to date on such innovations as computer-assisted telephone interviewing (CATI) or random digit dialing (RDD), are old favorites because of their broad and lucid coverage of fundamental methodological issues in survey research. At the top of the list is *Survey Methods in Social Investigation* by C. A. Moser and G. Kalton (2nd. ed., New York: Basic Books, 1972). This text addresses all phases of survey research in great detail. The book's only distraction is its use of examples from Great Britain, and the incorporation of British language customs in writing constructions. But beyond these distractions, the "beef" is plentiful and well served. *The Sample Survey: Theory and Practice* by D. P. Warwick and C. A. Lininger (New York: McGraw-Hill, 1975) also provides broad coverage of survey issues and constitutes an excellent, although dated, introductory text. The authors are particularly sensitive to problems encountered when conducting cross-cultural survey research. The book was originally written in Spanish and has its origins in a survey research center in Lima, Peru.

The Dynamics of Interviewing by R. L. Kahn and C. F. Cannell (New York: Wiley, 1957) is the classic, theory-grounded work on survey interviewing. Of course it omits 40 years of more recent research on interview techniques, but many of its recommendations are quite solid nonetheless. A more recent and delimited book on interviewing is *Survey Research by Telephone* by J. H. Frey (2nd. ed., Newbury Park, CA: Sage Publications, 1993). As the title suggests, this book is focused on interviews conducted by telephone. It provides a useful introduction to computer assisted interviewing techniques and computer-generated dialing algorithms for sample selection, among its more general coverage of survey issues, ranging from instrument development to the administration of telephone interview surveys.

Several books on method focus exclusively, or nearly so, on the design of survey instruments. Among these is the short, readable text by D. Berdie and

J. Anderson, titled *Questionnaire Design and Use* (Metuchen, NJ: Scarecrow Press, 1974). This book focuses on the construction of questionnaires for surveys conducted through the mail. It contains practical strategies for increasing the clarity of individual questions, designing effective letters to introduce a mailed survey, and building the interest of potential survey respondents. All three of these issues are critical when surveys are conducted through the mail, since printed materials must stand on their own in convincing potential respondents that they should respond and in conveying instructions and questions understandably. Another text on writing survey questions, titled *Survey Questions: Handcrafting the Standardized Questionnaire* by J. M. Converse and S. Presser (Beverly Hills, CA: Sage Publications, 1986), in contrast to the Berdie and Anderson text, focuses principally on the construction of questions for face-to-face or telephone interview surveys, where follow-up questions and oral clarification are possible. Another book that complements the Converse and Presser volume is W. Foddy's *Constructing Questions for Interviews and Questionnaires: Theory and Practice in Social Research* (Cambridge, UK: Cambridge University Press, 1993). This book is comprehensive in its coverage, and offers sound advice, but, as was true of the Moser and Kalton text, it has a British flavor.

A more recent introductory text on survey method is F. J. Fowler's *Survey Research Methods* (1993, Sage Publications). This book lacks the depth of Moser and Kalton's classic text. However, it is a very readable and useful introduction to a wide variety of issues on survey method, from questionnaire design to sampling to data analysis. It is an excellent source to begin one's reading on the methodology of survey research, but should not be regarded as comprehensive and definitive.

Although not in the least introductory, two books that address specialized topics in survey method deserve mention and the attention of readers seeking research-grounded advice on selected survey research topics. Both are edited compendia of specialized chapters. The first, edited by P. Rossi, J. D. Wright, and A. B. Anderson, is titled the *Handbook of Survey Research* (New York: Academic Press, 1983). This book addresses such topics as sampling theory, the management of survey organizations, the theory of measurement and its application to surveys (called response effects), planning and management of large-scale data collection projects, and a variety of advanced procedures for analyzing survey data. The second volume, edited by J. Tanur, is provocatively titled *Questions About Questions: Inquiries into the Cognitive Bases of Surveys* (New York: Russell Sage Foundation, 1992). In contrast to the Rossi et al. book, this volume addresses the ways in which survey questions and their presentation can influence the cognitive processing of survey respondents. A critical issue in survey research is the disjuncture or congruence between the meaning intended by a survey researcher and the meaning construed by a survey respondent. This book explores this issue, among others.

At the risk of appearing self-serving, I will mention my own specialized text, Richard M. Jaeger, *Sampling in Education and the Social Sciences* (New York: Longman, 1984). As the title implies, this book addresses alternative procedures for selecting survey samples. In addition, it provides strategies for esti-mating population parameters when various sampling procedures have been used. These issues are critical in the near-universal situation when survey data are collected from a sample of respondents, and not from the entire population of potential respondents that is of interest to the survey researcher. The book presumes little prior mathematical and statistical background on the part of the reader, and is comparatively accessible, apart from the fact that it is now out of print. However, it is available in numerous academic libraries.

Reports on Important Educational and Social Surveys

One of the most effective ways to learn about a research method is to study the results of exemplary practice. A number of impressive nationwide surveys have been conducted to examine various aspects of education and its function-ing within our society. Although they are not without fault, these surveys illus-trate the application of survey practice to research on issues that are fundamen-tal to the education of youth in the United States. The surveys are uniformly massive in scale and benefited from the skills of large teams of survey specialists over a period of months, if not years. Reports on many of the surveys men-tioned here can be obtained through federal government document reposito-ries at college and university libraries throughout the United States.

Equality of Educational Opportunity. This survey is now 30 years old, but its sheer magnitude, scope, and policy impact give it a place of prominence in the history of large-scale surveys on American education. The survey was con-ducted in 1965–66 as a result of the Civil Rights Act of 1964. That Act directed the (then) Secretary of Health, Education, and Welfare to report to the Congress, no later than July 4, 1966, on the status of racial isolation in the pub-lic schools of the United States. The survey was directed very broadly at the issue of school segregation, and attempted to investigate the effects of segrega-tion on the standardized test performances and attitudes of students enrolled in the early elementary grades through the last year of high school. A massive mail survey produced data collected from school superintendents, principals, teach-ers, and students in every state. Nearly half a million students were surveyed and tested in the study.

One of the objectives of the survey was to provide separate estimates of the degree of school segregation for rural and urban populations in various regions of the nation. In addition, the quality of schooling and the effects of schooling were to be estimated and compared for members of various racial groups.

These objectives resulted in the use of a complex sampling design and esti-mation of many different parameters of a number of subpopulations. The sam-pling design involved two stages, with counties and metropolitan areas as sam-pling units in the first stage. Secondary schools were sampled within selected counties and metropolitan areas at the second stage of sampling. All elementary schools that sent a large percentage of their students to the selected secondary schools were then added to the sample. Data were collected in 1,170 schools, of which 349 were in metropolitan areas and 821 were in rural areas. Both counties and schools were stratified, so as to ensure large minority representation in the final sample.

The "Coleman Survey," as the study has come to be known with reference to its first author, has been criticized at great length and for a variety of reasons, not the last of which are a response rate of 67 to 70% and the use of analytic procedures that resulted in erroneous causal interpretations. Despite these shortcomings, the *Survey on Equality of Educational Opportunity* warrants careful study. The survey report is titled *Equality of Educational Opportunity,* and was written by J. S. Coleman, E. 0. Campbell, C. J. Hobson, J. McPartland, A. M. Mood, D. Weinfeld, and R. L. York. It is currently out of print, but can be found in the Educational Resources Information Centers archives under document number ED012 275.

National Assessment of Educational Progress (NAEP). The purpose of this continuing survey is to asses changes over time in the educational achievement of four age groups of students throughout the United States and to produce comparative statistics on these changes for four geographic regions (northeast, southeast, central, and west), a number of racial/ethnic groups, and a number of categories of size and type of community.

Achievement test exercises in 10 subject areas have been administered at regular intervals (more frequently for reading and mathematics than for other subjects) for more than 25 years to children and young adults. Originally, NAEP was administered to examinees, both in and out of school, in four age groups: 9-year-olds, 13-year-olds, 17-year-olds, and young adults (ages 26–35). In more recent years, as federal appropriations for NAEP have waxed and waned, the testing focus has shifted to grades 4, 8, and 12, and solely to students in schools.

NAEP is designed so that no examinee is required to answer every test question or to complete every exercise. This use of multiple test booklets, coupled with a design for sampling examinees, is known as "multiple matrix sampling."

The design for sampling NAEP examinees includes three stages of sampling. At the first stage, counties or groups of contiguous counties are sampled. At the second stage, both public and nonpublic schools are sampled within selected first-stage sampling units. Finally, at the third stage, samples of students are selected within each sampled school, and then test booklets within a subject area are randomly assigned to sampled students.

Since 1992, several innovations have altered the impact and interpretation of NAEP results. First, Congress authorized a Trial State Assessment that permitted states to support the expansion of NAEP samples to sizes that permit reasonably precise estimation of state-level performance on NAEP for selected subject areas. The vast majority of states have voluntarily participated in the Trial State Assessment, and, as a result, comparisons of students' performances in different states have been prominently featured in reports of NAEP results. Second, the policy board that oversees the NAEP program has developed performance standards that permit estimation and reporting of the percentages of students nationwide, and in various subpopulations, whose performances on NAEP exceed specified performance standards.

The results of NAEP testing are reported regularly in newspapers, in news broadcasts, and in news magazines. In fact, NAEP is now termed "The Nation's Report Card." An abundance of reports on NAEP results and on the technical features of NAEP can be found in government reports and in professional journals on educational measurement. A listing of available NAEP reports can be found at the Gopher computer site of the National Center for Education Statistics. The address is gopher://gopher.ed.gov:10000/00/tab/address/naep/ncesea7. This site can be reached easily through any networked computer with access to the Internet. A partial listing of federal documents containing information on NAEP methodology and results, available from the U. S. Superintendent of Documents or in any academic library with a federal documents repository, is as follows:

America's Challenge: Accelerating Academic Achievement, A Summary of Findings from 20 Years of NAEP (September 1990)

The Civics Report Card (1990)

The U.S. History Report Card (1990)

Geography Learning of High School Seniors (1990)

Learning to Read in Our Nation's Schools (1990)

Learning to Write in Our Nation's Schools (1990)

The State of Mathematics Achievement, NAEP's 1990 Assessment of the Nation and the Trial Assessment of the States (June 1991) The State of Mathematics Achievement, *Executive Summary, NAEP's 1990 Trial State Assessment of the Nation and the Trial Assessment of the States* (various reports) (June 1991)

Individual Reports on Each of the 40 States and Jurisdictions Participating in the 1990 NAEP Trial State Assessment (June 1991)

The Technical Report of NAEP's 1990 Trial State Assessment (March 1991)

NAEP Facts: The Use of Calculators and Computers in School (March 1992)

The NAEP 1990 Technical Report (February 1992)

Trends in Academic Progress: Achievement of U.S. Students in Science, 1969–70 to 1990; Mathematics, 1973–1990; Reading, 1971 to 1990; and Writing, 1984 to 1990 (September 1991)

Trends in Academic Progress: Achievement of U.S. Students in Science, 1969–70 to 1990; Mathematics, 1973–1990; Reading 1971 to 1990; and Writing, 1984 to 1990: Report and Data Summary (November 1991)

The 1990 Science Report Card: NAEP's Assessment of Fourth, Eighth, and Twelfth Graders (March 1992)

School Effects on Educational Achievement in Mathematics and Science: 1985–86 National Assessment of Educational Progress (May 1992)

Reading In and Out of School: Factors Influencing the Literacy Achievement of American Students in Grades 4, 8, and 12 in 1988 and 1990 (May 1992)

Exploring New Methods for Collecting Students' School-Based Writing: NAEP's 1990 Portfolio Study (May 1992)

Challenges to Teaching Reading and Writing: 20 minute videotape available from National Audio-Visual Center.

The NAEP Guide: A Description of the Content and Methods of the 1990 and 1992 Assessments (November 1991)

Reading Framework for the 1992 National Assessment of Educational Progress (February 1992)

Questions Raised by the 1990 NAEP Trial State Assessment Results (August 1992)

1990 NAEP Summary Report (September 1992)

Mathematics Achievement and Classroom Instructional Activities, 1990 Trial State Assessment in Math (September 1992)

Mathematics Achievement and Individual Background (September 1992)

National Assessment of College Student Learning: Issues and Concerns (July 1992)

A Preliminary Report of National Estimates from the National Assessment of Educational Progress 1992 Mathematics Assessment (January 1993)

The National Longitudinal Studies of the National Center for Education Statistics. The U. S. Department of Education's National Center for Education Statistics has conducted a series of longitudinal studies of the operation and outcomes of public education since beginning with a study of over 21,000 high school seniors sampled from 1,200 high schools in 1972. A surprisingly high percentage of those students were surveyed at regular intervals, up to the age of 34. The resulting longitudinal data will support a vast array of research studies on the academic effects of schooling, the effects of school counseling on later career choices, and so on. Detailed information on the purposes, procedures, and outcomes of the National Longitudinal Study of the High School Class of 1972 are provided by the National Center for Education Statistics (NCES) at its World Wide Web site. The NCES description follows:

Young people's success in making the transition from high school or college to the work force varies enormously for reasons only partially understood. Some cling to dependency; others move into self-determination smoothly. The National Longitudinal Study of the High School Class of 1972 (NLS-72) base year study together with the five follow-up surveys attempted to provide data to allow researchers to study how these transitions evolve.

Design

NLS-72 was designed to produce representative data at the national level on the cohort of students who were in the 12th grade in 1972. The sample for the base year NLS-72 was a stratified, two-stage probability sample of students from all schools, public and private, in the 50 states and the District of Columbia with a 12th-grade enrollment during the 1971–72 school year. A sample of schools was selected in the first stage. In the second stage, a random sample of 18 high school seniors was selected within each participating school.

Data were collected by mail, telephone, and personal interviews. In addition, the survey obtained school transcript data on high school curriculum, credit hours in major courses, grade point average, standardized test scores, and related information for each senior. To conduct intensive studies of disadvantaged students, NCES oversampled schools in low income areas and schools with significant minority enrollments.

The size of the student sample was increased during the first follow-up survey because base year nonrespondents were recontacted at that time. Those who provided base year information were retained and included in later follow-up efforts. Consequently, in 1972 there were 16,683 respondents, but in the first follow-up in 1973 the number jumped to 21,350. The number of respondents in subsequent follow-ups in 1974, 1976, 1979, and 1986 were 20,872; 20,092; 18,630; and 12,841 respectively (only a subsample of the original sample was contacted in 1986).

In addition to the follow-ups, a number of supplemental data collection efforts were undertaken. For example, a Postsecondary Education Transcript Study was undertaken in 1984, and the fifth follow-up survey in 1986 included a supplement for those who become teachers.

The major components of the study are as follows: Base Year Survey:

Age; sex; racial/ethnic background; physical handicap; socioeconomic status of family and community; school characteristics; future education and work plans; test scores; school experience; school performance; work status; work performance and satisfaction. Follow-up Surveys (1973, 1974, 1976, 1979, and 1986):

Age; sex; marital status; community characteristics; education and work plans; educational attainment; work history; attitudes and opinions; postsecondary school characteristics; grade average; credits earned; financial assistance for postsecondary education.

Policy and Research Issues

NLS-72 can provide information about quality, equity, and diversity of educational opportunity and the effect of those factors on cognitive growth, individual development, and educational outcomes. It can also provide information about changes in educational and career outcomes and other transitions over time. The NLS-72 data cover the sampled cohort from 1972–86.

Additional surveys within the National Center for Education Statistics series of longitudinal surveys of elementary and secondary education include *High School and Beyond* and *NELS-88*. The first began in 1980 with a survey of 10th graders and secured data in a second wave 2 years later, when the students were 12th graders, and has collected data periodically since that time. The second began in 1988 with a survey of 8th graders, and collected data on those students at 2-year intervals through the remainder of their school experiences and beyond. Again, information on these surveys is available on the Internet site of the National Center for Education Statistics (reachable through gopher://gopher.ed.gov) and in any academic library that has a federal documents repository.

Study Questions

1. Survey research and experimental research are different in some important ways, yet they share some common characteristics. What would you say is the most important distinction between survey research and experimental research? Can you cite at least one objective that is common to survey research and experimental research?

2. If you want to estimate the characteristics of a population precisely, is it more important that your sample consist of a large proportion of the population, or that your sample be of a particular size?

3. If you wanted to conduct a survey that would yield information on the annual operating budgets of public colleges and universities in the United States, what issues would you consider when you defined your *target population*? Would you want to include 2-year community colleges? Would you want to include junior colleges? Would you want to include special-purpose institutions, such as medical and dental schools? Do you think that these issues would affect your results substantially?

4. Suppose you wanted to investigate the attitudes of the general public on the use of domestic animals (such as dogs and cats) in medical research. You might choose to conduct a mall survey, a telephone interview survey, or a face-to-face interview survey. Name at least one advantage and one disadvantage of each of these survey methods, considering your survey objective.

5. If you wanted to estimate the average arithmetic achievement of elementary school pupils in a large school system, do you think stratified random sampling would be better than simple random sampling? In what ways might stratified random sampling be better? What characteristics of the population could you use for stratifying the pupils?

6. Why is it usually necessary to "code" survey data that are collected through interviews? What is meant by "coding?" Suppose that in a household interview survey, the interviewers asked "What is the occupation of the person in this family who earns the largest amount of money?" Do you think it would be necessary to code responses to this question? How might responses to this question be coded?

7. Virtually all textbooks on survey research make a strong case for doing pilot surveys. What are some important questions that can be answered by conducting a pilot survey? In what ways do well-designed and well-conducted pilot surveys reduce the likelihood that a subsequent main survey will avoid major problems?

8. It has been said that statistical generalization of survey results is threatened by bias error and random error. What is the major difference between these two

kinds of error? Describe a survey situation that could result in substantial bias error. Describe a survey situation that could result in substantial random error.

9. What is the essential distinction between substantive generalization and statistical generalization in the interpretation of survey results? Can you think of any survey situations in which either type of generalization would be unnecessary?

10. Suppose you conducted a face-to-face interview survey for the purpose of determining the average household expenditure for food during a given week. What would be the likely impact on the validity of your conclusions if you failed to obtain data from 40% of the households you sampled? What type of error would likely result? What type of generalization would be threatened?

Reading

Introduction
A Report on a Prominent Survey in Education

Richard M. Jaeger

This section contains the full text of a survey report titled *The 26th Annual Phi Delta Kappan/Gallup Poll of the Public's Attitudes Toward the Public Schools.* As the title implies, this survey has been conducted annually for over a quarter century, under the joint sponsorship of Phi Delta Kappa (a nationwide honorary organization of professionals in education) and the Gallup Organization, a commercial provider of survey research services The report was published in the September, 1994 issue of the *Phi Delta Kappan,* the journal of the Phi Delta Kappa organization. It is reproduced here with permission.

This survey is presented as an exemplar of the genre for several reasons. First, it is among the most prominent of the regular, nongovernmental surveys on the public schools. It is widely cited, its results are noted in the popular press, and it is often used as a point of reference by local school systems when they survey parents or citizens in their districts. Second, its methodology, although not fully described, is well conceived and generally well executed. It thus provides a useful object of review and thoughtful critique.

The 26th Phi Delta Kappa/Gallup Poll sought opinions from a nationally representative sample of adults (18 years or older) toward a range of issues surrounding the public schools. Opinions were gathered through telephone interviews. Respondents were identified through a technique called "random digit dialing" by selecting telephone numbers at random, within randomly-selected area codes and exchanges. Area codes and exchanges were first selected by dividing the continental U. S. into four geographic strata, and then dividing each stratum into three size-of-community strata (see Frey, 1989 for an introduction to the random digit dialing technique). The resulting sample is claimed to be representative of all "telephone households within the United States." By design then, the survey excludes those few U. S. households that do not have telephones.

The topics that define the content of the Phi Delta Kappa/Gallup Poll are an interesting combination of "hot button" issues that reflect the latest concerns and fads that inevitably seem to dominate educational debate, and issues that are constants on the public education scene, such as parental satisfaction with the quality of the public schools. This combination ensures that the Poll is topical and provocative, but nonetheless supports analyses of trends on some pervasive, long-term issues. The list of topics for the Poll is proposed each year by a panel of prominent educators, typically in executive positions in local school systems, state departments of education, private foundations, major professional organizations, and academe.

In an important book published in 1969, Lee Cronbach and Patrick Suppes categorized research studies in education as "conclusion-oriented" or "decision-oriented." These categories were intended to distinguish more fundamental studies that are designed to contribute to a body of accumulated knowledge from studies that are designed to inform current policy questions facing decision-makers. In this typology, the Phi Delta Kappa/Gallup Poll would undoubtedly be considered a decision-oriented study. Yet among those who specialize in the study of public policy in education, the longitudinal information that the Poll provides on the public's view of the quality of the public schools might contribute to the formulation of fundamental theory.

It is suggested that you refer to the 26 questions that compose the *Short Checklist for Survey Evaluation* provided in the preceding chapter, and use the questions as a basis for evaluating the Phi Delta Kappa/Gallup Poll report. You will find that a number of the questions can be answered in the affirmative, but information for addressing others is wanting. For example, the report provides clear indication of the research issues the Poll was to address, although it does not contain an integrated list. The Poll is clearly organized by major topic, with related questions surrounding a single issue presented sequentially. Although the report identifies the desired target population, it does not provide an explicit description of the sampling frame that was used by the researchers.

This initial list is intended to help you begin a critical reading of the report. Try to determine which of the 26 questions on the Checklist can be answered confidently, which can be answered only in part, and which cannot be answered at all. When you finish this task, ask yourself the important questions: Does this report answer the research questions identified by the researchers? Are the conclusions presented believable? Should the Poll be considered successful, given its objectives and its results? What, if anything, could have been done to improve the Poll, or the report on its findings? By using the questions in the Checklist, you should have little difficulty evaluating the quality of the Poll, and you'll gain useful experience in learning to review survey reports critically and thoughtfully.

References

Cronbach, L. J., & Suppes, P. (1969). *Research for tomorrow's schools.* New York: Macmillan.

Frey, J. H. (1989). *Survey research by telephone.* Newbury Park, CA: Sage Publications.

The 26th Annual
Phi Delta Kappa/Gallup Poll
Of the Public's Attitudes
Toward the Public Schools

Stanley M. Elam, Lowell C. Rose, and Alec M. Gallup

Two problems—the growth of fighting/violence/gangs and poor discipline—are by far the most serious problems facing U.S. public schools today, according to the 26th annual Phi Delta Kappa/Gallup Poll of the Public's Attitudes Toward the Public Schools. Each of these problems was mentioned by 18% of the 1,326 adults surveyed. Lack of adequate financial support and drug abuse were also frequently mentioned.

People cited a web of causes for violence in and around schools, including the abuse of drugs and alcohol by students, the growth of gangs, the easy availability of weapons, and the breakdown of the American family. Remedies for most of these problems may be beyond the direct control of the schools, but people would like to see stronger penalties for student possession of weapons and more training for school personnel in how to deal with student violence. Other measures people consider potentially effective include more job training for students in the public schools, drug and alcohol abuse programs, courses in values and ethics, and education in ways to reduce the racial and ethnic tensions. Courses in how to be a good parent and in conflict resolution were judged less likely to be effective.

Other highlights of the 26th Phi Delta Kappa/Gallup education poll:

- People gave the school attended by their eldest child good grades—70% gave it an A or a B, and 92% gave it a passing grade. But they continue to give the nation's schools considerably lower grades: only 22% award the nation's schools an A or a B, while 49% give them a C.
- The vast majority of respondents looked favorably on such Clinton Administration initiatives as financial help with college expenses in return for public service; efforts to improve school-to-work transition

Stanley M. Elam is contributing editor of the *Phi Delta Kappan*. He was *Kappan* editor from 1956 through 1980 and has been coordinating Phi Delta Kappa's polling program since his retirement. Lowell C. Rose is executive director of Phi Delta Kappa. Alec M. Gallup is co-chairman, with George Gallup, Jr., of the Gallup Organization, Princeton, N.J.
Reprinted with permission of the *Phi Delta Kappan* (Volume 76, pp. 42–56, 1994).

programs; full funding of Head Start and concentration of the program in schools with the highest proportions of poor children; and the establishment of academic achievement goals for children, with financial help from the federal government so that states and districts can meet these standards.

- Americans reaffirmed their historic opposition to government assistance (in the form of vouchers) for those who choose nonpublic schools for their children's education. The 1991 Phi Delta Kappa/ Gallup education poll showed majority support for the voucher idea for the first time since 1983.
- The trend in opinion favoring character education in the public schools continues. Moreover, Americans also approve nondevotional instruction in the world's religions.
- Americans have decidedly mixed reactions to the recent flurry of interest in contracting with private corporations to operate public schools.
- Americans give mixed signals on Channel One, the plan whereby Whittle Communications provides free television equipment and 10 minutes of news programming to the schools in return for the right to include as much as 2½ minutes of advertising in the program. Those without knowledge of such a program in their community oppose it, while those with knowledge of such a program in their local schools support it.
- By a 3–1 majority, Americans believe that public schools should give equal emphasis to a common cultural tradition and to the cultural traditions of growing minorities in the U.S.
- People generally believe that the existing U.S. system of tax funding for public schools is unfair to the average taxpayer.
- A majority of respondents like the idea of charter schools that would be free to try out promising reform measures.
- More people are currently involved in local school activities and reform efforts than at any time in the past decade.
- People continue to believe that the traditional A to F or numeric grades are useful in reporting student progress, but they give even higher grades to two newer forms of reporting: written descriptions of students' progress and checklists indicating what students can and cannot do.

The report and tables that follow provide details about these and other findings of the 26th annual Phi Delta Kappa/Gallup poll.

Biggest Problems Facing Local Public Schools

For the first time ever, the category "fighting, violence, and gangs" shares the number-one position with "lack of discipline" as the biggest problem confronting local public schools. Why has this happened in 1994, only a year after inadequate financing and drug abuse were most frequently mentioned?

Is the current uproar about violence in the schools merely a media phenomenon? To some extent, yes. For all the hoopla in the national press, there is no crime wave in America—except among blacks. Although one-third of Americans rate crime as the nation's most important problem, crime statistics have been declining steadily since 1981, according to the Bureau of Justice. But not in the black community. Between 1968 and 1994 murder rates for whites actually decreased. By contrast, the rate among blacks increased by 65%. A black person is now seven times as likely as a white person to be murdered, four times as likely to be raped, three times as likely to be robbed, and twice as likely to be assaulted or to have his or her car stolen. The total number of murders in the U.S.—about 22,000 last year—has remained constant since 1980, but murder now disproportionately affects the black community.

Contrary to popular perceptions, cities with populations of one million or more experienced the greatest decline in serious crimes last year (5%), while suburban law enforcement agencies reported 3% fewer serious crimes and police in rural areas reported a 2% drop, according to a preliminary crime report issued by the Federal Bureau of Investigation in March.

A Louis Harris survey of U.S. public school teachers, students, and police department officials, conducted for the Metropolitan Life Insurance Company in the fall of 1993, showed 77% of the teachers feeling "very safe" in their schools, 22% feeling "somewhat safe," 1% feeling "not very safe," and less than 1% feeling "not at all safe."[1] A somewhat smaller majority of teachers (60%) in schools with all or many minority students felt very safe. Students felt less safe than teachers: 50% very safe, 40% somewhat safe, 4% not very safe, 3% not at all safe, and 3% not sure.

Among teachers and students overall, only small pluralities felt that violence has increased in the past year. However, among some schools dominated by minority and low-income students, the perception that violence had increased was considerably stronger. Law enforcement officers, especially those in urban areas, thought violence in schools had increased.

A majority of teachers and law enforcement officers believe that the major factors contributing to violence in the public schools include lack of supervision at home, lack of family involvement in the schools, and exposure to violence in the mass media. Students see a wider variety of sources, many related to peer relations.

The accompanying tables present 1994 Phi Delta Kappa/Gallup poll findings on the biggest problems facing the schools and compare the frequency with which certain problems have been mentioned in these polls over the past decade.

The question (see Table 1):

The table below shows how public perceptions of the biggest problems facing local public schools have fluctuated over the past decade, a period when four different problems have ranked number one at least once.

There was considerable uniformity among demographic groups as to the nature of local public school problems. However, these differences stood out:

	Percentages Mentioning Each Major Problem								
	1994 %	1993 %	1992 %	1991 %	1990 %	1989 %	1988 %	1987 %	1986 %	1985 %
Fighting/violence/ gangs	18*	13	9	3	2**	1**	1**	1**	2**	1**
Lack of discipline	18*	15	17	20	19	19	19	22	24	25*
Lack of proper financial support	13	21*	22*	18	13	13	12	14	11	9
Drug abuse	11	16	22*	22*	38*	34*	32*	30*	28*	18

*Indicates first rank (or tie)
**Category was "fighting."

TABLE 1. *What do you think are the biggest problems with which the public schools of this community must deal?*

Problems	National Totals %	No Children in School %	Public School Parents %	Nonpublic School Parents %
Fighting/violence/gangs	18	19	16	17
Lack of discipline	18	18	17	22
Lack of proper financial support	13	12	16	9
Drug abuse	11	11	13	7
Standards/quality of education	8	8	5	11
Overcrowded schools	7	5	11	10
Lack of family structure/problems of home life*	5	5	3	4
Crime/vandalism	4	5	4	3
Pupils' lack of interest/truancy/ poor attitudes	3	3	3	5
Parents' lack of support/interest	3	4	2	3
Difficulty in getting good teachers	3	4	2	2
Poor curriculum/low curriculum standards	3	2	3	2
Lack of respect	3	2	3	1
Integration/segregation, racial discrimination	3	3	2	2
There are no problems	1	1	2	2
Miscellaneous**	9	9	8	13
Don't know	11	12	9	11

*New category.
**A total of 33 different kinds of problems were mentioned by 2% or fewer respondents.
(Figures add to more than 100% because of multiple answers.)

fighting/violence/gangs was mentioned more often by residents of urban areas (27%), by nonwhites (31%), by 18- to 29-year olds (28%), and by people living in the West (23%) and South (21%).

Causes of and Cures for Violence

Note that if one combines "lack of discipline" with "fighting/violence/ gangs," the figure for total "net" mentions reaches 35% in 1994, whereas it was

27% in 1993. Something appears to have happened, and it was most likely a media creation. There is no gainsaying, however, that Americans live in a violent culture—four times more violent, some experts say, than that of Western Europe.

By coincidence, poll planners decided to ask 1994 respondents two questions: the first to judge the importance of several putative causes of violent behavior among schoolchildren and the second to make judgments about the effectiveness of certain measures the schools might take to combat or ameliorate violence.

To determine what the public believes to be the main causes for increased violence in the nation's public schools, respondents were asked to rate the importance of each of 13 possible causes of school violence. At least 70% of respondents rate the increased use of drugs and alcohol, the growth of youth gangs, the easy availability of weapons, and a general breakdown in the American family as very important causes of violence in the nation's schools.

The first question (see Table 2):

Obviously, such a list of causes ignores the relationships between various causes and makes no attempt to distinguish between root causes and immediate causes of violence among young people. But the strength of the responses indicates that the public sees youth violence as part of the larger problem of social breakdown in America, a breakdown that is the subject of countless seminars, sermons, and sociological studies.

The role of the schools in combating or ameliorating this breakdown is being sorted out by policymakers in thousands of settings. However, considering just the causes of school violence deemed most important by the public, we must go to the seventh on the list before we find one that attributes responsibility to the school. The schools have little control over the first six.

Analysis of the findings by population group reveals that public school parents are about as likely as are other groups to rate these causes of school violence very important. However, blacks are substantially more likely than whites to judge the following causes very important: easy availability of weapons (88% to 69%); shortages in school personnel (76% to 49%); increased cultural, racial, and ethnic diversity among student populations (63% to 39%); cutbacks in school support programs (67% to 42%), and increased poverty among parents (65% to 41%). There is little difference between blacks and whites with regard to the importance of drug and alcohol use and the growth of youth gangs.

The second question (see Table 3):

People tended to be hopeful about all the measures proposed. Not a single one was judged likely to be "not very effective" or "not at all effective" by a majority of respondents. In fact, majorities rated all but one of the remedies likely to be "very effective."

There were virtually no differences in the responses of public school parents and those with no children in schools. It is interesting to note that better-educated respondents were somewhat more skeptical of the likely success of every measure proposed than were the less-educated respondents. In addition, by an

TABLE 2. *As you probably know, there has been an increase in violence in the nation's public schools over the last decade. How important do you consider each of the following as a cause for this increased violence—very important, quite important, not very important, or not at all important?*

Cause	Very Important %	Quite Important %	Not Very Important %	Not at All Important %	Don't Know %
Increased use of drugs and alcohol among school-age youth	78	17	3	2	*
Growth of youth gangs	72	19	4	3	2
Easy availability of weapons (guns, knives)	72	15	6	6	1
A breakdown in the American family (e.g., an increase in one-parent and dysfunctional families)	70	20	7	2	1
Schools do not have the authority to discipline that they once had	65	22	9	3	1
Increased portrayal of violence in the media (especially in movies and on TV)	60	20	14	5	1
Inability of school staff to resolve conflicts between students	59	26	11	3	1
Shortages in school personnel	52	26	15	5	2
Trying to deal with troubled or emotionally disturbed students in the regular classroom instead of in special classes or schools	51	27	16	4	2
A school curriculum that is out of touch with the needs of today's student	48	28	17	4	3
Cutbacks in many school support programs	45	27	18	6	4
Increased poverty among parents	44	29	20	6	1
Increased cultural, racial, and ethnic diversity among the public school student population	43	26	22	7	2

*Less than one-half of 1%.

average margin of about 20 percentage points, more blacks than whites felt that the following measures would be very effective ways to curb school violence: courses in how to be a good parent (70% to 48%), more vocational or job-training courses (85% to 64%), conflict education to reduce racial and ethnic tensions (65% to 42%), and drug and alcohol abuse programs (82% to 64%).

TABLE 3. *How effective do you think each of the following measures would be in reducing violence in the public schools—very effective, somewhat effective, not very effective, or not at all effective?*

Measure	Very Effective %	Somewhat Effective %	Not Very Effective %	Not at All Effective %	Don't Know %
Stronger penalties for posses- sion of weapons by students	86	8	3	2	1
Training school staffs in how to deal with student violence	72	20	5	2	1
More vocational or job-training courses in public schools	67	25	7	1	*
Drug and alcohol abuse pro- grams for students	66	23	7	3	1
Values and ethics education for students	60	27	9	3	1
Education designed to reduce racial and ethnic tensions	57	27	10	4	2
Courses offered by the public schools in how to be a good parent	51	28	15	5	1
Conflict education for students	45	35	11	3	6

*Less than one-half of 1%.

The People Grade Their Schools

Ever since 1974 respondents to the Phi Delta Kappa/Gallup education poll have been asked to rate their local public schools' performance on a scale of A to F. Over the years related questions have been added, including one that secures judgments about the performance of public schools nationally. The most revealing question, however, was one first asked of public school parents in 1982: What grade would you give the school your oldest child attends? Parents' responses make it clear that the more one knows about a school, the more likely one is to think well of its performance. (Certainly, parents have more direct information than nonparents.)

In 1994 more than four Americans in 10 (44%) give the public schools in their community an A or a B, about the same proportion as reported in every Phi Delta Kappa/Gallup survey since these ratings were introduced two dec- ades ago. Three-quarters of the public (74%) award their local public schools at least a grade of C. Only 7% say their local schools deserve a grade of F. These relatively high grades are awarded despite the fact that the grading is strongly based on the views of the large majority of the public (70%) with no children in school or with children enrolled in nonpublic schools.

The first question (see Table 4):

The second question (see Table 5):

When respondents likely to be most familiar with the schools—i.e., public school parents—are asked to grade the school their oldest child attends, seven

TABLE 4. *Students are often given the grades A, B, C, D, and FAIL to denote the quality of their work. Suppose the public schools themselves, in this community, were graded in the same way. What grade would you give the public schools here—A, B, C, D, or FAIL?*

	National Totals %	No Children in School %	Public School Parents %	Nonpublic School Parents %
A & B	44	39	57	28
A	9	8	12	4
B	35	31	45	24
C	30	30	30	39
D	14	16	9	16
FAIL	7	8	3	13
Don't know	5	7	1	4

Ratings Given the Local Public Schools

	1994 %	1993 %	1992 %	1991 %	1990 %	1989 %	1988 %	1987 %	1986 %	1985 %	1984 %
A & B	44	47	40	42	41	43	40	43	41	43	42
A	9	10	9	10	8	8	9	12	11	9	10
B	35	37	31	32	33	35	31	31	30	34	32
C	30	31	33	33	34	33	34	30	28	30	35
D	14	11	12	10	12	11	10	9	11	10	11
FAIL	7	4	5	5	5	4	4	4	5	4	4
Don't know	5	7	10	10	8	9	12	14	15	13	8

in 10 (70%) would award that school a grade of A or B. This has been true for the last decade. More than nine in 10 public school parents (92%) give the school their oldest child attends at least a passing grade of C. Public school parents' tendency to rate their children's schools high extends to their perceptions of local schools. For example, 57% of public school parents give the local public schools a grade of A or B, and 87% give the local public schools at least a C.

The third question (see Table 6):

There were few demographic differences in parental ratings. However, parents of children in elementary schools were more likely to give high grades than parents of children in high school. This is consistent with poll reports in other years.

This year the poll planners added another question to the series on grading the public schools. People were asked to grade the public schools "in their neighborhood." The ratings of neighborhood schools were higher than those for the nation's schools and for schools in the community. While 44% of respondents gave schools in the local community a grade of A or B, 50% of respondents gave schools in their neighborhood similarly high grades. These results should not be too surprising, because a "community" may have a great many schools about which respondents know little more than they do about the nation's

TABLE 5. *How about the public schools in the nation as a whole? What grade would you give the public schools nationally—A, B, C, D, or FAIL?*

	National Totals %	No Children in School %	Public School Parents %	Nonpublic School Parents %
A & B	22	23	19	18
A	2	2	2	4
B	20	21	17	14
C	49	50	48	45
D	17	14	22	23
FAIL	6	8	4	6
Don't know	6	5	7	8

	Ratings Given the Nation's Public Schools										
	1994 %	1993 %	1992 %	1991 %	1990 %	1989 %	1988 %	1987 %	1986 %	1985 %	1984 %
A & B	22	19	18	21	21	22	23	26	28	27	25
A	2	2	2	2	2	2	3	4	3	3	2
B	20	17	16	19	19	20	20	22	25	24	23
C	49	48	48	47	49	47	48	44	41	43	49
D	17	17	18	13	16	15	13	11	10	12	11
FAIL	6	4	4	5	4	4	3	2	5	3	4
Don't know	6	12	12	14	10	12	13	17	16	15	11

TABLE 6. *Using the A, B, C, D, FAIL scale again, what grade would you give the school your oldest child attends?*

	Ratings Given School Oldest Child Attends								
	1994 %	1993 %	1992 %	1991 %	1990 %	1989 %	1988 %	1987 %	1986 %
A & B	70	72	64	73	72	71	70	69	65
A	28	27	22	29	27	25	22	28	28
B	42	45	42	44	45	46	48	41	37
C	22	18	24	21	19	19	22	20	26
D	6	5	6	2	5	5	3	5	4
FAIL	1	2	4	4	2	1	2	2	2
Don't know	1	3	2	*	2	4	3	4	3

*Less than one-half of 1%.

schools, whereas respondents are most likely to be familiar with the schools attended by children from the more limited area of their own neighborhood.

The question (see Table 7):

The most significant demographic differences in responses to this question were found in the category of community size. More than 50% of people living in suburban and rural communities give schools attended by neighborhood

TABLE 7. *How about the public schools attended by children from your neighborhood? What grade would you give them—A, B, C, D, or FAIL?*

	National Totals %	No Children in School %	Public School Parents %	Nonpublic School Parents %
A & B	50	46	60	39
A	12	10	16	11
B	38	36	44	28
C	30	30	29	35
D	9	10	7	12
FAIL	6	7	3	8
Don't know	5	7	1	6

children a grade of A or B, while only 43% of those living in urban areas give similarly high grades.

Have Schools Improved or Deteriorated?

In three of the last seven Phi Delta Kappa/Gallup education polls, people have been asked whether they think that their local public schools have improved, deteriorated, or stayed about the same over the previous five years. This year, as was the case when the question was last asked in 1990, more people perceived deterioration (37%) than saw improvement (26%); in 1988, more people saw improvement than deterioration.

The question (see Table 8):

Poll interviewers followed the question about improvement/deterioration of *local* public schools with the same question about the *nation's* schools. The findings were far more negative. For every individual who believed that the nation's public schools have improved (16%), there were three (51%) who thought they have deteriorated.

The question (see Table 9):

But when *parents* were asked the same question about public schools their children attended, the findings were nearly reversed. For every parent who believed that the school attended by his or her oldest child had gotten worse in the past five years (15%), there were more than two (36%) who thought it had improved.

The question (see Table 10):

What can one make of these responses? It seems likely that the general public has come to believe public education's critics regarding the state of the *nation's* schools, which have been blamed for everything from ignorance of geography to economic recession. Parents with children in school know better; a comfortable majority of them believe that the schools their children attend are improving.

Clinton's Education Initiatives

When President Clinton signed his education reform strategy into law in March 1994, he called the Goals 2000: Educate America Act a "new and dif-

TABLE 8. *Just your own impression, would you say that the public schools in your community have improved from, say, five years ago, gotten worse, or stayed about the same?*

	National Totals %	No Children in School %	Public School Parents %	Nonpublic School Parents %
Improved	26	23	32	20
Gotten worse	37	39	30	43
Stayed about the same	33	33	34	33
Don't know	4	5	4	4

	National Totals		
	1994 %	1990 %	1988 %
Improved	26	22	29
Gotten worse	37	30	19
Stayed about the same	33	36	37
Don't know	4	12	15

ferent approach for the federal government." He said that the measure would establish "world class" national education standards and rely on school districts at the grassroots to help students achieve them.

The centerpiece of Goals 2000 is a new program, authorized at $400 million a year (appropriations to come later) that would provide grants to states and districts that adopt reform plans consistent with the legislation. The plans must call for setting high standards for curriculum content and student performance, as well as opportunity-to-learn standards or strategies for insuring adequate school services.

Enactment of Goals 2000 was the culmination of a process begun in 1989 when the National Governors' Association and President Bush agreed at an education summit to set six national goals for education. Clinton, then governor of Arkansas, was a key player in drafting the goals. The current version of

TABLE 9. *What about public schools in the nation as a whole? Would you say they have improved from five years ago, gotten worse, or stayed about the same?*

	National Totals %	No Children in School %	Public School Parents %	Nonpublic School Parents %
Improved	16	15	18	18
Gotten worse	51	51	51	55
Stayed about the same	26	28	24	20
Don't know	7	6	7	7

TABLE 10.   *Would you say the public school your oldest child attends has improved from five years ago, gotten worse, or stayed about the same?*

	Local Schools %	Nation's Schools %	School Attended By Oldest Child %
Improved	26	16	36
Gotten worse	37	51	15
Stayed about the same	33	26	41
Don't know	4	7	8

this ambitious strategy includes two additional goals, dealing with teacher training and parent participation.

Three major initiatives of the Clinton Administration were already in place: increases in Head Start funding, with more of it targeted directly to children living in poverty; a modest program that will allow a limited number of students to earn money for college by performing public service; and a school-to-work bill authorizing $300 million a year to help high schools create work-based learning programs for students who do not go to college.

Respondents to the current poll were asked to indicate approval or disapproval of four of the Clinton Administration initiatives. All four proved highly popular.

The question (see Table 11):

Strong majority support for these initiatives was registered in all demographic groups. Young adults (aged 18–29) and blacks were particularly enthusiastic about improved funding for early childhood education. The percentages in favor were 90% and 84%, respectively. There was even considerable bipartisan support for all four of the measures.

National Curriculum and National Assessment

The question about federal initiatives was followed by another focusing on the idea of a national curriculum and national assessment of achievement. Once again, as in earlier polls, people made clear their approval of a basic curriculum of subject matter for all schools (read "national curriculum") and of standardized national examinations that students must pass for grade promotion and high school graduation.

Although most respondents probably do not understand the full implications of such a significant change in U.S. tradition, every poll in this series that has explored the idea shows strong support for it. In 1989, for example, poll respondents favored national standards and goals for schools by a 70% to 19% margin. In the same poll, 69% said that they favored the use of a standardized national curriculum in the local public schools, while only 21% opposed the idea. The same questions asked in 1991 yielded similar results.

The current poll examined these issues using questions that were worded somewhat differently, but the results only confirm the earlier findings. For example, instead of being asked whether they favored or opposed a national

TABLE 11. *Here are some education programs currently being advanced by the federal government. As I read off each program, would you tell me whether you favor or oppose it?*

	National Totals		
	Favor %	Oppose %	Don't Know %
Assistance with high school students' college expenses in return for performing some kind of public service	81	17	2
Greater emphasis on, including additional money for, work-study vocational programs for high school students who do not plan to go to college	79	20	1
A large increase in funds for early childhood education in those public schools with the highest percentage of children living in poverty	74	22	4
More effort to reach agreement on academic achievement goals for children at various stages of school, without specifying how the schools should reach these goals	63	32	5

	Those Who Favor These Initiatives			
	National Totals %	No Children in School %	Public School Parents %	Nonpublic School Parents %
Assistance with high school students' college expenses in return for performing some kind of public service	81	80	83	83
Greater emphasis on, including additional money for, work-study vocational programs for high school students who do not plan to go to college	79	78	82	74
A large increase in funds for early childhood education in those public schools with the highest percentage of children living in poverty	74	74	75	66
More effort to reach agreement on academic achievement goals for children at various stages of school, without specifying how the schools should reach these goals	63	62	66	56

curriculum and standardized national exams for grade promotion and high school graduation, respondents were asked how important they considered each factor to be as a way to improve the nation's public schools.

More than eight in ten (83%) responded that a standardized national curriculum was either very important or quite important; similarly, about seven in ten (73%) thought standardized national exams were either very or quite important.

The question (see Table 12):

TABLE 12.   *How important do you think each of the following is as a way to improve the nation's public schools: very important, quite important, not too important, or not at all important?*

	Very Important %	Quite Important %	Not Too Important %	Not at All Important %	Don't Know %
Establishing a basic curriculum of subject matter or program of courses for all schools	49	34	12	4	1
Establishing standardized national examinations, based on a national curriculum, that students must pass for grade promotion and for high school graduation	46	27	18	7	2

	Those Who said "Very Important"			
	National Totals %	No Children in School %	Public School Parents %	Nonpublic School Parents %
Establishing a basic curriculum of subject matter or program of courses for all schools	49	47	54	58
Establishing standardized national examinations, based on a national curriculum, that students must pass for grade promotion and for high school graduation	46	46	45	44

School Choice and Vouchers

Since 1970, these polls have traced trends in opinion about government financial aid to parochial schools, about the use of government-issued vouchers that would help parents finance a private or church-related school for their children, and about public school choice proposals. People have consistently opposed any form of government aid to nonpublic schools and have favored public school choice by sizable margins. But no consensus has developed on the voucher question.

Here in a table form is the history of responses to a question worded as follows: "In some nations the government allots a certain amount of money for each child for his education. The parents can send the child to any public, parochial, or private school they choose. This is called the 'voucher system.' Would you like to see such an idea adopted in this country?"

	National Totals							
	1991 %	1987 %	1986 %	1985 %	1983 %	1981 %	1971 %	1970 %
Favor	50	44	46	45	51	43	38	43
Oppose	39	41	41	40	38	41	44	46
Don't know	11	15	13	15	11	16	18	11

Over the past two or three years, Oregon, Colorado, and California have held referendums on various forms of vouchers. Although all three referendums were defeated by sizable majorities, voucher proponents vow to keep trying. Californians may vote on the proposition again as soon as next year.

In the current poll the issue was presented again, without mentioning the word *vouchers* but making clear that government money would pay "all or part" of a child's tuition if the parents chose to send the child to a nonpublic school.

Presented with this somewhat different question, the public opposes the voucher idea by a 54% to 45% majority. The response to this year's question suggests that opinion for and against the voucher idea has begun to crystallize. For example, when the long-term trend question was asked most recently (in 1991), 11% of the public had no opinion. In response to the new question, however, only 1% of respondents expressed no opinion.

In only two demographic groups did majorities favor the voucher idea as stated. Not surprisingly, nonpublic school parents (representing 9% of Americans) supported vouchers by more than a 2–1 margin (69% to 29%). In addition, Catholics (24% of Americans) approved the idea by a 55% to 44% majority.

The question (see Table 13):

Support for Character Education

"The fundamental tragedy of American education is not that we are turning out ignoramuses but that we are turning out savages," says Frederick Close, director of education for the Ethics Resource Center in Washington, D.C. Close would institute moral education or character education in the schools in an effort to counteract what he calls "a continuously rising crime wave among the

TABLE 13. *A proposal has been made which would allow parents to send their school-age children to any public, private, or church-related school they choose. For those parents choosing nonpublic schools, the government would pay all or part of the tuition. Would you favor or oppose this proposal in your state?*

	National Totals %	No Children in School %	Public School Parents %	Nonpublic School Parents %
Favor	45	42	48	69
Oppose	54	57	51	29
Don't know	1	1	1	2

younger generation." He echoes the sentiments found in a growing body of literature that includes the best-selling *Book of Virtues*, by William Bennett, who used his office as secretary of education in the late eighties to campaign for "moral literacy" in the public schools. (*The Book of Virtues* is subtitled *A Treasury of Great Moral Stories* and is intended for home and school use.) Like many of his fundamentalist backers, Bennett believes we must recover paradigms that we once shared as a nation "before the triviality of television absorbed most of children's attention and before a prevailing cynicism made virtue seem laughable."

Kevin Ryan, a professor of education at Boston University, points out that public schools have bent over backwards in their efforts not to offend anyone about anything. To make themselves inoffensive and studiously neutral, they have all but cleansed the curriculum of religious and ethical content. He speaks of schools as "morally dangerous places for children."[2]

It was Thomas Jefferson who first used the phrase "the wall of separation between church and state" in 1802, and it describes one of the most settled doctrines in American constitutional law. In his majority opinion in *Everson* (1947), Justice Hugo Black repeated Jefferson's phrase in a case that blocked out some of the last vestiges of religion in the public schools. Has the doctrine designed to protect the individual from tyranny diminished the role of virtues and values in civic life? Many people are beginning to think so.

In last year's poll Americans said that they believe their local communities could agree on a set of basic values, such as honesty and patriotism, that could be taught in the public schools. This year poll planners framed three questions related to issues of character education and the teaching of moral values in the schools.

The first question, repeated from the 1987 Phi Delta Kappa/Gallup education poll, asked respondents whether ethics should be taught in the public schools or left to parents and religious institutions. As in 1987, when 43% favored ethics and character education courses and 36% opposed them, in 1994 a small plurality of the public supported such courses (49% in favor, 39% opposed). Support was a good deal stronger among public school parents, however (57% in favor, 34% opposed).

The first question (see Table 14):

To find out what personal traits or virtues the public believes should be taught as part of character education courses, survey respondents were asked to indicate whether each of nine virtues should or should not be included in such courses. The vote in favor of teaching these virtues was practically unanimous, with the single exception of "thrift"—and even this old-fashioned virtue was judged worthy of inclusion by 74% of respondents.

The second question (see Table 15):

In the 1993 poll, a different list of character traits (some better described as attitudes) was offered, with the following results: honesty, 97%; democracy, 93%; acceptance of people of different races and ethnic backgrounds, 93%; patriotism or love of country, 91%; caring for friends and family members, 91%; moral courage, 91%; the golden rule, 90%; acceptance of people who hold different

TABLE 14. *It has been proposed that the public schools include cou:ses on "character education" to help students develop personal values and ethical behavior. Do you think that courses on values and ethical behavior should be taught in the public schools, or do you think that this should be left to the students' parents and/or the churches?*

	National Totals %		No Children in School %		Public School Parents %		Nonpublic School Parents %	
	'94	'87	'94	'87	'94	'87	'94	'87
Yes, schools	49	43	44	42	57	45	54	54
No, parents and/or churches	39	36	42	36	34	38	38	31
Both (volunteered)	12	13	14	13	8	13	8	11
Don't know	*	8	*	9	1	4	*	4

*Less than one-half of 1%.

TABLE 15. *Now, here is a list of personal traits or virtues that might be taught in the public schools in your community. As I read off each item, would you tell me whether you think it should be taught or should not be taught in the local public schools?*

Should Be Taught	National Totals %	No Children in School %	Public School Parents %	Nonpublic School Parents %
Respect for others	94	94	93	91
Industry or hard work	93	93	93	95
Persistence or the ability to follow through	93	92	94	94
Fairness in dealing with others	92	93	92	90
Compassion for others	91	91	91	89
Civility, politeness	91	91	90	91
Self-esteem	90	90	92	80
High expectations for oneself	87	87	88	82
Thrift	74	73	74	71

religious beliefs, 87%; acceptance of people who hold unpopular or controversial political or social views, 73%; sexual abstinence outside of marriage, 66%; acceptance of the right of a woman to choose abortion, 56%; acceptance of people with different sexual orientations (i.e., homosexuals or bisexuals), 51%.

The third question (see Table 16):

There were few significant demographic differences in the responses to this question. However, respondents living in the South (71%) and Midwest (69%) were slightly more likely to favor nondevotional religious instruction than those in the East (59%) or those in the West (62%).

TABLE 16. *The public schools in America are constitutionally prohibited from teaching any particular religion. Would you favor or oppose nondevotional instruction about various world religions in the public schools in your community?*

	National Totals %	No Children in School %	Public School Parents %	Nonpublic School Parents %
Favor	66	65	67	61
Oppose	33	33	32	39
Don't know	1	2	1	*

*Less than one-half of 1%.

Jury Still Out on Privatization

In a development reminiscent of the ill-fated experiments with performance contracting in the early 1970s, public school boards in several U.S. cities have recently contracted with private companies to manage some of their schools. For example, nine Baltimore schools are now being run by Education Alternatives, Inc., of Minneapolis. The same company was hoping to operate as many as 15 schools in Washington, D.C., but that plan has been put on hold for further study. The Baltimore and Washington superintendents have said that they sought contracts with private firms because they were frustrated by bureaucracies so complex and cumbersome that they could not get leaking roofs repaired or teachers transferred from under- to overenrolled schools in a timely way.

The Edison Project, established in 1991 by Whittle Communications, Inc., and now based in New York City, expects to begin operating the first of several hundred public schools in the fall of 1995, investing its own capital. Meanwhile, former Yale University President Benno Schmidt, Jr., who heads the Edison Project, hopes to contract with the board of education in Chicago to operate a number of that city's public schools. Schmidt has hinted that Edison schools will have a student/teacher ratio of about 17 to 1, that students will be organized in "houses" of about 100 each with a team of teachers to stay with them for three years, and that schools will be open from 7 a.m. to 6 p.m., including an optional 1½ hours at the beginning and end of the day for families who need child-care services.

To determine public acceptance of the concept of privatization of some facets of the public school system, respondents were asked whether they favored or opposed the idea of private, profit-making companies operating the schools. Opinion is almost evenly divided on the privatization idea.

The question (see Table 17):

There were few significant demographic differences in the responses. However, younger respondents and Republicans show considerably more support for this form of privatization than do older respondents and Democrats. Among those under 50 years of age, 50% support the idea, while only 39% of those older than 50 do. Fifty-one percent of Republicans favor the idea, while 38% of Democrats do.

TABLE 17. *Do you favor or oppose an idea now being tested in a few cities in which private, profit-making corporations contract to operate schools within certain jurisdictions?*

	National Totals %	No Children in School %	Public School Parents %	Nonpublic School Parents %
Favor	45	46	43	50
Oppose	47	46	49	41
Don't know	8	8	8	9

More 'Basics' But Broader Curriculum

In several previous Phi Delta Kappa/Gallup education polls, a majority of respondents favored more emphasis on curriculum "basics," which people generally conceive to be "reading, writing, and arithmetic," often with science and history/U.S. government included. Generally, people do not think that the public schools pay enough attention to these subjects. Nevertheless, the 1990 poll (whose results for the "basics" are reported in the accompanying table) showed that people also want more emphasis on computer training (79%), vocational education (65%), health education (62%), business (60%), and even physical education (32%).

To determine the public's preferences concerning curriculum content, respondents to this year's poll were asked whether they would favor more, less, or about the same emphasis in eight subject areas. Music, art, and foreign language have posted remarkable gains since 1990. Nonwhites are more likely than whites to say they desire more emphasis on most of the the subjects listed. The differences are largest in the case of music and art.

The first question (see Table 18):

Are Students Capable of Learning More Math and Science?

Do some students avoid math and science simply because they don't want to invest the effort to master these subjects? Or does mastery elude them despite their efforts? To ascertain whether Americans believe that public school students can learn more about these subjects, survey respondents were asked two questions.

The questions (see Table 19):

The answers reveal that virtually the entire U.S. public believes that most students are capable of learning more math and more science than they generally do.

Support for and Opposition to Channel One

Channel One, the 12½-minute news and information program (with commercials) produced by Whittle Communication, Inc., for the past four years, is the subject of considerable debate in educational circles. But it has gained only modest media attention.

TABLE 18. *As I read off each high school subject, would you tell me if you think that subject should be given more emphasis, less emphasis, or the same emphasis it now receives in high school, regardless of whether or not you think it should be required?*

	More Emphasis %	Less Emphasis %	Same Emphasis %	Don't Know %
Mathematics	82	1	17	*
English	79	2	19	*
Science	75	3	22	*
History/U.S. government	62	6	31	1
Geography	61	7	31	1
Foreign language	52	16	32	*
Music	31	22	46	1
Art	29	24	46	1

	1990 Results			
	More Emphasis %	Less Emphasis %	Same Emphasis %	Don't Know %
Mathematics	80	3	14	3
English	79	3	15	3
Science	68	11	18	3
History/U.S. government	65	9	23	3
Geography	53	18	25	4
Foreign language	37	34	25	4
Music	13	39	43	5
Art	12	42	40	6

*Less than one-half of 1%.

TABLE 19. *Do you believe that most public school students have the capacity to learn more math than they generally do today? Do you believe that most public school students have the capacity to learn more science than they generally do today?*

Yes, Have Capacity	National Totals %	No Children in School %	Public School Parents %	Nonpublic School Parents %
Math	89	88	90	94
Science	88	88	88	92

To determine how the public feels about the Whittle experiment, survey respondents were first read a description of the Whittle program and asked whether they were aware of any such arrangement in their own communities. Those who thought the Whittle experiment was in effect in their local public schools were then asked whether they were in favor of or opposed to it.

Those respondents who thought the experiment was not in operation in their communities or who did not know whether or not it existed there were asked whether they would be in favor of or opposed to having such an arrangement in their local schools.

The survey findings reveal that the relatively few (11% of respondents) who are aware of the use of the Whittle program in their local schools *favor* it by more than a 2–1 margin. (Channel One is now employed in more than 12,000 schools, most of these with high concentrations of poor students.) By contrast, those who are unaware of such a program in their communities oppose the introduction of the experiment into their schools by a substantial 57% to 38% margin.

The first question (see Table 20):

The second question (asked of those who indicated awareness of the arrangement) (see Table 21):

The third question (asked of those "not aware" of any local arrangement) (see Table 22):

Those *unaware* of the Whittle experiment registered opposition by substantial majorities in most demographic groups. However, there were two notable exceptions: young adults (ages 18–29) favored the Whittle experiment (60% to 37%), whereas those 30 and older opposed it (63% to 31%); and nonwhites were evenly divided between support and opposition (48% to 49%), whereas whites were opposed to the program (36% in favor, 58% opposed).

TABLE 20. *A company has been loaning TV sets and satellite dishes to public schools that agree to show their students daily 10-minute news and feature broadcasts from this company. Each broadcast includes two to 2½ minutes of commercial advertising directed to the students. The company makes money by selling this television time to advertisers. Do you happen to know whether any of the public schools in your community have entered into an arrangement of this kind, or not?*

	National Totals %	No Children in School %	Public School Parents %	Nonpublic School Parents %
Yes, have arrangement	11	11	13	10
No, do not have	48	46	51	55
Don't know	41	43	36	35

TABLE 21. *Are you in favor of this arrangement in the local public schools or opposed to it?*

	National Totals %
Yes, favor	66
No, opposed	30
Don't know	4

TABLE 22. *Would you be in favor of your local public schools' entering into this kind of arrangement, or opposed to it?*

	National Totals %	No Children in School %	Public School Parents %	Nonpublic School Parents %
Yes, favor	38	39	36	34
No, opposed	57	56	58	54
Don't know	5	5	6	12

Unmotivated High School Students

Educators often speculate about reasons for the lack of academic motivation that afflicts many high school students. There appears to be no consensus among them about causes.

To obtain some idea of the public's perceptions on this topic, respondents were presented with a question offering three possible explanations. Respondents were asked how important they considered each explanation. The public considered *all of them* important; between seven and eight in 10 respondents felt that each of the three explanations was either very important or somewhat important.

The question (see Table 23):

Monoculturalism or Multiculturalism?

The long-running debate over multiculturalism in the schools has heated up in recent years, as some groups protest a tendency to abandon the melting-pot metaphor in favor of "tossed salad" and as the number and size of racial and ethnic minority groups increase. In Lake County, Florida, for example, fundamentalists holding a 3–2 edge on the school board voted in May 1994 to teach students that American culture and institutions are "superior to other foreign or historic cultures."

Answers to the following two questions in the current poll suggest that there is a commodious middle ground on the issue of multiculturalism, and, as the first table shows, three out of four Americans choose to occupy it.

The first question (see Table 24):

The second question (asked of the 75% who said that schools should promote both one common tradition and diverse traditions of different peoples— (see Table 25):

As the first table above shows, about one citizen in five (18%) would agree that the public schools should promote only a single common cultural tradition. (Those most in favor of monoculturalism are Republicans [23%] and those 65 years of age and older [24%].) The great majority of Americans think that the public schools should advocate a diversity of traditions—although with varying emphases. One American in 10 believes that, while diverse traditions should be taught, the common cultural tradition should be emphasized; a similar number

TABLE 23. *Many high school students are not motivated to do well academically. To indicate why you think this is the case, would you rate each of the following reasons as very important, somewhat important, not very important, or not at all important?*

	Very Important %	Somewhat Important %	Not Very Important %	Not at All Important %	Don't Know %
The negative attitudes of fellow students about high academic performance	63	25	7	3	2
The fact that employers of high school graduates seldom seem to care about high school records	49	29	15	5	2
The fact that many colleges will admit any student with a high school diploma, regardless of his or her high school record	49	28	15	6	2

Rated Very Important	National Totals %	No Children in School %	Public School Parents %	Nonpublic School Parents %
The negative attitudes of fellow students about high academic performance	63	64	61	59
The fact that employers of high school graduates seldom seem to care about high school records	49	50	49	44
The fact that many colleges will admit any student with a high school diploma, regardless of his or her high school record	49	52	45	47

(11%) believe that, while both the common culture and diverse cultures should be taught, diversity should be given more emphasis. Roughly half (53%) of those polled believe that a common cultural tradition and diverse traditions should be given equal attention.

Tax System for Schools

Many questions in past Phi Delta Kappa/Gallup polls have shown that people are unhappy with the forms of taxation used to support U.S. public schools, and they are particularly disturbed by the inequalities in funding that result from features of the tax system in most states. Tax revolts occur with some regularity. Among the most recent was last year's upheaval in Michigan, which led to the virtual abandonment of the local property tax, backbone of school finance in most states for generations, in favor of a massive state sales tax increase and new mechanisms to equalize funding among districts.

TABLE 24. *In your opinion, which should the public schools in your community promote—one common, predominant cultural tradition only, or both a common cultural tradition and the diverse cultural traditions of the different population groups in America?*

	National Totals %	No Children in School %	Public School Parents %	Nonpublic School Parents %
Promote one common tradition only	18	18	19	19
Promote both one common tradition and diverse traditions of different populations	75	74	76	72
Don't know	7	8	5	9

A question in the current poll shows that the U.S. public, by a 54% to 43% majority, regards tax policies that fund education in the U.S. as unfair to taxpayers.

The question (see Table 26):

Bare Majority for Charter Schools

A charter school is a tax-funded school given broad freedom from state regulations in exchange for such favorable "outcomes" as improved test scores, attendance rates, dropout rates, and the like. Most charter contracts provide for the loss of the charter, typically granted by a public school board, if results aren't evident within a specified period.

In Minnesota, whose pioneering legislation was passed in 1991, charter schools include one with a year-round program for 35 students between the ages of 13 and 21, a private Montessori school, and a school for deaf students. In California, where 1992 legislation authorized 100 charter schools, one will have an English-as-a-second-language curriculum, and two will be resource centers for home schooling.

TABLE 25. *Which one do you think should receive more emphasis—one common cultural tradition, diverse cultural traditions, or should both receive the same emphasis?*

	National Totals %	No Children in School %	Public School Parents %	Nonpublic School Parents %
More emphasis on one common cultural tradition	10	10	9	11
More emphasis on diverse cultural traditions	11	11	11	9
Equal emphasis on both	53	53	56	51
Don't know	8	8	5	10

(Figures add to 100% when those who believe that the schools should promote one common culture *only*—see responses to the first question in this series—are included.)

TABLE 26. *In your opinion, is the existing system of funding public education in this country fair or unfair to the average taxpayer?*

	National Totals %	No Children in School %	Public School Parents %	Nonpublic School Parents %
Fair	43	48	36	30
Unfair	54	50	61	65
Don't know	3	2	3	5

Despite growing support for charter schools among state governing bodies, some people fear that the movement is a step on the road to vouchers for private schools, which many believe would create a two-tiered education system that would shut out the poor, since private schools would raise tuition beyond the value of the vouchers.

The current poll shows that a 54% to 39% majority of the public favors charter schools.

The question (see Table 27):

Majorities in virtually every demographic group support the idea of charter schools. Age is a key determinant, however. Those between the ages of 18 and 29 favor the idea (66% to 31%), as do those between the ages of 30 and 49 (57% to 37%). But those over age 50 oppose charter schools (47% to 42%).

Citizen Contact with the Schools

Recent emphasis on the importance of parental knowledge about and involvement in the life of the public schools may be paying off. Over the last decade the frequency of many forms of public contact with the schools has doubled or

TABLE 27. *A number of states have passed, or are considering, legislation that frees some public schools from certain state regulations and permits them to function independently. Some people say that these charter schools would be a good thing because, with fewer regulations, they would be able to try out new ideas for improving education. Others say charter schools would be a bad thing because regulations are necessary to guard against inferior or poor educational practices. Which position do you agree with more—that charter schools are a good thing for education or that they are a bad thing for education?*

	National Totals %	No Children in School %	Public School Parents %	Nonpublic School Parents %
Charter schools are a good thing for education	54	53	55	60
Charter schools are a bad thing for education	39	39	39	32
Don't know	7	8	6	8

nearly so. Areas showing the greatest gains are attendance at school board meetings, attendance at meetings dealing with school problems, and attendance at plays, concerts, and athletic events. Even adults with no children in school now claim to participate in the life of the schools to a considerable degree.

The question (see Table 28):

New Formats for Reporting Student Progress

The always-simmering dissatisfaction with time-honored forms of reporting student progress has resulted in much experimentation in recent years. To the

TABLE 28. *Since last September, which of the following, if any, have you yourself done?*

	National Totals %	No Children in School %	Public School Parents %	Nonpublic School Parents %
Attended a school play or concert in any local public school	54	43	79	51
Attended a local public school athletic event	53	46	70	59
Met with any teachers or administrators in the local public schools about your own child	31	6*	87	48
Attended any meeting dealing with the local public school situation	28	18	51	34
Attended a PTA meeting	21	7	49	50
Attended a meeting to discuss any of the school reforms being proposed	20	13	35	34
Attended a school board meeting	16	10	27	38
Been a member of any public-school-related committee	15	8	31	18

	National Totals			Public School Parents		
	1994 %	1991 %	1983 %	1994 %	1991 %	1983 %
Attended a school play or concert in any local public school	54	30	24	79	56	42
Attended a local public school athletic event	53	30	25	70	49	42
Met with any teachers or administrators in the local public schools about your own child	31	27	21	87	77	62
Attended any meeting dealing with the local public school situation	28	16**	10	51	36**	18
Attended a PTA meeting	21	14	14	49	38	36
Attended a school board meeting	16	7	8	27	13	16

*Parents of a child approaching school age might consult school personnel about enrolling him or her.
**In 1991 this category was worded: "Attended any meeting dealing with the local public schools."

discomfiture of college admissions officials, a growing number of high schools have even abandoned calculating rank in class, which depends on letter grades that can be converted to numbers.

To determine which format for reporting students' progress was considered preferable, parents of public school children were asked how useful they found each of the following systems: A to F or numeric grades to denote excellent to failing achievement, A to F or numeric grades to describe the student's efforts, a written description of the student's progress, or a checklist that indicates what the student knows and is able to do. Parents felt that the two newer formats were preferable to the more traditional A to F systems. For example, about seven in 10 called both the written description and the checklist "very useful." Two more traditional A to F grading systems, by contrast, were judged very useful by smaller percentages.

The question (asked of parents of public school children—see Table 29):

Interesting Cross Comparisons

Some of the most interesting information in the Phi Delta Kappa/Gallup education poll comes from cross comparisons that can be made among the various subgroups in the sample. (Care should be taken, of course, to observe the confidence intervals described in the table of sampling tolerances that appears elsewhere in this report). A sampling of some interesting cross comparisons follows.

- Of those surveyed, 18% mention fighting/violence/gangs as the biggest problem facing the public schools; however, this figure rises to 31% among nonwhites.

TABLE 29. *Here is a list of different types of reports that the public schools use to inform parents of their children's progress in school. As I read off a description of each type, would you tell me if you consider it very useful, quite useful, not very useful, or not useful at all for informing you about the progress of your child?*

	Very Useful %	Quite Useful %	Not Very Useful %	Not Useful At All %	Don't Know %
A written description of the student's progress in a number of areas	74	20	5	*	1
A checklist which indicates what the student knows and is able to do in each subject	70	22	6	1	1
A to F or numeric grades in each subject to denote excellent to failing achievement	58	32	8	1	1
A to F or numeric grades to describe the student's *effort* in each subject	56	32	9	1	2

*Less than one-half of 1%.

- Of those living in the West, 35% give the public schools in their communities an A or a B. This compares to 52% in the Midwest and 48% in the East.
- Of nonpublic school parents, 69% favor allowing parents to send their school-age children to any public, private, or church-related school (with the government paying all or part of the tuition for those who choose nonpublic schools). This percentage falls to 48% among public school parents and to 42% among those with no children in school.
- Men and women differ over the teaching of "character education" in the schools, with 54% of women—but only 43% of men—in favor.
- Of young respondents—in the 18–29 group—52% favor private, profit-making corporations contracting to operate schools within a certain jurisdiction. However, only 33% of those 65 and older are in favor.

Cross comparisons of this kind can be produced from the data contained in the 415-page document that is the basis for this report. Persons who wish to order this document should write to Phi Delta Kappa, P.O. Box 789, Bloomington, IN 47402. Ph. 800/766-1156. The price is $95, postage included.

Sampling Tolerances

In interpreting survey results, it should be borne in mind that all sample surveys are subject to sampling error, i.e., the extent to which the results may differ from what would be obtained if the whole population surveyed had been interviewed. The size of such sampling error depends largely on the number of interviews.

The following tables may be used in estimating the sampling error of any percentage in this report. The computed allowances have taken into account the effect of the sample design upon sampling error. They may be interpreted as indicating the range (plus or minus the figure shown) within which the results of repeated samplings in the same time period could be expected to vary 95% of the time, assuming the same sampling procedure, the same interviewers, and the same questionnaire.

The first table on the next page shows how much allowance should be made for the sampling error of a percentage:

The table would be used in the following manner: Let us say that a reported percentage is 33 for a group that includes 1,000 respondents. We go to the row for "percentages near 30" in the table and across to the column headed "1,000."

The number at this point is 4, which means that the 33% obtained in the sample is subject to a sampling error of plus or minus four points. In other words, it is very probable (95 chances out of 100) that the true figure would be somewhere between 29% and 37%, with the most likely figure the 33% obtained.

In comparing survey results in two samples, such as, for example, men and women, the question arises as to how large a difference between them must be before one can be reasonably sure that it reflects a real difference. In the tables

Recommended Allowance for Sampling Error of a Percentage

In Percentage Points
(at 95 in 100 confidence level)*
Sample Size

	1,500	1,000	750	600	400	200	100
Percentages near 10	2	2	3	3	4	5	8
Percentages near 20	3	3	4	4	5	7	10
Percentages near 30	3	4	4	5	6	8	12
Percentages near 40	3	4	5	5	6	9	12
Percentages near 50	3	4	5	5	6	9	13
Percentages near 60	3	4	5	5	6	9	12
Percentages near 70	3	4	4	5	6	8	12
Percentages near 80	3	3	4	4	5	7	10
Percentages near 90	2	2	3	3	4	5	8

*The chances are 95 in 100 that the sampling error is not larger than the figures shown.

below, the number of points that must be allowed for in such comparisons is indicated.

Two tables are provided. One is for percentages near 20 or 80; the other, for percentages near 50. For percentages in between, the error to be allowed for lies between those shown in the two tables.

Here is an example of how the tables would be used: Let us say that 50% of men respond a certain way and 40% of women respond that way also, for a dif-

Recommended Allowance for Sampling Error of the Difference

In Percentage Points
(at 95 in 100 confidence level)*

TABLE A Size of Sample	Percentages near 20 or percentages near 80					
	1,500	1,000	750	600	400	200
1,500	4					
1,000	4	5				
750	5	5	5			
600	5	5	6	6		
400	6	6	6	7	7	
200	8	8	8	8	9	10
TABLE B Size of Sample	Percentages near 50					
	1,500	1,000	750	600	400	200
1,500	5					
1,000	5	6				
750	6	6	7			
600	6	7	7	7		
400	7	8	8	8	9	
200	10	10	10	10	11	13

*The chances are 95 in 100 that the sampling error is not larger than the figures shown.

ference of 10 percentage points between them. Can we say with any assurance that the 10-point difference reflects a real difference between men and women on the question? Let us consider a sample that contains approximately 750 men and 750 women.

Since the percentages are near 50, we consult Table B, and, since the two samples are about 750 persons each, we look for the number in the column headed "750," which is also in the row designated "750." We find the number 7 here. This means that the allowance for error should be seven points and that, in concluding that the percentage among men is somewhere between three and 17 points higher than the percentage among women, we should be wrong only about 5% of the time. In other words, we can conclude with considerable confidence that a difference exists in the direction observed and that it amounts to at least three percentage points.

If, in another case, men's responses amount to 22%, say, and women's to 24%, we consult Table A, because these percentages are near 20. We look in the column headed "750" and see that the number is 5. Obviously, then, the two-point difference is inconclusive.

Research Procedure

The Sample. The sample used in this survey embraced a total of 1,326 adults (18 years of age and older). A description of the sample and methodology can be found elsewhere in this report.

Time of Interviewing. The fieldwork for this study was carried out during the period of 10 May to 8 June 1994.

The Report. In the tables used in this report, "Nonpublic School Parents" includes parents of students who attend parochial schools and parents of students who attend private or independent schools.

Due allowance must be made for statistical variation, especially in the case of findings for groups consisting of relatively few respondents, e.g., nonpublic school parents.

The findings of this report apply only to the U.S. as a whole and not to individual communities. Local surveys, using the same questions, can be conducted to determine how local areas compare with the national norm.

Design of the Sample

For the 1994 survey the Gallup Organization used its standard national telephone sample, i.e., and unclustered, directory-assisted, random-digit telephone sample, based on a proportionate stratified sampling design.

The random-digit aspect of the sample was used to avoid "listing" bias. Numerous studies have shown that households with unlisted telephone numbers are different in important ways from listed households. "Unlistedness" is due to household mobility or to customer requests to prevent publication of the telephone number.

To avoid this source of bias, a random-digit procedure designed to provide representation of both listed and unlisted (including not-yet-listed) numbers was used.

Telephone numbers for the continental United States were stratified into four regions of the country and, within each region, further stratified into three size-of-community strata.

Only working banks of telephone numbers were selected. Eliminating non-working banks from the sample increased the likelihood that any sampled telephone number would be associated with a residence.

The sample of telephone numbers produced by the described method is representative of all telephone households within the continental United States.

Within each contacted household, an interview was sought with the youngest man 18 years of age or older who was at home. If no man was home, an interview was sought with the oldest woman at home. This method of respondent selection within households produced an age distribution by sex that closely approximates the age distribution by sex of the total population.

Up to three calls were made to each selected telephone number to complete an interview. The time of day and the day of the week for callbacks were varied so as to maximize the chance of finding a respondent at home. All interviews were conducted on weekends or weekday evenings in order to contact potential respondents among the working population.

The final sample was weighted so that the distribution of the sample matched current estimates derived from the U.S. Census Bureau's Current Population Survey (CPS) for the adult population living in telephone households in the continental U.S.

As has been the case in recent years in the Phi Delta Kappa/Gallup poll series, parents of public school children were oversampled in the 1994 poll. This procedure produced a large enough sample to ensure that findings reported for "public school parents" are statistically significant.

Conducting Your Own Poll

The Phi Delta Kappa Center for Dissemination of Innovative Programs makes available PACE (Polling Attitudes of the Community on Education) materials to enable nonspecialists to conduct scientific polls of attitude and opinion on education. The PACE manual provides detailed information on constructing questionnaires, sampling, interviewing, and analyzing data. It also includes updated census figures and new material on conducting a telephone survey. The price is $55.

For information about using PACE materials, write or phone Neville Robertson at Phi Delta Kappa, P.O. Box 789, Bloomington, IN 47402-0789. Ph. 800/766-1156.

How to Order the Poll

The minimum order for reprints of the published version of the Phi Delta Kappa/Gallup education poll is 25 copies for $10. Additional copies are 25 cents each. This price includes postage for delivery (at the library rate). Where possible, enclose a check or money order. Address your order to Phi Delta Kappa, P.O. Box 789, Bloomington, IN 47402. Ph. 800/766-1156.

Composition of the Sample

Adults	%	Income	%
No children in school	66	$40,000 and over	34
Public school parents	30*	$30,000–$39,999	15
Nonpublic school parents	6*	$20,000–$29,999	16
		$10,000–$19,999	17
Sex	**%**	Under $10,000	9
Men	47	Undesignated	9
Women	53		
		Region	**%**
Race	**%**	East	24
White	83	Midwest	25
Nonwhite	14	South	31
Undesignated	3	West	20
Age	**%**	**Community Size**	**%**
18–29 years	23	Urban	33
30–49 years	44	Suburban	35
50 and over	33	Rural	23
		Undesignated	9
Occupation	**%**		
(Chief Wage Earner)		**Education**	**%**
Business and professional	34	Total College	52
Clerical and sales	10	College graduate	22
Manual labor	29	College incomplete	30
Nonlabor force	2	Total high school	47
Farm	2	High school graduate	33
Undesignated	23	High school incomplete	14
		Undesignated	1

*Total exceeds 34% because some parents have children attending more than one kind of school.

If faster delivery is desired , do not include a remittance with your order. You will be billed at the above rates plus any additional cost involved in the method of delivery.

Acknowledgments

The authors of this report gratefully acknowledge the assistance of the following advisory panel in originating and prioritizing questions for the 26th Phi Delta Kappa/Gallup survey. The panel should not be held responsible, however, for the final form in which the questions were asked or for the way in which answers were interpreted.

Douglas Bedient, president of Phi Delta Kappa and professor of curriculum and instruction, Southern Illinois University; David L. Clark, Kenan Professor of Education, University of North Carolina, Chapel Hill; Chester E. Finn, Jr., founding partner and senior scholar, the Edison Project; Pascal D. Forgione, Jr., state superintendent of public instruction, Delaware; Betty Hale, vice president and director, Leadership Programs, Institute for Educational Leadership;

Katie Haycock, director, Education Roundtable, American Association for Higher Education; Vinetta Jones, national director, Equity 2000 Program; James A. Kelly, president, National Board for Professional Teaching Standards; Sally B. Kilgore, senior fellow and director of educational policy studies, Hudson Institute; Joanne Kogan, communications manager, National Board for Professional Teaching Standards; Anne Lynch, past president, National Congress of Parents and Teachers; Gene Maeroff, senior research associate, Carnegie Foundation for the Advancement of Teaching; John Merrow, executive officer, Learning Matters; Richard A. Miller, executive director, American Association of School Administrators; John Murphy, superintendent, Charlotte-Mecklenburg (N.C.) Schools; Joe Nathan, director, Center for School Change, University of Minnesota; Peter J. Negroni, superintendent, Springfield (Mass.) Schools; Ted Sanders, superintendent of public instruction, Ohio; Gilbert T. Sewall, director, American Textbook Council, and editor, *Social Studies Review;* Thomas A. Shannon, executive director, National School Boards Association; and Brenda Wellburn, executive director, National Association of State Boards of Education.

Section VIII
Comparative Experimental Methods in Educational Research

Comparative Experiments in Educational Research

Andrew C. Porter
University of Wisconsin-Madison

Overview

Of all empirical work, comparative experiments provide the strongest evidence about the effects of education interventions. Unlike other empirical methods, these comparative experiments can supply answers to questions like the following: Does site-based decision making result in increased student achievement? Does the Cognitively Guided Instruction project increase primary school students' ability to use their mathematical knowledge to solve novel problems?

Comparative experiments also provide the best answers to theory-driven questions about cause and effect. What are comparative experiments and why are they so useful in determining whether or not causal relationships exist?

This introduction to comparative experiments in educational research is organized into four main sections. First, experiments are presented as one formal method for investigating whether or not a specific set of actions causes predictable changes in behavior. Key terms necessary for understanding experiments are defined. In the second section, requirements for arguing cause are considered, and experiments are defined in light of these requirements. Illustrations are provided of both experimental and nonexperimental research, making clear that experiments represent only one form of research.

In the third section, criteria are presented for judging the quality of an experiment. The first criterion concerns the ambiguity in deciding which of several possibilities were the causal factors in an experiment. The criterion is called internal validity. The second criterion, precision, reflects a concern for the accuracy of experimental results. The third criterion is called external validity and reflects the fact that a good experiment provides results that can be generalized for use elsewhere.

Having defined what an experiment is and how to judge its quality, the role of experiments in educational research is considered in the fourth and final section of the paper. Here, the strengths and limitations of experiments are outlined.

Starting With a Question

Much of what educators do they do with the belief that through their actions students will profit in some way. Not surprisingly, therefore, a great deal of educational research is conducted with an eye toward seeing whether beliefs about alternative educational practices are correct. For example, is cooperative learning to be preferred over whole-group instruction? Should basic skills be mastered before students learn to apply knowledge, or is instruction more effective when basic skills and applications are integrated? These questions have in common a concern for choosing among alternative educational practices. If I do this, will the result be better than if I do something else? Experiments represent one formal method for investigating the relative merits of educational practices.

Most experiments begin with just such a broad and general question as, Which is better, cooperative learning or whole-group instruction? Certainly it would be nice to know the answer to this general question, but unfortunately the question has many interpretations. Each interpretation might result in a different answer. For example, what exactly is meant by cooperative learning? Does it mean students work in groups where each group member plays a unique role (Aronson, Blaney, Stephan, Sikes, & Snapp, 1978)? Are students graded according to the quality and quantity of group products, or are grades based only on independent individual work (Slavin, 1983)? And what is meant by whole-group instruction? Are you imagining teacher lectures, or are you imagining group discussions? Any of these alternative interpretations would be consistent with the initial question, and the goals of instruction have still to be considered. Are cognitive skills of interest and, if so, in what subject? Some people would be equally interested (or even more interested) in student affect, such as self-concept and how the student feels toward school and learning. Finally, under what conditions are cooperative learning and whole-group instruction to be compared? Is the interest in school learning something else, such as military training? If the initial general question brought school learning to your mind, what types of teachers and students did you imagine?

From a general question about which alternative educational practice is preferred follow a very large number of interpretations, each of which might lead to a different specific question and so a different answer. If there are different answers depending upon the specific interpretation, then the general question has no answer.

Hypotheses

Thus, a very important part of experimental research is restating the general question into one or more of its specific interpretations. Each specific interpretation is then translated into a statement of belief about alternative practices. These statements of belief are *hypotheses*. To illustrate, a researcher might start with the general question, "Which is better, cooperative learning or whole-group instruction?" A specific question might be, "Which is better, education in which students work in groups and each student plays a unique role or education in which there is group discussion?" The resulting hypothesis might be "Education in which students work in groups and each student plays a unique role is better than education in which there is group discussion."

In hypotheses, the alternative practices would represent what is called the independent variable. A variable is simply something that can differ, for example, from student to student, teacher to teacher, or school to school. Because students might be taught by either cooperative learning or by whole-group instruction, those two methods of instruction represent a variable. The goals of the methods of instruction represent what are called dependent variables. In the example about cooperative learning and whole-group instruction, the goal might be to increase reading comprehension. Reading comprehension would then be the dependent variable in the hypothesis. Because reading comprehension differs from student to student, reading comprehension is a variable.

Independent and Dependent Variables

To reiterate, experiments begin with a general question that is then made into a specific statement of belief called a hypothesis. Two important parts of a hypothesis are the independent variable and the dependent variable. Both the independent and the dependent variables represent characteristics that can be used to describe differences of interest, for example, differences among students. The *independent variable* is something that is believed to predict or bring about other differences (e.g., method of instruction). The resulting differences represent the *dependent variable* (e.g., reading comprehension).

Experiments are conducted to check the validity of a hypothesis. For example, it might be hypothesized that: Cooperative learning results in better reading comprehension than does whole-group instruction. Still, the independent variable, type of instruction, and the dependent variable, reading comprehension, need more explicit definition prior to conducting an experiment. The objective is to state a hypothesis that is specific enough that it can be shown to be either generally true or generally false.

The idea of a statement being either generally true or generally false is very important to experiments. It must be possible to imagine a study that could lead you either to believe more strongly in your original hypothesis or to reject that hypothesis and so come to change your original belief. In short, a hypothesis must be testable. The original question about cooperative learning and whole-group instruction was not directly testable because it was too general. To answer the original question would have required considering all the different methods of cooperative learning and all the different methods of whole-group instruction. Similarly, all of the different possible conceptions of reading comprehension would need to be considered.

Population

Even given explicit definitions for the types of instruction and reading comprehension, the hypothesis remains ambiguous about the conditions for which it is to be true. The validity of the hypothesis may depend on answers to such questions as: What types of students? What types of teachers? In what types of physical arrangements will students be learning? The answers to these and similar questions must be provided before the hypothesis is complete. The answers define what is called the *population* for the hypothesis. A *population* is the collection of instances for which the statement about independent and dependent variables is believed to hold. When an experiment is done to test a hypothesis, it is done with the intention of concluding that the hypothesis is either true or false for a well-defined population (e.g., all fourth graders in the state of Wisconsin who are in public schools and who have teachers with three or more years of teaching experience).

You may think that cooperative learning versus whole-group instruction is a positively awful example for an introduction to the concept of experiments in education. After all, doesn't everybody know that cooperative learning is superior to whole-group instruction? But the evidence makes clear that the benefits of cooperative learning depend on the particulars (see Good & Brophy's *Educational Psychology*, 1990, for a summary of this point and supporting research).

Arguing Cause

At a minimum, then, a hypothesis specifies an independent variable, a dependent variable, and a population. But experiments are not appropriate for testing all hypotheses. Experiments are limited to testing hypotheses about independent variables that cause changes in dependent variables. The important word is "cause." When contrasting cooperative learning and whole-group instruction, the interest is in whether a student will read with better comprehension if he or she is taught with one method rather than the other. In short, does the method of instruction *cause* changes in reading comprehension?

Some Necessary Conditions

While philosophers debate the precise meaning of the word *cause*, there are three conditions that are commonly held as necessary for arguing that an independent variable causes predictable changes in a dependent variable. First, changes in the independent variable must precede changes in the dependent variable. Second, the independent and dependent variables must be correlated. *Correlated* simply means that the experimental condition a subject experienced (in this example, cooperative learning or whole-group instruction) is useful in predicting the subject's performance on the dependent variable (reading comprehension). For example, if one observed that the average achievement in reading comprehension of students who received cooperative-learning instruction was higher than that for students who received whole-group instruction, then knowledge of type of instruction received predicts student achievement. The independent variable, type of instruction, is correlated with the dependent variable, student achievement. Third, there must be no plausible third variable that explains why a correlation was found between the independent and dependent variables. The independent variable alone must be the reason that a correlation was found. For example, it should not be the case that higher achieving students were more likely to receive cooperative-learning instruction than they were to receive whole-group instruction because differences in the achievement of students would then be a plausible third-variable explanation for the correlation observed.

Clearly it is difficult to design and conduct a study that will provide a convincing argument of cause. For example, many nonexperimental studies have found that students who have relatively positive self-concepts of academic ability have also achieved relatively well on cognitive skills in school. But these nonexperimental studies leave ambiguous which came first, positive self-concept or high achievement. Even when it seems clear that the independent variable preceded differences in the dependent variable, there are an infinity of "third" variables that singly or in combination might have been responsible for a correlation between the independent and dependent variables. To further complicate matters, a lack of correlation can also result from the effects of "third" variables. For example, many people have argued that evaluations conducted to investigate the effects of Title I programs were biased in that only students most in need were eligible to participate in Title I. Because students in Title I programs started out behind, they would have done well just to catch up with students not in Title I. Campbell and Erlebacher (1970) claim that evaluations reporting no difference between students in Title I and not in Title I were really evidence in favor of program success.

Because a great deal of educational research (not just experiments) is used to support statements of cause, the three conditions for cause just given (i.e., temporal antecedence, correlation of experimental conditions and outcomes, and the lack of plausible alternative explanations) are useful in planning and understanding educational research, beyond just experiments. Even when the word *cause* is not used explicitly, researchers and individual readers of a research report may still infer causality in the report. For example, all educational evaluations conducted to assess an innovation or to aid decisions about a preferred educational practice are attempts to establish a causal link between practice and outcomes. Some researchers go out of their way to avoid use of the word *cause* because the criteria for arguing a cause are so demanding. But many words carry the connotation of cause: produce, create, induce, evoke, elicit, affect, institute, bring about. If cause is of interest, then arguing cause should be one of the explicit goals of the research. The reporting of results and the critiquing of their validity would then be done with both eyes open for plausible alternative explanations of results.

So experiments are done to test hypotheses about causal relationships between independent and dependent variables. But what are experiments and what are they not?

Experiments: A More Formal Definition

The word *experiment* is used a great deal, and in a number of different contexts. For purposes of describing educational research methods, placing some limits on what is meant by an experiment is useful. First, an experiment is comparative. It includes at least two different conditions represented by the independent variable, as in the example, cooperative learning versus whole-group instruction.

Second, the independent variable is under the direct control of the researcher. For purposes here, an experiment is not the study of naturally occurring changes in the independent variable; rather, it is the study of planned changes. Simply locating 20 teachers who said they were using cooperative learning and comparing the achievement of their students to that of students of 20 teachers who said they used whole-group instruction would not be an experiment. In the words of the famous statistician George Box (1966), "To find out what happens to a system when you interfere with it you have to interfere with it (not just passively observe it)."

Third, the decision about which subjects will receive which experimental condition is made randomly. Random assignment is a process that gives each subject an equally likely chance of experiencing any one of the experimental conditions under investigation. These three limits are motivated by the three conditions described earlier for establishing cause.

Experiments: An Illustration

An illustration may help. A study was conducted to investigate the accuracy of diagnoses of school psychologists (Frame, Clarizio, & Porter, 1984). Briefly, it was hypothesized that the diagnosis of a student as learning disabled depends on the student's race (black/white) and socioeconomic status (high/low) and on the general achievement level of the school the student attends (high/low). The school psychologists were all from the state of Michigan and were experienced professionals. The experimental task did not involve diagnoses of actual students. Rather, a single student was represented by a file containing the full range of information that school psychologists attempt to collect prior to making a diagnosis. Thus, the main difference between actual practice and the experimental conditions was that, in the experiment, the school psychologists requested information from the experimenters about a simulated child instead of working with a child.

As you have probably concluded, the independent variables of the study were the simulated case's race and socioeconomic status and the school's achievement level. Sometimes when the independent variables of interest are difficult to bring under experimental control, a simulation can be used to address questions of cause and effect. As is usually true, there were several dependent variables including the nature of the diagnosis and the extent to which diagnoses among school psychologists were in agreement.

By considering all possible combinations of race, socioeconomic status, and school achievement, eight experimental conditions were created. For example, one such condition was a white student from a family with high socioeconomic status who attends a school where achievement is high. Because a simulated student was used, it was possible to keep all information about the student the same for each of the eight experimental conditions except, of course, the three independent variables. School psychologists were then randomly assigned to diagnose one of the eight simulated students, and their diagnoses were recorded.

Consider again the three requirements placed on experiments. The study was comparative for each of the three independent variables. Each of the independent variables was under the direct control of the researcher. Finally, the decision about which school psychologists would diagnose which experimental conditions was made randomly. The study was an experiment. Incidentally, diagnoses were found to differ according to experimental conditions. For example, school psychologists were less likely to prescribe special class instruction for the black simulated student than for the white simulated student. Of course, the questions remain about whether or not the results from school psychologists diagnosing a simulated child represent what school psychologists do in the field.

To further understand what experiments are, consider some types of research that are not experiments. First, only research studies designed to test the validity of statements about independent variables causing changes in dependent variables are candidates for consideration as experiments. This immediately rules out large classes of research studies. For example, studies done to investigate the utility of the Graduate Record Examination for predicting success in graduate school are not experiments. In general, studies that investigate the utility and fairness of criteria used for making decisions about educational opportunities are not experimental studies. Studies with the purpose of describing education as it is are not experiments either because they lack an interest in causal relationships. A well-known example is the Gallup poll of public opinion about education.

Even research to investigate causal relationships between independent and dependent variables is not always experimental. For example, most research on the effectiveness of education programs has not been experimental, though there are exceptions. The typical study of the effects of programs involves comparing schools or classrooms using a specific program to schools or classrooms not using the program. Those using the program typically made that decision themselves, just as those in the comparison group decided not to use the program. In this research the independent variable is not under the control of the researcher, and there is no random assignment of students, classrooms, or schools. The research is not experimental. Still the interest is in determining whether or not the program produced the benefits anticipated, a causal question. Nonexperimental studies of causal relations must find ways to rule out "plausible third variable" explanations of results. For example, if the program schools look better, is it because of the program or is it because the program schools were volunteers anxious to improve in whatever ways they could?

Another common method of investigating program effects is to test student performance against the goals of an innovation, give the students the innovation, and then test the students a second time. For example, the innovation might be some form of computer-aided instruction. Although such a study gives the researcher direct control over the independent variable (before innovation versus after innovation), it does not involve random assignment of students to those two conditions. Because most students benefit at least to some extent from any reasonable type of instruction, the question of cause must be, did students gain more in achievement from the computer-aided instruction than they would have gained otherwise? Because all students are first without the innovation and later all students receive the innovation, the design fails to provide an estimate of what students would have gained from "regular" instruction. An experiment would randomly assign some students to receive the innovation and other students to receive regular instruction.

Three Goals of Experimental Design

Simply being able to distinguish between what is and what is not an experiment is not terribly useful. What is more important is knowing how to assess the strengths and weaknesses of an experiment.

To understand the advantages and difficulties of experiments for testing hypotheses about cause-and-effect relationships, it is useful to understand three goals of experimental design. The first goal is directly related to the interest in cause and is sometimes stated as, an experiment should have internal validity. Consider again the hypothesis that cooperative learning results in better reading comprehension than does whole-group instruction. To test this hypothesis, a researcher might have some students taught by a particular method of cooperative learning and some other students taught by a particular method of whole-group instruction. Students in both groups would then be given a test of reading comprehension. If method of instruction is the only plausible interpretation for any differences in reading comprehension between the two groups of students in the study, then method of instruction must be the cause of those differences. If the independent variable is the only reasonable explanation for differences in the dependent variable, the study is said to have internal validity.

The second goal of experimental design reflects the possibility that differences among individual students on reading comprehension may be considerable, regardless of the method of instruction used to teach these skills. For example, even if cooperative learning was somewhat better than whole-group instruction, it would be quite likely that several of the best students who received whole-group instruction would have better reading comprehension skills than several of the poorest students who received cooperative-learning instruction. The test results for these students would make more difficult the objective of determining whether whole-group instruction or cooperative learning was better. The second goal of experimental design, then, is to conduct a study in which even small differences caused by the independent variable are measured with sufficient accuracy that they will not be overlooked, even though they are embedded in relatively large individual differences among subjects. This goal is called precision.

The third goal of experimental design is that valid generalizations can be made from the study. For example, if cooperative-learning instruction were superior to whole-group instruction in a particular study, the next question would be, Does the finding generalize to other students, teachers, and conditions? To the extent that the study had external validity, at least some of these desired generalizations would be appropriate. The issue of external validity was raised with the results from the simulation experiment of diagnosing learning disabilities given earlier.

When interpreting the results of an experiment or when designing an experiment, the experiment should be considered from the perspectives of internal validity, precision, and external validity. Each of these three goals is discussed separately in greater detail.

Internal Validity

Judging the extent to which you believe an experiment has internal validity is equivalent to deciding how much of the correlation between the independent and dependent variables you believe was caused by the independent variable. How effective was the design of the experiment in allowing you to rule out explanations, other than the independent variable, for differences between experimental conditions on the dependent variable? Clearly, if the brightest students received cooperative-learning instruction and the poorest students received whole-group instruction, a finding in favor of cooperative learning would be suspect.

Confounding Variables

The most important concept for judging the internal validity of an experiment is the concept of confounding variables. A variable is said to be confounded with the independent variable of a study if the two variables are inseparable. In the example above, the brightness of students was confounded with the method of instruction. Students' brightness is then an explanation for differences between the two groups of students taught by different methods of instruction. Because method of instruction is also an explanation, the two explanations are confounded. An experiment has internal validity, therefore, to the extent that no variables are confounded with the independent variable.

Random Assignment

As stated previously, a crucial part of the definition of a comparative experiment is that the experimenter uses random assignment in determining which subjects will experience which experimental condition. (Subjects need not be individual students and can be classrooms or even whole schools.) The essential idea behind the process of random assignment is that, for an initial pool of subjects, each has an equally likely chance of being assigned to any one of the experimental conditions to be compared. Random assignment is, therefore, a way of guarding against confounding variables.

Before considering the strengths and weaknesses of random assignment of subjects to experimental conditions, a brief description of the process is appropriate. Imagine that you have 40 subjects that you wish to randomly assign to one or the other of two experimental conditions. You need a process that gives each of the subjects an equal chance of being assigned a particular experimental condition. One method for random assignment is to use a table of random numbers. The method begins by putting the subjects' names in a list in alphabetical order. A subject can then be represented by a number indicating that subject's position on the list. The table of random numbers has been prepared such that each number has an equally likely chance of having been placed anywhere in the table. The researcher begins reading the table in any row and any column. Reading from the table of random numbers, the first 20 numbers between 1 and 40 indicate the positions of subjects on the list of subjects to be assigned one of the two experimental conditions. The remaining subjects are assigned to the other experimental condition. Random assignment is a process that ensures each subject's having an equally likely chance of being assigned to each experimental condition. Random assignment is not accidental, fortuitous, or casual.

In thinking about the value of random assignment in eliminating confounding variables, a few points are worth emphasizing. First, random assignment takes place at the beginning of an experiment and is followed by the experimental conditions. The dependent variable is not observed until the end of the experiment. Thus, for experiments, the independent variable precedes the dependent variable. The temporal antecedence requirement for arguing cause is unambiguously established. In this sense, all experiments include at least three sequential activities: (a) random assignment, followed by (b) application of experimental conditions, and finally, (c) observation of the dependent variables. Second, randomization is a process of assignment and not a result of assignment. It is virtually impossible to look at the composition of experimental groups created by someone else and from that to judge accurately whether or not they were created randomly. Third, randomization creates comparison groups at the outset of the experiment that differ only by chance on all possible confounding variables. Randomization not only eliminates the confounding variables that the researcher may have considered, but it also eliminates the confounding variables the researcher may have overlooked. This is the real power of random assignment.

The utility of random assignment for controlling confounding variables must, of course, be tempered by the realization that the process is based on chance, and by chance alone experimental groups will differ at least to some extent. For example, an experiment used to compare cooperative learning and whole-group instruction would begin by identifying a large enough pool of classrooms to institute both methods of instruction. If the initial pool for assignment consisted of only two classrooms, however, the two groups would differ at the outset of the experiment to the same degree that the two classrooms differed (and that might be considerable). In such a case, many characteristics of the two classrooms would be totally confounded with the independent variable and would constitute a major threat to the goal of providing a strong statement about cause. If there were four classrooms in the initial pool, the chances would be a little less that the best students (or the best teachers) would end up in a single group. The more classrooms in the initial pool, the smaller the chance that there will be worrisome differences between experimental groups at the outset of the experiment. Still, chance plays a part in the final results of any experiment.

Assessing the Utility of Random Assignment

Imagine 20 students randomly assigned to receive a version of cooperative learning and 20 students to receive a version of whole-group instruction. One method for delivering the two modes of instruction would be to form two experimental classes of 20 students each and then have one teacher teach the cooperative-learning instruction class while another teacher taught the whole-group instruction class. Even though students were randomly assigned to the two classes and even if the two teachers were randomly assigned to classes, the characteristics of teachers would be confounded with methods of instruction. For most people, this would represent a serious threat to internal validity. One teacher might be more effective, regardless of method of instruction.

To unconfound teachers from experimental conditions would require identifying several existing classrooms of students each with a different teacher and then randomly assigning classrooms to methods of instruction. Each method would then be represented by several teachers. Of course, the need for several teachers increases the cost of the experiment. You may wonder why one teacher couldn't teach both classrooms. Although using one instructor would prevent teachers from being confounded with the method of instruction, the strategy introduces another confounding variable. If one teacher taught both classrooms, then one classroom would have to be taught first and the other second. Among other difficulties, this confounds both order of presentation and time of day with the independent variable, methods of instruction. The possibilities for confounding variables to enter a design are virtually unlimited.

The internal validity that is gained through random assignment of subjects to experimental conditions is the real strength of experiments, compared to other research methods. Consider a typical study of teaching practices. Several classrooms and their teachers are recruited, and students are tested on school achievement variables in both fall and spring of a school year. The researcher observes teaching practices during the school year and attempts to relate them to student gains in achievement. Useful as these studies may be, they always suffer from the presence of confounding variables. There is always ambiguity in deciding whether teaching practices caused the relationships between teaching practices and student achievement. What confounding variables are you imagining? Probably the first one that came to your mind was student aptitude. The most able students will probably have the biggest achievement gains regardless of the quality of the instruction they receive. There will be a tendency for the teaching behaviors of teachers who have the most able students to appear as though they produced the greatest gains in student achievement. Teachers of the most able students may have actually employed the most effective teaching methods, or whatever teaching practices were used with the most able students appeared to be most effective. It might even be that able students cause teachers to follow certain instructional practices (e.g., teaching at a faster pace or giving more frequent positive feedback to students). The implications for practice are quite different if one believes that faster paced instruction produces more student learning than if one believes that teachers who have more able students cover more content. There are, of course, many other potentially confounding variables for this nonexperimental design.

The ever-popular pretest/posttest design is yet another context in which to understand the implication of confounding variables. One group of students takes a test on the dependent variable, it then receives an educational innovation, and finally the students are tested once more on the dependent variable.

The researcher is interested in student gains on the dependent variable and would like to attribute those gains to the innovation. But what are the possibilities for confounding to have occurred between the two times of testing? Campbell and Stanley (1963), in their classic chapter on experimental and quasi-experimental designs, provided a taxonomy of the types of possible confounding. Students may do better on the second test because they learned from taking the first test; the second test may be different from the first in some way that makes it easier; the students themselves are older and more mature; or during the course of the study the students may have received some experiences (other than the experimental condition) that changed them and improved their performance on the dependent variable.

Experiments are the single most effective method for ruling out confounding variables, but experiments are not infallible indicators of the presence or absence of causal relationships. Randomization only starts experimental groups out in the right way. Absence of confounding variables at the beginning of an experiment does not guarantee absence of confounding variables at the end of an experiment. There are plenty of opportunities for important confounding variables to creep into the design while the study is being conducted. Subjects may drop out of the experimental groups at different rates or for different reasons. Observations on the dependent variables may inadvertently result in observers being confounded with experimental conditions or even reflect experimenter bias. Data can be incorrectly coded in ways that create confounding. In fact, anything that happens systematically during the course of the study and results in a different treatment of subjects in one experimental condition from subjects in another must either be included in the definition of a treatment or become a confounding variable.

There is no foolproof method for insuring internal validity. Experiments are a big help, but even experiments differ greatly in their ability to convince. One hopes that, as confounding variables are identified (usually in retrospect), their probable effects can be judged either by common sense or from the research literature and in that way be taken into account.

Precision

For an experiment to have internal validity is important, but that alone is not enough. An experiment must also be designed so that, if the independent variable causes differences in the dependent variable, those differences will be detected. In short, the experiment must have precision.

Because of random assignment, chance plays a part in the results of any experiment. Through random assignment there is always the chance that by bad luck all students of a particular type will be assigned to the same experimental condition. One way to think about precision is that the more precise an experiment, the less likely it is that the experiment will yield large chance differences between experimental groups.

To better understand the concept of precision, it may be useful to digress a bit and consider the typical ways that results of experiments are reported. At its simplest, an experiment can be thought of as describing the average difference between two experimental conditions on a dependent variable (e.g., student achievement). Thus an experiment might report that, on the average, students who received cooperative-learning instruction scored four points higher on a particular test of reading comprehension than did students who received whole-group instruction. Because classrooms were randomly assigned to experimental conditions, an important question remains. Is it reasonable to believe that cooperative-learning instruction was more effective than whole-group instruction, or should the experimenter conclude that the four-point difference was likely to happen by the chance results of random assignment? Deciding between these two alternative interpretations of the four-point difference is an important aspect of experimental research.

Statistical Significance

The results of an experiment are often reported as statistically significant or not. If they are statistically significant, the researcher decided that the difference between experimental conditions did not happen by chance. If they are not statistically significant, the study failed to provide evidence of the superiority of one experimental condition over another. The rules for deciding whether or not the results of an experiment were statistically significant are called the procedures of inferential statistics.

Briefly, experimenters use the rules of statistical inference to decide for their particular studies how large the observed difference between experimental conditions must be to be judged statistically significant. Of course, the more certain the experimenter wishes to be that a difference called statistically significant was not due to chance, the larger the required difference must be. Without going into details, the procedures of statistical significance begin with an experimenter stating how willing he or she is to make a mistake when concluding that a difference does exist. A common criterion is to take a 5% chance of making such a mistake.

Returning to the concept of precision, sometimes experiments result in quite large differences between experimental conditions, and still the rules of statistical inference lead to a decision of no significance. This is a particularly frustrating situation. Even if the difference appears large, if it is no larger than might be expected by chance, the researcher is forced to conclude that the independent variable did not affect the dependent variable. The only information gained is that the experiment lacked precision. The experiment should not have been conducted because the unacceptable precision could have been predicted.

In short, the second goal of experimental design is to conduct a study such that if a "large difference" is found between experimental conditions, that difference will also be judged by the rules of statistical inference to be significant.

Judging the Importance of a Difference

Before considering ways in which the precision of an experiment can be enhanced, a comment on the cavalier use of the term *large difference* is in order. What may be a large difference in the eyes of one person may not be a large difference in the eyes of another. How would you go about deciding what constitutes a large difference in average reading comprehension between cooperative learning and whole-group instruction? Would you consider the four-point difference I mentioned earlier to be important if you knew it had been caused by differences in the method of instruction? Of course you can't say. You are probably wondering about the types of items on the test of reading comprehension. You may also be wondering what types of decisions are to be made about school practices based on the four-point difference. You may even be wondering what types of students were involved in the study. Deciding what constitutes large or important differences is a highly personal activity. There is no right or wrong answer.

Saying that a difference between experimental conditions was statistically significant is not synonymous with saying that a difference was large or important. Using statistical significance as an indication of importance is a common mistake that should be avoided. Statistical significance only indicates that a difference was *not* due to the chances of random assignment. A statement of statistical significance leaves completely unanswered the question, How important was the difference that can be attributed to experimental conditions? It is possible to design a study that is so precise that a difference as small as a fraction of a test score point would be judged significant by methods of statistical inference.

Confidence Intervals

Although it has been common practice to report the results of an experiment as simply statistically significant or not, many argue that this practice does not go far enough (e.g., Carver, 1978). First, that kind of reporting encourages the belief that statistical significance implies importance, which isn't true. Second, a researcher is not likely to be satisfied by knowing simply whether or not a difference happened by chance. A researcher will probably want to have some idea about how big the difference was. For these reasons, many researchers prefer to report the size of difference found between experimental conditions and then to indicate that because of random assignment the difference might have been a little higher or a little lower. The procedure of establishing upper and lower limits on an observed difference between experimental conditions is called building a confidence interval. Confidence intervals represent an alternative to reporting results as simply statistically significant or not.

Basically, the same procedures are used to build confidence intervals as are used to decide whether or not a difference was statistically significant. Returning to the example of a four-point difference between cooperative learning and whole-group instruction, a confidence interval could have indicated that the true difference between instructional methods might be as low as three points or as high as five points. This information indicates that there was a statistically significant difference between methods of instruction and also provides a range of values, three to five, for thinking about how big the difference actually was. Alternatively, had the interval included zero (i.e., no difference between methods), the conclusion would have been that the difference was not statistically significant. Just as deciding on statistical significance requires setting a criterion level for chance errors, so does building a confidence interval. If a researcher were willing to take a 5% chance of mistakenly thinking a difference was real, this same researcher might decide instead to build a 95% confidence interval.

If a confidence interval is used to report the results of an experiment, precision can be thought of in terms of the width of the interval. The narrower the interval, the more precise the experiment is. An experiment with perfect precision would yield a confidence interval with no width at all. The interval would be a single point.

Improving Precision

So precision is an important attribute for any experiment to have. Without precision, even an internally valid experiment may fail to detect important differences between experimental conditions and leave the mistaken impression that the various conditions lead to equivalent results. But how can the precision of an experiment be made acceptable?

The most direct method for increasing the precision of an experiment is to increase the number of subjects assigned to each experimental condition. As indicated earlier, the larger the number of subjects to be randomly assigned, the less likely it is that random assignment will result in unusual groups of subjects. Increasing the number of subjects is often expensive, however, and there are other ways to improve precision.

A straightforward way to make sure that not all of the most able students (or classrooms) are assigned to a single experimental condition is first to group students according to aptitude. Then, for each group of students at a specified aptitude, randomly assign equal numbers to each experimental condition. This insures that each experimental condition has subjects with similar aptitude levels. The procedure is called blocking and is one way to improve precision.

There are several other ways to improve precision, some of which are quite complicated and technical. For illustration, consider just one more. Clearly, if all subjects for an experiment were identical, random assignment could not result in an unusual composition of experimental groups. Precision would be assured. You are probably saying that identical subjects are an impossibility. In a sense you are right. Still, some researchers have used identical twins as subjects in an attempt to improve precision. My earlier example of an experiment to study the accuracy of school psychologists provides another illustration. In that study school psychologists diagnosed a single simulated student. Using a simulated student increased precision over what it would have been had each psychologist diagnosed a different actual student.

External Validity

The first two goals of experimental design, internal validity and precision, are primarily concerned with interpreting the results of a particular study as it was conducted. But an experiment would have little utility if the results only revealed what was true for that particular study. The third goal of experimental design, then, is to have an experiment from which it is possible to make valid generalizations. The goal is called external validity. The word *external* indicates an interest in concluding that the findings of a particular study have validity beyond or external to that study.

One way to think about external validity is to imagine a particular experiment and then attempt to identify situations in which you believe the results might not apply. To illustrate the point, consider again the experiment to investigate the accuracy of school psychologists' diagnoses. The experiment used a simulated learning-disabled student to investigate the effects of student race, socioeconomic level, and school general achievement level have on school psychologists' diagnoses. The school psychologists in the study were experienced professionals recruited from school districts in Michigan. School psychologists were randomly assigned to diagnose one of the eight versions of the simulated student. To what situations would you be willing to generalize the significant finding from this study that school psychologists were less likely to prescribe special class instruction for the black simulated student? To the extent that you would be unwilling to generalize the result, the experiment lacked external validity for you.

In the words of Bracht and Glass (1968):

> Threats to external validity appear to fall into two broad classes: (1) those dealing with generalizations to populations of persons (What population of subjects can be expected to behave in the same way as did the . . . experimental subjects?), and (2) those dealing with the "environment" of the experiment (Under what conditions . . . can the same results be expected?). (p. 438)

The results of the school psychologist experiment may be valid for school psychologists outside of Michigan and for inexperienced school psychologists, but there is no evidence from the experiment that this is so. If generalizations are to be made to other states or to inexperienced school psychologists, the grounds for such generalization would need to be based on information not provided by the experiment.

Random Selection

Depending on how school psychologists were recruited, it might not even be appropriate to generalize the results of the experiment to all experienced school psychologists in Michigan. In an ideal experiment, all experienced school psychologists in Michigan would have been identified and put on a list. The list would represent the population of school psychologists referred to in the hypotheses for the experiment. Participants in the experiment would then be selected from the list, using a process that gave each person on the list an equally likely chance of being selected and ultimately included in the study. The process is called random selection. Random selection from a well-defined population is ideal, because the process insures, within the limits of chance, that the participants in the study are representative of the population from which they were selected. Had random selection been used to select school psychologists, the results of the study could be straightforwardly generalized to the population of experienced school psychologists in Michigan.

Do not confuse random selection with the earlier concept of random assignment. Random selection and random assignment serve two distinctly different purposes. Random assignment is motivated by internal validity, and random selection is motivated by external validity. Random assignment is an essential ingredient of an experiment, but because of costs and subject availability, random selection is almost never part of an experiment's design. Rather, subjects are recruited as best they can be. In the case for the experienced school psychologists, volunteers were recruited from the pool of graduates from several different degree programs.

Generalizing Across Subjects

How then should the external validity of the experiment with school psychologists be thought about? Is generalization limited to the subjects immediately involved? More generally, because random selection is rarely used in experiments, are the results of experiments typically limited to the subjects used? Most people answer these questions with a decided, "No." People who are willing to generalize from an experiment, however, require a careful description of the subjects. The description defines a hypothetical population to be used for purposes of interpreting results.

We already know that the subjects were experienced school psychologists working in Michigan. But clearly we need to know more about these psychologists if we are to generalize the results of the experiment. What was meant by the word *experienced*? What were the theoretical persuasions of the school psychologists? In general, the more complete the description, the easier it becomes to think about the range of external validity of the experiment. Given a thorough description of the subjects in the experiment on school psychologists, people will differ in their willingness to generalize the results. Some people will conclude that the results are even valid for states other than Michigan.

So the results of an experiment may be valid for types of subjects that were not included in the experiment. There is another way, however, that external validity may be threatened even for the types of subjects used. Imagine that the experienced school psychologists could be categorized into two groups. For example, half the school psychologists may have received their training from one institution and the other half from another institution. School psychologists from both institutions are represented in the study, and so, on the surface, it would appear that the results can be generalized to both types of school psychologists. But the results of experiments are reported as averages across all subjects. An experiment may indicate no *average* difference between experimental conditions when in fact there was a difference between experimental conditions for each of two types of subjects. This apparent paradox will occur when the difference between experimental conditions was in a different direction for each type of subject. The two differences simply cancel each other when the averages are computed. When the size and/or direction of an experimental effect depends on some characteristics of the subjects (e.g., the institution from which they received their training), there is said to be a *treatment* by subject characteristic interaction. More generally, interactions limit (or at least describe) the external validity of an experiment. When interactions are hypothesized, the experiment should be designed so that the interaction hypothesis can be tested. The straightforward way to test for interaction is to first block on the subject characteristic and then, within each block of subjects, to randomly assign subjects to experimental conditions. In the school psychologist example, subjects could have been blocked by the institution from which they received their training and then for each block separately randomly assigned to the eight experimental conditions.

Generalizing Across Experimental Conditions

Threats to external validity are not limited, however, to concerns about types of subjects. One must also consider the conditions under which the experiment was conducted.

The school psychologist experiment provides fertile ground for illustrating several ways in which experimental conditions can limit external validity. Remember that school psychologists diagnosed a simulated student who was the same in all eight experimental conditions. Clearly, only one example of learning disability was considered. If the results of the study are to be generalized, one would need to know the nature of that specific example of learning disability. The experiment provides no direct evidence about whether the same results would have been obtained for a different type of learning disability.

The school psychologist experiment is also an example of what might be called a laboratory study. The subjects were not working in their natural environment with real students. There is no question but that they realized they were in an experiment, although they were not told the purposes of the experiment. Still, one must at least raise the question of whether their behavior in the simulation was representative of how they would behave as psychologists in their school districts. Did the subjects merely respond as they felt they should have responded and not as they would ordinarily? Because they were confronted with only a single student, did they perform their work more carefully than when they are under the pressure of a heavy work schedule? Did the experimenter inadvertently reveal a desired set of responses? Unfortunately, the experiment did not provide answers to these questions. Each of us must decide the answers on our own. The point is that these and similar questions should be raised when judging the external validity of any experiment.

More generally there can sometimes be tension between designing an experiment that has good internal validity and precision and designing an experiment that has good external validity. In the school psychologist experiment, a simulated case increased internal validity through increased experimenter control and increased precision by using a single simulated case to control variance. At the same time, the simulation aspect of the experiment raised a number of serious questions about whether the results could be generalized to practice. Every empirical investigation suffers from some weaknesses that call into question the results, no matter how carefully designed and conducted. Experiments are no exception, even though experiments have unique strengths for investigating causal relationships. The best way to deal with the tensions among internal validity, precision, and external validity is to conduct multiple experiments, all of which investigate the same general question but each of which is designed to have unique strengths and few if any overlapping weaknesses.

Generalizing Across Outcomes

External validity can also be limited to the extent that results apply for only certain narrowly defined dependent variables. To illustrate this point, consider again the example of cooperative learning and whole-group instruction. The dependent variable was reading comprehension, but how reading comprehension was to be measured was not made explicit. Suppose the task for each subject was to read some short paragraphs and then to answer a series of multiple-choice questions. If so, how difficult were the passages to be read? What vocabulary was included in the tasks? What was the nature of the multiple-choice questions? Was the subject also asked to demonstrate reading comprehension of longer passages, perhaps a whole book? What type of book? Was comprehension assessed through an oral examination? Was the subject asked to demonstrate that the information acquired from a passage could also be put to use in solving problems? Reading comprehension can mean many different things. A good experiment would include several definitions of reading comprehension as multiple dependent variables so that external validity could be assessed directly.

Experimental conditions can also lead to unintended results. The method of instruction that promotes greatest gains in reading comprehension might at the same time leave subjects with a distaste for reading. Thus, an experiment should reflect a concern for unintended results by including appropriate dependent variables.

Finally, differences on a dependent variable (e.g., student achievement) observed immediately following the experiment may not be present one year later. Education is typically interested in practices that promote sustained effects. It may not be valid to generalize from measures taken immediately at the end of an experiment to what will be true weeks, months, or even years later.

Of course, it is impossible to measure subjects on everything that might be of interest. Nevertheless, one should be cautious about generalizing the results of experiments using one dependent variable to what is true for another.

Limitations to Experiments

Now you know what experiments are and how to think about their quality against the three criteria: internal validity, precision, and external validity. What remains to be done is to provide a sense of the role of experiments in educational research.

Among all the methods of educational research, experiments provide the most unimpeachable evidence of whether or not an independent variable causes differences in a dependent variable. The key to the internal validity of experiments lies with random assignment. Without random assignment there will always be variables that are confounded with the independent variable and, therefore, offer alternative explanations of results. Explanations of cause have greater ambiguity when random assignment is not used.

But comparative experiments are not the sole methodology of educational research. One obvious reason is that not all educational research is interested in questions about what causes what. Even if cause is of interest, however, research methods other than comparative experiments are frequently used. The reasons for this lie primarily with the nature of the research questions asked.

By definition, experiments involve random assignment to experimental conditions. Thus to conduct any experiment, the researcher must first create experimental conditions. Experiments are anticipatory, not retrospective. They are not appropriate for investigating the antecedents of a historical event. For example, at this time, experiments cannot be used to investigate the effects of the "new mathematics" curriculum reform.

Even when an educational event has been anticipated, experiments are not always possible. The researcher must have the authority to randomly assign subjects. Imagine that a teacher strike is anticipated in a school district, and you are interested in determining the effects of the strike on student achievement, teacher/principal relations, and the like. An experiment would require a comparison of striking teachers and nonstriking teachers, and the comparison would need to be built through randomly assigning teachers (or school districts) to the two conditions. Can you imagine an experimenter having the authority to tell some teachers to strike and others not to strike? Here, the requirements of an experiment are clearly impossible.

Finally, experiments necessarily focus on a few selected variables. Because creating experimental conditions and random assignment is difficult to accomplish, the typical experiment investigates the causal effects of only a single independent variable. (There may, of course, be other independent variables in the design of the study for purposes of testing interactions that describe the range of external validity.) Even the selection of dependent variables is restricted by the requirement that they be formally observed in a way that is common to all subjects. Experiments attempt to facilitate understanding of a few variables well. Sometimes the goal of educational research is to understand a community or a school so completely that, regardless of the situation, it would be possible to accurately predict the actions of the individuals involved. Anthropologically oriented research of this type requires the consideration of many variables simultaneously. Potentially, many of the variables have causal influences on the behaviors of individuals involved. Experiments do not lend themselves well to answering questions about complicated causal models that involve many independent variables, which are all believed to influence a dependent variable, some directly and some indirectly through influencing other independent variables.

Using Experiments

If one defines educational research as that research of potential relevance to improving understanding of the processes of education, then presumably a considerable portion of research conducted in the following disciplines is of interest: psychology, sociology, anthropology, economics, history, philosophy, and political science. Of these disciplines, psychology stands out as the predominant user of comparative experiments.

Moving beyond the disciplines, a great deal of important educational research is conducted within an educational context by educators. Much of this research has been conducted with an eye toward developing new programs, curricula, and teacher training procedures. Historically, these efforts have been heavily influenced by psychology, and not surprisingly they evidence considerable use of comparative experiments. However, there has been a strong tendency to drop the requirement of random assignment, leading to a distinction between true experiments, the topic here, and quasi-experiments, which are comparative studies without random assignment. Educational researchers have been too quick to conclude that random assignment was not possible. The overreliance on nonrandomized quasi-experiments has led to a great many results that leave ambiguous the causal antecedents of behavior.

It is impossible to define the range of educational research questions that might profitably be addressed through experiments. Experimental studies have been conducted to investigate the effects on achievement of peer tutoring, teacher questioning techniques, sequencing of instructional material, types of teacher lecture notes, different types of feedback on past achievement, and self-pacing versus instructor pacing. Experimental studies have investigated the effects on reading comprehension of positioning of questions in text; organization of prose using semantic, temporal, and random strategies; and different types of pictures to accompany the text. There have been experimental studies of the effects of biracial learning teams on race relations as well as experimental studies on the effects of achievement and aptitude testing on a variety of dependent variables, including teachers' expectations for student achievement.

Experiments have been used to determine the effects of education programs. (An example is provided in the reading that follows this chapter.) Unfortunately, experiments to determine the effects of education programs are not as prevalent as needed. The result has been the widespread promotion of education programs without solid evidence that they have the touted effects. Today school restructuring provides a disappointingly large number of examples. Hopefully, many of these "name brand" school improvement efforts are effective. If they are not, most will ultimately be tossed on the garbage pile of education fads, but not without having first wasted the time, energy, and money of a good many well-intentioned educators. A strong commitment to requiring that education innovations first prove themselves through experimental validation might slow the reform process a bit, but at the same time make the reform process much more effective.

Summary

The term *experiment* means many different things to many different people. In this chapter the term has been limited to a rather narrow, but useful, definition—an investigation, involving random assignment, of the causal relationship between one or more independent variables and one or more dependent variables. The methodological quality of an experiment should be judged against three standards: (a) internal validity, (b) precision, and (c) external validity. No experiments are perfect according to these criteria. When critiquing an experiment, however, a single flaw should not be sufficient, in and of itself, to dismiss the results. An attempt should be made to estimate, on the basis of common sense and other research, the likely effect of the flaw. Unless there is reasonable evidence to the contrary, the conclusion of the experiment should be tentatively held as correct.

An experiment is a highly focused investigation, the details of which are specified in advance—this is potentially one of its greatest strengths and one of its greatest weaknesses. The strength is that carefully specified experimental procedures allow rigorous control and provide relatively unambiguous results for a limited set of questions. By concentrating on only a few variables, the difficult measurement problems of each can be given careful attention. The weakness is that the original questions may have been misguided. The method is not well suited for midstudy corrections. Further, the highly focused nature of experiments, which facilitates control and precise measurement, may blind the researcher to recognizing difficulties or findings that might have been obvious with a less structured approach.

This brief introduction to experiments in education has touched on a broad number of issues, including defining, conducting, and interpreting educational experiments. My hope is that you have acquired a slightly better appreciation for what experiments can and cannot accomplish in educational research. Perhaps you will even consider undertaking the study necessary to acquire the skills and knowledge that will enable you to critique and conduct experiments in education.

References

Aronson, E., Blaney, N., Stephan, C., Sikes, J., & Snapp, M. (1978). *The jigsaw classroom*. Beverly Hills, CA: Sage.

Box, G. E. P. (1966). Use and abuse of regression. *Technometrics, 8,* 625–629.

Bracht, G. H., & Glass, G. V. (1968). The external validity of experiments. *American Educational Research Journal, 5,* 437–474.

Campbell, D. T., & Erlebacher, A. E. (1970). How regression artifacts in quasi-experimental evaluations can mistakenly make compensatory education look harmful. In J. Hellmuth (Ed.), *Disadvantaged child, Vol. 3. Compensatory education: A national debate* (pp. 185–210). New York: Brunner/Mazul.

Campbell, D. T., & Stanley, J. C. (1963). *Experimental and quasi-experimental designs for research*. Chicago: Rand McNally.

Carver, R. P. (1978, August). The case against statistical significance testing. *Harvard Educational Review, 48*(3), 378–399.

Frame, R. E., Clarizio, H. F., & Porter, A. C. (1984). Diagnostic and prescriptive bias in school psychologists' reports of a learning disabled child. *Journal of Learning Disabilities, 17,* 12–15.

Good, T. L., & Brophy, J. E. (1990). *Educational psychology: A realistic approach* (4th ed.). White Plains, NY: Longman.

Slavin, R. (1983). *Cooperative learning*. New York: Longman.

Suggestions for Further Reading

A great deal has been written that is relevant to acquiring a better understanding of experiments in educational research. Virtually all textbooks designed to provide an introduction to research methods in education contain a chapter on experiments or experimental methodology. The following list contains some of the better known introductions to educational research. I suggest that you read the chapters on experimental research in two or three of them.

Ary, D., Jacobs, C., & Razavieh, A. (1990). *Introduction to research in education* (4th ed.). New York: Holt, Rinehart & Winston.

Best, J. W. (1989). *Research in education* (6th ed.). Englewood Cliffs, NJ: Prentice Hall.

Borg, W. R., & Gall, M. D. (1989). *Educational research: An introduction* (5th ed.). New York: Longman.

Cohen, L., & Manion, L. (1994). *Research methods in education* (4th ed.). New York: Routledge.

Crowl, T. K. (1993). *Fundamentals of education research*. Madison, WI: Brown & Benchmark.

Fraenkel, J. R., & Wallen, N. E. (1993). *How to design and evaluate research in education* (2nd ed.). New York: McGraw-Hill.

Kerlinger, F. N. (1973). *Foundations of behavioral research* (2nd ed.). New York: Holt, Rinehart & Winston.

McMillan, J. H., & Schumacher, S. (1993). *Research in education: A conceptual introduction* (3rd ed.). New York: HarperCollins College.

Tuckman, B. W. (1994). *Conducting educational research* (4th ed.). New York: Harcourt Brace College.

Wiersma, W. (1995). *Research methods in education* (6th ed.). Philadelphia: Lippincott.

Many textbooks on statistics in psychological or educational research contain chapters or sections that are relevant to the design of educational experiments. Some of these textbooks even contain the words *experimental design* in their title although, in my opinion, they are more textbooks on statistics than they are textbooks on experimental design. Although knowledge of statistics is extremely useful for designing or interpreting educational experiments, a separate body of knowledge is appropriately labeled experimental design. Following is a list of some statistically oriented textbooks for educational researchers as well as some of the classics on experimental design. These references will be of interest if you have some background in inferential statistics and if you plan to conduct experiments in the future.

Cochran, W. G., & Cox, G. M. (1957). *Experimental designs* (2nd ed.). New York: Wiley.

Dayton, C. M. (1970). *The design of educational experiments*. New York: McGraw-Hill.

Fisher, R. A. (1935 and subsequent editions). *Design of experiments*. Edinburgh: Oliver and Boyd.

Kempthorne, O. (1952). *Design and analysis of experiments*. New York: Wiley.

Kirk, R. E. (1982). *Experimental design: Procedures for the behavioral sciences* (2nd ed.). Belmont, CA: Wadsworth.

Mendenhall, W. (1968). *Introduction to linear models and the design and analysis of experiments*. Belmont, CA: Wadsworth.

A most important part of becoming familiar with experiments in educational research is to read reports of studies that have used comparative experiments as at least one aspect of their design. The following reading provides one opportunity. The best approach, of course, is to look for examples of experiments that have been conducted in your substantive areas of interest. A good exercise would be to select a few issues that seem to be of interest and see if you can identify examples of comparative experiments in the journals that dominate your field of work. For the experiments identified, see if you can judge their quality against the three main goals of experimental design.

Study Questions

1. What is a hypothesis and how is a hypothesis used in experimental research?

2. Define the terms *independent variable, dependent variable,* and *population.*

3. What is meant by a causal relationship? What are the requirements for arguing cause?

4. What is an experiment? Give an example of an experiment and an example of a study that is not an experiment.

5. State the three criteria for judging experimental research and define what is meant by each.

6. Why are confounding variables of concern to experimenters?

7. What is random assignment, and why is it useful?

8. What is meant by the description of a difference as statistically significant? Why is statistical significance not synonymous with importance?

9. State at least two ways to improve the precision of an experiment.

10. What is random selection, how does it differ from random assignment, and why is random selection important?

11. Describe at least three threats to the external validity of an experiment. How can an interaction between the treatment independent variable and another independent variable help to define the range of external validity?

12. Give two illustrations of when experiments would be an appropriate research method.

13. Give two illustrations of when experiments would not be an appropriate research method.

Reading

Introduction
A Comparative Experiment in Educational Research

Andrew C. Porter
University of Wisconsin-Madison

In the following reprint of an article from the *American Educational Research Journal*, Carpenter, Fennema, Peterson, Chiang, and Loef report findings from a well-designed and well-executed experiment to test the effects of Cognitively Guided Instruction (CGI), a teacher education program designed to improve student achievement in the areas of addition and subtraction. The article is an excellent illustration of how research builds upon results from previous research and also the progression from basic research to increasingly more applied research and, ultimately, into classroom practice. Incidentally, the article also illustrates that education experiments are sometimes planned, carried out, and reported by a team of researchers and that sometimes education experiments are supported by federal funds. Most important to purposes here, however, the article illustrates many of the concepts and terms introduced in the preceding chapter on comparative experimental methods in education research.

Perhaps unfortunately for purposes here, the article illustrates that data from experiments are typically analyzed with fairly sophisticated statistical procedures. Clearly, now is not the time or place for a minicourse on inferential statistics. Still, it may be helpful to know the following:

- Reliability (Cronbach's Alpha) indicates the extent to which a variable has been measured with precision (in the sense that if the same subject were measured in the same way again, the same results would be found). Reliability can be any value from 0.0 to 1.0, with higher values meaning better reliability.
- Standard deviation is a descriptive statistic indicating the amount of variability or dispersion in scores on a variable. For example, in Table 4, CGI classrooms spent, on average, 60 percent of time in whole-class instruction. Around this average, however, classrooms differed considerably. The reported standard deviation was approximately 23. For most distributions, a range around the mean of ± 2 standard deviations includes 90% or more of the observations.

- Several different tests of significance were used, depending on the dependent variables that were analyzed. *T* tests were used for observation data, analysis of variance was used for teacher belief data, and analysis of covariance was used for student achievement data.

Each technique is used to decide whether mean differences between CGI and control classrooms were sufficiently large that they could not be dismissed as simply having occurred by chance. Results were reported at both 0.05 and 0.01 levels of significance, allowing readers to decide which of the two chances they want to take in concluding that the treatment had an effect, when in fact it did not.

The study of Cognitively Guided Instruction is of interest in its own right, but the purpose here is to illustrate the methodology of comparative experiments. With that in mind, the following may be worth thinking about while reading the article:

1. Like most experiments, the researchers were originally motivated by a general question, "Whether providing teachers access to explicit knowledge derived from research on children's thinking in a specific content domain would influence the teachers' instruction and their students' achievement." The researchers move from there to testable hypotheses. What are the hypotheses tested? What are the independent variables, the dependent variables, the population?

2. Are the hypotheses (or the initial motivating question, for that matter) about causal relationships of independent variables on dependent variables? In short, are the purposes of the study consistent with the purposes of comparative experiments?

3. Does the study satisfy the requirement of a comparative experiment, as presented in the preceding chapter? Where did random assignment enter the design?

4. Internal validity is one of three main criteria for judging the quality of an experiment. Beyond random assignment, were any measures taken to see that confounding variables did not occur? For example, is it possible that the observations of classrooms and/or the interviews of students and teachers, might reflect an experimenter bias in favor of CGI? The possibilities of experimenter bias entering a study during measures of dependent variables are often controlled through using observers that are "blind" as to whether or not they are observing a person in the treatment group or the control group.

5. Most of the conclusions reached in the study are based on comparisons between CGI and a control group. In the discussion section, however, the following is stated: "Both CGI and control teachers increased in their agreement with the perspective that children construct mathematical knowledge. These results suggest that both the CGI workshop and the problem-solving workshop for the control teachers had an effect on teachers' beliefs about children's problem solving." Is this conclusion based on the experimental portion of the study, or is it represented on a weaker pretest/posttest comparison? What, if any, confounding variables might offer an alternative interpretation to the data?

6. Another criterion for judging the quality of an experiment is precision. Clearly, the study had sufficient precision for achieving statistically significant results for some but not all of the dependent variables. Several techniques were used to give the study good precision: relatively large sample sizes (e.g., 40 classrooms with 12 target students from each), highly reliable measures of dependent variables (most of the reliability coefficients were above 0.80), blocking on schools when assigning teachers to experimental conditions, and using prior achievement as control variables in analysis of covariance when analyzing achievement test results.

7. The authors reported CGI and control means on each dependent variable and tests of statistical significance. They did not report confidence intervals. Do you believe the authors provided sufficient help to the readers to judge for themselves whether the statistically significant differences among treatment conditions were also important in some educational sense (as opposed to real but trivial differences)?

8. Did the researchers randomly select subjects from well-defined populations? Regardless of your answer, how would you judge the quality of this study against the criterion of external validity? One of the strengths of the study was the inclusion of several types of dependent variables (across types of outcomes). A similar strength was that the authors checked for an interaction between treatment conditions and prior levels of student achievement. Good experiments should contain design features that help test the limits of external validity in just this way. Reports should also describe the research procedures in sufficient detail that readers can make educated guesses about external validity on other dimensions not explored systematically in the design. Did you feel that the descriptions of students, teachers, and experimental procedures were adequate? In what ways, if any, did the experimental conditions differ from those of regular school settings?

9. Sometimes education interventions have unanticipated effects, and occasionally these are negative. The experiment checked to see whether the problem-solving orientation of CGI might have led inadvertently to weaker student achievement on computational skills. Perhaps surprisingly the results were just the opposite. CGI students surpassed control students in performance on computational skills of addition and subtraction. Might CGI have caused teachers to spend more time on mathematics instruction of addition and subtraction than they had in the past and less time on other subjects and other mathematics? Presumably, the observation data would have allowed the experimenters to check whether CGI teachers spent more time on addition and subtraction than did control teachers, although these results were not reported. The experimenters investigated whether, within the amount of time allocated to instruction of addition and subtraction, CGI teachers spent more on problem solving than did control teachers, and that was found to be the case.

Don't be discouraged when reading the following article. Few people understand exactly everything they read in a report of an experiment, not even seasoned veterans of education research. Don't dwell on what seems beyond your present grasp. Rather, concentrate on any new understandings of comparative experiment methodology that may occur. Don't be embarrassed if some parts of the article need more than one reading; some parts did for me. Finally, don't be surprised if you spot what appear to be flaws in the study (beyond those few hinted at already). There is no such thing as a perfect experiment. A flaw in one experiment is simply a motivation for another slightly different experiment. Empirical studies are not meant to stand alone but rather to serve as pieces of the puzzle.

American Educational Research Journal
Winter 1989, Vol. 26, No. 4, pp. 499–531

Using Knowledge of Children's Mathematics Thinking in Classroom Teaching: An Experimental Study

Thomas P. Carpenter and **Elizabeth Fennema**
University of Wisconsin—Madison
Penelope L. Peterson
Michigan State University
and
Chi-Pang Chiang and **Megan Loef**
University of Wisconsin-Madison

This study investigated teachers' use of knowledge from research on children's mathematical thinking and how their students' achievement is influenced as a result. Twenty first grade teachers, assigned randomly to an experimental treatment, participated in a month-long workshop in which they studied a research-based analysis of children's development of problem-solving skills in addition and subtraction. Other first grade teachers (n = 20) were assigned randomly to a control group. Although instructional practices were not prescribed, experimental teachers taught problem solving significantly more and number facts significantly less than did control teachers. Experimental teachers encouraged students to use a variety of problem-solving strategies, and they listened to processes their students used significantly more than did control teachers. Experimental teachers knew more about individual students' problem-solving processes,

Assisting in all phases of the research were Deborah Carey, Janice Gratch, and Cheryl Lubinski. Both the experimental treatment and the data collection were facilitated by Glenn Johnson and Peter Christiansen III of the Madison, Wisconsin, Metropolitan School District and Carolyn Stoner of the Watertown, Wisconsin, Unified School District. The research reported in this paper was supported in part by a grant from the National Science Foundation (MDR-8550236). The opinions expressed in this paper do not necessarily reflect the position, policy, or endorsement of the National Science Foundation. A previous version of this paper was presented at the annual meeting of the American Educational Research Association, New Orleans, April 1988. More detailed information about the instructional treatment can be obtained from the authors.

and they believed that instruction should build on students' existing knowledge more than did control teachers. Students in experimental classes exceeded students in control classes in number fact knowledge, problem solving, reported understanding, and reported confidence in their problem-solving abilities.

One of the critical problems facing educators and researchers is how to apply the rapidly expanding body of knowledge on children's learning and problem solving to classroom instruction. Implications for instruction do not follow immediately from research on thinking and problem solving, and explicit programs of research are needed to establish how the findings of descriptive research on children's thinking can be applied by teachers in actual classrooms with all the complexity that is involved (Romberg & Carpenter, 1986).

The purpose of this study was to investigate whether providing teachers access to explicit knowledge derived from research on children's thinking in a specific content domain would influence the teachers' instruction and their students' achievement. We hypothesized that knowledge about differences among problems, children's strategies for solving different problems, and how children's knowledge and skills evolve would affect directly how and what teachers did in classrooms. We also hypothesized that such knowledge would affect teachers' ability to assess their own students, which would be reflected in teachers' knowledge about their students. Knowledge about their students would allow teachers to better match instruction to students' knowledge and problem-solving abilities. As a consequence, students' meaningful learning and problem solving in mathematics would be facilitated.

Background

Research on children's addition and subtraction concepts. Many of the recent studies on children's thinking have focused on a specified content area, and the analysis of the task domain represents an important component of the research. This study draws on research on the development of addition and subtraction concepts and skills in young children. (For reviews of this research see Carpenter, 1985; Carpenter & Moser, 1983; or Riley, Greeno, & Heller, 1983). Within this domain researchers have provided a highly structured analysis of the development of addition and subtraction concepts and skills as reflected in children's solutions of different types of word problems. In spite of differences in details and emphasis, researchers in this area have reported remarkably consistent findings across a number of studies and have drawn similar conclusions about how children solve different problems. This research provides a basis for studying how children's thinking might be applied to instruction.

The research is based on a detailed analysis of the domain. Addition and subtraction word problems are partitioned into several basic classes, which distinguish between different types of action or relationships that represent different interpretations of addition and subtraction. Within each class three distinct problem types can be generated by systematically varying the unknowns. This scheme provides a highly principled analysis of problem type such that knowledge of a few general rules is sufficient to generate the complete range of problems.

The analysis is consistent with the way children think about and solve problems. Empirical research on children's solutions of addition and subtraction problems has shown that children initially solve word problems by directly representing the action or relationships in the problems. Research also has identified the major levels that children pass through in acquiring more advanced procedures for solving addition and subtraction problems. These more advanced procedures include counting strategies, use of derived facts, and recall of number facts. Thus, the taxonomy of problem types provides a framework for identifying the processes children are likely to use to solve different problems and to distinguish between problems in terms of their relative difficulty.

When children enter first grade, most of them are able to solve a variety of problems, and the processes they initially use to solve problems do not appear to have been learned through formal instruction. However, this informal knowledge may provide a basis to give meaning to the formal operations and symbol systems that are taught in school, provided that children are able to make the connections between their informal knowledge and the formal mathematics of school.

A cognitive view of the teacher. Consistent with the emerging cognitive view of the learner reflected in the research on addition and subtraction, those conducting research on teaching have begun to have a cognitive perspective on the teacher (Clark & Peterson, 1986; Peterson, 1988). Like their students, teachers are thinking individuals who approach the complex task of teaching in much the same way that problem solvers deal with other complex tasks. However, previous research on teachers' decision making suggests that teachers do not tend to base instructional decisions on their assessment of children's knowledge or misconceptions (Clark & Peterson, 1986). Putnam (1987) and Putnam and Leinhardt (1986) proposed that assessment of students' knowledge is not a primary goal of most teachers. They argued that keeping track of the knowledge of 25 students would create an overwhelming demand on the cognitive resources of the teacher. Putnam and Leinhardt hypothesized that teachers follow curriculum scripts in which they make only minor adjustments based on student feedback. The evidence is far from conclusive, however, that teachers do not or cannot monitor students' knowledge and use that information in instruction. Furthermore, Lampert (1986) has argued that a concern for monitoring students' knowledge should be related to a teacher's goals for instruction. Although teachers may be able to achieve short-term computational goals without attending to students' knowledge, they may need to understand students' thinking to facilitate students' growth in understanding and problem solving.

Researchers have begun to investigate how teachers' knowledge of and beliefs about their students' thinking are related to student achievement. In an earlier study, we measured 40 first grade teachers' knowledge of students' knowledge and cognitions through questionnaires and an interview (Carpenter, Fennema, Peterson, & Carey, 1988). We found that these first grade teachers were able to identify many of the critical distinctions between addition and subtraction word problems and the kinds of strategies children use to solve such problems. However, teachers' knowledge was not organized into a coherent network that related distinctions between types of word problems to children's solution strategies for solving the problems, nor to the difficulty of the problems. In the same study, we found that teachers' knowledge of their own students' abilities to solve different addition and subtraction problems was significantly positively correlated with student achievement on both computation and problem-solving tests. Similar results were reported by Fisher et al. (1980), who found that teachers' success in predicting students' success in solving specific problems on a standardized test was significantly correlated with their students' performance on the test.

In a related study (Peterson, Fennema, Carpenter, & Loef, 1989), we found a significant positive correlation between students' problem-solving achievement and teachers' beliefs. Teachers whose students achieved well in addition and subtraction problem solving tended to agree with the cognitively based perspectives that instruction should build on children's existing knowledge and that teachers should help students to construct mathematical knowledge rather than to passively absorb it.

In none of the studies cited above did researchers address the critical question, "How might knowledge of the very explicit, highly principled knowledge of children's cognitions derived from current research influence teachers' instruction and subsequently affect students' achievement?" Research provides detailed knowledge about children's thinking and problem solving that, if available to teachers, might affect their knowledge of their own students and their planning of instruction. Shulman (1986) called this type of knowledge *pedagogical content knowledge*, and Peterson (1988) referred to it as *content-specific cognitional knowledge*.

Research Questions

The purpose of this investigation was to study the effects of a program designed to provide teachers with detailed knowledge about children's thinking. In this study we addressed the following questions about teachers and their students.

1. Did *teachers* who had participated in a program designed to help them understand children's thinking (a) employ different instructional processes in their classrooms than did teachers who had not participated in the program? (b) have different beliefs about teaching mathematics, about how students learn, and about the role of the teacher in facilitating that learning than did teachers who did not participate in the program? and (c) know more about their students' abilities than did teachers who did not participate in the program?

2. Did the *students* of teachers who participated in a program designed to help them understand children's thinking (a) have higher levels of achievement than did the students of teachers who did not participate in the program? (b) have higher levels of confidence in their ability in mathematics than did the students of teachers who did not participate in the program? and (c) have different beliefs about themselves and mathematics than did students of teachers who did not participate in the program?

Method

Overview

Forty first grade teachers participated in the study. Half ($n = 20$) were assigned randomly by school to the treatment group. These teachers participated in a 4-week summer workshop designed to familiarize them with the findings of research on the learning and development of addition and subtraction concepts in young children and to provide them with an opportunity to think about and plan instruction based on this knowledge. The other teachers ($n = 20$) served as a control group who participated in two 2-hour workshops focused on nonroutine problem solving. Throughout the following school year, all 40 teachers and their students were observed during mathematics instruction by trained observers using two coding systems developed especially for this study. Near the end of the instructional year, teachers' knowledge of their students was measured by asking each teacher to predict how individual students in his or her class would solve specific problems and if correct answers would be obtained. Teachers' predictions were then matched with students' actual responses to obtain a measure of teachers' knowledge of their students' thinking and performance. Teachers' beliefs were measured using a 48-item questionnaire designed to assess their assumptions about the learning and teaching of addition and subtraction. Students in the 40 teachers' classes completed a standardized mathematics achievement pretest in September and a series of posttests in April and May. The posttests included standardized tests of computation and problem solving as well as experimenter-constructed scales that more precisely assessed students' problem-solving abilities. At posttest time, students were also interviewed as they solved a variety of problems to assess the processes they used to solve different problems. Finally, students completed several measures of attitudes and beliefs developed for this study.

Subjects

The subjects in the study were the teachers (39 women and 1 man) and their students in 40 classrooms in 24 schools located in Madison, Wisconsin, and in four smaller communities near Madison. Two Catholic schools and 22 public schools were included. All the teachers in the sample volunteered to participate in a 4-week in-service program during the summer, to be observed during their classroom instruction in mathematics during the following year, and to complete questionnaires and interviews in May of 1986 and 1987. The sample included about a fourth of the first grade teachers in the participating districts. Each participating teacher received $100 as an honorarium for each year of the study. The mean number of years of elementary teaching experience for the teachers in the sample was 10.9, and the mean number of years teaching first grade was 5.6. Two of the teachers had just completed their first year of teaching. None reported participating in any training in which recent research on addition and subtraction was discussed. During the instructional year of the study, 36 teachers taught first grade classrooms and 4 taught first/second grade combinations.

Teachers were assigned randomly to treatments by school. Twelve first grade students (six girls and six boys) were selected randomly from each class to serve as target students for observation and the interviews. There were fewer than 12 first grade students in two of the first/second grade combinations. In those classes, all first grade students were included in the sample. Children with special learning needs were omitted from the sample. Although all first grade students in each class completed the written posttests, the analyses were based on data from target students so that all comparisons of treatment effects were conducted on the same sample of students.

Cognitively Guided Instruction (CGI) Treatment

Goals of the workshop. The goal of the workshop for the treatment group was to help teachers understand how children develop addition and subtraction concepts and provide them the opportunity to explore how they might use that knowledge for instruction. We called the program Cognitively Guided Instruction (CGI). Much of the workshop was devoted to giving teachers access to knowledge about addition and subtraction word problems and how children think about them. The initial goal of instruction was to familiarize teachers with research on children's solutions of addition and subtraction problems. Teachers learned to classify problems, to identify the processes that children use to solve different problems, and to relate processes to the levels and problems in which they are commonly used. Although the taxonomy of problem types and the models of children's cognitive processes were simplified somewhat, each teacher showed evidence of understanding of the problem types and related solution strategies. This knowledge provided the framework for everything else that followed, and 1½ weeks of the 4-week workshop was spent on it.

During the remainder of the workshop, teachers discussed principles of instruction that might be derived from the research and designed their own programs of instruction on the basis of those principles. Although instructional practices were not prescribed, broad principles of instruction were discussed. One guiding principle was that instruction should develop understanding by stressing relationships between skills and problem solving, with problem solving serving as the organizing focus of instruction. A second principle was that instruction should be organized to facilitate students' active construction of their own knowledge with understanding. Third, each student should be able to relate problems, concepts, or skills being learned to the knowledge that he or she already possessed. Fourth, because instruction should be based on what each child knows, it is necessary to continually assess not only whether a learner can solve a particular problem but also how the learner solves the problem. The most effective way to analyze children's thinking is by asking appropriate questions and listening to children's responses. Research on children's thinking provided a framework for this analysis and a model for questioning.

Specific questions were identified for teachers to address in planning their instruction, but teachers were not told how they should resolve them. The following questions were included: (a) How should instruction build initially on the informal and counting strategies that children use to solve simple word problems when they enter first grade? (b) Should specific strategies like "counting on" be taught explicitly? and (c) How should symbols be linked to the informal knowledge of addition and subtraction that children exhibit in their modeling and counting solutions of word problems?

Another goal of the workshop was to familiarize teachers with curricular materials available for instruction. Teachers were encouraged to evaluate these materials on the basis of the knowledge and instructional principles they acquired earlier in the workshop.

Format of the CGI workshop/treatment. The CGI workshop was conducted during the first 4 weeks of the teachers' summer vacation. The workshop was taught by Carpenter and Fennema with the assistance of three graduate students. Two mathematics supervisors from the Madison Metropolitan School District, and one curriculum supervisor from the Watertown, Wisconsin, Unified School District, also attended. The workshop involved 5 hours of participation each day, 4 days a week for 4 weeks.

Although teachers were told that they could complete all work during the 20 workshop hours each week, some teachers did take work home.

Teachers were provided with readings prepared for the workshop that presented the problem type taxonomy, synthesized the results of research on children's solutions of addition and subtraction word problems, and discussed how these findings might be applied in the classroom. Numerous videotapes of children solving problems were used to illustrate children's solution strategies, and teachers had the opportunity to interview one or two young children. Various instructional materials were also available for the teachers to review, including textbooks, manipulatives, and enrichment materials.

A typical day included an hour of lecture and discussion led by Carpenter or Fennema. During the first 6 days, these discussions focused on the findings from research on addition and subtraction. Discussions during the next 4 days explored ways that these findings might be implemented in the classroom. Each day the teachers could also participate in a small-group seminar led by one of the graduate students. The purpose of these seminars was to examine different curricula or enrichment materials and to discuss how these materials might be used to facilitate children's problem solving following principles of CGI. During the rest of the time, teachers were free to read, to plan the following year's instruction, to study video-tapes of children solving problems, to talk with other participants and the staff, and to examine textbooks, manipulatives, or enrichment materials.

Teachers were given a great deal of freedom to monitor their own progress and to select and work on activities that facilitated their own learning. Although they were given no specific written assignments, teachers were asked to plan a unit to teach during the following year, as well as a year-long plan for instruction based on principles of CGI. Most teachers developed units around a theme. For example, one teacher adapted a story about a friendly forest with a number of different animal characters. Using the problem taxonomy, she wrote a variety of different problems related to this story. Each week teachers met with one of the staff to discuss their progress for the week and to clarify their ideas about their plans. Teachers either worked alone or with others as they desired.

Because we hypothesized that teachers' knowledge about their students' thinking about addition and subtraction would develop during the instructional year, we conceptualized the treatment as including the following instructional year. However, after the workshop, our formal contact with the CGI teachers was limited. We met one time with them in October, when they discussed with us what they had done to that point with CGI. One of the staff also served as a resource person and responded to any questions that CGI teachers posed to her throughout the year. Each teacher who participated in the workshop received 3 university credits and was given $50 to buy materials.

Control Group

Teachers in the control group participated in two 2-hour workshops that were held in September and February during the instructional year. The control group workshops were in no way comparable to the CGI workshops in duration or extent of coverage, and the purpose was not to provide a contrasting treatment. The goal was to provide control teachers with some sense of participation in the project and give them some immediate reward for their participation. The problem-solving focus of the control group's workshops was different from that of the CGI workshop. Whereas the problem-solving emphasis of CGI was on story problems that were relevant to the children, the problem-solving emphasis of the control group's workshop was on mathematical problems that were intriguing and of a more esoteric nature. Such problems are often designated as nonroutine problems. During the control group workshops, no discussion occurred about how children think as they solve problems, nor was any specific framework given for how to understand children's cognitions. Rather, the discussion focused on the importance of children learning to solve problems and the potential use of nonroutine problems to motivate students to engage in problem solving.

The control workshops were taught by a graduate student who was a member of the CGI staff. Teachers were first asked to solve a nonroutine problem themselves, and then they discussed the various heuristics they used as they found a solution. This problem-solving activity was followed by a discussion of various heuristics that children might use to solve a problem, such as charting, making a diagram, drawing a picture, or making a list. Teachers were given access to materials that provided examples of nonroutine problems and to trade books that contained problem-solving activities for children. They also discussed how they might use their own mathematics textbook to provide problem-solving experiences for children.

Classroom Observations

We constructed two observation systems: one that focused on the teacher and one that focused on the student. In both systems, observers used a 60-second time-sampling procedure in which they observed for 30 seconds and, then, for the next 30 seconds, they coded the behavior and activities of either teacher or the target student, depending on the system. The teacher observer focused on the teacher from the beginning of the time that the teacher taught mathematics to the end of the mathematics period. The student observer focused on each of the target students, in turn, until all 12 students had been observed. The observer then returned to the first target student and rotated through the same 12 students as long as class time allowed. Target students were observed in a different order each day.

Observation categories. Observation categories were selected carefully by considering the literature and the purpose of the study. From a previous study (Peterson & Fennema, 1985), we adapted the major category of *setting* (*whole class, medium group, small group, teacher/student,* and *alone*) because we believed that CGI teachers might vary the instructional setting to adapt to students' knowledge and abilities. To compare possible differences in CGI teachers' instruction with the *lesson phases* of active mathematics teaching (Good, Grouws, & Ebmeier, 1983), we coded the phases of *review, development, controlled practice,* and *student work* (seatwork) in the student system.

The *mathematics content* was a primary category in both systems. The major categories of addition and subtraction content were *number facts, represented problems, word problems,* and *other addition and subtraction.* Number facts focused on the knowledge and use of simple computations using addition number facts up to $9 + 9$ or corresponding subtraction number facts. Represented problems were problems presented pictorially or with counters whose solution did not require any additional representation by the students. Included in this category were typical textbook problems in which pictures show children, animals, or objects joining or leaving a group to illustrate an addition or subtraction problem. Word problems were problems presented either verbally or written in story form that required the student to use addition or subtraction to solve them. Other addition and subtraction included problems or activities, other than those described thus far, that required the student to use addition or subtraction. Student *nonengagement* with mathematics was coded in the student system (Peterson & Fennema, 1985).

Subcategories under *teacher behavior* were derived from CGI principles and findings by Fennema and Peterson (1986) indicating that students' problem solving was positively related to teachers' feedback to the process of obtaining the answer rather than to the answer itself, so *feedback to process* and *feedback to answer* were coded. In addition, both cognitive research on children's learning and CGI principles suggest that it may be important for the teacher to *pose problems* to students and to *listen to process,* which involves listening to a student working a problem aloud or listening to a student describe the way he or she solved a problem.

Building on the research on children's learning and cognitions, we coded both the strategy that the teacher expected or encouraged the students to use in solving problems and also the strategy that students actually appeared to be using. Strategies coded in both systems included *direct modeling, advanced counting, derived facts,* and *recall.* The direct modeling strategy was coded when students used counters or fingers to model directly the action in a word problem or calculate the answer to a computation problem. Advanced counting was coded when students counted on or counted back from a given number without using counters to model the numbers in the problem. Derived facts were coded when students used relations between number facts to generate their answers. For example, 6

+ 6 might be used to find the answer to 6 + 7. Recall was coded when students were expected to recall a number fact from memory and no opportunity was provided for modeling or counting. In the teacher system, if the teacher appeared to expect no particular strategy, then *no clear strategy* was coded. If the teacher encouraged or expected use of more than one of these strategies, *multiple strategies* was coded. In the student system, if the observer could not determine what strategy the student was using, then *no clear strategy* was coded.

In summary, in the teacher system for each 60-second time sampling interval when addition and subtraction instruction was occurring, the observer checked one subcategory within each of the following major categories: *setting, content, expected strategy*, and *teacher behavior.* In the student system, for each 60-second time sampling interval when addition and subtraction instruction was occurring, the observer checked *one* subcategory within each of the following categories: *setting, content* (including *nonengaged* with content), *strategy used*, and *lesson phase.* Table 1 shows the specific observation categories in each system.

Interobserver agreement was estimated by having a reliability observer code with the assigned observer at specified times during the study. A sample of these data was used to calculate interobserver agreement. For the teacher system, agreement estimates were calculated for a pair of observers who coded the same two teachers on each of 4 days during the study. For the student system, estimates were based on the coding of three teachers on each of 2 days by the regular coder and a reliability coder. An estimate of agreement for each category was made by comparing the coding of the two observers for each coding interval. Thus, for each coding category and interval, observers might have agreed or not agreed to check or not to check a given category. Percentage of interobserver agreement was calculated for each category by dividing the total number of agreements by the total agreements plus disagreements for the intervals coded. Table 1 presents the estimates of interobserver agreement for each coding category in the teacher and student observation systems.

Observation procedures. In September and October observers were hired and trained in a 2-week training session following procedures used previously by Peterson and Fennema (1985). Observations manuals were developed for each system (Peterson, 1987). Training involved a week of coding transcripts and videotapes followed by a week of practice coding in first grade mathematics classrooms that were not part of our study. At the end of the training period, each observer completed a written test that assessed content knowledge and coded a videotape of a first grade classroom that assessed coding ability. Observers who achieved the criterion levels on both tests were judged sufficiently knowledgeable and skilled to begin actual classroom observations.

Each teacher and class was observed for four separate week-long periods

TABLE 1

Interobserver agreement on teacher and student observation categories

Teacher observation category	Interrater agreement (%)	Student observation category	Interrater agreement (%)
Setting		Setting	
Whole class	98	Whole class	90
Medium group	96	Medium group	99
Small group	98	Small group	97
Teacher/student	96	Teacher/student	99
Alone	99	Alone	88
Content		Content	
Number fact problem	97	Represented problems	94
Represented problem	96	Word problems	97
Word problems	93	Number fact problems	94
Other addition/substration	99	Other addition/subtraction	99
		Nonengaged with content	95
Expected strategy		Strategy used	
Direct modeling	90	Direct modeling	90
Advanced counting	98	Advanced counting	99
Derived facts	100	Derived facts	100
Recall	91	Recall	82
Multiple	82	Not clear	89
Not clear	90		
Teacher behavior		Lesson phase	
Poses problem	87	Review	95
		Development	94
Process focus		Controlled practice	99
		Student work (seatwork)	88
Questions process	95		
Explains process	96		
Gives feedback to process	95		
Listens to process	98		
Answer focus			
Questions answer	87		
Explains answer	95		
Gives feedback to answer	92		
Listens to answer	88		
Checks/monitors	98		

(a minimum of 16 days) from November through April. During each scheduled observation period, a student observer and a teacher observer coded together in the same classroom. During the observations, the teacher wore a wireless microphone, and the teacher observer listened to the teacher through earphones to aid in understanding the teacher's private interactions with students.

Teachers' Knowledge Measures

Three separate measures were constructed to assess teachers' knowledge of their students. Procedures were adapted from a similar test used in an earlier study (Carpenter et al., 1988). For each of the three measures, teachers were asked to predict their target students' solution strategies or answers on specific problems. The teachers' knowledge scores were based on the match between their predictions for each target student and that student's actual response.

For the knowledge of *number fact strategies*, teachers were asked to predict the strategy that each of their target students would use to answer each of the five items on the students' number facts interview. The teachers' scores were calculated by comparing each teacher's predicted strategy with the strategy that the given target student actually used. For each item for each student the teacher received one point for each correct match between predicted and actual strategy, and zero points for no match.

For the knowledge of students' *problem-solving strategies*, teachers were asked to predict the strategy that each of their target students would use to solve each of the six problems on the students' problem-solving interview. Because students frequently use several different strategies to solve a given problem at different times, teachers were allowed, but not required, to identify as many as three strategies that a given student might use for a particular problem. Teachers were encouraged to identify only strategies they thought the student might actually use. The teacher's response was scored as a match and given one point if the student solved the given problem on the problem-solving interview using any one of the strategies identified by the teacher.

For the knowledge of *problem-solving abilities*, teachers were asked to predict whether each of the target students could answer correctly specific problems on the written tests. Teachers were not required to specify what strategy the student used. Eight problems were selected from the complex and advanced problem scales described below. The teacher's response for each student for each item was scored on the basis of the match between the teacher's prediction and the target student's actual answer to the given problem. The teacher received one point for each correct match for each student and each item. A teacher's prediction could match the students' actual response by predicting accurately whether or not a student would answer a given problem correctly.

The number fact strategies and the problem-solving strategies tests were administered individually by trained interviewers using similar procedures and coding criteria to those used for the student interviews described below. For the problem-solving abilities test, interviewers gave teachers a list of the target students and a list of the eight problems. Interviewers asked teachers to predict which of the problems each of the target students could solve correctly. The Cronbach alphas were .57, .86, and .47 ($n = 40$)

for teachers' number fact strategies, problem-solving strategies, and problem-solving abilities tests, respectively.

Teachers' Belief Instrument

Teachers' beliefs about the learning and teaching of addition and subtraction were assessed using four 12-item, experimenter-constructed scales. Peterson et al. (1989) have provided a complete description of these scales and have demonstrated the reliability, construct validity, and predictive validity of teachers' scores derived from them.

For each item teachers responded on a five-point Likert scale by indicating *strongly agree, agree, undecided, disagree,* or *strongly disagree.* Half of the items on each scale were worded such that agreement with the statement indicated agreement with a cognitively guided perspective. The remaining six items were worded so that agreement with that item indicated less agreement with a cognitively guided perspective. Scale 1, The Role of the Learner, was concerned with how children learn mathematics. A high score indicated a belief that children construct their own knowledge, whereas a low score reflected a belief that children receive knowledge. Scale 2, Relationship Between Skills, Understanding, and Problem Solving, dealt with the interrelationships of teaching various components of mathematics learning. A high score indicated a belief that all components should be taught as interrelated ideas, whereas a lower score indicated a belief that lower level skills are prerequisites to teaching understanding and problem solving. Scale 3, Sequencing of Mathematics, assessed teachers' beliefs about what should provide the basis for sequencing topics in addition and subtraction instruction. A high score indicated a belief that the development of mathematical ideas in children should provide the basis for sequencing topics for instruction, and a low score indicated a belief that formal mathematics should provide the basis for sequencing topics for instruction. Scale 4, Role of the Teacher, assessed teachers' beliefs about how addition and subtraction should be taught. A high score reflected a belief that mathematics instruction should facilitate children's construction of knowledge, whereas a low score reflected a belief that instruction should be organized to facilitate teachers' presentation of knowledge.

Sample items included "Most young children can figure out a way to solve simple word problems" (Scale 1); "Children should not solve simple word problems until they have mastered some basic number facts" (Scale 2); "The natural development of children's mathematics ideas should determine the sequence of topics used for instruction" (Scale 3); and "Teachers should allow children to figure out their own ways to solve simple word problems" (Scale 4). Cronbach alpha estimates for teachers' scores in this sample ($N = 40$) were .93 for the combined scales and .81, .79, .79, and .84 for Scales 1 through 4, respectively.

Student Achievement Measures

At the beginning of the year, students' achievement was measured using a standardized achievement test as a pretest. Posttests, given near the end of the school year, included three written tests and individual interviews. Written posttests include a standardized test of computational skills, a standardized test of problem solving, and an experimenter-developed problem-solving test. From the two problem-solving tests, three scales were constructed: Simple Addition and Subtraction Word Problems, Complex Addition and Subtraction Word Problems, and Advanced Word Problems. Posttest interviews assessed each student's recall of number facts (a computational skill) and identified the strategies used to solve addition and subtraction word problems. Thus, there were two posttest measures of computational skills—one based on a written test and one from the interview—and five posttest measures of problem solving—the standardized test, the three problem-solving scales, and the interview of problem-solving strategies. The internal consistencies of the tests were estimated using Cronbach's alpha and are reported in Table 2.

Written achievement tests. The Mathematics subtest of the Iowa Test of Basic Skills (ITBS), Level 6, was used as the pretest. The Computation subtest of the ITBS, Level 7, was used as the written posttest of computation. Three posttest problem-solving scales were constructed using items selected from the Mathematics Problems subtest of the ITBS, Level 7, and experimenter-designed items that included a broad range of more difficult problems. The three scales, listed below, represent different levels of problem-solving ability.

The Simple Addition and Subtraction Word Problems scale included 11 word problems involving simple joining and separating situations with the

TABLE 2

Reliabilities of student achievement measures (N = 40)

Test	Cronbach's alpha
Pretest	
ITBS (Level 6)	.84
Computation posttests	
ITBS (Level 7)—Computation	.89
Number facts interview	.83
Problem-solving posttests	
ITBS (Level 7)—Mathematics Problems	.90
Scale 1: Simple Addition and Subtraction Word Problems	.72
Scale 2: Complex Addition and Subtraction Word Problems	.91
Scale 3: Advanced Word Problems	.90
Problem-solving interview	.66

result unknown. The Complex Addition and Subtraction Word Problems scale included 12 more difficult addition and subtraction word problems based on the analysis of problem types by Carpenter and Moser (1983) and by Riley et al. (1983). The Advanced Word Problems scale included multi-step problems, grouping and partitioning problems, and problems involving extraneous information. Table 3 shows representative examples from each scale.

Student interviews. At posttest time, target students were interviewed individually to determine the strategies they used to solve certain problems and to assess their recall of number facts. The number facts interview involved five addition number facts with sums between 6 and 16. The problem-solving interview consisted of six addition and subtraction word problems involving simple joining situations and missing addend situations with the change unknown. Responses were coded by the interviewer using a coding system developed by Carpenter and Moser (1983).

Students' Confidence and Beliefs

Students' confidence. Students were asked to indicate whether they thought they could solve 12 word problems. They were asked to circle "yes" if they thought they could solve the problem and to circle "no" if they did not think they could solve the problem. One item read, "Dorothy has 6 stickers. How many more stickers does she need to collect to have

TABLE 3

Representative items from problem-solving scales

Scale 1: Simple Addition and Subtraction Problems
> Garcia had 5 guppies. He was given 7 more guppies for his birthday. How many guppies did he have then?
> Maria had 13 balloons. 5 balloons popped. How many balloons did she have left?

Scale 2: Complex Addition and Subtraction Problems
> Pat has 6 baseball cards. How many more baseball cards does she need to collect to have 14 altogether?
> Larry had some toy cars. He lost 7 toy cars. Now he has 4 cars left. How many toy cars did Larry have before he lost any of them?
> John has 12 rings. Amy has 7 rings. How many more rings does John have than Amy?

Advanced Problems
> Jim needs 11 dollars to buy a puppy. He earned 5 dollars on Saturday and 2 dollars on Sunday. How much more money does he need to earn to buy the puppy?
> Ann had 11 pennies. Candies cost 3 pennies each. Ann spent 6 pennies on candies. How many pennies does Ann have left?
> Mary has 3 packages of gum. There are 6 pieces of gum in each package. How many pieces of gum does Mary have altogether?

---

14 altogether?" The items were read to children in a group setting. Students were given one point for a yes answer and zero points for a no answer. The Cronbach alpha internal consistency estimate for students' scores was .91 ($N = 40$).

Students' beliefs. Students were interviewed about their beliefs on the same four belief constructs described above for teachers. Items from the teachers' belief scales were reworded to make them understandable to children. A 16-item interview scale was constructed with 4 items for each scale. Students were asked to respond to the interviewer on a 3-point Likert scale (*yes, maybe,* or *no*). Students' responses were scored *yes* = 3, *maybe* = 2, and *no* = 1 for positively stated items and the opposite for negatively stated items. Sample items included "The teacher should tell kids exactly how to solve story problems in math" (Scale 4) and "Most kids can solve easy story problems by counting their fingers or something else before the teacher teaches them how to solve the problem" (Scale 2). (See *Teacher Belief Instrument* above for descriptions of each construct.) Cronbach alphas for students' scores on each of the four belief scales were .63 ($N = 40$ classes) for the total scale and .52, .19, .45, and .68 ($N = 40$ classes) for Scales 1, 2, 3, and 4, respectively. Because of the low internal consistency for student beliefs on individual scales, which may be due to the small number of items per scale, only the total scale score was used in subsequent analyses.

Students' attention and understanding. Students' reports of attention and understanding were assessed in an interview using questions developed and used previously by Peterson, Swing, Braverman, and Buss (1982) and Peterson, Swing, Stark, and Waas (1984). Peterson et al. (1982, 1984) provided empirical data that demonstrated the reliability and validity of students' reported attention and understanding on these questions. The interviewer asked students to "think back to the last time you were in math class at school" and answer the following questions: "During that math class, when you were supposed to be paying attention to the teacher or your work, were you paying attention all of the time, most of the time, some of the time, or not very much of the time?" "During that same math class, how well were you understanding the math that you were doing? Were you understanding all of it, most of it, some of it, or not very much of it?" Students' responses were scored as follows: *all* = 4; *most* = 3; *some* = 2; and *not very much* = 1.

Testing and Interview Procedures

Student data. The students' written tests were administered by trained testers following written protocols. Target students who were absent on the day of testing were tested after they returned to school. The pretest was administered during September. In each class the written posttests and student confidence and belief measures were administered on 2 consecutive days in April or May 1987. On the first day the ITBS problem-solving test and the ITBS computation test were administered consecutively. On the second day the experimenter-designed problem-solving items and the Confidence Scale were given.

The student interviews were also conducted during April and May 1987 by trained interviewers. The problem-solving interview was conducted first, followed by the number fact interview, the beliefs scales, and, finally, questions on student's attention and understanding.

Teacher data. In May 1986, before the workshop began in June, teachers completed the belief questionnaire, and these data are reported in Peterson et al. (1989). In May 1987, after the student data were collected, we again assessed teachers' beliefs. Within 1–2 days after their children's interviews were conducted, trained graduate assistants conducted the teacher knowledge interview and administered the teacher belief instrument to individual teachers.

Results

In this section we describe the results of the four major analyses we conducted. First, we examine how CGI and control classrooms differed in the content, activities, behavior, learning, and instruction in which teachers and students were observed to be engaged. Second, we describe differences between CGI and control teachers in their knowledge and beliefs. Then we examine effects on students' achievement, including students' problem solving and knowledge of number facts at a recall level. Finally, we describe effects on students' confidence, beliefs, and reported attention and understanding. For all analyses, the class or the teacher served as the unit of analysis.

Classroom Observations

We computed means, standard deviations, and t tests between groups for each of the categories on the teacher observation system and the student observation system. Table 4 presents the results for the teacher system, and Table 5 presents the results for the student system. For most measures in both tables the numbers within each major category represent the mean proportion of time spent on that activity within the total time spent on addition and subtraction instruction. Thus, total time spent on addition and subtraction was used as the denominator for most of the proportions in these two tables.

Although the focus of the observation—the teacher or the student—differed between the two observation systems, the results showed consistent and complementary patterns between CGI and control teachers for similar observation categories in the two systems. Although some differences were significant in one system but not in the other, the same trends appeared consistently in both systems. The differences that exist can generally be

TABLE 4

Means and standard deviations of proportions of CGI and control teachers' time spent on addition and subtraction instruction for each teacher coding category (N = 40)

Teacher observation category	CGI		Control		$t(38)$
	M	SD	M	SD	
Setting[a]					
Whole class	59.95	22.97	61.29	18.07	−.20
Medium group	11.31	18.47	3.00	4.47	1.95
Small group	6.20	8.23	5.12	5.45	.49
Teacher/student	20.60	12.85	28.03	14.15	−1.74
Alone	1.93	3.10	2.55	4.17	−.53
Content[a]					
Number fact problems	25.95	13.63	47.20	21.22	−3.77**
Represented problems	9.70	8.33	8.18	5.50	.68
Word problems	54.58	18.84	36.19	21.92	2.84**
Other addition/subtraction	9.77	8.97	8.44	6.38	.54
Teacher behavior[b]					
Poses problem	16.96	6.22	10.43	4.64	3.76**
Focuses on process	24.96	7.10	22.78	4.43	1.17
Questions process	5.91	2.96	4.85	2.95	1.13
Explains process	6.78	2.49	8.24	3.44	−1.54
Gives feedback to process	4.81	2.89	5.71	2.48	−1.05
Listens to process	7.46	3.88	3.97	2.11	3.54**
Focuses on answer	28.63	5.06	30.85	5.58	−1.32
Questions answer	11.94	3.32	11.34	4.26	.49
Explains answer	1.67	1.07	2.33	1.24	−1.80
Gives feedback to answer	8.04	3.10	10.51	3.27	−2.45*
Listens to answer	6.97	3.10	6.66	2.67	.34
Checks/monitors	10.89	6.21	13.11	6.35	−1.12
Expected strategy[c]					
Direct modeling	29.85	16.10	29.05	16.46	.16
Advanced counting	4.65	4.18	10.72	12.67	−2.04*
Derived facts	3.19	4.38	1.43	3.21	1.44
Recall	14.82	8.83	18.48	11.24	−1.15
Multiple	32.29	15.51	21.93	10.89	2.45*
Not clear	5.43	5.91	9.95	10.11	−1.73

* $p < .05$; ** $p < .01$.

[a] Proportions within this category sum to 100% because one of each of the subcategories was coded for each time the teacher engaged in addition and subtraction instruction.

[b] Proportions within this category do *not* sum to 100% because for each time the teacher engaged in addition and subtraction instruction, some additional subcategories of teacher behavior were coded but are not reported here.

[c] Proportions within this category do *not* sum to 100% because the additional content category of "other addition and subtraction" might have been coded when the teacher engaged in addition and subtraction instruction.

TABLE 5

Means and standard deviations of proportions of CGI and control students' time engaged in addition and subtraction instruction/activities for each student coding category (N = 40)

Student observation category	CGI		Control		t(38)
	M	SD	M	SD	
Setting[a]					
Whole class	51.79	24.38	53.25	18.58	−.21
Medium group	6.56	12.91	1.67	2.83	1.65
Small group	5.92	4.39	7.72	7.25	−.95
Teacher/student	1.47	1.18	1.59	1.07	−.34
Alone	34.26	16.67	35.76	16.45	−.29
Lesson phase[b]					
Review	4.49	2.78	8.04	4.44	−3.03**
Development	19.10	12.06	19.71	10.20	−.17
Controlled practice	37.50	18.93	30.14	14.51	1.38
Student work (seatwork)	38.44	17.88	41.42	17.18	−.54
Content[a]					
Represented problems	7.56	5.99	7.23	5.82	.13
Word problems	39.93	15.90	31.44	18.64	1.55
Number facts problems	26.90	13.52	37.19	17.58	−2.08*
Other addition/subtraction	7.80	6.76	6.81	5.33	.51
Nonengaged with content	17.81	7.10	17.23	8.00	.24

Content by lesson phase[b]

Review, development, and controlled practice					
Represented problems	4.84	4.72	5.49	5.34	−.40
Word problems	36.13	15.13	23.27	13.00	2.88**
Number facts	9.03	5.61	18.81	10.81	−3.59**
Other addition/subtraction	4.61	5.78	4.92	4.20	−.20
Student work					
Represented problems	2.67	2.73	1.79	2.18	1.13
Word problems	3.67	4.33	8.06	8.15	−2.13*
Number facts	17.78	12.58	18.05	11.09	−.07
Other addition/subtraction	3.19	2.83	1.85	2.14	1.65
Strategy used[c]					
Direct modeling	24.40	12.70	26.46	12.24	−.52
Advanced counting	8.35	6.58	8.93	7.95	−.25
Recall	19.91	5.91	20.72	9.89	−.31
Derived facts	1.63	2.06	1.25	2.36	.54
Not clear	20.10	10.58	18.60	10.99	.44

$* p < .05; ** p < .01.$

[a] Proportions within this category sum to 100% because one of each of the subcategories was coded for each time the student was expected to be engaged in addition and subtraction instruction or activities.

[b] Proportions within this category do *not* sum to 100% because for each time the student was engaged in addition and subtraction instruction or activities, some additional subcategories were coded but are not reported here.

[c] Proportions within this category do *not* sum to 100% because the additional content category of "other addition and subtraction" and "nonengagement" might have been coded for content.

explained by the fact that the focus of the observation, teachers or individual students, were not always engaged in the same activity. For example, for the *alone* category under *setting* the teacher was seldom observed to be working alone (approximately 2% of the time, as shown in Table 4), but students frequently worked alone (about 34% of the time, as shown in Table 5). Similarly, although the teacher engaged in one-to-one interaction with students about 20% of the time, individual students were observed to be engaged in one-to-one interaction with the teacher only about 1% of the time.

Setting. No significant differences appeared between CGI and control teachers in their grouping patterns, as measured by the coding of the setting in the two systems.

Content and lesson phase. CGI students and control students did not differ in the proportion of time in which they were engaged with addition and subtraction content, but teacher observations showed significantly different content emphases between CGI and control teachers when teaching addition and subtraction. During addition and subtraction instruction, CGI teachers spent significantly more time on word problems than did control teachers. In contrast, control teachers spent significantly more time on number facts problems than did CGI teachers (Table 4). A similar pattern was observed for the student observations, although the difference in time spent on problem solving by students was not statistically significant (Table 5).

In the student observations the differences in content coverage varied over different phases of the lessons (Table 5). Control students were more likely to be given word problems to work on during seatwork, which was more apt to be done alone. CGI students were more likely to work on word problems during review, development, and controlled practice, which was generally done in a large-group setting. In contrast, during the large-group lesson phases, control students were more likely than CGI students to be working on number facts. Although CGI and control teachers did not differ in time spent on *development, controlled practice,* or *seatwork,* control teachers and students did spend more time on review. Taken together, these findings for review and for content by lesson phase suggest that control students were more likely than CGI students to be spending time in a large-group setting on drill and review of number facts, whereas CGI students were more likely to be solving problems in a large-group setting.

Teacher behavior. CGI teachers more often posed problems to students and more frequently listened to the process used by students to solve problems. In contrast, in giving feedback on students' solutions to problems, control teachers focused more frequently on the answer to the problem than did CGI teachers.

Strategy. Although no overall differences appeared between CGI and control classes in the strategies students actually used during class (Table 5), CGI teachers allowed students to use a variety of different strategies during instruction more often than did control teachers (Table 4). Control teachers appeared to provide more explicit instruction in a particular strategy and expected the students to use that strategy. This pattern is illustrated by the different results for the advanced counting strategy on the two observation systems. Although results from the teacher observation system showed that control teachers expected students to use advanced counting strategies significantly more often than did the CGI teachers, results from the student observations showed no difference in the students' actual use of advanced counting strategies. It appears that CGI teachers provided as much opportunity for students to use advanced counting strategies, but they allowed the opportunity for students to use other strategies as well.

Teachers' Knowledge

Table 6 presents means, standard deviations, and *t* tests between groups for scores on the tests of teachers' knowledge. CGI and control group teachers differed significantly in their knowledge of student strategies for both number facts and problem solving. However, CGI and control teachers did not differ significantly in their knowledge of students' problem-solving abilities in which teachers predicted students' performance on complex addition and subtraction word problems and on advanced problems.

Generally, control group teachers overestimated the use of number fact recall by their students by factors of two or three to one. In contrast, CGI teachers' predictions for the level of recall of number facts by their students generally did not deviate by more than 10% to 20% from the actual level of use by their students. Although CGI students actually used recall strategies significantly more than did control group students, control group teachers predicted higher levels of recall of number facts for their students.

TABLE 6

Means, standard deviations, and t tests for teacher knowledge tests

Test	Maximum possible	CGI M (SD)	Control M (SD)	t(38)
Number fact strategies	5	2.81 (.46)	2.25 (.58)	3.51*
Problem-solving strategies	6	2.97 (.87)	2.08 (.71)	3.56*
Problem-solving abilities	8	5.40 (.75)	5.25 (.51)	.74

*$p < .01$.

TABLE 7

Pretest means, posttest means, standard deviations, and ANOVA results for teachers' beliefs (N = 39)[a]

Belief scale	CGI M (SD)	Control M (SD)	F tests		
			Group	Time	Group by time
		Scale 1			
Pretest	40.15	39.05			
	(7.52)	(6.24)			
Posttest	45.20	42.11			
	(4.82)	(7.08)	1.18	27.65**	1.68
		Scale 2			
Pretest	48.75	50.26			
	(5.80)	(6.62)			
Posttest	53.80	50.16			
	(4.48)	(6.85)	0.38	9.01**	9.79**
		Scale 3			
Pretest	45.60	45.00			
	(5.83)	(6.01)			
Posttest	47.75	44.63			
	(5.12)	(5.06)	1.28	1.87	3.74
		Scale 4			
Pretest	44.00	44.79			
	(6.10)	(5.42)			
Posttest	50.85	47.37			
	(5.78)	(5.51)	0.37	25.68**	5.26*
		Total			
Pretest	178.50	179.11			
	(22.11)	(20.30)			
Posttest	197.60	184.26			
	(16.27)	(20.95)	1.13	27.73**	9.16**

* $p < .05$; ** $p < .01$.
[a] Pretest belief scores unavailable for one teacher.

Teachers' Beliefs

Table 7 presents the means and standard deviations for CGI and control teachers' beliefs at pretest and posttest. Group × Time analyses of variance (ANOVAs) were computed to examine treatment effects on each of the teacher belief scales from pretest (before the workshop) to posttest (after a year of teaching). Table 7 summarizes the ANOVA results. A significant time by treatment interaction indicated that after the treatment for Scales

2, 4, and total, CGI teachers were significantly more cognitively guided in their beliefs than were control teachers. Both groups of teachers increased significantly in their agreement with the perspective that children construct mathematical knowledge (Scale 1), and at posttest the CGI and control teachers did not differ in their agreement with this perspective.

Student Achievement

Analyses of covariance (ANCOVAs) between groups were computed on each of the student achievement measures controlling for prior mathematics achievement as measured by the pretest. The ANCOVA was not computed on scores on the Simple Word Problem scale because tests for homogeneity of regression revealed a significant prior achievement by treatment interaction. Table 8 presents means, standard deviations, adjusted means, and *t*-values for the ANCOVAs for the posttest student achievement measures. Although students in CGI teachers' classes and

TABLE 8

Means, standard deviations, adjusted means, and t-values for student achievement measures (N = 40)

| Test | Maximum Possible | CGI | | Control | | $t(37)^a$ |
		M (Adjusted *M*)	*SD*	*M* (Adjusted *M*)	*SD*	
Computation						
ITBS (Level 7)	27	20.95 (20.91)	2.08	20.05 (20.10)	1.81	1.40
Number facts	5	2.26 (2.25)	.49	1.80 (1.81)	.78	2.23*
Problem solving						
ITBS (Level 7)— Problems	22	17.28 (17.20)	1.83	16.42 (16.50)	1.89	1.62
Simple addition/ subtraction[b]	11	9.87	.40	9.63	.67	
Complex addition/ subtraction	12	8.60 (8.53)	1.56	7.80 (7.87)	1.51	1.99*[c]
Advanced	13	8.40 (8.32)	2.02	8.05 (8.13)	1.29	.52
Interview	6	5.62 (5.61)	.28	5.37 (5.38)	.37	2.51*

* *p* < .05.

[a] *t*-values calculated following ANCOVA approach.

[b] Interaction present so ANCOVA could not be calculated.

[c] One-tailed test.

students in control teachers' classes did not differ significantly in their performance on the ITBS Computation Test, CGI students demonstrated a higher level of recall of number facts on the number facts interview than did control students.

A significant prior achievement by treatment interaction was found on the Simple Addition and Subtraction Word Problem scales. For classes who scored at the lower end of the scale on the ITBS pretest, CGI classes scored higher on the Simple Addition and Subtraction Word Problem posttest than did control classes. For classes at the very top of the scale on pretest achievement, control group classes scored higher than CGI classes. Figure 1 shows the interaction and the regions of significance that were computed using the Potthoff (1964) extension of the Johnson-Neyman technique. The regions of significance included six CGI classes and six control group classes at the lower end on pretest achievement and three CGI classes and one control class at the upper end on pretest achievement.

On the test of Complex Addition and Subtraction Word Problems, students in CGI teachers' classes outperformed students in control teachers' classes. CGI and control classes did not differ significantly in their achievement on Advanced Problems. On the problem-solving interview, students in CGI classes used correct strategies significantly more often than students in control classes. No significant differences appeared between the groups in the students' use of any strategy.

Students' Confidence, Beliefs, Understanding, and Attention

Table 9 presents the means, standard deviations, and *t* tests between groups for students' confidence, beliefs, and reports of understanding and attention. CGI students were more confident of their abilities to solve mathematics problems than were control students. Like their teachers,

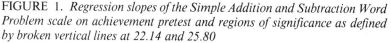

FIGURE 1. *Regression slopes of the Simple Addition and Subtraction Word Problem scale on achievement pretest and regions of significance as defined by broken vertical lines at 22.14 and 25.80*

TABLE 9

Means, standard deviations, and t tests for CGI and control students' confidence, beliefs, reported attention, and understanding (N = 40)

Student measure	CGI M (SD)	Control M (SD)	$t(38)$
Confidence	10.34 (.87)	9.77 (1.14)	1.79*[a]
Student beliefs	31.12 (2.01)	29.61 (1.09)	2.97**
Reported understanding	3.30 (.28)	3.16 (.22)	1.73*[a]
Reported attention	3.43 (.30)	3.50 (.24)	−0.82

* $p < .05$; ** $p < .01$.
[a] One-tailed test.

students in CGI classes were significantly more cognitively guided in their beliefs than were students in control teachers' classes. In addition, CGI students reported significantly greater understanding of mathematics than did control students. CGI and control students did not differ in the extent to which they reported that they paid attention during mathematics class. These latter findings are consistent with the classroom observations that showed that CGI and control students did not differ in the amount of time they were judged to be engaged with the addition and subtraction content.

Discussion

The results of this study provide a coherent picture of teachers' knowledge and beliefs, classroom instruction, and students' achievement and beliefs that is consistent with the assumptions and principles of Cognitively Guided Instruction. Two major themes are reflected in the guiding principles of CGI. One is that instruction should develop understanding by stressing the relationships between skills and problem solving, with problem solving serving as the organizing focus of instruction. This suggests that CGI classrooms would be characterized by a greater emphasis on problem solving than would be found in traditional classrooms. The second major theme is that instruction should build on students' existing knowledge. This implies that teachers regularly assess students' thinking and the processes that students use to solve different problems so that teachers understand students' knowledge and capabilities and can adapt instruction appropriately. We use these two themes in our discussion of the results.

The Role of Problem Solving

Both CGI and control teachers increased in their agreement with the perspective that children construct mathematical knowledge. These results suggest that both the CGI workshop and the problem-solving workshop for the control teacher had an effect on teachers' beliefs about children's problem solving. However, in contrast to control teachers, CGI teachers agreed more with the belief that instruction should facilitate children's construction of knowledge. CGI and control teachers differed significantly in their beliefs about the relationship between skills and problem solving. In particular, CGI teachers agreed more than control teachers with the belief that skills should be used on understanding and problem solving.

The instruction of CGI and control teachers represented by the classroom observation data reflected the picture portrayed by the belief scales. Although the difference between groups in the total time that students spent on problem solving was not significant, CGI teachers spent significantly more instructional time interacting with students about problems than did control teachers. CGI teachers also allowed students to use multiple strategies more frequently. Thus, it appears that CGI classes spent more time talking about problems and discussing alternative solutions than did control classes. In contrast, control classes spent proportionally more time working on problems alone during seatwork.

Although differences in student achievement were modest, the differences found consistently favored the CGI treatment group. No overall difference appeared between the CGI and control classes in students' ability to solve simple addition and subtraction word problems. Performance on the Simple Addition and Subtraction Word Problem scales was near the ceiling for both groups (means of 9.87 and 9.63 out of a maximum score of 11), so there was little room for treatment effects. However, a significant prior achievement by treatment interaction appeared. In classes with low levels of achievement on the pretest, CGI students scored higher at posttest on the test of Simple Addition and Subtraction Word Problems than did control students. The reason for this interaction may have been that the test allowed more room for lower achieving classes than higher achieving ones to move up on the test.

The types of problems on the Simple Addition and Subtraction Word Problem scale represent the treatment of word problems typically found in most first grade mathematics textbooks and programs. The Complex Addition and Subtraction Word Problem scales included problems from the more comprehensive analysis of addition and subtraction problems that was discussed in the CGI workshop, and such problems are not typically included in a first grade program. Although the effect size was relatively small, performance of CGI classes was significantly higher on these complex problems than was performance of control classes. These significant differences did not transfer, however, to the advanced problems that involved multiple steps, extraneous information, or grouping and partitioning.

It might be argued that the differences in problem-solving performance simply reflected a greater emphasis on solving problems. Increasing instructional time devoted to problem solving is not, however, a simple matter. In the past, teachers generally have been reluctant to sacrifice time traditionally devoted to teaching computational skills to teach more problem solving or to spend more time developing understanding (National Advisory Committee on Mathematical Education, 1975; Romberg & Carpenter, 1986).

Teachers may be reluctant to place a greater emphasis on problem solving for several reasons. One is that teachers may fear that many problems are beyond the capabilities of their students and that students must master number facts first in order to solve word problems (Peterson et al., 1989). The research that CGI teachers studied during the summer workshop provided convincing evidence that a wide variety of problems are not beyond the abilities of most first grade students. Furthermore, this knowledge provided CGI teachers with a basis for assessing their own students to find out their students' actual problem-solving capabilities. Consequently, CGI teachers may not have been reluctant to emphasize problem solving.

Another related concern of teachers may be that time spent on problem solving will detract from their students' learning of computational skills. First grade teachers and students are held accountable for students' learning addition and subtraction number facts to a requisite level of automaticity. The results of this study document that a focus on problem solving does not necessarily result in a decline in performance in computational skills. In spite of the emphasis on problem solving in CGI classes and the corresponding decrease in time spent on computational skills, CGI classes and control classes performed equally well on a standardized test of computational skill. Furthermore, students in CGI classes actually had a higher level of recall of number facts than did control students. Because CGI teachers were able to accurately assess their children's knowledge, they may have been aware that their children were learning number facts, so the concern of not meeting expectations for their children's competency in computation was alleviated.

Because most first grade children use a variety of counting and modeling strategies to generate number facts, standardized tests often provide a better measure of the speed with which children can apply counting and modeling strategies than of children's actual recall of number facts. On tests such as the ITBS computation test, children often use these counting and modeling strategies so rapidly that it appears that they are recalling as they solve number fact items (Steinberg, 1985). Because CGI students actually used a recall strategy during the interview more than did control children, it might be argued that CGI students actually demonstrated higher levels of number fact knowledge and skills than did control students.

In summary, in contrast to control teachers, CGI teachers expressed beliefs that were more consistent with the principle that problem solving should be the focus of instruction in mathematics. CGI teachers spent more instructional time than control teachers on problem solving and spent less time teaching number facts. Differences in students' achievement on both problem solving and recall of number facts favored the CGI group.

Assessing Students' Thinking and Building on Their Knowledge

In contrast to control teachers, CGI teachers' knowledge, beliefs, and instructional practices were more consistent with the principle that it is important to assess children's thinking. The observation data showed that CGI teachers posed problems and listened to the processes students used to solve problems significantly more often than did control teachers. CGI teachers also allowed students to use a variety of strategies to solve a particular problem more frequently than did control teachers. Both posing problems and listening to process provided the opportunity for teachers to assess students' knowledge. By allowing students to use any strategy they chose, the teacher was able to assess how each student was thinking about the problem rather than requiring the student to imitate one strategy that the teacher specified. This approach was also more consistent with the belief expressed by CGI teachers that instruction should facilitate children's construction of knowledge rather than present information and procedures to children.

A typical activity that was observed in CGI classes was for a teacher to pose a problem to a group of students. After providing some time for students to solve the problem, the teacher would ask one student to describe how he or she solved the problem. The emphasis was on the process for solving the problem rather than on the answer. After this student explained his or her problem-solving process, the teacher would ask whether anyone had solved the problem in a different way and give another student a chance to explain her or his solution. The teacher would continue calling on students until no student would report a way of solving the problem that had not already been described. This approach might have served at least two purposes. First, the CGI teacher was able to assess the problem-solving processes of a number of students in the group, thus giving the teacher knowledge of each student's problem-solving abilities and strategies. Second, students were allowed to solve the problem at a level that was appropriate for them. In other words, the teacher facilitated students' learning by encouraging each student to construct a solution to the problem that was meaningful to him or her.

Control teachers' instruction was characterized by more control over the content of instruction and less assessment of students' thinking. In contrast to CGI teachers, control teachers less often (a) posed problems, (b) listened to students' strategies, and (c) encouraged the use of multiple strategies to solve problems. They spent more time reviewing material covered previously, such as drilling on number facts, and more time providing feedback to students' answers.

What CGI teachers learned by posing problems and listening to their children solve problems was reflected in their knowledge of their students. CGI teachers identified the strategies that their students would use to solve a problem or generate a number fact significantly more accurately than did control group teachers. Control group teachers consistently overestimated their students' ability to recall number facts. By better understanding the processes that children were using, CGI teachers may have been able to adapt instruction so that more appropriate activities were provided to children who were ready to learn number facts at a recall level. Recall of number facts was higher in CGI classes.

Although we had anticipated that the observation data might show treatment differences in grouping practices because CGI teachers would attempt to adapt instruction to individual students, we found no significant differences between CGI and control teachers in their use of medium groups, small groups, or individual instruction. Thus, whereas CGI teachers may have greater knowledge of the individual differences between students, this knowledge did not appear to influence their grouping practices. Most teachers in both groups used whole-class and individual seatwork as the primary instructional settings.

Conclusions

The results of this study suggest that one effective approach for using the results of research on children's thinking and problem solving to improve classroom instruction is to help teachers understand the principal findings of the research so that teachers can use this knowledge to evaluate more effectively their students' knowledge and make more informed instructional decisions. Contrary to previous findings that teachers do not use knowledge of their students to make instructional decisions (Clark & Peterson, 1986; Putnam, 1987), the experimental teachers in this study did attend to their students' thinking. Providing teachers access to explicit knowledge derived from research on children's thinking did influence their instruction and their students' achievement.

In this study we provided teachers with explicit knowledge about children's thinking in a well-defined domain. We speculate that giving teachers knowledge of broad principles of learning and problem solving would have had less effect on teachers' instruction than giving teachers' access to more specific knowledge about children's problem solving in the particular content domain that was the basis for this study. In the workshop we provided teachers with explicit examples of children's problem solving in addition and subtraction that the teachers could relate directly to their own students, and we also discussed examples of assessment techniques the teachers could apply in their classrooms. As one of the CGI teachers in our study commented: "I have always known that it was important to listen to kids, but before I never knew what questions to ask or what to listen for."

A key feature of this study that distinguishes it from other studies of classroom teaching was that the mathematics content was critical. Cognitive researchers' analysis of content, which was the basis for the research on addition and subtraction, provided a link between the psychology of children's thinking and the mathematics curriculum so that teachers could apply what they learned about children in their teaching. The cognitive analysis also provided us, as researchers, with a framework for thinking about and for assessing teachers' knowledge, beliefs, and classroom instruction and for evaluating students' achievement and beliefs. Although many unanswered questions remain, our results suggest that giving teachers access to research-based knowledge about students' thinking and problem solving can affect teachers' beliefs about learning and instruction, their classroom practices, their knowledge about their students, and most important, their students' achievement and beliefs.

References

Carpenter, T. P. (1985). Learning to add and subtract: An exercise in problem solving. In E. A. Silver (Ed.), *Teaching and learning mathematical problem solving: Multiple research perspectives* (pp. 17–40). Hillsdale, NJ: Lawrence Erlbaum.

Carpenter, T. P., Fennema, E., Peterson, P. L., & Carey, D. (1988). Teachers' pedagogical content knowledge in mathematics. *Journal for Research in Mathematics Education, 19*, 345–357.

Carpenter, T. P., & Moser, J. M. (1983). The acquisition of addition and subtraction concepts. In R. Lesh & M. Landau (Eds.), *The acquisition of mathematics concepts and processes* (pp. 7–44). New York: Academic Press.

Clark, C. M., & Peterson, P. L. (1986). Teachers' thought processes. In M. C. Wittrock (Ed.), *Handbook of research on teaching* (3rd ed., pp. 255–296). New York: Macmillan.

Fennema, E., & Peterson, P. L. (1986). Teacher-student interactions and sex-related differences in learning mathematics. *Teaching and Teacher Education, 2*(1), 19–42.

Fisher, C. W., Berliner, D. C., Filby, N. N., Marliave, R., Cahn, L. S., & Dishaw, M. M. (1980). Teaching behaviors, academic learning time, and student achievement: An overview. In C. Denham & A. Lieberman (Eds.), *Time to learn* (pp. 7–32). Washington, DC: United States Department of Education.

Good, T., Grouws, D., & Ebmeier, H. (1983). *Active mathematics learning.* New York: Longmans.

Lampert, M. (1986). Knowing, doing, and teaching multiplication. *Cognition and Instruction, 3*, 305–342.

National Advisory Committee on Mathematical Education. (1975). *Overview and analysis of school mathematics, grades K–12.* Washington, DC: Conference Board of the Mathematical Sciences.

Peterson, P. L. (1987). Observation manual. In E. Fennema, T. P. Carpenter, & P.

L. Peterson (Eds.), *Studies of the application of cognitive and instruction science to mathematics instruction* (Technical Progress Report, August 1, 1986 to July 31, 1987). Madison: Wisconsin Center for Education Research.

Peterson, P. L. (1988). Teachers' and students' cognitional knowledge for classroom teaching and learning. *Educational Researcher, 17*(5), 5–14.

Peterson, P. L., & Fennema, E. (1985). Effective teaching, student engagement in classroom activities, and sex-related differences in learning mathematics. *American Educational Research Journal, 22*, 309–335.

Peterson, P. L., Fennema, E., Carpenter, T. C., & Loef, M. (1989). Teachers' pedagogical content beliefs in mathematics. *Cognition and Instruction, 6*, 1–40.

Peterson, P. L., Swing, S. R., Braverman, M. T., & Buss, R. (1982). Students' aptitudes and their reports of cognitive processes during direct instruction. *Journal of Educational Psychology, 74*, 535–547.

Peterson, P. L., Swing, S. R., Stark, K. D., & Waas, G. A. (1984). Students' cognitions and time on task during mathematics instruction. *American Educational Research Journal, 21*, 487–515.

Potthoff, R. F. (1964). On the Johnson-Neyman technique and some extensions thereof. *Psychometrika, 29*, 241–255.

Putnam, R. T. (1987). Structuring and adjusting content for students: A study of live and simulated tutoring of addition. *American Educational Research Journal, 24*, 13–48.

Putnam, R. T., & Leinhardt, G. (1986, April). *Curriculum scripts and adjustment of content to lessons.* Paper presented at the annual meeting of the American Educational Research Association, San Francisco.

Riley, M. S., Greeno, J. G., & Heller, J. I. (1983). Development of children's problem-solving ability in arithmetic. In H. Ginsburg (Ed.), *The development of mathematical thinking* (pp. 153–200). New York: Academic Press.

Romberg, T. A., & Carpenter, T. C. (1986). Research on teaching and learning mathematics: Two disciplines of scientific injury. In M. C. Wittrock (Ed.), *Handbook of research on teaching* (3rd ed., pp. 850–873). New York: Macmillan.

Shulman, L. S. (1986). Those who understand: Knowledge growth in teaching. *Educational Researcher, 15*(2), 4–14.

Steinberg, R. M. (1985). Instruction on derived facts strategies in addition and subtraction. *Journal for Research in Mathematics Education, 16*, 337–355.

Authors

THOMAS P. CARPENTER, Professor, University of Wisconsin—Madison, 225 N. Mills St., Madison, WI 53706. *Specialization:* mathematics education.

ELIZABETH FENNEMA, Associate Professor of Education, University of Wisconsin—Madison, 225 N. Mills St., Madison, WI 53706. *Specialization:* teachers' knowledge and beliefs.

PENELOPE L. PETERSON, Associate Professor, Michigan State University, 510 Erickson Hall, East Lansing, MI 48824. *Specialization:* teachers' knowledge.

CHI-PANG CHIANG, Assistant Professor of Psychology, National Chengchi University, Taipai, Taiwan, Republic of China. *Specialization:* research design.

MEGAN LOEF, Graduate Student in Educational Psychology, University of Wisconsin—Madison, 225 N. Mills St., Madison, WI 53706. *Specialization:* teachers' knowledge.

Section IX
Quasi-Experimental Methods in Educational Research

Interrupted Time-Series Quasi-Experiments

Gene V Glass
Arizona State University

Researchers seek to establish causal relationships by conducting experiments. The standard for causal proof is what the psychologist Donald Campbell and educational researcher Julian Stanley (1963) called the "true experiment." Often, circumstances will not permit meeting all the conditions of a true experiment, and a quasi-experiment is then chosen. Among the various quasiexperimental designs is one that rivals the true experiment in validity: the interrupted time-series design. It has become the standard method of causal analysis in applied behavioral research.

Just what is a "cause" is a matter of deep philosophical debate. Perhaps I can safely ignore that debate and appeal to your intuitive understanding that renders meaningful such statements as "The nail caused the tire to go flat" or "Owning a car causes teenagers' grades to drop." If every relationship were causal, the world would be a simple place; but most relationships are not. In schools where teachers make above-average salaries, pupils score above average on achievement tests. Despite the seeming connection between these events, it would not be correct to say that increasing teachers' salaries will cause an increase in pupils, achievement. Similarly, business executives who take long, expensive vacations make higher salaries than executives who don't. But will taking the summer off and touring Europe increase your salary? Try it and find out.

Relationships: Causal and Spurious

Relationships may fail to be causal for two principal reasons: a third variable or an ambiguous direction of influence. The third-variable situation occurs when two things are related only because each is causally related to a third variable and not because of any causal link between each other. The example of teachers, salaries and pupil achievement is probably an instance of the third-variable situation. In this case, the third variable might be the wealth of the community; rich communities pay teachers more and have pupils who score higher on achievement tests for a host of reasons connected to family wealth but not to teachers' pay. Teachers are professionals who want to be paid well and deserve to be, but I doubt if they try any harder to teach pupils because they earn a few hundred dollars more after their salary negotiations are finished. So the relationship of teachers' salaries and pupil achievement—a relationship that is an empirical fact, incidentally—is due to common relationships to a third variable.

The business executive's vacation is an example of ambiguous direction of influence. A travel agent might advertise that executives who take longer vacations earn more than those who don't, but the relationship doesn't show causality. A simple relationship of earnings and vacations doesn't mean that long vacations cause higher salaries (presumably through improving morale and vitality and the like) or that higher salaries cause long, expensive vacations. The truth is obvious in this case, and it is quite the opposite of the direction of influence that the travel agent wants people to believe. But many other examples are less clear. Does enhanced motivation cause pupils to learn successfully in school, or does success in learning increase their motivation to learn? The truth is probably some of each in unknown amounts, which goes to show how ill-advised one is to think of each relationship as if it were a causal relationship. Experimenters describe as "spurious" relationships that would not stand the test of a true experiment.

Experimenters have devised a methodology that lays to rest both the problem of the third variable and of the ambiguous influence of direction. They contrive two or more sets of circumstances that are alike in all respects except for the phenomenon that is being tested as a possible cause. Then they observe whether the expected effect ensues.

For example, an experimenter might take a large sample of teachers and their pupils and divide them into two identical groups except that one group's teachers receive a $1,500 raise and the other group's do not. A year later the experimenter measures the pupils' achievement to see whether it has been affected to see whether it is different in the two groups. If it is, the difference must be attributable to the monetary increase. By setting up two identical groups of teachers and their pupils, the experimenter rules out all possible third variables as explanations of the eventual difference in pupil achievement. Can it be said that an achievement advantage for the pupils of the better paid teachers is not really a result of increased pay because the better paid teachers might have had older pupils or smarter pupils or the better paid teachers might have had more experience? In other words, might not there be some third-variable problems here? No, because the teachers and pupils were equivalent in all respects at the beginning of the year. Can it be said that the direction of influence between salaries and achievement is ambiguous in this experiment? No, because the different salaries were set by the experimenters before pupil achievement was observed. Hence, the differences in achievement could not have caused the differences in teacher salaries; the only possible direction of influence is that the differences in teachers' salaries caused the differences in achievement.

This style of experimental thinking has been around for well over 150 years. Its original conception (due primarily to John Stuart Mill) was relatively impractical because it held that the conditions compared in an experiment had to be identical in all respects except for the hypothesized cause. That is, all third variables were to be ruled out by ensuring that they did not vary between the conditions. But all the possible third variables could not be known, and, even if they could be, they couldn't possibly be equated. Imagine having to equate the high-paid and low-paid teachers on their age, sex, height, weight, IQ, experience, nationality, and on and on.

Randomized or "True" Experiments

The experimental method received a big boost in the 1920s when Ronald Fisher, a young Englishman, devised an ingenious, practical solution to the third-variable problem-using chance. Fisher reasoned that if chance alone were used to determine, for example, which teachers in the experiment were paid more and which less, then any of an infinite number of possible third variables would be equated in the two groups. The variables would not be numerically equal but they would be equated within the limits of chance, or randomly equated, as it has come to be known. If a coin flip determines which teachers enter the high-pay group and which the low-pay group, then with respect to any third variable you can imagine (such as eye color or shoe size) the two groups will differ only by chance. Fisher then reasoned as follows: After the experiment if the only observed differences between the conditions are no larger than what chance might account for, then those differences might well be due to the chance differences on some third variables. But if the differences are much larger than what chance might produce (e.g., if all of the pupils of well-paid teachers learn much more than the pupils of poorly paid teachers), then chance differences in third variables could not account for this result (differences in teacher pay must be the cause of the large differences in pupil achievement). Because experimenters must calculate the size of differences that chance is likely to produce and compare them with the differences they actually observe, experimenters necessarily become involved with probability theory and its application to statistics.

Fisher's modern experimental methods were applied in agricultural research for 20 years or so before they began to be applied in psychology and eventually in education. In the early 1960s, Campbell and Stanley (1963) published a paper that was quickly acknowledged to be a classic. They drew important distinctions between the type of experiments Fisher devised and the many other designs and methods used by researchers who aspired to perform experiments but failed to satisfy all of Fisher's conditions. Campbell and Stanley called the experiments that Fisher devised "true experiments." The methods that fell short of satisfying the conditions of true experiments they called "quasi-experiments," quasi meaning seemingly or apparently but not genuinely so.

True experiments satisfy three conditions: the experimenter sets up two or more conditions whose effects are to be evaluated subsequently; persons or groups of persons are then assigned strictly at random, that is, by chance, to the conditions; and the eventual differences between the conditions on the measure of effect (for example, the pupils, achievement) are compared with differences of chance or random magnitude.

The most common substitute for a true experiment is what Campbell and Stanley labeled a "pre-experimental design." In the most common example, two groups of people—a treatment group and a control group—are compared on a dependent variable "after the fact" of their having found their way into these two groups through no intervention of the experimenter. This "ex post facto" experiment usually involves an attempt to correct statistically for differences between the treatment and control groups on a succession of "third variables" through such devices as analysis of covariance. For example, a group of students who report watching more than 100 hours of television per month is compared with a group that watches fewer than 20 hours; the dependent variable is success in school. The researcher might try to equate the groups after the experiment has run its course by adjusting school success averages for differences in intelligence and social-economic status. The adjusted differences in this pre-experimental design were long thought to be dubious, but never more so than after Cronbach (1982) explained the many and varied deficiencies of this method of testing causal claims. Nothing so recommends the techniques of quasi-experimentation presented below as does Cronbach's critique of the fatally flawed ex-post facto preexperiment.

A Quasi-Experimental Design: The Interrupted Time Series

Quasi-experiments cannot be so easily described. There are many varieties of them, and the various species arise from different ways of attempting to control for third variables without actually using random assignment. One of the most promising quasi-experimental designs is known as the interrupted time-series experiment.

In Figure 1 appears a graph of the number of depressed thoughts (the solid black line) a mildly depressive young woman recorded for 49 consecutive days. On the first day, she counted about 70 depressed thoughts; on the second day,

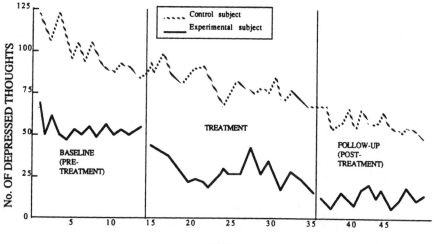

FIGURE 1. *Incidence of depressed thoughts for an experimental subject receiving behavioral therapy and for a control subject.*

about 55. After 14 days of recording (after the first solid vertical line in Figure 1) the woman was placed on a behavioral modification therapy designed to eliminate depression. The therapy was continued for 21 days and then terminated (at the second vertical line), and the recording of depressed thoughts continued for an additional 14 posttreatment days.

By studying the pattern of the graph, paying particular attention to what happens to the series precisely at the point of shifting from no-treatment to treatment or vice versa, one hopes to learn something about the effect of the therapy on depressed thoughts. In general terms, the therapy is called a treatment or an intervention, and depressed thoughts are the outcome or dependent variable.

You might often find that a time-series experiment is a workable alternative when the conditions of a true experiment cannot be met; for example, when you have only one or two units (persons or classrooms) instead of a substantial number, or when different units cannot be treated in different ways (methods A and B) at the same time. But the time-series experiment imposes its own requirements, the foremost of which is that it sometimes requires that data be recorded for many consecutive points in time before and after a treatment is introduced. How many is "many"? We'll return to this important question later.

Time-series experiments might also be used to assess the effect of treatments that use naturally occurring interventions, which are measured with data from archives. These interventions are made by someone other than the researcher and are not normally made for experimental purposes, although researchers make use of them for causal analysis. The data to evaluate the impact of the interventions come from archives-collections of data gathered routinely across time for administrative purposes. An example of this type of archival time-series experiment appears as Figure 2. Here you see a graph of the traffic fatality rate in Great Britain, by month, from 1961 through 1970. The dependent variable

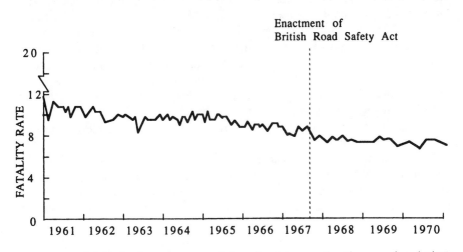

FIGURE 2. *British fatality rate corrected for miles driven and with seasonal variations removed.* (Source: Ross, 1973)

is the number of traffic deaths in a month divided by the number of miles driven in Great Britain, in units of 100 million. For example, there were about 12 deaths per 100 million miles driven in January 1961; that is, if the total mileage driven in Great Britain in January 1961 was 300 million, then there were about $3 \times 12 = 36$ traffic deaths that month. In October 1967, the British Road Safety Act of 1967 instituted a variety of measures designed to reduce traffic accidents, foremost among which was setting up road blocks and administering breath tests to discover drunken drivers. This intervention is indicated by the vertical line in Figure 2.

The simple logic of the time-series experiment is this: If the graph of the dependent variable shows an abrupt shift in level or direction precisely at the point of intervention, then the intervention is a cause of the effect on the dependent variable. In the two examples presented thus far, the causal questions are these: "Did the behavioral psychotherapy reduce the rate of depressed thoughts?" and "Did the British Road Safety Act of 1967 reduce the traffic fatality rate?"

The effect of an intervention on an outcome variable can assume a variety of forms. Some of these are depicted in Figure 3. Having detailed expectations about how the graph should change in response to an intervention is the best protection against deluding oneself and being led astray by extraneous influences and chance occurrences. For example, suppose that a highway safety law required a safety check of car tires and replacement of worn tires. Because not all tires would have worn treads at the moment the law was enacted, and because perhaps 10% of the worn tires might be detected and replaced monthly for about the first year, an intervention effect like that in case E in Figure 3 might be anticipated. If an abrupt level change-case A-were observed in the data instead, the chain of causal reasoning from tire inspection to reduced accidents would be weakened, even though the possibility of an effect due to some unknown cause remained strong.

Carefully spelled out expectations for the form of an effect are crucial where delayed effects might exist (for example, cases B and F in Figure 3). Delayed effects occur frequently and are perfectly plausible. For example, the Mental Health Act of 1965 authorized construction of community mental health centers that couldn't possibly have begun to function significantly before 1967. An experimenter who does not have definite expectations about the form of an effect may interpret as an effect every little ephemeral and irrelevant jump or wiggle in the curve.

Graphs of time-series data can change level and direction for many reasons, only some of which are related to the intervention. Separating potential reasons for effects into those essentially related to the intervention and those only accidentally related is the principal task in analyzing time-series experiments. You might recognize the time-series experimental design as an extension in both directions (the past and the future) of the old and disreputable pretest-posttest experiment. In the pretest-posttest design, a group of persons is observed, a treatment is applied to them, and then they are observed a second

A. Abrupt change in level

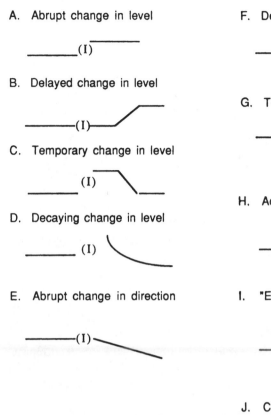

B. Delayed change in level

C. Temporary change in level

D. Decaying change in level

E. Abrupt change in direction

F. Delayed change in direction

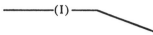

G. Temporary change in direction

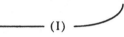

H. Accelerated change in direction

I. "Evolutionary operations" effect

J. Change in variability

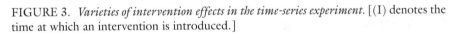

FIGURE 3. *Varieties of intervention effects in the time-series experiment.* [(I) denotes the time at which an intervention is introduced.]

time. An increase (or a decrease) of the group average from the first observation to the second is taken to be the effect of the independent variable (the treatment) on the dependent variable that was observed. The pretest-posttest design has such a bad reputation because so many influences other than the treatment can account for a change in scores from pre to post. The person or persons in the experiment could grow tired, smarter, or less cooperative from the single premeasure to the postmeasure. Likewise, two less-than-identical tests might be given before and after, or the experimental units could have been chosen because they fell so far from the average on the pretest thus greatly increasing the odds of their regression (i.e., movement) toward the mean of the posttest. Each of these influences can cause increases or decreases in scores that are confounded with whatever effects the intervention or treatment might have. The pretest-posttest design deserves its bad press.

The time-series experiment adds many preintervention and postintervention observations and thus permits separating real intervention effects from other long-term trends in a time series. Consider Figure 1 again. The series of depressed thoughts for the control subject shows a gradual, regular decline from Day 1 to Day 49. The course that the graph follows shows no abrupt shifts at those points in time when the experimental subject, represented by the solid black line, is put on treatment and taken off. There is no evidence of an intervention effect on the control subject's graph, as there ought not to be, because this subject was given no therapy but merely recorded the rate of depressed thoughts for 49 days. But notice how, if a single premeasure had been taken on the control subject around Day 5 and a single postmeasure around Day 25, it would have appeared as though this subject had experienced a sizable reduction in depressed thoughts because of treatment. To be sure the control subject's graph shows a decline across time, but the decline could be due to many extraneous factors, including becoming bored with counting depressed thoughts, a shifting standard for what constitutes a depressed thought, hormonal changes, and the like.

There are many different ways to arrange experimental units and to plan one or several interventions. Some ways may be cheaper or safer than others. In Figure 4, several possible alternative time-series designs are sketched. They are special purpose designs, each created for reasons of economy or validity. The Os in the diagrams stand for observations or measurements and are taken repeatedly over time. The Is stand for interventions, that is, the introduction of a treatment. The "1" and the "2" subscripts are added to the Is to indicate that two different treatments were introduced into the series.

Time-series experiments differ in important ways depending on whether the "experimental unit" is a single person or a group of persons. If the unit is a large group of persons, one can either measure each person in the group at each point in time or subsample different persons at each point. For example, in Figure 5 appear the results of a time-series experiment on the effects Outward Bound, a wilderness camping experience, has on participants' self-confidence. Several hundred participants were available for study, but it would have been unnecessary and too costly to test each person each week of the 11-month study. By randomly sampling a new group of 20 persons each week, no participant was burdened by the testing, and yet an accurate picture was obtained of the group's response to treatment.

Statistical Analysis of the Time-Series Experiment

Although operant psychologists made extensive use of the time-series design for years before methodologists christened it as such, they have remained resistant to most considerations of statistical analysis, preferring to rely on visual inspection of the graphs to judge the presence of an effect. Even though the methods of analyzing time-series experiments have been in the literature for nearly three decades, those who could benefit most from their application refuse to employ them. Indeed, one can scan volumes of applied operant liter-

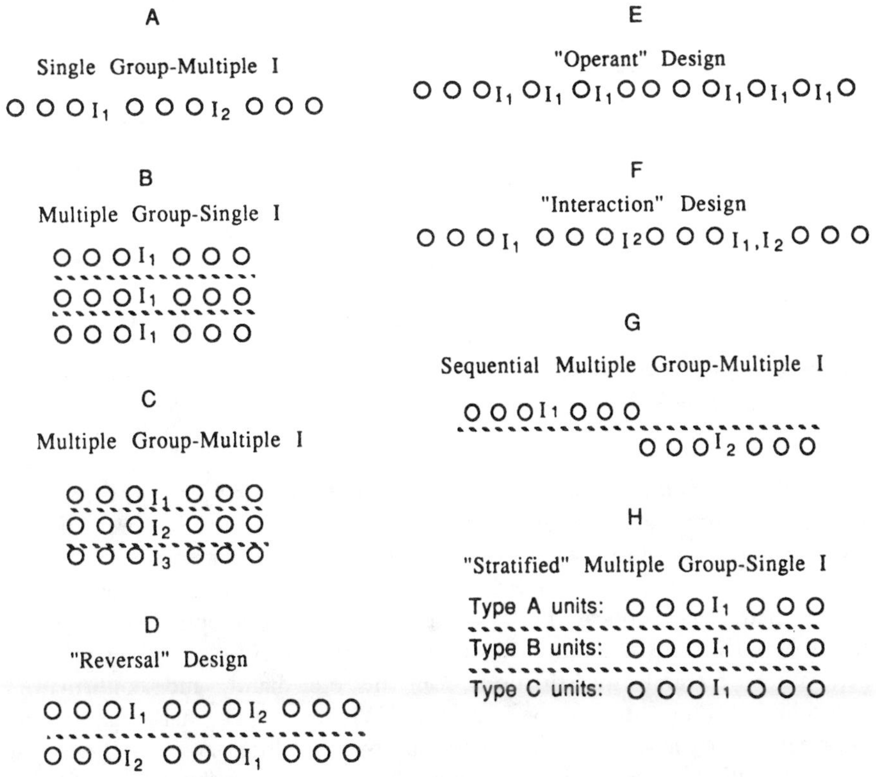

A

Single Group-Multiple I

O O O I_1 O O O I_2 O O O

B

Multiple Group-Single I

O O O I_1 O O O
O O O I_1 O O O
O O O I_1 O O O

C

Multiple Group-Multiple I

O O O I_1 O O O
O O O I_2 O O O
O O O I_3 O O O

D

"Reversal" Design

O O O I_1 O O O I_2 O O O
O O O I_2 O O O I_1 O O O

E

"Operant" Design

O O O I_1, OI_1, OI_1, O O O O OI_1, OI_1, OI_1, O

F

"Interaction" Design

O O O I_1, O O O I_2 O O O I_{1},I_2 O O O

G

Sequential Multiple Group-Multiple I

O O O I_1 O O O
O O O I_2 O O O

H

"Stratified" Multiple Group-Single I

Type A units: O O O I_1 O O O
Type B units: O O O I_1 O O O
Type C units: O O O I_1 O O O

FIGURE 4. *Variations on the basic time-series experimental design.* (O represents an observation or measurement of the dependent variable; I represents an intervention.)

ature, such as the *Journal of Applied Behavior Analysis,* and never encounter statistics more complex than means and graphs. And yet, the statistical problems of interpreting time-series experiments are sufficiently complex that merely eyeballing graphs and drawing conclusions are not enough.

The operant psychologists' position on the application of statistics to time-series experiments was possibly never stated more emphatically and directly than it once was by an anonymous reviewer of a manuscript submitted to an applied behavioral analysis journal 25 years ago:

Applied behavior analysis doesn't need sensitive statistics to salvage small effects. The field needs basic effects, that is, effects that are large, reliable, powerful, clear, and durable. Such basic effects will give us strong principles. The field doesn't need dubious, small, and ephemeral but statistically significant results, because these would result in the development of more and weaker principles. Behavior modification became a technology by ignoring small effects. The sort of eyeball analysis that has been done has acted as a filter, weeding out the small effects. . . . In the reviewer's opinion, the development of sensitive statistics appropriate for the research designs of applied behavior analysis would be bad for the field.

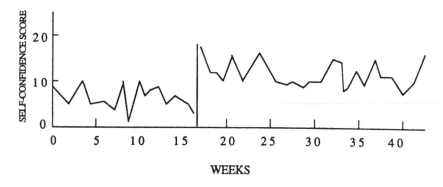

FIGURE 5. *Self-confidence scores of a large group of participants before and after an Outward Bound experience.* (Source: Smith et al., 1976).

The above opinion is not merely a relic from a discarded past. As recently as 1992, Parsonson and Baer were arguing for the superiority of impressionistic, visual examination of timeseries experiments over statistical analysis. Their position prompted this mild rebuke from Levin (1992), who edited the book in which their paper appeared: ". . . it is the author's opinion that many researchers cannot (or do not) distinguish between exploratory (hypothesis-generating) research investigations, on the one hand, and confirmatory (hypothesis-testing) studies, on the other. Whereas visual analysis and other informal inspection methods represent legitimate exploratory-research vehicles for communicating what 'is interesting to the eye' or what 'merits further study,' corroborating predicted outcomes on the basis of formal statistical analysis is often mandatory for confirmatory research studies" (p. 221).

Of course, everyone would like "large, reliable, powerful, clear and durable effects." But perusal of the *Journal of Applied Behavior Analysis* will show that its authors are more than willing to investigate and report small, weak, and ephemeral effects, or effects that are entirely illusory. Such perusal will also reveal that the "eyeball" test is applied very differently by different persons-some seeing effects, some seeing none at all. Consider the study published by Gettinger (1993) on the effects of two methods of spelling instruction in a regular second-grade classroom. Four boys, two above average spellers and two below average spellers, were alternately taught to spell a targeted set of words by either the direct instruction method or the so-called invented spelling method, wherein words are spelled phonetically at first in context then eventually replaced with conventional orthography. The different methods were applied in a multiple-group ABAB design. The results of the study appear as Figure 6, in which the series have been averaged for each group of spellers. Gettinger (1993) wrote this about the data on which Figure 6 is based: "As predicted, children spelled more of the six words correctly when they received direct instruction and practice on words in isolation than during the invented spelling condition" (p. 287). I know of no legitimate statistical analysis that

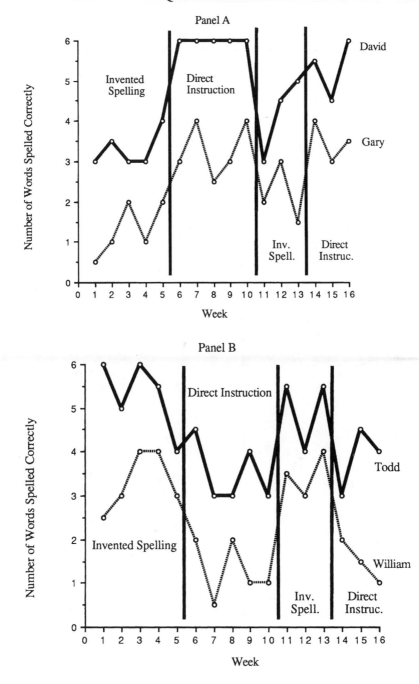

FIGURE 6. *Number of words spelled correctly by four boys* (two good spellers–panel A; two poor spellers–panel B) *under two methods of spelling instruction* (after Gettinger, 1993).

would support the conclusion that the ABAB design in Figure 6 shows a differential effect for direct instruction versus invented spelling. Judge for yourself.

The graph of a real time-series will show a good deal of fluctuation quite apart from any effect an intervention might have on it. Consider, for example, the graph of the series in Figure 7, where the number of anxious thoughts of a neurotic patient is recorded for 10 days before psychotherapy and for 21 days during therapy. The graph was shown to 13 researchers, and they were asked to judge whether the roughly 7-point drop at the intervention point was merely a random fluctuation, unaccountable for in terms of the intervention (like the 9-point increase between days 5 and 6 or the more than 9-point rise from day 29 to day 30, for example) or whether it was evidence of a true intervention effect. Five of the researchers judged the intervention of therapy to be effective and eight judged it to be ineffective. Jury analysis by visual inspection proved to be inconclusive in this instance.

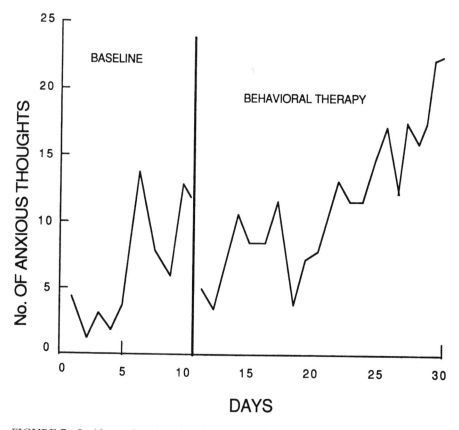

FIGURE 7. *Incidence of anxious thoughts for a single subject before and during behavioral therapy* (after Komechak, 1974).

Stationary Versus Nonstationary Series

A key distinction has to be drawn between two types of series: those that are stationary and those that are nonstationary. The distinction makes all the difference in the world when it comes to inspecting graphs and analyzing whether or not an intervention had an effect. The difference between stationary and nonstationary time series is the difference between graphs that fluctuate around some fixed levels across time and graphs that wander about, changing their level and region haphazardly. The graph of British traffic fatalities in Figure 2 is reasonably stationary, with most of the preintervention observations contained in a region between 8 and 11.

It is far easier to detect an intervention effect in a stationary process than in a nonstationary one. Intervention effects are seen as displacements of the curve, and as you can see, nonstationary processes are, by definition, curves that are subject to displacements of level and slope at random points in time. The trick with a nonstationary time series is to distinguish the random displacements from the one true deterministic displacement caused by the intervention. And that's not easy.

If a process is basically nonstationary, one needs to establish that fact and, furthermore, be able to estimate the degree of nonstationarity before you can decide how much displacement of the curve precisely at the point of intervention is convincing evidence of an effect. Behavioral psychologists have long (since Skinner) recognized this fact in their advice to establish a stable baseline for the organism before intervening; unfortunately, as one moves out of the laboratory into the world, one often encounters baselines that are not so accommodating and would never settle into being stationary no matter how long they are observed. Nonstationarity is a fact of life in the world. It must be dealt with, not wished away.

How can one establish the fact and character of nonstationarity? They can do so by patiently watching the series before intervening. This is why the researchers who looked at Figure 7 and tried to guess whether the intervention was really effective did such a bad job. The preintervention period, the "baseline" if you will, simply wasn't long enough to establish the character of the process and give researchers a good idea of how the series should behave in the absence of an intervention. The circumstances in Figure 2 are quite different. The British fatality rate can be expected to be about 8 to 10 after mid-1967, as it was for several months before.

Once again, the statistician must act as a messenger of the doleful news: The single most important thing to remember about time-series experiments is that they require long baseline periods for establishing whether the process is stationary or nonstationary.

How long is "long"? Once again, the statistician must, in honesty, give a vague answer where a precise one is expected. It is difficult to say exactly how long a baseline must be for a time-series experiment to be safe. The answer depends in part on how much one knows in advance about the process being studied. If a researcher has studied extensively a particular phenomenon-like "out-of-seat time" for pupils in a classroom-and has never seen much nonstationarity, it's conceivable that a satisfactory baseline can be established in relatively short order in a time-series experiment, a dozen or so points in time, say. But when a series is quite nonstationary, 40 or 50 baseline time points may be needed before the process is sufficiently understood that one would attempt to assess the effects of an intervention. We have found that time-series of observations of a single individual are often stationary, particularly if you discard the first few points during which the subject may be acclimating to the equipment or observation procedures. On the other hand, time-series based on large groups of persons-like classrooms, cities, or the population of an entire nation-are often nonstationary. I hasten to point out that this generalization isn't always true even in the examples presented here.

Few statisticians would insist on more than 100 points in time, but some of the more rigid ones might not accept fewer. Fifty time points (25 pre and 25 post) is a good round number, provided you make a definite hypothesis about the form of the intervention effect and stick with it. In other words, 50 pre and 50 posttime points are sufficient if you don't succumb to the temptation of fishing around in the data after you see it and taking second and third guesses at the form of the intervention effect. Fifteen preintervention points are certainly cutting things thin, and even then so short a baseline is only safe if you know far in advance about the probable statistical character of the series. If you're held to fewer than 10 preintervention points, then you shouldn't be performing a time-series experiment unless you have an intervention so potent that it will work huge effects, in which case you'll probably know it without an experiment. If you attempt time-series experiments with too short baselines, you're likely to end up with data like those in Figure 8. There the incidence of child molestation is graphed for a 12-year period around the enactment of three regulations that made pornography easily available to adults. The time series is simply too short to permit any kind of conclusion.

Time series nearly always evidence a form of statistical correlation that is quite unlike what we are accustomed to in working with random samples. For many reasons, today's score is more highly correlated with either yesterday's or tomorrow's score than it is with either the score from a week ago or a week hence. This condition of correlation within the series wreaks havoc with ordinary statistical techniques; it's about the only violation of standard statistical assumptions (normality, equal variance, and independence) that is worth worrying about. The proper means are known of taking account of this form of correlation, but the methods are complex by elementary textbook standards. At the end of this paper, I've given references in which you can pursue these more technical questions on your own. Suffice it to say that proper statistical analysis involves very complex methods now relegated to computer programs. Among the best of these for analyzing time-series experiments is a series of computer programs produced by Quantitative Micro Software (Quantitative Micro Software, 1994). For an explanation of the state-of-the-art analysis methods on which such programs as the Micro TSP program is based, see McCleary and Welsh (1992).

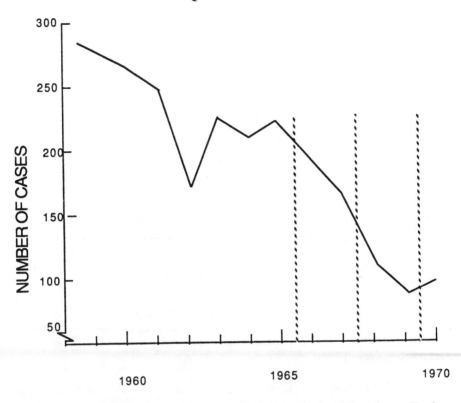

FIGURE 8. *Child molestation (offenses against girls) in the city of Copenhagen.* (Broken vertical lines represent successive liberalizations of Danish pornography laws.) (Source: Kutchinsky, 1973).

Investigation and Detective Work

In some time-series experiments, it frequently happens that subsections of a large data pool reveal intervention effects that are not apparent in the complete body of data. Consider the data in Figure 2, for example. If there is any effect of the British Road Safety Act of 1967 on the traffic fatality rate, it certainly isn't very apparent in the graph in Figure 2. But look at the graph in Figure 9 to see what happened when the fatalities on weekend nights were singled out of the total body of data. There we see a huge, more than 50%, reduction in fatalities coincident with the implementation of the Road Safety Act in October 1967. We can move from the equivocal results of Figure 2 to the clear certainty of Figure 9 merely by separating the larger body of data.

Why is the effect so apparent in Figure 9 when it was barely discernible (or not discernible at all) in Figure 2? As was mentioned earlier, an essential feature of the Road Safety Act was a program of roadblocks where drivers were tested for blood alcohol level. And what time is better for finding drunks on the road

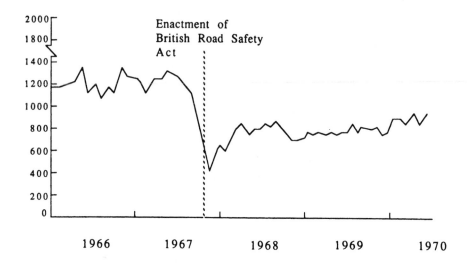

FIGURE 9. *Fatalities for Friday nights, 10:00 p.m. to midnight; Saturday mornings, midnight to 4:00 a.m.; Saturday nights, 10:00 p.m. to midnight; and Sunday mornings, midnight to 4:00 a.m.; corrected for weekend days per month, seasonal variations removed.* (Broken vertical line represents implementation of the Road Safety Act.) (Source: Ross, Campbell, & Glass, 1970)

than weekend nights? The picture is completed in Figure 10, which shows the fatalities curve for the hours commuting to and from work in the morning and late afternoon when there are few drunken drivers. Sorting the data in Figure 2 into two different series in Figures 9 and 10 not only has revealed the intervention effect but also has illuminated the whole question of how the Road Safety Act worked its effect.

Opponents of the antidrunk-driver features of the Road Safety Act argued that other features of the law were actually responsible for the decrease in fatalities: for example, the construction of more and better traffic signals, a tire inspection program, and a reduction in the numbers of motorcycles and mopeds on the road. The pattern of the time series in Figures 9 and 10 refutes these claims because each of them would lead one to expect an effect that was initially small then grew and was of equal size for commuting hours and weekend nights.

Consider Figure 11 as a final example of an experiment in which the answers aren't so clear. The figure is a graph of the enrollment of the Denver Public Schools from 1928 to 1975, and the experimental question concerns forced racial integration and so-called White flight. In 1969, in the Federal District court, Judge Doyle rendered a decision in the Keys versus Denver Public Schools case that represented the first forced integration decision in a major northern city. The question is, "Was there a resulting flight of White families to the suburbs to escape racially integrated schools?"

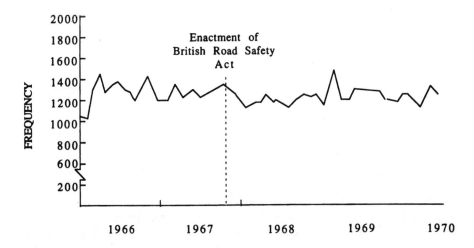

FIGURE 10. *Fatalities for Mondays through Fridays, 8:00 a.m. to 10:00 a.m. and 4:00 p.m. to 5:00 p.m., corrected for weekdays per month, seasonal variation removed.* (Broken vertical line represents implementation of the Road Safety Act.) (Source: Ross, Campbell, & Glass, 1970)

The total enrollment of the Denver Public Schools dropped from 1970 on, but it had been dropping since 1960. The question is whether the enrollment declined faster after 1969 than before, and it appears that it has, but the situation is hardly unequivocal. The enrollment grew as fast during the 1950s as it fell in the early 1970s, but no one has implicated racial strife or harmony in the earlier acceleration. Moreover, the national birthrate was falling sharply in the

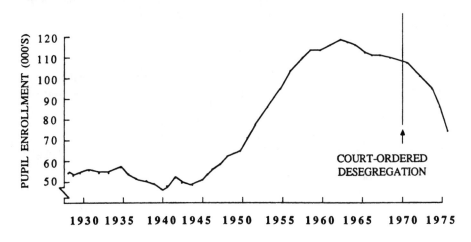

FIGURE 11. *Enrollment of Denver public schools from 1928 to 1975.*

late 1960s, exactly 5 years ahead of what looks like a sharp decline in Denver School enrollment in the 1970s; and for all that Judge Doyle's decision might have done, it is stretching things to believe that it could have affected the birthrate 5 years before it was handed down.

The effect of the Denver case on enrollment, as shown in Figure 11, has to remain uncertain. But I suspect that it could be resolved fairly conclusively by breaking down and plotting in several alternative ways the total enrollment series in Figure 11. Breaking the enrollment data down by grade might cast a little light on things. If White flight were causing the decline, one might expect a larger decline at the elementary grades than at the secondary grades, particularly grades 11 and 12 where parents would likely decide to stick it out for the short run. If enrollment data existed separately for different ethnic groups, these time series would provide a revealing test. If they showed roughly equal declines across all ethnic groups, the White-flight hypothesis would suffer a major setback. Data on enrollment that could be separated by individual school, neighborhood, or census tract would be exceptionally valuable. These various units could be ranked prior to looking at the data on their susceptibility to White flight. Such a ranking could be based on variables like pre-1969 ethnic mixture, percentage of change in ethnic-mixture of the school under the desegregation plan, or mobility of families based on percentage of housing values mortgaged or amount of disposable income. If the large enrollment declines fell in the highly susceptible regions, the pattern would constitute some degree of support for the White flight hypothesis.

Conclusion

At their easiest, time-series experiments require little more than good graphing skills, a skeptical attitude toward one's pet hypotheses, and the capacity to subdivide the data to locate hidden effects. At their most complex, time-series experiments involve complicated statistical analyses to separate the unaccountable variation of indexes across time from the significant effects of planned interventions.

References

Campbell D. T., & Stanley, J. C. (1963). Experimental and quasi-experimental designs for research on teaching. In N. L. Gage (Ed.), *Handbook of research on teaching* (pp. 171–246). Chicago: Rand McNally.

Cronbach, L. J. (1982) Designing evaluations of educational and social programs. San Francisco: Jossey-Bass.

Gettinger, M. (1993). Effects of invented spelling and direct instruction on spelling performance of second-grade boys. *Journal of Applied Analysis of Behavior, 26*, 281–291.

Glass, G. V, Willson, V. L., & Gottman, J. M. (1975). Design and analysis of time-series experiments. Boulder: Colorado Associated University Press.

Komechak, M. G. (1974). Thought detection as a precipitator of anxiety responses. Unpublished doctoral dissertation, North Texas State University. Dallas, TX.

Kutchinsky, B. (1973). The effect of easy availability of pornography on the incidence of sex crimes: The Danish experience. *Journal of Social Issues, 29,* 163–181.

Levin, J. R. (1992). Single-case research design and analysis: Comments and concerns. In T. R. Kratochwill & J. R. Levin (Eds.), Single-case research design and analysis: New directions for psychology and education (pp. 213–224). Hillsdale, NY: Lawrence Erlbaum.

McCleary, R., & Welsh, W. N. (1992). Philosophical and statistical foundations of time-series experiments. In T. R. Kratochwill & J. R. Levin (Eds.), *Single-case research design and analysis: New directions for psychology and education* (pp. 41–91). Hillsdale, NY: Lawrence Erlbaum.

Parsonson, B. S., & Baer, D. M. (1992). The visual analysis of data, and current research into the stimuli controlling it. In T. R. Kratochwill & J. R. Levin (Eds.), *Single-case research design and analysis: New directions for psychology and education* (pp. 15–40). Hillsdale, NY: Lawrence Erlbaum.

Quantitative Micro Software. (1994). Micro-TSP: Version 7. Irvine, CA: Quantitative Micro Software (4521 Campus Drive, Suite 336, Irvine, CA 92715).

Ross, H. L., Campbell, D. T., & Glass, G. V (1970). Determining the social effects of a legal reform. In S. S. Nagel (Ed.), *Law and social change* (pp. 15–32). Beverly Hills, CA: SAGE.

Smith, M. L. et al. (1976). Evaluation of the effects of Outward Bound. In G. V Glass (Ed.), *Evaluation studies review annual: Vol. 1.* Beverly Hills, CA: SAGE.

Suggestions for Further Reading

The following references deal with general questions of the design of time-series experiments and their application to specific fields of study.

Campbell, D. T. (1969). From description to experimentation: Interpreting trends as quasi-experiments. In C. W. Harris (Ed.), *Problems in measuring change* (pp. 212–242). Madison: University of Wisconsin Press.

Campbell, D. T. (1969). Reforms as experiments. American *Psychologist, 24,* 409–429.

Campbell, D. T., & Stanley, J. C. (1966). *Experimental and quasi-experimental designs for research.* Chicago: Rand McNally.

Cook, T. D., & Campbell, D. T. (1979). *Quasi-experimentation: Design and analysis issues for field settings.* Chicago: Rand McNally.

Glass, G. V, Willson, V. L., & Gottman, J. M. (1975). *Design and analysis of time-series experiments.* Boulder: Colorado Associated University Press.

Kratochwill, T. R., & Levin, J. R. (Eds.). (1992). *Single-case research design and analysis: New directions for psychology and education.* Hillsdale, NY: Lawrence Erlbaum.

The following references deal with problems in the inferential statistical analysis of time-series experiments. Unfortunately, they are not simple. Each requires some background in statistics and a good deal of dedication to extracting its message.

Box, G. E. P., & Tiao, G. C. (1965). A change in level of nonstationary time-series. *Biometrika, 52,* 181–192. (The first rigorous treatment of the intervention problem. Provides the accepted solution for the most commonly encountered nonstationary process.)

Glass, G. V, Willson, V. L., & Gottman, J. M. (1975). Design and analysis of time-series experiments. Boulder: Colorado Associated University Press. (Presents a solution to the intervention analysis problem in the general case.)

Gottman, J. M., & Glass. G. V (1979). Analysis of the interrupted time-series experiment. In T. R. Kratochwill (Ed.), Strategies to evaluate change in single subject research (pp. 151–178). New York: Academic Press. (Further applications of the techniques derived in Glass, Willson, & Gottman, [1975].)

McDowall, D., McCleary, R., Meidinger, E. E., & Hays, R. A. (1980). *Interrupted time series analysis.* Beverly Hills, CA: SAGE.

Study Questions

1. What is one basic difference between experimental and nonexperimental research?

2. Describe two problems that interfere with causal interpretation of the relationship between two variables.

3. Describe the major difference between experimental and quasi-experimental research designs.

4. Why might a researcher choose to use an interrupted time-series design instead of a true experimental design?

5. Try to think of some readily available data that could be analyzed using an interrupted time-series design. What kinds of educational data are routinely collected by most school systems or colleges, year after year?

6. Is there any way to rule out the potential effects of all third variables?

7. How do researchers identify or demonstrate the effects of experimental interventions when they analyze data from time-series experiments?

8. How do carefully delineated hypotheses help a researcher to demonstrate the effect of an intervention in a time-series design?

9. What is the difference between stationary and nonstationary time series?

10. Can standard statistical procedures typically be used when analyzing data from time-series experiments? Why or why not?

11. How do long baselines of data aid in interpreting the results of time-series experiments?

12. If a school system abandoned ability grouping in April and a long-standing time-series on average reading achievement increased sharply from the previous June to the following June, could the change be used as evidence of the causal effect of the policy shift? Would the evidence be strong and convincing? What additional data might be required?

13. Why is it frequently useful to develop separate time series for subgroups of large populations? Give an example to illustrate your reasoning.

Readings

Introduction
An Application of Time-Series Models to an Educational Research Study

Richard M. Jaeger

These two readings illustrate an application of the time-series analysis procedures described in the preceding paper by Glass. Both readings were selected by Gene V Glass. The first, by Mayer and Kozlow (1980), illustrates the use of what Glass (Figure 4) called the "multiple-group, single- intervention design." The researchers examine changes in the average achievement of two eighth grade classes on a science concepts test, as a result of instruction on a science concept called "crustal evolution." The second reading, by Willson (1982), contains a reanalysis of the Mayer and Kozlow data. Willson uses some sophisticated statistical analysis procedures that were specially developed for the examination of data collected in time series. In addition, the Willson reading provides an illuminating discussion on the kinds of models that can be used to describe expected patterns of student achievement that might result from the use of an instructional treatment.

There are several reasons that these articles were selected to illustrate the use of time-series models in educational research. First, they illustrate an objective that is common in educational research studies—trying to determine the effects of an instructional treatment. Second, they are clearly written and, with the exception of the "Analysis" section of Willson's reading, avoid the use of complicated technical vocabulary. In other words, you should find these readings understandable even if your education in statistics is limited. Finally, these readings will add to your understanding of the practical application of time-series methods, since they show you how a real time-series study is designed, and how the results of such a study can be interpreted.

The Mayer and Kozlow Reading

In reading Mayer and Kozlow (1980), you should pay particular attention to the research questions the authors attempted to investigate. First, you must realize that observation in elementary or secondary school classrooms is both intrusive and time consuming. Whether a data collector merely sits in the back of a classroom and records what takes place, or asks students to provide specific information, the act of data collection is very likely to interfere with the principal instructional purpose of the class. In time-series research, data must be collected on a regular basis—such as daily or weekly—over an extended period of time. The danger of intrusion is thus far greater than would be the case if a more traditional research design were used, for example, one that required collection of data only twice (just prior to an intervention and just following an intervention). So one objective of the Mayer and Kozlow research was to determine whether a time-series study could be conducted in a typical classroom setting without upsetting instruction or taking too much class time.

Second, Mayer and Kozlow wanted to investigate the kinds of learning patterns a time-series study would show, and, in particular, to determine whether students' average achievement would increase during instruction and decrease (through forgetting) once instruction had ended. Note that Mayer and Kozlow had specific expectations about the pattern and shape of their time series, assuming their intervention was effective. They expected what Glass (Figure 3) termed "an abrupt change in direction" when their intervention was introduced and when it was removed.

Figures 1 and 2 in the Mayer and Kozlow reading illustrate the actual patterns of average student achievement they observed in two classrooms. When you study these figures, you should consider the question of whether these time series are stationary or nonstationary. Do you think that data have been collected at enough time points to tell? Just by looking at the figures, would you conclude that students' average achievement increased during instruction and then decreased after instruction stopped?

You might be tempted to conclude that Figure 1, which shows data for Class A, is more convincing than Figure 2, which shows data for Class B. Note that students' average achievement scores appear to vary more from day to day in Class B than in Class A, thus making it more difficult to identify a pattern. In Class B, students answered different achievement test items from one day to the next, and these items differed in their difficulty. In Class A, most of the same test items were used each day, although a given student answered different test items. Thus the pattern of achievement scores shown for Class B must be attributed, in part, to differences in the tests used each day, as well as to changes in students' actual learning. This third variable was not well controlled in Class B, and thus it muddies the interpretation of the time series.

Mayer and Kozlow used very simple, but intuitively appropriate, statistical analyses in trying to interpret the results of their time-series research. As shown in their Table I, they correlated students' average scores on the achievement test with the sequence numbers of the days on which they collected data. That is, they paired students' average achievement on Day 1 with the number 1, students' average achievement on Day 2 with the number 2, etc. For students in each class, they computed one correlation coefficient for Days 1 through 8 (the baseline period), another correlation coefficient for Days 9 through 18 (the intervention period), and a third correlation coefficient for Days 19 through 26 (the follow-up period). If the patterns of students' achievement scores followed their expectations, Mayer and Kozlow reasoned that the baseline correlations would be close to zero, that the intervention-period correlations would be positive (since they expected students to show increasing achievement as they were exposed to more instruction), and that correlations from the follow-up period would be negative (since they expected students to forget more of what they had learned as the time following instruction increased). Think about these expectations as you review the data in Table I, to see what really happened.

Notice that students' average achievement in Class A increased during the two days immediately following the end of instruction (Figure 1). In Class B, students' average achievement dropped a little on the day immediately following instruction, and then increased on the second day. Mayer and Kozlow interpreted these patterns as a "momentum effect," thus suggesting that students' cumulative learning continued to build for a couple of days after instruction ended, as a result of their having "put it all together" or having become enthusiastic about the instructional material. Table II contains the results of data analyses that reflect this supposition. When you read this section of Mayer and Kozlow, think about what Glass said in his paper concerning after-the-fact interpretations of time series. Do you think the "momentum effect" is a plausible explanation? What do you think of an interpretation that is based on only two data points?

In his paper, Glass told you a lot about the promises and pitfalls of time-series research designs. When you consider fundamental issues concerning the Mayer and Kozlow reading—Did they achieve their research objectives? Do you agree with their conclusions?—think about Glass's advice concerning the data requirements of stationary and nonstationary time series, the importance of specifying the time series' expected response to intervention, and the likely influence of third variables.

The Willson Reading

You should approach the Willson (1982) reading with the objectives of learning a bit more about the methodology of time-series research and trying to understand Willson's reanalysis of the Mayer and Kozlow data.

In his Figure 1, Willson illustrates two time-series patterns that might result from an instructional intervention, and two time-series patterns that might model students' forgetting after instruction has ended. His "Increasing Ramp Function" (1a) and "Declining Ramp Function" (1c) correspond to Mayer and Kozlow's expectations concerning the general patterns of their time series.

Willson notes the importance of having an observation for *every* time period (e.g., day or week) in a time series, and gives advice on how to estimate missing data, in case some days or weeks have been omitted. You should realize that having complete data is far more important if sophisticated statistical procedures are going to be used for analysis than if the time series is to be analyzed solely by inspecting a graph. Thus the two data points that are missing in the Mayer and Kozlow data (Friday of the second week during the baseline period and Monday of the third week during the intervention period) are far more troublesome for Willson's analysis than for Mayer and Kozlow's.

You might find Willson's "Analysis" section to be hard reading. He uses many statistical terms such as "parametric," "nonparametric," "frequency domain," "time domain," and probably worst of all, "autoregressive integrated moving average model (ARIMA)." Although this section would be a good bit clearer to you if you knew the definitions of these terms, you can get the general idea even if you know none of them.

Willson has assumed that the data collected by Mayer and Kozlow fit a specific statistical model, and has analyzed their data as though his assumptions were correct. Assuming a specific model is always a more powerful approach to data analysis than is the alternative, and it is a particularly useful procedure when the assumptions can be validated. Willson assumed that the data collected by Mayer and Kozlow for each class during the baseline and intervention periods would satisfy a statistical equation that, if graphed, would look like the "Ramp Function" of Figure la. He also assumed that the data collected during the baseline and forgetting periods, if analyzed together, would look like the "Declining Ramp Function" of Figure 1c. He further assumed that the differences between students' actual average achievement scores, and the average achievement scores predicted by these models, would be related to each other on successive days. By using statistical procedures that are consistent with these assumptions (called autoregression analysis), Willson was able to show that the Mayer and Kozlow data fit his models. When he conducted his analyses of the data for Class A, Willson decided that the extremely high average achievement score earned by students on the first day of the baseline period was the result of factors that were unrelated to the rest of the time series. In other words, he decided that the first day's data produced an "oddball score" that would best be ignored. Screening data for outlying and seemingly uninterpretable scores prior to analysis is in the best traditions of statistical practice, and can often save researchers from totally misleading interpretations of results.

Although based on more powerful statistical procedures, Willson's conclusions are quite similar to those of Mayer and Kozlow. In both classes, the "Ramp Function" (Figure 1c) appears to provide a good description of students' average achievement during the intervention period. However, substantial loss of achievement during the follow-up period was not confirmed for either class.

This summary and interpretation of the Willson reading has been provided as an aid to your understanding of the original. Now that you've read the summary, the reading should be far easier to comprehend. By approaching the reading with the summary in mind, you should learn some important new concepts and some fundamental terms in the language of time-series research.

AN EVALUATION OF A TIME–SERIES SINGLE–SUBJECT DESIGN USED IN AN INTENSIVE STUDY OF CONCEPT UNDERSTANDING

VICTOR J. MAYER

The Ohio State University

M. JAMES KOZLOW

University of British Columbia, Vancouver

Introduction

Time-series single-subject designs for use in intensive studies in learning were introduced in a report of an investigation by Mayer and Lewis (1979). That report includes a rationale for use of such designs in science education studies. It also describes an evaluation of the use of time-series single-subject designs in an intensive testing situation. The dependent variable used was student attitude toward the science class and the independent variable, teaching methods. The major conclusions were that a five-item semantic differential could be developed to be reliable when used in the design, and that the design could produce valid information on variation in student attitudes due to instructional methodologies. The relative success of this first full-scale effort to use the design in a classroom situation encouraged the first author to modify the design for measuring concept learning as well as attitudes.

The study reported here is the development and evaluation of an intensive single-subject time-series design for use in studying learning of concepts. It focuses on answering two questions: (1) Can procedures for measuring concept learning on a daily basis be devised that will interfere little with the normal classroom routine and take a minimum of time away from instruction? (2) Can such procedures yield valid information on the learning of a science concept? To answer these questions an intensive descriptive study was designed to investigate learning of the concept of crustal evolution.

Procedures

The two subjects chosen for the study were two eighth-grade earth-science classes in a junior high school situated in a central Ohio suburban community. The students were from families representing a broad range of socioeconomic backgrounds. The two classes were taught by the same teacher, the science department chairman. He normally maintained a very informal classroom with almost all instruction of a student-centered, small group, laboratory, or activity-oriented nature.

A multiple-group single-intervention design was adapted from that defined by Glass, Willson and Gottman (1975; pp. 39–41):

$$\text{Class A} \ldots O_5\ O_6\ O_7\ O_8\ O_9\ I\ O_{10} \ldots I\ O_{17}\ O_{18}\ O_{19}\ O_{20}\ O_{21} \ldots$$
$$\text{Class B} \ldots O_5\ O_6\ O_7\ O_8\ O_9\ I\ O_{10} \ldots I\ O_{17}\ O_{18}\ O_{19}\ O_{20}\ O_{21} \ldots$$

Daily observations (O) were made in each of the subjects (Class A and Class B) for a period of 26 days. The intervention (I) stage, days 9 to 18, consisted of instruction using a 10-day unit on crustal evolution. The eight days prior to the intervention constituted the baseline stage, which was established to identify any systematic variation in student knowledge of the concept of crustal evolution. The eight days following the end of the intervention constituted the followup stage.

In designing the procedure for the collection of data on changes in understanding of the concept of crustal evolution, multiple-choice items were chosen. According to Ebel (1972; pp. 187–188), they are the most highly regarded and widely used form of objective testing. He states that they are adaptable to the measurement of most important educational outcomes including knowledge, understanding, and judgment, the expected levels of learning science concepts. Experience with the use of multiple-choice items also indicated that students were able to respond to them rapidly. Two approaches for collecting data were developed using multiple-choice items. The first required all students to respond to the same three items on a given day, with different three-item tests given on successive days. The advantages over the second method were that it was much simpler and less time-consuming to develop the instrument. And, since all students took the same test on the same day, their scores could be compared. The second method required students to respond to one item, with every student getting a different item on a given day. Using this method, the effects of any inherent differences in the difficulty of items upon the data could be minimized. Also, it would take the least student time for completion.

The concept of crustal evolution was chosen for instruction during the intervention; this was the independent variable. It was appropriate for the earth science classes involved in the investigation and yet the concept was relatively unfamiliar to students in those classes. Three broad objectives were defined, encompassing crustal evolution. Each of these was further subdivided into two to four specific objectives for the purpose of developing an instructional unit and test items.

An attempt was then made to generate an item universe, that is, all of the items possible that would measure understanding of the concept, the dependent variable. Three individuals, a graduate student in earth science education, a teacher teaching eighth-grade earth-science, and the first author, independently developed as many items as possible relating to the specific and general objectives. The resulting items were examined for duplication, consistency with objectives, wording, and structure. An item pool of 48 items was the result.

A unit was developed concurrent with the development of the item pool. The objectives were used to identify appropriate teaching materials for 10 days of instruction. They were grouped such that a two- or three-day instructional sequence focused on a single group of objectives. Instruction was carefully structured through the use of student guides to activities and discussions and teachers guides.

When the unit was completed it was carefully compared with the item pool to ensure content validity. The unit was then piloted with four eighth-grade earth-science classes. The item pool was randomly divided into two parts. Each part was given to two of the classes (about 50 students) as a posttest of the unit. The unit was redesigned as a result of teacher feedback. The item pool was extensively modified from item-analysis information. Some items were deleted and others were revised. Additional items were developed through word substitution in existing items. An effort was also made to insure that there was an equal number of items relating to each of the three broad unit objectives. The final item pool consisted of 54 items.

The two approaches described earlier were used to obtain daily measures of student understanding of crustal evolution. Class A responded to the *one-item instrument*, which consisted of a single item for each student, randomly drawn from the item pool. Each student was assigned a different item on a given day. A new random assignment of items was made each day and no student was given the same item more than once throughout the 26 days of data collection. Class B responded to the *three-item instrument*, in which one item was drawn randomly from items representing each of the three unit objectives. Every student was given the same three-item test on a given day and different tests were given on successive days.

Two forms of a *crustal evolution posttest*, to be administered at the end of the intervention, were generated from the item pool. Each form consisted of 32 items, including 10 items that were common to both forms. The 10 common items were randomly selected from the complete pool and the remaining items were then randomly assigned to alternate forms one item at a time. The KR 20 reliabilities were Form 1 (Class A), .77 and Form 2 (Class B), .71.

An individual from the research project staff observed both classes every day during the intervention. Information was recorded on the concurrent use of the unit in the two classes and on the time taken for the administration of the data-collecting instruments.

Analysis and Interpretation of Data

Were procedures for measuring concept learning developed that interfered little with normal classroom routine and that took a minimum of class time? This, of necessity, is a judgmental question. However, the log of classroom observations indicated that the one-item procedure took an average of less than two minutes of class time to administer and the three-item instrument only slightly longer. Once the teacher grew accustomed to administering the instruments, it became a part of the daily classroom routine, and therefore, resulted in minimum disruption.

Did the data collecting result in valid data? To determine this a form of concurrent validity was used. Any standard psychology text illustrates learning curves where the amount of information learned increases over the period of time during which instruction takes place. After cessation of instruction, the curve drifts downward due to forgetting. If the data collection techniques are valid, similar patterns should be noted—during intervention, a growth in learning, and during the followup, a downward drift in the learning curve. The data obtained from the daily administration of the multiple-choice instruments were analyzed to answer this question.

Data for those students who had missed three or more days of intervention were omitted from the analysis, leaving data for 19 students in Class A and for 21 students in Class B. The total enrollments in Classes A and B were 24 and 25 respectively.

The data were reduced to a single score for each class for each day. For Class A, which received the one-item tests, the number of students who responded correctly to their item was divided by the total number of students present. For Class B, which received the three-item tests, the student scores were first converted to a proportion by dividing the number correct by three and then the class mean was computed. The class scores for each day are plotted in Figure 1 for Class A and in Figure 2 for Class B. A visual examination of the two graphs reveals a positive trend during the intervention and a negative trend during the followup. The very high score on day 1 in Class A is very puzzling and thus far unexplained. Although not repeated with Class B, the first-day score in that class is also higher than would be anticipated.

To determine the significance of these patterns, correlation coefficients between day and class score were calculated for each of the three stages of data collection in each class. The means, standard deviations, and correlations for each stage for each class are included in Table I.

During baseline, Class A had a negative though not significant correlation of scores with

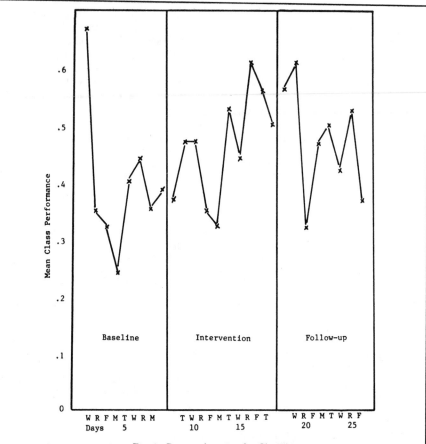

Fig. 1. Data on learning for Class A.

time, whereas Class B has a positive correlation significant at the .1 level. If the first-day scores are eliminated, both baselines have positive but not significant correlations with time. In both classes, there was a significant ($p \leqslant .05$) positive correlation of class score with time during the intervention stage, indicating an increased understanding of crustal evolution. Neither correlation during the followup stage was significant.

The data for Class A are those one might expect to reflect a typical learning curve. The data in the baseline do not exhibit any pattern or trend. The intervention data show a gradual positive and significant drift, and the followup data exhibit a gradual decline. This pattern demonstrated the validity of the one-item technique for obtaining data on knowledge acquisition using the intensive time-series design.

The data for Class B, however, though exhibiting the expected pattern during the intervention stage, do not for the other two. The baseline data have a positive, significant ($p \leqslant 0.1$) drift and there is an absence of drift in the followup data.

In order to investigate the possibility that daily fluctuations in performance may have been partially due to differences in the difficulty levels of the test items, the mean difficulty of all items used each day was calculated. Item difficulty indexes were obtained from the results of the crustal evolution posttests which were given at the end of the intervention stage. Since both classes did not respond to all items and since the two classes did not perform at the same level (Class A, $\bar{X} = 6.11$; Class B, $\bar{X} = 4.67$) on the 10 common items, it was necessary to make an adjustment for some items. The arbitrary decision was made to use Class B performance as the standard of item difficulty. The observed difficulty levels for the 32 items on the Class B form were used as difficulty indexes for these items. An adjustment was made to the 22 items which were on the Class A form but not on the Class B form. The relative performance of the two classes on the 10 common items was used to make the adjustment. The mean difficulty of these 10 items was .61 for Class A and .47 for Class B. The difference (.14) was substracted from the difficulty levels of the 22 items which were on the Class A form only, to get an estimate of what the difficulty levels for these items might have been if they had been given to Class B.

These difficulty indexes were used to calculate the mean difficulties of all items used each day with each class.

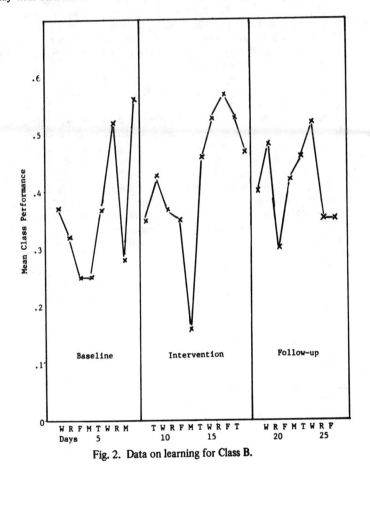

Fig. 2. Data on learning for Class B.

TABLE I
Correlations (r), Means ($\bar{x}$), and Standard Deviations (σ) for the Three Stages

Stage (days)	Class A			Class B		
	BL (8)	IN (10)	FU (8)	BL (8)	IN (10)	FU (8)
r (p<)	−.33(0.21)	.58(0.04)	−.47(0.15)	.51(0.10)	.55(0.05)	−.12(0.39)
$\bar{x}$	.40	.46	.47	.37	.42	.41
σ	.13	.09	.10	.12	.12	.07

One possible reason for the differences in the obtained learning curves for the two classes is that the daily fluctuations in mean item difficulty are more pronounced for Class B than for Class A. The mean difficulties for Class A range from .43 to .56, but for Class B they range from .30 to .66. The positive trend during the baseline stage for Class B could be due to the fact that the items used toward the end of this stage tended to be less difficult than those used at the beginning. The absence of a negative trend during the followup stage for Class B could be due to this same effect. Only 18 three-item tests were generated. The tests given during the followup stage were the same as those given during the baseline stage. This fluctuation of difficulty level from day to day is a serious limitation to the use of the three-item instrument for data collection.

The relatively high means during the first two days of the followup in both classes seem to indicate the occurrence of some type of "momentum effect" with the classes continuing to increase their knowledge about the topic after instruction in crustal evolution had ended. To determine the likelihood of a "momentum effect," the first two days of the followup were added to the intervention data for both classes. Table II summarizes the correlations and means. For Class A, the positive correlation for intervention plus two days was much higher than for the intervention alone and the negative trend for the followup minus two days was not as pronounced as it was for the eight days of followup. This would support some type of "momentum effect" occurring in the learning of concepts. The absence of these shifts in Class B could be due to the large fluctuations in item difficulty from day to day.

Could familiarization of students with the items account for the apparent learning curve? An examination of student data for Class A indicated that no student received the same item twice. In Class B, students did receive the same items in the baseline and followup

TABLE II
Correlations (r), Means ($\bar{x}$) and Standard Deviations (σ)
of Days 9–20 and 21–26

Days	Class A		Class B	
	9–20	21–26	9–20	21–26
r (p<)	0.71(.005)	0.23(0.33)	0.46(.07)	0.07(0.45)
$\bar{x}$	0.48	0.44	0.43	0.40
σ	0.10	0.09	0.11	0.08

EVALUATION OF TIME-SERIES DESIGN

stages. Students apparently did not learn the items, however, since Class B exhibited a greater decline in performance than Class A during the followup stage. It might be possible for item familiarity to result from discussion about items among class members. Since the items were not used for grading purposes, however, the major motivation for this would not be present. Also, neither the teacher nor the classroom observers noticed the occurrence of any discussions of items during the class period. It is possible that such discussions occurred after class, but this was fully 45 minutes after the items had been seen by the students. It seems most likely then that the curve represented by the data are indeed learning curves and not the result of item familiarization.

Conclusions

The results of this study demonstrate that a data-collecting procedure can be developed for measuring concept understanding in an intensive single-subject time-series design. The procedure took a minimum of class time, resulted in little disturbance of the usual class routine, and provided valid measurement of learning of the concept of crustal evolution. The results indicate that the one-item data collection procedure is more valid than the three-item procedure. The main problem with the three-item procedure is the large fluctuation in difficulty level of items from day to day.

References

Disinger, J. F., & Mayer, V. J. Student development in junior high school science. *Journal of Research in Science Teaching*, 1974, **11**, 149-155.

Ebel, R. L. *Essentials in educational measurement*. Englewood Cliffs, N.J.: Prentice-Hall, 1972.

Glass, G. V., Willson, V. L., & Gottman, J. M. *Design and analysis of time-series experiments*. Boulder, Colo.: Colorado Associated University Press, 1975.

Mayer, V. J., & Lewis, D. K. An evaluation of the use of a time-series single-subject design. *Journal of Research in Science Teaching*, 1979, **16**, 137-144.

Manuscript accepted November 20, 1979

MORE ON TIME SERIES DESIGNS:
A REANALYSIS OF MAYER AND KOZLOW'S DATA

VICTOR L. WILLSON

*College of Education, Texas A&M University,
College Station, Texas 77843*

Abstract

A recent article by Mayer and Kozlow introduces a time series experiment to science education researchers. This article examines in greater detail design considerations and reanalyzes their data using time series analysis.

The first applications of time series experimental methodology to science education research were reported by Mayer and Lewis (1979) and by Mayer and Kozlow (1980). This article discusses Mayer and Kozlow's work and presents a reanalysis of their data which is intended to be heuristic, not critical. (All data were supplied by Dr. Mayer and permission was granted to use the data.) Both design and analysis will be examined. It is important to distinguish time series experimental design from time series analysis. The former, as presented by Campbell and Stanley (1966) and detailed by Glass, Willson, and Gottman (1975), is concerned with structuring treatment conditions and observations over time to make causal inferences. Time series analysis is a set of statistical techniques from which an appropriate technique can be selected to analyze collected data in the framework of a time series design. Just as data from in a randomized experiment might be analyzed using a one-way analysis of variance or a Kruskal-Wallis *H*-test, data from a time series design may be subjected to several alternative analysis techniques.

Design Considerations

The design employed by Mayer and Kozlow is a multiple-group single intervention design with baseline, treatment period, and post-treatment follow-up. This design is eminently practical for school settings and can be set up and conducted easily by the classroom teacher. The independent variable is an indicator variable time series consisting typically of the value zero for each observation (daily in Mayer and Kozlow) during baseilne and nonzero during treatment. The values during treatment depend on the nature of the treatment. In the typical educational setting, knowledge gained through a curriculum is expected to follow an upward trend. In Figure 1 are various time series that might model educational treatments. The simplest are the ramp function in which knowledge is gained at a constant rate [Fig. 1(a)] and the step function [Fig. 1(b)] in which knowledge is gained in a short period (in a day, perhaps) and is maintained at a constant level. Forgetting during a post-treatment

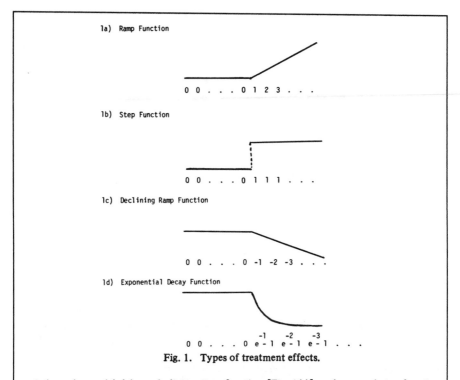

Fig. 1. Types of treatment effects.

period can be modeled by a declining ramp function [Fig. 1(c)], a downward step function, or an exponential decay [Fig. 1(d)] which is suggested by the psychological literature (Kintsch, 1970). More sophisticated learning curves employing logarithms or exponents can also be easily constructed. The dependent variable in a science education time series experiment is likely to be a cognitive or attitude measure. The dependent variable for time series analysis must be an interval or ratio score measured at approximately equal intervals (daily, weekly, etc.). When data "holes" occur, such as a holiday, the best procedure is to forecast a score for that time from the remaining data. Data points before and after the hole can be analyzed independently, each providing an estimate. These estimates are then weighted and averaged to produce the final estimate. Only data in a given treatment condition should be used to avoid confounding of treatment condition with the estimate. It is necessary to use a full data set since the statistical structure of time series analysis requires regular measurements, and parameters are conceived and estimated under this assumption. As long as the number of holes is small in relation to the total number of observations (perhaps less than 5%), no problem is likely to occur in this data estimation.

A practical need to maintain regularity in data points occurs when there is a recurrent, or seasonal effect: For example, in daily measurement of pupils it is not uncommon to have a correlation between scores five days apart, assuming five observations per week (weekends do not exist in education), which reflects activities, attitudes, and learning interests that vary during the week. It means that Mondays are more similar to each other than to any other days; the same is true for each other day. Removing even one day from such a series destroys this regularity and introduces spurious correlation between data at other intervals. In Mayer and Kozlow's data, two days were missing and should be estimated.

The construction of the dependent variable tests in science education was discussed well by Mayer and Kozlow. Since the use of the same tests or items on a daily basis is ruled out by memory effects, the use of item sampling is needed. Cooney and Willson (Note 1) presented a method to solve this problem: the application of matrix sampling of test items and students. In this solution not all children need to be tested each day (or whatever period is being used). Mayer and Kozlow chose to test each child each day with one item (class A) or three items (Class B) working from a fifty-four-item pool. An alternative is to allocate students and items randomly using a matrix sample. For example, using Mayer and Kozlow's classes, each class of about twenty-five students would be randomly split each week into five groups of five students. The pool of fifty-four items would be reduced to fifty and randomly split into five subtests. One group of students each day would receive a subtest for the five-day school week. The next week, items and students would be rerandomized until the testing period of six weeks was over. Cooney and Willson (Note 1) showed that this procedure produces a virtually identical time series to that which would have been produced if all students took each item each day.

Item difficulty variance can be controlled either by stratifying the item pool or by allowing items to vary randomly across the matrix sample. While the latter will increase error variance, it will be cheaper and simpler if attention is paid to the item generation. Thus, poor items are removed before conduct of the experiment, as was done in Mayer and Kozlow's study.

Attitude items may be similarly treated, but there should be greater concern for homogeneity or factorial simplicity of the pool of items. Use of Thurstone-scaled statements may have a real advantage since the matrix sample may be stratified by range of scale values.

Ratings by observers, performance counts, or sociometric measures may also be used in a time series design. One caveat about counts is that currently used time series analysis techniques do not work well with rare frequency distributions, so dependent variables which are expected to be constant much of the time are not compatible with time series analysis. Other techniques based on the Poisson distribution may eventually be refined for use with time series data.

Analysis

Time series analysis techniques can be classified first as parametric or nonparametric. Since little has been published on nonparametric techniques, only parametric techniques will be discussed further. With these techniques data may be described in a time domain or frequency domain. Frequency domain models are based on spectral analysis, which typically requires 100 or more observations, making spectral analysis inappropriate for Mayer and Kozlow's study. Time domain models for time series analysis have been treated in a general case, called the autoregressive integrated moving average (ARIMA) model, by Box and Jenkins (1976). Other treatments of the ARIMA model have been given by Glass, Willson, and Gottman (1975) and McCleary and Hay (1980).

In this section, a reanalysis of Mayer and Kozlow's (1980) knowledge data collected on two classes over a 26-day period is presented. Their treatment was a junior high unit on crustal evolution presented to two classes. The program used is PROC AUTOREG of the Statistical Analysis System (Barr et al., 1979). The SAS procedure does not handle the entire ARIMA class of time series models (see Glass et al., 1975) but proved adequate for Mayer and Kozlow's data.

The Mayer and Kozlow (1980) study was analyzed using a regression model relating daily achievement to treatment condition (baseline or treatment) and forgetting condition (baseline or forgetting). The treatment condition was assumed to produce a ramp function for learning [Fig. 1(a)] and the forgetting condition a declining ramp function. In addition, error in the regression model was assumed to follow the form of a simple ARIMA process, an autoregressive process of order 1. This means that the errors are treated as if correlated, each with its successor. The need to account for such correlation has been detailed in Glass et al. (1975) and mainly concerns obtaining correct denominators for tests of hypothesis of the regression weights for the treatments.

A check on the adequacy of the autoregressive model for errors is conducted through examination of residuals of fit to the regression model, which form a new time series. If the model is correct, the residual time series should consist of random, uncorrelated scores. A time series analysis of these scores assumes a zero mean and no correlation between any score and any successors beyond that likely by chance.

The analysis discussed above was applied to Mayer and Kozlow's (1980) data. Several details must be discussed before results are given, however. In their class A data, the first data point is greater than any other and quite extreme, as it was over four standard deviations from the mean (see Mayer & Kozlow, 1980, p. 458). It was considered an outlier in this analysis and discarded as completely atypical. Consequently, one might apply windsorized t-distributions to all that follows (Winer, 1971, pp. 51–53). This would reduce degrees of freedom by 2. For this analysis, it was assumed that the series for class A began one day later than that in Mayer and Kozlow (1980).

A second point is that significance tests in an experiment such as this should be directional. That is, the slope of the ramp function for treatment is expected to rise, not fall, so that the alternative hypothesis to no change is a significant, positive slope. Similarly, only a negative forgetting curve slope is tested. This greatly increases the power for the tests, which is important when there are few data points, as in the Mayer and Kozlow study.

Results

In class A in Mayer and Kozlow's study (1980), each student got one item of the crustal evolution item pool each day and the gain in knowledge from beginning of treatment to end has a significant slope ($t = 1.959$, $df = 22$), at $p < 0.01$, while the slope for forgetting, although in a downward direction, was not significant ($t = 1.163$, $df = 22$). The estimate of pretreatment test knowledge was about 41%, with a 0.7% average gain per day.

For class B, which received three item tests each day from the item pool, the treatment gain was significant at $p < 0.10$ ($t = 1.35$, $df = 22$) with an average daily gain of 0.6% and the forgetting slope parameter was nonsignificant ($t = 0.20$, $df = 22$). The pretreatment knowledge on the test items averaged 38%, not significantly different from the other class. There was greater variability in the difficulty of items used in class B (Mayer & Kozlow, 1980, p. 460) than in class A. This is expected to produce greater daily variation and will reduce the power of detect effects, which apparently occurred with the class B data.

This analysis generally supports the analysis performed by Mayer and Kozlow but puts the results on a somewhat firmer statistical footing. Mayer and Kozlow chose to examine correlation coefficients (standardized slopes) for the three intervention conditions. In general, it is hazardous to do this since any statistical comparison of the slopes depends on the degree of correlatedness of the residuals, as noted earlier. In this particular study, the autoregressive parameters were nonsignificant (class A, $t = 0.68$, $df = 24$; class B, $t = -0.65$, $df = 25$), and the residuals were uncorrelated. This means that ordinary least squares regression was used to analyze the data. It is never safe to assume, however, that this condition holds. Glass et al. (1975), for example, reported that over three-quarters of a sample of 100 behavioral time series they examined required time series analyses because of autocorrelation of some form.

Discussion

This article is designed to further familiarize science education researchers with the utility of time series designs and to present an example of formal analysis. It has not been presented as a primer on time series design or analysis. Glass et al. (1975), Cook and Campbell (1979), or McCleary and Hay (1980) should be studied for that purpose. Time series experimental design can be readily mastered by a careful reader. Time series analysis is quite complex in the general case and requires grounding in statistics. It is further complicated by the lack of easily accessible software. Major statistical packages are adding time series analysis programs, and this restriction will soon be lifted. Analysis will then be simpler. It is well to remember in this field that analysis should be as simple as possible, but no simpler, else it becomes simpleminded.

Acknowledgment

Thanks are given to Dr. V. J. Mayer for his assistance in providing the data and in explaining their collection and layout.

Reference Note

1: Cooney, J., & Willson, V. L. The use of time series designs and multiple matrix sampling as evaluation tools. Paper presented at AERA Annual Meeting, Boston, April 10, 1980.

References

Barr, A. J., Goodnight, J. H., Sall, J. P., Blair, W. M., & Chilko, D. M. *Statistical analysis system user's guide 1979 edition.* Raleigh, NC: ASA Institute, Inc., 1979.

Box, G. E. P., & Jenkins, G. M. *Time-series analysis: Forcasting and control.* San Francisco: Holden-Day, 1976.

Campbell, D. T., & Stanley, J. C. *Experimental and quasi-experimental designs and research.* Chicago: Rand-McNally, 1966.

Glass, G. V., Willson, V. L., & Gottman, J. M. *Design and analysis of time series experiments.* Colorado Associated University Press, 1975.

Kintsch, W. *Learning, memory, and cognitive processes.* New York: Wiley, 1970.

Mayer, V. J., & Lewis, D. K. An evaluation of the use of a time-series single-subject design. *Journal of Research in Science Teaching,* 1979, **16**, 137–144.

Mayer, V. J., & Kozlow, M. J. An evaluation of a time-series single-subject design used in an intensive study of concept understanding. *Journal of Research in Science Teaching,* 1980, **17**, 455–461.

McCleary, R., & Hay, R. A., Jr. *Applied time series analysis.* Beverly Hills, CA: Sage Publications, 1980.

Winer, B. J. *Statistical principles in experimental design.* New York: McGraw-Hill, 1971.

Manuscript accepted April 21, 1982

American Educational Research Association

MEMBERSHIP APPLICATION
(may be photocopied)

Please type/print.

Name: _____   ☐ New
      Last   First   Middle initial   ☐ Renewal

Mailing address: _____ E-mail: _____

_____
     City   State   ZIP or foreign postal code

Organization/School: _____ Telephone: _____

Type of Membership Requested

	1-Year	2-Year
☐ Voting	$45.00	$85.00
☐ Student	$20.00	—
☐ Associate	$45.00	$85.00
☐ International Affiliate	$45.00	$85.00

If you reside outside the United States, please add $9.00 per year to dues for postage and handling ($18.00 for 2 years).

Publications

In addition to the *Educational Researcher* and the *Annual Meeting Program*, I wish to receive as part of my membership dues the following two publications:

☐ *American Educational Research Journal* (quarterly)
☐ *Review of Educational Research* (quarterly)
☐ *Journal of Educational and Behavioral Statistics* (quarterly)
☐ *Educational Evaluation and Policy Analysis* (quarterly)
☐ *Review of Research in Education* (annual, casebound)

In addition to these two, I wish to subscribe at the special member rate of $15 each per year to the folllowing:

☐ *American Educational Research Journal*
☐ *Review of Educational Research*
☐ *Journal of Educational and Behavioral Statistics*
☐ *Educational Evaluation and Policy Analysis*
☐ *Review of Research in Education*

Divisional Membership Requested

Divisional memberships are $5.00 each per year ($10.00 each for 2-year memberships). Divisional memberships for students are $2.00 each per year.

☐ A—Administration
☐ B—Curriculum Studies
☐ C—Learning and Instruction
☐ D—Measurement and Research Methodology
☐ E—Counseling and Human Development
☐ F—History and Historiography
☐ G—Social Context of Education
☐ H—School Evaluation and Program Development
☐ I—Education in the Professions
☐ J—Postsecondary Education
☐ K—Teaching and Teacher Education
☐ L—Educational Policy and Politics

Applicant's
Signature: ___ _____

Student Membership

Proof of graduate student status or the endorsement of a voting member who is a faculty member at the student's institutution is required.

Signature of
endorser: _____

Printed name
of endorser: _____

Payment Enclosed

Membership dues $ _____

International postage & handling*   _____

Additional subscriptions*   _____

Additional Divisional affliations*   _____

Total $ _____

*For 2-year memberships, double the fees (international postage and handling—$18.00, additional subscriptions—$30.00, additonal divisonal affiliations—$10.00 each).

For members with a foreign address only:
MasterCard   Exp.
or VISA No. _____ Date _____

Dues include a subscription to *Educatonal Researcher* (valued at $12.00) and two additional publications (valued at $15.00 each).

Mail this form with your check to:
   AERA - Member Application
   1230 17th St., N.W.
   Washington, DC 20036-3078